We work with leading authors to develop the strongest educational materials in Economics, bringing cutting edge thinking and best learning practice to a global market.

Under a range of well-known imprints, including Financial Times Prentice Hall, we craft high quality print and electronic publications which help readers to understand and apply their content, whether studying or at work.

To find out about the complete range of our publishing please visit us on the World Wide Web at: www.pearsoneduc.com

Industrial Organisation

An Analysis of Competitive Markets

JOHN LIPCZYNSKI
JOHN WILSON

FT Prentice Hall
FINANCIAL TIMES

An imprint of **Pearson Education**

Harlow, England • London • New York • Boston • San Francisco • Toronto
Sydney • Tokyo • Singapore • Hong Kong • Seoul • Taipei • New Delhi
Cape Town • Madrid • Mexico City • Amsterdam • Munich • Paris • Milan

Pearson Education Limited
Edinburgh Gate
Harlow
Essex CM20 2JE
England

and Associated Companies throughout the world

Visit us on the World Wide Web at:
www.pearsoned.co.uk

First published 2001

© Pearson Education Limited 2001

ISBN 0-273-64620-6

British Library Cataloguing in Publication Data
A catalogue record for this book can be obtained from the British Library

Library of Congress Cataloging-in-Publication Data
A catalog record for this book can be obtained from the Library of Congress

10 9 8 7 6 5 4
07   06   05   04

Typeset by 35 in 9/12 pt Stone serif
Printed in Malaysia, PP

Contents

Preface

We wrote *Industrial Organisation* with a number of objectives in mind. First and foremost we have attempted to write a book which will appeal to second- and third-year undergraduates on economics, business and management related courses. We have assumed that readers have a reasonable knowledge of basic economic and statistical theory. An introduction to regression analysis is included as an appendix for those readers who have not studied the topic at a formal level. We also believe that the book will be of use to managers of businesses wishing to develop their understanding of strategic issues in the context of industrial organisation theory. The nature of the subject requires a balance to be struck between abstract theory, econometric analysis and an appreciation of real-world case study material. Different topics discussed in the book require a slightly different emphasis on these three ingredients. When we felt it necessary to stress abstract theory, as for example in the chapter on oligopoly, we did so. We have used many cases drawn from the pages of the *Financial Times*. These have helped to complement our text with vivid and entertaining descriptions of industrial market structures and patterns of firm and industry behaviour. We also felt that the book should provide a convenient springboard for readers wishing to pursue the subject at a higher level. We have therefore provided numerous journal, monograph and book references throughout the text, further reading at the end of each chapter, and an extensive bibliography. In contrast to the numerous US textbooks in the field of industrial organisation, the final objective was to write a book from a European perspective, focusing on European research and case studies. However, we have not ignored the importance of many of the seminal and sub-sequent US contributions to the field.

We would like thank to John Goddard, David Glenn, Bob Greenhill, Mark Wronski and three anonymous reviewers for useful comments and suggestions. Any remaining errors are of course the authors' responsibility.

We would also like to thank our wives Nicole and Alison for their patience, encouragement and support throughout the writing of this book. Finally, it remains for us to thank our mothers for being an important part of our lives.

John Lipczynski
John Wilson

Acknowledgements

We are grateful to the following for permission to reproduce copyright material:

Figure 2.15 from The Uses of Game Theory in *Management Science*, (Shubik, M., Cowles Foundation, 1975); Figures 3.7, 3.8 and 8.5, adapted from *Industrial Market Structures and Economic Performance, 3e*, Houghton Mifflin Company, (Scherer, F.M. and Ross, D. 1990); Table 4.7 from 'Census of Production PA1002 (1995)', National Statistics © Crown Copyright 2000; Case Study Table 5.1 adapted from *The Economics of 1992: The EC Commission's Assessment of The Economic effects of Completing the Single Market*, Oxford University Press, (Emerson, M. 1988); Table 6.1 from Industry Structure, Market Rivalry and Public Policy in *Journal of Law and Economics*, Table 2, p.6 (Demsetz, H. 1973); Tables 7.1 and 7.2 from *Advertising Statistics Yearbook*, (The Advertising Association, 1998); Case Study 7.4, Tables 1 and 2 from OFT Research Paper Number 11, Office of Fair Trading, 1997, pp.109–110; Table 8.1 from *Management and Innovation in High Technology Small Firms*, Continuum International Publishing Group Ltd., (Oakey, R., Rothwell, R., & Cooper, S. 1988); Tables 8.2, 8.3 and Figure 8.10 © European Communities, 1995–2000; Case Study 8.3 from *The Financial Times*, (Kay, J. 1999); Figure 9.9 reprinted from *Research Policy*, Vol 24, Robertson *et al.*, pp.543–563; Table 10.2 from Large firm diversification in British manufacturing industry in *Economic Journal*, Blackwell Publishers Ltd, adapted from Utton, M.A. 1977); Table 10.3 from *Industrial Organisation in the European Union*, (Rondi, L., Sembenelli, A. and Ragazzi, E. 1996) by permission of Oxford University Press.

We are grateful to the Financial Times Limited for permission to reprint the following material:

Case Study 2.1 from Strategic complements and substitutes (abridged), © *Financial Times*, 8 November, 1999: Case Study 2.2 from BskyB offer set to spark digital TV price war, ©

Financial Times, 6 May, 1999; Case Study 2.3 from The prisoner's dilemma in practice, ©
Financial Times, 18 October, 1999; Case Study 3.1 from Competition rankles Amsterdam
cab drivers, © *Financial Times,* 22 January, 2000; Case Study 3.2 from Brewers raided on
suspicion of French cartel, © *Financial Times,* 29 January, 2000; Case Study 3.3 from The
king of diamonds attempts to polish its rough edges, © *Financial Times,* 2 June, 2000; Case
Study 5.3 from Investing in communications companies, © *Financial Times,* 24 November,
1999; Case Study 5.4 from A blueprint for constructing defensive walls, © *Financial Times,*
30 May, 2000; Case Study 8.1 from Getting a grip on innovation, © *Financial Times,* 15
June, 2000; Case Study 8.2 from Strategy for creativity, © *Financial Times,* 11 November,
1999; Case Study 9.1 from Business and the law, © *Financial Times,* 24 June, 1997; Case
Study 9.2 from Vertical integration sets building material debate, © *Financial Times,*
17 December, 1999; Case Study 9.3 from UK retail group seeks review of PC pricing, ©
Financial Times, 10 April, 2000; Case Study 10.1 from Larger British and German companies
are using mergers and acquisitions to specialise and internationalist as the conglomerate
model loses its appeal, © *Financial Times,* 9 May, 2000; Case Study 10.2 from Life sciences
and pharmaceuticals, © *Financial Times,* 6 April, 2000; Case Study 10.3 from Mogul in a
slicker mould, © *Financial Times,* 22 May, 2000; Case Study 11.7 from Brussels launches
Microsoft probe, © *Financial Times,* 10 February, 2000; Case Study 12.1 from Welcome to
the ways of the market, © *Financial Times,* 12 November, 1999; Case Study 12.2 from
Pressure rises in least competitive utility, © *Financial Times,* 12 January, 2000; Case Study
12.3 from Current developments in rail franchising, © *Financial Times,* 20 January, 2000;
Case study 5.1 adapted from Emerson: *The Economics of 1992: The EC Commissions Assessment of the Economic Effects of Completing the Single Market* published by Oxford University
Press from a report entitled: *A Survey of the Economies of Scale,* prepared for the EC Commission, Brussels, by C. Pratten (1987).

Whilst every effort has been made to trace the owners of copyright material, in a few cases
this has proved impossible and we take this opportunity to offer our apologies to any copyright holders whose rights we may have unwittingly infringed.

Dedicated to our wives, Alison and Nicole

CHAPTER *1*

Industrial organisation: an introduction

Learning objectives

After reading this chapter the student should be able to:

- Define the concept of competition

- Explain the difference between static and dynamic views of competition

- Explain and analyse the Structure–Conduct–Performance paradigm

- Analyse the Chicago school approach to the study of competition

- Discuss the role of transactions costs in the modern economy

1.1 Introduction

This book provides an overview of the economics of industrial organisation. It will cover many of the main topics in industrial organisation such as oligopoly, concentration, barriers to entry, innovation and technical change, product differentiation, vertical integration, diversification, competition policy and regulation. The aim is to provide an overview of industrial organisation for the specialist and non-specialist student. We have attempted to write in a concise manner and assumed only a general knowledge of microeconomics and quantitative methods.[1]

---

[1] The Appendix outlines the basics of regression analysis for those students with little or no knowledge of quantitative methods.

1

Given the scope of the subject area, we have included examples from the UK and other European countries, and augmented these with case study material where appropriate. Questions for discussion and references to guide the student to additional reading have been provided. In the subsequent sections of this chapter, we provide a brief discussion of competition analysis, introduce a framework for analysing firms and industries and outline how the rest of the book is organised.

1.2 Competition analysis

This section discusses the basic microeconomic theory that underpins competition analysis. It begins by providing an overview of the historical development of competition analysis. Vickers (1995) defined three general ideas underlying the analysis of competition, namely that it:

● leads firms to become more efficient;
● allows efficient firms to gain market share from others; and
● through innovation, it leads to increases in firms' productive efficiencies.

It is possible to trace the roots of industrial organisation back to basic microeconomic theory. There are four main theoretical industry structures outlined in microeconomic theory: **perfect competition**, **monopoly**, monopolistic competition and oligopoly.

The basic components of market structure include:

● The number and size distributions of firms.
● The type of product produced (homogeneous or differentiated).
● The extent of control over prices by established firms.
● The ease with which firms can enter or exit markets.
● The ease with which information flows between buyers and sellers.

Competition analysis began using a static framework first developed by Cournot (1838), who suggested that as the number of sellers in an industry rises so price falls until price equals marginal cost. Drawing on Cournot's exposition, Jevons (1871/1970), Edgeworth (1881/1932), Clark (1899) and Knight (1921) developed the model of perfect competition.[2]

A perfectly competitive industry has five main characteristics. These are:

● Many buyers and sellers. This means that the action of any individual buyer or seller has almost no influence on the market price.
● Producers and consumers have perfect knowledge. This is used to make rational choices between the goods and services on offer.
● The products sold by firms are identical. This means that consumers are indifferent between each producer's product.
● Firms act independently of each other and aim to maximise profits.
● Firms are free to enter or exit and to supply markets with the quantities they wish.

If these conditions are satisfied, a competitive equilibrium exists in which all firms earn a normal profit. Figures 1.1 and 1.2 show equilibrium under perfect competition in the short and long run, respectively. In the short run, firms can earn supernormal profits, defined as

---

[2] Stigler (1957) discusses the development of the theory of perfect competition.

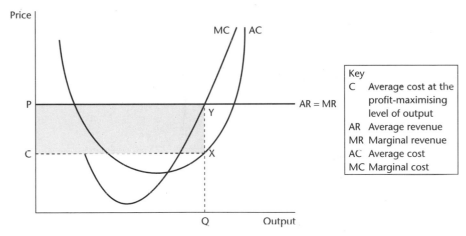

Figure 1.1 Short-run equilibrium under perfect competition. The shaded area PCXY is the total supernormal profits, equal to total revenue (PY) minus total cost (CX)

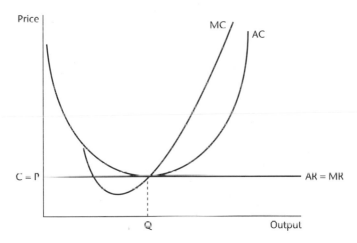

Figure 1.2 Long-run equilibrium under perfect competition

returns in excess of normal profits, which latter are the minimum amount of profit necessary to induce the firm to remain within the market it occupies. The shaded area (PCXY) in Figure 1.1 shows these supernormal profits. However, in the long run, new firms attracted by the supernormal profits enter the market and compete these profits away (C = P in Figure 1.2), so eventually all firms earn normal profits, where average revenues (AR) equal average costs (AC). If the firm is unable to earn normal profits then in the long run the firm exits the market.

The theory of perfect competition assumes that all firms are free to enter and exit markets, which ensures that large numbers of small firms make normal profits. In reality, competitive conditions often give rise to many industries consisting of a few large firms which may have considerable influence over the prices charged, enabling these firms to earn abnormal profits.

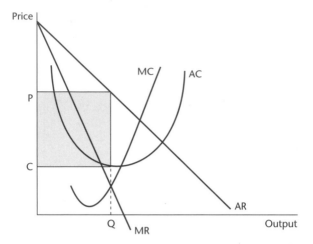

Figure 1.3 Equilibrium under monopoly

Marshall (1961/1890) and Sraffa (1926) amongst others formulated a theory of monopoly. They argued that as firms grow in size so they enjoy lower average costs through economies of scale, which ultimately lead to an industry structure consisting of a small number of large firms. In the extreme, the industry could become a monopoly in which a single firm can charge high prices and earn abnormal profits (shaded area in Figure 1.3).

Influenced by Marshall and Sraffa, Chamberlin (1933) and Robinson (1933) brought together the previously separate theories of monopoly and perfect competition, to formulate theories of oligopoly and monopolistic competition. Under the theory of monopolistic competition, markets contain elements of monopoly and competition. This theory emphasises non-price as well as price competition.[3]

Chamberlin also contributed to the theory of oligopoly. Under oligopoly, firms realise that their actions are interdependent (i.e. a change in output by one firm will alter the profits of rival firms and cause them to adjust their output). Competitive behaviour under oligopoly ranges from vigorous price competition, which can often lead to competing firms making substantial losses, to collusion. Firms can collude either tacitly (through a dominant firm or barometric price leadership) or explicitly through a formal cartel.[4]

Austrian school

In the twentieth century, many researchers turned away from the static view of competition and attempted to develop a more realistic dynamic view. One school of thought that is prominent in this respect is the **Austrian school**. A closely related view is that of Schumpeter who emphasised the dynamic process of competition but who has a different view of the entrepreneurial role in the competitive process. Both the Austrian school and Schumpeter believed that competition could not be analysed using the traditional approach.

[3] Chamberlin's work is covered in more detail when we examine advertising decisions in Chapter 7.
[4] Theories of competitive and collusive oligopoly are discussed in Chapters 2 and 3.

Abnormal profit was not evidence of potential market power (monopoly) but an important part of the competitive process guiding entrepreneurs to a resource allocation determined by consumer demand.

Schumpeter and the Austrian school both recognised that competition is a dynamic process and not a particular state. Their concern is with the roles of the entrepreneur and knowledge in a dynamic system.[5] Schumpeter (1950) saw the competitive process as being driven by non-price competition (i.e. innovation) and strategic decisions emanating from entrepreneurs. He adopted a broad definition of innovation, which encompassed not only the introduction of new products and processes, but also the conquest of new markets for supplies or products, and the reorganisation of some existing market structure (for example through entry or takeover). By initiating changes from within the economy by means of innovation, the entrepreneur is seen as the key to economic progress. The entrepreneur's actions propel industries from one equilibrium to another by means of innovation. This innovative activity leads to a revolution in existing economic conditions by destroying old production techniques and creating new ones. Entrepreneurs introducing innovations which create monopoly profits drive this process of 'creative destruction'. These monopoly profits encourage entrepreneurs in related industries to innovate as well. Recent examples of such a competitive process can be found in the information technology industry with developments in computer operating systems and communications systems, for example mobile telephones and digital television. The clusters of innovations have the effect of propelling the economy towards a higher state. However, following a brief 'catching up' period, imitators start to flood the market with similar innovations. This has the effect of undermining any monopoly profits, eventually bringing industries to a new period of relative tranquillity.

Abnormal profits are both the reward for past innovation and the incentive for future innovative activity. The source of any monopoly profits is the superior productivity achieved by entrepreneurial innovation. Any monopoly profits can therefore be thought of as a disequilibrium phenomenon. These profits do not persist because of imitation, and eventually dissipate before a new cluster of innovations appears and the process begins again. Therefore, there is no role for government intervention to ensure competitive outcomes (Mueller, 1986).

The Austrian school viewed competition as a dynamic process, and saw the market as consisting of an interaction of decisions made by consumers, entrepreneurs and resource owners (Kirzner, 1973). Entrepreneurs play a crucial role by noticing missed opportunities. They discover new pieces of information, which they spread to other decision-makers who can adjust their plans in order to improve on past performance. Kirzner (1997a) argued that market disequilibrium results from the general ignorance of buyers and sellers operating in a particular industry. Thus, potential buyers were unaware of potential sellers and vice versa, so scarce resources are often used to produce goods for which there is no market. However, the entrepreneur can step in and remedy the situation by helping to bring the two together by noticing these missed opportunities. This differed from the Schumpeterian view of the entrepreneur.

---

[5] Under the static conception of competition the entrepreneur is unimportant because in long-run equilibrium all buyers and sellers have perfectly anticipated all changes in supply and demand. The entrepreneur is not needed to co-ordinate activities and price is seen as the only form of rivalry.

Schumpeter saw the entrepreneur as a disequilibrating force that interrupts the circular flow of the economy via innovatory activity. Therefore, in a dynamic economy, Schumpeter's entrepreneur initiates change while Kirzner's entrepreneur merely responds to changes which arise for 'exogenous' reasons. The Austrian definition of competition is closer to its everyday usage in society (i.e. it conjures up a picture of individual firms battling against each other using entrepreneurial skills in an attempt to obtain larger profits). As we have seen above, in standard economic theory any firm which has market power and can obtain supernormal profits is regarded as monopolistic. However, according to the Austrian definition of competition, these firms are only engaging in competition. According to Austrian economists, a monopoly position can be won by originality and competitiveness through the foresight of the entrepreneur rather than by destroying competition by restrictive practices. However, this is not to say that monopoly profits necessarily persist for long periods. When other firms notice that the entrepreneur is earning monopoly profits they are likely to imitate by switching from the old products to the new ones. This increase in output reduces the entrepreneur's price. Therefore, the competitive process ensures that no one firm can make monopoly profits in the long run by the existence of imitative forces.

1.3 Approaches to industrial organisation

The static and dynamic theories discussed above have found an empirical counterpart in the field that has become known as industrial organisation. Early work in this area concentrated on empirical rather than theoretical studies (Bain, 1951). Later work focused on competitive behaviour, using theoretical models which utilised the tools of **game theory** (Tirole, 1988).[6] However, in the 1980s there was an increased interest in empirical research (Bresnahan and Schmalensee, 1987). In the main, the field of industrial organisation analyses empirical data and, by a process of induction, develops theories to explain the real-world behaviour of firms and industries (Schmalensee, 1988).

The seminal writers in the field of industrial organisation were Mason (1939, 1949) and Bain (1951, 1956, 1959), who developed the **Structure–Conduct–Performance** (SCP) model. This model analysed competitive conditions in industries by examining how the structure of industry related to the behaviour and performance of firms.

The approach was considered useful for analysing industries in several respects and forms the foundation of the analysis of industries. Stigler (1968, p.1) argued that the field of industrial organisation is interested in investigating 'the size structure of firms (one or many, "concentrated" or not), the causes (above all the economies of scale) of this size structure, the effects of concentration on competition, the effects of competition on prices, investment, innovation and so on.'

At its most basic, the SCP approach is useful in several ways:

- It allows the researcher to reduce all industry data into meaningful sections (Bain, 1956).
- On the basis of microeconomic theory there should be a relationship between structure, conduct and performance. As a consequence, conduct and performance are likely to be determined by structure (Caves, 1980).

---

[6] Game theory and its applications to the study of decision making in oligopolistic industries industries are examined in Chapter 2. Fudenberg and Tirole (1989) provide an extensive review of the applications of game theory to oligopolistic industries.

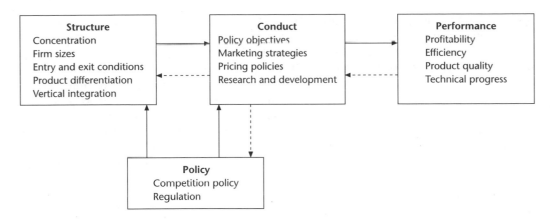

Figure 1.4 The Structure–Conduct–Performance paradigm

- On the basis of 'workable' or 'acceptable' performance we may accept an 'imperfect' market structure (Clark, 1940). By implication we can alter structure to improve conduct and performance (Sosnick, 1958). This is an issue for government regulation.[7]

A schematic representation of the SCP approach is presented in Figure 1.4.

The conditions of supply and demand in any given industry will characterise the structure of that industry. Supply conditions include the availability and cost of raw materials, the prevailing state of technology and the price elasticity of supply. Demand conditions include industry size, methods of procurement and elasticities of demand. These conditions will have a direct effect on industry structure. Let us now examine the factors that constitute the division of industry data into structural, conduct and performance variables. The basic supply and demand conditions of an industry will determine the structure, which in turn has fundamental effects on the conduct and performance of firms within any given industry.

Structure

Structural characteristics often change slowly and can be regarded as fixed over time. Government policies can alter significantly various structures to improve performance. We can identify the following as some of the more important structural variables:

- *Concentration.* This refers to the amount of market power held in the hands of a few firms. This is normally measured by the share of total industry sales, assets or employment controlled by the largest firms in the industry.[8]
- *Product differentiation.* This refers to the nature of the product. To what extent is the product identical to those produced by other firms? To what extent is it unique? If

---

[7] We discuss government regulation of private and publicly owned monopolies in Chapters 11 and 12.
[8] There are many measures of industrial concentration; they are explored in Chapter 4.

there is no product differentiation, then perfect competition will prevail; if the product is unique, monopoly prevails. Any change in the nature of the product, whether real or imagined, will alter the demand conditions facing the firm.[9]

● *Size of firm.* Firm size plays an important role in defining the structural characteristics of an industry. The larger the firm, the more likely it will be able to exploit technical efficiencies. Equally, large firms are much more likely to exercise market power advantages.[10]

● *Entry conditions.* According to Bain (1951), an entry barrier was anything that placed a potential entrant at a competitive disadvantage when compared with the established firm. The important issue is the relative ease or difficulty that firms may experience when entering an industry. If entry is difficult, then established firms are sheltered from outside competition and are likely to be able to raise prices to make abnormal profits (Neven, 1989).[11]

● *Vertical integration and diversification.* The extent to which firms are involved in many stages of the production process (vertical integration) or in producing different types of goods and services (diversification) will also have implications for the conduct and performance of firms and industries. Vertically integrated firms will have greater certainty in obtaining supplies of raw materials, and are more likely to have guaranteed distribution outlets for their manufactured products. Diversified firms are less exposed to risk than their non-diversified counterparts, as losses made in one market can be recouped by profits in another.[12]

Conduct

Conduct refers to the behaviour of firms under a given set of circumstances and is normally determined by the structural characteristics of industry. Several issues are important here:

● *Policy objectives.* The objectives which firms follow often flow from the inherent structural characteristics of an industry. Objectives may include the pursuit of profit, growth or sales maximisation or the utilisation of managerial discretion to pursue non-financial objectives. The overall business objective of a given firm is likely to determine how the firm behaves when formulating price and non-price strategies.

● *Pricing objectives.* The extent to which firms follow a given price strategy may also flow from industry structure. Under perfect competition, firms price products at competitive levels (i.e. where prices equal marginal costs), while under monopoly, prices exceed marginal costs. Possible pricing strategies which firms may follow include cost-plus, marginal cost, entry-deterring price, collusive pricing, price leadership and price discrimination.

● *Marketing strategies.* Such strategies may include product differentiation of various types. Although included under the structural heading above, firms may also wish to actively pursue strategies of vertical integration and diversification.[13]

---

[9] This is discussed further in Chapter 7.

[10] The implications of differing size distributions of firms for the evolution of an industry are discussed in Chapter 4.

[11] The role of entry barriers in deterring actual and potential competition is explored in Chapter 5.

[12] Vertical integration and diversification are discussed in Chapters 9 and 10.

[13] These issues are covered in Chapters 7, 9 and 10.

● *Research and development.* Drawing on the work of the Austrian school, many researchers have argued that research and development leading to technical advances through the introduction of new products and processes drives the evolution of industries from one state to another. Firms may undertake basic applied research and development work in order to produce innovative commercial products and processes which will give them advantages over rivals. The diffusion of these new products and processes will ultimately determine the performance of industries and economies. The size of firms and industry structure will determine the importance of research and development as a strategic variable.[14]

Performance

When trying to gauge performance, economists focus on profitability, efficiency, product quality and technical progress. Traditional analysis assumes that high profits are the result of established firms pursuing anti-competitive practices aimed at distorting or eliminating competition. However, some evidence suggests that high profits are the consequence of efficiency differences across firms, while others contend that high profits are the returns appropriated from innovatory behaviour. We examine in Chapter 6 how economists have measured profits, and whether high profits are the result of superior efficiency or established firms pursuing anti-competitive practices.

Overall, the SCP approach attempts to explain and predict the performance of an industry as a consequence of market structure. The emphasis is therefore on the structure of industry and how it influences conduct and performance. This is shown by the solid arrows in Figure 1.4. The approach assumes that the smaller the number of firms in an industry, the greater the likelihood of the abuse of market power and the greater the profitability of these established firms. However, it is possible that conduct and performance can have feedback effects on the structure of an industry. Phillips (1976) pointed out the severe limitations of performance flowing from structure. He makes a strong case that performance itself can lead back to changes in conduct and structure. Clarke (1985) gave the example of expenditures on research and development affecting costs and demand, which may affect structure in the long run.

The dashed arrows in Figure 1.4 show feedback effects of performance and firm behaviour on industry structure. This finding to some extent led to a shift away from the presumption that structure was the most important variable in driving the competitive process. Instead, many researchers argued that the strategies (conduct) of individual firms were important in determining industry structure and thus the SCP process (Scherer and Ross, 1990). This type of research was subsumed under the general heading of the 'new industrial organisation'.[15] Under this approach, firms were not seen as passive entities alike in all respects bar size. Instead they were seen as active entities that often followed different strategies. Researchers adopted dynamic approaches to modelling the competitive process using game theoretic analysis. In these games, firms could choose from a plethora of strategies over finite and infinite time periods. Although many authors argued that game theory strengthened the theoretical framework upon which industrial organisation is based (for example, Tirole, 1988), others were extremely critical of the approach. Schmalensee (1990, p.140) noted

[14] We examine innovation in Chapter 8.
[15] Schmalensee (1982) provides a detailed discussion of the new industrial organisation.

that when utilising game theory for competition analysis, 'Anything can happen!' He goes further (pp.141, 6) and argued that:

> Game theory has proven better at generating internally consistent scenarios than at providing plausible and testable restrictions on real behaviour . . . Until game-theoretic analysis begins to yield robust, unambiguous predictions or is replaced by a mode of theorizing that does so, any major substantive advances in industrial organization are likely to come from empirical research.

Most early research that applied the SCP approach focused on the extent to which markets become concentrated, and how this affects performance. Therefore, a positive correlation between concentration and profits is caused by firms acting in a collusive manner to achieve high profits. Later research contended that high profits were achieved through economies of scale and other advantages held by large firms. This particular issue is explored in Chapter 6.

In cases where an industry is composed of a few large firms, it is argued that competition is likely to be stifled. This may lead to a fall in product quality, lack of choice and an increase in prices charged. As a consequence, policy-makers have been interested in pursuing policies aimed at promoting competition. In the UK, as in most developed countries, governments have attempted to promote competition by pursuing policies and passing legislation aimed at altering the structure of industries and the behaviour of firms in these industries (shown by solid arrows in Figure 1.4). Strict regulation of prices and rates of returns often accompany this type of policy for firms operating in industries that can be regarded as natural monopolies. It is possible, however, that large firms can use their influence to alter government policy towards industry (shown by dashed arrows in the figure). We examine competition policy and regulation in Chapters 11 and 12.

There are several qualifications to the view that competition policy and regulation are required to ensure that competition prevails and that firms are unable to weld market power.

Chicago school

The **Chicago school** approach in common with the Austrian school is generally against government intervention in the marketplace to promote competitive outcomes (Reder, 1982). Their approach is that the best thing government can do is to allow market forces to take place to bring about desirable performance outcomes (Posner, 1979). For example, there is no point in having laws against collusive agreements as these agreements are inherently unstable. This means that industries will tend towards competition.

Contestable markets

Another qualification to the SCP approach has been proposed by Baumol *et al.* (1982) with the **contestable markets** approach. A contestable market is one where the threat of entry exists, i.e. potential rivalry. A perfectly contestable market is one where there are very low entry barriers and entry or exit is costless. Thus a contestable market does not have to be made up of a large number of firms to generate competition, as is the case in the standard model of perfect competition. We examine the importance of contestable markets in Chapter 5.

Transaction cost analysis

In this text, the main focus is on how firms behave within the industry setting. We tend to view firms as units, which use factors of production to produce goods and services. One school of thought takes a different approach and asks why firms exist. Under this approach there are two ways within which resources can be allocated, namely through exchange in the market or co-ordinated through the firm. This approach to assessing resource allocation has become known as **transaction cost analysis.** Transaction cost analysis examines the efficiency of trade when resources are allocated either through the market or the firm. Under this type of approach, information is assumed to be imperfect. In other words, trade does not take place in a world of certainty. As a consequence, economic agents cannot behave in a fully rational manner because they do not have access to all available information, and they find it difficult to process all pieces of information that are available. In other words, there are bounds on rational behaviour (bounded rationality). Given that information is often one-sided, opportunities are available for individuals to act in an opportunistic manner.[16] They can do this by failing to disclose facts that would make the transaction more efficient. The seminal work in this area is attributed to Coase (1937). Coase argued that there are costs of using the market to conduct transactions and allocate resources. These costs are known as transaction costs. These costs include the time spent collecting information about the prices and qualities or products and services under offer, drawing up detailed proposals and contracts for transactions, and ultimately enforcing the contract in a court of law if need be. These ideas have been subsequently developed in a series of articles and books (Williamson, 1971, 1975, 1979, 1985). When transaction costs are high, Williamson argues that it is more efficient to bring the transaction/activity within the bounds of a firm. Firms are likely to be a more efficient medium of trade when the transaction is complex, carried out frequently and involves the utilisation of a specific asset. By bringing these types of transaction within the firm, savings can be made through specialisation in production leading to technical and learning economies of scale and scope. However, many of the savings achieved by conducting trade using the firm rather than markets are offset by monitoring costs specific to the firm. In other words, firms have to monitor the behaviour and performance of employees and ensure that the quality of goods and services produced is to a given specification. We do not provide a detailed treatment of transaction costs analysis in this chapter. However, we utilise the approach to explain why firms adopt collusive agreements and vertically integrated organisational structure in Chapters 3 and 10, respectively.

1.4 Structure of the book

The remainder of the book is structured as follows. Chapter 2 deals with theories of oligopolistic behaviour. The chapter examines the behaviour of firms in oligopoly under conditions of competition by utilising well established tools of analysis such as the kinked demand curve and game theory. Chapter 3 examines the factors which lead firms to collude explicitly. Chapters 4 and 5 deal primarily with structural aspects of industry. In Chapter 4, we examine the topic of industry concentration, where we look at the various ways in which researchers have attempted to measure concentration. The chapter also examines how industries evolve into concentrated market structures. In Chapter 5 we discuss barriers to entry. The chapter deals with how researchers have identified and quantified barriers to entry, and the implications of such barriers for the performance of new and established firms. Chapter 6 discusses the empirical work that has aimed to test the Structure–Conduct–Performance paradigm and related hypotheses. The chapter provides an overview of selected

---

[16] The implications of imperfect information for the prices and quality of goods and services traded are examined in Chapter 7.

literature and discusses the models estimated and the results obtained along with some of the debates arising from the empirical findings reviewed. Chapter 6 can be excluded to some extent while retaining continuity of discussion.

Chapters 7 to 10 examine many of the conduct variables outlined in Figure 1.4. In Chapter 7, the economics of advertising are examined. The chapter discusses the various ways in which product differentiation can occur, and examines the controversy surrounding whether advertising can be regarded as informative or persuasive. The chapter also examines the advertising and the competitive environment by examining the relationships between advertising, and profitability and concentration. Chapter 8 discusses innovation, focusing on the stages of the research and development process. The chapter also examines the relationship between market structure and the incentive to innovate. Various factors relating to marketing, production, finance and time are thought to affect the firm's decision to innovate, and are highlighted. In Chapters 9 and 10 we examine the motives for vertical integration and diversification, respectively, and the implications for the competitive process of firms engaging in such activities.

Chapter 11 examines the rationale for competition policy. We examine the main legislative measures which have been passed in the United States, UK and the European Union to promote competition in industries where privately owned firms operate, and assess the effectiveness of such policies. Chapter 12 examines regulation of natural monopolies. The chapter examines how control of natural monopolies can take place through public ownership, privatisation accompanied by deregulation and reregulation, and franchising and competitive tendering.

Key terms

Austrian school
Chicago school
Contestable market
Game theory
Monopoly

Perfect competition
Structure–Conduct–Performance paradigm
Transaction cost analysis
Workable competition

Questions for discussion

1. Why is the Structure–Conduct–Performance paradigm so widely used in the study of firms and industries?
2. List the factors that describe market structure.
3. Give examples of how market structure affects conduct.
4. Outline briefly the Phillips argument as regards the SCP approach.
5. Discuss the Chicago approach to the study of industry.
6. Assess the contribution of transaction cost analysis to the understanding of firms.
7. Compare the traditional approach to competition analysis with that advocated by the Austrian school.

Further reading

Bresnahan, T.F. and Schmalensee, R.C. (1987) The empirical renaissance in industrial economics: an overview, *Journal of Industrial Economics*, **35**, 371–8.

Caves, R.E. (1980) Corporate strategy and structure, *Journal of Economic Literature*, **28**, 64–92.

Fudenberg, D. and Tirole, J. (1989) Noncooperative game theory for industrial organization: an introduction and overview, in Schmalensee, R.C. and Willig, R. (eds) *Handbook of Industrial Organization*. Amsterdam: North-Holland.

Kirzner, I. (1997) Entrepreneurial discovery and the competitive market process: an Austrian approach, *Journal of Economic Literature*, **35**, 60–85.

Posner, R. (1979) The Chicago school of anti-trust analysis, *University of Pennsylvania Law Review*, **127**, 925–48.

Reder, M.W. (1982) Chicago economics: permanence and change, *Journal of Economic Literature*, **20**, 1–38.

Scherer, F.M. and Ross, D. (1990) *Industrial Market Structure and Economic Performance*, 3rd edn. Boston: Houghton Mifflin, chapter 1.

Schmalensee, R.C. (1988) Industrial economics: an overview, *Economic Journal*, 643–81.

Schmalensee, R.C. (1990) Empirical studies of rivalrous behaviour, in Bonanno, G. and Brandolini, D. (eds) *Industrial Structure in the New Industrial Economics*. Oxford: Clarendon Press.

Vickers, J. (1995) Concepts of competition, *Oxford Economic Papers*, **47**, 1–23.

Williamson, O.E. (1981) The modern corporation: origins, evolution and attributes, *Journal of Economic Literature*, **19**, 1537–68.

CHAPTER 2

Oligopoly

Learning objectives

After reading this chapter the student should be able to:

● Appreciate the various forms of oligopolistic behaviour

● Understand the construction of reaction functions and appreciate how they help to explain oligopolistic equilibria

● Evaluate the contribution of various models which attempt to explain oligopolistic interdependence

● Appreciate the contribution game theory has made to the study of oligopoly

2.1 Introduction

At the beginning of the twentieth century, standard classical microeconomic analysis had traditionally focused on an analysis of the models of perfect competition and pure monopoly in its attempt to cover the behaviour of producers in a typical market economy. While no one pretended that what was being presented was a copy of real business behaviour, it was felt that the two extremes sufficiently defined a spectrum on which reality could be comfortably located. It almost seemed that what was being argued was that defining the colour white and the colour black will somehow determine other colours such as yellow and purple. It soon became apparent that these two models were unable to explain such business conduct as product differentiation, advertising, price wars, parallel pricing, and tacit and explicit collusion, which increasingly characterised modern firms and industries.[1] What was needed was an additional theory to deal with this vast area of industry structure covering the ground between perfect competition and monopoly. This middle ground, which can be referred to as imperfect competition, can be divided into two: monopolistic competition, occupying the analytical space just after perfect competition, and oligopoly, taking up the remaining large portion of the spectrum.

The basis of all oligopoly theory must rest on the acceptance of the importance of two structural characteristics, namely the number of firms in the industry and the nature of the product. In essence the two are related. An industry is defined according to the nature of the product it supplies. Thus firms producing highly differentiated products may lack self-identification with a particular industry, whereas, the more homogeneous the output, the greater the awareness of 'others' in the industry. Oligopolistic markets are defined on the basis of the recognition that a 'few' sellers account for a substantial proportion of total sales. Thus the relative fewness of firms is the chief identifying characteristic of such markets. In fact the word is derived from the Greek *oligoi* meaning 'a few' and *poleo* 'to sell'.[2]

As a result of the fewness of firms within a clearly defined industry, i.e. where output is fairly homogeneous, the central problem of oligopoly will focus on the recognition of mutual interdependence. Asch (1964, p.54) summed it up as:

> 'I' (an oligopolist) cannot define my best policies unless I know what 'You' (my rival) are going to do; by the same token, however, you cannot define your best move unless you know what I will do.

It is this 'circular dependence' that provides the real challenge for oligopoly analysis. In the oligopoly context, optimal behaviour will depend on assumptions of rivals' likely reactions, and even assumptions about rivals' assumptions. Interdependence means that a firm is aware that its actions affect the actions of its rivals and vice versa. Oligopolists are 'outward turning'. They cannot confine themselves to their own internal cost structures. They must concern themselves with every action and future action of their rivals. Profit maximisation and survival in an oligopoly depends on how a firm reacts to the strategies of its rivals.

The central characteristic of oligopoly, that of two or more rivals' recognition of mutual dependence, gives rise to a potential bargaining situation. This situation may be expressed in explicit negotiations or clouded in tacit behaviour, where individual firms 'reveal' their offers, reactions and counter-offers through various recognised moves in the market. If bargaining does exist in some form, then one can expect some agreement on the co-ordination of activity as a likely outcome. The directions that oligopolistic markets may take are analysed below.

---

[1] See, for example, Joan Robinson's arguments in the preface to the second edition of her *Economics of Imperfect Competition*, Robinson (1969).

[2] Chamberlin (1957) describes how the word came into use. He claims to have been the originator in 1929, naming one of his articles 'Duopoly and oligopoly'. Unfortunately the editor of the *Quarterly Journal of Economics* (F.W. Taussig) thought the word was monstrous and crossed it out. The amended article was 'Duopoly and value where sellers are few'. When Chamberlin published his book *Monopolistic Competition* in 1933 he included his original word. Chamberlin noted that the word did appear in Thomas More's *Utopia*: 'quod si maxime increscat ovium numerus, precio nihil decrescit tamen; quod earum, si monopolium appellari non potest, quod non unus uendit, certe oligopolium est' (Chamberlin, 1957, p.213) ['But if the number of sheep increases greatly, the price does not fall, because, even though it cannot be called a monopoly, since there is not just one person selling, we have an oligopoly'].

Some oligopoly typologies

It is often implied that the solution to the oligopoly problem is one of two extremes: either pure independent action or pure collusion in which independent action has been extinguished. This popular approach is at variance with reality. Both independent action and collusive behaviour are a matter of degree, and while examples may be found that conform to the polar cases, the great majority of outcomes fall somewhere within these extremes. Thus the typical oligopoly solution will contain elements of both independence and collusion. For the purpose of developing and identifying various stages along the spectrum of oligopolistic behaviour, it will be useful firstly, to define the limits as clearly as possible. Secondly, we shall trace the various forms of behaviour that tend towards 'independent' courses of action. 'Collusive' activity, in its various guises, is examined in Chapter 3.

Pure independent action implies that a firm reaches a unilateral decision on a course of action with no prior contact with its rivals. Since this definition alone could still result in collusion-type behaviour (if the firm were to revise its decisions in the light of rivals' reactions), the definition is somewhat incomplete. We must add that we expect the firm to assume that its rivals will not react. What this implies is that pure independent action can only exist in either a state of unnatural ignorance or in an atomistic market structure, where the actions of one firm are too insignificant to have any effect on rivals.

Collusion exists where an agreement or an undertaking is reached regarding the level of output and/or price. Bain (1959, p.272) defined collusion in its purest form as consisting of the following features: all sellers in the industry would be covered by the agreement; the agreement is specific and enforceable; the agreement clearly states the price to be charged and outputs to be allocated to each member so as to minimise total industry costs; the existence of a formula as to the distribution of benefit to the members of the agreement, and all members rigidly adhere to the terms of the agreement. What Bain had in fact suggested is a prescription for a successful cartel. Thus we have a model similar to that of a single monopolist, where all independent action, including the striving for individual benefit, has been checked. Let us now turn to an analysis of the type of behaviour that might, in practice, be considered as independent action.

Independent action in oligopoly

We will try to analyse the possible actions of interdependent sellers who do not resort to any recognised agreement, whether written or spoken. This type of behaviour has attracted many diverse labels and no satisfactory terminology exists. Thus the terms 'imperfect collusion', 'unorganised oligopoly' and 'interdependent conduct with no agreement' have been used by economists to discuss similar sets of observations. Differences between terminologies do exist, but there is sufficient overlap to regard the terms as synonymous.

The starting point must inevitably be that type of behaviour which is characterised by truly independent action. True independent action can be defined simply as a state of affairs where collusion or co-ordination is absent. The result will be competitive activity in varying degrees of severity. Machlup (1952a, pp.504–11) describes four types of conduct that he terms as 'uncoordinated oligopoly'. The first is referred to as a 'fighting oligopoly'. Some reasons why oligopolies may slide into economic warfare are the existence of surplus stocks and limited storage facilities which lead to near-ruinous price wars (seen in the global petroleum industry in the mid-1980s). On the whole, economists have tended to restrict themselves to analyses of rational behaviour, termed 'vigorous' price competition, and ignore other, more extreme forms of conduct. Firms that wish to hurt others, firms that harbour resentments or firms that enjoy a 'scrap' are difficult to accommodate within the standard methodology. Machlup believes that there are sufficient constellations within oligopolistic structures to determine such behaviour.

The second model is termed the 'hyper-competitive oligopoly'. The structural characteristic would be of a considerable number of firms selling a fairly homogeneous product in an imperfect market. Imperfection is due to lack of precise knowledge as to future prices, sales, changes in quality, and so on. Decisions are thus taken on the basis of rumours. Although conscious of rivals, the typical seller is not inhibited by their presence as it strives for a greater market share, believing rival firms to be as aggressive as itself. This belief is confirmed by the firm's observations that buyers are quick to play one seller against another. It is a structure that accepts entrants and where individuality and non-conformity preclude co-operation. Although this model approaches perfect competition, the presence of interdependence sharpens the potential gains and losses. Business might regard this type of market as 'demoralised, unhealthy and chaotic' (Machlup 1952a, p.508).

Thirdly, Machlup suggested a 'chain oligopoly'. Some firms in a relatively competitive industry will, by nature of small qualitative differences, find themselves in smaller subsets. Where these subsets are linked to one another, interdependence will result. Thus, for example, M is an oligopolist as regards L and N, while L is an oligopolist as regards K and M, and so on. Every firm is thus, to some extent, within an oligopolistic subgroup. With increases in the number of firms in the industry, oligopolistic pressures will tend to ease. One could argue that within large numbers of sellers, all characterised by roughly the same production function, any small oligopolistic subgroups could exploit their position with collusive action. However, should they attempt this strategy they would soon be swamped by potential entrants. Thus the unconcentrated nature of the industry guarantees relative competitive behaviour.

Lastly, Machlup suggested the 'guessing-game oligopoly', which refers to a small group of firms that would normally result in some form of collusion were it not for a few stubborn characters who refuse to 'play ball'. This will result in firms having to guess the likely reactions of rivals. In reality these guesses will not be too difficult as a tendency to play safe develops, which lessens the degree of uncertainty and the amount of guesswork undertaken.

The analysis in this section encounters one obvious contradiction: that once sellers recognise interdependence, no true independent action can occur. Each seller will take into account the likely reaction of rivals. The effect will be that the amplitude of price and output changes will be dampened by the constraint of potential rivalrous reaction. In essence one would expect more co-ordinated or parallel behaviour the more interdependent and uncertain the industry.

Methods to reduce the degree of uncertainty often involve movements towards various forms of collusion. Some economists (Machlup 1952a, p.439) thus see all oligopoly behaviour as collusive to some extent. The unfortunate conclusion of such a view is that it would become impossible to discuss any effect of such behaviour if there were no non-collusive point of comparison.[3]

---

[3] See, for example, Asch and Seneca (1976), p.2.

However, Bain (1959, p.208) has described possible scenarios in which interdependent sellers can still act independently. The first of these he referred to as 'implicit bargaining', whereby every announced price and output change is implicitly an offer or invitation to one's rivals to act in an 'acceptable' way. If such acceptable behaviour results, we have a weak form of tacit collusion. It is not tacit collusion in the generally understood sense, since no regular routine action or uniformity of behaviour is detected. Secondly, on the basis of a game theory approach, Bain suggests that there are many possible outcomes that do not fall into the pure collusion or pure independence definition, one of which would inevitably satisfy the above criteria. This conclusion, though logically correct, seems weak in that it does not provide any precise explanation of how such a state of affairs may have come about or indeed why it should persist. It simply states the obvious conclusion that between the two extremes we would find many in-between models of behaviour.

Finally, Bain outlines the case where interdependent firms will exchange market information on, for example, prices, sales, future plans. On the basis of this 'open competition', firms will act independently when fixing their output and price. Again, the explanation is weak in that no obvious distinction is made between what is and is not independent action. Does a firm truly act independently if it has to rely on information from its rivals before it can decide on the most appropriate strategy?

Another frequently observed and well documented phenomenon in oligopolistic markets is price leadership, whereby one firm announces a price change and soon all other firms in the industry follow suit. There are various types of price leadership; some fall within our category of independent action and others do not. These are covered later in the chapter.

Interdependence

The structure of this chapter will reflect the development of oligopoly theory as it has grappled with the central issue of **interdependence**. In non-collusive oligopoly, firms must make some guesses or conjectures as to the likely actions of rivals. (Though even in collusive oligopolies firms may still be uncertain as to the action of fellow colluders and they may also be forced to make such guesses.) Thus each firm must determine its price or output on the basis of its rivals' reactions to such strategies. The term used to describe this is 'conjectural variation', which reflects the output or price adjustments a firm will make following real or expected changes made by its rivals. We begin our analysis in section 2.2 by examining early classical models of duopoly and oligopoly that simply 'assumed away' the problem of interdependence. Such a state of affairs would be described as a 'zero conjectural variation'. While this would appear to be highly improbable and unrealistic, a modern approach might be to suggest, tentatively, that interdependence is relatively weak in the area of non-price competition, such as product quality and advertising. Decisions on changes in advertising strategies take time to develop, to analyse and to put into operation. There is evidence that American business people have an unwritten code that, within their industries, non-price competition is seen as 'cricket' and price competition as 'not playing the game' (Shonfield 1965, p.336). Hence interdependent action in oligopolistic markets would only be identified in the area of pricing policy. Haskel and Scaramozzino (1997) have suggested that conjectural variations depend largely on the *ability* of firms to respond, which in turn will depend on factors such as physical capacity and profitability.

As the chapter progresses we will examine models that begin to recognise the importance of interdependence. One such theory was developed by Chamberlin (1933, pp.46–51) who outlined an approach where, 'mutual dependence was recognised'. Although some very broad theorising ensued, the process was valuable in the sense that it asked the right questions concerning short- and long-run problems, time-lags, imperfect knowledge, irrational conduct, and so on. Another example of an attempt to introduce a greater degree of reality into oligopoly theory was Sweezy's (1939) kinked demand curve hypothesis. Although challenged on empirical grounds, the model was built on the core assumption that firms' behaviour was determined by expectations as to what actions rivals would take. In this respect it did provide a major contribution to the development of more realistic and pertinent oligopoly theories. The final part of the chapter focuses on game theory. Game theory is the study of decision-making in conflict situations and is thus potentially well suited to determine oligopolistic outcomes. Theoretically it is the strongest of all the models when we consider the issues of interdependence.

What is apparent from this brief introduction is that oligopolistic markets can generate a multitude of scenarios and an equal multitude of possible outcomes. It seems that almost anything can happen in an oligopoly context, from outright collusion to bitter price wars. As a result some economists (for example, Rothschild, 1947) have suggested that oligopoly theory is indeterminate. The consensus however is still largely in favour of developing better theory and better models. Scherer (1980, p.152) made the following case for the study of oligopoly theory:

> But it would be misleading to conclude that we cannot develop theories which predict oligopolistic conduct and performance with tolerable precision. A more constructive interpretation is this: to make workable predictions we need a theory much richer than the received theories of pure competition and pure monopoly, including variables irrelevant to those polar cases. In our quest for a realistic oligopoly theory we must acquire Professor Mason's 'ticket of admission to institutional economics', at the same time retaining the more sharply honed tools with which economic theorists have traditionally worked.

2.2 Classical models

Augustin Cournot (1838)

Although Cournot's approach to the determination of the oligopoly problem is simplistic and hardly covers the rich spectrum of behaviour found in such market structures, this model was the first successful attempt to describe an oligopoly equilibrium.

At its most simple the model assumed a two-firm duopoly operating at zero marginal cost. Cournot suggested a market made up of two proprietors, A and B, both selling mineral spring waters. To ensure that both 'firms' operated at zero marginal cost, we assume that they are situated side by side and that customers arrive at the spring with their own glasses. Thus we have the following analysis as illustrated by Figure 2.1.

Assume that firm A is the first to open up for business. At a zero price the total market demand (Q) is OQ. A fixes output and price where marginal revenue (MR) is zero since marginal cost (MC) is zero. Output is OQ_1 (half of OQ)[4] and price is OP_1. Total revenue (TR) is also maximised since at price P_1, price elasticity of demand (η) equals unity:

---

[4] OQ_1 is exactly $1/2 OQ$, since if we assume the demand curve to be linear, then $AR(P) = a - bQ$; $TR = P \times Q = aQ - bQ^2$ and $MR = dTR/dQ = a - 2b$, thus the MR curve falls twice as steeply as the AR curve and therefore intersects the quantity axis at exactly the mid-point.

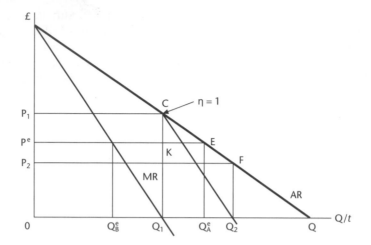

Figure 2.1 The Cournot duopoly

$$TR = \pi_{max}$$

$$= OP_1 \times OQ_1$$

In this situation, A is acting as a monopolist.

Let us now assume that B enters the market. B sees that A is supplying OQ_1 of the total market. Thus B can try to meet some of the unfulfilled demand Q_1Q. B now has to decide how A will *react* to its entry into the market. Cournot assumed a zero **conjectural variation**. B believes that A will continue to sell its existing quantity of OQ_1 and will not change this as a result of B's entry.

Thus as B enters he expects that A will keep selling OQ_1 glasses of mineral water. CQ is the demand curve that B faces. To maximise profit, B sells Q_1Q_2 (which again is *half* of Q_1Q) at price OP_2. B's profit is Q_1Q_2FK, and A's profit falls to OQ_1KP_2. A in turn now expects B always to sell Q_1Q_2, and since $Q_1Q_2 = Q_2Q$ the total market facing A is now OQ_2. Again, assuming a linear demand function, A will sell $\frac{1}{2}OQ_2$, thus reducing output and causing the price to rise. After this B will also readjust, as more of the market opens up, i.e. $OQ - \frac{1}{2}OQ_2$. B thus increases output to $\frac{1}{2}(OQ - \frac{1}{2}OQ_2)$ and the price falls, a little. Again A reacts in the belief that B will maintain output at $\frac{1}{2}(OQ - \frac{1}{2}OQ_2)$ and reduces sales; and so on. A is gradually reducing output while B is increasing output. The eventual solution is that each sells one-third of the total output, i.e. Q_A^e and Q_B^e at the market price OP^e. Under perfect competition where $P = MC$, output would be OQ. Under monopoly, OQ_1 ($\frac{1}{2}OQ$) is sold and profit is OQ_1CP_1, while with a duopoly, output is OQ_A^e ($\frac{2}{3}OQ$) and profit is $OQ_A^eEP^e$.

Let us explain why each firm produces one-third of the total output. We have assumed a linear demand curve $Q = a - bP$, and that firm A sells Q_A and firm B sells Q_B. Total output, Q, is thus $Q_A + Q_B$. Market demand is therefore:

$$Q_A + Q_B = a - bP \qquad (a > 0 \text{ and } b > 0)$$

$$P = \frac{a}{b} - \frac{Q_A}{b} - \frac{Q_B}{b}$$

Total revenue for firm A (TR_A) is PQ_A, thus by substitution:

$$TR_A = \left(\frac{a}{b} - \frac{Q_A}{b} - \frac{Q_B}{b}\right)Q_A$$

Marginal revenue will thus be:

$$MR_A = \frac{a}{b} - \frac{2Q_A}{b} - \frac{Q_B}{b}$$

Since marginal cost is assumed to be zero, firm A will determine its output Q_A where MR_A is zero. Solving for Q_A we will have:

$$Q_A = \frac{1}{2}(a - Q_B)$$

The above equation tells us how much firm A will produce *given* firm B's output and is commonly referred to as a **reaction function**. By similar reasoning, firm B's reaction function will be:

$$Q_B = \frac{1}{2}(a - Q_A)$$

The simultaneous solution to the two reaction functions is when each produces one third of total output.

Reaction functions

It is important to fully understand the construction of the reaction curves.

The dashed, concave curves in Figure 2.2 represent firm A's isoprofit curves: each curve represents the combinations of A and B's output that generate the same level of profit for A. Note, that the isoprofit curves represent higher levels of profit for A as they approach the horizontal axis. For any given level of output for firm A, a lower isoprofit curve for A will imply a lower output for B and thus greater profits for A. In Figure 2.2, π_2 represents a higher profit level than π_1. We begin by assuming that A sees that B is producing Oq_B^1 and further that A assumes that B will *maintain this output* regardless of what A produces. Thus A sees $q_B^1 R_B^1$ as B's horizontal reaction function, albeit erroneously. Firm A will produce q_A^1 which is the point of tangency of firm A's profit π_1 and B's 'reaction function' $q_B^1 R_B^1$. Had A

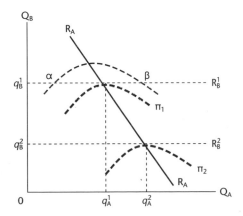

Figure 2.2 Construction of reaction functions

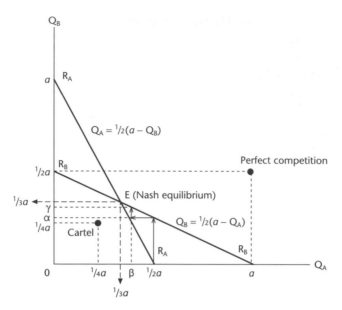

Figure 2.3 Cournot–Nash equilibrium

reacted with any other level of output, profits would have been *lower*, for example at outputs α and β. If B changes its output to q_B^2, firm A will maximise its profits where B's horizontal reaction function is tangential to A's lowest isoprofit curve, i.e. at π_2. Connecting the points of tangency will determine the reaction curve for A. Output reaction curves can be similarly constructed for B.

The task now is to find the outputs Q_A and Q_B that will determine an equilibrium. One such equilibrium condition can be defined as the 'Nash equilibrium' which requires that each firm is doing the best it can, given what its rival is doing. This is shown in Figure 2.3.

The horizontal axis refers to A's output and the vertical axis to B's output. The reaction function R_AR_A, tells us how much A will produce and sell given the output decisions of B. Thus if B is not in the market, i.e. $Q_B = 0$, A is a monopolist and produces at $\frac{1}{2}a$. (Quantity a refers to the competitive output.) Similarly, the reaction curve R_BR_B tells us how B will react to the output decisions of A. If B is the sole seller, i.e. $Q_A = 0$, then B produces at $\frac{1}{2}a$ as well.

Suppose then that A is a monopolist and produces at $\frac{1}{2}aQ_C$ and that B enters the market. Seeing that A is producing $\frac{1}{2}a$, B decides to produce at point α. A now reappraises the situation; if B is producing at α, A reacts by producing at β. B then reacts by increasing output to γ, and so on. In time we will reach an equilibrium point at E. At E both A and B will each produce $\frac{1}{3}a$. Point E is also the Nash equilibrium, where both firms behave optimally. No matter where we start, equilibrium will be determined at E. The analysis can be extended to include any number of firms in our oligopoly and the formula for the equilibrium solution is:

$$Q_I = Q_C \frac{n}{n+1}$$

where Q_I the equilibrium output in the industry, Q_C the competitive output and n the number of firms. Thus in a monopoly situation:

$$Q_I = Q_C \frac{1}{1+1}$$

$$= Q_C \left(\frac{1}{2}\right)$$

For a duopoly, the industry output will be two-thirds of the competitive output and for a three-firm oligopoly (triopoly) the industry output will be three-quarters of the competitive output, and so on. As the number of firms approaches infinity so industry output approaches the competitive output.

We can identify other potential equilibria from Figure 2.3. If both firms were to collude and agree to produce jointly one-half of the industry output – the monopoly output – each would produce $\frac{1}{4}a$ as shown in the diagram. This would have the effect of increasing price and increasing profits for both firms. With a monopoly output equal to $\frac{1}{2}a$, we can substitute this into our linear demand curve of $P = a - bQ$ and determine the monopoly price of $a/2b$. The total revenue (PQ) will then be $a^2/4b$ and each firm will enjoy half that revenue, $a^2/8b$. In the duopoly case, industry output is $\frac{2}{3}a$ and the oligopoly price is $a/3b$. This means that total revenue will be $2a^2/9b$, with each firm receiving $a^2/9b$, *less* than the cartel solution. However, the cartel solution is not feasible under Cournot assumptions, in that one firm, believing that the other will not change its output of $\frac{1}{4}a$ will be tempted to *increase* its output (as shown by the reaction function) to maximise its own profits. Such action will naturally lead to the collapse of any jointly agreed output. We can also identify the competitive output in Figure 2.2. On the assumption that marginal cost is zero, price will be set to zero and both firms produce $\frac{1}{2}a$, for an industry output of a.

What can we conclude from the Cournot model? The model can be criticised in three ways. Firstly, it is based on a naive and unrealistic assumption that each firm believes its rival will never alter output (zero conjectural variation), in spite of each firm observing constant, contradictory behaviour. This type of criticism dates back to the nineteenth century:

> no businessman assumes either that his rival's output or price will remain constant any more than a chess player assumes that his opponent will interfere with his effort to capture a knight. On the contrary, his whole thought is to forecast what move the rival will make in response to his own.[5]

A little support is provided by Scherer (1980, p.155) who claims that 'some decision-makers do exhibit myopic tendencies in certain rivalry situations'. This is also echoed by Martin (1988, pp.109–10):

> the assumption that each firm believes that its rival will hold output constant – is implausible. But the general prospect that in oligopoly firms will misunderstand the way rivals behave is quite plausible.

Secondly, Cournot seems to ignore the possibility that firms may wish to seek co-operative or collusive solutions to maximise their joint profits. This is, and almost certainly was in Cournot's time, a fact of economic life in oligopolistic markets, and to ignore it is to ignore

[5] Fisher (1898), p.126.

a substantial part of oligopoly behaviour. Finally, Cournot has been criticised for focusing on output-setting and ignoring price-setting as an oligopolistic strategy. Prices in the Cournot model are the consequence of output rather than being primary courses of action.

Nonetheless we can point to some positive contributions of the theory. It did provide important tools of analysis, such as conjectural variation and reaction functions that helped to develop subsequent analyses of duopoly and oligopoly behaviour. It also determined an oligopoly equilibrium that was set reassuringly between that of perfect competition and monopoly. It can also be viewed as the 'starting-point' in all discussion of oligopoly, as Fellner (1949, p.57) remarked,

> A realistic approach to oligopoly problems cannot be based on Cournot's theory. Yet now, after more than a century, it is still difficult to see what is involved in an oligopoly theory without showing how the theory is related to Cournot's basic construction.

Bertrand (1883)

Bertrand criticised Cournot for his zero conjectural variation assumption as well as the emphasis Cournot placed on output-setting. He proposed that prices rather than output should be the key decision variable, but he too then assumed a zero conjectural variation as regards prices, assuming that each firm believes its rivals will maintain a constant price. The model rests on the implicit assumption that the output of the two firms is homogeneous and that there are no transaction or search costs, so that customers will flow effortlessly to the firm that is offering the lowest price. The solution can be shown by Figure 2.4 with the use of price reaction functions, which show the prices that a firm will charge in order to maximise its profits, given a price set by the other firm.

The reaction function $R_A R_A$ shows the prices which maximise the profits for A for all prices set by B, and $R_B R_B$ performs the same function for B. The two firms arrive at the equilibrium point E by successive movements along their price reaction curves. Since both firms

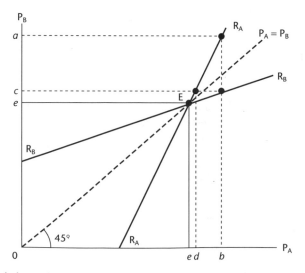

Figure 2.4 Bertrand duopoly

produce identical goods, any divergence in price can only be temporary. Equilibrium will occur where both prices are equal, which will be along the dashed 45° line. The reaction functions have a positive slope since if a firm is to compete it must set a price below that set by the rival firm. If firm A believes that firm B will set a price at *a*, it will react by setting its price at *b*, which is below that set by B. All the customers will move to firm A and the firm will enjoy abnormal profits. B now considers its pricing strategy and, in the belief that A will maintain prices at *b*, will react by undercutting that price, to set price *c*. A will react to this price by setting *d*, an so on. Both firms edge towards the competitive equilibrium, where each will charge price *e* and earn normal profits. In this case consumers will be indifferent regarding from whom they buy, and each firm will supply half the market. If we were to relax the assumption that both firms produce homogeneous goods and assume product differentiation then we may achieve equilibria that do not lie on the 45° line.

The model can be criticised in three ways. Firstly the general criticism regarding the zero conjectural variation applies to the Bertrand model as much as it did to the Cournot model. Secondly, it could be argued that where outputs are not differentiated, output-setting would seem a more realistic strategy than price-setting. Finally, the model concludes that the market will be shared equally, but in practice such neat outcomes may not be realised for a variety of non-economic factors.

Edgeworth (1897)

Edgeworth based his model on Bertrand's price-setting, zero conjectural model. However, the conclusions he reached were very different from that of Bertrand. Edgeworth considered a market evenly divided between two sellers, though no one firm is able to meet total demand. Each tries to undercut the other's price until the point of competitive equilibrium is reached ($P = MC$). At this price, one of the firms, believing its rival will not alter price, will itself now charge a monopoly price. Since the rival is producing at full capacity and thus unable to supply any more consumers, remaining consumers are forced to pay this higher price. This action will in turn trigger another price war. This is explained in Figure 2.5.

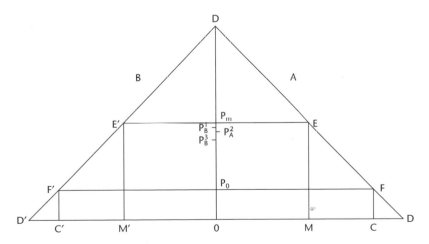

Figure 2.5 The Edgeworth duopoly

Let us assume a zero MC. The market is evenly divided between A and B. DD is A's demand curve and DD' is B's demand curve. There is a limit to the productive capacity of A and B, which is set, for example, at C' and C. Thus the maximum output B can supply is OC' and A can supply only OC. OD is the price axis.

If A enters the market first, it sells OM at OP_m which gives A maximum monopoly profit $OP_m EM$.[6] B enters and believes A will not alter price. B thus sets price OP_B^1, a little below A's and thus sells *all its output* of OC', since most of A's customers will now buy from B at the lower price. A will not lose all its customers since B cannot meet total market demand by assumption.

A now considers B's price and assumes that it will not change and thus resets its price a little below B's, at OP_A^2. A then recaptures its market and most of B's. B now reduces price to OP_B^3, and so on. Prices will keep falling till OP_0 is reached, where both A and B sell their maximum output. At this point, however, one of the firms will see the other selling all its output at price P_0. It knows that the rest of the market must buy from it. Having a zero conjectural variation (rival will not alter price), the firm decides to set its price at OP_m and sell OM (if A) or OM' (if B), thus reaping monopoly profits. Assume A does this. B now sees that it can charge a price just below OP_m which is higher than OP_0 and *still sell* OC'. And so it goes on, prices fluctuating between OP_0 and OP_m. The solution is unstable and indeterminate.

Again, we can criticise the model for its naive assumptions of zero conjectural variation. The model seems to be built around the idea that firms' conjectures are *always* wrong. There seems no attempt on the part of firms to learn from the lesson of instability. We may also criticise the model for the assumption that firms can continually and effortlessly adjust to new prices and outputs. A charitable assessment of the model is to see it as an improvement on the previous models discussed, in that it identifies the possibility of *instability* in oligopolistic markets. Some economists argue that oligopolies are inherently unstable. Although prices may at times appear stable, often one finds that the stability is imposed on the market by either tacit or explicit collusion. The model will at least show that the temptation to collude may be irresistible under such Edgeworthian fluctuations. Solberg (1992, pp.603–4) suggested that Coca-Cola and Pepsi Cola, both subject to capacity limits in local markets, have frequently resorted to aggressive price-cutting strategies, as suggested by the Edgeworth model.

The above models are some of the earliest attempts to theorise about the behaviour of oligopolists. The one major drawback to all three models is the assumption of zero conjectural variation: the belief that rivals will not respond to any price or output change by altering their own prices or output, *despite* continually observing such behaviour. We now turn to an examination of models where this assumption is relaxed and firms become very much aware that their actions will prompt rivals to reconsider their strategies.

2.3 Models of mutual interdependence

Chamberlin (1933)

Chamberlin's suggested solution to the oligopoly problem was initially based on Cournot's model of two proprietors of mineral spring waters, operating side by side at zero MC. The

---

[6] This is where A's marginal revenue curve (not drawn) intersects the output axis, at exactly the mid-point of OD. Read the Cournot model analysis to understand why the output will be at half of OD.

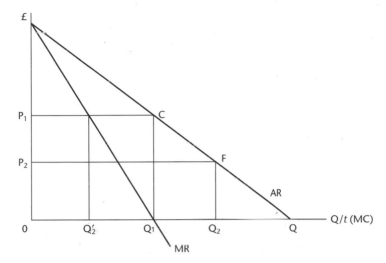

Figure 2.6 Chamberlin's model where mutual interdependence is recognised

difference, however, lies in the fact that Chamberlin assumed that *mutual interdependence was recognised.*

Chamberlin's model, as illustrated in Figure 2.6, is identical to Cournot's but for the final solution. As before, we assume that A enters the market, and on the assumption of a linear demand curve will proceed to sell OQ_1, which is half of OQ (where marginal revenue equals zero). A will enjoy monopoly profits OP_1CQ_1. B enters the market and seeing that A is producing OQ_1 knows that the best it can do is to sell $\frac{1}{2}Q_1Q$ (half of the remaining market). Price falls to OP_2 and total industry profit is OP_2FQ_2.

A now recognises mutual interdependence and realises that sharing the monopoly profit OP_1CQ_1 is the best that both can do. A reduces output to $OQ_2' = \frac{1}{2}OQ_1$. B also recognises the optimum solution and maintains output at $Q_1Q_2 = \frac{1}{2}OQ_1$. Thus A and B together supply just half the total market and consequently share the monopoly profit.

This model is an improvement on the older models in the sense that the firm recognises the reality of the situation. Both firms accommodate reality and achieve an equilibrium solution that generates a higher payoff than the earlier scenarios. Unfortunately the model determines an unrealistically *quiescent* industry, allowing for no unilateral aggression, cheating or backsliding – a state of affairs rarely found in oligopolistic markets. It is also important to note that Chamberlin did not suggest that firms determine this solution through collusion. The outcome rests on the belief that both firms recognise that the monopoly ideal can be achieved through *independent action* and that this view is shared by rivals. This, too, is a somewhat unrealistic assumption in the context of modern oligopolies.

Stackelberg (1934)

Stackelberg refined the Cournot duopoly model to include the idea of 'first-mover advantage'. The traditional Cournot model gives both firms equal status as they play out a ritual step-by-step progress to final equilibrium. If both firms were aware of their reaction functions, they could solve the problem and move immediately to the Nash equilibrium. The

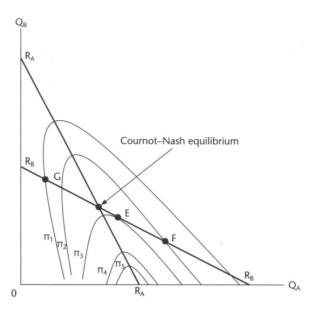

Figure 2.7 The Stackelberg duopoly

advantage of this *simultaneous* action as opposed to the long-winded sequential action is that both firms can avoid the benefits of first-mover advantage accruing to their rival. This advantage simply means that to be first in the market, with a higher output and higher profits, will confer benefits on the leader. The follower may well have to accept the status quo and produce an output below that of the leader's. The equilibrium is illustrated in Figure 2.7.

Stackelberg used the same duopoly model as that developed by Cournot, a linear demand curve and zero marginal costs and with an implicit assumption that the moves are sequential rather than simultaneous. Let us assume that firm A is the leader and sets an output. Firm B is the follower and takes firm A's output as given and determines its best reaction, which is shown by reaction function $R_B R_B$. Firm A knows that for any output it sets, B will choose that output which will determine its best response. A will therefore select an output that corresponds to point E as this will maximise its profits, given B's expected reactions. Note that firm A, as leader, is not on its reaction function. Isoprofit curve π_3 is the lowest A can reach (hence greatest profit), given $R_B R_B$. By moving first, A can in effect choose where to be on B's reaction function. Point E is the Stackelberg equilibrium and any other point is suboptimal. If we were to consider points F or G, these would be on higher isoprofit curves π_2 and π_1 respectively, and hence imply lower profits. Firm A cannot realise higher profits as shown by isoprofit curves π_4 and π_5 as B's reaction function does not intersect these curves.

From the above discussion we can deduce four possible outcomes in the Stackelberg model. These are shown in Figure 2.8.

Firstly we can identify the equilibrium as discussed in Figure 2.7, where firm A was the leader and firm B was the follower. The equilibrium in this case is shown by point S_A. The second case is the case where firm B is the leader and firm A the follower and the equilibrium is the mirror image at point S_B. The third possibility is that both firms are followers

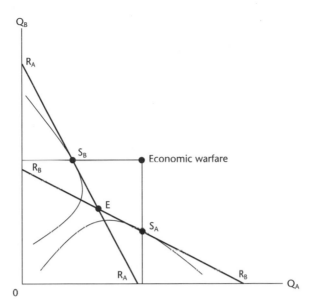

Figure 2.8 Four possible outcomes in the Stackelberg model

and both reach the Cournot–Nash equilibrium at point E. There is the final possibility, quite real in oligopolistic markets, that both firms wish to be the leader and both stick to their outputs as leader and we end up at a 'Stackelberg disequilibrium' or economic warfare. This conflict point in the diagram implies that both firms will be on higher isoprofit curves and thus suffer lower profits than would have been the case under a Cournot equilibrium. This costly process of attrition may eventually determine a winner and a loser but it is equally likely that firms may soon realise the futility of conflict and seek co-operative solutions.

Kinked demand curve

This now famous model was developed almost simultaneously by Sweezy (1939) and Hall and Hitch (1939). The *raison d'être* of the model was to explain the observed price rigidity in oligopolistic market structures. Sweezy tried to fit this observed behaviour into standard price theory.

Sweezy's solution, shown in Figure 2.9, was based on the assumption that firms will not initiate a price rise. They believe that if they did so, rivals will *not* follow and consequently they would lose a sizable share of the market. However, firms will always follow a price fall, so as to protect their market share. Prices will still be subject to large changes in demand and supply conditions in the long run.

Curve dP is the firm's demand curve. The kink is at price P, the price at which the firm is selling OQ_0. Above P the demand curve, as perceived by the firm, is dP, which is relatively elastic and MR is positive. Curve dP is elastic because the firm believes that rivals will not follow a higher price and consequently the fall in sales will be high. PD is less elastic (inelastic) because the firm believes that a reduction in price will be matched. Although it may temporarily enjoy an increase in sales, eventually all the other firms will follow the price fall and the firm will suffer lower sales and lower profits.

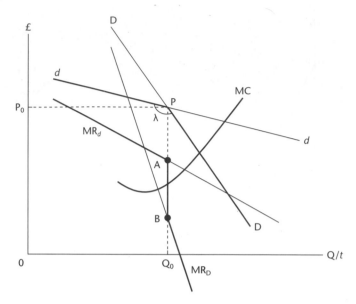

Figure 2.9 Sweezy's kinked demand curve hypothesis

The gap between A and B, which the MC curve intersects, can be regarded as the vertical section of the MR function. Profits are maximised where MC = MR. To the left of Q_0, MR > MC and the right of Q_0, MR < MC, thus profit will be maximised where the MC curve intersects the vertical discontinuity, which can be seen analytically as an extension of the marginal revenue function. We can now see that if MC rises or falls within the discontinuity, as shown by points A and B, *price and output will remain constant*. Thus Sweezy was able to demonstrate **price rigidity** or 'sticky' prices. One can go further and show that even if demand were to increase, prices may still not be affected.

Figure 2.10 shows an increase in demand from dD to d'D', which generates a new marginal revenue function MR_D. The marginal cost curve intersects both the old and the new vertical discontinuities and prices remain static at P_0.

The degree of price rigidity will depend on the length of the discontinuity AB, which in turn depends on the angle of the kink (λ), which can be referred to as the 'barometer of price rigidity'. Stigler (1947) identified various factors that might affect the angle of the kink:

- Where there are few rivals, price increases are more likely to be followed since any gains from lower prices may be quickly eroded. If there are many rivals, they are more likely not to follow a price rise, but equally they may not follow a price reduction either. Stigler thought that an intermediate number of firms would generate the longest discontinuity.

- The size of the rivals may also affect the size of the kink. If there is one large firm, or a clique of firms, it may act as a price leader and all rivals follow price increases and decreases. In this extreme case there will be no kink. This will equally apply to a situation where collusion takes place.

- Where goods are homogeneous with a high positive cross-elasticity of demand the discontinuity will be longer as consumers are more likely to shift to the low-price firms.

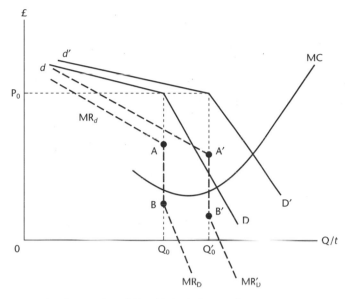

Figure 2.10 Increases in demand and the kinked demand curve

Other issues that might be added to the list were suggested by Cohen and Cyert (1965, p.251).

● Where entrants are unsure about the market structure, or existing firms are unsure about the intentions of entrants, firms may adopt a wait-and-see attitude and be reluctant to initiate price rises.
● A similar analysis can be applied to a new industry in which firms are in the process of 'sizing' each other up.
● One might argue that where there is substantial shareholder control, managers may be risk averse and decide to play safe.

All the above features (except the last point) simply reinforce the feeling of mutual interdependence and the desire for stability. In contrast, the absence of a kink implies a normal demand curve, which is independent of any conjectural variation between firms. This could occur as suggested above where we have a price leader or collusion. This may be termed a 'well behaved' industry.

Critique

The model can be attacked for not explaining how prices are formed at the kink. The model begins with price as a given variable. It does not tell us how prices are determined in an oligopoly context. It explains the existence of kinks but not their location. It is an *ex post rationalisation* rather than *ex ante explanation* of market equilibrium. Secondly one could argue that price rigidity can be explained in other ways. Firms may be reluctant to increase price for fear of alienating their consumers. Firms may wait for a convenient time to introduce one large price increase rather than revise prices continuously, the latter

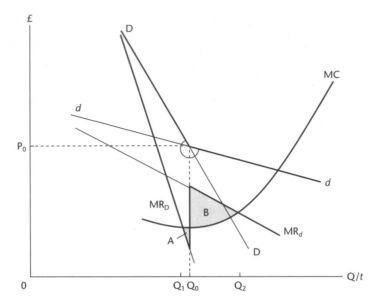

Figure 2.11 The reflexive kinked demand curve

being a strategy which may negatively affect buyer psychology. There is also evidence that changing prices itself is a costly and complex process and that in businesses where such 'menu costs' are high, changes in price are less frequent.[7]

Thirdly, Sweezy's argument that price increases will not be followed and that all decreases will, can also be challenged. A price reduction need not signal to rivals that a firm has introduced an aggressive strategy to capture a larger share of the market. Rivals may reason that the products being sold are of lower quality, or that the firm has financial problems. Rivals will react according to *how they interpret* the price reduction. Likewise, price increases may be followed if firms believe that market conditions warrant such an increase, or if they face temporary shortages in capacity and are unable to meet increases in demand. It has been argued by some that in times of inflationary demand, as a firm approaches capacity, additional output increases a firm's short-run AC curve.[8] Thus the firm is faced with a great many orders that it is unwilling to fulfil. It may thus be eager to follow a rival's price *rise* and reluctant to follow a price fall, which would only increase demand. The implication of this is that the angle of the kink becomes reflexive. This is shown in Figure 2.11.

The MC curve passes through the vertical discontinuity of the MR curve. The profit maximisation point is not necessarily below the kink. There are three possible equilibria, where MC = MR. Area A represents the loss in total revenue by moving from Q_1 to Q_0, i.e. where MC > MR. Area B represents a gain in total revenue when increasing output from Q_0 to Q_2, where MR > MC. The firm will not produce at OQ_0 since it incurs a loss equal to area A and denies itself a gain equal to area B. Since area B is greater than area A, the firm will select output OQ_2.

---

[7] See Levy *et al.* (1997).
[8] See Brofenbrenner (1940) and Efroymson (1955).

During times of inflation MC will tend to rise. If the increase in MC is greater than the increase in demand, i.e. area B becomes smaller than area A, the profit-maximising firm will switch to the lower of the three output possibilities. This analysis was challenged by Cyert (1955) who, on the basis of three industries, concluded that price behaviour was independent of business cycles.

Stigler (1947) found little evidence for price rigidity. Having examined the evidence in seven oligopolistic markets (cigarettes, automobiles, anthracite, steel, dynamite, refining and potash) he claimed that price changes in oligopolistic market were frequent; though the evidence tended to suggest that the more oligopolistic the market the less frequent the price changes. He concluded:

> But is this adverse conclusion really surprising? The kink is a barrier to changes in prices that will increase profits, and business is the collection of devices for circumventing barriers to profits. That this barrier should thwart businessmen – especially when it is wholly of their own fabrication – is unbelievable.[9]

In a later article, Stigler (1978, p.188) said he was amazed at the continuing popularity of the model, which he saw as performing, at best, 'only ceremonial functions!' He noted, somewhat acidly: 'The theory has received no systematic empirical support and virtually no theoretical elaboration in these decades, but these lacks have been no handicap in maintaining its currency' (1978, p.183).

There has however also been a steady stream of evidence that would seem to back the initial hypotheses. Kashyap (1995) examined price changes for twelve retail goods over a period of 35 years and found that prices were typically fixed for more than a year. Domberger and Fiebig (1993) found that price decreases were more readily followed than price increases in 'tight' oligopolies, drawn from their sample of 80 industries over an 11-year period. Finally, in its defence, one can say the model is an improvement on some of the earlier classical models that failed to cope with the issue of interdependence. For all its faults, the kinked demand curve at least recognises that firms are making strategic decisions *vis-à-vis* rivals.

Price leadership models

Let us turn to one further analysis of oligopoly models where interdependence is recognised, namely **price leadership** models or 'parallel pricing'. It is a frequently observed phenomenon that firms in oligopolistic markets will change prices in tandem. One firm announces a price change and soon all the other firms follow suit. There are three types of price leadership.

Dominant price leadership

As the word suggests the industry is dominated by one firm, owing to its greater efficiency (lower costs) or possibly its aggressive behaviour. The firm sets the price and other firms follow through convenience, ignorance or fear. In fact there is no oligopoly problem as such since interdependence is absent. The dominant firm could act as a monopolist and eliminate many rivals through a price war, though this would clearly attract the attention of the government anti-monopoly agencies. A better name for this type of behaviour could be 'partial monopoly' price leadership. The model below can help to explain this type of

---

[9] Stigler (1947), p.435.

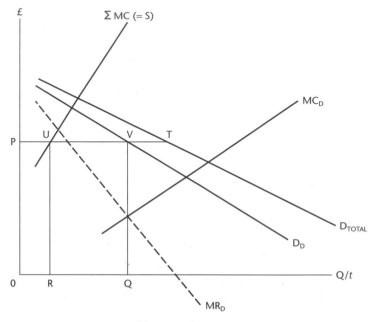

Figure 2.12 Dominant firm price leadership

behaviour. It is assumed that the dominant firm controls the market price and that the followers are price takers, hence they face a perfectly elastic demand curve. It is also assumed that the dominant firm has complete information regarding its demand and cost curves as well as those of its smaller rivals. The market is analysed as if it were a duopoly comprising the dominant firm and the others (the smaller rivals). This is shown in Figure 2.12.

The curve D_{TOTAL} is the total market demand which includes the demand curve of the dominant firm D_D and all the other firms. Profit-maximising output and the market price is fixed by the dominant firm at OQ and OP, respectively. The sum of all the marginal cost curves of all the other firms is ΣMC, which is also their supply curve (S). As price-takers they will sell output OR at price OP. Total market demand at price OP is PT, of which PU is supplied by the smaller 'other' firms and UT is supplied by the dominant firm (UT = OQ).

Will the smaller firms always follow the leader? It may be possible that when demand is depressed, there will be a great temptation among some of the smaller firms to lower prices. The small firms will have to gamble on the hope that the dominant firm may be reluctant to discipline the smaller firms with yet more price-cuts, possibly throwing the whole market into turmoil. However, if sufficient numbers were to ignore the lead of the dominant firm, there may come a point when the leader must act to restore market discipline.

Barometric price leadership

Barometric price leadership exists where a firm announces a price change that would, in time, be set by the forces of competition. It is simply the first to announce a price change. The leader is not necessarily the dominant firm in the market. Indeed, one would expect the identity of the leader to change over time. The leader acts as a barometer for the market and if it fails to interpret market conditions correctly, leadership will pass to other firms.

Effective price leadership

Markham (1951) believed that barometric price leadership was of two types: the competitive type and the more dangerous monopolistic type, which he named 'effective' price leadership, though it has often been referred to as 'collusive price leadership'. The benign, competitive type was characterised by:

- frequent changes in the identity of the leader;
- no immediate, uniform response to price changes, i.e. a lagged response as followers consider the suitability of a price change; and
- variations in market share.

Markham claimed that effective price leadership was characterised by the following market conditions:

- small number of firms, all fairly large;
- substantial entry barriers;
- absence of marked product differentiation, to reinforce the feeling of interdependence;
- low elasticity of demand, to prevent price-cutting; and
- similar cost functions.

The above characteristics are not too dissimilar to the characteristics of successful cartels, as we shall see in the next chapter.

As the agreed leader changes price, all the other firms follow suit. There is no overt or explicit collusion. All firms act *independently*. They realise that it is better to tacitly co-operate in an orderly market than to slide into the anarchy of a price war. The effect nonetheless is similar to overt price agreements, as Bain (1960, p.198) remarked: 'The monopolistically barometric form of price leadership is dire, and it may serve all the ends of a strong trade association or a closely knit domestic cartel.'

2.4 Game theory

Methodology

This approach to decision-making was developed by von Neumann and Morgenstern (1944). The object of any game is to determine solutions to different outcomes based on the actions of independent players. A game is a situation where two players, or firms compete, for example for market share. Courses open to the players are known as strategies, and all strategies for all players are known. It is possible to relax this assumption in which case we will have different outcomes. Strategies open to oligopolistic firms can refer to changes in product, pricing policies, advertising, output, public relations, and so on. Each firm will then face a 'payoff' for every given set of strategies. This can be illustrated by the use of a simple matrix.

Figure 2.13 illustrates the payoff matrix for two firms A and B. Firm A's strategies are α and β, whilst firm B's are γ and δ. The elements in the matrix represent the payoffs (for example profits) to the two firms. The first figure refers to A's payoff and the second to B's payoff. Thus if firm A selects strategy β, whilst firm B selects strategy γ, A's payoff (profit) is 6 and B's payoff is 0, i.e. no profit. Each firm will then select that strategy that gives it the best outcome, *given the likely strategies of the other firm*. If this is completed we have a

Firm B

		γ	δ
Firm A	α	4, 4	0, 6
	β	6, 0	2, 2

Figure 2.13 Payoff matrix

Nash equilibrium, which means that no firm can improve its payoff, given the actions of the other firm. We first considered this type of equilibrium when discussing the Cournot duopoly model. In Figure 2.13 we have four possible strategy pairs (αγ, αδ, βγ and βδ) and thus four possible outcomes to the game:

● Strategy pair αγ cannot be a Nash equilibrium, since firm A can improve its payoff from 4 to 6 by selecting strategy β.
● If we consider strategy pair αδ, again, firm A can improve its payoff from 0 to 2 by selecting strategy β. Thus this cannot be a Nash equilibrium.
● Strategy pair βγ is also not a Nash equilibrium since firm B can improve its payoff from 0 to 2 by selecting strategy δ.
● The fourth option, strategy pair βδ is an outcome that no firm can better. Thus, *given* the fact that firm B has selected δ firm A cannot do better than strategy β. Likewise, given the fact that firm A has selected strategy β firm B cannot do better than strategy δ.

It is interesting to note that in the above game, both firms would have been better off had they chosen strategy pair αγ. This is known as a prisoners' dilemma game and is discussed below.

Types of game

Broadly speaking, games fall into two categories: **co-operative** and **non-cooperative** games. In the case of a co-operative game, it is assumed that firms can negotiate a binding agreement. Thus when a seller and a buyer haggle over the price of a good we are faced with a 'game', which can be solved by an agreement (whether verbal or written) over a mutually beneficial price. Equally, when two producers decide to collude over prices or output, we also have a *de facto* binding agreement. However where agreements are not possible, for example when two firms fight for market share, we are faced with non-cooperative games. Games can also be classified according to their outcomes. A 'constant-sum game' occurs when the sum of the payoffs to both players is always equal. Thus, if a game concerns strategies to divide a market worth £200 million, then all strategy pairs for the firms will sum to that figure. A game may be 'non-constant' when the outcomes vary with different strategies. A 'zero-sum game' occurs where one firm's gain is exactly equal to another's loss. A game of poker is a zero-sum game in that one player's winnings will be exactly matched by the losses of the rival player. Finally, we can distinguish games that are 'positive-sum games', where both players are better off after the game, for example an exchange between a producer and a consumer, and 'negative-sum games', where both players are

A's strategies	B's strategies				Row minima
	w	x	y	z	
a	10	(9)	14	13	**9**
b	11	8	4	15	4
c	6	7	15	17	6
Column maxima	11	**9**	15	17	9 = 9

Figure 2.14 Payoff matrix

worse off after the game. This may occur in situations of 'ruinous competition' where firms force losses on each other by setting lower and lower prices. Although both lose profits in the short run, both hope that they will emerge victorious and recover these losses in the long run.

Equilibrium

The solution to a game was briefly outlined in Figure 2.13. Let us turn to a more formal analysis of how an equilibrium can be determined. An equilibrium is defined when no firm will wish to change its strategy given the strategy selected by its rival. Let us consider the game as illustrated in Figure 2.14.

Assume that firm A can choose one of three strategies, a, b, c, while firm B can choose from four, w, x, y, z. These strategies are shown in the payoff matrix of Figure 2.14. The elements in the matrix refer to A's payoff, say market share, for each possible combination of strategies. We further assume that the constant value of the game (here the size of the market) is 20. If A chooses strategy c and B chooses strategy w, then A wins 6 and B wins 14 (the constant value of the game less A's winnings). Therefore B chooses strategy w because it yields the greatest payoff, given A's choice.

Alternatively, if we assume that B chooses strategy y, A would choose strategy c to maximise its gain. A realises that for any strategy (row) it selects, B will select that strategy (column) which minimises A's winnings (and maximises B's winnings). Thus A has to be aware of the row minima, the *worst possible outcomes* of each strategy. Faced with row minima of 9, 4 or 6, A will select strategy (row) a since it guarantees the largest return. Had it selected any other strategy (row), B could have forced a lower payoff on A. In all cases A selects that strategy that corresponds to the maximum of the row minima: a procedure referred to as 'maximining'. This represents A's dominant strategy. In a similar way, B is interested in column maxima, which represent its worst outcomes. To ensure the best payoff, B will select the strategy which corresponds to the minimum of the column maxima: B 'minimaxes'. Strategy pair (a,x), the 'saddle-point', is determined: A wins 9 and B wins 11.

The above game is known as a *two-person, strictly determined, constant-sum game*. It is strictly determined since it has a unique solution or saddle-point, two-person since only two players are involved, and constant-sum since the sum of the shares of the two players is always the same (in this case 20).

A's strategies	B's strategies			Row minima
	x	y	z	
a	−5	3	6	**−5**
b	6	3	−5	**−5**
Column maxima	6	**3**	6	3 ~ −5

Figure 2.15 Payoff matrix with no saddle-point

Mixed strategies

In reality most games are not strictly determined, i.e. there is no convenient saddle-point. Consider the payoff matrix in Figure 2.15, which is a zero-sum game.[10] The elements in the matrix refer to A's profits.

There is no unique solution to this game since the column maxima and the row minima do not coincide. A is now in a difficult position. If it chooses strategy a, B can respond with strategy x and A suffers a loss of 5. If A selects strategy b it again could face a similar loss when B reacts with strategy z. The solution lies in the concept of a mixed strategy, developed by von Neumann and Morgenstern (1944).

Assume A assigns strategy a with a probability of x_1 and strategy b with a probability of $(1 - x_1)$. Assume that B assigns strategy x with a probability of y_1, strategy y a probability of y_2 and strategy z a probability $(1 - y_1 - y_2)$. The expected value of the game is then calculated by:

● multiplying the elements of the matrix by the compound probability of each one's being selected, and
● summing these products for all elements in the matrix.

Thus the expected payoff for A if B selects strategy x is:

$-5x_1 + 6(1 - x_1) = 6 - 11x_1$

If B had selected strategy y, A's expected payoff would be:

$3x_1 + 3(1 - x_1) = 3$

If B chose strategy z, A's expected payoff would be:

$6x_1 - 5(1 - x_1) = -5 + 11x_1$

We can map A's expected payoffs against the different values of x_1 for the three possible strategies open to B (see Figure 2.16).

If A selects a value for x_1 that is less than $1/2$, then the worst outcome for A would be if B selects strategy z. If A assigns a value for x_1 greater than $1/2$ then the worst outcome facing A would be if B selected strategy x. If B selects that strategy which A regards as the worst, the expected payoff for each value of x_1 is bounded by the triangle ABC. If A wishes to ensure the minimisation of the worst possible outcome, it will choose a value of $1/2$ for x_1 and achieve a payoff at the apex of triangle ABC.

[10] Example taken from Mansfield (1975), p.331.

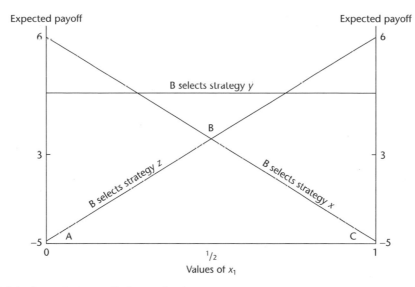

Figure 2.16 Expected payoffs in a mixed strategy game

Thus a probability of $1/2$ is attached to strategy a and $1/2$ to strategy b. A will then guarantee itself a payoff of at least $1/2$. This is referred to as the optimal mixed strategy for A. It can be shown that the optimal mixed strategy for B is to assign probability values of $1/2$ for strategy x, 0 for strategy y and $1/2$ for strategy z ($y_1 = 1/2$, $y_2 = 0$). Von Neumann and Morgenstern (1944) showed that a pair of mixed strategies will always exist and that they are an equilibrium pair, i.e. no firm can improve its position when it selects its optimum mixed strategy. A cannot better its guaranteed expected gain if it selects a value for x_1 other than $1/2$.

Prisoners' dilemma

A prisoners' dilemma is said to exist when there are gains to be made by players colluding. However, the collusive solution is unstable since greater gains can be made if one player moves independently (cheats), on the assumption that its rival will stick with the agreement. Let us consider a situation where two prisoners are separated physically and that no communication between them is possible. Each is told the following:

● If you both confess you will receive the normal punishment, 5 years in prison.
● If neither of you confesses you will both go free.
● If you confess and your fellow prisoner does not, you will go free and receive an extra benefit of £500,000.
● If you do not confess and your fellow prisoner confesses you will receive a sentence of 20 years.

The strategies open to both prisoners can be illustrated by the payoff matrix shown as Figure 2.17. The matrix shows the payoffs to both prisoners in the form of a hypothetical utility measure. In each case A's payoff is first, followed by B's.

Prisoner A's strategy	Prisoner B's strategy		Worst outcome for A
	Confess	Don't confess	
Confess	(–2, –2)	(+4, –4)	**–2**
Don't confess	(–4, +4)	(+2, +2)	–4
Worst outcome for B	**–2**	–4	

Figure 2.17 Prisoners' dilemma game

Firm A's strategy	Firm B's strategy		Worst outcome for A
	Collude	Cheat	
Collude	(160, 160)	(2, 200)	0
Cheat	(200, 0)	(100, 100)	**100**
Worst outcome for B	0	**100**	

Figure 2.18 Prisoners' dilemma game – unstable collusion

A considers his position and determines a strategy. If he confesses and B confesses he loses 2 (5 years in prison). If he confesses and B does not confess he gains 4. This is preferable to his other strategy which is not to confess, in which event he loses 4 if B confesses and gains 2 if B does not confess. Thus faced with the worst possible outcomes of –2 and –4 he will select the 'best of the worst' and confess. Similar reasoning applies to B. Thus both prisoners will confess (the shaded strategy) even though it was *mutually desirable for neither to do so*.

This type of game can be applied to oligopolies where firms decide to collude. In this case, the firms' mutual interest might be to abide by the terms of the oligopoly agreement, yet the temptation to cheat may be too great to achieve such a solution.

The matrix in Figure 2.18 shows the payoffs to both firms. As before, A's payoff is shown first and B's is second. It is clear that it is mutually beneficial for the firms to collude, which would result in each gaining 160. However each realises that to stick to the collusive agreement will invite the rival to cheat and result in a zero return. Both decide to cheat and both lose by determining a suboptimal solution. For a prisoner's dilemma game to be resolved in the oligopoly context, the agreement may have to be accompanied by an enforceable contract (legal or otherwise) to keep members to the 'collude, collude' strategy pair. Equally, prisoners are more likely not to confess to crimes if they know that to confess might impose greater costs in the long term in the form of a 'contract' on their life.

Not all prisoners' dilemma games generate suboptimal solutions, especially when one relaxes the assumptions. The reasons for more stable, more beneficial outcomes may depend on the following factors.

Firstly, an optimal solution can be achieved if there is a high degree of information and communication between the rivals. If firms meet frequently they will be able to exchange information and monitor each other's actions. If our two prisoners were not segregated they could determine their best strategies by a continual examination of their options. The nuclear war 'game' played by the United States and the Soviet Union in the 1960s and 1970s was likened to a prisoners' dilemma game. The choices were whether to attack the rival with a pre-emptive strike or whether to stick to the 'non-first use' agreement. One reason why the optimal solution (sticking to the agreement) was followed was the installation of the telephone hotline between Washington and Moscow to allow the two countries to exchange regular information at the highest level of government.

Secondly, an important feature regarding the solution to the game is the length of the reaction lags. The longer the reaction lag the greater the temptation for a player to act as an aggressor. This is especially true in cartels, where the greatest deterrence to cheating is immediate discovery and punishment. In the nuclear war game, reaction lags were crucial to ensuring that both sides kept to the agreement. Each side boasted that it could retaliate within minutes if attacked by the other, thus ensuring that there was no first-mover advantage. This policy became known as mutually assured destruction or MAD.

Finally we must also take into account the dynamics of rivalry. Is the rivalry continuous or a 'one-off' affair? If rivalry is continuous players learn over time that co-operation is preferable to outright rivalrous behaviour. Professional criminals have no problem with the prisoners' dilemma: experience has taught them that silence is the best option. In the context of an oligopoly, firms change prices, alter product lines, determine advertising strategies, continuously. Thus many firms learn over time that aggressive behaviour will lead to tit-for-tat reactions from rivals that cancel out any short-term gains (see below). Thus a price reduction will not benefit a firm for very long as the rival will respond with its price-cut, with the result that both firms will be worse off. Firms will soon learn to accommodate rivals and attempt to seek optimal solutions. These sorts of game are referred to as 'repeated games'.[11]

Sequential games

Most of the above games have focused on rivals acting simultaneously, but as in the case of a tit-for-tat game, there are games that follow a sequence. One firm may decide to increase its advertising budget and the rival has to decide how best to react. Choices facing a firm can then be mapped in the form of decision trees. Consider the following example.[12]

Assume that two breakfast cereal producers are considering a new product launch. They have a choice of launching one of two products. One product's focus is on its sweetness characteristics, whilst the other is on its crispiness. We also assume that the sweet cereal is more popular with consumers. Figure 2.19 illustrates the outcome if both firms move simultaneously, ignorant of what their rival is planning. Once again A's payoff is first and B's is second.

If both were to launch the breakfast cereal simultaneously, both would probably opt for the sweet variety. This would result in a loss for both firms. If, however, we consider

[11] See, for example, Kreps *et al.* (1982).
[12] Pindyck and Rubinfeld (1992), pp.481–3.

Firm A's strategy	Firm B's strategy	
	Crispy	Sweet
Crispy	(−5, −5)	(+10, +20)
Sweet	(+20, +10)	(−5, −5)

Figure 2.19 The breakfast cereal game

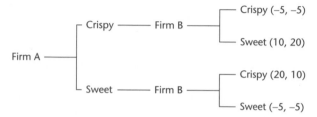

Figure 2.20 The breakfast cereal game as a sequential game

a sequential game, where firm A is the first to launch the new product, a different outcome will result. A realises that whatever product it launches the rational response of B is to launch the alternative. It will therefore decide to launch the sweet cereal knowing that B will react by selecting the crispy cereal. A will gain 20 and B will gain 10. This outcome can be illustrated with the use of a decision tree in Figure 2.20.

In Figure 2.20 the outcomes of the strategies are shown at the end of each branch. For firm A the best outcome would be to win 20. To achieve this, firm A will launch the sweet cereal knowing that firm B will produce the crispy cereal. As in the case of the Stackelberg duopolist, firm A has first-mover advantage.

Conclusion

Game theory has undoubtedly added to the analytical toolkit of the microeconomist and the industrial economist. Nonetheless there are two general criticisms. Firstly, the games suggest that firms should always assume the most pessimistic of reactions from their rivals and thus follow a mimimax (or maximin) strategy. There may be instances where such behaviour is not seen in oligopolistic markets and to pursue a minimax strategy while a rival does not, would imply lost profits. Secondly, the games do not generate unique solutions, since strategic decisions and outcomes are dependent on sociological, psychological as well as economic variables. The analyses develop a better understanding of oligopolistic behaviour but are weak at predicting that behaviour. Finally, since it is difficult to observe information that shapes bargaining behaviour in practice a new branch of economics has been developed to test the predictions of game theory. This is referred to as *experimental economics*, whereby laboratory experimentation allows economists to control the games and to test deduced hypotheses. Issues such as risk aversion, incomplete information and auction behaviour, can be explored and analysed. Some economists, such as Roth (1991, p.107) are particularly optimistic about the future of this development:

> a hundred years from now, game theory will have become the backbone of a kind of micro-economics engineering that will have roughly the relation to the economic theory and laboratory experimentation of the time that chemical engineering has to chemical theory and bench chemistry.

2.5 Conclusions

It is clear from the discussion that oligopoly theory is inconclusive. We have no clear and unambiguous solutions to the central issue of interdependence. Firms and individuals react in many different ways and this is reflected by the great number of models that occupy the analysis of oligopolistic markets. Each of the models we have covered, and indeed many others, reveals but a small part of wide-ranging oligopoly behaviour and we are far from developing a general theory of oligopoly. It is important to remember that a proper analysis of such structures must recognise the role of rivals and that firms are dependent on these rivals. This is echoed by Schick (1997, pp.82–3) in his book on decision theory:

> For Sartre, hell is dependence on others . . . In every room of Sartre's hell, each person wants something he cannot get except from certain others, who refuse. People sometimes avoid frustration; sometimes, in real life, the others consent. But people are always dependent on others and so they are always vulnerable.

It is the presence of 'other' firms in oligopolies that creates uncertainty which in turn makes oligopoly theory so difficult and challenging.

Key terms

Conjectural variation	Non-cooperative games
Co-operative games	Price leadership
Game theory	Price rigidity
Interdependence	Reaction function

Case study 2.1
Strategic complements and substitutes (abridged)

Understanding competition and how to influence it can significantly improve decision making in markets where there are few major competitors. In seeking to predict a competitor's response it helps to know which game you are playing – strategic substitutes or complements. The tools discussed by the author are relatively simple but they represent a critical building block for more elaborate game theory tools. What makes competitive strategy difficult is that the other forces in the environment are live – they can change their strategies at any time. A manager therefore has to chart the best course for the corporate 'ship', avoiding fixed hazards like rocks while trying to avoid collisions with other moving vessels. Before making a strategic decision in such a setting, it is crucial to understand how your rival will respond to an action. Advertising may be answered with more advertising, expanding capacity may cause a rival to build less capacity. Clearly, the advantages of a particular strategy will partially depend on reaction by others.

The essence of strategic thinking is to anticipate your competitor's moves in advance. Knowledge of your competitor's reaction, or likely reaction, dramatically improves your ability to choose a strategy that will be successful. Some competitor reactions enhance your own profit, while others reduce it. The economic tools described below allow a manager to determine what a competitor's reaction will be and what kinds of initial action generate positive or negative feedback. Informed managers understand and can affect competitive interaction to their advantage. This analysis only applies in markets where there are few major competitors – an environment in which the actions of any one company can noticeably affect the profits of the others. Such markets are known as oligopolies. Competitive interaction can get complicated and very sophisticated. The models in this article are the basics, the first steps required before moving on to advanced competitive strategy. While they may seem simplistic in some regards, they make basic and fundamental points about how competition works. More elaborate strategies build on these insights, so it is important to understand them.

To figure out the most likely competitive response, a manager needs to know the rival's goal (this is usually to maximise profit), the possible actions available to that rival (enter a new market or not, raise or lower price), and the gains to the rival from choosing one action over another. While to an outsider, many of these concepts seem difficult to estimate, competitors within an industry often have very good estimates of technical options, costs, and profitability of their competitors. Identifying a goal such as profit maximisation is important because that is how we will predict a company's choice: if, for example, we know approximately what level of profit will result from two different actions, and the company's management team steadfastly pursues profit, we can guess that they will choose the higher-profit alternative. How are profits determined? The 'game' being played by the industry is of crucial importance. There are two basic economic models of competition, price games and quantity games, which I will discuss below. Both models are short term; they are specifically designed to reflect the profitability of competitive tactics today. Dynamic concerns such as building market share today in order to reap profits from it tomorrow are advanced refinements of these models.

The most common kind of competitive interaction is in prices. Coca-Cola and Pepsi, for example, are substitutes yet consumers have different preferences for each. If Coke lowered its price in a particular city, some Pepsi customers would switch to Coke at that moment, while others will prefer Pepsi enough to pay its higher price. Coke will gain some customers who, until the price declined, were outside the soft drink market; it will also attract some former Pepsi customers. In 1883 Joseph Bertrand developed an expression for the profits of a company based on this type of consumer demand. He showed that any company engaged in price competition – in our case Pepsi – has a best (profit-maximising) response to competitor price changes. If Coke lowers its price, Pepsi does best by lowering its price also, although it may not match Coke's decrease in full. Why? Pepsi will lose customers to Coke when Coke's price falls. By lowering its own price, it prevents some of those customers from leaving. However, a lower price means a lower margin, so Pepsi finds it is not worth exactly matching Coke's price drop, but prefers to preserve some margin on its existing customers instead. Suppose the opposite case whereby Coke raises its price. Pepsi would find it could raise profits by partially matching Coke's increase. It could steal some customers from Coke – and serve them at a higher margin than before – if it matches only part of the price increase. This example illustrates that the best response in a price game is to imitate the original move of your rival. In a price game a lower price inspires a lower price, while raising a price causes the other company to raise price; competitors' prices move together. A key feature of these markets is that both companies' choices and profits move together. Industry prices and profits rise or industry prices and profits fall. In some sense, everyone is in the same boat. This is known as a strategic complements market.

The other type of action is a strategic substitute. The classic example of a strategic substitute is a company's choice of production quantity. Clearly, if companies choose the quantity they will put on the market, they cannot also force a particular price. (Think of OPEC's decisions over production, not price.) Instead, consumer demand determines the price. Another Frenchman, Augustin Cournot, showed more than a century ago that in a quantity game you should do the opposite of what your competitor does. For example, if your competitor decreases the quantity he puts on the market, you should increase yours if you want to maximise profit. Why? Because your competitor's decrease drives up the (common) market price, which raises your margin on every unit. It is now worth producing more units. For example, when OPEC organises lower production, the best response by other oil-producing countries is to produce more. While quantity competition is the classic parallel to price competition, it is not very common. Commodity markets are some of the only examples. The most important strategic complements action is capacity choice. For example, increased levels of computer memory-chip capacity by one player lead others in the industry to scale back. This is because increased chip production due to increased capacity will lower market prices. Lower prices lower the return on the capacity investment planned by other companies. Notice that in contrast to the first type of market, the best response to a competitor's move in a strategic substitutes game is to do the opposite. The pattern of profit changes is also different. Lower quantity goes hand-in-hand with lower profits; higher quantity with higher profits. When a rival increases output, your profits fall. While you can improve them somewhat by reducing your own output, you are still worse off, on balance. On the other hand, if a competitor lowers his capacity, your profits rise and will rise further if you increase your capacity.

How do you tell when you are playing a price game rather than a quantity game? Simply that the company chooses to set the price component of the demand curve. Coke and Pepsi choose the price at which their products sell. In a quantity game a company chooses what quantity (or capacity) to place on the market, but it is the market demand curve for the product itself that determines price.

Case study 2.2
BSkyB offer set to spark digital TV price war: group to give away set-top boxes in battle for subscribers

British Sky Broadcasting, the satellite broadcaster, armed itself for a fierce battle for digital television subscribers yesterday when it said it would give away the £200 set-top boxes needed to receive the new services. BSkyB, which launched 140 digital channels last year, said it would give away the equipment from next month to 'remove all possible barriers to digital take-up'. It also intends to stop broadcasting using analogue technology by 2002. The move looks set to spark a price war in the industry. On Digital, BSkyB's rival, which launched 30 digital terrestrial channels via roof-top aerials last year, confirmed it planned to give away its own set-top boxes for a month. Analysts said yesterday On Digital would have to extend that offer to match BSkyB's. A feeling that BSkyB would win the battle for digital subscribers sent its shares soaring 65.5p to 607p. Meanwhile, shares in Carlton Communications and Granada Group, the two ITV companies that own On Digital, closed down 48.5p at 544.5p and down 24p at £13.43 respectively. BSkyB also announced it would offer free internet access via personal computers from June 1 and a 40 per cent discount on British Telecommunications telephone calls. In addition, it revealed it had signed up 551,000 digital customers by May 3. Mark Booth, BSkyB's chief executive, said the announcements were aimed at competing more effectively with the cable industry, which has yet to launch a digital service. Cable customers have discounted phone calls and will not have to pay an upfront charge for digital boxes. Mr Booth brushed off suggestions that BSkyB was feeling threatened by competition from On Digital. 'On Digital will be a successful niche player but it will always be in a niche,' he said.

Stephen Grabiner, chief executive of On Digital, welcomed BSkyB's plans. He said BSkyB's decision to cease analogue transmissions would enable the government to feel more comfortable about switching off the terrestrial analogue signal. He hinted that On Digital would match BSkyB's offer.

BSkyB said the cost of acquiring each new subscriber would be £155. It is suspending dividend payments in favour of investing in digital. BSkyB is setting aside £315m to pay for the free transfer of its analogue subscribers to digital. However, Martin Stewart, chief financial officer, said switching off analogue transmissions would give BSkyB annual savings of £50m. BSkyB is increasing the monthly charge for many of its channels.

Cable & Wireless Communications, the UK's biggest cable operator, said its 200-channel digital television service would be launched in Manchester and the north west on July 1. It hoped to sign up about 200,000 customers during the first year and said it would always be able to charge less than BSkyB. But it warned that launching the channels would hit pre-tax profits.

© The Financial Times Limited, 6 May 1999. Reprinted with permission.

Case study 2.3
The prisoner's dilemma in practice: tit-for-tat in the First World War trenches

The 'price war game' is an example of a general game known as a prisoner's dilemma. In these games, the individual incentive of each player to defect (in the pricing game, to reduce prices) leads both players to a situation that leaves them collectively worse off. The original story involves two criminals who are arrested after committing a serious crime. The police have no proof of their involvement except for a minor infraction. The prosecutor offers them a deal whereby the one who implicates the other escapes all punishment and the other gets a heavy prison sentence. If both implicate the other, both end up in prison for a long time. The dominant strategy is for each criminal to implicate the other. Consequently they both end up getting relatively heavy prison sentences. When the game is repeated, however, co-operation can be sustained implicitly through dynamic strategies. In his classic book, *The Evolution of Co-operation*, University of Michigan political scientist Robert Axelrod studied empirically and experimentally the strategies that lead players involved in prisoner's dilemma type situations to co-operative outcomes. His starting point was an unexpected experimental result. When experts were asked to submit strategies for repeated prisoner's dilemma games and these strategies were matched with each other in a computer tournament, tit-for-tat, the simplest strategy, won. This was a strategy that simply started co-operating and then did to the other player what that player had done to it previously. Axelrod's analysis of the data found that tit-for-tat had four properties making a strategy successful. A successful strategy should be nice: confronted with a co-operative player, it should reciprocate. It should also be provocable: faced with an uncalled defection, it should respond. It should be forgiving: after responding to a defection, it should go back to co-operation. And it should be easy to understand: other players should be able to anticipate the consequences of their actions. Axelrod presents a surprising example of the usefulness of a variant of this strategy: First World War trench warfare. Here is a summary of his account.

The historical situation in the quiet sectors along the Western Front was a (repeated) prisoner's dilemma. At any time, the choices of two small units facing each other are to shoot to kill or deliberately to shoot to avoid causing damage. For both sides, weakening the enemy is important because it promotes survival. Therefore, in the short run it is better to do damage now whether the enemy is shooting back or not. What made trench warfare so different from most other combat was that the same small units faced each other in immobile sectors for extended periods of time. This changed the game from a one move prisoner's dilemma in which defection is the dominant choice, to an iterated prisoner's dilemma in which conditional strategies are possible. The result accorded with the theory's predictions: with sustained interaction, the stable outcome could be *mutual co-operation based upon reciprocity* (emphasis added). In particular, both sides followed strategies that would not be the first to defect, but that would be provoked if the other defected. As the lines stabilised, non-aggression between the troops emerged spontaneously in many places along the front. The earliest instances may have been associated with meals which were served at the same times on both sides of no-man's land. An eyewitness noted that: 'In one section the hour of 8 to 9 a.m. was regarded as consecrated to private business, and certain places indicated by a flag were regarded as out of bounds by the snipers on both sides'. In the summer of 1915 [a soldier noted that] 'It would be child's play to shell the road behind the enemy's trenches, crowded as it must be with ration wagons and water carts, into a bloodstained wilderness but on the whole there is silence. After all, if you prevent your enemy from drawing his rations, his remedy is simple: he will prevent you from drawing yours. The strategies were provocable. During the periods of mutual restraint, the enemy soldiers took pains to show to each other that they could indeed retaliate if necessary.

For example, German snipers showed their prowess to the British by aiming at spots on the walls of cottages and firing until they had cut a hole. (Extracted from Chapter 4 of *The Evolution of Co-operation*, by Robert Axelrod.)

Questions for discussion

1. Try to find examples from the real world that reasonably match any one of the classical models of oligopoly.

2. Give examples of firms that have benefited from first-mover advantage in oligopolistic markets.

3. Why is price leadership important in oligopoly and how are price leaders chosen?

4. Repeated games suggest that rivals are more likely to co-operate than to compete. Can you think of situations where firms are likely to compete in repeated games?

5. With reference to case study 2.2, discuss which oligopoly model best explains the behaviour of firms in the market for digital television subscribers.

Further reading

Asch, P. and Seneca, J. (1976) Is collusion profitable? *The Review of Economics and Statisitics*, **58**, 1–10.

Hall, R.L. and Hitch, C.J. (1939) Price theory and business behaviour, *Oxford Economic Papers*, **2**, 12–45.

Haskel, J. and Scaramozzino, P. (1997) Do other firms matter in oligopolies? *Journal of Industrial Economics*, **45**, 27–45.

Kashyap, A. (1995) Sticky prices: new evidence from retail catalogues, *Quarterly Journal of Economics*, **110**, 245–74.

Machlup, F. (1952) *The Economics of Sellers' Competition*. Baltimore: Johns Hopkins University Press.

Robinson, J. (1969) *The Economics of Imperfect Competition*, 2nd edn. London: Macmillan.

Roth, A.E. (1991) Game theory as a part of empirical economics, *Economic Journal*, **101**, 107–14.

Stigler, G.J. (1978) The literature of economics: the case of the kinked oligopoly demand curve, *Economic Inquiry*, **16**, 185–204. Reprinted as reading 10 in Wagner, L. (ed.) (1981) *Readings in Applied Micro-economics*. Oxford: Oxford University Press.

Collusion

3.1 Introduction

One aspect of business behaviour in industrial organisation which seems to attract much attention from the public, the press and government is that of collusive practices. Price-fixing is an easily understood strategy and one that will often have a direct consequence on the welfare of consumers. With such a high profile, it is not surprising that so much has been written about this subject. This chapter tries to order the literature and the ideas surrounding collusion in such a way as to develop the fundamental argument that almost all such practices are inherently unstable. Whenever possible we attempt to complement the theoretical models with examples drawn from diverse businesses and industries.

The chapter begins by examining some general reasons why firms may be attracted to collusion and the different forms collusion may take. In section 3.3 we focus on the institutions that help to shape and determine collusion. Many people seem to regard all collusion as being organised by cartels, which is a great oversimplification. In section 3.4 we discuss the various economic models of cartel and quasi-cartel behaviour. In section 3.5 we examine specific factors that will force firms to consider co-operative action. This is followed in section 3.6 by an analysis of market variables that are conducive to the establishment of a cartel. The last section examines the most important aspect of cartels and other co-operative ventures: their fundamental impermanence. The pressures facing cartel operations are divided into three parts. The first deals with internal pressures, such as numbers of firms, degree of product homogeneity, divergent goals of firms and effectiveness of sanctions for cheating. External pressures which stem from factors outside the direct control of firms in the industry, such as changes in demand, the entry of new firms and buyer concentration, are examined in the second part of section 3.7. Finally we analyse pressures that can be referred to as non-economic factors. These cover aspects such as leadership, trust and social cohesion. This issue is frequently ignored in an economic analysis of collusion.

3.2 Collusive action and collusive forms

In the idealised free market, all firms are assumed to act independently in their desire to seek the highest economic return. As we saw in Chapter 2, in oligopolistic structures, which are characterised by interdependence and uncertainty, such independent action is what most firms will attempt to avoid. It is the uncertainty and risk of independent action which act as a spur to firms to arrange some form of collusion in their industry. This desire was well summarised by Machlup (1952a, p.434):

> Unlimited competition may be a fine thing from the point of view of the political philosopher speculating about the welfare of people, but surely it is a nuisance from the point of view of most businessmen. There may be a few hardy individualists among them who enjoy vigorous competition as long as they are stronger than their opponents, can take pride in their success, and make enough money for comfort. But those that are losing ground and those that are losing money, or fear that they may lose, and all those who prefer an easy life to one of strain and strife – the majority, I dare say – regard unrestrained competition as an uncivilised way of doing business, unnecessarily costly of nervous energy and money, and disruptive of friendly relations with their fellow men.

A similar view was expressed by Whittlesey (1946, pp.19–20):

> The conventional picture of a typical businessman as a bold adventurer always on the alert for larger profits is a questionable abstraction. A more accurate characterisation of many established businessmen would be a comfortable middle-aged squire who would rather ride than walk, somewhat distasteful of elbowing the crowd, and more disposed to leave well enough alone than to run the risk of having his hat knocked off. Because cartels [collusion] are a means of softening the rigours of competition, they [it] could exist independently of any design to increase profits or raise prices.

Thus collusion is seen as a way of easing the pressures of competition by unified action rather than just a strategy to maximise joint profits. It has often been claimed that the collusive solution to the oligopoly problem is the most obvious solution. As Asch (1969, p.5) wrote:

> What, then, do oligopolists really do... Undoubtedly they do many things, but the specific suggestion offered here is that they frequently 'collude', 'conspire', or, otherwise 'agree' on coordinated policies.

Furthermore, Asch advanced three reasons for suggesting why oligopolists would follow such a strategy. Firstly it is plausible. Collusion does obviate the uncertainties of independent action and in some weak forms it need not be illegal or at least not easily detected, for example price leadership. Secondly it is realistic. Evidence shows that throughout the world anti-trust authorities are never short of work in investigating the sharper end of collusive practices. Thus it seems probable that the weaker forms abound. Collusion is a fact of economic life in oligopolistic markets. Lastly, Asch believed that collusion is simple. Co-operation reduces the complexities of interdependence. Firms no longer need to enter conjectural commitments, i.e. to speculate about the likely reactions of rivals.

Let us now discuss some general factors that may tempt firms into collusive activity. The most often quoted reason for collusion is that by decreasing the amount of competition, the firms can determine monopoly solutions and thus increase their profits. However, other issues, such as the problems of risk, market position, security and the need for information, can also be solved by a collusive strategy. The higher profits resulting from near-monopoly power can be adequately explained by traditional microeconomic models which are discussed later in the chapter. We focus now on the other points.

To some, risk was the major influence in the setting-up of co-operative structures. Some of the earliest writers placed a great emphasis on this specific point. MacGregor (1906, p.46) wrote: 'it is the pressure of risk which first arouses producers to the possibilities of another method of organisation'.

The risk facing firms is twofold. The first stems from the variability of demand:

> No method of industrial organisation will standardise the consumer. His demand for even such routine goods as food and clothing changes both quantitatively and qualitatively by accidents of time, place and value of money. Even a whole industry must face these changes, and provide whatever defences may lessen their influence.[1]

The second factor is the risk resulting directly from the competition within the industry. In the absence of any central control, firms may tend to overproduce and drive price below average cost:

> The market may be able to bear the increment of supply caused by himself [the firm]; but not an equivalent increment from all his rivals, if they retaliate by his own means, or if even they communicate panic to each other. This is the road which leads to crises.[2]

Under this dual pressure, MacGregor felt that the natural outcome would be an environment of insecurity brought about by firms speculating about rivals' behaviour, prices and outputs. This could generate 'secret and corrupt practices' for firms to hold onto their market shares. MacGregor concluded somewhat colourfully: 'There is some ground for saying that the lack of a well coordinated system of control makes industry resemble a mob rather than an army' (1906, p.53).

---

[1] MacGregor (1906), p.51.
[2] Ibid., p.52.

The one possible escape from these risks would be for the firm to develop market power independently on the basis of product differentiation, product innovation or vertical integration (issues that are explored in subsequent chapters of the book). But such a strategy would be costly and highly uncertain. Collusion is thus an obvious alternative solution to these risks.

Liefmann (1932) saw the development of combination or collusion as a result of the increased divergence between what he called the 'risk of capital' and the 'profit of capital'. He noted that modern mass production produced a potential risk to an entrepreneur's fixed capital if he were unable to keep his plant in continuous operation. He would also risk his working capital if he were unable to find sufficient customers for his finished goods. Combined with these pressures and risks on capital, the modern entrepreneur had seen a steady erosion of profits due to the intensification of competition as a result of the technology of mass production available to entrants. Liefmann claimed that this divergence reached a critical point when the capital risks could no longer be offset by profits earned. As soon as this occurred, common agreements became an accepted solution. Thus he concluded, 'competition had killed competition.'[3]

Nevertheless, both pre-war and more recent evidence provided little support for this view. Industries prone to rigorous competition are not necessarily made up of sickly firms, limping their way towards various agreements: 'Thus claims that competition has cutthroat and destructive propensities, and hence that cartelisation [collusion] is warranted, deserve to be taken with several grains of salt.'[4]

A more common thesis is that both position and security matter to oligopolists, and any move towards a guarantee of status and security, via collusive action, will be readily adopted. Perfect competition and monopoly, as theoretical ideals, are not concerned with market position. A perfectly competitive firm will regard itself as too insignificant to be concerned with status. In theory, a monopolist, as a sole supplier will not consider its position as a goal or objective. It cannot better its position. On the other hand, an oligopolist is aware of market share, for share defines its status in the industry. The oligopolist may wish to improve market share or at least to ensure that it is not eroded. In either event, the firm cannot ignore its position, and its position forms a central plank for strategic decision-making.

The above arguments are related to security. So long as the firm in perfect competition maximises profits, it will enjoy maximum security. The monopolist in the pure form fears no one and is consequently rewarded with absolute safety. The oligopolist does not enjoy such peace of mind. It faces the ever-present challenge to its position, both internally from rivals and externally from potential entrants.

Much of what has been discussed can be dealt with in a slightly different way. Collusion may be spurred by the existence of risks, the fear of loss of position, security and profit. All these risks can be very much lessened by the provision of useful market information. Thus the desire for information may itself be the powerful drive towards an agreement. We need therefore to develop a theory of information exchange. What follows is an outline of one such approach, that developed by O'Brien and Swann (1969).

[3] Liefmann (1932), p.21, who attributed this famous remark to Proudhon (1888).
[4] Scherer and Ross (1990), p.305.

O'Brien and Swann argued that all firms require information on which to base their decisions. The importance of such information will depend on the degree of interdependence in an industry, or the extent to which firms are 'vulnerable to damage' by the actions of other firms. This vulnerability is in essence the types of risk outlined above. The greater this vulnerability, the greater is the need for information. Firms are most vulnerable when undertaking investment decisions. A firm will not wish to suffer the consequences of over- or underinvestment. It may also be in the interests of other firms that a firm invests wisely, since miscalculations can lead to price-cutting or other 'panic' measures that could threaten group stability.

The type of information, its timing (whether pre-notification or post-notification), the means of communication (whether trade gossip or more formal, detailed memoranda), whether written or oral, will depend on the required degree of stability. Thus strict pre-notification agreements, identifying individual parties and their terms of sale, will result in greater uniformity and stability than if information were to be supplied annually in some general aggregate form.

The effect of such information exchange is to reduce firms' vulnerability and to increase group cohesiveness, since firms can react more efficiently when informed of some potentially destabilising event. Firms will also become more sensitive to one another and more aware of their relative market positions. It is also evident that information itself can drive firms towards greater co-operation and collusion. Once the above benefits are seen to exist, an *esprit de corps* may develop and there will be little desire to threaten group stability with overtly competitive behaviour. Thus it could be argued that the provision of information acts as the gelling agent for collusion.

Degrees and forms of collusion

Collusion is not a homogeneous form of behaviour. Very different degrees and forms can be observed. In this section we will identify and comment on some suggested classifications. According to Machlup (1952a) the difference between **degrees of collusion** and **forms of collusion** rests on the notion that *expectations* as to likely behaviour will define the likely degree of collusion, whereas the *basis for such expectations* will define the form of collusion.

The first degree of collusion, the weakest, is the expectation that rivals will not act independently unless the level of business activity warrants such action. We can move up several degrees to identify states where firms, even those suffering from slack business, will refrain from independent action. The '100th degree of collusion', the strongest, represents a state where each firm has a complete trust that rivals will stick to all agreements and rules of conduct, so long as the firm itself abides by such codes. Within this spectrum one can speculate where specific cases of collusion can be found. Thus, for example, Machlup suggested various scenarios for a '39th degree' and a '68th degree of collusion'.

When we examine the form of collusion, we do not necessarily recognise any close correlation between it and the degree of collusion. Collusion of a high degree may be based on a very informal understanding. Conversely it is possible that highly structured forms of collusion may be developed to determine some relatively low degree of collusion. Machlup separates the forms of collusion into two: those that rely on no formal agreement or communication and those forms of collusion that are based on explicit agreements.

Six forms of collusion are identified as belonging to the former group:

- The existence of an industry tradition. The belief, due to observations of consistent behaviour, that rivals will act or react in a predictable way.
- Informal expressions of opinion within the industry regarding trade practices, with a clear implication that firms will adhere to these expressed beliefs.
- Sales representatives from different firms exchange information about strategic decisions taken by their firms.
- Trade association announcements regarding proposed courses of action to be taken by firms. The implication is that firms will honour these commitments.
- Similar announcements made by individual firms, again with the clear understanding that firms will adhere to such announcements.
- The active participation of firms in trade association activities, which implies an adherence to codes of conduct.

Although the methodology used in the above classification system for an ascending order of collusion is a little unclear, one could argue that the six forms are differentiated by the degree of expectation as to likely conduct, the first form reflecting greater uncertainty than the second, the second being of greater uncertainty than the third, and so on. If the above argument is correct then the 'forms of collusion' could be interpreted as simply 'degrees of collusion' and negate much of Machlup's desire to keep the two apart.

Collusion which requires no formal agreement and takes the above forms will have developed from factors such as personal contacts, a group ethos and live-and-let-live attitudes. These factors will have added the necessary social lubrication for successful informal collusion. Personal and social contacts among competitors lessen rivalrous attitudes. One does not undercut or poach customers from people with whom one socialises. It will be argued later that social groupings, whether by ethnic origin, social class or even religion, have provided a powerful cement to otherwise potentially unstable collusive activities. This feeling of belonging, or an *esprit de corps*, can be strengthened by the existence of trade associations, trade journals, conferences and social activities. Judge Gary, president of US Steel, once explained: 'close communication and contact among the members of his industry had created such mutual "respect and affectionate regard" that they regarded themselves as honor-bound to protect one another, and that each felt that this moral obligation was "more binding on him than any written or verbal contract".'[5] Such feelings of geniality would undoubtedly foster the live-and-let-live attitude amongst rivals or what was referred to as 'considerate competition'.

Turning our attention to collusion based on explicit agreements, our first form is the *gentlemen's agreement*. This refers to an agreement that is purely oral, or where written notes are at a minimum. This form of collusion has many examples. A frequently quoted example is that of the Gary Dinners, where the top firms in the US steel industry met between the years 1907 and 1911. Although the dinners were social occasions, they were, more importantly, a vehicle for fixing prices and outputs through verbal communication. The colluders also believed that they were within the law if no formal agreement existed.

Written agreements could be regarded as higher forms of collusion. Formal contracts, stipulating rights and obligations, sanctions, fines, deposition of collateral and so on would

[5] See Machlup (1952b), p.87.

characterise these forms. The exact degree of the 'explicitness' of the agreement would depend on the number of issues covered by the agreement.

Finally, Machlup identified the highest form of collusion, which revolved around the sphere of governmental influence and guidance. Recognised (or tolerated) national and international cartels fall within this category. It is important to note that although this form of collusion may appear highly formalised there is no guarantee of a successful outcome. Inherent instabilities within the industry may more than outweigh any sophisticated organisational structure used to promote the collusion.

We have seen that collusive activity is a probable outcome in many oligopolistic markets, though it may take many different forms. In the next section we examine the various institutions which have been set up to promote and organise co-operative activities.

3.3 Collusive institutions

Alchian and Allen (1969, Chapter 18) used the term 'effective collusion' to refer to successful collusion.[6] Many attempts at collusion fail owing to the profusion of inherent problems, as will be seen later in the chapter. Parallel behaviour itself is not particularly good evidence of effective agreements. Alchian and Allen claimed that the existence of an 'enforcement technique' is better evidence. If costs are incurred to enforce parallel behaviour, there is a prima facie case for 'effective' collusion, since the costs of enforcement would implicitly be outweighed by the benefits of collusion: 'an effective collusion will be associated with some organisation in which membership is essential if one is to stay in business.'[7]

These organisations can take many forms. Our preoccupation will be with an examination of **trade associations** and **cartels**, since it is these types of institution which occur most frequently in oligopoly markets. Our first task will be to differentiate the two. We then discuss trade associations and cartels separately. Finally, we identify and discuss other institutional forms such as joint ventures and government-sponsored agreements.

Trade associations and cartels

What differences, if any, exist between cartels and trade associations? Both could be regarded as a collection of independent firms pursuing a joint course of action. In many books and reports, the two appear as almost synonymous terms. For example, the Board of Trade *Survey of Internal Cartels* discussed the role and activities of trade associations under the heading of 'cartels'.[8] In a practical sense, the difference often seems to rest on a legal interpretation. Thus trade associations, when seen as co-operative ventures which foster competition (for example by providing market information) or at least as organisations that do not frustrate the competitive ambitions of their members, are generally tolerated by legal authorities. An example of this view was presented by Dolan (1977): 'Unless trade associations promote competition and except as they do, there is little justification for their existence.'[9]

---

[6] Other authors have used the term to mean different things, for example Howard (1954), p.198, defined effective collusion as 'close collusion on price . . . but it permits nonprice competition'.

[7] Alchian and Allen (1969), p.406.

[8] Board of Trade (1944), p.iv.

[9] Oppenheim and Weston (1968) cited in Dolan (1977), p.273.

The implication is that once trade associations have been purged of any anti-competitive practices they undergo a metamorphosis to become the champions of greater competition. In reality, trade associations which were historically based on anti-competitive objectives may find it hard to adapt to new circumstances. This indeed, was one of the conclusions reached by Cuthbert and Black (1959, p.52):

> Many entrepreneurs, having grown up in this tradition of cooperation, will find it difficult to adjust themselves to different conditions. It may take more than the formal determination of agreements by the Restrictive Practices Court to ensure that they act competitively.

The term 'cartel' refers to a form of organisation adopted by firms in an oligopolistic industry in a clear attempt to effect a collusive set of decisions. The essential distinction is that a cartel's objective is to ensure a collusive outcome, whereas trade associations can be differentiated from cartels in so far as trade associations do not obviously pursue such ambitions. The dividing line is fine and in many cases can be blurred. The practical division of competitive or non-competitive activity is generally left to a legal interpretation. It is in this sense that people often conclude that trade associations are the 'legal' form of co-operation, and cartels, unless specifically tolerated by governments, are their 'illegal' counterpart.

Earlier writers have grappled with similar problems of distinction. Liefmann (1932) saw cartels as organisations with a purpose, the purpose being to 'achieve monopolistic control'.[10] To achieve this aim, most firms in the industry would have to be included within the agreement. Liefmann believed that about three-quarters of all firms should be included for effective monopolistic action. This fact alone is the distinguishing feature of cartels. In order to operate effectively, as many firms as possible have to be involved. Trade or professional associations, which attempt to improve the economic situation of their members do not require monopolistic control to achieve that objective.

Trade associations

Although it may be difficult to state clearly the precise function of trade associations, there certainly exist many idealised pictures of their role, for example:

> Trade associations can be enormously helpful to their memberships. They can expand and upgrade education and consumer information programs, launch new research and development programs, encourage ethical business practices and communicate the viewpoint of business in the political forum.[11]

What is it that trade associations actually do and to what extent can these actions be regarded as competitive or anti-competitive? One of the chief functions of trade associations is to provide members with industry information on sales, productive capacity, employment, creditworthiness of customers, quality of products and innovatory activity. They will also promote activities intended to reduce inefficiencies and promote better relations with customers, trade unions and governments. To achieve this goal they often publish trade journals, stimulate co-operative research programmes, instigate market research surveys, define trade terms and recruit lobby teams. In all these respects, so long as the trade

[10] Liefmann (1932), pp.8–9.
[11] Clanton (1977), p.307.

association does not attempt to frustrate the independent decision-making of its members, the association can be accepted as an organisation quite separate from a cartel. If trade associations undertake other activities, such as the fixing of prices, restriction of output and allocation of territories, they can no longer be regarded as non-collusive organisations. What behaviour constitutes legitimate action or collusive action is open to interpretation. For example, the objective of trying to standardise output could be seen either as a desire to improve the quality of the industry's product or alternatively as a means of ensuring price discipline by reducing the ability of firms to price differentially.

Another example concerns the issue of price reporting schemes or open-price associations. Through these schemes or associations, members inform one another, as well as outsiders, of the current and future prices for their products. The justification is that this ensures a model of fairness in competition in so far as it delivers the ideal of perfect knowledge, the necessary ingredient for a perfectly competitive market. However, for this to be so, a number of industry characteristics must be present. Wilcox (1960, p.77) identified the following: sellers must be numerous and relatively small, there must be no sizable entry barriers, prices should be fairly stable over time, output should be homogeneous and in small units, and demand should be relatively elastic. If these characteristics are not present, any price reporting agreement may simply provide cover for price controls. Furthermore, Wilcox added the proviso that the price reporting scheme itself, should not, be doctored in any sense, nor prevented from being disclosed to all parties, buyers included. No comments or suggestions as to likely future price policy should accompany such reports. They must remain neutral and informative. Whether in practice trade associations could so divorce themselves from such self-interest is doubtful.

Mund and Wolf (1971) and Machlup (1952b) suggested additional tests for the legitimate use of price reporting agreements. Mund and Wolf believed that agreements could be tolerated if they were limited to 'closed transactions'. Thus reported prices would be the actual prices. To report 'quoted' prices could open firms to pressure from the more dominant or militant members, to standardise all offer prices. Machlup stated that where 'waiting periods' were stipulated in the agreements, i.e. each member undertook to maintain the old price for a given period before announcing a new one, open-price agreements were similar to price-fixing agreements. A waiting period allowed firms to plan a price policy, confident in the knowledge that their rivals will not reduce their prices.

The popularity of price reporting systems reached a peak in the United States in the early years of the twentieth century, where they were welcomed variously as the 'new competition', 'open-door competition', 'open-price competition' and 'co-operative competition'. Many of the schemes were developed by a lawyer, Arthur Jerome Eddy, and became known as the Eddy Plan. Associations which undertook such plans became known as open-price associations. Nelson (1922, p.9) defined these associations in the following way:

> an organisation which provides a medium for the exchange of business information among members of a given industry whereby they may arrive at an intimate acquaintance with competitive conditions as they exist among themselves and in the whole industry.

Nelson saw these organisations as very different from 'ordinary trade associations' which were characterised by fairly loose structures with only very general aims. He quoted the case of the American Hardwood Manufacturers' Association which was very open in its price deliberations, inviting its customers, the press and any other interested parties to its meetings. Above all, it was felt that the most important of the objectives was the promotion of better relations amongst members, through regular and frequent meetings, than those achieved in the traditional trade associations. One cannot help but refer to Adam Smith's statement in 1776 as to the consequences of regular meetings between business people:

> people of the same trade seldom meet together, even for merriment and diversion, but the conversation ends in a conspiracy against the public, or in some contrivance to raise prices.[12]

As an interesting conclusion to our discussion on price reporting schemes we can refer to the Danish ready-mix concrete industry in the early 1990s. The Danish anti-trust agency, the Competition Council, decided to gather and publish market prices for three regional markets of Denmark. It believed that the provision of such price information would provide greater transparency in the market and thus greater competition. Albaek *et al.* (1997) found that as a consequence of the reporting scheme, average prices rose by some 15–20 per cent in one year. Having examined all possible explanations, the authors concluded that the rise was due to the 'improved scope for tacit collusion' following such price information. They also discovered that the relevant trade association would have been unable to provide such a price reporting scheme as there was insufficient trust amongst the members. Without a costly monitoring of members' price reports the system would not have been seen as credible.

To reach a conclusion as to whether a trade association is acting competitively or not, Herold (1977) and Dolan (1977) identified seven areas which could be examined:

● An examination of the association's pricing activity. Any agreement amongst trade association members to fix prices or allow courses of action which resulted in stable prices and inhibited market mechanisms was an obvious restraint of trade.

● The exclusivity of membership could serve as an indicator of specific economic advantage to existing members. Any association which barred or impeded membership to some firms would be deemed to be acting anti-competitively.

● The provision of statistical data should not be used as a vehicle for uniformity of action.

● The trade association's wish to standardise output by various certification procedures. As previously mentioned, this might have been aimed at maintaining minimum standards of product quality, but it could also have ensured either further symmetry of strategic decision-taking or a boycott of uncertified producers.

● The nature of the lobbying undertaken by associations. This activity could be viewed only as an indirect contributor to anti-competitive behaviour. There is no reason why lobbying *per se* should be anti-competitive, but it could provide the means for determining such a result.

● The involvement of associations in labour negotiations, whereby information exchanges led to price-fixing in the labour market.

● Any agreement over joint research could have been instrumental in weakening the competitive pressures to innovation, rather than being a spur to the development of new products and ideas.

One can conclude that the effects of trade associations are uncertain. They have in many cases been instrumental in creating strong collusion. The advantage of price information

---

[12] Smith (1937), p.128.

for stronger competition may be undermined by the use of such services to reinforce and police collusive agreements. Our conclusion will be that only a case-by-case approach could possibly establish the direction a trade association has decided to take. However, we can safely conclude that their organisational forms can provide the necessary stepping-stones to full-blooded collusion.

Cartels

Cartels are associations of independent firms in the same industry that are formed to increase their joint profits by restricting their competitive activities. To many people, cartels or cartel behaviour implies action taken by small groups of firms determined to exploit their market power to the full. In this sense they are seen as champions of rigid monopolistic ambitions and enjoying maximum profits. Furthermore, to the man in the street the word 'cartel' tends to connote something evil. Benton (1943, p.1) saw the term surrounded 'with a strange aroma suggesting some new social disease'. For the *New York Times*, 'The word cartel has become the label for something "bad". As an emotional symbol, it calls for the response of a "secret", "un-American", "contact with foreigners".'[13]

In reality, evidence shows that firms enter cartel type agreements to protect themselves rather than because of a desire to exploit the market.[14] Agreements tend, on the whole, to keep out or keep under control potential entrants and new products that could threaten the stability of existing firms. Price-fixing seems only to be of secondary importance, and usually as a means to support the less efficient members. Profits are not spectacularly higher than one would suppose, thus supporting the view that firms may aim at reasonable profits rather than maximising joint profits.[15] Fog (1956, p 22) echoed similar conclusions:

> it seems that the main purpose of many cartels is to obtain security rather than maximum profit *per se*. Of course, 'security' requires a good profit; but not necessarily maximum profit. From my own interviews I got the definite impression that the participants did not meet at the negotiations with any ideas about which cartel price would give the best profit. But each of them had an idea about a certain minimum price that nobody should be allowed to cut.

Since cartels reflect so many different forms and objectives, it is important to discuss some workable definition of a cartel. The word 'cartel' derives from the German word *kartelle* meaning a producers' association. Liefmann (1932) claimed that the term was coined to describe phenomena first observed in Germany. He also discovered that the word was first used publicly on 5 May 1879 in the Reichstag, by a certain Eugen Richter. The word *kartelle* is itself derived from the Latin *charta*, which means a paper or letter. The word was generally used in a military context referring to a written agreement for an exchange of prisoners. Thus this type of temporary truce led to the modern derivation of the word to apply to a truce amongst producers. Though it is interesting to note that the reference is to a 'truce' and not 'peace'.

The simplest and most concise definition was the one put forward by Liefmann (1932), who saw cartels as associations with 'monopolistic aims'. This, Liefmann considered was the necessary and sufficient definition. Other authors, he noted, wrote of cartels as associations

[13] *New York Times*, 14 September 1943, quoted in Hexner (1946), p.7.
[14] Hunter (1954), p.587.
[15] See, for example, Asch and Seneca (1976).

aiming to increase their profits. In fact cartels may often simply be attempting to prevent profits from falling too low. The idea of monopolistic intent as the essential constituent of a cartel definition caused much controversy. The word 'monopoly' itself has emotional connotations which may blur a reasonable application to collective action. Secondly, monopolistic behaviour can be so diverse and complex that it cannot provide sufficient precision to the cartel concept. Finally, some saw the monopolistic result of cartels as simply the consequence of the restriction of competition. It was this, according to Piotrowski[16] that gave a cartel its power in the market and it was this that had to be stressed in any definition.

Examples of more detailed definitions are those submitted by Hexner (1946) and Brems (1951). Hexner described a cartel as:

> a voluntary, potentially impermanent, business relationship among a number of independent, private entrepreneurs, which through coordinated marketing significantly affects the market commodity or service.[17]

He identified four elements that define a cartel. Firstly, the 'plurality of independent entrepreneurs'. This ensures that cartels are a 'collective' marketing control, rather than a marketing control exercised by one entrepreneur. The firms must also be effectively independent, rather than merely legally independent. If firms are very close then they may already form one large interest group, and thus cartelisation may not generate anything new in the market. Similarly, different divisions and subsiduaries within one parent company cannot be regarded as independent. Secondly, the cartel must be voluntary. There is a distinction between free and compulsory cartels. Hexner cites the case where the German Nazi Party abolished free cartels in the 1930s and transformed them into compulsory ones to ensure that they acted in accordance with specified social and macroeconomic objectives. The leadership within such compulsory cartels was directed and controlled by government regulations. Thirdly, a cartel must be of 'at least potential impermanence', i.e. a cartel is characterised by its temporary nature. Certainly much of the discussion later in the chapter supports this view. Finally, the cartel should serve the interests (whether real or imagined) of its members.

Brems (1951, p.52) defined cartels in the following way:

> A cartel is a voluntary, written or oral agreement among financially and personally independent, private, entrepreneurial sellers or buyers fixing or influencing the values of their parameters of action, or allocating territories, products or quotas, for a future period of time.

Brems adds a few more ideas. 'Personal independence' is included to ensure that interlocking directorships are excluded from cartel definitions. 'Private' ensures that cartels are limited to non-governmental organisations. 'Entrepreneurial sellers' is intended to excluded trade unions; and finally, the word 'or' in 'sellers or buyers' is designed to eliminate vertical integration from the definition.

It is interesting to note that Piotrowski's (1932) key concept of the definition of cartels, i.e. that of 'restriction of competition', does not appear in many definitions, especially the ones selected above. The reason for this is that competition may indeed survive within cartels, albeit in a different form. Competition in the marketplace could be replaced by

---

[16] Piotrowski (1932), pp.46–7.
[17] Hexner (1946), p.24.

competition around the negotiating table as part of the cartel bargaining process. This was part of Fog's (1956, p.23) conclusion:

> But even in a well established cartel the members may retain a competitive and even hostile attitude towards one another and all the time be on their guard – first of all the cartel may be dissolved again and be replaced by competition. This fact definitely limits the potentialities of a cartel. In the extreme case there may still be a high degree of competition even within a well organised cartel . . . [It] is possible under the guise of a well-established cartel to have competition so strong that it may be termed price warfare.

Cartels should not be thought of as a homogeneous form of organisation nor do they have similar ambitions. Observers have tried to classify many types of cartel. The OECD (1965) identified seven types: price cartel, quota cartel, allocation cartel, standardisation agreement, specialisation agreement, costing agreement and a rebate agreement. Wilcox (1960) identified four main categories according to the methods they employ: those that control the conditions surrounding a sale; those that attempt to fix costs, prices and profit margins; those that allocate particular territories and customers; and finally those that award members a fixed share of the productive capacity of the industry.[18] Many cartels fall into several categories or types.

Joint ventures and semi-collusion

So far, we have discussed trade associations and cartels, but we should mention briefly two other possible institutional developments: **joint ventures** and **semi-collusion**. A joint venture is an ad hoc association between two or more otherwise competing firms. Their form varies from country to country, even industry to industry. They can be referred to as a consortium or a syndicate, although the latter is generally applied to the fields of banking and insurance. Consortia are usually found where firms undertake activities that involve very high risks: sufficiently high to discourage any individual undertaking. In so far as such joint ventures may prevent or distort competition by coalescing the interests of existing firms, they approach the cartel model of behaviour. It could be argued, however, that they may provide innovatory stimulus and promote competition with the emergence of new products. Secondly, joint ventures may allow small firms to band together and overcome entry barriers in concentrated industries. Finally, sharing arrangements can generate the necessary economies to keep rivals in business.

Joint ventures have often been sponsored by governments and international bodies. The European Commission (1985, p.34) stated: 'Community action must . . . create an environment or conditions likely to favour the development of cooperation between undertakings.' However in a more recent report, the European Commission (1997a) was concerned that this type of co-operation could lead to a lessening of competition. It identified three main reasons why firms were keen to form joint ventures: to combine their resources in such a way as to achieve industry efficiencies, to enter a market, and lastly to develop joint research and development programmes. The report found that it was only the latter motive that provided 'convincing efficiency justifications for cooperation'.[19]

---

[18] Wilcox (1960), p.73.
[19] European Commission (1997a), p.175.

Not all joint ventures result in co-operative outcomes. Minehart and Neeman (1999) noted that partnerships such as joint ventures and strategic alliances may face problems when managers behave non-cooperatively so as to advance the interests of their firms. The issue is then how best to determine contracts that ensure that managers will maximise total partnership profits.

Semi-collusion occurs in markets where collusion cannot be determined in all aspects of firms' behaviour. Research and development, advertising, capital investment strategies are all difficult to subject to common agreements as it will be difficult to monitor compliance. It has thus been argued that firms may opt to collude in some activities and compete in others. Matsui (1989) argued that where the collusion took place in the product market and competition existed in other areas of business activity, then firms could be worse off and consumers better off. On the basis of a study of Japanese cartels in the 1960s, Matsui argued that firms accumulated excess capacity in the belief that cartel quotas would be based on capacity. The combination of cartelisation and excess capacity led to increased output and a reduction in firms' profits. Similar conclusions were reached by Steen and Sørgard (1999) when they examined semi-collusion in the Norwegian cement market. However, Brod and Shivakumar (1999) showed that where the non-production (competitive) activity was research and development, then spillovers could lead to either both producers and consumers being worse off or both being better off.

In our discussion of cartels we have concentrated on voluntary organisations, i.e. organisations free of any government control or intervention. Government-sponsored cartels or 'forced cartels' are a variation of the theme. Governments may either acquiesce to the demands of an oligopolistic group, or they may enforce cartelisation on reluctant firms. The justification for this has usually been to effect rationalisation, for example Britain and Germany in the 1930s, or to encourage 'orderly marketing' – the objective behind the UK's Agricultural Marketing Acts of 1931 and 1933.

3.4 Economic models of cartels

We now turn to an examination of the models that have been developed by economists to explain the goals, mechanics and problems faced by cartels. These models can range from the very simple to the complex, although the elegance of the exposition is not necessarily correlated with the degree of complexity. We begin by examining some general models and the treatment of cartel problems that are popular with authors of standard micro-economic textbooks. We also briefly discuss the contributions of Stigler (1964), Williamson (1975), Osborne (1976) and Von Neumann and Morgenstern's (1944) game theory. Finally, an attempt is made to outline some additional observations to the formal theory of oligopoly drawn from the study of social psychology.

Collusion occurs when, as a strategy, to collude is seen to be more profitable than to compete. For this to occur, not only must the maximised collusive profit be greater than the total combined maximised profits of the independent firms, but no individual firm must be allowed to extract a greater benefit should it follow an independent strategy based on an expectation that other firms will adhere to the agreement. Where such conditions cannot be met, competition will dominate collusion.

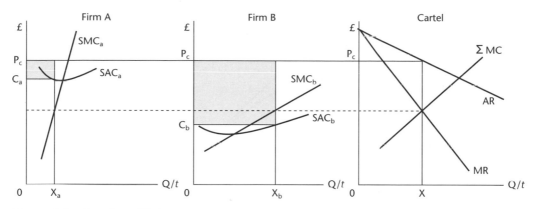

Figure 3.1 Cartel equilibrium

General models

The general model has many variants. We consider the simplest case, where a centralised cartel has complete control over price and output decisions and allocation of profit. We assume that entry into the industry is successfully deterred and that every firm's output is homogeneous. The maximisation of the cartel's profits is thus seen as a monopoly problem and resolved by determining output and price where the industry's marginal revenue equals the industry's marginal cost. The latter is the horizontal summation of all the short-run marginal cost curves of individual members.

Figure 3.1 represents a simplified two-firm case. Total industry costs are minimised by allocating quotas in such a way that the short-run marginal costs (SMC) of each firm, when producing its quota, are equal to the SMC of all other firms. Thus the inefficient firms, those with a steeper SMC, will be assigned a lower output quota than if they were independent. The reduction in output of the inefficient firms is made up by an increase in the output of the efficient firms. This rationalisation ensures that the rate of increase in total cost due to increased output of the efficient firm is less than the rate of decrease in total cost due to the decrease in output of the inefficient firms. The profit maximising price set by the cartel is P_c and total industry output is OX, of which OX_a is supplied by firm A and OX_b by firm B. As mentioned above, this type of static model is simplistic and many of the real-life problems of risk, conflict and the nature of costs have been ignored.

An alternative approach to cartel price determination is to focus directly on the divergent interests of members in a cartel. A model is developed on the recognition of the need to negotiate a mutually acceptable cartel price, rather than assume away any potential conflict. One such model has been outlined by Fog (1956).

Three firms A, B and C wish to fix a cartel price. All produce homogeneous goods. Figure 3.2 shows the profit curves for the three firms to reflect the expected profit at every cartel price. The horizontal axis measures the excess of the cartel price over the competitive price. Thus the intercept on the vertical axis represents the expected profit under conditions of competition, i.e. where the cartel price is equal to the competitive price and thus the difference between the two is zero.

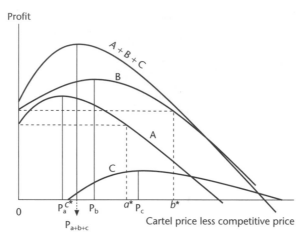

Figure 3.2 Fog's cartel model

At the competitive price we see that firms A and B enjoy a positive profit, whereas C makes a loss. Curve A + B + C represents joint profits. In Figure 3.2, firms A, B and C would favour cartel prices P_a, P_b and P_c, respectively. Room for manoeuvre is restricted by the following constraints: A will not accept a price above a^* since in that event its profits would fall below those realised at the competitive price level. Naturally C cannot accept a price below c^*. B would not wish to see a price above b^*. The scene is set for negotiations to determine some mutually beneficial outcome. It would seem that C is in a weak position and must accept the solution imposed by A and B. Fog assumed that C could threaten the position of A and B by 'active price competition'. This seems doubtful since any move towards a competitive price would see C suffer losses. We will have to assume that A and B are aware of C's poor position and consequently C is unable to bluff in any way. The joint profit-maximising price would be at P_{a+b+c} and indeed all three firms would benefit. Negotiations are complicated by such factors as different aspirations or goals of the firms, government policies and existence of potential entrants. Large firms will have large resources invested in the industry and will act to protect them from external threat. In essence this commitment broadens a firm's time horizon. A large firm will take a long-term view of the industry. It may well be reluctant to set up a high cartel price as this may attract the attention of potential entrants and government action.

As we have already suggested the idealised solution to the cartel problem as presented by Figure 3.1 is unlikely to be achieved in reality. Negotiations that include bluff, counter-bluff, give-and-take and compromise will dictate the exact nature of the solution. There may be no reason to suppose that the cartel will act in the same way as the monopolist: firms that dominate cartel negotiations may impose suboptimal outcomes. For example, they could secure larger output quotas at points where their marginal costs may be increasing at a faster rate than those of other firms. These issues are often difficult for theoretical models to explain. However, there are aspects of the cartel problem that can be tackled with tolerable precision.

The first major problem facing cartels is cheating or chiselling. Since price is raised above marginal cost, there is a temptation for firms to sell more than their allocated quotas. Price

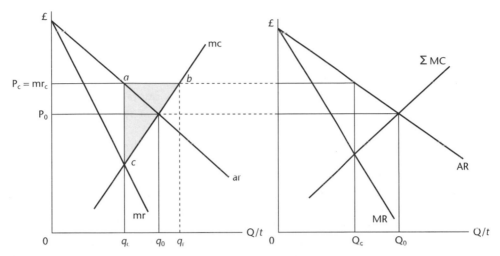

Figure 3.3 Stigler's recalcitrant firm

is maintained at the higher level because of the imposition of quotas, and hence any successful large-scale cheating will eventually lead to the collapse of the cartel. This is referred to as the 'free-rider' problem. The cheat hopes to profit at the expense of the loyal firms who maintain the high price through the sacrifice of their reduced output. This can be illustrated with reference to Stigler's 'recalcitrant firm' example.[20]

Figure 3.3 refers to an industry of n equal firms. The left-hand diagram represents one firm, which under conditions of competition produces Oq_0 at price OP_0. Total industry output is OQ_0 ($= n \cdot Oq_0$), i.e. where $\Sigma MC = AR$. After cartelisation the industry equates marginal cost with marginal revenue and sets the cartel price at P_c. Each firm is assigned quota Oq_c. This is similar to the previous analysis in Figure 3.1. Assume we have a firm that stays outside the agreement, or contemplates cheating. Its potential output is Oq_r at the cartel price OP_c. As a *price-taker* the firm is facing a perfectly elastic demand curve at the price OP_c, which also equals its marginal revenue. By equating the new MR with its MC, the firm produces at Oq_r. The output of each of the other members is then $(OQ_c - Oq_r)/(n - 1)$, which, if the number of loyal firms is large, is very little less than Oq_c. The effect on loyal members of the cartel is small, and they may tolerate the situation, since any costs of disciplining the recalcitrant firm may be greater than profits lost through such deviant behaviour. The cheat receives additional profits equal to the shaded area *abc* per unit of time. As Stigler concludes:

> And this is the first difficulty of forming a cartel. Every firm would prefer to be the outsider, and yet if enough stay outside, the cartel becomes futile: a large group of free riders will find that the streetcar won't run.[21]

The second problem that stems from the free-rider problem is that of potential entry. If sufficient outsiders enter an industry to exploit the higher prices, output will expand and prices fall, destroying the cartel. The cartel may well have to modify its pricing policy to

[20] Stigler (1966), p.233.
[21] Ibid.

exclude potential entrants; or if entrants are persistent, the cartel may seek some form of accommodation. This latter point is well discussed by Patinkin (1947).

The third problem facing the cartel is administrative. How should quotas be determined and profits divided? As already shown in Figure 3.1, quotas can be fixed by equating marginal costs across all firms. However, with a given cartel price, this implies that member firms will earn different levels of profit. Any move to equalise quotas and hence profits may reduce the total profit. One proposal for a solution could be a system of side-payments to compensate low profit earners. However, this solution implies a great degree of complex negotiations, policing and sanctions for non-compliance. Administration costs may far outweigh any benefit. Quotas could be set at suboptimal levels (less than those necessary to maximise industry profits) to make mutual compliance more likely; for example, quotas could be fixed according to capacity or pre-cartel output. However, as Stigler pointed out, quotas based on capacity levels may also lead to instability.[22]

The conclusions of economic theory as to the output policy of cartels have been frequently attacked. For example, Patinkin's (1947) conclusions – that output quotas will be determined on the basis of minimising total industry costs, and that the firms in the cartel will accept different quota levels or even accept a complete close-down of plants in return for an equitable slice of the profits – were criticised by Bain (1948). Bain argued that Patinkin's conclusions must be based on assumptions that cartels possess 'workable mechanisms' to distribute revenues to member firms on some basis other than quotas, and that mutual trust exists in the industry in sufficient strength to damp down individual profit considerations. Profit-pooling, the inevitable ingredient of a successful Patinkin strategy, was, according to Bain, markedly absent in American industry.

We can conclude that a failure to maximise joint industry profits could be due to any one or a combination of factors. These are: the inability to solve the administrative problem; the fear that success may encourage new entry; the disproportionate benefits that accrue to disloyal members; the problem of product differentiation; different cost conditions; and the different discount rates, whereby different firms place different weights on short-run and long-run profits. If one also considers that such a strategy may have to be conducted in an environment of secrecy, to avoid legal detection, the problem is deepened.

Some additional approaches

Stigler (1964) explored the factors that facilitated effective collusion. The core of his argument was that collusion is successful when it is accompanied by an efficient method of policing the agreements. He focused less on the problem of determining the collusive price and output, and more on the detection of potential violators. He argued that because cheating on an agreement will bring about a positive benefit to disloyal firms, some machinery of enforcement must be present. Efficient enforcement of the agreement is therefore a crucial determinant of successful collusion. The method of enforcement proposed by Stigler was to detect 'significant deviations from the agreed-upon prices'. If a firm is detected, the violation will cease, since otherwise the loyal firms will retaliate. The speed of retaliation will thus implicitly define the strength or weakness of the conspiracy. The most effective method of determining secret price-cutting is to check the transaction prices in the market.

---

[22] Ibid., p.235. Stigler argued that revenues flowing from quotas based on capacity levels would simply stimulate investment rivalry amongst the cartel members.

Notwithstanding the practical difficulties of such audits[23] there is still no guarantee that a detailed inspection will be able to detect violations.[24]

Stigler argued that evidence of cheating was inferred from unplanned changes in the market shares of individual firms. If a firm discovers that it is systematically losing business that it would normally expect to secure, only one conclusion is possible. All markets are subject to normal variability, but the size of this 'market-share variability'[25] will depend on such factors as the size and number of firms in the industry, as well as the degree of homogeneity of output and number of buyers. The greater the market-share variability, the greater the potential for secret price-cuts, since it would take longer for loyal firms to observe marked changes in market shares. Stigler's approach led to the following conclusions. Collusion was more effective where actual transaction prices were correctly reported, as in government contracts. Collusion was less effective where the identity of the buyers changed frequently. Finally, success of collusion varied inversely with the numbers of sellers and buyers and entry of new buyers.

Stigler's approach can be criticised in some respects. It is not particularly obvious that detection is a sufficient deterrent, as Yamey (1970) noted: '[I]n Stigler's analysis, the detected offender suffers no penalty other than that of having to discontinue his cheating'. Furthermore, Stigler ignored much else about collusive agreements by concentrating on the detection of cheating. Stigler's approach can at best be regarded as a partial theory of collusion. Williamson (1975, p.244) argued:

> Stigler's analysis runs almost entirely in terms of prices. Moreover, he takes as given that the collusive agreement has already been reached. Attention is focused instead on cheating and on statistical inference techniques for detecting cheaters. While this last is very useful and calls attention in an interesting way to aspects of the oligopoly problem that others have neglected, it is also incomplete . . . monitoring is only one of a series of contracting steps, and not plainly the one that warrants priority attention.

Williamson's (1975) approach was to view collusion as a problem of contracting. His model assumed agreements to be lawful, though participants could not rely on the courts to enforce the terms of the agreements and firms would have to develop their own armoury of weapons to cope with the problems of enforcement and punishment of deviant behaviour. Entry was assumed to be difficult. The efficiency of contractual agreement for collusive activity would depend on a number of factors. These were:

- *The ability to specify contractual relations correctly.* Williamson believed that a 'comprehensive joint maximising statement' would be difficult to achieve. The chief reason was that such a statement would entail a great amount of information, for example production costs of each firm, the nature of the product, the degree of innovation invested by individual firms, their selling costs, financial strategies as well as the 'interaction effects between the decision variables within and between firms'.[26] Not only would this information be

---

[23] As Stigler (1968), p.44, commented: 'The detection of secret price cutting will of course be as difficult as interested parties can make it. The price cutter will certainly protest his innocence, or, if this would tax credulity beyond its taxable capacity, blame a disobedient subordinate.'

[24] There were, for example, some sophisticated methods of cheating on price agreements by recourse to reciprocal trade. See Stocking and Mueller (1957).

[25] Term used by Yamey (1970).

[26] Williamson (1975), p.240.

expensive to amass, interpret and to transform into specific policies for each firm, but it would also be necessary to place these policies into an unknown future context. If the contract was to be specified correctly, all future contingencies had be anticipated. Joint profit maximisation cannot be easily translated from theoretical abstraction to the operational problems one meets in practice: 'the resulting complexity becomes impossibly great in addition, when . . . the optimisation problem is cast in a multiperiod framework under conditions of uncertainty, abstract analysis breaks down.'[27]

● *The extent to which agreement can be reached over joint gains.* Even if joint profit maximisation could be specified contractually, a number of problems would immediately arise. Joint profit maximisation entails the reduction of output of some firms and the expansion of output of others. Since the firms that have expanded output are in a relatively powerful position, their rivals, faced with demands to reduce their output, may be reluctant to agree to, or tolerate such 'manufactured' dominance in the marketplace. Simply put, some firms fear that if the agreements were to break down then they would be left in a less powerful position than before the agreement.

● *Uncertainty.* The agreement is also subject to various uncertainties. Firms must thus agree on how to tackle any changes in the economic environment. This may bring about costly haggling if the firms see an opportunity to profit from any such changes.

● *Monitoring.* In Williamson's terminology, cheating was seen as 'the pairing of opportunism with information impactedness'.[28] Individual firms may not be able to detect fellow conspirators' price cuts, i.e. information is impacted, and if one were to add the widely held belief that cheating will confer benefits, cheating may be inevitable. Monitoring was obviously necessary to detect and deter any such deviations. Monitoring or the policing of agreements will be made more complex where non-price competition exists.

● *Penalties.* Effective collusion must eventually rest on the presence of available sanctions against deviant behaviour. In the absence of any legal protection for cartels, the cartel must impose penalties 'in the marketplace', such as a reduction in price to the cheat's level, cease inter-firm co-operation and raid key employees. However, the success of these penalties must depend on the effectiveness of the deterrent as well as the willingness of the loyal firms to impose them. The enforcers, i.e. the loyal firms, will also incur costs by introducing such sanctions. Indeed, some of the firms may defect from the loyal group and secretly aid the cheat if a benefit can be realised, for example selling any necessary supplies at a premium price. All these questions must be considered by the colluding group if it wishes to ensure success.

Some people tend to regard oligopolistic collusion as an attempt to achieve a monopolistic solution and then treat successful cartels as effective monopolies. Williamson's contracting approach clearly underlines the difference between the problems that a monopolist faces and those that the interdependent oligopoly faces:

> The monopolist . . . enjoys an advantage over oligopolists in adaptational respects since he does not have to write a contract in which future contingencies are identified and appropriate adaption thereto devised. Rather, he can face the contingencies when they arise; each bridge can be crossed when it is reached, rather than having to decide *ex ante* how to cross all bridges that one may conceivably face. Put differently, the monopolist can employ adaptive, sequential

[27] Ibid.
[28] Ibid., p.242.

decision-making procedure, which greatly economises on bounded rationality demands, without exposing himself to risks of contractual incompleteness which face a group of oligopolists.[29]

Game theory was discussed in the previous chapter. It can be simply summarised as a method for the 'study of decision-making in situations of conflict'.[30] The approach is in essence concerned with analysing strategic interaction. As we saw in Chapter 2, the prisoners' dilemma game is a popular model used to explain suboptimal outcomes, i.e. where a Nash equilibrium does not necessarily lead to a Pareto optimal outcome.[31] This particular game is often used to explain why cartels are inherently unstable. Firms are faced with two choices: whether to collude or whether to cheat. If a firm believes its rival will remain loyal to the agreement, it will profit the firm to cheat. If the firm believes the rival will cheat, then the firm will cheat as well. Thus both firms cheat and earn a return which is less than the collude–collude strategy. The game can be modified if one were to consider the game as a 'one-shot affair' or whether it would be repeated an infinite number of times.

Experiments have shown that the dynamics of rivalry is an important issue.[32] Continuous rivalry teaches firms that co-operation is the optimal outcome. To cheat invites immediate retaliation and no long-term rewards. It was claimed in Porter's (1983) paper that such implied tit-for-tat behaviour helped a railroad cartel of the 1880s to maintain its stability. While game theory hasn't provided economics with a general theory of oligopoly it has helped to explain some real-life issues. It has illustrated the strong incentive for collusion under certain conditions. Playing 'oligopoly games' with computers, based on payoff matrices, has provided useful insights into the behaviour of decision makers under conditions of uncertainty. However it may be true to say that Hurwicz's (1945, p.924) critique of von Neumann and Morgenstern, seems appropriate even today:

> The potentialities of von Neumann's and Morgenstern's new approach seem tremendous and may, one hopes, lead to revamping, and enriching in realism, a good deal of economic theory. But to a large extent they are only potentialities: results are still largely a matter of future developments.

Osborne (1976) developed an interesting model that reflects the prisoners' dilemma game and can also be applied to an analysis of how a cartel can discourage cheating. This latter point is explored towards the end of this chapter. The model makes use of isoprofit curves, which can illustrate the rivalry between oligopolists. We assume a duopoly of firm A and firm B and that their appropriate strategy is to vary their level of output.

We discussed the derivation of isoprofit curves in Chapter 2. An isoprofit curve is a set of points that yield the same level of profit for a given firm for given level of outputs. In Figure 3.4 these curves, labelled A_1, A_2, and A_3, are concave to their respective axis and curves nearer the axis represent higher levels of profit. Thus $A_3 > A_2 > A_1$.

If we assume that B produces Q_1^B, the highest profit that A can make is at output Q_1^A. No other level of output will generate as much profit. If B were to reduce output to Q_2^B then A could increase profits (to A_2) by increasing output from Q_1^A to Q_2^A. This is so since A and B are rivals who produce goods that are substitutes. If B abandons a segment of the market, A will profit by this. Similar reasoning will apply to points Q_3^B and Q_3^A. A

---

[29] Ibid., p.245.

[30] Shubik (1959), p.8.

[31] Pareto optimality is said to exist when resources are so allocated that it is not possible to make anyone better off without making someone else worse off.

[32] See Axlerod (1984) for an extended discussion.

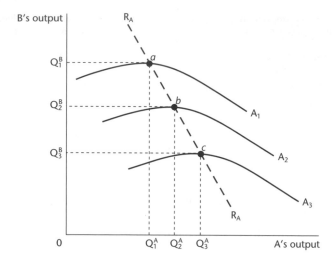

Figure 3.4 Isoprofit curves

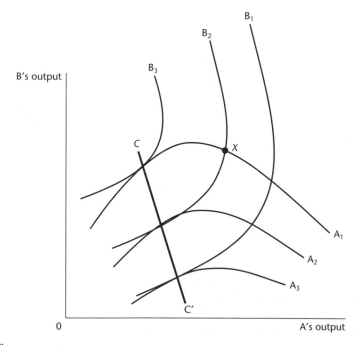

Figure 3.5 The contract curve

curve ($R_A R_A$) linking points *a*, *b* and *c* traces the reactions of A to changes in B's output. It is a locus of profit maxima points associated with B's output and it is referred to as A's reaction curve.

If we combine the isoprofit curves of A and B we can trace out a contract curve of optimal outputs, CC′, shown in Figure 3.5. Any point off the contract curve is non-optimal, for example point X, since it would be possible to improve one firm's profit position

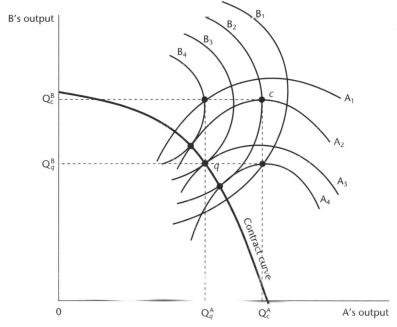

Figure 3.6 Cartel stability

without harming the profit position of the other. If one is off the contract curve it is always possible to move back to the curve in such a way as to benefit at least one firm and to harm nobody. We can employ this model to illustrate the problem of cartel stability.

In Figure 3.6 we assume the cartel selects point q on the contract curve. B's output quota is Q_q^B and A's is Q_q^A. If A expects B to keep to the (agreed) quota, A maximises profits at output Q_c^A. In a similar way, B maximises profits at output Q_c^B if he expects A to stick to the agreement. If both cheat, both will end up at point c, which is off the contract curve and both are worse off. It is also clear that if one firm cheats then the other is better off cheating as well, rather than sticking to the cartel quota. This type of solution reflects the prisoners' dilemma conclusion: that, in the absence of an enforceable contract, firms will cheat.

Oligopoly – an interpretation from social psychology

In addition to mainstream economic theories there have been some notable attempts to integrate the study of oligopoly with other disciplines such as sociology and psychology.[33] These attempts have tried to present a more realistic theory of oligopoly, stressing that firms in an oligopoly belong to a group and that oligopoly decisions are in essence group decisions. Group behaviour exhibits quite different traits from individual behaviour, and yet economic theory seems almost totally concerned with the latter. If economists make certain assumptions about the reactions of 'rational economic man' and for which sociologists and psychologists find no evidence, it might be argued that newer theories should be built on the basis of

[33] See, for example, Phillips (1962), Cyert and March (1964), Stern (1971) and *Economist* (2000), p.112.

sociology and psychology: 'If economic theories are at variance with the postulates of other social sciences, it then becomes essential to reinvestigate the fields involved in order to construct a theoretical framework that will be consistent with all levels of investigation.'[34]

One interesting contribution to group dynamics in an oligopoly context has been provided by Benz and Wolkomir (1964), who based their work on Sherif and Sherif (1956). The analysis proceeds as follows. Individuals frequently come into contact with each other as a result of some focal issue, for example university course, football team, stallholders in a market. If this focal issue helps to develop common goals, such as attending good lectures, securing a share of a transfer fee, maximising takings, then an informal group will develop. Sherif and Sherif define the group as:

> [a] social unit which consists of a number of individuals who stand in (more or less) definite status and role relationships to one another and which possesses a set of values or norms of its own regulating the behaviour of individual members, at least in matters of consequence to the group.[35]

Naturally, conflict will arise when groups with mutually exclusive goals meet. If subordinate goals can be introduced that require 'collective interaction', conflict will be reduced and co-operative action will result. When firms compete for a market share, inter-firm conflict results. Firms initially view rivals as members of an out-group. In fact, any individual or firm that generates a cost of production to the firm, for example raw material suppliers, labour and governments, as well as rival firms, will be regarded as members of the out-group. In time, certain norms of behaviour and attitudes will arise owing to the similarity of the economic environment that each firm is facing – the same technology, customer behaviour, government action, labour demands, and so on. The firms in the industry will move closer together and will begin to view the industry as a reference group, i.e. they sense a mutual feeling of belonging. This may lead firms once regarded as part of the out-group, to be included within the in-group.

The focal issue or common goal that unites firms is the desire to organise their environment. The initial impetus comes from the inherent conflict present in the oligopolistic industry. Thus in a contradictory manner, conflict may bring about the necessary cohesion for group solidarity. For example, independent firms, in effect members of different out-groups, may unite to form an in-group to put an end to price-cutting which becomes their common (uniting) goal. Conflict may then be channelled into what is regarded as the less disruptive areas, perhaps product differentiation or research and development. The cohesiveness of the group will be even stronger where the conflict is seen to stem from outside the industry. The common goal, in the face of external threat, is then simply survival. Furthermore, we could add that the greater the threat of conflict, the greater is the group bond and the less likely the chance of deviant behaviour.

While the above approach does suggest an alternative to standard economic theory, there are obvious difficulties in attempting to develop an experimental model to test the relationship between group structures in various industries and any resultant behaviour. Indeed, one would have to redefine whole industries, not according to output, but perhaps according to group affinities. To develop meaningful structures in which groups function, an exhaustive and difficult firm-by-firm and industry-by-industry analysis would be essential.

---

[34] Benz and Wolkomir (1964), p.291.
[35] Sherif and Sherif (1956), p.144.

3.5 Factors encouraging firms to seek cartel solutions

Some of the factors encouraging firms into cartels have already been briefly examined in the previous section when we discussed the reasons why firms felt it necessary to collude. In order to avoid duplication of prior arguments we will focus on just three issues: unsatisfactory performance, the level of risk and uncertainty, and the similarities in costs amongst members.

Unsatisfactory performance

Firms are naturally concerned with profitability. Years of poor profitability caused by an ever-increasing competitive industry with frequent price-cutting can eventually prompt firms to explore strategies that might establish an accommodation with rivals. It was this sort of pressure which forced the American Plumbing Fixtures Manufacturers to develop price-fixing agreements in the 1960s. The price conspiracy was rationalised by the executives of the fifteen companies involved as not '"gouging" the public, just seeking an adequate profit'.[36] Profits may also be low as the result of a general depression in the industry. The frequently quoted examples of price agreements in the American bleachers, electrical equipment and pipe industries all followed periods of decline and poor performance in those industries. As one economist noted: 'Certain economic conditions – depressions, recessions, or downward movements in industry demand – provide both a favourable climate and a powerful incentive for conspiracy.'[37]

Further evidence is provided by Asch and Seneca (1976). They attempted to estimate the effect that collusion had on the profitability of American manufacturing corporations between 1958 and 1967. In the second part of their paper they reversed the causality, to examine the effect profitability had on the level of collusion. They found that collusion and firm profitability were negatively related. They argued that this result was consistent with the hypothesis that unsatisfactory profits would force firms to collude. An alternative explanation of the correlation was to suggest that their sample was largely made up of collusive-prone firms, and since the data were based on unsuccessful examples of collusion, a poor collusive performance was more likely to be discovered.[38] Nevertheless, this does tend to reinforce the initial argument, that poor profit performance may induce collusion, which then proceeds under conditions unfavourable to its success. The bleacher manufacturers suffered lower profits during the Second World War owing to their inability to obtain steel and other materials. The formation of price and tendering agreements in the industry could not of itself solve the underlying problem, that of supply shortages. Consequently, the agreements were unstable.

Schmitt and Weder (1998) examined the factors that propelled firms in the Swiss dyestuff industry into cartel agreements after the First World War. Two major factors were identified. Firstly the drop in foreign demand owing to increased protection and an increase in productive capacity in those countries; secondly the entry of German firms on

---

[36] *Fortune* (1969), p.96.

[37] Erickson (1969), p.83.

[38] Their sample was made up of companies that were found guilty of collusion or had entered 'nolo contendere' pleas, in response to the Sherman Act conspiracy charge.

to the world market. Scmitt and Weder quote the view of the Ciba representative from the minutes of the first cartel meeting in 1918, who:

> pointed to the necessity to establish some close form of cooperation among the Basle dye factories, in order to successfully meet the competition from the established German firms as well as from the new producers in all countries . . . which would arise once normal circumstances return.[39]

A firm's growth record can also reflect the extent to which a firm has achieved a satisfactory performance. In an earlier paper Asch and Seneca (1975) suggested that growth and profits could be correlated, and thus growth as a variable could be included when examining factors encouraging firms to collude. One could argue that firms in a declining industry are more likely to collude in an attempt to restore rates of return to some historical level. Declining industries may also see the breakdown of 'orderly marketing' or other forms of **tacit collusion**, as firms begin to undercut rivals in a desperate bid to maintain their positions. This sudden lack of industry discipline may encourage firms to suggest more overt and specific forms of collusion. Palmer (1972) attempted to test the hypothesis that firms in declining industries are more likely to collude than firms in expanding industries. Using US data he examined the growth rates of industries that were subject to anti-trust suits between 1966 and 1970. He found that the declining industry hypothesis was consistent with the evidence.

Risk and uncertainty

Risk is an important and indeed a central characteristic of oligopoly. The presence of interdependence, requiring each firm to ascertain likely reactions of its rivals, implies uncertainty and risk. We saw earlier in the chapter that risks emanating from variable levels of demand and the actions of rivals often forced firms into collective solutions. In this section we suggest some additional specific factors.

One important source of uncertainty is a firm's exposure to 'lumpiness' and infrequency of orders. Scherer and Ross (1990) put forward two arguments why the presence of large, infrequent orders may destroy some degree of tacit collusion and may force firms to consider overt collusion. Any price reduction from some tacitly agreed norm involves a cost in the form of lower future profits owing to retaliation from the other firms. This cost is independent of the size of the order, whereas the short-term benefit depends on the size of the order. Hence, owing to this 'cost versus benefit' imbalance, undercutting will more likely occur where orders are large and irregular, rather than small and regular. Furthermore, some firms may be operating under very short-run time horizons and therefore willing to accept the immediate gain of a large order rather than worry about the cost of future retaliations that may or may not occur. Firms with large overheads or sudden excess capacity may well be tempted into breaking rank and undercutting some tacit price agreement. Scherer and Ross quoted examples from the cast-iron pipe, electrical equipment and antibiotics industries, to show that the risk and uncertainty of such industries, characterised by large, infrequent orders, led to the formation of 'bidding cartels to restrain industry members' competitive zeal'.[40]

---

[39] Schmitt and Weder (1998), p.211.
[40] Scherer and Ross (1990), p.307.

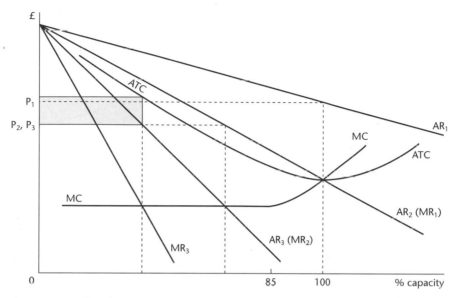

Figure 3.7 Firm A, low fixed-cost producer

In his study of pricing in the UK electrical equipment industry, Richardson (1966) found that the industry suffered badly from excess capacity, due to the variability of the government's electricity investment programmes, technical advances, and lack of any co-ordination on the part of the independent manufacturers. He concluded, as many firms would have done, that price competition would not solve the above problem, and argued in favour of price agreements amongst the manufacturers and with government. Agreed prices would guarantee a reasonable return to firms, who had installed capacity to meet the variable government demand.

An additional source of instability for tacit collusion would be the presence of a high ratio of fixed to variable costs. Typically, firms dependent on heavy investment in the extraction of natural deposits and capital-intensive methods of production (petroleum, coal, chemicals, steel, cement, paper) are susceptible to these pressures. To explain why, we can refer to the Scherer and Ross (1990) model.[41] We compare two firms. Firm A is a low fixed-cost producer and firm B is a high fixed-cost producer. A's fixed costs account for a small proportion of average total costs (ATC) at, for example, the 85 per cent level of planned output; whereas B's fixed costs account for around one-half of average total costs at the 85 per cent planned output level. It is further assumed that marginal costs are constant up to the 85 per cent capacity level and that the average costs of both firms are equal at the 100 per cent capacity level. This model is shown in Figures 3.7 and 3.8.

Both firms face the same three linear demand curves, one for each phase of the business cycle: prosperity being represented by AR_1, gentle recession by AR_2 and a severe recession by AR_3. Each lower demand curve is so drawn that it is half the slope of the preceding one, enabling it to serve additionally as the marginal revenue function for the preceding demand curve. It can also be shown that the demand curves have the same elasticity at any

[41] Scherer and Ross (1990), pp.285–94 for a full discussion.

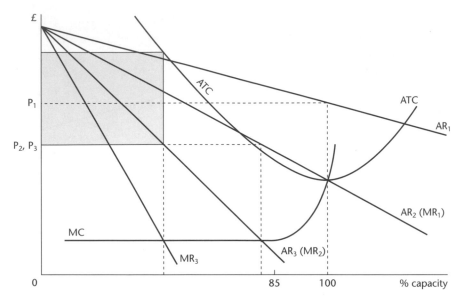

Figure 3.8 Firm B, high fixed-cost producer

price. If each firm operates at 100 per cent capacity, then during prosperity each will sell at price OP_1 and enjoy profits. As a result of a gentle recession, firm A must reduce output substantially and make a small price change to OP_2. (We also assume that rivals match all price reductions, so that market shares will remain constant.) Faced with the same scenario, B's strategy is for a smaller reduction in output, but a larger reduction in price. Consequently it can be shown that B's profits fall proportionately more than those of A.

If we now consider a severe recession in which demand drops to AR_3, A's price is unchanged as is B's.[42] We conclude that for joint profit maximisation, little if any price reduction is called for. However, the profit positions of the two firms are very different. If one compares the two shaded areas, A is only just incurring a loss, whereas B is suffering a much larger loss. B is facing a crisis of survival. It will consider any strategy to extricate itself from its predicament. It will consider moving off any 'constant-shares' demand curve onto a 'rival's price constant' demand curve, i.e. undercutting its rivals. This strategy may in time lead to further price reductions, well away from any joint profit-maximising price OP_3, as rivals begin to react to their diminishing market shares. Thus the higher the fixed cost relative to total costs, the greater the risks of price warfare. Scherer and Ross conclude that: 'the probability of price discipline breakdowns increases with the burden of fixed costs borne by sellers *ceteris paribus*, but that recognition of this danger may stimulate institutional adaptations nullifying the tendency'.[43]

The degree of collusion as a function of the level of risk in an industry would appear to be difficult to measure. High risk may bring about collusion, but the intended result of such collusion would be to reduce such risks. Ambiguity as to the direction of causation

---

[42] In fact Scherer and Ross's model shows a very small reduction in price, since their demand curve (D3) does not intersect the horizontal portion of the marginal cost curve.
[43] Scherer and Ross (1990), p.290.

is obvious. Asch and Seneca (1975) measured risk as the standard deviation of residuals from a trend fitted to each firm's profits over a period of time. They found little systematic evidence either way, a finding consistent with the above argument.

Similar cost functions

Firms that enjoy similar costs will tend to find it easier to collude than those whose differences in costs are pronounced. A firm which is faced with a declining cost function as output is increased, owing to economies of scale, may be reluctant to restrict its output as a condition of cartel membership. Indeed, in the absence of side-payments that offset the opportunity costs incurred by membership of the cartel, a firm will be reluctant to join the cartel in the first place.

If quotas are determined by the cartel on the basis of *equal* percentage cutbacks from prior 'competitive' output levels; then, on the assumption of different marginal costs, unequal shares of cartel profits will result. Much of the discussion surrounding the foundation of the uranium cartel in 1980 rested on the realisation that in the mining of uranium there are a wide variety of deposits, at different depths and thicknesses and consequently a wide variety of marginal costs (Rothwell, 1980). Quotas, devised to ensure an equitable distribution of cartel profits, were thus an important precondition of success in this particular cartel. Furthermore, the strategy of lower output may run counter to a firm's long-run ambitions of eventually challenging the larger firms. This can only be achieved by the expansion of sales and not by moves to restrict them. We can thus safely conclude that firms are discouraged from joining or establishing a cartel because of a marked difference in their costs. Some of the above issues were explored by Rothschild (1999) from the point of view of different firm costs threatening the stability of the cartel.

3.6 Market variables conducive to cartel formation

Market variables conducive to cartel-like organisations are numerous. We begin our study with an analysis of the level of industrial concentration and the numbers of firms involved. Most economists would place these two variables in a prominent position. Collusion would be facilitated by the high level of concentration of a few firms, since the lines of communication between the existing and potential cartel members are small. The expected relationship would therefore be a positive one between concentration and collusion, and negative between the number of firms and collusion. Other factors, which may help to determine collusive solutions, which are examined in this section, are the lack of product differentiation, inelastic demand, the degree of asymmetry of market shares, vertical integration and the existence of strong, unified trade associations.

Industrial concentration and the number of firms

A common hypothesis is that firms will find it easier to establish collusive solutions to their oligopoly problem in industries characterised by high levels of concentration. The hypothesis is based on theories of group and coalition behaviour that show that, as numbers increase, the unanimity of goals will diminish. With a dilution of this unanimity, the group will incur greater enforcement (or transactions) costs. As the number of firms grows so the costs of monitoring and adjusting to other firms' behaviour will grow at a disproportionately fast rate. Throughout the literature on cartels, this variable crops up most often. In 1906, MacGregor wrote: 'The formation of a Trust or Cartel requires in the first place that the parties shall be few enough to come to terms readily.'[44] More recently Erickson (1969, p.84) provided a good example of the conventional wisdom.

> the single most important factor in the development of collusive pricing is the structure of the industry, particularly the number of firms. Studies of specific industries have revealed again and again the significance of structure here. In bleachers, an industry where there was a particularly successful conspiracy, the market was dominated by four, then six, and finally eight firms. In electrical equipment, another industry that had a particularly successful set of conspiracies, the various markets were again dominated by a very few firms.

A systematic theory of how numbers affect the extent of collusion is provided by Phillips (1962) and Scherer and Ross (1990). As the number of sellers increases, the importance of each of the firms to total output will diminish and firms are more likely to ignore the possible effects of any independent action by a rival. Secondly, as the number of sellers increases there is a greater temptation for a 'rogue' firm deliberately to undercut the cartel price as it feels the risk of detection is less. Finally, since firms will often have different views as to the optimal cartel strategy, a process of inter-firm communication to reconcile these differences will be necessary. This co-ordination is made more difficult if the number of sellers increases. In the absence of a strong selling agency or trade association, the number of channels of communication rises exponentially with the number of sellers. Thus one channel will suffice for two firms, but six are required for four firms, fifteen for six firms, and so on.[45] A breakdown in any one channel may precipitate retaliation and turmoil well beyond the two parties.

The above hypothesis seems to be borne out by the empirical evidence. Hay and Kelley (1974) found that of 50 cases of reported conspiracy for which four-firm concentration ratios could be calculated, 38 had a value greater than 50 per cent. They also found that the average number of firms involved in a conspiracy was 7.25, and in 79 per cent of all conspiracies examined, 10 or fewer firms were involved:

> The number of firms is a variable which was very much on the minds of the potential conspirators; in one of the case studies the product which was to be subject to agreement was deliberately defined narrowly in order to keep the number of participants small.[46]

The relatively high level of concentration will also ensure that the fringe of non-colluders will be kept as small as possible. If the non-colluding fringe of sellers makes negligible inroads into the markets of colluding firms, it will be tolerated. Indeed, any other action might run the risk of alerting the anti-competition authorities. However, if the fringe of sellers begins to make serious inroads into market shares, then defensive strategies such as price reductions

---

[44] MacGregor (1906), p.120.
[45] Based on the expression $N(N - 1)/2$.
[46] Hay and Kelley (1974), p.23.

may be instigated.[47] We can conclude that if there is a sizable fringe of firms that cannot be induced to join the cartel, there is little chance of success in maximising joint profits. Bain (1959) noted that the tacitly set collusive price (though this would apply equally to an explicitly set price) in the American tobacco industry was:

> Significantly influenced and limited by the threat of aggressive independent competition. Cigarette prices, though collusively determined, appear to have been held below the industry profit-maximising level in part because of the rivalry and independence of action of a limited group of independents.[48]

Similarly, Armentano (1975) found that price-fixing conspiracies in the electrical equipment industry were always threatened by small 'non-national' firms, who, when geographically close to potential customers, would, in times of falling demand, quote a price just to cover costs. The industry was also threatened by a fringe of so-called tin-makers, i.e. firms who produced inferior equipment and would regularly underbid any nationally agreed price.

An additional, related variable to the level of concentration can be the level of past concentration. It might be expected that the more stable the level of concentration over time, the more collusive the behaviour. Little research has been done in this area and most of the evidence is based on casual empiricism.[49] One historical example of such stability was the collusion in the heavy woollen industry, observed by Glover (1977, p.231):

> The number of firms regularly engaged in heavy woollen cloth contracting does not seem to have varied greatly in the period 1820–50 except during the years of deep general depression in the early 1840s, which brought many desperate bidders into this market, and structurally the trade had the appearance of a concentrated core of enterprises of efficient size with a more or less competitive fringe of smaller firms continuously fluctuating in size and composition.

One should, however, not expect the positive relationship between collusion and concentration to be continuous. There are many cases where high seller concentration did not invariably lead to collusion. Asch and Seneca (1975) found no significant association between the number of firms in the industry and the degree of collusion. In addition, they found that there was no significant difference between collusive and non-collusive firms, based solely on their industry's concentration ratios.

To resolve this contradiction one could argue that very high concentration may lead to tacit co-operation, but that at slightly lower levels of concentration, as group numbers increase, a more formal, overt type of collusion is required. An industry comprising three or four firms may well be able to organise itself informally. If the industry experiences changes in structural conditions such as the entry of new firms, this tacit form of collusion may no longer work. Fraas and Greer (1977) postulated that at one very favourable extreme, for example two firms selling a homogeneous product, **explicit collusion** is possible but hardly necessary. At the other extreme, i.e. many firms selling differentiated products at

---

[47] An example of such conduct was the allegation by the liquidator of Laker Airways (later to be proved largely correct by the American courts) that the major airlines (British Airways, Lufthansa, Swissair, Pan Am and TWA) conspired to drive Laker out of business by reducing their fares. Laker was regarded by one airline chairman (Thompson of British Caledonian) as 'the most disruptive airline on the North Atlantic' (*Sunday Times*, 3 April 1983).

[48] Bain (1959), p.307.

[49] See, for example, Adams (1981).

irregular intervals, explicit collusion is much more difficult but nonetheless essential for the success of joint profit maximisation. It is in the intermediate conditions that one would expect to find more collusive-prone industries.

On testing just such a hypothesis, Fraas and Greer found that:

> the evidence indicates that as the number of parties increases and/or as the structural conditions become increasingly complex, conspirators must increasingly resort to arrangements of more elaborate design or greater efficiency if they are to achieve their joint maximising objectives.[50]

Asymmetry of market shares

The asymmetry of market shares, i.e. the size distribution of firms, is yet another variable that can affect the ability of firms to collude. It is commonly argued that, where firms in an industry are of roughly equal size, the chance of collusion, *ceteris paribus*, is enhanced. One of the earliest proponents of this argument was MacGregor (1906), who regarded it as one of his six necessary conditions for the formation of a cartel. He argued that the large firms would probably already have eliminated the smaller firms through the usual process of independent competition. Substantial asymmetry thus implies a divergence of views between the large and the small firms. The small firms may, for example, be reluctant to adopt quotas based on existing market shares, while the large firms may use the collusive agreement as a springboard for increased dominance.

However, there is a degree of ambiguity over this particular variable. It could be argued that market asymmetry enhances the ability of a few large firms to initiate and enforce a profitable agreement. Phillips (1962) argued that unequal market shares can create a degree of stability and order in the industry. Some firms will act as leaders, others will accept the role of followers. The leaders will have the necessary authority to lead the group towards the realisation of co-operative ventures. Smaller firms will follow through the knowledge that as high-cost producers they can easily be punished by the larger firms in the form of price reductions. If the large firms are vertically integrated they may also punish the smaller firms by affecting their supply and demand conditions. The fear of economic loss need not be the sole reason for co-ordination in asymmetrical market structures. Phillips noted: 'A number of other factors might be mentioned, going to such vague influences as historical prominence and a reputation for wisdom and fairness. But whatever the source of power, it tends to diminish the degree of rivalry.'[51]

Product differentiation

Homogeneity of output or lack of **product differentiation** is also seen as an important factor in facilitating efficient collusion. One would expect, all other things being equal, that price-fixing would be more difficult where there was marked product differentiation. Firms selling homogeneous goods need only focus on a narrow range of pricing decisions. The greater the number of variables affecting any real or perceived differences in the output, the greater complexity for price-fixing. Thus, Armentano (1975, p.307) noted that: 'Consumer goods industries, with their usual emphasis on diversity and differentiation, would appear

---

[50] Fraas and Greer (1977), p.43.
[51] Phillips (1962), pp.31–2.

to be poor candidates for successful price collusion.' This was also the conclusion reached earlier by MacGregor (1906, pp.122–3):

> [C]ombination is much easier if there is some degree of uniformity in the products of the firms ... There is also abundant evidence that the process of formation is impeded by differences in quality ... and for this reason finishing industries are not easily combined. Thus the German Steel Cartel has not yet been able to take complete control of finished products, which are still sold by the individual works. Syndication is as a rule possible only for raw material and half-finished goods.

In theory, product heterogeneity can be measured by the degree of cross-elasticity of demand between the various products. However, products, while homogeneous in this sense, may still be supplied under many varied conditions and specifications. Thus a product such as steel springs for upholstery seems at first sight to be fairly homogeneous. The price list used by the Spring and Interior Springing Association recorded over four hundred separate prices, according to height, thickness of spring, alloys used, status of buyer and so on.[52] Negotiating, monitoring and renewing such an array of prices will naturally increase the complexity of the collusion.

A further complication could rest on the degree of homogeneity over time. If a product is subject to change, due to frequent technological improvements, or changes in consumer tastes, a price agreement would be all the more difficult to negotiate and sustain. Thus one would expect collusion to be more difficult to arrange in an industry characterised by high rates of technological change or subject to fashions.

Measuring the effect that product differentiation has had on collusion is particularly difficult and most empirical work has relied on measures indirectly related to product differentiation. Asch and Seneca (1975) divided their sample into producer goods and consumer goods industries, on the assumption that the former are more homogeneous than the latter. The implication was that producer goods industries would thus be more collusion-prone. Such a relationship, although weak, was demonstrated. A second test was based on examining the advertising-to-sales ratios and collusion for all industries, on the assumption that advertising intensity is associated with perceived differences of the products. They found that. 'Advertising intensity by itself ... is significantly related to collusive behaviour as firms in low-advertising industries are associated with collusion.'[53] This conclusion is clouded by the expectation that high advertising is a potential entry barrier, which itself could also affect the level of collusion. (We turn to the question of entry barriers when we examine cartel stability.) More recently, Symeonidis (1999) argued that product differentiation through investment in advertising or research and development will frustrate collusion since the 'low-quality' firms are less likely to collude with the 'high-quality' producers. He found that UK firms in the 1950s with high R&D/sales and high advertising/sales ratios were less likely to be involved in collusive pricing.

Kantzenbach et al. (1995) suggested that one could modify the general conclusion that greater product differentiation hampers effective collusion. They argued that where firms could not reduce such product differentiation, this could lead to a change in the *form* of collusion rather than a total inability to conclude an agreement. Firms could abandon any hope of fixing prices and instead attempt to divide the market by product type or geography.

[52] Office of Fair Trading (OFT) Register, Agreement no. 1132.
[53] Asch and Seneca (1975), p.232.

They also believed that cheating would be less likely as, firstly, the price elasticity of demand would tend to be low: firms would have to make substantial price reductions to increase their market shares. Secondly, punishment would be more effective in that the price-cuts need only be concentrated in a few market segments. This general conclusion has also been supported by Davidson (1983) and Ross (1992).

Inelastic demand

Collusion is far more likely to be attempted where demand is inelastic. If higher prices are to lead to higher revenues it is implicit that demand will be inelastic. The cost of not fixing a high price when the demand curve is inelastic is the higher profit forgone. The implication is that the price agreement must cover all substitute goods, i.e. include most of the firms in the industry. There is much circumstantial and subjective evidence that inelastic demand was indeed present in many cases of collusion.[54] A note of caution is provided by Posner (1976). He claims that there is some ambiguity surrounding the relationship of inelasticity of demand and the propensity to collude. Elastic demand could imply that the sellers have forced the price up to the elastic region of the demand curve, so as to maximise monopoly profit. Indeed, it is thus possible to infer that inelastic demand at current prices is evidence that sellers are not colluding.

Vertical integration

The success of cartel operations will depend on the ability of member firms to be reassured that fellow members are abiding by the terms of the agreement. They must therefore be in a position to monitor deviations from such agreements. If one of the members is vertically integrated downstream, for example it owns retail outlets, it may be able to undercut the cartel price by reducing its transfer price to its retail outlets. Unless the members are fully aware of the true costs involved in retail operations, they may be unable to detect such cheating. This state of affairs would then compromise the efficiency of the cartel. Rothwell (1980), however, added a rider to this argument. It may often be a condition of cartel formation that firms should be integrated, though this appears to be the case where most of the potential members are already integrated.

Strong trade association

The existence of a strong and efficient trade association will provide the necessary operational mechanism for setting up the cartel. A trade association can gather, process and disseminate information, and this function can form the basis of an agreement. Erickson (1969, p.87) found that: 'In both the electrical equipment and bleacher industries, and in the earlier cases as well, conspiratorial meetings were held at, or immediately after, the regular trade association meetings.'

The vast majority of price and other cartel agreements in the UK prior to their abandonment or modification, in the late 1950s, were operated through the relevant trade

---

[54] See, for example, Erickson (1969), p.86.

association. This factor was also one of MacGregor's (1906) necessary preconditions for the successful formation of a cartel. He wrote:

> [T]he process of formation is easier if there have been already opportunities for communication between the parties which combine. Such opportunities furnished by Chambers of Commerce, by associations of masters with reference to the demands of labour, by Institutes and Congresses, or by temporary associations such as are formed to make representations to the Legislature regarding the claims of an industry.[55]

More recently the report by the Organisation for Economic Co-operation and Development (OECD, 1999, p.8) into oligopolies also highlighted the role of trade associations:

> Participating in industry associations could also be regarded as a facilitating practice especially where associations are used to promote or disguise the exchange of sensitive information, adoption of anti-competitive standards, or changes in government regulations which would facilitate co-ordinated interaction.

Allied to a strong trade association one could briefly add the role of a strong individual leadership in the development of cartels. (This factor is discussed in more detail towards the end of the chapter.) Erickson (1969) found that in the bleacher industry, one forceful executive took such a strong exception to the proposed conspiracy that it was doomed from the outset. Fog (1956) quoted the views of some Danish cartel members which seem to support the notion that while it is difficult to estimate leadership's true contribution to effective collusion, it is, nevertheless, very important.

3.7 Pressures on cartel stability

The lack of long-run cartel stability has characterised most, if not all agreements in oligopolistic markets. Writers have frequently given examples of the inevitable short-run nature of all cartels. One such typical comment is: 'Many of them lasted a day, some of them lasted until the gentlemen could go to the telephone from the room in which they were made.'[56]

Where agreements appear to have lasted for some period of time, their effectiveness in promoting joint profit maximisation may have been negligible. One sales executive once remarked on the near-impossibility of fixing anything worthwhile:

> If you are talking about meeting to increase the 'book' price of a transformer, that's one thing. If you meet to increase the 'market' price of a transformer, you can talk all week and you can't get to first base, because nobody in a meeting has control over the market price.[57]

Brozen (1975), a supporter of the Chicago school, devoted a whole section of his book to seven readings on the instability of price conspiracies, with each reading dwelling on the ineffectiveness and fragility of agreements not to compete.

The reason that so many cartels fail to live up to expectations is that the 'obvious' solution to oligopolistic interdependence is far more complicated than it may at first appear. The complication is that what appears optimal for the group may not be optimal for

[55] MacGregor (1906), p.123.
[56] Davis (1974), p.351.
[57] Sultan (1974), pp.52–3.

each of the individual members. This divergence of interests necessitates some method of bargaining to reconcile these differences. Fellner (1965) believed that the basic reason for the instability of co-ordinated action was that the bargaining strength of members would change in unpredictable ways. The consequence of these changes is that the group must create outlets for these changes, which in turn can be regarded as mutually acceptable forms of competition within the group. These outlets could, for example, allow firms some individual control over cost-saving innovations, to pursue product differentiation or to invest in innovatory activity. There would thus be a recognition that superior skills must somehow be rewarded. These outlets would diminish the ability of the group to maximise joint profits, but, more importantly, Fellner saw that these outlets might not be sufficient to channel and control the competitive zeal of members. As a result, skirmishes and wars would break out from time to time. Since firms were aware of these possibilities they would wish to stay 'armed'. Since joint profit maximisation required disarmament (i.e. the reduction of productive capacity), such a goal could be difficult to realise.

One other general issue that might affect stability was the suggestion by Prokop (1999). This was the neglected topic of the *process* of cartel formation. Two models of cartel formation were suggested by Prokop. The first was a 'sequential-moves game'. In this game, each firm had in turn to decide whether to join the cartel or whether to remain with the non-cartel fringe. The alternative model was the 'simultaneous-moves game', in which all firms had to decide simultaneously whether to join the cartel or not. Prokop also showed that cartel stability was more likely in the first model than in the second.

In this chapter we examine some of the specific factors which can lead to the frustration of long-term co-operation. These factors have been classified into three groups: those that spring from the internal pressures or constraints facing the firm, for example the number of firms and different goals of members. Factors that spring from the external environment can generally be regarded as producing an external threat to industry stability, for example entry and changes in demand. Finally, we examine some variables usually considered beyond the scope of economic analysis but nonetheless crucial to the survival and effectiveness of group co-ordination: the issues of leadership, trust and social homogeneity.

Internal pressures on stability

Seller concentration and fewness of number

As we saw in the previous section, seller concentration and the number of firms was important to the establishment of effective cartels. Understandably, the same force which may help the creation of such organisations will help to sustain them. Nonetheless, it is possible that cartels have been formed with a level of concentration unsuitable to the actual day-to-day running of such an operation. Indeed, it may be argued that where structural conditions are perhaps not particularly favourable to collusion, such as a substantial number of firms, a formal cartel is necessary to effect such an end. Since the structural conditions will remain unfavourable, it is logical to assume that the cartel will be undermined by argument and cheating.

The degree of seller concentration affects the stability of collusion on the assumption that communication amongst the colluders detection of cheating is easier the more concentrated the industry. Furthermore, if the number of firms is small, retaliation, (the deterrent to cheating), is much quicker. If the retaliation lag is lengthy, the payoff from cheating becomes more attractive since the short-run gains from cheating outweigh the long-run losses of lower future profits. If, on the other hand, the retaliation lag is short, the expected net effect would be for a loss. This, according to Spaan and Erickson (1970), was the reason for the failure of many of the railroad cartels in the United States.

Research in the field of 'experimental oligopoly' has supported the above notion that price and profit stability is affected by the number of firms. Dolbear *et al.* (1968, p.259), for example, concluded: 'The number of firms in the market had a significant effect upon average profit and price under both information states [incomplete and complete information] . . . Finally, stability increased as N [number of firms] decreased.'

Different goals of members

When faced with a heterogeneous collection of firms existing in an uncertain coalition, it is more than probable that the individual firms will have substantially different goals. Thus, there may be an inherent internal goal conflict which can either remain lightly buried in the interests of group solidarity, or rise to the surface at any time. Members may disagree over such issues as short- and long-run policies, the due regard that should be paid to potential competition and how best to treat the risks of any government reaction to anti-competitive behaviour. Cartel literature is full of examples of conflict amongst firms.

Fog (1956) noted that larger firms tended to seek stable, long-run policies, while smaller firms were more interested in exploiting short-run opportunities. Pindyck (1977) found that members of the International Bauxite Association in Australia, faced with high transport costs and excess capacity, had an incentive to sell bauxite 'outside the cartel boundaries'. In his research on the baseball industry, Davis (1974, p.356) found that within the leagues some firms were less concerned with profit than others:

> Agreement within the cartel is also hampered by the fact that not all members are profit maximisers. Some owners view baseball as largely a sporting activity, with profitability at most a secondary concern. Even today, teams like the Red Sox and the Cubs behave quite differently from teams like the Dodgers. Given the relatively small size of the cartel and the protected positions of its members, this divergence of goals tends to produce instability.

Davis noted a further divergence of goals between the rich and the poor clubs over methods of redistributing gate receipts. In 1901, a plan had been agreed to ensure that visiting teams received 30 cents for each grandstand ticket sold and 20 cents from every 'bleacher' ticket, roughly 40 per cent of the gate. By 1953, the increase in ticket prices had reduced the share of the gate to 21 per cent:

> In that year Bill Veeck argued for a return to the old percentage but was voted down. In his words, 'Five clubs voted for the change I suggested and three voted against it. Since it takes six to make a change, I was licked. And who do you think lined up against me? You're right – the rich ones. The Yankees, Tigers and Red Sox.'[58]

A further example is Sultan's (1974) work on the famous American electrical equipment conspiracy. In one documented bid in 1958, to supply turbine generators to the New England Power Company, two of the largest firms badly needed the order. Westinghouse had not had a new order in 1958 and Allis–Chalmers was anxious to establish a foothold in

---

[58] Davis (1974), p.357.

that part of the United States. Both were willing to undercut any established price to secure the order. Westinghouse was given the 'start' position, but to ensure the success of their bid, their bid was some US$200,000 lower than it had promised to bid. On hearing of this 'deception', General Electric, a third member of the group, undercut that bid and secured the contract. A similar case occurred in a Tennessee Valley Authority (TVA) order. Westinghouse and General Electric agreed that one of them should provide a technically more efficient generator, while the other would submit a lower price. General Electric cheated in both respects, providing a more sophisticated unit and deducting US$90,000 from the bid, claiming that the deduction was for factory tests as permitted by the TVA. Recounting the subsequent meeting between the firms, one Westinghouse executive said: 'The only [thing] that happened was this obscene remark at quite great length, "screwed again" or something like that, and with that I left.'[59]

Extent of non-price competition

A cartel will be more unstable if there are possibilities for non-price competition. If the elimination of price competition leads to the development of alternative forms of competition, such as product innovation and advertising, any advantage of co-operative action could be dissipated away by these competitive outlets. An effective cartel must thus ensure that firms do not gain an edge over their rivals by non-price strategies. Thus, for example, a cartel may attempt to enforce **basing-point pricing**, whereby the transport cost component of any price is calculated from one fixed point so as to eliminate regional competition. The cartel may also attempt to standardise the quality of the product. Naturally, in markets where only price competition can exist, such as in 'fungible commodities',[60] where small price reductions can capture large proportions of rivals' market, the elimination of such reductions will ensure a great degree of stability.

Sanctions

The ability of a cartel to employ effective sanctions against cheats can also ensure cartel discipline and stability. It is a fact of cartel life that if additional profits can be realised by cheating, then cheating will occur, unless some policy of deterrence is adopted. Stigler (1968, p.42) made the following observation: 'It is surely one of the axioms of human behaviour that all agreements whose violation would be profitable to the violator must be enforced.'

There are many sanctions which can be applied against cheats. In their study of restrictive practices in the food trades, Cuthbert and Black (1959) found two types of sanction in use: the fine and the expulsion. Any member who broke the terms of the agreement would be fined, and in some cases fines were regarded as heavy. Expulsion, as a sanction, implies that any advantage of belonging to an association or cartel is lost. This consequence may be very serious if raw material suppliers co-operate with the association and agree not to supply non-members.

A common sanction is the matching of price-cuts. There is a large quantity of empirical evidence and elegant theorising for the use of such strategies. Stigler (1968, p.42) wrote:

---

[59] Quoted in Sultan (1974), p.69.
[60] Term used by Posner (1976), p.60, meaning products that have a high positive cross-elasticity of demand.

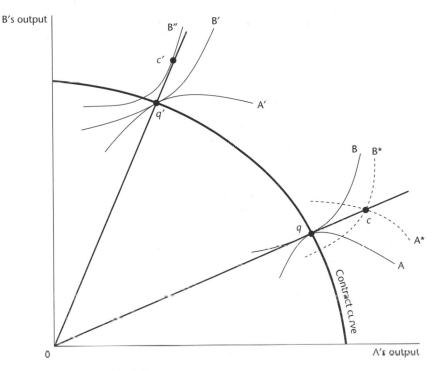

Figure 3.9 Osborne's cartel stability

Enforcement consists basically of detecting significant deviations from the agreed-upon prices. Once detected, the deviations will tend to disappear because they are no longer secret and will be matched by fellow conspirators if they are not withdrawn.

Examples of such actions can be found in studies of the railroad cartels in the United States.[61] Rees (1993a) found that in the British salt duopoly any gain from cheating was outweighed by losses from 'credible' short-term price-cuts. Levenstein (1996, 1997) also observed such use of effective short-term price-cutting in the bromine cartel prior to the First World War, though she argued that severe price wars could signal a new round of price bargaining and the determination of a fresh set of rents. Further theoretical analyses, as regards factors generating effective sanctions, have been provided by Osborne (1976) who argued that an optimally set quota level would itself solve the problem of cheating. The model was introduced earlier and we can use it to develop the above argument.

In Figure 3.9, A's output can be read as the output of the loyal firms in the cartel and B's output as the output of the potential cheat. As we saw in Figure 3.5, the contract curve is traced out by the points of tangency of the isoprofit curves of the two parties.

Assuming cross-effects to be similar (i.e. the marginal effect on B's price of an increase in the output of A is equal to the effect on A's price of an increase of B's output), Osborne shows that the optimum location on the contract curve would be on a ray from the origin,

---

[61] See, for example, the actions proposed by the Western Traffic Association in 1885, in Orr and MacAvoy (1965), p.186.

where it is tangential to the two isoprofit curves. Such a point is labelled q. The potential cheat is then informed that if it expands output the cartel will react by expanding its output by that proportion necessary to maintain its market share. The implied threat is that point c will be reached. At this point the cartel and the cheat suffer lower profits (A*, B*). This, according to Osborne, will deter cheating.

However, if the cartel makes a mistake and allocates quotas according to point q', where a ray from the origin is not tangential to the two isoprofit curves, then the strategy is doomed. The potential cheat has an incentive to expand its output. If the cartel maintains its market share (staying on the ray), a point such as c' is reached, where the defector's profits are higher (B''). The implication of Osborne's thesis is that, for success, a cartel must choose carefully where to be on the contract curve. It must have exact information as to total industry output and the shares of all the members. It must also act quickly to negate any potential gains arising from cheating.

Allied to this question of effective sanctions we can introduce the issue of **sealed bidding**. Sealed bid competition occurs when a buyer (frequently the government) requests bids for a contract, and subsequently announces the result publicly. The firms submit their bids secretly. This situation may encourage the bidding firms to meet and discuss their bids and decide which of them should win the contract. If a firm should decide to cheat on this arrangement, i.e. submit a lower than the prearranged bid, it will immediately be detected, and thus the incentive to do so is substantially reduced. 'The system of sealed bids, publicly opened with full identification of each bidder's price and specifications, is the ideal instrument for the detection of price cutting. There exists no alternative method of secretly cutting prices . . .'.[62]

Indeed, sealed bidding may be so effective in ensuring discipline, that the collusion may be limited to the sealed bid part of the relevant market. An interesting account of how sealed bidding worked in practice can be found in Herling's (1962) work on the electrical equipment conspiracy,[63] although a note of caution was sounded in the work of Hay and Kelley (1974). Hay and Kelley found that, in some cases, bids to government agencies were actually excluded from any agreement in the belief that such a collusion could easily be detected by the government.

As well as financial penalties such as fines and forced profit reductions, a cartel may attempt to use the services of third parties as possible solutions to cheating. A joint sales agency through which all output is channelled will naturally overcome the problem of price-cutting, though allocative problems might soon surface. An agreement may also rely on some independent arbitration,[64] and, in the case of legal agreements, the help of legal penalties and pressures could also provide the necessary stability. Lastly, one should be aware that some firms have used or threatened physical injury to keep cartel members 'in line'. It has been argued, and indeed, some evidence has been found, that organised crime can be effective in policing cartel agreements.[65]

In examining the importance of sanctions, one should bear in mind that if it appears to be in the economic interests of a firm to break an agreement, no sanction is likely to be

---

[62] Stigler (1968), pp.44–5.

[63] Herling (1962). See page 72 for an account of such an agreement. In this case, sealed bidding was insufficient to prevent serious undercutting and subsequent chaos in the industry.

[64] This was a common feature of agreements registered at the Office of Fair Trading.

[65] See, for example, Kuhlman (1969).

effective. At best, sanctions should be viewed as an additional constraint on potential independent action and not the prime force for stability.

External pressures on stability

Entry

In the long run, the stability and profitability of collusion will depend on the ease or difficulty of entry into the industry. If a cartel can shelter behind effective entry barriers, it may enjoy the necessary time and space to prosper and solve the often conflicting demands of its members. If, on the other hand, entry barriers are low, the cartel will face pressure from potential entrants. As discussed earlier, under most conditions, collusive agreements may provide great rewards for one firm, acting independently. In a similar way, an incentive will exist for a domestic or foreign firm to enter the industry and charge a price just below the cartel price. Entrants that remain outside the colluding group will increasingly encroach on the profits of the group and may eventually compete them away altogether. An example of such an irritating fringe of competitors was observed by Briggs (1996). Briggs referred to the famous Joint Executive Committee, an American railroad cartel of the 1880s, which fixed the price for the transportation of grain. The cartel, originally made up of three members (the New York Central, the Penn and the Baltimore and Ohio) and later expanded to include other American and Canadian 'roads', always faced competition from steamship and sail companies, transporting grain through the Great Lakes to the eastern seaboard. The existence of such non-cartel members is discussed in the next section.

The result of unrestricted entry will lead to the ultimate destruction of the cartel agreement. It therefore follows that, in most cases, some policy of entry prevention must be instituted. The term 'entry barrier' is used loosely in this context. Posner (1976, p.57) argued that an entry barrier implies that the entrant faces costs of gaining a foothold in the market, costs which existing firms have managed to avoid. Posner believed that barriers of this type were rare. Small entrants will be incurring disadvantages because of their scale of operations; but their scale may eventually increase and efficient organisation may result. Thus, a more valid approach in this context would be to consider the factors that lead, not to increasing the height of an entry barrier, but lengthen the time necessary to achieve successful entry. We shall thus use the term 'barrier' in both senses, as forestalling entry totally or retarding the rate of entry.

Entry barriers are discussed fully in Chapter 5. They can be regarded as falling into two main categories: natural and artificial. Natural barriers may be regarded as inevitable and permanent, given the state of an industry; whereas artificial barriers could, in theory, be removed. One such natural barrier is the small size of the market in relation to the minimum efficient size of plant in an industry, which may well dissuade profit-maximising entrants. Another natural barrier could be the problem of setting up a large-scale and complex operation. The huge capital investment may deter all but the largest of firms. An example of such a barrier, surrounding cartel operations, is provided by Noll (1977) in his study of professional sport in America. Noll found that the building of stadia and the acquisition of a team of 'recognisable stars' can deny an entrant access to a major league. The most effective of artificial barriers are those enforced by the government, such as patent rights and licences, the latter occurring frequently in the field of transportation.

Secondly, existing firms may be able to control a sizable proportion of raw materials, usually where they are geographically concentrated. A third artificial barrier can refer to 'unfair' or even illegal methods of discouraging the entry of competitors, such as the lowering of prices temporarily, or increasing raw material prices, a strategy pursued by the American tobacco companies in the 1930s.[66] In his book on shipping cartels, Marx (1953, p.263) gave an account of the testimony submitted to the Supreme Court in 1932 regarding entry prevention tactics of conference members; these included:

> giving rebates; spreading false rumours and falsely stating that the petitioner is about to discontinue its service; making use of their combined economic bargaining power to coerce various shippers, who are also producers of commodities used in large quantities by respondents, to enter into joint exclusive contracts with them; and threatening to blacklist forwarders and refuse to pay them joint brockerage fees unless they discontinue making or advising shippers to make shipments in petitioner's ships.

A further potential barrier to entry is the effect of product differentiation. Customers may so closely identify a product with a producer or group of producers that entry may be effectively deterred. It is not clear to what extent a cartel can sufficiently differentiate its product in the minds of consumers, but what it may attempt to do is to standardise the output. This would help the cartel to monitor and police the arrangements by restricting the power of individual firms to follow an independent pricing policy on the basis of differentiated output. The cartel would justify such standardisation on grounds of maintaining the 'quality' of the output. Nonetheless many associations did, and indeed do, spend money on public relations exercises to maintain a distinct image of quality and service to the public.[67]

An important factor determining an entry-deterring strategy is the status of the entrant. Powerful firms attracted to the industry because of higher than expected prices and profits will not be easily discouraged by the presence of entry barriers. Scott Morton (1997) found that, in the case of British shipping cartels in the early part of the twentieth century, the attitude of the dominant cartel to potential entrants depended on the financial resources of the entrants. Examining 47 cases of entry she concluded that the weaker entrants were resisted whereas the stronger firms were not.

Entry that may threaten cartel stability need not emanate only from rival firms and industries. The entry of new products can have a similar destabilising effect. One example of this was the American incandescent lamp industry in the 1930s. General Electric controlled the industry under a system of licence agreements and quota allocations. One of the minor firms, Sylvania, which had been allocated a 5.5 per cent quota, decided to market the new fluorescent lamp without a General Electric licence. Within years it had captured a 20 per cent share of that market.[68] Sultan (1974) noted similar destabilising effects in the electrical equipment industry when, in 1959, General Electric, without prior notification to its competitors, announced the development of a new transformer.

One important aspect of entry, often ignored in the literature is the impact of foreign competition on the survival of a domestic cartel. Esposito and Esposito (1971) drew attention to the distinction between potential foreign entry and potential domestic entry by

[66] Bain (1959), pp.306–8.
[67] Almost all of the agreements registered at the OFT mentioned that one of the objective was to spread positive information about the industry to the market, the government and the public.
[68] Brems (1951), p.58.

discussing their relative advantages and disadvantages. In many cases, potential foreign competitors were able to purchase their inputs at lower factor prices and thus enjoy lower long-run average costs. Thus the Bainsi absolute cost barrier will be lower to foreign entrants than domestic entrants. Lower factor prices may also result in a lowering of the minimum efficient size of firm, and entry may well be attempted at a smaller level of output than that considered possible by the domestic entrants. This 'economies of scale' barrier will be lessened still further if we consider foreign firms that already sell at their minimum efficient size output in their own domestic market or world market. As regards product differentiation barriers, the foreign firms may face lower entry barriers if the foreign output is considered superior to the domestic output. Naturally, if the reverse were true, the barrier would be higher. Finally, Esposito and Esposito note that the rate of entry may depend on the time it would take for foreign firms to respond to favourable prices, by either expanding capacity or by diverting sales from current markets.

A further barrier that might be faced by foreign firms is that of government restrictions such as tariffs and quotas. Undoubtedly, the political climate of the late 1980s and 1990s has promoted the reduction of such restrictions, and thus the competition faced by the domestic industry in the UK and other European countries has certainly been much greater. Research by Esposito and Esposito (1971) and later by Turner (1980) supported the view that the existence of foreign competition did constrain the power of oligopolies and monopolies.

Existence of non-cartel firms

The prior discussion assumed implicitly and explicitly that cartels are always threatened by the existence of firms competing outside the cartel organisation. Much of the literature rests on the belief that non-cartel firms, enjoying profits higher than the loyal cartel members, will tempt the latter to desert the cartel and undermine its existence.[69] In most cases, however, when analysing agreements at the OFT, it became apparent that cartels did tolerate often sizable portions of the industry outside the cartel. (Lipczynski, 1994). One possible explanation for this 'equilibrium' was provided by d'Aspremont et al. (1983) and refined by Donsimoni et al. (1986). D'Aspremont et al. developed an argument based on a collusive price leadership model to show that members of a dominant cartel can earn higher than competitive profits; that members of the competitive fringe can earn profits higher than firms in the cartel; and that we can have stability or equilibrium in so far as no cartel member will wish to join the competitive fringe.

Assuming a fixed, finite number of firms, producing a homogeneous good and facing identical cost conditions, the situation can be illustrated by Figure 3.10. AB is the demand curve facing each cartel member, i.e. total demand less that demand met by the competitive fringe, divided by the number of cartel members. CD is the associated marginal revenue curve. The profit-maximising price and output is thus P* and OQ*. The competitive fringe firm, as a price-taker will equate P* (its marginal revenue) with marginal cost and produce OQ_c. It is clear that, since the cartel price is above the competitive price, profits for the cartel members are greater than if the industry were competitive. It is also clear that the competitive fringe firms can earn higher profits than the loyal cartel members by virtue of their greater output. D'Aspremont et al. also show that if the cartel were to attract more

---

[69] See, for example, Posner (1976) and Kleit and Palsson (1999).

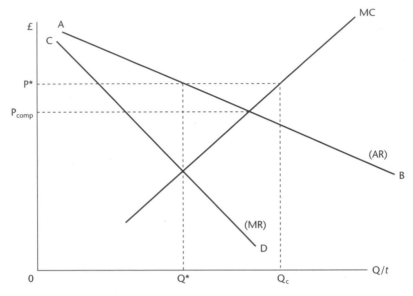

Figure 3.10 The cartel and the competitive fringe

members, profits per firm in the cartel would increase. Stability is considered in two ways. Internal stability is present if a cartel member were to leave the cartel and the resultant fall in prices were to depress profits for the competitive fringe, so that the firm would be no better off. External stability exists when there is no incentive for a firm to join a cartel since the increase in price would not be sufficiently high to increase profits above that earned as a member of the fringe. A cartel both internally and externally stable is thus in equilibrium. The theory shows that a stable cartel will always exist if there is a finite number of firms. Furthermore, the larger the industry, the smaller will be the effect of one firm's exit or entry on prices and profits, thus leading one to expect that cartels are more likely to be unstable. Stability thus depends on the effect on prices and profits resulting from the exit or entry of firms.

Changes in demand

A reduction in market demand places strains on an agreement.[70] As demand falls, sales drop and firms are tempted to undercut the cartel price in a bid to keep their remaining customers. The temptation need not affect all firms equally. Some, who may enjoy relatively high profits, may regard the recession in sales as temporary and may urge all firms to keep their nerve and ride out the squall; others, who are earning lower profits, may view the decline as a real threat to their future and will attempt any strategy to survive. The climate of falling demand may thus create mutual suspicion and fear which will eventually lead to the breakdown of the price agreement.

Cartels are no different from other business organisations in the market. They too, must adapt to fluctuating demand. If they decide to fix prices, they will have to accommodate

[70] See, for example, Briggs (1996), p.560.

changes in production and employment. If, on the other hand, they decide to fix output quotas, they will have to bear the cost of falling prices. No cartel has complete control over demand. In boom times, cartels may well be able to control their eagerness to exploit their monopoly power, largely so as not to attract entrants. In depression, the apparent inability of the cartel to control market prices will lead to instability. History is full of cases of cartels and agreements that fell apart in the face of changing demand. In the early 1920s, the demand for timber in Scotland fell, owing to the adoption of new styles in house-building. Soon after, the agreement amongst timber firms in north Scotland, which had endured for thirteen years, fell apart (Perren, 1979). A further example is the famous Addyston Pipe case, documented by Armentano (1975, p.310), who concluded: 'The probable reason for the inability of the conspiracy to increase and sustain high and unreasonable prices is not difficult to discover . . . the one crucial nonfavourable factor was the level of demand.'

The presence of excess capacity in a colluding firm, where the capital assets (fixed costs) tied up in a firm form a large proportion of total costs, has already been shown to lead to cartel instability. Faced with the additional pressures of falling demand, such firms will be severely tempted to reduce price in an attempt to expand output so as to cover their costs. Some writers have claimed that the presence of excess capacity allows for greater stability, so long as the excess capacity is under the control of the loyal cartel members. By increasing production and reducing the market price, a dominant cartel member can use such excess capacity as a method of keeping order and discipline in the market. The case of Saudi Arabian crude oil producers doing just that in 1986 is often quoted as evidence for such a hypothesis (Youssef, 1986). This can only work if the costs of keeping such an economic weapon are not excessive. It is questionable whether many cartel members would deliberately keep excess capacity as a means of keeping order in the industry.

A note of caution is added by Erickson (1969) who found that, in some agreements, price falls were associated with periods of demand growth. Posner (1976) believed that collusion was more difficult to enforce in times of increasing demand. A firm, facing an expanding market and at the same time being undercut by rivals may not be in a position to detect such cheating, since its own sales are rising. It would have to determine whether its sales were growing in the same proportions as those of its rivals. Suspicion that other firms may be stealing a more than proportionate share of the expanding market may force a firm to abandon the agreement. This view was supported by Rotemberg and Saloner (1986), though their model was challenged by Ellison (1994) and Bagwell and Staiger (1997).

A later contribution to the analysis of likely cartel reaction to variability in demand was presented by Porter (1983) and Green and Porter (1984). Green and Porter argued that cartel breakdowns or 'reversionary episodes' occur when firms detect an unanticipated change in demand, evidenced by unusually low market shares of at least one firm, rather than a general long-term decline in market demand. Demand can vary for a number of predictable reasons. However, at some critical level, when no rational explanation can be deduced for the falling sales, firms will take action. Green and Porter argued that if prices drop beyond a certain level (a trigger price) then firms who have been behaving monopolistically will revert, for a time, to Cournot behaviour. Firms will not move from their monopolistic share so long as the expected marginal loss in future profits from triggering a 'Cournot reversion' is greater than the gain from over-producing.

Buyer concentration

One would generally expect that cartel stability will be enhanced by the lack of market power of buyers. If the buyers are powerful, they may well threaten agreed prices by moving to alternative sources of supply or by suggesting reciprocal transactions with individual firms. In his general discussion on the external threat to inter-firm organisations, Phillips (1962, p.35) suggested an apt maxim that can be applied to many external organisations such as trade unions, suppliers and potential entrants, as well as buyers who face colluding firms: '[T]he better organised and more efficient are the other groups with which an interfirm organisation has conflict relations, the greater the tendency for rivalry within the interfirm organisation'.

Erickson (1969) found no obvious evidence that powerful buyers had a significant effect on stability, although this conclusion was reached on the basis of examining only two cases. However, the overall impression is that when an industry faces a few, large buyers, orders are 'lumpy', large and infrequent. Under these conditions there is a great temptation for colluders to offer secret price reductions to secure large and infrequent contracts. An added incentive would be that detection and punishment may take much longer to determine. Dennis (1992, p.9) pointed out:

> The relevance of big buyers to co-ordinated interaction does not stem from their sophistication or self-proclaimed ability to protect themselves. Instead, the issue is whether sellers will have the incentive to deviate from terms of co-ordination because the gains from securing a large long-term contract outweigh any losses from being caught after the fact.

An atomistic group of buyers would help to maintain stability amongst the colluders by virtue of the difficulty of sellers to cheat on the established price. The more buyers there are, the greater is the chance of being found out. 'No one has yet invented a way to advertise price reductions which brings them to the attention of numerous customers but not to that of any rival.'[71] This assertion is based on Stigler's view that as the number of customers increases the chance of detecting a cheat is enhanced. Thus, if detection is easy, the conspiracy will either collapse or the cheating will cease. The probability that a firm will learn of a least one price reduction given to n customers by a rival is $1 - (1 - p)^n$, where p is the probability of learning of one such cut. Thus even if p is very small, e.g. 0.01, and n equals 100, the probability of detection is still 0.634. If the number of firms rises to 1,000, the probability becomes 0.99996, i.e. almost certain. Additionally, the costs of bargaining so many individual transactions may outweigh the benefit of cheating.

The non-economic factors of stability

When attempting any classification of factors that determine the degree of cartel stability, variables such as leadership, trust and social background must also be considered. It is important to include these variables if we wish for a complete picture of cartel operations. Machlup summed this up well:

> [A]ssumptions about how much fun a man will get out of being in a good scrap with a competitor; how quickly a man will get tired and will acquiesce in a position he first vigorously rejected; how conscientiously a man, when he is in a pinch, will adhere to a gentleman's agreement to maintain prices; how good a man's political connections are enabling him to bring off or to stop some

---

[71] Stigler (1968), p.44.

governmental intervention in the industry. A thousand and one of such things may be the crucial factors in an oligopolistic situation. Disregard them – and the solution may be indeterminate.[72]

Yamey (1973, p.315) presented a similar argument:

> In my view the propensity of an oligopoly to behave monopolistically or competitively is unlikely to depend upon industry characteristics alone. The 'personalities' of the oligopolists, the presence or absence of an *esprit de corps* or sense of group loyalty or mutual confidence and trust among them . . . may in some cases be as important as industry characteristics.

Cowen and Sutter (1999) developed the notion of 'co-operative efficacy', which they defined as a belief in the benefits of co-operation. They claim that there has been a decline in such co-operation in American society, using the metaphor that Americans prefer to bowl alone rather than join leagues. In respect of cartels, they believe that a major threat to their stability is this lack of co-operative efficacy.

Leadership

Most economists would naturally shy away from considering a variable such as leadership. Theory, with its emphasis on structural characteristics, tends to sit uncomfortably with such sociological aspects of organisational behaviour. The development of an agreement, nevertheless, requires that someone takes the lead and organises the initial meetings. People will need to be persuaded, coaxed or even threatened to join the cartel. Thus someone must possess the leadership qualities necessary to form and control such a group. Likewise, a strong personality set against the idea of co-operation may frustrate any attempt at such a strategy.

Thus, when recording and commenting on specific cases, writers have frequently noted the large contribution made by individuals in ensuring organisational stability. For example, Glover's (1977, p.241) work on collusion in the nineteenth century heavy woollen industry often referred to the power of individual leaders: 'Although tacit agreements operated sporadically for a few "seasons" after 1848, the overt collusion between Cook and the Earlys was terminated in that year. The death of Jeremiah Carter was the initial precipitating cause of the break.'

Phillips's (1962) commentaries on price-fixing also contain many examples of the importance of leadership. In the Trenton Potteries Case, Phillips noted that the president of the Association of Sanitary Earthenware was reduced to pleading with his members to be honourable in maintaining Association prices: 'This attitude, coupled with the persistence of price cutting, the lack of any evidence of threats, coercion or pressure on any member, demonstrates that no one in the market had enough power to lead the group effectively.'[73]

In his analysis of the Chrome Cartel, Phimister (1996) drew special attention to the role played by Edmund Davis in developing a successful world cartel in the early twentieth century. It seemed that Davis's talents were also put to good use in the exploitation of other extractive industries in Africa:

> Davis increasingly devoted his time to constructing cartels. Monopoly or near-monopoly control over large sections of the base mineral industry was a key to much of his subsequent success. It was a strategy which he employed to marked effect in coal, asbestos, chrome, copper, tungsten and tin mining.[74]

[72] Machlup (1952a), p.423.
[73] Phillips (1962), p.174.
[74] Phimister (1996), p.79.

Trust

As Yamey (1973) stated above, one of the central questions surrounding successful collusion is whether the colluders can trust one another. If this trust is lacking, no number of sophisticated price and output agreements will prevent the group from being under continual pressure. The lesson is obvious: if trust is absent, it must be built.

This was put into practice by Judge Gary, president of US Steel in the early 1890s. Through the medium of his famous dinners, Judge Gary attempted to develop a spirit of mutual co-operation and an *esprit de corps*. Thus if a firm was to consider a change of market strategy, it would feel duty-bound to inform the other firms in the industry. As Gary claimed: 'They were not obligated to do it except as two men who profess to be friends, or professing to give information to one another as to what they were doing, naturally ought to tell the truth about it.'[75]

Again, economic literature in this field is rich in examples of trust, or, more commonly, lack of trust, in various cartels. Sonkondi (1969, p.100) quoted the views of one cutlery manufacturer, who did not wish to attend his trade association meetings, claiming that:

> I don't go because the fellows there are too insincere. A manufacturer gets up and makes a speech condemning the prices we are getting. We all ought to agree to charge, say, 19s. a dozen. There are cries of Hear! Hear! all round. The speaker finishes, walks into the next room and takes up the telephone – Get out a new price list! We are charging 18s. 6d.

A similar example was quoted in *Fortune* magazine regarding the plumbing fixtures conspiracy in the late 1960s. One executive claimed: 'The trouble was . . . we couldn't trust each other outside the damn room.'[76]

James (1946) found a lack of trust amongst the late nineteenth century lumber manufacturers in the United States. Effective collusion was often held back by the strong individualism which, he claimed, was a characteristic of the frontier spirit. Trade associations were inevitably places full of mistrust.

Social homogeneity

If the participants to an agreement share the same social background, their group adhesion will go some way to ensure stability and trust. An example of such cohesion was provided by the *Wall Street Journal*'s account of the American electrical equipment conspiracy:

> The industry is tightly-knit with many friendships among the executives of competing firms; indeed, officials of smaller firms sometimes are former General Electric or Westinghouse Electric executives. The men involved oftentimes had similar educational backgrounds – college graduates in engineering with a rise through technical ranks into the world of sales. And the friendships were not only professional but often quite personal. Trade association meetings fostered these. It was perhaps easy in the camaraderie of these meetings at upper bracket hotels, amid speeches typical of any association lauding the industry's members and 'mission', to draw even closer than business and background indicated.[77]

To cheat on one's social group is to run the risk of suffering not only the economic loss of forgone future profits, but also the disutility of social stigmatisation. The cheat is branded

---

[75] Quoted from Nelson (1922), p.37.
[76] *Fortune* (1969), p.97.
[77] *Wall Street Journal*, 10 January 1962.

as the outsider and denied the support and comfort of the social group. Phillips (1972) made use of the concept of a firm's 'value systems'. As firms' value systems grow more homogeneous, owing to such things as similar products, similar customers, similar technical problems, so rivalry begins to lessen and co-operation results. An important contribution to firms' value systems is the homogeneity of managers and owners. Gupta (1995), in describing collusion in the Indian tea industry in the 1930s, found that the collusion was organised by managing agents. These agents belonged to a small and cohesive social group of British nationals. Any agent who violated the norms of business and social behaviour would have faced the sanction of social exclusion. According to Gupta, this was a powerful force for stability. Podolny and Scott Morton (1999) found that the social status of the entrant into the British merchant shipping industry would determine the level of predation effected. Entrants who exhibited a higher social class would, on average, be less likely to be faced with a price war than would entrants from a lower social class. It is interesting to note the methodology used to identify high and low social status:

> The writers of the historical sources we use . . . are actually attuned to this feature [social status] of owners. Many of the sources were written around the Second World War when social status still mattered. Consequently owners are described as from 'a prominent family in Yorkshire that founded the University of X' or a knight, or a member of Parliament. These owners were coded as high status . . . the lack of a description of family background or accomplishments probably indicates there were none . . . we therefore assume that entrants whose economic actions are described, but social background omitted, are not high status.[78]

Even where collusion would seem to be unenforceable, common backgrounds can help to establish effective joint action. It was claimed that, during the 1930s, many European medical schools barred Jewish applicants because of a fear of 'outsiders' who did not share their value systems and who could possibly even reduce medical fees to attract patients.[79] Common value systems are also built on efficient communications. Thus any conflict or potential conflict can be quickly resolved through the auspices of trade association meetings, clubs, lodges, and so on.[80]

Some empirical evidence of the effect that such homogeneous values have on price-fixing is provided by Phillips (1972). He used the number of trade associations in an industry as an indicator of homogeneity. The more trade associations the more separable are the values of the firms. His tentative conclusion was that price-fixing was more effective where there was a small number of trade associations, though there appeared to be a greater propensity to attempt price-fixing where there was a larger number of trade associations.

Williamson (1965) also examined the question of social cohesion in price-fixing agreements. He drew attention to three variables: a performance variable, the degree of adherence to group goals and the extent of interfirm communication. If we take π to represent performance, A to be the degree of adherence, C the effective level of communication, and E the exogenous economic environment, then:

$$\pi = \pi(A, E) \qquad \pi_A, \pi_E > 0$$

[78] Podolny and Scott Morton (1999), pp.54–5.
[79] Low (1970), p.260.
[80] Low (1970), p.260, quotes an example of a failed collusion in the US steel industry due to the exclusion, on religious grounds, of two Jewish executives from association meetings that were held in a 'waspish' country club in Pittsburgh.

Performance depends on the degree of adherence to group goals and on the economic environment. It will improve if either of these factors improves. Secondly:

$$\frac{dA}{dt} = f(\pi, C, A) \qquad f_\pi, f_C, f_A > 0$$

Thus group adherence will improve over time (t) with improved performance, more communication and more adherence, i.e. success will generate further success. Lastly:

$$\frac{dC}{dt} = g(A, C) \qquad g_c > 0;\ g_A > 0 \text{ for low A, but } g_A < 0 \text{ for high A}$$

That is, communication will increase with adherence at a low level but will diminish if adherence is high, i.e. there is less need to meet frequently if firms are loyal and stick to agreements. The above model can be used to develop further theoretical predictions, but to test empirically is difficult.

3.8 Conclusions

In this chapter we have discussed the meaning of collusion and the means by which firms organise themselves to pursue that objective. We have discussed the attempts of economic theory to model such complex and varied behaviour. In the second part of the chapter we analysed factors that encourage collusive strategies as well as those that can lead to instability. Failure or success can depend on many factors, some outside the control of the colluding firms.

Let us sum up the chief characteristics of a successful cartel. In the absence of legal sanctions, what factors would we most hope to see in an industry to ensure cartel success? Certainly, fewness of number will help in the handling and evaluation of information flows. Similar cost functions will tend to remove some of the potential conflict between firms of differing efficiencies. Attempts at an equitable and fair division of the profits should be seen to be attempted. Demand should be relatively inelastic at the pre-cartel price, to ensure increased revenues at lower levels of output. Potential members must be shown the benefits of co-operative action. The cartel must also ensure that entry is made difficult so as not to dilute too much of its gain. The cartel must guard against other external threats to its stability, notably any significant changes in demand and technology. In effect, the fewer decisions the members of a cartel are called upon to make in dealing with any structural imperfection or changes in internal or external conditions, the greater the chance of success.

Key terms

Basing-point pricing	Joint ventures
Cartels	Sealed bidding
Degrees of collusion	Semi-collusion
Explicit collusion	Tacit collusion
Forms of collusion	Trade association

Case study 3.1
Competition rankles Amsterdam cab drivers: the launch of a rival service has seen a taxi war erupt in the Dutch city

Taking a taxi in Amsterdam, often tricky, is becoming treacherous. Warring cabbies drag passengers bodily from their seats. Rival drivers overtake and then hit the brakes. Tyres are slashed, paintwork gouged, windscreens smashed – the list of incidents goes on. At issue in a conflict that has erupted this month are deregulation and competition. Drivers in what was once the European Union's most expensive metropolitan cab service have come to a junction, and they are as unwilling as ever to yield. Alone among Dutch cities, Amsterdam long had only one taxi operator. The launch of a rival service last year began a feud that has gained ferocity with the phased liberalisation of the sector nationwide from the beginning of this month. That forms part of a drive by the centre-left government to bring competition to a country where cartels and sole concessions are rife. Taxi Centrale Amsterdam (TCA), the former monopoly, has not taken kindly to the loss of its position. It is equally unhappy about the partial freeing of tariffs, which must be displayed in the window – and the right of customers to pick a vehicle from a taxi rank rather than taking the first in line. TCA drivers are furious that licences, for which they paid up to Fl 300,000 (£84,000) apiece, will in future be issued by the transport ministry virtually free. That wipes out a resale value many had regarded as a form of pension. They add that the government has not dealt fairly with their tax position. KNV Taxi, the employers' organisation for the sector, said: 'The ministry did not do its homework.' Not only fiscal but physical preparations have failed to keep up with the changes. Some main Amsterdam taxi ranks have barriers that force cabs into a single queue. The government is willing to pay for alterations allowing any vehicle to drive off, but the diagonal parking this requires will be difficult to achieve in the capital's narrow streets. Even where it is possible for cabs to pull away, established drivers have made clear they want to stick to the old system and are prepared to enforce it. A vehicle affiliated to TCA – grouping a few dozen big companies and hundreds of owner-drivers – was yesterday freed after being impounded last weekend. Its driver had hemmed in a car from the rival Taxi Direkt. That is the least of the miseries for cabbies from the upstart service, which so far has fewer than 100 vehicles compared with TCA's 1,300. Amsterdam business is aware it too is vulnerable. One hotelier said: 'If a TCA driver sees a cab from the other company pull up at the door to collect a guest, I fear he will tell colleagues by radio to blacklist the address.' City authorities have threatened to withdraw the radio licence if drivers continue to use it as a means of rallying the troops to an area where a clash has just broken out.

Residents have little sympathy with a service that makes them either phone for a cab and wait, or walk to one of the thinly spread ranks where vehicles sit in long lines with their engines running. Few drivers bother to cruise for fares. According to an international survey a few years ago, Amsterdam had the highest per-kilometre cab charges of any big city except Tokyo, Zurich and Lagos. Adding to costs, for driver and consumer, is a zoning system that means a city cab dropping someone at Schiphol airport has to return empty unless an arriving passenger has booked with the company in advance. That is not to change until 2002. The restriction adds to pollution and traffic congestion, at a time when the government plans to introduce road pricing to ease pressure on clogged highways. But TCA wants it preserved. The main advantage for locals so far is that TCA has been putting as many vehicles as possible on the streets, hoping strength of numbers will limit what others can earn. The chance of hailing a cab is improving by the day.

Case study 3.2
Brewers raided on suspicion of French cartel

European Commission investigators probing a suspected beer cartel in France have raided Kronenbourg, the French brewer, Danone, its parent company, and the French premises of Heineken, the Dutch brewer. It followed similar raids in neighbouring Belgium last year. The Commission raided the Leuven headquarters of Interbrew, the world's fourth largest brewer, last July, and in October raided the Belgian brewers' association and Alken Maes, also a subsidiary of Danone. In this week's raids on Tuesday and Wednesday inspectors were said to be looking for evidence of price-fixing arrangements or agreements to carve up distribution and exchange information. Commission officials said it was too early to say whether proof had been found. The two brewers dominate the French beer market with a combined market share of more than 70 per cent. Kronenbourg is the bigger, with more than 40 per cent, while Heineken has about a third of the market. Companies can be fined up to 10 per cent of turnover if guilty of operating a cartel. Officials declined to comment on whether the Belgian and French investigations were linked or whether the inquiry was likely to spread to other EU countries. Danone said Commission officials had visited its premises in Strasbourg and its headquarters in Paris but said it was confident of the results of any inquiry. 'We respect the rules,' the company said. The raid took place two days after Danone published better-than-expected 1999 results, with provisional net profits rising 13.8 per cent to €681m against market expectations of a 10 per cent rise. Heineken said the inquiry was 'apparently aimed at the application of competition rules at European level' and insisted: 'Heineken operates according to the law. We are confident about the outcome of the inquiry.' The Commission's raid on Interbrew last July was part of an investigation into claims that the company was abusing its position of strength in the Belgian beer market. This followed charges that the brewer had acted to exclude other beer brands and indirectly 'tied' pubs and wholesalers.

Case study 3.3
The king of diamonds attempts to polish its rough edges

Nicky Oppenheimer, scion of the South African mining dynasty and chairman of diamond giant De Beers, is trying his hardest to modernise an archaic company. The company plans to stop acting as buyer of last resort and financing stocks of rough – uncut – diamonds for the whole industry. It wants to use its funds to benefit its own shareholders and clients, and it hopes to get those clients to contribute to an enhanced advertising campaign. Instead of dictating prices, which are then carved in stone, it will operate a flexible pricing policy responding to market pressures. The company also wants to persuade the US Justice Department to allow it to trade in the US, the world's biggest market. These changes in business practice could, some analysts suggest, pave the way for parallel corporate changes: the elimination of its contentious cross-holdings with London-listed mining group Anglo American; and possibly a switch from Johannesburg to London for its stock market listing, to attract global investors.

Until recently De Beers used its diamond stockpile, which topped $5bn at the end of 1998 although it has since dropped to just below $4bn, as a buffer stock to prop up world diamond prices when demand flagged. That was fine when De Beers effectively was the diamond industry and handled up to 80 per cent of world production. Now it accounts for only 40 per cent of production and handles perhaps two thirds of the world supply of rough diamonds. (It does not deal in polished stones.) So its stockpile had also been financing its rivals at its shareholders' expense. De Beers has decided the cost to its shareholders was too high. It aims to refine its stockpile strategy so that its operations benefit De Beers and its customers and not the diamond industry at large. Quite how this fine-tuning will work is not clear. What is clear is that the emphasis has moved from maintaining prices to increasing sales, partly through market-sensitive pricing, partly through more advertising. It also expects its clients – the 125 wholesalers privileged to buy at its 10 annual 'sights' – to share the cost of promoting diamonds in return for a more customer-friendly attitude on De Beers' part.

This week it announced a more flexible and frequent pricing policy, in response to changing market conditions. Price movements for different types of diamond may vary. Thus in next week's 'sight', against a background of buoyant demand, the main adjustments will be on the smaller stones. On July 12 it is putting its proposals for the new relationship to its clients. Gary Ralfe, managing director, recently explained the thinking: 'We feel it necessary to formalise and make transparent the relationship between ourselves and our customers, we want to provide a globally recognised identity to our Diamond Trading Company customers . . . that protects themselves, the producers, the retailers and consumers.' But working together with clients is hard if you are not allowed into their country. About half of De Beers sales end up in the US, where they rose for the eighth consecutive year in 1999. But no De Beers director can even set foot in the US for fear of antitrust prosecution. In 1994 it was indicted, along with General Electric of the US, on charges of fixing industrial diamond prices. Although the case was dismissed in court, and charges against GE dropped, the indictment of De Beers remains in force. The US bar could become even more of a problem if, as expected, the company eventually finds a way of cashing in on its brand. This year Mr Oppenheimer made overtures to the US Justice Department. He made an abortive attempt to fix a meeting at the World Economic Forum in Davos.

Simultaneously the company is sprucing up its image in the emotive area of 'conflict diamonds' from war-torn African countries. It now issues certificates guaranteeing that the stones it sells at its sights are clean. The company is also hoping that its co-operative attitude towards the US State Department over conflict diamonds may help it with its attempted negotiations with the US Justice Department over the antitrust issues, even though it openly admits to being a monopoly. To date De Beers' attempts at building bridges with the Clinton administration have largely failed. Its planned overtures to antitrust officials backfired when plans for a meeting became public. Justice Department officials, who have taken a hardline approach to De Beers since the GE case, loathe any publicity in their negotiations and are understood to have refused to take part.

In spite of the collapse of their case in 1994, antitrust officials still want to negotiate an end to the cartel. Those discussing conflict diamonds with the company were angered by suggestions of a trade-off between the company's antitrust problems and its role in cleaning up the diamond trade. However, State Department officials have enthusiastically backed the company's plans to certify its diamonds' origins. But that does not satisfy the company's critics, including Tony Hall, a Democratic congressman from Ohio, who introduced legislation to certify diamonds last year. 'This is just a massive PR move,' said Deborah DeYoung, spokeswoman for Mr Hall. 'Until recently they were saying there is no way to tell where a diamond is from. If they want to credibly reassure consumers, they should have set up some independent, respected monitoring process.'

© The Financial Times Limited, 2 June 2000. Reprinted with permission.

Questions for discussion

1. Is parallel pricing evidence of some degree of collusion?

2. Why is it necessary to police cartel agreements? Who polices OPEC?

3. When a market is subject to sealed bidding it is often prone to collusion. Explain why this is so.

4. The major characteristics of industries prone to collusion are: high levels of concentration, substantial entry barriers, inelastic demand, many customers, homogeneous output and static demand. Give examples of some industries that fulfil some of the above characteristics.

5. Explain why some producers set recommended retail prices.

6. Given the difficulty in detecting overt acts of collusion, suggest evidence that might provide investigators with an *economic* proof of collusive behaviour.

7. With reference to the three case studies of alleged price-fixing and cartel behaviour, identify the factors that help and hinder collusion in the particular industry.

Further reading

Asch, P. and Seneca, J. (1975) Characteristics of collusive firms, *Journal of Industrial Economics*, **23**, 223–37.

Carlton, D.W. and Perloff, J.M. (1999) *Modern Industrial Organisation*. Harlow: Addison-Wesley, chapter 5.

European Commission (1997) *Competition Issues. Impact on Competition and Scale Effects.* Single Market Review, subseries V, vol. 3.

Jacquemin, A. and Slade, M.E. (1989) Cartels, collusion and horizontal merger, in Schmalensee, R. and Willig, R.D. (eds) *Handbook of Industrial Organization*. Cambridge, MA: MIT Press.

Osborne, D.K. (1976) Cartel problems, *American Economic Review*, **66**, 835–44.

Phlips, L. (ed.) (1998) *Applied Industrial Economics*. Cambridge: Cambridge University Press, sections II and III.

Podolny, J.M. and Scott Morton, F.M. (1999) Social status, entry and predation: the case of British shipping cartels 1879–1929, *The Journal of Industrial Economics*, **47**, 41–67.

Shepherd, W.G. (1997) *The Economics of Industrial Organization*. New Jersey: Prentice Hall, chapter 11.

Concentration

4.1 Introduction

An analysis of a firm's competitive environment usually involves quantifying elements of market structure. Having done this we can examine the effects of market structure on the behaviour and performance of firms. In the study of industries, market concentration has been the predominant measure of structure used. Any measure of concentration attempts to capture the prevailing structure and the extent of competitive forces operating in an industry. Industry structure can be characterised by the number of firms in the industry at a given moment in time, and whether or not there is mutual recognition of interdependence.[1] The structure of the industry is also characterised by the size distribution of firms. For example,

---

[1] A detailed discussion of interdependence between firms is provided in Chapters 2 and 3.

an industry consisting of ten equal-sized firms will be very different from an industry with a dominant firm and nine smaller firms. Therefore, any valid concentration measure should to some extent attempt to capture the importance of the number and relative sizes of firms within an industry. The more accurate the concentration measure, the clearer the picture of competition in any given industry. The extent to which industries become concentrated is governed by many factors. These include the ease of entry and exit, government policies and strategies followed by established firms.

Given the importance of concentration in empirical studies of competition, we devote an entire chapter to the discussion of the measurement and determinants of concentration. The rest of the chapter is structured as follows. Section 4.2 discusses how researchers have attempted to classify markets and industries. Any measure of concentration is dependent on how accurately the industry is defined. In Section 4.3, various measures of concentration are outlined. These include the concentration ratio, the Herfindahl–Hirschman index, the Gini coefficient and the entropy index. We also highlight the problems associated with each of these measures. Section 4.4 provides some factual discussion of the level and trends in concentration in various industries. Section 4.5 examines the various factors that have been found to change the level of concentration in industries, and the role that these factors play in the evolution of industry. These factors include economies of scale, industry size and growth, mergers, government regulation, entry and exit barriers and stochastic influences.

4.2 Classification of industries

In any analysis of competitive conditions, the researcher frequently comes across the concepts of **industries** and **markets**. Most of the discussions in this book focus on industries. This immediately presents a definitional problem. What do we understand by the term 'industry'? In the microeconomic theory discussed in earlier chapters, an industry is seen as a collection of firms producing and selling a similar product, using the same technology and competing for factors of production in the same factor market.

Although the terms 'market' and 'industry' are often used interchangeably, there is a distinction. Markets can be defined in terms of geographic and product areas that firms cover. In these markets, firms produce similar goods and services from the buyer's perspective. In this case, close substitutes exist on the demand side of the industry. For example, the tea industry is composed of many different markets which include fruit, herbal, loose and granulated teas. It is often difficult for economists to arrive at a precise definition of a market. For example, when defining geographic markets, it is often difficult to assess whether the market should be viewed from a local, regional or national perspective.

The industry can be referred to as a group of products, which are close substitutes from the suppliers' point of view. Thus all telecommunications equipment can be grouped together in the same industry. This is because they use the same raw materials, technology, labour skills and so on. In most cases we would expect industries to be of a wider grouping than a market.

It is important not to confuse the two when analysing various relationships. For example, price/output decisions may be more relevant to the concept of 'the market', whereas entry decisions will be relevant to 'the industry' (Nightingale, 1978). However, many economists do appear to have used the terms 'market' and 'industry' interchangeably. For example, Stigler (1955, p.4) noted that:

An industry should embrace the maximum geographical area and the maximum variety of productive activities in which there is strong long-run substitution. If buyers can shift on a large scale from product or area B to area A, then the two should be combined. If producers can shift on a large scale from B to A, again they should be combined. Economists usually state this in an alternative form: All products or enterprises with large long run cross elasticities of either supply or demand should be combined into a single industry.

From a theoretical perspective we can define an industry in one or more of the following ways:

● *Type of product produced*. Economists have tended to focus on product pricing policies of firms, which has led to a definition of industry where there is a close substitutability of demand. This can be calculated by the using the cross-elasticity of demand formula which examines the percentage change in the quantity demanded of one good when the price of another good changes. This can be expressed as follows:

$$\text{CED} = \frac{\% \text{ change in quantity demanded of good } a}{\% \text{ change in price of good } b}$$

A high, positive cross-elasticity of demand would indicate that the two goods in question are close substitutes (for example butter and margarine) and as a consequence should be grouped in the same industry. In contrast, a high negative value would indicate goods are close complements (for example camera and film), which may again imply they belong in the same industry. However, it is difficult to assess what constitutes a high positive or negative value. For example, should we refer to a 'cotton industry' or would the 'textile industry' be more relevant? Is there a 'whisky industry' or should we focus on the 'spirits industry'? Answers are likely to depend on the nature of the problem we are trying to solve.

● *Type of production process used*. The type of production process used to produce goods and services may provide an appropriate variable from which to classify firms into a given industry. However, this may cause industries to be defined too widely. For example, if 'engineering' were defined as 'a process using lathes', then this would classify aircraft and bicycle manufacturers within the same industry

● *Type of raw material input*. The type of raw material may provide a useful yardstick for grouping firms into a particular industry. However, again there are potential pitfalls with this type of measure. For example, the approach would suggest that woollen gloves and leather gloves belong to different industries, while soap and margarine belong to the same one.

In reality even the above approaches are an obvious oversimplification. Many firms are multi-product operations, diversified over many industries, selling in many different markets. Nonetheless, for practical reasons, some operational classifications have to be made.

However, does the concept of 'industry' exist in reality? Andrews (1951, p.168) contended that:

> an individual business must be conceived as operating within an 'industry' which consists of all businesses which operate processes of a sufficiently similar kind . . . and possessing sufficiently similar backgrounds of experience and knowledge so that each of them could produce the particular commodity under consideration and would do so if sufficiently attractive.

Table 4.1 ● The UK Standard Industrial Classification, 1980 (by division)

Division	Description
0	Agriculture, forestry and fishing
1	Energy and water supply industries
2	Extraction of minerals and ores and other fuels; manufacture of metals, mineral products and chemicals
3	Metal goods, engineering and vehicle industries
4	Other manufacturing industries
5	Construction
6	Distribution; hotels and catering; repairs
7	Transport and communication
8	Banking, finance, insurance, business services and leasing
9	Other services

Kay (1990a, p.3) introduced the concept of a strategic market, which he defines as the smallest geographic or product area that a firm can successfully compete in. Given that markets focus on demand conditions, while industries focus on supply conditions, the strategic market is a combination of both. Kay summed this up by stating that:

> The characteristics of the strategic market are influenced both by those demand factors which determine the economic market which the firm serves, and by those supply factors which determine the boundaries of the industry within which the firm operates.

Elzinga and Hogarty (1973, 1978) forwarded an empirical test of market boundaries. This test examined whether geographical markets are properly defined. The test was conducted by assessing the extent to which consumers in a regionally defined market, purchase products from regional producers (i.e. internal transactions) or from producers outside the market boundaries (i.e. external transactions). If the ratio of internal to total transactions is high (exceeding 75 per cent), the market is properly defined. However, if the ratio is low, then the market is mis-specified and should be redefined.

Although there are inherent problems in trying to define industries, some government decisions with regard to classification must be taken. As a consequence, policy-makers have defined industries at varying levels depending on the type of economic analysis being conducted. The official classification of industries in the UK is referred to as the Standard Industrial Classification (SIC). This system was introduced in 1948 and updated in 1980 and 1992. The 1980 classification was divided into ten divisions, each assigned a digit from 0 to 9. These are reproduced in Table 4.1.

The ten divisions can be further subdivided by the addition of digits, to provide definitions at the class, group and activity level, respectively. Consider Division 3, 'Metal goods, engineering and vehicle industries', which can be broken down in the following manner:

Division	3	Metal goods, engineering and vehicle industries
Class	34	Electrical and electronic engineering
Group	345	Other electronic equipment
Activity	3454	Electronic consumer goods

Table 4.2 ● The EU Standard Industrial Classification, 1992 (by division)

Section (SIC 1992)	Description	Division (SIC 1980)
A	Agriculture, hunting and forestry	0
B	Fishing	0
C	Mining and quarrying	1, 2
D	Manufacturing	1, 2, 3, 4
E	Electricity, gas and water supply	1
F	Construction	5
G	Wholesale and retail trade; repair of motor vehicles and household goods	6
H	Hotels and restaurants	6
I	Transport, storage and communication	7, 9
J	Financial Intermediation	8
K	Real estate, renting and business activity	8, 9
L	Public administration and defence, compulsory social security	9
M	Education	9
N	Health and social work	9
O	Other community, social and personal service activities	9
P	Private households with employed persons	9
Q	Extra-territorial organisations and bodies	9

The more digits there are the finer the definition of the industry. The 1980 SICs are still found in many textbooks and government reports.

In 1992, the European Union (EU) introduced a new industrial classification system that was to be used across the whole of the Union. The aim was to standardise industry definitions across member states. This made inter-country comparisons easier and laid the foundation for the harmonisation of competition and industrial policies across member states. The EU approach adds a fifth digit to the numbering system where it was felt necessary. The seventeen sections replaced the ten divisions that had been used under the UK 1980 classification. These sections were identified by letters from A to Q (see Table 4.2). The table also provides a comparison with the UK classification.

One major difference between the 1980 and the 1992 classifications is a more detailed breakdown of the services industries in the 1992 version. This reflects the growing importance of the service sector in European economies (European Commission, 1997c).

The sections can be subdivided into subsections by the addition of another letter. (Not all sections are subdivided; for example, fishing (section B) has no subsections, whereas manufacturing (section D) has 14. Subsections are then broken down into two-digit divisions, three-digit groups, four-digit classes and five-digit subclasses. For example, in the case of manufacturing sector we can define down to the subclass as follows:

Section	D	Manufacturing
Subsection	DA	Manufacture of food products, beverages and tobacco products
Division	15	Manufacture of food products

Group	15.1	Production, processing and preservation of meat and meat products
Class	15.13	Production of meat and poultry products
Subclass	15.13/1	Bacon and ham

The industry classifications outlined above have provided clear definitions for economists and governments when carrying out competition analyses of particular industries.

4.3 Measurement of concentration

Researchers and policy-makers use various **concentration indices** to capture industry structure. The extent to which industries are concentrated provides useful information on the extent and nature of competitive forces acting upon firms in a particular industry at any given time. The measures employed provide useful information on the competitive conditions in any given industry. This section examines the more commonly used measures of concentration. These include concentration ratios, Gini coefficient, Herfindahl–Hirschman index, Hannah and Kay index, entropy coefficient and the variance of logarithms in firm size.

Concentration ratio

The concentration ratio (CR) measures the market share of the top N firms in an industry, where N is normally taken to be 3, 4 or 8.[2] It is expressed in the form:

$$CR_N = \sum_{i=1}^{N} x_i$$

where x_i is the market share of firm i. For example, a four-firm concentration ratio measures the sum of the shares of the top four firms. Traditionally, market share is measured as

Table 4.3 • Calculation of the concentration ratio

Firm	Sales	Market share (x_i)
1	2,500	25
2	2,000	20
3	1,500	15
4	1,000	10
5	900	9
6	700	7
7	700	7
8	500	5
9	200	2
Total	10,000	100
CR3 = 60%	CR4 = 70%	CR5 = 79%

[2] Bailey and Boyle (1971) find a strong correlation between concentration ratios using varying numbers of firms.

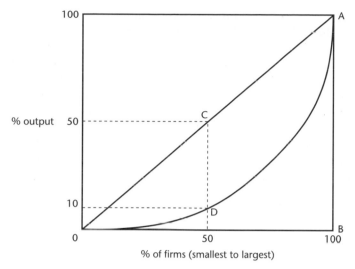

Figure 4.1 Lorenz curve

value of sales or assets, or number of employees.[3] White (1981, pp.223–4) argued as follows regarding the appropriate measure of firm size.

> In the case of concentration in individual markets, we are searching for some inferences as to the likelihood of oligopolistic co-ordination concerning prices and sales. The [sales] shares of the oligopolists themselves will be a prime determinant of the likelihood of that co-ordination. Hence, industry sales are the proper measure of concentration calculations in individual industries.

The concentration ratio measure suffers from the problem that it only focuses on the top firms in the industry and takes no account of the distribution of remaining firms. Table 4.3 calculates the measure for the top 3, 4 and 5 firms in a 9-firm industry using hypothetical data.

As a result of some of the difficulties associated with the concentration ratios, many researchers have adopted summary measures of concentration, which take into account all firms.

Lorenz curve and the Gini coefficient

A Lorenz curve is used to show the share of the industry accounted for by various proportions of firms.[4] An example of a Lorenz curve is shown in Figure 4.1. The vertical axis shows the percentage of industry output under consideration (ranging from 0 to 100 per cent), while the horizontal shows the percentage of firms cumulated from smallest to largest (cumulated from 0 to 100 per cent). The line OA is referred to as the line of absolute equality. If firm sizes are distributed along this line then all firms are of equal size. For example, at point

---

[3] Smyth *et al.* (1975) examine the correlation between various measures of firm size and their correlation with profits. They find that the various size measures are closely correlated. However, there is a stronger correlation of sales with profits than any of the other size measures. Shalit and Sankar (1977) also provide a discussion of the measurement of firm size.

[4] After the statistician Lorenz (1905).

C we can see that 50 per cent of firms account (cumulated from smallest to largest) for 50 per cent of industry output. The implication is then that the other 50 per cent of firms (cumulated from smallest to largest) account for 50 per cent of industry output. It is assumed in this case that competition prevails as all firms are of equal size. However, if firm sizes are distributed along a curve, and deviate from the line of absolute equality then firm sizes are not equal. At point D, for example, we can see that now the smallest 50 per cent of firms account for only 8 per cent of the total industry output, implying that the largest 50 per cent of firms account for the other 92 per cent of output.

A concentration measure known as the Gini coefficient[5] can be derived from the Lorenz curve. From Figure 4.1, the Gini coefficient could be calculated by dividing the deviation from the 45° line by the area AOB. In other words:[6]

$$G = 1 - \left\{ \sum_{i=1}^{N} \sum_{j=1}^{i} x_j \middle/ 0.5N \sum_{i=1}^{N} x_i \right\}$$

The value of the Gini coefficient is determined by the extent to which the Lorenz curve deviates from the line of absolute equality. A value of zero indicates that all firms are of equal size, while a value of unity indicates that a single firm dominates the industry.

This measure tends to focus on firm inequalities, and subsequently ignores the number of firms in an industry. For example, an industry with two equal-sized firms would have the same Gini coefficient as an industry with 100 equal-sized firms. However, the competitive structure of these two industries is likely to be completely different.

Herfindahl–Hirschman index

The Herfindahl–Hirschman index (HH) uses every point in the firm size distribution. It is determined by the sum of the squares of the market shares of each firm:[7]

$$HH = \sum_{i=1}^{N} (x_i)^2$$

where x_i is the market share of firm i. As a result of summing the market shares of each individual firm the larger firms receive higher weighting to reflect their relative importance in the industry. The higher the value of the index, the less likely a given industry will exhibit competitive behaviour. A reciprocal measure, the 'numbers equivalent', can be calculated as 1/HH, which gives the number of equal-sized firms that an industry can sustain. Table 4.4 calculates the Herfindahl–Hirschman index and its numbers equivalent. For example, in the table, the HH index is found to be 0.1558. Therefore, the numbers equivalent is 6.4 (i.e. 1/0.1558). This means that an industry with approximately six equal-sized firms would generate an index of 0.1558.[8]

---

[5] Due to Gini (1912).

[6] x_i = market share of the ith firm, when firms are marked in ascending order of market share. N is the total number of firms in the industry.

[7] This measure is due to Hirschman (1945) and Herfindahl (1950).

[8] In other words, the numbers equivalent is subject to a maximum value of N, the actual number of firms. If all N firms have equal size, the numbers equivalent equals N. So the actual value of the numbers equivalent (between 1 and N) tells us how close we are to an industry of equal-sized firms.

Table 4.4 ● Calculation of the Herfindahl–Hirschman Index

Firm	Sales	Market share (x_i)	(Market share)^2 (x_i^2)
1	2,500	0.25	0.0625
2	2,000	0.20	0.0400
3	1,500	0.15	0.0225
4	1,000	0.10	0.0100
5	900	0.09	0.0081
6	700	0.07	0.0049
7	700	0.07	0.0049
8	500	0.05	0.0025
9	200	0.02	0.0004
Total	10,000	1.00	0.1558

HH Index = 0.1558; numbers equivalent = 6.4

Hannah and Kay index

Using a similar measure to the Herfindahl–Hirschman Index, Hannah and Kay (1977) argue that firm market shares can be given weights ranging from $\alpha = 0.6$ to 2.5 depending on the importance one wishes to attach to the larger firms in the industry. The index can be expressed as follows:

$$HK = \sum_{i=1}^{N} (x_i)^{\alpha}$$

where x_i is the market share of firm i. The larger the value of α, the more importance is given to larger firms. Davies (1989) points out that if $\alpha = 0$, then only firm numbers are important, but as α approaches 1, size inequalities across firms become more relevant. If $\alpha = 2$, then the Hannah and Kay index becomes the Herfindahl–Hirschman index. A numbers equivalent version of this measure can be calculated as 1/HK.

The entropy coefficient

The entropy coefficient (E) is a measure that quantifies the degree of uncertainty in a given industry (Hart, 1971). This measure has been used in information theory to assess the level of certainty attached to any decision. It is determined by the sum of each firm's market share multiplied by the natural logarithm of its reciprocal, as follows:

$$E = \sum_{i=1}^{N} x_i \cdot \log \frac{1}{x_i}$$

where x_i is the market share of firm i. The lower the value of the coefficient, the greater is the certainty of the established firms' future relationships with buyers in the market. A value of E = 0 indicates a monopoly position, which will ensure that the firm will have a captive market, as no substitute goods exist. Table 4.5 illustrates the calculation of the

---

Table 4.5 ● Calculation of the entropy coefficient

Firm	Sales	Market share (x_i)	$\log \dfrac{1}{x_i}$	$x_i \cdot \log \dfrac{1}{x_i}$
1	2,500	0.25	1.386	0.3465
2	2,000	0.20	1.609	0.3218
3	1,500	0.15	1.897	0.2846
4	1,000	0.10	2.303	0.2303
5	900	0.09	2.408	0.2167
6	700	0.07	2.659	0.1861
7	700	0.07	2.659	0.1861
8	500	0.05	2.996	0.1498
9	200	0.02	3.912	0.0780
Total	10,000	1.00	21.829	1.9999

$E = 1.9999; \quad RE = \dfrac{1.9999}{9} = 0.2222$

---

entropy coefficient. The value of the measure is to some extent determined by the number of firms in the industry. When comparing two industries with different numbers of firms, a relative measure (RE) equal to

$$RE = \left(\frac{\displaystyle\sum_{i=1}^{N} x_i \cdot \log \frac{1}{x_i}}{N} \right)$$

can be used, where N is the number of firms. A numbers equivalent measure can be calculated by taking the anti-log of E.

Variance of logarithms of firm sizes

Many industries have firm size distributions that correspond closely to the log normal distribution, with large numbers of small firms, fewer medium-sized firms and small numbers of large firms. As a result, many researchers have used the variance of the logarithms of market shares to measure the inequality in firm sizes (Aitchison and Brown, 1966). The variance of logarithms (VL) can be expressed as follows:

$$VL = \frac{\displaystyle\sum_{i=1}^{N} (\log X_i - \bar{x})^2}{N} \quad \text{where } \bar{x} = \frac{\displaystyle\sum_{i=1}^{N} \log X_i}{N}$$

If all firms are of equal size then VL = 0. The greater the dispersion in firm sizes, the more concentrated the industry; thus the greater the value VL takes. This measure suffers from the same limitations as the Gini coefficient in that it focuses on inequality of firm sizes but ignores the importance of firm numbers.

Table 4.6 • Calculation of the variance of the logarithms of firm sizes

Firm	Sales	Market share	log	log − $\bar{x}$
1	2,500	0.25	−1.386	1.080
2	2,000	0.20	−1.609	0.666
3	1,500	0.15	−1.897	0.2788
4	1,000	0.10	−2.303	0.0149
5	900	0.09	−2.408	0.00029
6	700	0.07	−2.659	0.0548
7	700	0.07	−2.659	0.0548
8	500	0.05	−2.996	0.3260
9	200	0.02	−3.912	2.2112
Total	10,000	1.00	−21.829	4.6868
			$\bar{x} = $ 2.425	0.5207

Problems with using concentration indices

Economists and policy-makers have faced several problems when using concentration ratios to assess the competitive structures of industry:[9]

- *Correct definition of the industry.* When compiling industry concentration statistics we have to rely on economic data that sensibly reflect economic power. A properly defined industry should contain all substitutes within the industry. For example, the 'sugar beet industry' may be too weak (or narrow) a definition for calculating concentration indices as it excludes the sugar cane industry. The problem is to know where to draw the line. By defining the limits very tightly almost any firm could be described as a monopoly. In one case in the United States the relevant market was described as 'the industry supplying paint to General Motors'. Since only DuPont supplied paint to General Motors the definition instantly made DuPont a monopolist in this particular case. Overall, the finer the industry definitions (greater number of digits), the greater the concentration measure is likely to be.
- *Size of the market.* This will affect the importance of a firm and the industry. The relevant market for a firm may only be on a local scale. National concentration ratios will tend to be smaller than regional ones. For example, the bus industry tends to consist of local monopolists, but the national concentration ratios for such an industry would tend to be small.
- *Omission of imports and exports.* If imports are excluded from domestic production, sales, etc., the concentration measures will overstate the degree of importance of the top firms. Thus if we had a CR4 equal to 0.6 and a foreign firm imported goods that accounted for 40 per cent of the market, then the 'true' CR4 would be 0.36 (0.6 × 60%). The opposite would apply if exports were excluded. Utton (1982) provides a discussion of this issue.

[9] See Curry and George (1983) for a full discussion of the problems associated with various measures of concentration.

- *Multi-product operations.* Government industry statistics may ignore the fact that firms are diversified and have multi-product operations. A plant or firm is regarded as part of the census industry to which its main product belongs. For example, if a firm produces 60 per cent of its output for industry A and 40 per cent for industry B, then the whole of that firm (size, capacity, output, labour and so on) is allocated to industry A. Thus a CR computed from this type of data may over- or underestimate the extent of concentration in the industries under consideration.
- *Internal size distribution.* The CR may not be able to distinguish between the size dispersion within the top firms. If CR4 = 1, this could be made up of four equal-sized firms or one giant and three smaller ones.
- *Changes in concentration.* Again the CR statistic may be insensitive to changes within the top N firms. Thus, if in the above case the four equal-sized firms evolved into the one giant and three smalller ones, the CR4 would be unable to detect this fundamental change in the structure of the industry. In this case, measures which capture the turnover of firms in the top part of the size distribution would have to be employed (Geroski and Toker, 1996).

Although most of these measures have their limitations they normally tend to correlate highly with one another (Davies, 1979; Kwoka, 1981). Vanlommel *et al.* (1977) compared 11 measures of concentration for 119 industries based in Belgium. They found that most measures were correlated. However, they contended that no one measure captured the true competitive nature of an industry. They argued that: 'no single concentration measure [out of the 11 studied] effectively considers the three underlying determinants of competition: sector size, inequality of market shares and coalition potential'.[10]

Hannah and Kay (1977) argued that if a measure is to capture the structure of an industry it must satisfy the following criteria:

- Concentration measures should rank one industry as more concentrated than another if the cumulative share of output of the largest firms is everywhere greater than the shares of the other firms.
- A transfer of sales from smaller to larger firms should increase concentration. Entry of smaller firms should decrease concentration, while exit of small firms should increase concentration.
- The merger of two firms within an industry should increase concentration.
- Random influences on firms' growth should increase concentration. If firms have the same chance of growing by any given proportionate amount in any one period, then any growth will affect large firms' size to a greater degree than it affects smaller firms', and so will increase the level of concentration.

In isolation, concentration indices cannot tell us accurately the degree of competition that exists in any given market. There may be few firms in an industry but they may disagree about the future and disregard interdependence. Attention must also be paid to industry traditions, background, and objectives of management. None of these issues can be measured by concentration indices.

---

[10] Vanlommel *et al.* (1977), p.15.

Table 4.7 ● UK concentration ratios for selected industries, 1992

Industry	Five-firm concentration ratio
Tobacco	99
Iron and steel	95
Motor vehicles and engines	83
Pharmaceuticals	51
Grain milling	63
Footwear	48
Brewing	38
Clothing	21
Printing and publishing	16

Source: 'Census of Production PA 1002 (1995)', National Statistics © Crown Copyright 2000.

4.4 Trends in concentration

Concentration varies considerably from industry to industry. Economists have generally been more interested in concentration in manufacturing industries where large-scale production techniques became prevalent from the 1930s onwards (Chandler, 1990). However, many service industries have become increasingly concentrated in recent years. Table 4.7 shows the five-firm UK concentration ratios in selected industries in 1992. Industries that are concentrated at the UK level tend also to be concentrated at a European level. Davies and Lyons (1996) provided estimates of concentration for various industry groupings for 1987. The European Commission (1994) noted that concentration increased in 12 of the 16 industries sampled over the period 1986–91.

Taking such industries together it is possible to examine what has happened to concentration at an aggregate level over time. Several researchers have investigated trends in **aggregate concentration**. Hart and Prais (1956) studied concentration trends for the period 1895–1950. The period was partitioned into ten-year intervals and changes in concentration examined. They found that concentration increased up to 1939, but declined between 1940 and 1950. Evely and Little (1960) supported this finding in a similar study. Hannah and Kay (1977) examined trends in concentration for four separate periods: 1919 to 1930, 1930 to 1948, 1948 to 1957 and 1957 to 1969. The authors found that concentration (measured by the proportion of assets accounted for by the top 100 firms) increased over the period 1919 to 1930, declined during 1930 to 1948 and increased again in 1950s and 1960s. The increased levels of concentration in the periods 1919–30 and the 1950s and 1960s are attributed to the substantial merger activity that took place in these periods. The decline in concentration in 1930 to 1948 was attributed to the rapid growth of medium-sized firms at the expense of their larger counterparts. Shepherd (1972) compared aggregate concentration levels in the UK and the United States. He found that the average concentration was lower in the UK (52.1 per cent against 60.3 per cent). He attributed these results to differences in technologies (used to produce products), more intense competition in UK industries and greater competition policy constraints in the UK.

Hart and Clarke (1980)[11] found that concentration increased throughout the 1970s (partly as a consequence of large-scale merger and increased competitiveness of large UK manufacturing firms), but declined in the 1980s. Clarke (1993) suggested that the observed fall in concentration in the 1980s might have been caused by several factors including:

● Nationwide recession which affected many parts of UK industry. This meant that the demand for the goods and services produced by many firms declined, leading to an observed fall in the size of firms, and consequently concentration.
● Intensified competition from foreign firms led to increased imports and decreased exports and ultimately to the decline of many UK firms.
● Large-scale reduction in production facilities of large firms seeking to make productivity gains.

Aggregate concentration figures should be treated with some caution. Clarke (1993) pointed out that although the general trend in concentration was downwards, some industries (such as stoneworking and leather increased in concentration in the 1980s). Overall, concentration has declined in many industries in recent years because of increased competition and entry of foreign firms. However, the 1990s saw a revived interest in mergers as many industries consolidated to meet the challenges of globalisation which may lead to increased concentration in many industries.

4.5 Determinants of concentration

As we have seen, market concentration is the proportion of an industry's total assets, sales or employment that is controlled by its largest firms. Traditional industrial organisation literature suggests a number of systematic factors can cause industries to be dominated by a few large firms. The factors thought to influence the level and change in concentration include economies of scale, entry and exit barriers, government regulation, and successful pricing and non-price strategies adopted by established firms. This systematic view suggested that large firms are likely to gain a competitive advantage through enhanced efficiency or by exercising market power. These advantages enable them to grow at faster rates than their smaller rivals, and leads to a market structure in which a few large firms dominate. An alternative (stochastic view of the determinants of concentration) suggests that firm size does not necessarily enhance a firm's growth prospects. In this case the observed concentration and size distribution in any particular period is the result of a number of cumulative shocks which act on firm sizes in a stochastic (random) manner. Through the workings of this stochastic process, a size distribution will emerge over time that exhibits a positive skew with a few large firms and a long tail of smaller firms. This section discusses these two views of concentration by discussing the research that has examined the determinants of concentration. Waterson (1993) noted that there has been a revival of interest in analysing the determinants of concentration as researchers have sought to explain why industries tend to evolve where a few large firms dominate.

[11] See also Clarke (1985, 1993).

Systematic determinants of concentration development

This section examines the systematic determinants thought to affect concentration. These factors include economies of scale, firm and industry lifecycles, innovation, industry growth and size, product differentiation, mergers, regulation, entry and exit barriers, and the distinctive capabilities of established firms. Each of these factors is deemed important in determining the market share of individual firms and the subsequent level of concentration observed in any given industry. Drawing on empirical evidence from various countries and industries, we discuss briefly each of these systematic factors.

Economies of scale

The costs of production affect the structure of industries and the behaviour of firms. An analysis of firm costs can yield useful information for a number of reasons. These are as follows:

● It can aid firms in making pricing and output decisions at the point where average costs of production are at a minimum. In other words, it determines the most efficient size of production for established firms, and the numbers of firms which can successfully operate in a particular industry.
● High average costs of production and distribution can increase the costs of entry to a given industry. If entry of new firms is slow, concentrated industry structures may evolve.[12]
● Cost information can aid firms in taking long-term strategic decisions such as whether to expand existing levels of services into new areas or to acquire another firm to make gains in efficiency.

The first part of this section examines the role of costs in determining the structure of industries, by considering economies of scale. The assumption is that firms seek to become large to achieve cost efficiencies, which may ultimately lead to a concentrated market structure.

Economies of scale result from cost savings that occur as firms change in size (i.e. the greater the size, the lower the average cost of production). Most economic textbooks provide their own particular classification of economies of scale. Most fall broadly into two categories: real and pecuniary. The former is associated with changes in the physical input quantities, whereas the latter refers to changes in prices paid by the firm for its factors of production. These categories can be further divided according to whether they arise from more efficient labour usage, technology, marketing, transport or managerial functions. These economies of scale can be at the level of the factory or the firm. Firms can be broken down into many factories, processes and divisions. Some factories may benefit from economies of scale, some may have excess capacity, and some may suffer diseconomies of scale. Firm-level economies of scale are thus the sum of all of the factory-level economies. Economies of scale may also be identified at the industry level, for example if improvement in technology and automation leads to lower costs for all firms. We will not cover the sources of economies of scale in depth here; an extensive review can be found in Koutsoyannis (1979).

[12] The extent to which absolute costs of production and economies of scale act as a barrier to entry for new firms is discussed in Chapter 5.

Diseconomies of scale may arise from managerial inefficiencies. Williamson (1975) argued that as firms become larger, so managerial hierarchies become more complex. This makes it difficult for managers to receive, process and transmit information signals. As a consequence of the complex hierarchy which exists in large firms, distortions in information flows take place that lead to inefficiencies and thus diseconomies of scale. Overall, large firms increase the costs of formulating and implementing managerial tasks leading to increases in the average cost of production.

Economies of scale can often help to explain why some industries are inherently more concentrated than others. These economies of scale depend on the state of technology prevailing in an industry. The minimum efficient scale in the industry to some degree determines the scale at which firms would wish to produce products. The extent to which there is a unique firm size depends on the slope of the long-run average cost curve. If the curve is steep, and U-shaped, there is one optimum size of firm where costs are minimised. A firm that does not operate at this scale will incur higher average costs. However, if the long-run average cost curve is flat, firms can operate at various points without incurring substantially higher average costs.

The relationship between the minimum efficient scale and industry size gives an indication of the number of efficient sized firms an industry will tolerate, and so the likely level of concentration which will yield efficient production. If the minimum efficient scale is large relative to industry size, then the industry will have a natural tendency to become concentrated. For example, suppose we have two industries, A and B. For A the total market size is equal to 10,000 units, while the minimum efficient scale of production is 2,000 units. This means that the industry will support only five efficient firms. In contrast, in industry B, the total market size is again equal to 10,000 units, but the minimum efficient scale is at 100 units of production. This means that the industry will support 100 efficient firms. Therefore, as a consequence of the relationship between the minimum efficient scale and market size, industry A is naturally more concentrated than industry B.

Learning economies may also lead to firms achieving reductions in average costs, thus boosting profitability and growth. Spence (1981) argued that learning economies of scale arise as firms become more experienced in the production and management processes relating to various goods and services. Furthermore, the advantages associated with learning can lead to large, powerful firms and concentrated industries.

A concept related to economies of scale is economies of scope. If a firm can widen the scope of its activities by engaging in related types of production, then average costs may fall. Economies of scope are cost savings arising when a firm produces two or more outputs using the same set of resources, hence the cost of producing the group of goods or services is less than the sum of the costs to produce them separately.

Economies of scope permit the firm to spread fixed costs across a larger product range. In particular, the increased use of computing and telecommunications is an important source of economies of scale and scope in many industries. For example, the use of computing facilities means large firms can handle thousands of transactions, making the average cost of a single transaction low. Economies of scope can be realised because most computing systems possess excess capacity, so the information collected on clients can be used to offer and provide additional services.

Several methods have been proposed to test for the existence of economies of scale. Traditional methods include the engineering, survivor and statistical cost techniques. The engineering method uses questionnaire analysis to gain information on costs. The researcher questions engineers and other industry experts to gain estimates of costs for producing at various levels of output given existing technology (Bain, 1954). The minimum cost of producing at a given level of output is found by multiplying input combinations by input prices. This approach uses hypothetical instead of actual data. Problems with the approach include:

- It tends to be expensive in terms of time and resources.
- An engineer may find it difficult to estimate non-productive activities such as advertising costs.
- If the expert has no prior experience of estimating costs for a given size of firm, he may produce misleading estimates.
- The estimated costs are crucially affected by the quality of factors of production such as labour and capital.
- Industry experts may give biased statements on what constitutes the minimum efficient scale in an industry based on their personal experiences.

An early study which applied this approach to UK manufacturing industries is that of Pratten (1971). Pratten used the engineering method to find the minimum efficient scale for a sample comprising 25 UK industries. He defined the minimum efficient scale as the point at which cost savings arising from increased production are exhausted. He specified this point as occurring where, even when output is doubled, costs fall by less than 5 per cent. Pratten found that in industries such as commercial aircraft and diesel engines, the minimum efficient scale was large relative to industry output, implying that these industries should be concentrated if firms operate at an efficient scale. For industries such as machine tools and iron foundries, the minimum efficient scale was found to be small relative to industry output.[13] A more recent study by Emerson *et al.* (1988) followed this work to find similar results.[14]

The statistical cost analysis method uses actual data to examine the relationship between input costs and output volumes. Average costs are calculated for each firm, and an industry cost curve is derived from these. Johnston (1960) found that economies of scale often prevailed at very low levels of output. Many authors have drawn on this basic approach to develop sophisticated econometric techniques to test for economies of scale.

Weiss (1963) used data on 87 US industries between 1947 and 1954 to investigate whether proportionate changes in industry concentration could be explained by proportionate changes in the ratio of the minimum efficient scale plant size to industry size. Median plant size was used to proxy for the minimum efficient scale. Weiss investigated how the CR4 (concentration ratio for the top four firms) changed as the ratio of industry minimum efficient scale to industry size changed. He found a significant positive relationship between changes in concentration and the minimum efficient scale. This implied that industries with large minimum efficient scales became more concentrated over time.

---

[13] Scherer *et al.* (1975) carried out a similar study for twelve US manufacturing industries. This involved interviewing a large sample of workers drawn from six countries. In general, the authors found that larger firms had market shares greater than those required for efficient production to take place. This provides some indirect evidence that firms become large for reasons other than to maximise efficiency.

[14] Emerson *et al.*'s study is discussed in Chapter 5 when we examine barriers to entry.

For the UK, Hart and Clarke (1980) used data on 76 industries to examine the extent to which changes in market concentration over the period 1958–68 could be explained by economies of scale. Using a simple regression model they tested for a relationship between the CR5 and several independent variables which included the minimum efficient scale, market size and the plant size to firm size ratio (which was used to proxy for firm-level economies of scale). They found a positive relationship between changes in the concentration ratio and the minimum efficient scale and between the concentration ratio and the plant/firm ratio, while that between the CR and market size showed a negative coefficient. This implied that concentration tends to be higher if firms have to attain large size to realise economies of scale, and lower if the market is large.

Another technique that has been used by researchers to test for economies of scale is the survivor technique. This technique is based on the Darwinian notion of survival of the fittest. In other words, firms that belong to efficient size classes within an industry will increase their market share, while those operating at suboptimal scales will lose market shares. Stigler (1958, p.56) suggested that:

> The survivor technique proceeds to solve the problem of determining the optimum firm size as follows: Classify the firms in an industry by size, and calculate the share of industry output coming from each class over time. If the share of a given class falls, it is relatively inefficient, and in general is more inefficient the more rapidly the share falls.

An example of an application of this technique can be found in Scherer *et al.* (1975). The authors carried out a survivor analysis on the US brewing industry. They found that the minimum efficient scale is approximately 4.5 million barrels per year.

In reality most researchers have found difficulty in applying the technique, often finding that the most efficient firms in terms of growth often come from the largest and the smallest groups (Shepherd, 1967). George *et al.* (1991) argued that for the test to be a true indication of picking the most efficient firms, the market must be free from imperfections. The approach ignores that the distribution and market shares of firms can be affected by factors other than costs. These factors may include changes in technology, entry barriers, collusive practices of established firms and differences in objectives. For example, some firms may pursue expense preference behaviour in an attempt to maximise managerial utility (Williamson, 1963).[15] However, the method does equate efficiency with survival of the fittest (Marshall, 1961).

The scale economies hypothesis concerns the number of firms that can operate given existing cost and demand conditions. However, it says little about the inequalities between firm sizes, suggesting that other forces may also be important in shaping industry structure. These are discussed later in the chapter.

Firm and industry lifecycles
Some economists have argued that concentration development occurs as industries and firms follow an aging process or natural lifecycle. Stigler (1951) examined the interaction

---

[15] In the modern firm the separation of ownership (shareholders) from control (management) means that firms often pursue non-profit objectives. These objectives may include the maximisation of size, growth or managerial satisfaction. Managerial satisfaction is often maximised by excess expenditures on staff and superfluous office equipment. This will affect the firm's costs and profits, and could lead to biased results when applying the survivor method of cost estimation.

between an industry's lifecycle and the extent of vertical integration. He contended that in the early stages there are no specialist suppliers of raw materials, so manufacturers engage in backward integration. Alternatively, they may integrate forward to ensure proper sales service. This leads to an industry which has high concentration. However, as the industry grows, specialists in the supply of raw materials and the distributions of goods and services appear, which leads to vertical disintegration and a subsequent fall in industry concentration. Finally, as the industry matures and demand levels off, firms again engage in vertical integration to protect declining market share, leading to an increase in concentration.

Mueller (1972) argued that firms go through a lifecycle of growth and profitability which can be split into four main phases: emergent, growth, maturity and declining. In the emergent phase, firms are often small entities reliant on single products and under the control of owner-managers. The firm often charges low prices to gain market share, and reinvests profits to facilitate expansion. At this stage it is critical that the firm makes enough revenue to meet immediate liabilities, otherwise it may decline and die. Marshall (1961, p.317) likened young firms to young trees in the forest, 'as they struggle upwards through the benumbing age of their old rivals. Many succumb on the way, and only a few survive.'

In the growth phase of the lifecycle, firms raise finance on the capital markets to aid expansion. This expansion gives the firm access to scale economies which lead to increased efficiency. Furthermore, the firm may often diversify into new product areas in order to reduce the risks associated with any single product or service. During the maturity phase, growth and profits level off as markets reach saturation, and the firm encounters diseconomies of scale associated with problems of managerial co-ordination (Penrose, 1959). In the declining phase, the firm's sales and profits fall, leading to a loss of confidence on the part of investors, falling share prices and eventually to bankruptcy. The firm lifecycle may have important consequences for concentration. If firms eventually cease to exist, the implication is that concentration cannot increase indefinitely (Geroski, 1999).

Innovation

Successful innovation can help firms to increase market share and achieve dominance. This is likely to have the effect of increasing concentration. Nelson and Winter (1982) used simulation analysis to identify the impact of different types of innovative behaviour by firms on industry structures. In their model, firms can invest either in innovation or in imitation, depending on which is more profitable. The model assumed that the more firms invest in research and development, the more likely they are to achieve success. By producing at high output levels to meet the demand for their product, successful firms will gain economies of scale advantages over rivals, enabling them to expand further, and leading ultimately to increased concentration.[16] Scherer and Ross (1990) contended that the speed at which a firm innovates will determine the success or otherwise of any investment. Early innovation allows the firm to exploit the market over a longer period of time, and improves the firm's position relative to its rivals. However, if the firm innovates too quickly, mistakes can follow which can lead to increasing costs. The relationship between concentration and innovation is explored in Chapter 8.

---

[16] Sutton (1998) examines the relationship between technology and market structure. Scherer (2000) provides a useful overview of this work.

Industry growth

The rate of growth of a market will influence the intensity of competition. Market concentration is likely to be inversely related to the industry growth rate. With rapid growth, incumbent firms are unlikely to be able to expand capacity sufficiently to satisfy demand, so the opportunity exists for smaller firms to enter, leading to de-concentration. If sales are static or declining, incumbents are likely to collude or exercise market power in order to protect current and future profitability, leading to increased concentration (Dalton and Rhoades, 1974). A notable contribution here is Kamerschen (1968) who examined the role of industry growth in explaining changes in the level of industry concentration over several time periods, using US industry data.[17] Regression analysis is used to examine changes in concentration arising from changes in the value of industry sales (the industry growth rate) and the number of firms in previous periods. He found that as industry sales and firm numbers decline, so concentration rises.

Industry size

Larger markets naturally support larger numbers of firms. As a consequence, concentration levels will tend to be lower in large markets, especially if the minimum efficient scale is small relative to industry size.

Recent research has emphasised the importance of the links between market size and concentration. Sutton (1991) defined two main industry types, now commmonly referred to as **Type 1** and **Type 2**.[18] In Type 1 industries, the size distribution of firms is determined by exogenous factors such as the state of technology, while in Type 2 industries endogenous factors embodied in the strategic behaviour of firms determine the concentration levels observed.[19]

In Type 1 industries, the industry evolves in response to prevailing cost and technological conditions. Products and services tend to be homogeneous, leading firms to compete often on price. Sutton argued that in these industries, as market size increases relative to the minimum efficient scale of production, the market shares of established firms will decline and the industry structure becomes more fragmented. This is what is termed the 'lower bound of concentration'. As a consequence, in Type 1 industries we would expect a negative relationship between market size and concentration.

Type 2 industries are industries where product differentiation is prevalent. Firms spend heavily on discretionary investments such as advertising and research and development. To some extent these costs are sunk and act as a barrier to exit which makes it difficult for established firms to leave the industry when faced with intensified competition. These sunk costs mean that firms are much more likely to take strategic actions to protect their market shares than are Type 1 firms. If industry size increases, established firms will

---

[17] The three time periods were 1947 to 1963, 1954 to 1963 and 1958 to 1963. The corresponding numbers of industries were 177, 197 and 212.

[18] Schmalensee (1992) gives a comprehensive account of the defining characteristics of Type 1 and Type 2 industries. Other extensive reviews of Sutton's work on sunk costs can be found in Bresnahan (1992) and Davies and Lyons (1996).

[19] Examples of Type 1 industries are household textiles, leather products, footwear, clothing, printing and publishing. Type 2 industries include motor vehicles, tobacco, soaps and detergents, pharmaceuticals and man-made fibres. A discussion of Type 1 and Type 2 industry classification is provided in Davies and Lyons (1996) and Lyons *et al.* (1997).

increase expenditure on discretionary investments, leading to an increase in the minimum efficient scale of production (and raising the barriers to entry facing potential entrants). As a consequence, concentration may increase as market size increases. These arguments have been confirmed empirically. Notable contributions include Robinson and Chiang (1996) and Lyons *et al.* (1997) who found a stronger negative relationship between concentration and market size for Type 1 industries relative to their Type 2 counterparts.

A recent study by the European Commission (1997b) examined the evolution of concentration in a sample of 71 industries. The industries were classified as Type 1, Type 2A, Type 2R and Type 2AR. Type 1 industries are defined as above. Type 2A industries are defined as those where competition through advertising takes place; Type 2R industries are where competition takes place through expenditures on research and development; and Type 2AR industries are those where firms compete on advertising and research and development expenditures. The study examined the changes in concentration between 1987 and 1993 for each of the four types of industry.

The study found that the level of concentration was substantially higher in Type 2 than in Type 1 industries.[20] In Type 2 industries, the rate of concentration change is more rapid than in their Type 1 counterparts. This is particularly prevalent in industries where the mode of competition is based primarily on research and development. This, the study contended, was a consequence of firms pursuing policies to increase size in order to exploit economics of scale arising from research and development activities.[21]

Product differentiation

Firms that can successfully differentiate their products, gain market share and raise barriers to entry will prevent new competition. This is likely to lead to high levels of industry concentration. Mueller and Hamm (1974) examined the extent to which product differentiation contributed to the level of concentration. Using data for 166 four-digit industries covering the period 1947 to 1970, they examined how the concentration ratio of individual industries was related to the extent of product differentiation, industry growth, industry size, initial concentration and net entry. They found a strong positive association between product differentiation and concentration. Industry growth, industry size, initial concentration and net entry were found to be inversely related to concentration. The analysis was repeated for the sub-periods 1947 to 1958 and 1958 to 1970 with similar results.

Mueller and Rodgers (1980) updated earlier work by examining the relationship between advertising and concentration in US manufacturing industry over the period 1947 to 1972. They found a positive relationship between advertising expenditure and changes in concentration. They then sought to distinguish between the effects of different types of advertising on concentration. Advertising through television and radio led to higher levels of concentration, while newspaper and outdoor advertising led to falling concentration.

---

[20] In 1993, concentrations for Type 1, Type 2A, Type 2R and Type 2AR were 14.4 per cent, 23.6 per cent, 38.9 per cent and 32.4 per cent, respectively.

[21] The estimated increases in concentration for Type 1, Type 2A, Type 2R and Type 2AR were 1.2 per cent, 1.2 per cent, 6.1 per cent and 2.3 per cent, respectively. A full explanation of the results is provided in European Commission (1997b), table 4.5b, p.68.

Caves and Porter (1980) investigated the extent to which firm turnover determines con-centration for a sample of 166 US manufacturing industries observed over various periods spanning 1954 to 1972. Changes in concentration were linked to changes in the number of firms, industry size, the extent of diversification, minimum efficient scale and cost dis-advantage. Caves and Porter estimated this model for industries where concentration had increased or decreased by two percentage points over the sample period. They found a positive relationship between the minimum efficient scale and concentration, and a negative relationship for changes in cost disadvantage, industry growth and changes in the number of firms. In industries in which concentration was increasing, they found that entry and industry growth became insignificant, while changes in economies of scale and cost dis-advantage became significant. For industries that experienced decreasing concentration, rapid growth was the most significant variable. The relationship between advertising and market structure is explored in Chapter 7.

Mergers

There are three main types of merger: horizontal, vertical and conglomerate. Horizontal mergers occur when firms combine their resources at the same stage of production and similar products and services are produced: in other words, where firms producing the same products merge. This type of merger may lead to a reduction in costs as the production and distribution facilities of firms are combined. However, it may also lead to less choice and higher priced products, since the merger in effect reduces competition. The extent to which a merger increases efficiency or reduces competition will have direct effects on the welfare of the economy. These issues are examined in Chapter 11.

Vertical mergers occur when firms combine their resources at different stages of production. These types of merger involve firms that are in both supplier and manufacturer or manu-facturer and retailer relationships, respectively. These mergers may reduce uncertainty for firms in their supplier relationships by assuring supplies, or they may reduce the costs of monitoring complex relationships with retailers. This integration of operations may also lead to technical economies of scale. However, these types of merger also increase a firm's market power, which may allow it to follow anti-competitive strategies such as exclusive dealing, tying, price discrimination and resale price maintenance. We discuss these issues in Chapter 9.

Conglomerate mergers occur when firms combine their resources that are producing different goods and services. Benefits may arise from the rationalisation of management and more effective controls over costs by central management. Competition between divisions may also lead to a fall in costs. However, given that the new firm is diversified, it now may have the power to engage in anti-competitive strategies such as predatory pricing or even reciprocal deals. These issues are explored in Chapter 10.

In the UK, certain periods or 'waves' of mergers have taken place. These have been in the 1920s (to achieve economies of scale associated with new mass production techniques), the 1960s (where mergers were actively encouraged by the government), 1980s and 1990s (in response to the increased integration and globalisation of world markets).[22] Such merger activity can increase efficiency through lower costs and increased revenues or bring enhanced market power to the new merged entity.

---

[22] Griffiths and Wall (1999), chapter 5, provide a discussion of the evolution of mergers in the UK.

Firms may decide to merge for several reasons. These are:

● to achieve economies of scale and scope through the increased size and possibly diversity of operations;
● to gain enhanced market power by eliminating competitors in the short run, so prices can be raised in the long run;
● to pursue managerial objectives such as growth and size maximisation;
● to meet changes in customer attributes; for example, the firm may have to grow to meet commitments to large customers.

Mergers can lead to increased concentration, as firms continue either to exploit technical economies of scale or exercise market power advantages. In a seminal work, Weiss (1965) examined the effects of merger on industry concentration over the period 1926 to 1959 for six US manufacturing industries.[23] A merger was defined as having taken place when a plant in operation in the start of the period was taken over by an existing firm before the end of the sample period. Weiss calculated changes in plant size for four separate years at approximately ten-year intervals.[24] He decomposed changes in the concentration ratio into changes arising from merger, internal growth of firms, exit of existing firms and changes in the identity of the top firms in the industry. He found that internal growth and exit had a large effect on concentration, while mergers played a lesser role.

For the period 1957 to 1969, Hannah and Kay (1981, p.312) found that mergers play a crucial role in raising concentration in the UK.[25] Furthermore, if growth attributable to merger is ignored, then smaller firms grew more than large firms did over this period. They argued that: 'Merger has been the dominant force in increasing concentration in the UK since 1919 . . . Its role has been growing and it now accounts for essentially all of currently observed net concentration increase.' However, Hart (1981, p.318) suggested that Hannah and Kay exaggerated the role of mergers in raising concentration. Drawing on government statistics, he found that: 'even if all the 122 large mergers [involving over £5 million] had been prohibited, aggregate concentration would have continued to increase'. Although mergers are an important source of increases in concentration, Hart argues, they are less important than internal growth by individual firms. A more recent study by the European Commission (1994) found that mergers had increased concentration in several industries, including rubber, plastics, chemicals and pharmaceuticals.[26]

Regulation

Government policy can also influence levels of concentration. Strong policies aimed at increasing competition by discouraging restrictive practices and disallowing mergers, which may be against the 'public interest', tend to inhibit concentration.[27] Conversely, policies which impose restrictions on the number of firms allowed to operate in specific industries

[23] These industries consist of steel, cars, petrol, cement, flour and brewing.
[24] The sample periods for the six industries are as follows: steel, 1926–57; cars, 1948–58; cement, 1928–58, brewing 1947–58; flour, 1932–59; and petrol 1946–56.
[25] Utton (1971), Aaronovitch and Sawyer (1975), and Hannah (1983) confirmed this finding.
[26] Other notable studies of the effects of mergers on concentration in the UK include Utton (1971, 1972), Hart et al. (1973), Aaronovitch and Sawyer (1975), Hart and Clarke (1980) and Kumar (1985).
[27] We define the public interest in Chapter 11.

and grant exclusive property rights to selected firms tend to encourage concentration (Burke, 1991). Government policy is examined in Chapters 11 and 12.

Entry and exit barriers

Traditional microeconomic literature viewed entry as an important component in the process of market price adjustment towards equilibrium. More dynamic approach (for example the Schumpeterian and Austrian schools) viewed entry as an innovative process reflecting the interaction of decisions made by consumers, entrepreneurs and resource owners. Kirzner (1973) argued that entry is instrumental in driving industry evolution. Empirical evidence on the determinants of entry suggests that entry is higher in profitable industries or in industries enjoying high average growth rates (Baldwin and Gorecki, 1987; Geroski, 1991a,b). Entry of new firms is much slower for industries where established incumbents hold advantages over potential entrants. Baumol (1982) argued that exit is easy if established firms have no sunk costs. Empirical evidence suggested that exit was higher from industries in which profits were low, and in which sunk costs were insignificant (Dunne *et al.*, 1988). Porter (1980 p.110) noted that: 'When exit barriers are high, excess capacity does not leave the industry, and companies that lose the competitive battle do not give up. Rather they grimly hang on.'

The extent to which entry and exit affect levels of industry concentration depends crucially on the association between entry and exit rates (Caves, 1998). Using US manufacturing data over the period 1963 to 1982, Dunne *et al.* (1988) found a negative correlation between annual entry and exit rates. Industries where new entry takes place were likely to experience declining rates of concentration. However, if diversified entry takes place by large, established firms, concentration is likely to increase. We examine the importance of entry in Chapter 5.

Distinctive capabilities

Kay (1993) argued that firms can draw on what he terms 'distinctive capabilities', including architecture and reputation, in order to achieve competitive advantage and growth. Architecture refers to the firm's internal organisation, and its relationships with suppliers, distributors and retailers. For example, knowledge of the industry may yield substantial advantages that allow the firm to grow over successive periods. This may in turn allow established firms to follow aggressive pricing strategies aimed at preventing or eliminating the entry of new firms. However, if market structure or production technologies change, this advantage may be quickly eliminated.

Reputation effects can also provide advantages over competitors. If a firm has a reputation for providing high quality and service, this will help to add value and generate more sales. Kay argues that reputation can be sustainable over long periods, making it difficult for entrants to compete on equal terms with a reputable incumbent. Overall, Kay (1993) argued that in industries in which selective firms can draw on distinctive capabilities, these firms are likely to grow and achieve dominance for long periods.

Singh *et al.* (1998) assessed which strategies were most used by UK firms to gain competitive advantage in the food, electrical engineering, chemicals and pharmaceuticals industries. From data gathered from questionnaires sent to a random sample of marketing executives drawn from these industries, Singh *et al.* found that spending on research and development and advertising was the most prevalent strategy used by firms to gain an advantage over

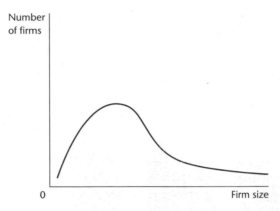

Figure 4.2 Skewed distribution of firm sizes

competitors. Little evidence was found to suggest that firms used the pricing and patenting of new products as strategies.

Stochastic determinants of market structure

Most research into the determinants of concentration has tended to emphasise the role of systematic factors in determining the structure of industry. This research implicitly assumes that size confers advantages to large firms over their smaller counterparts. Consequently, the research largely ignores the role of stochastic (chance) factors in determining the size configurations and growth of firms within industries. However, the importance of stochastic factors unrelated to firm size can have implications for concentration. This assertion is now examined.

Industries may evolve into concentrated structures even if size does not enhance a firm's growth prospects. Some evidence suggests that industries may evolve into concentrated market structures through a sequence of random shocks to individual firm sizes. These arguments are embodied in the law of proportionate effect. This approach contested that growth of demand, managerial talent, innovation, organisational structure and luck, are distributed across firms in a random manner. If, then, firms' growth rates are determined in a random fashion, this will result in a firm size distribution that becomes increasingly skewed towards a small number of large firms. This is illustrated in Figure 4.2.

Research has found that this process is consistent with the actual size distribution of firms observed in many industries.[28] Gibrat (1931) was the first author to investigate the implications for concentration development if each firm's growth in any year is determined

---

[28] Quandt (1966), Silberman (1967), Clarke (1979) and Stanley et al. (1995) carried out statistical tests to assess how closely the actual size distribution of firms in particular industries conforms to a family of skewed distributions including the log normal, Yule and Pareto distributions. These studies had some difficulties in assessing exactly which type of distribution industries followed. However, skewed distributions of firm sizes were observed in all of these studies. Collectively, these results suggest that a common underlying stochastic process is instrumental in generating firm size distributions. More recently, Goddard and Wilson (2000) make a useful contribution to the theoretical literature an growth and convergence.

randomly, and is therefore independent of its size and its growth in previous years. His general findings became known as Gibrat's law or the **law of proportionate effect** and stimulated a body of empirical research that has continued for over sixty years. However, this explanation of concentration development has to some extent been overshadowed by the systematic explanation of industrial concentration, which was discussed above.

Several economists have noted the importance of random factors in determining the growth of firms. Sherman (1977) used Schwed's (1965) 'great coin flipping contest' to illustrate how inequalities can arise over time. In this example, participants must choose heads or tails from a coin toss. Those who have guessed correctly go through to the next round of the contest, while those who have guessed incorrectly are eliminated. After several rounds only a few lucky participants are left. Schwed (p.161) argued that these participants 'are regarded as the experts, the greatest coin flippers in history, the men who never lose, and they have their biographies written'.

Sherman (1977) argued that it is important not to regard all large firms as successful and efficient; to do so is like treating coin-flippers as skilled. In many cases, luck may have a significant effect on the growth of firms.

Prais (1976) argued that random shocks can lead to a greater dispersion of firm sizes over time even if large firms are not growing any faster than small firms.[29] He constructs a simple numerical example to compare the implications of two growth processes for the development of industry concentration. In the first, all firms have an identical chance of achieving any given amount of absolute growth in any period. In the second, all firms have an equal chance of achieving any given proportionate growth rate in any period. The second case corresponds to the law of proportionate effect.

The numerical example involves a hypothetical industry that consists of 128 firms, each employing 100 people. Under the equal-absolute-growth model, 50 per cent of the firms remain the same size, 25 per cent increase in size by 10 workers, and 25 per cent decrease in size by 10 workers. Under the equal-proportionate-growth model, 50 per cent of firms in any period stay the same size, while 25 per cent grow by 10 per cent, and 25 per cent decline by 10 per cent. In both cases, concentration tends to increase. From an initial value of 7.8 per cent in year zero, concentration levels of around 9.5 or 9.6 per cent are reached by the end of year three. 'The dispersion of the distribution thus grows inexorably as time proceeds as a result of spontaneous drift (the sizes of firms follow a random walk, as sheep which have no shepherd).'[30]

In the long term, however, the equal-proportionate-growth model leads to a faster increase in industry concentration than the equal-absolute-growth model. If the process Prais described continued for long enough, the size distribution of firms will approximate a skewed distribution which is close to the size distribution of firms observed in many industries.

Hannah and Kay (1977, p.103) used the following gambling analogy to describe the above process:

> [I]f a group of rich men and a group of poor men visit Monte Carlo, it is likely that some of the rich will become poor and some of the poor become rich: but it is also probable that some of the rich will get richer and some of the poor will get poorer, so that the extent of inequality

---

[29] See Prais (1976), chapter 2, for an extended discussion and explanation.
[30] Prais (1976), p.26.

within each group and over the two groups taken together is likely to increase. The process works to increase industrial concentration in much the same way.

Empirical research that has tested the law of proportionate effect has used comprehensive data sets and various econometric techniques. In most cases the law of proportionate effect is tested via the following simple equation:

$$s_{it} = \beta_1 + \beta_2 s_{it-1} + u_{it}$$

where the dependent variable s_{it} is a measure of the size of firm i at time t (converted to natural logs). Coefficient β_1 is the intercept term, and β_2 denotes the relationship between firm size in the current (s_{it}) and the previous period (s_{it-1}). If $\beta_2 = 1$, there is no relationship between firm size and growth. In other words, a firm's size today is not determined by its past size, but by a 'shock' which is distributed across all firms in a random fashion. A value of $\beta_2 = 1$ implies that the law of proportionate effect holds. This means that all firms have an equal proportionate chance of growing in any period. However, over time some firms will have a run of years of positive growth and become large. This eventually leads to an industry where a few large firms will dominate. If $\beta_2 < 1$, then small firms will tend to grow faster than larger firms. This means that any tendency towards increased concentration may be offset by the superior growth of small firms. If $\beta_2 > 1$, then large firms are expected to grow faster than their smaller counterparts. This may be the case if large firms have advantages associated with economies of scale. u_{it} is the error term.

Researchers have tested the law of proportionate effect for manufacturing and service firms in the UK and United States, and there is also some evidence for Germany, Austria and Italy and Japan. Results have been mixed. Early studies found either no relationship or a positive relationship between firm size and growth. More recent studies found that small firms grew faster with more variable growth rates. Table 4.8 provides an overview of the research that has tested the law of proportionate effect. The following paragraphs discuss some of the major studies.

Hart and Prais (1956) tested the law of proportionate effect for the period 1885 to 1956, using a sample of firms quoted on the London Stock Exchange. The number of firms varied over time, ranging from 60 firms in 1885 to 2,103 firms in 1956. Firm size was measured as the Stock Exchange valuation of the firm.

Hart and Prais carried out a regression analysis of the logarithm of opening firm size on closing firm size for the periods 1885 to 1896, 1896 to 1907, 1907 to 1924, 1924 to 1939 and 1939 to 1950. The model used was similar in structure to the equation above. For periods up to 1939, the authors found that firm size was unrelated between the two periods. This implied that the law of proportionate effect held. However, from 1939 they found that smaller firms grew proportionately faster than larger firms. The authors argued that industry concentration in the UK increased between 1885 and 1939 through the operation of the law of proportionate effect, but stabilised after this point as the growth of smaller firms offset the process by growing faster than their larger counterparts.

Singh and Whittington (1975) tested the law of proportionate effect for a sample of 2,000 firms, which were divided into 21 industry groups. They argued that one would expect smaller firms to grow faster than large firms because smaller firms will seek to increase their outputs in order to reach the minimum efficient scale, and thus take advantage of any potential scale economies.

Table 4.8 ● Tests of the law of proportionate effect (LPE): a selective review

Study (chronological order)	Sample characteristics	Results
Hart and Prais (1956)	UK data covering period 1885 to 1950. Firm size measured as the Stock Exchange valuation	Split sample into five sub-periods, and found that LPE holds until 1939. From 1939 to 1950 negative relation between size and growth. Overall, accepted LPE
Hart (1962)	UK data covering period 1931 to 1954. Sample comprises brewing, spinning and drinks firms. Size measured as gross profit – depreciation	LPE tested for various time periods. Found equal mean growth rates in all periods considered. However, found large brewing firms had more variable growth rates than small. Overall, accepted LPE
Hymer and Pashigian (1962)	US data covering period 1946 to 1955 for 1,000 largest manufacturing firms. Size measured as assets	Average mean growth rates were unrelated to firm sizes. Variations in firm growth rates were inversely related to firm size. Overall, rejected LPE
Mansfield (1962)	US data covering period 1916 to 1957 for firms in steel, petroleum and tyre industries covering various sub-periods. Size measure is firm output	Tested the LPE for all firms, for surviving firms only, and for firms operating above the industry minimum efficient scale. LPE accepted only for firms operating above the minimum efficient scale. Dispersion of growth rates found to be greater for smaller firms. Overall rejected LPE
Samuals (1965)	Data covered period 1951 to 1960 for 322 UK manufacturing firms. Size measured by net assets	Larger firms grew faster than smaller firms through economies of scale advantages. Overall, rejected the LPE
Samuals and Chesher (1972)	UK data for 2,000 firms drawn from 21 industry groups. Size measured as net assets	Large firms grew faster than small firms. Variation in growth rates declined with size. Departures from LPE were greatest in industries characterised by an oligopolistic structure. Growth rates persisted through time
Utton (1972)	Data on 1,527 UK manufacturing firms drawn from 13 industries covering the period 1954 to 1965. Size measured as net assets	Large firms grew faster than smaller firms in five industries, while smaller firms grew faster in one industry. Overall, rejected LPE
Aaronovitch and Sawyer (1975)	UK data on 233 quoted manufacturing firms over the period 1959 to 1967	LPE holds
Singh and Whittington (1975)	Approximately 2,000 UK firms in 21 industry groups over the period 1948 to 1960	Large firms grow faster than small firms. Variation in growth rates tends to decline with firm size. Average firm growth rates are related through time
Chesher (1979)	Data covered the period 1960 to 1969 for 183 UK manufacturing firms	No relationship between firm size and growth. Growth rates persisted from one period to the next
Kumar (1985)	UK data covering the period 1960 to 1976. The sample is split into three sub-periods: 1960–65 (1,747 firms), 1966–71 (1,021 firms), 1972–1976 (824 firms). Net assets, fixed assets, total equity, employees and sales measure firm size	12% of growth persisted from one period to the next. Negative relationship between size and growth for 1960–65 and 1972–76, but accepted LPE for the period 1966–71. Growth rates were inversely related to firm size. Overall, rejected LPE

Evans (1987a)	US data for 42,339 small firms over the period 1976 to 1980. Size measured by number of employees	Failure of firms decreased with age, as does growth and variability of growth. Overall, rejected LPE
Evans (1987b)	US data for 17,339 small manufacturing firms covering the period 1976 to 1982	Found an inverse relationship between firm size vs growth and age
Hall (1987)	US data covering the period 1972 to 1983. Three samples of firms: 1972–83 (962 firms); 1972–79 (1,349 firms); 1976–83 (1,098 firms). Size measured by number of employees	Negative relationship between firm size and growth for all samples. Small firms had more variable growth rates than large firms
Dunne et al. (1988)	US data for 200,000 manufacturing plants over the period 1967 to 1977. Size measured by number of employees	Growth declined with plant size. Growth declines with age for multi-plant firms. Variability of growth declines with plant size.
Contini and Revelli (1989)	Italian data for 467 small manufacturing firms covering the period 1973 to 1986. Size measured as number of employees	Overall, younger, smaller plants have faster, more variable growth rates than large firms. Rejected LPE
Acs and Audretsch (1990)	US data aggregated at the industry level for 408, 4-digit industries. Size measured as number of employees	Presented results for 1973–81 and 1981–86. LPE is accepted for larger firms for 1977–81. LPE is rejected for small firms in all industries sampled. Overall, small firms grew faster than larger firms
Reid (1992)	UK data for 73 small firms covering the period 1985 to 1988. Size measured by sales and employees	Accepted LPE in 245 of the 408 industries sampled. Overall, LPE was accepted
Wagner (1992)	German data on 7,000 small firms. Sample period covered 1978 to 1989. Size measured by the number of employees	Negative relationship between size and growth. Also found younger firms have higher growth rates. Overall, rejected LPE
Dunne and Hughes (1994)	UK data comprising 2,149 firms. Split into time periods 1975–80 and 1980–85. Size measured as assets	Found no relationship between size and growth. However, growth rates of firms are correlated over time leading to a rejection of LPE. LPE accepted for majority of size classes in 1980–85, but rejected in all classes 1975–80
Hart and Oulton (1996)	UK data on 87,109 small independent firms covering the period 1989 to 1993. Size measured as net assets, employees and sales	Negative relation between firm growth and size implying that the smallest firms grow the fastest. This finding is robust with respect to size category of firm examined, and size measure used
Hart and Oulton (1999)	UK data on 29,000 small independent firms covering the period 1989 to 1993. Size measured as number of employees	Overall, a negative relationship between firm growth and size implying that the smallest firms grew the fastest. However, this relationship did not hold for the largest firms in the sample
Wilson and Morris (2000)	UK data on 264 manufacturing and 163 service firms covering the period 1991 to 1995	Negative relationship between growth and size for manufacturing and service firms. Small firms from both samples had more variable growth than their larger counterparts. Some evidence of growth persistence for manufacturing firms
Wilson and Williams (2000)	Data on over 400 banks from France, Germany, Italy and the UK, covering the period 1990 to 1996	For Italy, small banks grew faster than larger banks. No relationship found for France, Germany and the UK. Small banks had more variable growth rates than their larger counterparts
Goddard, Wilson and Blandon (2000)	Data on 443 manufacturing firms from Japan covering the period 1980 to 1996.	Using cross-sectional and panel techniques of estimation, the authors find strong evidence of convergence in growth rates toward firm specific average values.

To test for differences in growth rates, Singh and Whittington grouped the sample into six size classes for the two sub-periods and the sample period as a whole,[31] and found a positive relationship between growth and size. They augmented these tests by carrying out a regression of closing on opening size, and found that in the majority of industries, large firms grew faster than smaller firms.

Values of the $\hat{\beta}_2$ coefficient were found to be highest in the industries with the slowest growth rates. This finding implies that large firms are likely to grow faster in industries where they are protected by entry barriers and operate in an environment of implicit or explicit co-operation.[32]

Dunne and Hughes (1994) added to the evidence on size-growth relationships using a large sample comprising 2,149 firms. The size measure adopted for the study was net assets.

Using a model similar in structure to the equation above, Dunne and Hughes tested the law of proportionate effect for two sub-periods (1975 to 1980 and 1980 to 1985). These tests were carried out for different size classes and industry groupings. The law of proportionate effect was accepted for the majority of classes for the period 1980 to 1985 (with the exception of the smallest categories of firms, and for the sample as a whole). The authors argued that this provides evidence of a size threshold below which the law of proportionate effect does not apply. The law of proportionate effect was rejected for all size classes for the period 1975 to 1980. Dunne and Hughes extended the analysis to examine the size/growth relationship within individual industries. For the period 1980 to 1985, small firms grew fastest in sixteen of the nineteen industries sampled. However, this relationship is significant in only four cases. For 1970 to 1975 small firms grew fastest in sixteen industries, and significantly so in eight. Dunne and Hughes also concluded that large firms have less variability in their growth rates over time than their smaller counterparts. This was because large firms are more likely to be diversified, and as such can spread risk across many product areas, making them less susceptible to large fluctuations in growth. Overall, the results showed that small firms grew faster than large firms and had more variable growth rates. However, there is evidence of a threshold effect, and the law of proportionate effect can be said to hold for firms above a certain size.

Hart and Oulton (1996) added to the evidence on size/growth relationships for a sample of 87,109 independent firms for the period 1989 to 1993. They examined whether the observed size/growth relationships held by individual size class. The sample of firms was split into nine sub-classes based on initial size.[33] They found that small firms grew faster than their larger counterparts for all size bands, and that this was particularly pronounced in the smallest size category of firms. The authors concluded that very small firms grew proportionately faster in terms of employment than their larger counterparts. However, the authors acknowledge that the results do not take into account firms that have either entered or exited the industry during the sample period.

---

[31] The time period under investigation is 1948 to 1960, which is split into two sub-periods (1948 to 1954 and 1954 to 1960). The sample was drawn from manufacturing, construction, distribution and miscellaneous services, food, non-electrical engineering, clothing and footwear, and tobacco industries.

[32] Chapter 3 discusses why collusive agreements are likely to be more stable in industries where growth is slow.

[33] The number of employees in the opening period is used as the ranking measure. The size bands ranged from firms employing fewer than 4 employees to firms employing more than 1,024 employees.

Hart and Oulton (1999) tested the law of proportionate effect for a sample of 29,000 UK firms over the period 1989 to 1993. Number of employees was the size measure adopted. Regression analysis was used to examine the relationship between size and growth for the entire sample and for ten size classes. For the sample as a whole, small firms grew faster than their larger counterparts. This result is found for the majority of the size classes, with the exception of the largest sized firms where large firms grew fastest.

Clearly, the systematic and stochastic approaches to explaining the level of concentration in a given industry have some merit. Few authors have attempted to combine explicitly these two schools of thought. One notable exception is a study by Davies and Lyons (1982). Systematic and the stochastic explanations of concentration. Their systematic explanation emphasises firm numbers, economies of scale and barriers to entry; the stochastic explanation emphasises random factors. Davies and Lyons specify a model in which firms either operate at the minimum efficient scale, or expand output in order to reach this level. Once firms reach the minimum efficient scale, random shocks to firm sizes becomes important. The implication of this model is that systematic factors are important in determining firm growth and concentration only up to the point at which economies of scale are exhausted. After this point stochastic factors become important in determining future growth and concentration.

4.6 Conclusions

This chapter has examined the importance of concentration as a measure of market structure. The extent to which markets are concentrated has important implications for the way in which markets perform. Any measure of concentration attempts to capture the prevailing structure and the extent of competitive forces operating in an industry. Various measures of concentration have been examined and their relative merits discussed. We argued that concentration alone is not a sufficient indicator of competitive conditions in any particular industry. An analysis of industry traditions and the organisational structures and objectives of firms is required to built a meaningful picture of competitive conditions in a market.

An examination of the determinants of concentration has shown that both the level and rate of change in market concentration can be explained by the existence of economies of scale, entry and exit barriers, and strategic behaviour, mergers, government regulation and technological change. The importance of stochastic factors in determining concentration has also been highlighted with reference to a body of influential empirical research. Overall, the evidence suggests that economies of scale, high levels of product differentiation and advertising, slow industry growth, small firm numbers and the operation of stochastic factors lead to increased industry concentration, while high entry rates and industry growth lead to falling levels of concentration. Future research in the area of concentration is likely to look for ways to combine elements of the systematic and stochastic approaches to further explain the evolution of market structures.

Key terms

Aggregate concentration	Law of proportionate effect
Concentration indices	Market
Industry	Type 1 and Type 2 industries

Case study 4.1
The evolution of market structure: a simulation approach

The effects of stochastic factors on market structure and concentration can be examined via the use of simulation analysis. For example, Scherer (1980) traced the evolution of a hypothetical industry by constructing an industry made up of 50 equally sized firms. Each firm's growth rate in each year was drawn from a normal probability distribution whose parameters (mean and variance) were calibrated using a sample of 369 firms drawn from the 500 largest US firms over the period 1954 to 1960. The growth process was carried out 16 times over a 140-year time period and the average concentration ratio calculated. The results showed that the concentration ratio increased from 8 per cent in year 1 to approximately 58 per cent in year 140.[1]

This case study carries out a simulation exercise to examine the effects on market structure when firm sizes are subject to cumulative random shocks. In other words, it examines what happens to industry concentration when the law of proportionate effect holds.

In the model the relationship between current size and growth is controlled by the parameter β_2 and it is assumed that u_{it} (firm growth rates) are drawn from a normal distribution. The simulation results are reported using three sets of measures reflecting the evolution of the size distribution of banks:

● Mean and standard deviation of firm size.
● One, two and five bank concentration ratios and the numbers equivalent of the Herfindahl–Hirschman index.
● The persistence of dominance, measured by the average number of periods as market leader achieved by the firm with most periods as market leader.

Table 1 reports the average results across 20 simulations of the evolution over 50 time periods of the sizes of a group of 20 firms. The firms begin equal in size (1 unit at time $t = 0$). Their subsequent evolution is driven by equation $s_{it} = \beta_1 + \beta_2 s_{it-1} + u_{it}$, where the standard deviation σ_{it} is set equal to 0.1. (σ_{it} measures the variability in growth rates of firms of different size. If small firms have more variable growth rates than large firms there will be a tendency for an increase in concentration to be offset over time. However, if large firms have more variable growth rates than their smaller counterparts, then any increases in concentration are reinforced.) u_{it} is the error term.

Table 1 shows the evolution of firm size over 50 periods. Through the working of the law of proportionate effect, the mean and standard deviation of firm size increases over the 50 periods. Concentration also increases using each of the five measures employed. For example, the combined market shares of the top five firms (CR5) increased from 25 per cent in period 0, to 49 per cent in period 50. This has direct implications for the numbers of equally sized firms that the industry can support (measured by the numbers equivalent version of the Herfindahl–Hirschman index), which falls from 20 firms in period 0, to 13 firms in period 50. The leading firm in the industry managed to retain its position as market leader in 27 of the 50 periods.

---

[1] McGloughan (1995) extended the assumptions underlying a stochastic model of growth to produce a model that incorporates growth, entry and exit processes.

Table 1 ● Evolution of firm size and concentration

Time t	Mean	SD σ	CR1	CR2	CR5	HH	Num. equiv. (1/HH)
0	1	–	5	10	25	0.05	20
1	1	0.1	6	11.7	28.2	0.05	20
2	1	0.14	6.4	12.4	29.1	0.051	19.6
5	1.02	0.23	7.5	14.2	32.4	0.052	19.2
10	1.03	0.33	8.7	16.1	35.4	0.055	18.2
15	1.05	0.41	9.6	17.7	38.3	0.058	17.2
20	1.10	0.49	10.5	19.1	40.0	0.06	16.7
25	1.14	0.59	11.7	20.8	41.9	0.063	15.9
30	1.18	0.67	12.7	21.8	43.5	0.066	15.2
35	1.21	0.74	13.3	22.6	45.4	0.068	14.7
40	1.22	0.78	13.8	23.6	46.2	0.07	14.3
45	1.22	0.83	14.3	24.5	47.1	0.072	13.9
50	1.26	0.91	15.1	25.7	49.0	0.076	13.2
Top	26.7						

Notes:
1. The results are generated from 20 replications of the development over 50 time periods of a market comprising 20 firms, each of which starts from an initial size of 1 unit.
2. Mean and SD denote the mean and standard deviation of actual firm size.
3. CR1, CR2 and CR5 are concentration ratios measuring the market share of the top 1, 2 and 5 firms, respectively.
4. HH is the Herfindahl–Hirschman Index.
5. Num. equiv. is the numbers equivalent version of the Herfindahl–Hirschman index.
6. Top denotes the number of periods in which one firm retains the largest market share through time.

Overall, the table shows that cumulative random shocks to firm sizes lead to increases in the average and standard deviation of bank size, and increased concentration. The stochastic process observed in Table 1 illustrates how industries evolve into concentrated market structures even in the absence of economies of scale, entry barriers, mergers and government regulation.

Case study 4.2
Concentration and competition in retail industry

The evolution of concentration in certain industries has generated interest in recent years. For example, in the UK, European and US retailing industries several studies have examined the causes and effects of increasing levels of concentration.[1]

The retailing industry is of significance given that it accounts for a sizable proportion of national income in many European countries. *The Economist* (1999) noted that 18 of the top 1,000 largest firms were retailers. In most countries the number of retailing firms

---

[1] Examples include studies by the Office of Fair Trading (1985, 1997b) for the UK, and Eurostat (1997) and Dobson and Waterson (1999) for Europe. Studies for the US include Connor *et al.* (1996), and Marion *et al.* (1979).

has declined, leading to increased concentration in the 1990s. For example, Dobson and Waterson (1999) examined the level and change in concentration for food retailing across six European countries (Belgium, Netherlands, France, Germany, Spain and the UK). They found that the UK had the highest level of concentration, while Spain had the lowest.

The causes of this increased concentration in retailing vary from market to market within the retailing industry. For example, a study by the Office of Fair Trading (1997b) noted that regulation has played a major role in markets such as pharmacies and betting establishments, where rules relating to licensing had prevented the entry of new firms and led to high levels of concentration. Economies of scale arising from bulk buying and distribution along with increased productivity have led to growth and concentration in the food retailing market. Dobson and Waterson (1999) noted that over the period 1980 to 1996, mergers significantly affected the level of concentration in many European retail markets, with deals totalling £24,950 million.

Overall, the increased levels of concentration have led to increased market power for the largest firms in retailing. The leading firms had exercised their market power by either obtaining favourable prices from suppliers, or vast expenditures on advertising, branding and promotion to build reputation advantages to ensure customer loyalty (Dobson and Waterson, 1997). These strategies had allowed the largest retailers to increase prices of products to customers. Dobson and Waterson (1999) noted that between 1984 and 1992 the profit margins of the 50 largest UK retailing firms grew on average by 10 per cent.

As a consequence of these increases in concentration, many researchers have argued for government policies to promote competition in retailing. In many markets these policies may involve measures to reduce barriers to entry, prohibit mergers and curb other abuses of market power by retailers. However, in some retailing markets, competition has intensified with the entry of new firms offering retail goods online. This has led to pressure on the profit margins of many retailers and may eventually reduce concentration in many markets.

Case study 4.3
Mergers, concentration and regulation[1]

Mergers often lead to increased concentration. The increased power of the largest firms in the industry can lead to a decline in competition, resulting in consumers being offered less choice at higher prices.

In 1998, the Monopolies and Mergers Commission produced a report which resulted from the investigation of a merger between Tomkins Plc and Kerry Group Plc. The merger led to an increase in concentration in the flour milling industry. The investigation had arisen when bread-makers had complained that the increased concentration in the flour-producing industry would lead to less choice and higher prices in the flour market.

Before the merger, Rank Hovis Limited (a Tomkins subsidiary) produced 24 per cent of the flour milled in the UK, while Spillers Milling (a Kerry subsidiary) accounted for 11 per cent. Both companies were also involved in the production and sale of flour to commercial companies and the production of bread. The merger gave Tomkins control of six Spillers' flour mills. After the merger the new firm accounted for 60 per cent and 55 per cent of output in both these respective markets.

[1] A more detailed discusion of this case is given in Monopolies and Mergers Commission (1998).

The companies argued that the merger would lead to substantial cost savings which would be passed on to consumers in the form of lower prices. Furthermore, the two firms argued that they would not have the market power to charge high prices, given that many of their customers were large, powerful retailers who could, if need be, seek alternative sources of supply.

The investigation argued that there would be no significant competitive pressure on the firms to reduce prices and that the merger would lead to a decline in competition, increased concentration and higher prices. As a remedy to the increased concentration that had taken place, the Commission recommended that Tomkins sell four of the six flour mills it had acquired from the merger.

Questions for discussion

1. Why has concentration interested researchers?

2. Examine the differences between industries and markets.

3. Discuss the relative merits of the concentration ratio. What variables have been used to construct such measures?

4. Explain the significance of the numbers equivalent measures of the Herfindahl–Hirschman index.

5. Discuss how the relationship between the minimum efficient scale and industry size can determine the level of observed concentration in a given industry.

6. Discuss the difference between Type 1 and Type 2 industries. What are the implications for concentration of these industry types?

7. Examine the proposition that firms and industries follow a lifecycle of growth, and examine the implications of this for the evolution of concentration.

8. Discuss the view that industries become concentrated through time by chance.

Further reading

Caves, R.E. (1998) Industrial organization and new findings on the turnover and mobility of firms, *Journal of Economic Literature*, **36**, 1947–1982.

Curry, B. and George, K. (1983) Industrial concentration: a survey, *Journal of Industrial Economics*, **31**, 203–55.

Davies, S.W. (1989) Concentration, in Davies, S. and Lyons, B. (eds) *The Economics of Industrial Organisation*. London: Longman.

Davies, S.W. and Lyons, B.R. (1996) *Industrial Organisation in the European Union*. Oxford: Clarendon Press.

Geroski, P.A. (1999) *The Growth of Firms in Theory and Practice*, Centre of Economic Policy Research Discussion Paper Series, No. 2092.

Sutton, J. (1991) *Sunk Costs and Market Structure*. London: MIT Press.

Sutton, J. (1997) Gibrat's legacy, *Journal of Economic Literature*, **35**, 40–59.

Utton, M.A. (1970) *Industrial Concentration*. Harmondsworth: Penguin.

CHAPTER 5

Barriers to entry

Learning objectives

After reading this chapter the student should be able to:

- Define the concept of an entry barrier

- Explain and analyse the sources of entry barriers

- Analyse entry-deterring strategies

- Discuss the role of contestable markets theory and the importance of potential entry

- Appreciate the empirical evidence for the importance of entry barriers in different industries and different countries

5.1 Introduction

The traditional approach to the analysis of industry structure assumes that the smaller the number of firms operating in a market, the more likely it is that competition will be restricted. This implies that barriers to entry contribute to profitability in such markets. Barriers to entry can be defined in several ways. Bain (1956) defined barriers to entry as factors which allow established firms in an industry to earn supernormal profits without attracting entry. Stigler (1968, p.67) defined barriers to entry as: 'a cost of producing (at some or every rate of output) which must be borne by a firm which seeks to enter an industry but is not borne by firms already in the industry'. Demsetz (1982) asserted that barriers persist in the long run only if they are erected and supported by the state. Caves and Porter (1977) argued that entry barriers apply not only to entrants, but also between different groups of established firms within industries. Groups may arise from differences in products produced or ownership structure.

We will see in this chapter that entry barriers are central to any analysis of industry structure, and that their role helps to define the competitive conditions within industries. Before we examine entry barriers in detail, it is useful to discuss the effect that entry plays in the traditional market structures. We consider perfect competition, monopolistic competition, monopoly and lastly oligopoly.

Perfect competition

Free entry and free exit is an important assumption in the model of perfect competition. If price lies above average cost, the firm will realise abnormal profit. It is this abnormal profit which will attract the attention of firms, which will enter without any barrier. Over time, this entry will increase supply, which will depress price sufficiently for firms to earn only 'normal' profits. As abnormal profits are competed away, entry will cease. This long-run equilibrium will also coincide with the minimum point of firm's average costs and thus firms will be using all their resources in the most efficient manner.

In perfect competition, entry can be viewed as an 'equilibrating force', resulting in normal profits and allocative efficiency. It is implicit in the notion of easy entry that firms have access to the necessary resources, which implies that a perfectly competitive market is characterised by the free flow of labour, capital, knowledge and all other inputs. The assumption of free exit is equally important. If exit is costly then firms might be reluctant to enter an industry in the first place, and risk losing their sunk costs.

Monopolistic competition

Monopolistic competition differs from perfect competition in that firms in the former structure produce goods and services that can be seen as broadly similar, or substitutable for one another, yet sufficiently differentiated in the minds of consumers to allow individual firms a degree of discretion over price. This then implies that firms face a downward sloping demand curve for their outputs and the ability to earn abnormal profits. Again, as in perfect competition, it is entry that brings about an equilibrium where only normal profits are earned. Thus entry guards against the entrenchment of monopoly power.[1] It might also be possible for entry to occur even after abnormal profits have been competed away. Some entrepreneurs may have a strong wish to be independent and to own their own firms. Even if profits are low, factors such as independence, status and leisure may be sufficiently attractive for owners of firms to consider entry into certain industries.

Monopoly

At first glance, one might assume that entry is not an issue as, in theory, monopoly represents a long-run equilibrium. However, there are three ways in which the power of a monopolist may be threatened by entry considerations. Firstly, a monopolist may be faced by potential entry. Thus, while there may be only one firm operating in a given market,

---

[1] However, the firm does not operate at its lowest average cost.

there may be a number of potential entrants, who may have been temporarily deterred from entry by the actions of the incumbent monopolist. In effect, this potential competition constrains the actions of the monopolist and may result in a more competitive equilibrium. The market structure could be seen as being closer to oligopoly, since it is characterised by interdependence and uncertainty.

Secondly, the monopolist may be unable to prevent the development and entry of new products that could reduce its market power. This is part of the Schumpeterian argument discussed in Chapter 8 on innovation. Schumpeter (1928) saw technical change as exerting a disruptive force on market equilibria, arguing that the introduction of new products and new practices destabilised markets. This he referred to as 'creative destruction', a process by which innovation would lead not only to new goods, new services and new methods of production but also to a weeding-out of the older, less efficient firms. Stigler (1952, p.222) echoed this point:

> There are no permanent barriers to the invention of substitute products, the discovery of alternative resources, and the like . . . we should not seek for permanent barriers to the entry of rival firms; the fundamental problem is how entry is retarded.

The final way in which a monopoly can be affected by entry is if it has been created and sponsored by government action. Government-created monopolies will fear no rival as long as government protection remains in place. If the government follows a policy of denationalisation and deregulation, then the firm will be faced with greater competition. This issue is discussed at length in Chapter 12.

Oligopoly

One can argue that it is in oligopoly that the conditions surrounding entry become important in determining the nature of market competition. Whilst the market structures of perfect and monopolistic competition are affected by actual entry and the monopoly market is affected by potential entry, oligopolistic markets are affected by both types of entry. In oligopolistic markets, firms not only take into account the effects on entry conditions when making product differentiation, innovation and pricing decisions, but they may also erect obstacles to any potential threat of entry.

In this chapter we begin by classifying the various types of entry barrier which may arise from the fundamental structural conditions present in any given industry, and then examine various strategies that can be adopted by established firms to deter the entry of new firms. The role which potential entrants play in determining the behaviour and profitability of established firms is also examined. In this discussion, entry of new firms and exit of existing firms is seen as a potent force which helps industries to attain equilibrium such that all firms make average levels of profit. We then expand this view to highlight the role of entry in the evolution of industry structures.

5.2 Classification of entry barriers

This section provides a convenient classification of the different types of entry barrier. There is no one simple, agreed system of arranging the multitude of market variables that may provide impediments to the entry of potential firms.

Most commentators would agree that the study of entry barriers began formally with Bain's pioneering work in 1956, by identifying three main barriers to entry: economies of scale, absolute cost advantage and product differentiation. One should note that there were some notable earlier contributions to the theory of entry barriers. For example, Harrod (1952) analysed entry by identifying firms as either 'snatchers' – firms that are interested only in high prices and short-run profits and thus not worried about attracting entry – or the 'stickers' – firms that have committed long-term investments to the industry and do not wish to attract too many entrants by setting too high a price. The three barriers identified by Bain have been added to and refined. Shepherd (1997, p.210), for example, lists no less than 21 entry barriers under the title of 'common causes of entry barriers'. If one were to extend the list to cover 'uncommon causes', who knows how long and how complex the list would be. What this implies is that we have to arrange such barriers into meaningful groups to allow for more useful analysis.

Broadly speaking barriers may be conveniently thought of as either stemming from the structure of the relevant industry, providing shelter for the incumbent firms, or those that are 'created' by the incumbent deliberately to keep potential entrants out or at least retard the rate of entry. Howe (1978, p.64) referred to the former type as 'natural' and the latter as 'artificial'. Shepherd (1997, p.210–11) also divides entry barriers into two types: 'Exogenous causes' which reflect the structural conditions of the market, such as technology, which are normally regarded as beyond the control of the existing firms, and 'endogenous causes' which identify the strategies that allow firms to erect barriers. It is possible to refine these basic definitions into further subsets. Jacobson and Andréosso-O'Callaghan (1996, p.93), for example, introduced the concept of 'barriers of the first order' to cover domestic entry barriers, while 'barriers of the second order' refer to the additional barriers firms face when trying to break into foreign markets.

Our approach is to follow broadly the traditional dichotomy. We examine first the structural barriers which both incumbents and potential entrants face in the industry and then we turn to an examination of entry-deterring strategies, i.e. barriers that have been deliberately created by existing firms. Before we commence, however, we must bear four points in mind:

● All groupings and definitions are not always clear-cut. Undoubtedly there is a great deal of overlap in many of the barriers we examine. Thus it is possible to argue that product differentiation can be both a structural barrier and an entry-deterring strategy.
● No particular degree of difficulty is attached to these barriers.
● The status of the entrant will often define the ease of entry. What may appear to be a formidable barrier to one entrant may appear less of a restriction to a large multi-product firm, dominant in other markets.
● The entry effects on existing firms may well depend on the speed at which entry is executed. Entry at a slow rate will alert existing firms to the danger of additional competition and allow them time to develop effective strategies to counter the threat. Faster entry may not allow firms to react as effectively.

5.3 Structural barriers

Structural barriers refer to all those barriers over which neither existing firms nor entrants have direct control. They arise from the conditions of the industry structure. Under this heading we consider three broad categories of barriers: legal barriers, the traditional 'Bain' barriers, and geographical barriers.

Legal barriers

Legal barriers are some of the most effective of all barriers as they are erected by government action and have the backing of the law to enforce potential exclusion. Both the Chicago and Austrian schools view legal barriers as the most difficult to surmount and thus the most damaging to competition. Economists sometimes refer to 'free entry' as entry that is free of government restrictions, and 'easy entry' which would imply that neither actual nor potential competitors have any cost disadvantages. Examples of such legal barriers are:

● *Registration, certification and licensing of businesses.* Many markets and industries are characterised by the need to seek official permission to trade, for example pubs, taxis, defence equipment, airlines. It has been claimed that existing firms in an industry may sometimes seek some form of government regulation in order to keep out firms that cannot meet the existing industry standards. Under this guise of 'maintaining standards', potential low-cost producers may be denied access to the market.

● *Monopoly rights.* Monopoly rights may be granted by legislation. Governments may allow certain firms sole rights in the provision of goods and services for a limited or unlimited time. A common example of such sole rights is the awarding of franchised monopolies in a variety of markets, such as the railways, mobile telephones and television stations. The argument put forward for these franchises is that these markets are either natural monopolies, where average costs can be minimised only if the firms operate at a sufficiently large scale, or industries that require a guaranteed share of the market to justify investment in technology and product development.

● *Patents.* Patents are the deliberate creation of a property right so as to stimulate and encourage innovatory activity. Ownership of a patent confers monopoly rights and the potential of monopoly profit. It is this temporary monopoly status that is the sought-after return on investments in research and development. The downside is that a patent grants firms exclusive control over the output of new products and denies new firms access to the market and retards the rate of diffusion of the product throughout the economy.

● *Government policies.* Government policies can also indirectly bring about various legal barriers. Friedman (1962, p.144) suggested three areas – tariffs, tax policies and labour laws – as creating such barriers. An example of such a barrier is the French tax policy of setting a car tax directly related to its engine capacity. This has the effect of increasing the price of American cars, which have a greater capacity.[2]

Bain barriers

Bain (1956) defined the presence of entry barriers in terms of the ability of incumbent firms to persistently raise prices above the competitive level without inviting entry of new firms. Bain identified three main barriers, examined below.

---

[2] Cook and Farquharson (1998), p.429.

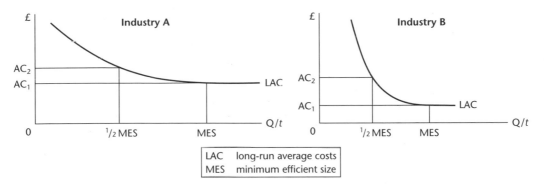

Figure 5.1 Economies of scale as a barrier to entry

Economies of scale

Barriers created by **economies of scale** will exist for two reasons. The first barrier is when the minimum efficient size of firm constitutes a large proportion total industry size. Minimum efficient size of firm is the level of output at which all potential scale economies have been exploited and the firm is operating under conditions of constant returns to scale. The nature of the technology may be such that firms must be large in relation to the market to be efficient. At the extreme, we can identify so-called natural monopolies, a condition where the market can tolerate only one firm. This is usually due to the very high fixed costs incurred in the industry.

Secondly, a barrier can exist when average cost at the *less than minimum efficient size (MES) level of output* is substantially greater than that at the minimum efficient size. This is illustrated in Figure 5.1. The penalty to a firm of entering at, for example, half the minimum efficient size is the additional unit costs it will face, i.e. the distance AC_1 to AC_2. Given the nature of the technology, these costs are much greater in Industry B than in industry A.[3]

Thus the entrant faces a dilemma. Either the firm faces high risks by entering at a large scale so as to avoid the penalty of higher average costs, or the firm enters at a smaller scale, which would mean that it incurs the penalty of a higher average cost. Large-scale entry is full of risks as the additional supply in the industry may disrupt the status quo by expanding industry capacity, depressing prices and inviting retaliatory action. The entrant's problems would be further exacerbated if there were significant economies of multi-plant operations and distribution networks. To compete with the existing firms in the first case, the entrant would be forced to enter as a horizontally integrated firm. In the second case the firm would have to be vertically integrated. Both these conditions may make it difficult for an entrant to compete on equal terms with the well integrated incumbents.

Absolute cost advantages

This barrier exists where the long-run average costs (LAC) of the entrant lie above those of the existing firm. Thus entrants will face higher average costs at every level of output.

There are many reasons why entrants face higher absolute costs. Firstly, established firms may be in control of superior production processes, own patents and be party to trade

---

[3] See Case study 5.1 at the end of the chapter.

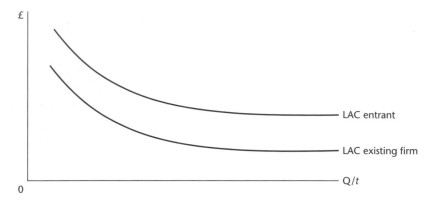

Figure 5.2 Absolute cost advantage as a barrier to entry

secrets. The Monopolies and Mergers Commission (1968) estimated that it would take an entrant in the cellulose fibre industry some five to seven years to catch up with the relevant technology. As noted earlier, patents are the deliberate creation of a property right for new knowledge, intended to protect an innovator from rivals. Although they may be regarded as an entry barrier they can also be viewed as increasing consumer welfare. Their existence will encourage firms to invest in research, with the promise of monopoly profits for successful innovations and these will increase consumer choice and consumer utility. However, patents can also be used as a strategy to deter entry and can thus be seen as an endogenously caused barrier. In particular, this may be the case when a firm in possession of a new technology decides to apply for many patents to cover all possible spin-offs, so as to deny rivals the opportunity to 'invent around' the new technology to produce similar goods. This can happen in the chemical industry, where a variation in the molecular structure can produce different goods.[4]

Secondly, established firms may have the exclusive ownership of superior inputs. They may control the best raw materials and have recruited the best labour and management personnel. With the best inputs under the control of the existing firms, entrants will then be forced to turn to more expensive alternatives or to purchase lower-quality inputs. An example of this is the control that British Airways exercised over landing slots at Heathrow, forcing potential competitors to use less attractive airports.

Thirdly, existing firms may have access to cheaper sources for investment finance as they are seen to be of a lower risk than new firms. New firms will be viewed by the capital market as firms with an uncertain future and any funds lent to such firms would carry a risk premium. Some authors have identified this type of issue as a separate barrier, referred to as the 'capital requirements barrier' which might be regarded as an all-embracing barrier that covers the problems of securing sufficient finance to enter the market at a realistic level of production.

Fourthly, the existence of vertically integrated operations such as brewing, iron and steel, and chemical industries will force an entrant to operate at more than one level of production if it wishes to compete with the existing firms. Denying rivals access to customers

[4] For an example of such 'manipulated patents' see Scherer and Ross (1990) p.624.

or inputs through a variety of vertical exclusions can be classed as a restrictive practice (discussed in section 5.4 below and at length in Chapter 9). Finally, the entrant may have to incur greater costs in order to create a reputation in the market so as to tempt customers away from the existing firms. The absolute cost advantage barrier may not always operate in practice as it is possible that existing firms may have overpaid for their assets so that new firms are then at an advantage because their current asset prices are much lower. This might be true of an industry subject to rapid technical change, such as the computer software market. Equally, some entrants may be spared the costs of persuading the market to accept a new idea or a new product, costs that were incurred by the established firms.

Demsetz (1982) argued that Bain's absolute cost advantages simply reflect the scarcity of resources and associated scarcity rents rather than being caused by the power of the dominant (incumbent) firms. This comment does not invalidate the above discussion in so far as we are concerned with structural barriers. These additional costs are real enough to potential entrants and we have not suggested that they were the result of the exercise of monopoly power.

Product differentiation

A structural barrier will arise because the existing brands and reputations of the incumbents create loyal customers who will need to be prised away from their loyalty or possibly stirred out of their inertia. This can be achieved either by selling the same good but at a lower price or by outspending the existing firms in the promotion of new goods. Either way, whether due to increased costs or reduced revenue the entrant is faced with a squeeze on potential profits. A good illustration of how **product differentiation** can create barriers to entry through advertising was discussed by Comanor and Wilson (1967). They identified the following barriers:

- High advertising implies additional costs to entrants. Owing to either brand loyalty or customer inertia the new entrant must spend proportionately more on advertising per prospective customer. In other words, market penetration costs are high. This is an absolute advantage type of barrier.
- A new entrant, entering on a small scale, will not be able to take advantage of various economies of scale in advertising. The large-scale advertisers benefit from an increasingly effective message as well as decreasing average costs of such advertising.
- Investment funds needed to fund an advertising campaign will incur high interest rates as this type of investment carries high risks. Not only is the risk of failure high but these funds do not create any tangible assets that can be sold off in the event of failure.

This is a complicated barrier to analyse since successful differentiation can not only generate such barriers but also *stimulate* entry with the promise of higher profits in the market. In fact, an entry strategy would often have to rely on extensive product differentiation to gain a share of the market.[5] Thus Stigler (1968) argued that product differentiation was only a barrier to entry if the entrant faced higher costs of differentiation than the incumbent.

Bain (1956) argued that the three entry barriers of economies of scale, absolute cost advantage and product differentiation were generally considered to be stable and long term, thus being an important structural condition of market structure. However, this did not imply

[5] For an excellent discussion of these sorts of issues, see Needham (1976).

that these barriers should be regarded as permanent. Market structures can change over time and the height of entry barriers can rise or fall. For example, new deposits of a raw material can be discovered which will reduce the absolute cost advantage to an incumbent; a new technical process may result in changing the economies of scale facing both incumbent and entrant; and the launch of a newly advertised product may also reduce the product differentiation advantages of the existing firms. However, Bain believed that such changes were gradual and would not invalidate his general argument that the above barriers defined long-term structural conditions in a given industry.

A contrary view has been vigorously pursued by the Chicago school.[6] Proponents have argued that the Bain definition of a barrier, as anything that a new firm must overcome in order to enter a market, such as scale barriers or capital requirements, is meaningless in that all firms are faced by such barriers, including those that were once new to the industry. A better definition, in their view, is Stigler's definition of an entry barrier as anything that imposes a higher long-run cost of production on the entrant than on the incumbent. This implies that the incumbent can charge a higher price and not attract entry. This, the Chicago school would argue, is rare. What is important when considering entry is not the existence of entry barriers but how quickly these barriers can be surmounted. Thus a firm faced with high absolute cost disadvantages or scale economies, compared with a firm faced with lower barriers, will simply take a longer time to organise its resources efficiently to ensure profitable entry.

Geographical barriers

Geographical barriers refer to the restrictions faced by foreign companies attempting to enter a domestic market. Barriers that fall into this category are:

- *Tariffs and quotas.* We can also include strategies such as subsidies to domestic firms and public procurement policies designed to help only the domestic firms. All these policies will impede the free flow of goods, leaving the foreign firms at a disadvantage.
- *Physical barriers.* Physical barriers refer to frontier controls, which can lead to delays, customs formalities and expensive handling charges.
- *Technical barriers.* These barriers refer to many constraints faced by foreign firms in a domestic market. They include: the need to meet specific technical standards, labour market regulations, transport regulations, exchange controls, language and cultural differences.
- *Fiscal barriers.* These cover the many different indirect and direct tax regimes imposed in different countries, which may disadvantage foreign firms.

5.4 Entry-deterring strategies

We have considered the structural barriers, those that are present in the underlying conditions of the market. Fundamentally, these were causes that could not be altered readily. The barriers discussed below refer to those over which firms have some degree of control. Firms can thus erect or heighten such barriers through their own actions. It is interesting to note

[6] See, for example, the arguments of Posner (1976), p.59.

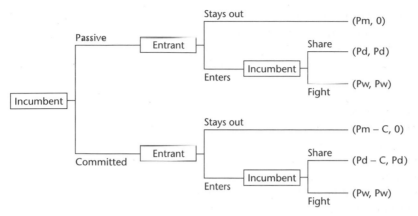

Figure 5.3 Game tree of an entry decision

that such barriers may exist even if the incumbent has not erected any such barrier. A credible threat of such action may be sufficient to warn off potential rivals. Most of these barriers will be a function of the degree of market power possessed by the existing firm or, put another way, the *degree of imperfection inherent in the market*.[7] There are many types of behaviour that could be included under this heading. We focus on some of the major strategies based on price, product differentiation and restrictive practices. However, before we do so, we examine how researchers have attempted to illustrate entry as a simple game between established firms and potential entrants. This type of approach to analysing entry deterrence emphasises the role of threats, commitments and sunk costs. Firms do not hold *a priori* beliefs about one another, but instead try to predict other firms' moves using knowledge of past encounters and assume that their rivals' decisions are rational.

An entry game

Dixit (1982) applied the game theoretic approach to entry deterrence. The following uses the Dixit methodology to analyse the strategic behaviour in a possible duopoly situation consisting of an incumbent monopolist and a potential entrant.

Figure 5.3 illustrates a series of outcomes which depend on whether entry to a market takes place. The outcome of this game depends on whether the incumbent firm is passive (does not prepare itself to fight entry) or committed (in which case it has prepared itself to fight entry by prior spending that will help it to avert entry). The top and bottom halves of the tree show the situations where the incumbent is **passive** and **committed**, respectively. We now examine the outcome of these two situations.

Passive incumbent

There are three outcomes if the incumbent has not prepared itself to fight in the event of entry. If the incumbent has not prepared to fight, and the entrant stays out of the market, then the incumbent continues to make monopoly profits (Pm) while the entrant earns zero, denoted by the tuple (Pm, 0). If entry does occur, the incumbent must decide whether

---

[7] Shepherd (1997), p.211.

to fight the entrant in a price war (in which case both firms make losses, Pw < 0), or divide the market (in which case both firms earn positive profits, Pd > 0). Dixit argued that the incumbent's threat to fight in the event of entry is not credible, as it has no incentive to fight. Therefore, the solution would be that the incumbent and entrant share the market, which is not as profitable as a monopoly, but more profitable than a price war (Pd, Pd).

Committed incumbent

If the incumbent is committed to the market by making a prior commitment (C), and the entrant knows this, the incumbent finds it optimal to fight entry through a price war (Pw), if this is more profitable than sharing the market (Pd – C, Pd). The rational entrant realises the threat of price war is credible and stays out of the market. Therefore, the solution occurs where the incumbent firm earns monopoly profits minus the cost of the commitment, while the entrant earns zero (Pm – C, 0). As long as the incumbent's commitment is visible and irreversible, the threat is credible. We can see from the Figure 5.3 that the committed incumbent is more profitable than the passive one.

Overall, the prior spending by established firms to raise entry barriers sends a clear signal to potential entrants of the likely behaviour of established firms if entry takes place. In the example above, the established firm has invested in specific assets to avert entry, and consequently has incurred costs that are likely to be unrecoverable (i.e. sunk costs). The existence of the prior irreversible commitment makes the threat of retaliation credible and indicates that the established firm is willing to fight a price war if entry takes place.

We now look at several strategies which established firms can adopt to erect entry barriers.

Pricing strategies

Fundamentally, incumbent firms enjoy sufficient cost advantages to earn abnormal profits at prices that also deter entry. The theory of **limit pricing** is one such illustration of this strategy. There are many variants of this theory in varying degrees of sophistication and attendant complexity. Here we develop just the simplest so as to capture the essence of the argument.

The strategy is designed to ensure that entry is unprofitable. It is the highest price that an established firm believes it can charge *without inviting entry*. The level of the limit price depends on costs of the potential entrant, the potential entrant's estimate of industry demand and eventual likely share after entry. Regarding the last point, the theory is built on the assumption (the Sylos Postulate) that potential entrants behave as though they expect existing firms to maintain output at the pre-entry level in the face of realised entry (Sylos-Labini, 1962). This means that any entry is a net addition to industry output.

Consider Figure 5.4, which shows the limit price in the case of an absolute advantage, i.e. the established firm enjoys average costs at AC_1, whereas the entrant faces an average cost schedule of AC_2. The demand curve faced by entrants is *dd*, which is that part of the market demand curve DD that is not served by the incumbent firms, who are producing output Q* at price P*. It could be thought of as the 'residual demand curve'. Since the entrant's average costs curve intersects the residual demand curve at P* the entrant will be unable to earn any profit. It is assumed that the established firms are forgoing profits to keep output and hence price at the entry-deterring level. P* is the limit price.

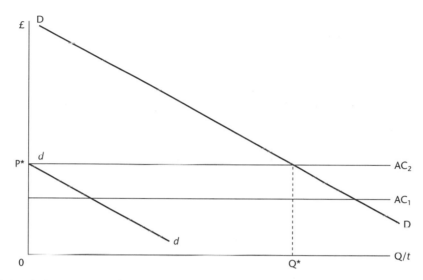

Figure 5.4 Limit pricing to deter entry

Little empirical evidence exists regarding the presence of limit pricing. What evidence there is tends to be anecdotal. Scherer and Ross (1990) observed that the pricing policy of the Reynolds Pen Corporation regarding the first ballpoint pens invited a massive entry. The price in 1945 was between US$12 and US$20, but by 1948 had fallen to 50¢ and Reynolds' market share was close to zero. As regards the existence of a limit price, Scherer claims that Xerox had a strategy of charging low prices to low-volume users (firms that used less than 5,000 copies a month) since there was an alternative technology (wet copying) available to low-volume users. Xerox wanted to keep these firms out of the market.

The theory has been heavily criticised. Stigler (1968, p.21) made the following points:

- Why is it more profitable to attempt to restrict all entry rather than retard the rate of entry?
- Why should the entrant not revise its belief that the incumbent firms will alter their price/output strategies after entry?
- If an industry is growing it may be difficult to dissuade a potential entrant that there is no market available to them if entry takes place.
- Industry structure is also ignored. The theory assumes that all oligopolists can carry out limit pricing. For the strategy to succeed there would have to be a high degree of collusion in the industry. As Stigler wrote: 'the theory of oligopoly is solved by murder'.

Further critical points were raised by Yamey (1972b):

- Could there not be a cheaper way of deterring entry, for example predatory pricing?
- The status of the entrant is all-important. Existing firms may wish to seek an accommodation with potential large entrants.
- Limit pricing implies perfect information regarding the industry demand curve, own costs, potential entrants' costs, and so on. This would be impossible to estimate with any degree of precision. Predatory pricing seems to offer an easier alternative: the firm would simply set a price below that of the new firm.

Predatory pricing

Predatory pricing is another strategy which can be used to deter entry. Strictly speaking this is a post-entry strategy but one that can be used to force recent arrivals out of the industry. Predatory pricing is designed to drive out new entrants by the incumbent setting prices at below average variable cost. Thus the incumbent may forgo short-run profits in order to reduce the profitability of entrants or existing competitors. This may force new firms out of the industry and constrain the ability of existing rivals to expand. The consequence is that the incumbent will enjoy greater market power and increased profits in the long run.

The Chicago school (the anti-interventionists) was rather sceptical about the reality of predatory pricing. Firstly, the predator would have to be certain that the gain in long-run profitability will offset short-run losses. There is little evidence that firms make such detailed analyses. Secondly, in the absence of any other entry barrier and in the possession of perfect information, there is no reason to suppose that further new firms will not enter the industry. This would imply that the predator would have to bear losses in the long run as well. A related problem for the regulators is to decide whether price-cutting constitutes illegal predation or is a legal business strategy designed to gain a competitive advantage.

Predation is not confined to pricing strategies but can use other strategies such as quantity and quality supplied. The Office of Fair Trading investigated such a strategy in the case of two bus companies in Scotland (OFT, 1994a). In 1990, Moffat & Williamson (M&W) won a contract to operate bus services that were subsidised by Fife Regional Council. On some of the routes M&W faced a competitor, Fife Scottish, which operated a commercial service. In 1992, Fife Scottish duplicated the subsidised service provided by M&W, by additional bus journeys. This had the effect of reducing market demand for M&W. The OFT held that Fife Scottish was a dominant local operator and was able to absorb losses. Predation was proven by Fife's ability to target that segment of the market where it faced a new rival.

Product differentiation

Product differentiation, especially advertising, can help to create or strengthen brand loyalties beyond what is natural to the market, thus reinforcing the structural barrier examined in the previous section. An example of this heightened barrier was the European Commission's investigation of the proposed merger between Kimberley-Clark and Scott Paper in the toilet tissues market. The Commission found that advertising in the UK was high and that the main objective of that advertising was to build brand loyalty, which would create entry barriers. The Commission concluded: 'The establishment of a new brand would require heavy investment in advertising and promotion in order to persuade brand loyal customers to switch away from their usual brand. Such expenditure is a sunk cost and adds to the risk of entry.'[8]

We can consider a few related strategies under this heading, which can lead to entry effects. *Brand proliferation*, common in, for example, the detergent market and the processed food market, can be an attempt by dominant firms to crowd the market with various brands and thus deny entrants sufficient market demand to recoup their sunk costs. In other markets, customers may face high *switching costs*, i.e. the cost of switching to another supplier. These customers are then 'locked in' with the existing firms. Examples are bank

---

[8] London Economics (1997), p.1.

accounts, computer software, hotels and stores (via loyalty cards). As a consequence, these customers cannot be easily lured to other firms. *Goodwill and reputation* may also help to strengthen the market position of incumbents, though this assumes that entrants from other industries do not have their own reputations.

Loyalty discounts, exclusive dealing, refusals to supply

Loyalty discounts, exclusive dealing and refusal to supply are all strategies intended to deny entrants access to supply of inputs or access to customers. An example was Capital Radio offering 'solus' advertising deals (OFT, 1994c). This meant that in return for agreeing to advertise exclusively on Capital Radio, the advertiser received a discount. The effect of these agreements was to place a share of the radio advertising market beyond Capital Radio's competitors. One of the most famous of solus tie contracts was in petrol retailing in the 1960s in which independent retailers in the UK agreed to a long contract for the supply of petrol from one particular supplier. Some of these issues are discussed at greater length in relation to vertical integration in Chapter 9.

5.5 Contestable markets

While the game theoretic approach to entry barriers demonstrates how incumbent firms can act to deter entry, the theory of **contestable markets** shows that under certain conditions incumbents may be forced to reduce their profits to a normal level.

Baumol *et al.* (1982) forwarded a theory of contestable markets, emphasising potential rather than actual competition. Contestable markets are those in which competitive pressures from potential entrants act as strong constraints on the behaviour of established firms. For a market to be truly contestable there must be no significant entry barriers. This is the case whether the market consists of a single supplier or large numbers of firms, because it is the potential rather than actual competition that constrains the behaviour of the established firms. Therefore, the theory of contestable markets excludes sunk costs and strategic behaviour of incumbent firms. When potential entrants have access to the same technology as incumbents and there is an absence of sunk costs along with free entry and exit before incumbents can react, the market is said to be perfectly contestable.

Baumol *et al.* introduced the idea of 'hit and run' entry based on three assumptions:

- A potential entrant can identify a clientele who will purchase its output at or below the current market price.
- The entrant has enough time to sell to these customers before the incumbent has time to react.
- At the prices quoted, the entrant earns enough revenue to cover all costs (fixed and variable).

When the investment is irreversible, the length of time the asset is used becomes very important. If the asset can be used solely in the current period, the sunk costs are in essence a current fixed cost. If, before the established firms can react, the entrant can sell enough output to cover all costs (sunk or otherwise), the firm finds entry profitable. Baumol *et al.* argued that covering all sunk costs in the first period is crucial, because after this period incumbent firms can act strategically by cutting prices to win back lost sales, thereby making the entrant's continuing operation unprofitable. If entry for one period is profitable the entrant can enter, take its profits and leave the market before the incumbent has time to react.

We now explore a number of criticisms of the theory of contestable markets:[9]

- The exclusion of sunk costs is unrealistic as most markets require a large amount of initial investment. Possible exceptions might be the commercial airline and bus industries, where a large proportion of total capital asset expenditure is not sunk. This is because these assets can easily be transferred from one route to another, thereby raising the possibility of 'hit and run' entry. However, if sunk costs are important then the possibility of hit and run entry is no longer possible. Coursey *et al.* (1984, p.69) noted that: 'Sunk costs are found to weaken the support for "strong" interpretations of the contestable market hypothesis and thus yield a wide diversity of dynamic patterns of market performance.'
- The theory does not take into account all possible reactions of the established firms. To deter hit and run entry the incumbent firm may threaten that any firm entering the market will face a price war, and so deter entry. Schwartz and Reynolds (1983) argued that an analysis of entry should focus not on the existing price charged by established firms before entry, but on the price charged after entry. Shepherd (1997, p.220) argued that: 'the theory is naïve and static, with only one price. It ignores possible strategic price discrimination by the incumbent, which would decisively defeat entry while permitting excess profits.'
- The assumption that the potential entrant faces no cost disadvantage relative to the established firm is unrealistic, as the established firm is likely to have built up goodwill and technical experience over time.

Much of the empirical testing for contestability has been in the airline industry, which had previously been put forward by Baumol *et al.* (1982) as a contestable market. Several studies have been carried out in this area.[10]

Hurdle *et al.* (1989) tested for contestability in 867 airline routes in 1985. The authors utilised a regression model which examined the effects which potential entrants and market concentration had on the level of fares charged on any given route. In general, they found that industry structure (measured by concentration) was the most important factor determining the level of fares charged, thereby refuting the contestability hypothesis.

Strassmann (1990) used quarterly data on 92 US airline markets in 1980 to test the contestability hypothesis. She argued that for the contestability hypothesis to hold there should be no relationship between prices charged and industry concentration. In addition, there should be no relationship between entry barriers and prices. Strassmann utilised a regression model that examined the effects of actual and potential entry, concentration and costs on prices charged. She found that structural variables such as concentration and entry barriers play an important role in determining the prices charged in individual airline markets. Overall, the results suggested that the airline markets sampled were not contestable.

[9] Schwartz and Reynolds (1983), Shepherd (1984) and Schwartz (1986) provide a detailed treatment of the issues raised here. Spence (1983) is also useful in this respect, as is Baumol and Willig (1986). Schotter (1994) outlines a simple game which illustrates the effects of potential entry on established firm pricing behaviour.
[10] Examples of such studies include Graham *et al.* (1983), Call and Keeler (1985), Moore (1986), and Morrison and Winston (1987).

The extent to which contestable markets exist is questionable. However, the theory does provide some predictions of what might happen to established firms' behaviour when threatened with entry. Empirical support for the theory is at best weak. Shepherd (1997, p.220) concluded that:

> As often happens, a bright idea has been exaggeratedly oversold by its enthusiastic authors. The ensuing debate trims the concept and claims to their proper niche, taking their place among all the other ideas. In this instance, contestability offers insights, but it does not affect the central role of market structure.

5.6 Market dynamics and entry

As we have seen, the analysis of the effects of entry and exit on the profitability of firms and industries has advanced since Bain. However, these advances have tended to be static in nature by concentrating only on before and after effects of entry. Even advances in game theory have concentrated on identifying types of game which can be played to bring markets into equilibrium. The approaches discussed above do little to explain the effects of entry and exit on profits in a dynamic economy.

Taking a dynamic approach, Geroski (1991a) analysed entry as an ongoing process as a once-and-for-all game, which we examined previously in Figure 5.3. He argued that the traditional view of entry is generally static, and is seen as correcting for positions of excess profitability. His argument is that entry does more than correct a period of disequilibrium, since it can actually be instrumental in the evolution of industries. Entry into industries by efficient firms can cause incumbent firms to lower costs or exit from the market, which forces remaining firms and industries towards some new average level of profit. Market dynamics do not describe the move to a specific equilibrium, but rather a movement between equilibria:

> Entry can also play a more creative role in markets, serving as a vehicle for the introduction and diffusion of innovations which embody new products or processes that fundamentally alter conditions of supply and demand. Further, the mere threat of entry of this type may induce incumbents to generate new innovations or to adopt existing ones more rapidly.[11]

Therefore, the turnover of entry and exit over time determines the profits of individual firms and industries. This turnover is likely to be higher in industries such as electronics and pharmaceuticals where non-price competition is prevalent. Firms in these industries will often experience extreme variations in profitability, arising from the uncertainties associated with the outcomes of product and process innovations.

We can split this concept of entry into two components:

● Imitative entry, which occurs when the entrant can make profits by copying the established firm's product or method of production. This type of entry is seen as an equilibrating force in that it competes away excess profits to an equilibrium level.

● Innovative entry, which occurs when an entrant finds new ways of producing more cheaply, to yield monopoly profits. This type of entry is seen as a disequilibrating force, which propels the industry from one equilibrium state towards another.

---

[11] Geroski (1991a), p.210.

Geroski also examined the role of entry on an industry's evolution. When markets are first created, there is considerable confusion with large numbers of competing firms, perhaps producing a proliferation of brands. As time passes, consumers assess the usefulness of competing brands, and eventually a 'core' product becomes established. This leads to some firms dominating the industry. However, domination does not last indefinitely because as the industry matures, consumer tastes change and the core products become obsolete. New firms enter by introducing new products and the market undergoes a new phase of expansion and moves towards another equilibrium. Therefore, past patterns of entry determine the structure of markets at any time.[12]

We can conclude that, within a static framework, entry (actual and potential) is seen as an equilibrating factor, which forces profits back from disequilibrium to an equilibrium level. On the other hand, the dynamic view of entry contends that innovative and imitative forces are instrumental in driving an industry from one equilibrium to the next.

5.7 Empirical evidence on entry

Entry and exit play an important role in the dynamic process of competition, since the level of profits of firms in an industry are determined by the extent to which other firms can enter the market and compete away excess profits.

Empirical evidence on the determinants of entry for manufacturing industries now forms a substantial literature. Most research suggests that entry is higher in profitable industries or in industries enjoying high average growth rates (Baldwin and Gorecki, 1987; Geroski, 1991a). In contrast, entry is slower for industries where incumbents hold absolute cost advantages over potential entrants, or where capital requirements for entrants are substantial (Orr, 1974). The evidence with regard to scale economies, excess capacity and restrictive pricing practices (i.e. limit and predatory pricing acting as entry barriers) is both limited and inconclusive (Baldwin and Gorecki, 1987; Geroski, 1991a).

Exit should be easy if established firms have no sunk costs. This is not often the case, given that many assets are specific, and as such cannot be transferred to other uses if the firms were to exit the industry (Harbord and Hoehn, 1994). Evidence for manufacturing suggests that exit is higher from industries in which profits are low, and in which sunk costs are insignificant (Dunne *et al.*, 1988). Duetsch (1984) argued that conflicting objectives of owners and managers often make it difficult for firms to take exit decisions. Schary (1991) found that profits are in fact unrelated to exit. She argued that other characteristics relating to the financial and operating structure to the firm are more likely to determine exit. It is also possible that there is an association between the entry and exit rates in any time period, if the entrants are displacing established firms by capturing market share. Using US manufacturing data over the period 1963 to 1982, Dunne *et al.* (1988) found a negative correlation between annual entry and exit rates.

The following section provides a discussion of a selection of empirical studies which have examined the determinants of entry and exit from industry. In a seminal study, Orr (1974) examined the determinants of entry for a sample of 71 Canadian manufacturing industries over the period 1963 to 1967. Orr estimated the following equation:

$$E = \gamma_1 + \gamma_2 \Pi_p + \gamma_3 Q + \gamma_4 X + \gamma_5 K + \gamma_6 A + \gamma_7 R + \gamma_8 r + \gamma_9 C + \gamma_{10} S$$

[12] Klepper (1996) provides an extensive treatment of these issues.

where E denotes the average number of entrants of the sample period, Π_p is the average of past industry profit rate, Q is past industry growth, X is the minimum efficient scale divided by industry sales (as a proxy for an economies of scale barrier to entry), K denotes the amount of fixed capital required to enter an industry (as a proxy for a capital requirement barrier to entry), A denotes advertising intensity (measured by dividing advertising expenditures by industry sales), R is research and development intensity (measured by research and development expenditures divided by industry sales), r denotes business risk (calculated by the standard deviation of industry profit rates over the sample period), C is the level of industry concentration (measured on an ordinal basis where low = 1 and high = 5, and S is industry size (measured by total industry sales); $\gamma_1, \ldots, \gamma_{10}$ are the estimated coefficients.

Orr estimated various specifications of the model outlined above. In general he found a positive relationship between E and each of Π_p, Q and S, implying that past profits and industry growth and size tended to encouraged entry into Canadian manufacturing industries. In contrast, Orr found a negative relationship between E and each of X, K, A, R, r and C. This implied that economies of scale, capital requirements, advertising and research and development intensity, business risk and high levels of industry concentration discouraged entry.

Smiley (1988) examined the types of strategy adopted by firms to deter entry in 'new' and 'existing' product markets. A total of 848 questionnaires were sent to product managers, brand managers, directors of product management, division managers and marketing managers. Of these 293 were completed and returned.

Smiley split the sample into 'new' and 'existing' products, and managers were asked to rate on a scale of 1 to 5 (where 1 denotes never and 5 denotes frequently) which types of entry-deterring strategy they employed. In the 'new' product sample, the entry strategies sampled included:

● Charging low prices combined with large expenditures on advertising and promotion.
● Building excess capacity as a signal to potential entrants that established firms are able to meet all future demand.
● Creation of brand loyalty by high levels of spending on advertising and other promotional activities.
● Pre-emptively patenting products in order to prevent potential entrants from producing identical or similar products.
● Using the media to signal to entrants that any entry would be met with retaliation.
● Engaging in limit pricing to make entry unprofitable.

Smiley repeated the last six strategies for a sample of existing products. In addition he attempted to assess the extent to which firms producing existing products:

● engaged in brand proliferation aimed at filling up product space, so that entrants could not produce anything different; and
● attempted to mask profitability of any single product by various reporting practices.

For the 'new' product sample, Smiley found that advertising and pre-emptive patenting strategies were the most popular methods of entry deterrence. These strategies were used by 78 per cent and 71 per cent of firms surveyed, respectively. Limit pricing was found to be the least used of the entry-deterring strategies. Smiley found little difference between manufacturing and service firms' strategies, except that manufacturing firms were more likely to use pre-emptive patenting than their service counterparts.

For the 'existing' product groups, brand proliferation, advertising and masking the profitability of individual product lines were found to be the most popular forms of entry deterrence, accounting for 79 per cent, 79 per cent and 78 per cent of respondents, respectively. In contrast, building excess capacity was found to be the least popular strategy. Some differences were found between manufacturing and service firms. For example, manufacturing firms were much more likely to mask the profitability of individual products or to engage in pre-emptive patenting than service sector firms. Service firms tended to concentrate on advertising and promotional expenditures aimed at ensuring brand loyalty and increasing product differentiation barrier to entry.

Khemani and Shapiro (1990) argued that entry takes place if a firm's profits at a given time are greater than the expected long-run equilibrium profits. Exit takes place if current profits are below expected long-run profits. The authors specified entry and exit equations as follows:

$$L_{ENT} = \alpha_1 + \gamma_1(\Pi_0 - \hat{\Pi}_p)^R + \beta_1 \ln N + e_1$$

$$L_{EXT} = \alpha_2 + \gamma_2(\Pi_0 - \hat{\Pi}_p)^R + \beta_2 \ln N + e_2$$

where L_{ENT} and L_{EXT} equal the logarithm of the number of firms which have entered or exited the industry, N is logarithm of the number of firms in the industry and R is a restriction depending on whether long-run profits are positive or negative. Unsurprisingly, Khemani and Shapiro found that established firms with high profits tend to encourage entry into any given industry. The opposite is found for exit.

Geroski (1991b) examined the extent of entry by domestic and foreign firms in the UK over the period 1983 to 1984. Using a sample of 95 manufacturing industries, he calculated the numbers of entering and exiting firms along with their respective market shares. For the entrant firms, Geroski found that the number of entrants was similar in both years sampled (on average 210 and 217 firms, respectively). He further found that the market share of these entrant firms was relatively small, on average accounting for only 7–8 per cent of total industry sales. Of the entrants, domestic firms were found to capture a higher market share from their established counterparts. Firms that exited UK industries were also found to be relatively stable over time, but did increase with the number of entrants, thus suggesting a displacement effect.

Drawing on the work of Orr (1974), Geroski examined the factors determining entry of domestic and foreign firms. For both domestic and foreign firms he found that profits and industry size encouraged entry, while industry growth (somewhat surprisingly) discouraged entry. The significance of each of these variables was found to be much more pronounced for domestic firms than for their foreign counterparts.

Sleuwaegen and Dehandschutter (1991) examined the determinants of entry and exit for a sample of 109 Belgian manufacturing industries over the period 1980 to 1984. They found that entry is positively related to expected profits and industry growth, but discouraged by barriers relating to initial capital requirements, and when established firms hold product differentiation advantages. In contrast, exit is discouraged when expected future profits and growth are low.

Schwalbach (1991) using a sample of 183 German manufacturing industries over the period 1983 to 1985 found that entry is encouraged when expected profits and industry growth are high, but discouraged when economies of scale barriers exist.

Overall, the rate of entry and exit across manufacturing industries from different countries tends to be strongly correlated. For example, Cable and Schwalbach (1991) found that in the early 1980s the rates of entry and exit from Belgium, Canada, Germany, Korea, Norway, Portugal, UK and the United States were around 6.5 per cent of the populations sampled.

Geroski (1995) presented a series of stylised facts which summarised much of the theoretical and empirical work surrounding entry barriers. Among these facts, he noted the following characteristics of entry in manufacturing industries:

● Entry of new firms is often substantial, but these entrants rarely capture a large proportion of market share.
● Entry of new firms often leads to the displacement and exit of existing firms.
● Small entrants are less likely to survive than established, larger counterparts.
● Entry by new firms is more common than entry by established firms pursuing strategies of diversification. However, diversified entrants are much more likely to successfully penetrate any given market.
● Entry is more likely to be large at an early stage of an industry's development, when consumers are unsure about preferences and brands and 'core' products and processes have yet to become established.
● Entry of new firms leads to increased competition, and often stimulates innovatory activity and encourages established firms to become more efficient.
● Established firms tend to use non-price strategies (in preference to price strategies) to deter entry.
● Larger, mature entrants are much more likely to succeed than smaller, young entrants.

5.8 Conclusions

This chapter has outlined the various entry barriers that may face firms wishing to enter an industry. The barriers discussed emphasise the role that the underlying structural characteristics of an industry can play in deterring entry, and highlight the ways in which established firms can actively deter entry. Often, the threat of entry is enough to alter the behaviour of firms already in a given industry.

Empirical evidence on the determinants of entry for manufacturing industries now forms a substantial literature. The rate of entry and exit is similar across different industries and countries. Most research suggests that entry is more rapid in profitable industries or in industries enjoying high average growth rates.[13] In contrast, entry is slower for industries where economies of scale, capital requirements, advertising intensity, research and

---

[13] Siegfried and Evans (1994) provide an extensive review of the empirical research which examines entry barriers.

development intensity, business risk and high levels of industry concentration predominate. Further literature examining entry as a dynamic process may provide some interesting insights into the nature and consequences of various barriers.

Key terms

Absolute cost advantages	Limit pricing
Contestable markets	Passive and committed incumbents
Economies of scale barriers	Predatory pricing
Geographical barriers	Product differentiation barriers
Legal barriers	

Case study 5.1
Economies of scale as a barrier to entry in EU manufacturing industries

The following example examines the extent to which economies of scale can act as a barrier to entry in many manufacturing industries. Using a sample of manufacturing industries drawn from Belgium, Denmark, France, Germany, Greece, Ireland, Italy, Luxemburg, Netherlands and the UK, Emerson *et al.* (1988) derived average cost curves to provide estimates of the minimum efficient scale of production (MES) in each respective industry. From this information the authors estimated the cost penalties which firms operating at half the MES would incur. The table can be used to show the additional costs, which would be imposed on firms if they were to enter a given manufacturing industry at half the MES.

The extent to which economies of scale act as a barrier to entry varies across industries. For example, the cost penalty which would be incurred by firms entering the motor vehicles industry at half the MES would be between 6 and 9 per cent, while for footwear and clothing the penalty would be only 1 per cent. This implies that the gradient of the AC curve would be steeper in motor vehicles than in footwear and clothing.

The sources of scale economies in each respective industry also differs. For example, in some industries such as transport, production techniques are particularly important, while for industries such as chemicals, research and development yields important economies of scale.

Economies of scale are most prevalent in industries (such as chemicals and electricals) where the products produced incorporate complex technological features, and involve established firms spending heavily on research and development. This implies that over the longer term established firms may enjoy absolute cost advantages over potential entrants arising from preferential access to skilled labour or the protection afforded by patented processes of products.

In contrast, in industries where the methods of production involve less complex goods (such as food) economies of scale act as less of a barrier. Overall, the table suggests that economies of scale act as a potent barrier to entry in most EU manufacturing industries.

Industry	Cost of entering at half MES	Remarks
Motor vehicles	6–9%	Substantial economies of scale (EOS) in production and development costs
Other transport	8–20%	Variable EOS: small for cycles and shipbuilding (although economies are possible through series production level), substantial EOS in aircraft development costs
Chemicals	2.5–15%	Substantial EOS in production. Research and development is an important source of economies of scale in pharmaceutical products
Man-made fibres	5–10%	Substantial EOS in general
Metals	>6%	Substantial EOS in general for production processes. Also possible in production and series production
Office machinery	3–6%	Substantial EOS at product level
Mechanical engineering	3–10%	Limited EOS
Electrical engineering	5–15%	Substantial EOS at product level and for development costs
Instrument engineering	5–15%	Substantial EOS at product level via development costs
Paper, printing and publishing	8–36%	Substantial EOS in paper mills and, in particular, printing
Non-metallic mineral products	>6%	Substantial EOS in cement and flat glass production processes; In other branches, optimum plant size is small compared with the optimum size for the industry
Metal articles	5–10%	EOS are small at the plant level, but possible at production and series production level
Rubber and plastics	3–6%	Moderate EOS in tyre manufacturing; small EOS in factories making rubber and moulded plastic articles, but potential for EOS at product and series production level
Drink and tobacco	1–6%	Moderate EOS in breweries; small in cigarette factories. In marketing, EOS are considerable
Food	3.5–21%	EOS at marketing and distribution level
Textile industry	10%	Limited EOS, but some possible through length of production runs and specialisation
Footwear and clothing	1%	Limited EOS, but some possible through length of production runs and specialisation

Source: adapted from Emerson *et al.* (1988), pp.129–30, table 6.1.1.

Case study 5.2
Three examples of barriers to entry

Examples of barriers to entry are not difficult to find. The Monopolies and Mergers Commission will frequently analyse the market structure of an existing monopoly or a market that might be affected by a proposed merger. The following three examples were taken from recent investigations carried out by the Monopolies and Mergers Commission.

In 1997, the Monopolies and Mergers Commission (1997a) investigated a proposed acquisition of one London casino company by another. Both firms controlled casinos in the relevant market, defined as the up-market segment of London casinos. Seventy-eight per cent of the 'drop' (money exchanged for chips) was controlled by these two firms. Entry barriers were considered to be high. Casinos had to be regulated by both the Gaming Board and local licensing authorities. To obtain a certificate from the Gaming Board, casinos had to show that there was an unsatisfied demand for their services. This was extremely difficult for a new entrant to show. Secondly, there were entry barriers due to location constraints. Potential sites for the location of up-market casinos could only be considered in the most expensive parts of London. Finally the Commission noted that regulation of the industry was strict. Gaming odds were fixed by law and no advertising was allowed. Again, these constraints would have deterred potential entrants. The merger was refused. One of the reasons cited was that the merger would result in the ability of the two firms to absorb any increase in demand and thus to prevent any 'gaps' in the market. Furthermore, it was concluded that the proposed merger was designed to send just such a message to all potential rivals with casino interests elsewhere.

In the second case, the Monopolies and Mergers Commission (1997b) investigated a proposed merger between two bus companies in Scotland in 1997. One of the companies served the Glasgow conurbation while the other had extensive interests in the north-east of Scotland, central Scotland and the Borders. The Commission believed that in the deregulated bus market, the main safeguard against abuse by a dominant supplier was the potential competition from adjacent suppliers. A contestable market was thus held to operate. The merger was refused because the Commission felt that the resulting merger had created a supplier of such scale and dominance that this would deter entry from the (smaller) adjacent bus companies.

In 1995, the Monopolies and Mergers Commission (1997c) was asked to investigate the monopoly situation in the 'white goods' market (supply of washing machines, fridges, freezers, dishwashers and tumble driers). While the main focus of the investigation was concerned with the issue of recommended retail pricing, the Commission did identify important entry barriers that operated in the industry. The most effective entry barrier was seen as the brand strength of the incumbent majors over a new entrant supplier. A further barrier was identified by the uncovering of a 'selective distribution service'. This was the practice whereby suppliers refused to supply certain retailers (such as discount clubs) under the pretext that the retailers were not offering a sufficiently high-quality pre-sales service. The Commission rejected this argument and concluded that this practice not only was designed to reduce consumer choice and maintain high prices but also had the effect of restricting entry into the industry.

Case study 5.3
Investing in communications companies

Investment in communications companies has been under the spotlight in recent months, with attention particularly focused on the remarkable performance of internet stock. The internet, while certainly a highly significant component of communications, is not, of course, the entire industry. But it is representative of the technological changes which are fuelling massive expansion in the communications business. 'The telecommunications industry ... will now be subjected to a virtual spiral of forces,' Pierre Brais, senior portfolio manager with the Swiss-based Pictet Telecom Fund, explained to participants of the 'Investing in communications companies' forum session, held at Telecom 99 in Geneva. He said: 'Technology is converging on digital transmission and merging with the computer industry. This is resulting in a huge decrease in the cost of installing lines. As a result, prices will drop, and this – combined with the demand for new services – is breaking down the old barriers to entry. The result will be a very different telecoms industry structure to the one which exists today.'

Successful providers will be those who invest wisely in new technology, new services and new markets. Innovation, quality of service, customer care and the ability to manage growth will become the new core skills of successful telecoms companies. Tadashi Sekizawa, chairman of Fujitsu, who delivered a keynote address to the 'investing' session, stressed: 'In this new communications era, we must face an information explosion when we make investment decisions regarding communications networks and services.' Such decisions, he explained, included recognising that while bandwidth and processing power were increasingly becoming 'abundant resources', the scarcest resource was the user's time. 'To solve this problem,' he said, 'future investment in communications networks must take user's time into consideration. This is the starting point for a user-friendly and knowledge-based communications system.'

There was consensus among speakers at the session – which also included representatives of venture capital firms in both the UK and the US – that this is a golden age for telecoms financing. Will Schmidt, managing director of London-based Advent International, said the communications industry was entering a better time for the generation of ideas, and for opportunities for young companies to carve out strong positions in a deregulated environment. He said: 'Conditions are also much better for venture capital investing, with positive changes in management culture, stock markets, and industry behaviour.' He pointed out that venture capital played a big role in the development of many telecoms, information technology and internet businesses, and stressed that the better venture capitalists were committed not just to providing finance and the passive harvesting of rewards, but also to bringing resources and guidance to enhance the prospects of success. 'Experience counts,' said Mr Schmidt. 'A communications entrepreneur may face a particular challenge for the first time – say negotiating with a large corporation or doing a cross-border acquisition – that the venture capitalist has seen dozens of times before.'

Pierre Brais said: 'Over the past five years, telecoms has been a good place for investors to be. It has yielded a compound return of over 21 per cent, much higher than the market return of 15 per cent, while exposing investors to less risk than the overall market.' He said that in a period of mergers, spin-offs and venture investments, 'the major players are attempting to reshuffle their assets and position themselves for the future at the same time as they try to retain the cash generation from their monopoly core businesses. Some countries are moving faster to liberalise, while others are working hard to maintain artificial barriers to entry to protect their national champions. We are certainly in a very turbulent time.'

Despite the turbulence, the telecoms industry remains attractive to private equity investors, according to Will Schmidt. 'Few sectors are as attractive as the telecoms services in Europe,' he said. 'Deregulation has opened the way to challengers, bringing prices down dramatically, and the market is expanding rapidly. Developments in technology and cheaper bandwidth have reduced barriers to entry. A young company with a good offering can achieve a fast revenue ramp and, with good customer care, recurring revenue streams. The current high demand for capital means that these exciting young companies often need private equity investors.'

The enthusiasm for the marketplace, while well-founded, should not cloud the importance of creating an effective Global Information Infrastructure (GII), according to Brian Thompson of Global Telesystems Group. Mr Thompson emphasised his belief that investing in the communications industry was a good thing, but added: 'Not all investments in communications companies are created equal. I'm not talking about good versus bad investments from the narrow perspective of profits or share price, but from the point of view of their impact on the development of the overall communications industry. More specifically on creating the GII.' He said that as co-chairman of the Global Information Infrastructure Commission (GIIC), an independent, non-governmental group of communications industry leaders from around the world, his remarks were likely to be coloured by the organisation's goals. These include the aim of strengthening the leadership role of the private sector in the development of an information infrastructure; and promoting the involvement of developing countries in the building of a truly global and open information infrastructure. 'I'm not saying that the investment impact on developing the GII should be the only factor in making an investment decision,' he said. 'I'm only suggesting that we begin to take developing a truly global information infrastructure into account: that we make it one factor among many to consider. Surely, that's not too much to ask.'

© The Financial Times Limited, 24 November 1999. Reprinted with permission.

Case study 5.4
A blueprint for constructing defensive walls

The construction industry has been shaken up by a series of large takeovers in recent months as the suppliers of basic materials get together and the merchants which serve the smaller builder merge. Lafarge has, for the time being, failed in its attempt to acquire Blue Circle but Anglo American bought Tarmac last November and Hanson recently paid £1.8bn for Pioneer of Australia. Among builders' merchants, St Gobain snapped up Meyer International while Travis Perkins bought two rivals. But away from all this activity two important sectors have remained stubbornly resistant to change. The contractors and the housebuilders have refused to consolidate despite pressure from investors wanting more easily tradeable stock. These sectors remain fragmented and many household-name companies have small market capitalisations. The six largest contractors, including Amec and

John Mowlem, have a combined market capitalisation of £1.5bn, less than half the values of Blue Circle or Hanson. The top six housebuilders, including Berkeley Homes and Barratt Developments, are together worth £3.23bn, less then either of the two building materials groups. 'Investors tend to want bigger companies because they want things that show up on the map,' says Mike Welton, chief executive of Balfour Beatty. 'But very few of the contractors can see a business advantage. This is a business where one plus one is one rather than three.'

A problem for the contractors is they have little asset backing so few economies of scale can be gained. There are also very low barriers to entry by newcomers. 'Consolidation usually occurs in markets where entry costs are high but that is not the case with construction,' says Sir Martin Laing, chairman of John Laing. 'You can't carve out a monopoly.' This is in contrast to the building materials sector, which is consolidating because high levels of investment required in assets such as cement plants do mean size can be an advantage. Housebuilding is also a sector where the barriers to entry are low and the benefits of scaling up activities are limited. It is a geographically diverse business taking place on dozens of sites around the country.

Efforts are being made to substitute factory-made walls and floors for the traditional on-site activities of bricklayers and plasterers but present methods allow few opportunities for savings from bulk buying. Another barrier to consolidation is the presence of strong-minded businessmen such as Tony Pidgley, managing director of Berkeley, and David Wilson, chairman and chief executive of Wilson Bowden. Many founded the companies they run and would be reluctant to work with, or for, rivals. Graham Cherry, chief executive of Countryside Properties and one of three Cherrys on the board, says: 'We want to be in charge of our own destinies. The Cherrys don't want to work for anyone else. The family involvement is a strength of the company.' In contracting, hostile takeovers are not a realistic proposition because of the opaque nature of the companies' order books. The assets of the contractors consist of hundreds of individual contracts, any one of which could wipe out the very thin margins earned elsewhere if it ran into difficulties. In operational terms, the contractors have found an alternative to consolidation in the shape of joint ventures. Carillion, a contractor, linked with Group 4, the security company, and British Telecommunications in its winning bid for an £800m contract to rebuild and manage GCHQ, the government's eavesdropping centre in Cheltenham. 'The pressure on the contractors is less intense because we have a number of partnerships with companies such as Balfour Beatty and Mowlem,' says Sir Fraser Morrison, chief executive of Morrison Construction.

Specialisation has also emerged as an alternative to consolidation because it gives critical mass in a particular field. As part of this trend Tarmac demerged its contracting activities under the Carillion label while Taylor Woodrow is disposing of its contracting and equipment trading activities to concentrate on housebuilding and property. The reluctance of the contractors and housebuilders to grow through mergers may irritate investors. But does it have more serious consequences? The low market ratings which result in part from the fragmented nature of the industry may not matter domestically but they expose British companies to bids from more highly-rated foreign companies. Contractors are also limited in their ability to provide financial guarantees when bidding internationally. This puts them at a disadvantage against continental European competitors.

Questions for discussion

1. Discuss the difference between free and easy entry.

2. Give examples of UK and European industries that are characterised by various legal barriers to entry.

3. Explain how advertising acts as a barrier to entry.

4. Explain how the height of an entry barrier can be measured.

5. Assess the extent to which limit pricing provides a valuable contribution to the theory of entry prevention.

6. Using empirical evidence to substantiate your arguments, discuss the factors which are most likely to deter entry.

7. Explain the theory of contestable markets and assess the extent to which it improves our understanding of entry barriers and competition.

8. With reference to Case studies 5.3 (communications) and 5.4 (construction), analyse the effect that barriers to entry have on determining market structure.

Further reading

Bain, J.S. (1956) *Barriers to New Competition*. Boston: Harvard University Press.

Baumol, W.J., Panzer, J. and Willig, R.D. (1982) *Contestable Markets and the Theory of Industry Structure*. New York: Harcourt Brace.

Geroski, P.A. (1991) *Market Dynamics and Entry*. Oxford: Blackwell.

Geroski, P.A. (1995) What do we know about entry? *International Journal of Industrial Organization*, **13**, 421–40.

Neven, D.J. (1989) Strategic entry deterrence: recent developments in the economics of industry, *Journal of Economic Surveys*, **3**, 213–33.

Siegfried, J.A. and Evans, L. (1994) Empirical studies of entry and exit: a survey of the evidence, *Review of Industrial Organisation*, **9**, 121–55.

CHAPTER 6

Market structure and profitability: a review of the empirical evidence

---

Learning objectives

After reading this chapter the student should be able to:

- Discuss the advantages and disadvantages of various measures of profitability

- Explain how to test empirically the Structure–Conduct–Performance model

- Critically assess the contribution of the Structure–Conduct–Performance model to our understanding of firm and industry behaviour

- Appreciate the empirical controversies surrounding the application of the Structure–Conduct–Performance model

- Explain the importance of strategic groups in determining competition within industries, and the factors that determine profitability differences between such groups

- Assess the extent to which profitability differences between firms and industries persist

---

6.1 Introduction

This chapter discusses the empirical work in industrial organisation that has examined the links between market structure and performance of firms and industries. Given the central importance of the Structure–Conduct–Performance model in the study of firms and industries, we aim to give the reader an overview of the research that has tested this, and related hypotheses. In particular we discuss early research, introduce the types of model and hypothesis tested, identify some of the controversies, and examine some recent work in the area. We do not provide by any means an exhaustive review of previous research, but instead adopt a selective approach to examine some of the major studies that have helped to illuminate our understanding of the ways in which firms and industries behave and perform. The overall aim of this chapter is to give the reader an appreciation of how researchers have analysed competitive conditions in various industries over the past half century.

The chapter is structured as follows. In section 6.2, we examine the difficulties that researchers have faced in defining profits. Section 6.3 discusses industrial organisation research which placed emphasis on the Structure–Conduct–Performance model.[1] This research examined the links between structure, conduct and performance. The main argument highlighted is that imperfect competition generally leads to firms outperforming their counterparts in more competitive industries. Section 6.4 discusses whether any observed abnormal profits in certain industries are the result of established firms colluding to raise industry prices or merely reflect efficiency differences across firms. Section 6.4 also introduces the intermediate concept of strategic groups, which is an approach that argues that variables specific to groupings of firms within industries could explain variations in performance. Section 6.5 examines a dynamic view of competition to analyse the extent to which profitability differences across firms persist.

6.2 Measurement of profitability

One fundamental problem faced by researchers in assessing competitive conditions of an industry is how to accurately measure firm performance. The most common measure used has been profits. However, the measurement of profitability has given rise to substantial controversy in the field of industrial organisation. This arose because of the practical difficulties in calculating an approximation to the theoretical concept of economic profitability. Many different measures have been used. The purpose of this section is to examine the concept of economic profitability and to appraise the alternative measures that have been proposed.

Bain (1951, 1956) defined monopoly power as the ability of firms to elevate price over marginal costs. In the short run, firms can earn abnormal profits, but in the long run these profits are eroded unless entry barriers exist.

Based on textbook models of profit-maximising behaviour under perfect competition and monopoly, the **Lerner index** (L) is a measure of monopoly power and specified as:

$$L = \frac{P - MC}{P}$$

where P denotes price charged and MC is marginal costs. L can take a value between zero and one. $L = 0$ denotes a perfectly competitive industry where all firms are of equal size and set prices equal to marginal costs, while values of $L > 0$ indicate an element of monopoly power, allowing firms to set price above marginal costs (Lerner, 1934).

The problem with this measure is that firms do not record marginal costs in financial reports.

---

[1] This model for the study of firms and industries was discussed in detail in Chapter 1.

Scherer and Ross (1990) noted that economists have opted for three different types of profitability measure:

● Measures based on the market value of the firm
● The price–cost margin
● Accounting rates of profit

The following discusses the relative merits of each.

Measures based on the market value of the firm

Schwert (1981) argued that market value measures are attractive because if capital markets are efficient, the market value of a firm's shares reflects all available information about its future profitability.

An early study by Stigler (1963a) used the ratio of the market value of a firm's equity to its inflation-adjusted book value. Two other measures based on the market valuation of the firm are **Tobin's q** and the excess value ratio (EVR).

Tobin's q was originally used to analyse the investment decision of the firm and its implications for the national income of a given economy.[2] The measure is defined as the ratio of the market value of the firm to the replacement cost of capital to the firm. This can be expressed as:

$$q = \frac{M_c + M_p + M_d}{A_r}$$

where the numerator is the sum of the market value of a firm's common and preferred stock ($M_c + M_p$) plus the total value of outstanding debt (M_d) and the denominator is the cost of replacing total assets (A_r). In a purely competitive environment, we should find that q is equal to 1. A value of 1 means that the market value of the firm is equal to the capital resources owned by the firm; $q > 1$ exists under conditions of monopoly, where firms make abnormal profits; and $q < 1$ means that firms are declining in value.

Lindenberg and Ross (1981) argued that under perfect competition q should be close to 1. However, if the firm grows larger, the value of q increases. If there is free entry, other firms can enter the industry and compete away any excess returns. However, if barriers do exist, q should persistently exceed 1.

Smirlock et al. (1984) argued that by using a capital market valuation, firm risk is incorporated thereby minimising distortions introduced by accounting practices and tax laws. Shepherd (1986) argued that the numerator of Tobin's q (the market value of the firm) depends upon expectations of future profits, and is therefore subjective. This means that the measure can be volatile and prone to fluctuations caused by rumours. Shepherd also pointed out that it is often difficult to measure the replacement cost of assets and obtain share price data for smaller firms.

Another measure of profitability based on the market value of the firm is the excess value ratio (EVR). Thomadikis (1977) defined the ratio as follows:

$$\text{EVR} = \frac{\text{Market value of assets} - \text{Book value of assets}}{\text{Sales revenue}}$$

[2] See Tobin and Brainard (1968).

This measure has been criticised for not calculating the replacement cost of capital to the firm.

Price–cost margin

Many studies of firm and industry performance have employed the price–cost margin (PCM).[3] This is defined as the ratio of profit to sales revenue and can be written as:

$$PCM = \frac{P \cdot Q - AC \cdot Q}{P \cdot Q}$$

$$= \frac{P - AC}{P}$$

where P denotes price, Q quantity and AC average costs. If a firm's average costs are constant, the price–cost margin is equal to the Lerner index of monopoly power (outlined above). If the firm operates in a perfectly competitive industry in equilibrium, the price–cost margin is equal to zero. The value of the price-cost margin increases if the firm or industry can elevate prices above average costs. This implies that some element of monopoly power exists.

The price–cost margin has some associated problems, as follows:

● The price–cost margin is not an accurate measure of monopoly power in the absence of constant returns to scale. In other words, if average costs are not constant, then they will not equal marginal costs. As a consequence, the greater the positive or negative difference between average costs and marginal costs, the more the price–cost margin overstates or understates the Lerner index of monopoly power.
● The treatment of research and development and advertising as current selling costs understates profit in the numerator but not sales in the denominator. This problem is particularly acute if the benefits of such discretionary expenditures accrue over more than one period.

Accounting rate of profit

Accounting rate of profit measures are frequently used in studies of competition, as data are readily available from annual reports. Scherer and Ross (1990) identified three main definitions of accounting rates of profit, as follows:

● Accounting rate of profit on capital = $\dfrac{\text{Accounting profit} + \text{Interest payments}}{\text{Total assets}}$

● Accounting rate of profit on equity = $\dfrac{\text{Accounting profits}}{\text{Book value of shareholders' equity}}$

● Accounting rate of profit on sales = $\dfrac{\text{Accounting profits}}{\text{Sales revenue}}$

---

[3] For example, Collins and Preston (1966) used this measure of profitability in their study of food manufacturing industries.

Bain (1951) used the return on shareholders' equity in his early structure–performance studies of industry. Stigler (1963a, p.54) used a return on capital measure. He argued that: 'There is no more important proposition in economic theory than that under competition, the rate of return on investment tends towards equality in all industries.'

The problem with accounting data is that bias can arise from methods used to value assets. There are at least four ways in which such bias may arise. These are related to the treatment of mergers, inflation, discretionary expenditures and deprecation, as follows:

- When firms are involved in mergers, it is often difficult to value the assets of the new, combined firm. Ravenscraft and Scherer (1987) argued that accounting bias arises when a merger has taken place. Their main argument can be explained as follows. Suppose a firm takes over another firm with some degree of monopoly power, thereby enabling that firm to elevate price above marginal costs. The predator firm may pay more for the assets in this case than if no monopoly power is held by the acquired firm. As a consequence, assets are overvalued and the return on capital on the new firm is biased downwards. This is likely to be the case if the acquiring firm brings the acquired firm's assets into its accounts at market value rather than book value (as in merger accounting). Therefore, if an industry undergoes a period of merger activity, expectations of monopoly profits become capitalised. This results in accounting rates of return on capital being biased downward

- Inflation can also create bias in accounting measures, as most firms value assets using historical cost conventions. If inflation occurs, the historical values understate the value of older capital. Therefore, older assets are undervalued relative to newly acquired capital. Stigler (1963a) argued that this causes an overvaluation of firm returns with slow growth relative to companies with a rapid growth of assets.

- A third problem with accounting rates of return is the treatment of discretionary expenditures such as advertising and research and development as current costs. Such costs are in essence investments that yield benefits in the future. If they are treated as current costs, the firm's returns are undervalued (assuming that investments in research and development etc. yield some benefits).

- Differing practices regarding the treatment of depreciation can create problems in valuing capital, as some firms may choose to pursue a policy of accelerated depreciation. Stauffer (1971) argued that a complex form of economic depreciation should be employed to remove these differences. The extent of bias created by differing depreciation policies when valuing assets is unclear.[4]

The use of accounting rates of profit to assess the competitiveness of markets has caused considerable controversy. Fisher and McGowan (1983) argued that serious errors arise when using accounting rates of profit to diagnose monopoly power. They contend:

> [I]t is clear that it is the economic rate of return that is equalised in an industry competitive equilibrium. It is an economic rate of return (after risk adjustment) above the cost of capital that promotes expansion under competition and is produced by output restriction under monopoly. Thus the economic rate of return is the only correct measure of the profit rate for economic analysis. Accounting rates of return are useful only insofar as they yield information as to economic rates of return.[5]

[4] A discussion of this type of excellent economic depreciation is beyond the scope of this book. However, Hay and Morris (1991) give an explanation of Stauffer's work.
[5] Fisher and McGowan (1983) p.82.

The authors defined these economic rates of return as the **internal rate of return** (IRR) on a single project. The internal rate of return does not seek to generate a cash figure to determine whether an investment should be undertaken, but instead attempts to find the discount rate at which the net present value of a project is zero.[6] In theory, it is the average value of this measure of profitability for a firm as a whole which we should be interested in. An investment opportunity is profitable if its net present value exceeds the cost of capital funds. If a firm persistently earns returns above the cost of capital, this would be an indication of monopoly power. However, the data needed to calculate the discount rate over the lifetime of a project are generally not available from company accounts.

Fisher and McGowan showed that the after-tax accounting rate of return on capital (ARR) for a single investment project can differ from the internal rate of return, depending on which type of depreciation method is used.

Kay and Mayer (1986) agreed that accounting rates of profit deviate from internal rates of return, but argued that these measures are fundamentally different. This is because they measure different things. Internal rate of return is the return which equates to zero the present value of the net cash flows (positive and negative) over the lifetime of the project. The capital outlay is treated as a negative cash flow and as a result no provision is made for depreciation. The accounting rate of profit (ARP) is defined as income (net of depreciation) earned in a single accounting period deflated by total assets minus depreciation.

The internal rate of return is calculated over the lifetime of a single project, while the accounting rate of profit relates to the return on a collection of projects in a single period (i.e. a year). These two measures describe totally different types of return over differing periods. Kay (1976) argued that only under certain circumstances will the two measures be equal: namely, if the rate of profit on capital is constant over the entire life of the project. The problem in calculating internal rate of return is that data are required over the entire lifetime of the project or firm, while most empirical research is limited to examining profitability at a single point in time or over a fixed period.

Edwards *et al.* (1987) acknowledged that internal rate of return is useful in providing information on investment projects, but are sceptical about its merits for an examination of market power. They contend that the internal rate of return cannot be used to examine a firm's performance over a finite period, but instead over its entire life. This information can only be known at the end of the firm's life.

Bosch (1989) examined the relationship between the accounting rate and internal rate of return for 1,030 large US industrial firms over a twenty-year period. He found a correlation coefficient of 0.63 between the two rates. He argued that this implies that accounting rates provide useful indicators of economic returns.

From Bosch's study we can conclude that accounting rates of return are a useful tool for diagnosing the extent to which monopoly power presents a danger to competition.[7] However, care must be exercised when drawing inferences from any analysis using accounting data.

---

[6] Brealey and Myers (1999) provide a standard textbook treatment of the internal rate of return.
[7] Martin (1984) also provided an extensive discussion in this area.

6.3   The Structure–Conduct–Performance model revisited

The empirical work that has tested the Structure–Conduct–Performance (SCP) approach tends to find that there is a positive relationship between the three dimensions. However, this relationship is often very weak. Much of the research reviewed examined the relationship between industry structure and performance, while assuming that a certain type of firm behaviour is given. For example, in industries where only a few large firms dominate, collusion was assumed to take place. A good example of early research carried out was an examination of profitability and concentration in the food industries by Collins and Preston (1966).

To measure profits, Collins and Preston (1966) used a variant of the price–cost margin as a percentage of sales revenue. In effect their dependent variable was:

$$\frac{\text{Total revenue} - \text{Total variable costs}}{\text{Total revenue}}$$

Their sample consisted of 32 four-digit (SIC) food manufacturing industries. Concentration was measured by a four-firm concentration ratio (see Chapter 4). The regression relationship between concentration and the profits was:

$$PCM = \alpha - CR + CR^2$$

where PCM refers to the price–cost margins for 1958, while CR refers to the 1958 concentration ratios in the respective industries. The CR^2 term is included to test whether there is a non-linear relationship between PCM and concentration. With an R^2 of 0.80 and statistically significant coefficients, on CR and CR^2, Collins and Preston concluded that one could accept a continuous, curvilinear relationship between concentration and profits.

Collins and Preston concluded that:

- There are no systematic increases in the price–cost margins accompanying increases in concentration in cases where concentration ratios are low (less than 30 per cent – slightly negative in fact).
- At the 30–50 per cent level, equal increases in concentration are associated with equal increases in the price–cost margin.
- Over 60 per cent the price–cost margin had reached 25 per cent and grew at an increasing rate. At about 85 per cent concentration, the price–cost margin was found to be around 45 per cent.

Much of this type of empirical work has been carried out, some of which is examined below. However, we should bear in mind some of the criticisms of this approach.

Critique

The following criticisms have been levelled at the SCP approach:

- The approach draws on microeconomic theory from which to examine the empirical behaviour of firms and industries. However, economic theory does not always give us exact relationships between structure, conduct and performance. The SCP approach has its roots in oligopoly theory discussed in Chapter 2. However, oligopoly theory can be seen as largely indeterminate, not generating any clear, unambiguous deductions.

● Structure can be measured by a multitude of indicators. Unfortunately, many economists tend to measure structure by concentration.[8] This is primarily because data are easy to find in government statistics. As a consequence, there is a danger of overemphasising the importance of concentration.

● The approach has been criticised for being too concerned with static short-run equilibrium. Sawyer (1985) argued that no explanation is offered as to the evolution of the structural variables, and how conduct and performance influence future changes. He argued that the approach is mainly a snapshot of the current state of industry conditions. This criticism is examined in section 6.5 of this chapter.

● It is often difficult to decide which variables belong to structure, which to conduct and which to performance. For example, the extent of advertising, vertical integration and diversification give useful information as to the structure of an industry; however, these are also strategies which firms can choose to follow.

● There are difficulties in measuring many of the variables. For example, how would one measure profitability, entry barriers or the rate of entry? How do we measure the extent of vertical integration?[9] The various methods economists have used for measuring profitability have already been examined in section 6.2 of this chapter. As we have seen these are not without problems.

● What exactly do we mean by performance? Performance is some measure of the degree of success in achieving desired goals. Is it possible to have a set of uniform performance indicators? Differences in firm objectives may make the SCP relationship tenuous. For example, if firms are sacrificing potential profits in order to reduce risk by investing in more certain activities, then researchers should be more interested in variability in profit rates and not profits levels *per se* (Schwartzman, 1963). Alternatively, if managers are maximising their own satisfaction through excess expenditures, then large firms in concentrated markets will not necessarily make abnormal returns (Williamson, 1963). Schmalensee (1990) lamented that:

> We have concentration measures for most manufacturing markets in many economies for instance, but little comprehensive information is available on more subtle aspects of market structure, and essentially no systematic data aside from accounting profit rates is available on conduct and performance. This leaves a factual vacuum in policy debates that is quickly filled by beliefs and assumptions.

6.4 Empirical tests of the SCP approach: a selective review

The underlying assumption of early SCP-based research was that there is a strong causal link between market structure and the performance of firms. However, it is questionable whether high profits enjoyed by established firms are a consequence of concentrated market structures and collusive price-setting behaviour, or of superior production and management techniques that allow larger firms to keep costs low and make high returns.

The SCP school viewed competitive market structures as imperfect, requiring government regulation to check the abuse of market power. However, the Chicago school argued

[8] Chapter 4 gives an extended discussion of the problems of using concentration indices to measure industry structure.

[9] Issues of measurement surrounding entry barriers and vertical integration are examined in Chapters 5 and 9, respectively.

that government interference leads to less competition (Stigler, 1968; Demsetz, 1973). Their approach argued that the best thing government can do in a market context is to allow market forces to bring about the desirable performance. For example, there is no point in having a cartel law as cartels are inherently unstable and a competitive equilibrium will eventually be re-established in industries where collusion is taking place. Therefore, the Chicago school holds that monopoly power is temporary (with the exception of government-created monopolies).

In the context of structure and profitability, a positive relationship between concentration and profits could be caused by two things:

- *Collusive behaviour.* As an industry becomes more concentrated, firms find it easier to collude and erect barriers to entry to earn excess profits. All firms are expected to earn similar profits if market power is shared. These findings have become known as the traditional concentration doctrine. In brief, the traditional view of industrial organisation focuses on industry-specific sources of market power. In this case all firms are treated as alike, and the industry is the appropriate unit of analysis.
- *Efficiency differences.* It may be that bigger firms are more efficient and make higher profits as a result. In this case, market structure affects profitability not through concentration, but by the association between market share and profitability. By definition, concentrated industries contain firms with high market shares, the average level of profit is greater in more concentrated industries. Therefore, a positive relationship between market share and profitability at the firm level implies a relationship between profit and industry concentration, even if higher concentration has no effect on conduct. Therefore, in markets with a small number of large firms, profits tend to be higher. If efficiency differences between firms are important, then the firm is the appropriate unit of analysis. This explanation has been termed 'revisionist'.[10]

Amato and Wilder (1990, p.93) provided a useful summary of the debate when they argued that:

> The debate between the revisionist and traditional schools can be summarised in terms of their differences regarding the appropriate unit of observation in industrial economics. The revisionist view is a story of industries consisting of both successful and unsuccessful firms, implying that there are important inter-firm differences in profitability. The traditional view focuses on industry effects which are assumed to be measured by concentration. The revisionist view thus focuses on the firm and firm-level efficiencies, while the traditional view focuses on the market and industry specific sources of market power.

These opposing views formed the basis for a substantial empirical debate.[11] Early research tended to find that concentration and industry-level variables were important in determining performance, while later work stressed the importance of efficiency differences between firms.

Bain (1951) tested the concentration hypothesis for 42 US manufacturing industries between 1936 and 1940. Profits were measured as return on equity, while concentration was measured by calculating the concentration ratio for the eight largest firms in each of

---

[10] This is a term first introduced by Schmalensee (1985).
[11] Martin (1993) provided a detailed discussion of many of the issues surrounding the specification of models used to test the SCP approach.

Table 6.1 ● Rates of return by size and concentration (weighted by assets)

CR4	Number of industries	R1 %	R2 %	R3 %	R4 %	R̄ %
10–20	14	7.3	9.5	10.6	8.0	8.8
20–30	22	4.4	8.6	9.9	10.6	8.4
30–40	24	5.1	9.0	9.4	11.7	8.8
40–50	21	4.8	9.5	11.2	9.4	8.7
50–60	11	0.9	9.6	10.8	12.2	8.4
Over 60	3	5.0	8.6	10.3	21.6	11.3

CR4 is the four-firm concentration ratio measured on industry sales in 1963.
R1 is average rate of return for firms with assets < US$500,000.
R2 is average rate of return for firms with at least US$500,000 assets but < US$5 million.
R3 is average rate of return for firms with at least US$5 million assets but < US$50 million.
R4 is average rate of return for firms with assets > US$50 million.
Source: Demsetz (1973), p.6, table 2.

the industries sampled. Bain found that in industries with eight-firm concentration ratios (CR8) of more than 70 per cent, profits were significantly higher than in those with CR8 less than 70 per cent. He split the sample of industries into two groups based on initial levels of concentration, the cut-off point defined at 70 per cent.

These results have been interpreted as supporting the hypothesis that concentration facilitates collusion and limits rivalry. Bain's findings were confirmed by numerous studies. As a consequence, these results have provided the empirical justification for government intervention aimed at increasing competition in concentrated industries.[12] Bain's findings went unchallenged for more than twenty years, until the early 1970s.

Demsetz (1973, 1974b) and others challenged this traditional view of industrial organisation.[13] They asserted that if the positive relationship between market concentration and profitability reflects the exercise of market power, then it should affect all firms equally. If large firms in concentrated industries have higher profits than small firms, then the correlation between profits and concentration is the result of the underlying relationship between profits and efficiency which has allowed these firms to become large.

Demsetz used data from the US Internal Revenue Service for 95 manufacturing industries. The data were classified by industry concentration and firm sizes. Rates of return were measured as profit plus interest divided by total assets. The results are shown in Table 6.1.

According to Demsetz, the association between collusion and concentration had little effect on the profits of firms in classes R1, R2 and R3. In other words, the profits of individual firms in these groups did not rise with concentration. However, in the largest class, R4, profits did increase with concentration, lending support to the efficiency hypothesis.

[12] For a summary of these studies see Weiss (1974), pp.204–15. Weiss reviews the results of a large number of concentration/profits studies, and finds that virtually all of these studies report a significant positive relationship between profits and industry concentration.

[13] For example, see Peltzman (1977).

Demsetz argued that these findings refuted the argument (of Bain) that competition does not prevail in high concentration industries. These results suggested that intervention by governments to promote competition in high-concentration industries was not necessary.

Smirlock et al. (1984) tested the efficiency against the collusion hypothesis using *Fortune* data on 132 US manufacturing firms covering the period 1961 to 1969. The estimated equation is:

$$q^* = \alpha_0 + \beta_1 MS + \beta_2 CR4 + \beta_3 HBTE + \beta_4 MBTE + \beta_5 MSG$$

where the dependent variable q^* is Tobin's q (as a proxy for performance) averaged over the sample period (q^* is defined as the ratio of the market valuation of the firm to replacement cost of its assets). The independent variables are: MS, market share; CR4, the concentration ratio of four largest firms; HBTE and MBTE, which measure the extent of entry barriers to an industry, classified as high or medium, respectively; MSG, the firm's growth over the period measured as the ratio of its market share in 1969 to its market share in 1961.

If the efficiency arguments are valid, one would expect to find a positive relationship between profits and market share, and no relationship between profits and concentration (i.e. $\beta_1 > 0$ and $\beta_2 = 0$). On the other hand, if the traditional concentration argument holds, one would expect a positive relationship between profits and concentration, and no relationship between profits and market share (i.e. $\beta_2 > 0$ and $\beta_1 = 0$).

Smirlock et al found a positive relationship between profits and market share, but no relationship between profits and concentration. In other words, β_1 is significantly greater than zero, while β_2 is also positive but not significant. These results provide some support for the efficiency hypothesis. The authors also found a positive relationship between firm profits and growth, perhaps because growth influences investors' expectations about whether the firm's profits will increase in the future (i.e. β_5 is significant). Finally, no relationship between profits and entry barriers is found (i.e. β_3 and β_4 are insignificant).

Clarke et al. (1984) also tested the collusion versus efficiency arguments for UK manufacturing. They argued that if the revisionist school argument holds, then one would expect to find differences in profitability between large and small firms in highly concentrated industries, thus reflecting efficiency differences. The authors used samples of 147 and 155 three-digit manufacturing UK industries for 1971 and 1977 to examine the profits in industries with above- and below-average concentration. Overall, little difference is found between the profits of large and small firms in high-concentration industries. These results provided substantial support for the traditional hypothesis that all firms are alike and the industry is the appropriate unit of analysis.

Schmalensee (1985) used US 1975 *Federal Trade Commission* for 456 firms in 261 industries to investigate the relative importance of firm and industry effects. The estimated equation is:

$$\Pi_{ij} = \mu + \alpha_i + \beta_j + \gamma S_{ij} + \varepsilon_{ij}$$

where the dependent variable Π_{ij} is the accounting rate of profit on an individual firm's production in a specific industry. Schmalensee incorporated several independent variables, which are defined as follows: S_{ij} is an individual firm's share in the market it produces for; α_i is the component of profits (Π_{ij}) which is specific to an individual firm (measured as the deviation of firm i's profits from the industry average); β_j is the component of profits (Π_{ij}) which is specific to industry j (measured as the average profits of the industry, and is the same for all firms which operate in industry j); and ε_{ij} is an error term to capture other influences on profitability not specified by the model. μ is the average profitability of the base category of firms.

If the traditional SCP hypothesis holds then only the industry-specific variable (β_j) would be important in determining profits. The efficiency view would hold if firm-specific effects (α_i) were important.

Schmalensee found that industry effects are very important, explaining 75 per cent of the variations in profits, while firm effects are less important.[14] In other words, he found that $\alpha_i = 0$ and $\beta_j \neq 0$. He argued that these results were supportive of the traditional view of industrial organisation. However, Schmalensee's study can be criticised for omitting important firm- and industry-level variables such as firm size, growth and concentration. This may have caused a bias in the observed results.

Drawing on Schmalensee's study, McGahan (1999) examined the extent to which industry and firm effects determined profitability for a sample of US firms over the period 1981 to 1994. Profits were measured using Tobin's q ratio and accounting profits. McGahan found that industry effects accounted for approximately one-third of variation in profitability, and that these effects tended to persist over time. Firm effects were found to be more important, but varied depending on the year under examination.

Eckard (1995) used US data for five cohorts of firms (based on size) to examine the relationship between changes in profits (measured by the price–cost margin), arising from changes in market share between 1967 and 1972, and between 1972 and 1977. If the efficiency hypothesis holds, a positive relationship should be observed between changes in profit and market shares, implying that profits change in response to changes in efficiency. He found a positive relationship between market shares and profits for all firm size bands. These results suggested 'a market process in which firms become large and profitable through superior efficiency'.[15]

Berger (1995) undertook an evaluation of the SCP relationship in the US banking industry.[16] He identified two 'market power' and two 'efficiency' theories of bank profitability. Banks can exploit market power by charging higher prices by differentiating products, or enter into collusive agreements to raise prices. Efficiency advantages can arise through superior management or innovative techniques or from advantages associated with producing at larger scale. As a consequence, banks that are efficient are likely to have large market shares.

Berger estimated a model to examine the determinants of profitability. Explanatory variables of profitability include market concentration, market share and efficiency. The data set comprises between 1,300 and 2,000 banks.

Berger used return on assets and return on equity as performance measures. Concentration was measured using the Herfindahl–Hirschman index. The efficiency variables were constructed to reflect advantages arising from scale economies and those arising from superior managerial talent. Berger found that banks which had superior management and innovative

---

[14] Schmalensee (1985), p.349.

[15] Eckard (1995), p.223.

[16] Schmalensee (1989), Britton *et al.* (1992) and Neuberger (1998) provide extensive discussions of applications of the SCP approach to the manufacturing, services and banking industries, respectively.

techniques earned higher profits. There was little evidence to support the proposition that banks which produced at a large scale made high profits. With reference to the market power theories, he found that profits are positively related to market share but not to concentration. This suggested that banks used differentiation advantages to raise prices and make high profits, but that collusion did not play a role in determining profits.

Although Berger had some success in discriminating between the various theories as explanations of bank profitability, the models estimated left large proportions of the variation in banks profit rates unexplained.

Berger and Hannan (1998) examined the relationship between operational efficiency and concentration. They tested the hypothesis that firms in concentrated markets exercise market power by not minimising costs. Using a sample of 5,263 banks, the authors examined the extent to which bank efficiency is determined by concentration and a number of variables that control for differences in ownership structure and geographical location. The evidence suggested that banks in highly concentrated markets are less efficient, implying some support for the view that firms in concentrated markets exercise market power.

The empirical evidence as to whether firms earn high profits through collusion, the exercise of market power or differential efficiencies appears to be inconclusive.[17] Of the nine studies discussed in this section, the evidence suggests that both concentration and efficiency differences between firms are important in determining profitability. The differences in results may be explained by the samples of firms and industries used, the time periods examined and the estimation methods employed. For example, the SCP approach has tended to focus on differences across large numbers of industries, while the efficiency view has emphasised examining differences between firms. More recent work by Berger (1995) focused on the behaviour of firms in a single industry.

Strategic groups

It has often been argued that neither the industry nor the firm should be used as the unit of analysis, but rather, the **strategic groups** which exist within an industry (Oster, 1999). A strategic group can be defined as a group of firms which follow similar behaviour. These firms tend to compete directly with other firms in the group. Firms within these strategic groups tend to recognise their interdependence and act accordingly. We briefly discuss the concept of the strategic group and highlight some of the key contributions in this area.

Porter (1979) argued that owing to the differing characteristics of strategic groups, the extent of entry barriers also differs between groups. These barriers to entering a group within an industry are defined as 'mobility barriers' which can vary between groups within a given industry. For example, the barriers to entering the UK medicines industry differ depending on whether the new firm wants to compete with branded or generic products. The higher the mobility barriers, the better protected are the firms within this strategic group from competition from other groups. This is why some groups of firms can earn higher profits than others within the same industry (Caves and Porter, 1977; Newman, 1978).

---

[17] Weiss (1989) provides an overview of more recent evidence. A discussion can also be found in *The Economist* (*Economist*, 1998).

The extent of the profitability differences amongst strategic groups depends on the following factors:

● *The number and size of groups.* This refers to whether strategic groups are numerous and similar in size. If this is the case, competition is likely to be more intense than if smaller strategic groups are attempting to compete with large groups.
● *The extent to which groups follow different strategies.* This refers to the extent to which groups differ on discretionary decisions such as research and development, and promotional expenditures.
● *The extent to which groups are interdependent.* This refers to the extent to which different strategic groups are competing for the same customers or whether some segmentation of the market takes place. This segmentation may arise naturally as industry evolves, or groups may attempt to divide the market.

Strategic groups can be delineated on the basis on similarities in market-related strategies, firm-specific factors and industry supply characteristics (McGee and Thomas, 1986):

● Market-related strategies include similarities in product quality, pricing practices, extent of product differentiation, branding and advertising.
● Firm-specific factors include the extent of vertical integration and diversification, ownership structure and firm size.
● Industry supply characteristics include economies of scale and scope, production processes and distribution methods and networks.

If strategic groups exist in an industry, then we would expect more variation in profitability between groups than within.

Porter (1979) attempted to identify strategic groups using US data for 38 consumer good industries. He split the firms in each industry into 'leaders' and 'followers' based on size of sales revenue, where leaders are defined as firms which account for 30 per cent or more of industry sales revenue, and followers as firms accounting for less than this figure. He found that the correlation between average rates of return for the two groups is low.

A cross-sectional analysis using average profits for the leader and follower firms and a set of structural variables was then undertaken. Porter found that for the leader group, concentration, economies of scale, advertising-to-sales ratio, capital requirements and industry growth were all positively related to profits. For the follower group, concentration is found to be negatively related to profits, while industry growth and capital requirements are positively related. Porter concluded by arguing that differences between the two groups of firms provided evidence of strategic groups in the US consumer goods industries.

Tremblay (1985) drew on Porter's findings to test for the existence of strategic groups in the US brewing industry. Using a sample of regional and national beer producers covering the period 1950 to 1977, he examined the determinants of demand by estimating an equation which incorporated variables to differentiate between the groups. He found that significant differences existed in the costs of marketing products between national and regional beer producers. Tremblay argued that mobility barriers existed between the two groups given that national producers could promote products at lower cost than could their regional counterparts.

Lewis and Thomas (1990) tested for strategic groups in the UK retail grocery sector. The authors used various methods to group a sample of 16 firms into strategic groups. Groupings were based on firm size. The authors also used statistical techniques such as cluster and discriminant analysis.[18] Different strategic groups were identified using each of the three methods. These groups consisted of major supermarkets, medium-sized supermarkets, and small independent stores and co-operatives. The authors found significant differences in capital intensity between the groups identified. An analysis of profits revealed that there is greater variation in profits within groups than across groups. The authors argue that this casts some doubt on the existence of strategic groups in UK retailing.

A major problem with the concept of the strategic group is the difficulty in identifying such groups. Barney and Hoskisson (1990) criticised researchers' attempts to analyse strategic groups. They argued that there is no theoretical basis for choosing variables to help identify strategic groups, or for determining whether such variables should be weighted and by how much. Most attempts at identifying strategic groups empirically have used cluster analysis which produced clusters of firms within industries. However, they argued that the detection of clusters did not necessarily imply the existence of a strategic group, but could just be a result of the testing procedure. Therefore they asserted that it is difficult to evaluate any empirical results derived from such techniques.

It is likely that strategic groups of firms do exist within most industries. However, finding reliable methods to identify such groups has proved difficult. As a consequence, economists have devoted little time to researching strategic groups; the approach has remained popular in the field of management science, however.

6.5 Dynamic views of competition

The SCP approach is built on a neoclassical microeconomic theory where the following assumptions are made:

- Participants are optimisers; that is, firms are seen as profit maximisers.
- The analysis focuses on equilibrium conditions – little is said about the 'process' by which these equilibria are realised.
- Ignorance and uncertainty are ignored.
- Efficient allocation of resources can only be achieved through perfect competition; in other words, perfect competition is seen as the ideal structure from a welfare perspective.

Empirical research that is in many ways sympathetic to the Austrian tradition has examined the time series behaviour of firm profits, consequently casting doubt on the static cross-sectional approach adopted by proponents of the SCP approach. Geroski (1990) argued that the SCP approach to examining competition provides only a snapshot at some point in time, and does little to explain the process of competition.[19]

There is no certainty that profits or other measures of performance observed at one point in time represent long-run equilibrium levels of the performance variable. An empirical

---

[18] Multiple discriminant analysis is used to find differences between groups based on several variables at once. These variables could include firm size, discretionary expenditures on advertising and research and development, geographical location, and so on. Cluster analysis is a multivariate technique which seeks to form groups based on similarities between several variables at once. As in the case of multiple discriminant analysis, such variables could include size, geographical location, and so on.

[19] Byers and Peel (1994) give a detailed discussion of the applications of time series econometrics to the empirical analysis of firms and industries.

association between concentration and high profits may result from observation during a period of disequilibrium. If so, the cross-sectional studies do not capture (unless by luck) the long-run equilibrium. Also, cross-sectional estimations usually do not contain enough information on which to base reliable policy decisions. For example, any monopoly profits found in one period could disappear in the next, rendering intervention by government or other regulatory organisations unnecessary.

Brozen (1971) criticised Bain's (1951) study, suggesting that a disequilibrium phenomenon was being observed (in the data used).[20] He argued that if high profits are the equilibrium result of monopoly power, then these returns should persist indefinitely. Brozen extended Bain's study to cover a later period (1953 to 1957) and found that concentrated industries were now earning only 0.6 per cent above the average and the unconcentrated industries earning 0.5 per cent below the average of the sample. He therefore argued that, over time, profits tend to fall in profitable industries and to rise in non-profitable industries, thus providing support for his disequilibrium hypothesis.

Brozen's findings prompted a body of empirical research at the industry and firm level of analysis which has examined the patterns of industry and firm performance over an extended period. Some of this research is now discussed in order to give the reader an appreciation of the dynamics of competition in an empirical context.

Industry-level studies

This subsection looks at five empirical studies of competition over an extended period. The focus is at the industry level.

Qualls (1974) used data on thirty industries over the period 1950 to 1965. He found no significant reduction in the concentration/profitability relationship over the period and so rejected Brozen's position. He also carried out an analysis using firm-level data for a sample of 220 firms over a twenty-year period (1951 to 1968). He again finds no evidence from the sample of any tendency for profit rates to converge.

Levy (1987), using a sample of 197 US industries for the years 1963, 1967 and 1972, applied a model to market structure variables using expected profits as a dependent variable. He argued that if profits are above future expected levels then there will be entry, which reduces these profits. This process would happen in reverse if profits were below future expected levels. Levy asserted that expectations of future profits are formed in with reference to market structure variables such as entry barriers, concentration, advertising intensity and industry growth, and how these change over time.

Levy found that if a firm earned profits above or below the long-run equilibrium in any year, the adjustment back to long-run equilibrium is almost complete after four years. He also found that industry-specific effects such as entry barriers, concentration and demand growth were important in determining such adjustments. Levy's results lend support to Brozen's critique of the SCP approach.

Coate (1989) uses a sample of 48 US industries over the period 1958 to 1982 to estimate the following equation, to test whether industry-level returns fall to average levels over time:

$$\Pi_{it} = \beta_0 + \beta_1 \Pi_{it-1} + \beta_2 \mathrm{GROWTH}_{it} + \beta_3 \mathrm{CR4}_{it}$$

---

[20] Bain's early work is discussed on pp.173–4.

where the dependent variable Π_{it} is the price–cost margin of an individual industry in a given year. The independent variables include previous profits (Π_{it-1}), industry growth (GROWTH$_{it}$) and the four-firm industry concentration ratio of industry i in year t (CR4$_{it}$).

The model was estimated to capture the effects of changes in profitability over time and between industries. Coate found that profits above or below the long-run equilibrium decayed towards long-run levels within ten years. This provided partial support for the Brozen critique.

Keating (1991) used a sample of 2,438 large companies in 230 industries covering the period 1969 to 1981. He found that profits in concentrated industries were less persistent than the returns in unconcentrated industries. By industry, he found that the profits of the top 50 of 261 industries declined on average for the following twelve years over the sample period. Keating found no evidence to support the view that industry-level profits persist over time.

Droucopoulos and Lianos (1993) studied the competitive process in the Greek manufacturing sector (20 industries) over the period 1963 to 1988 to analyse the convergence of industry profit rates to long-run values over time. The speed of adjustment towards long-run equilibrium were found to be slow for most industries. They found that 90 per cent of any excess returns earned in time t would persist into time $t + 1$. They further found that the level of industry concentration and advertising intensity slow the speed of adjustment to long-run values. These results suggested that the SCP hypothesis held over an extended period for Greek manufacturing.

Overall, most of the evidence at the industry level tends to find that profits persist for only short periods of time. Market structure variables such as concentration, industry growth and entry barriers are often found to be instrumental in adjusting industry profits towards equilibrium levels.

Firm-level studies

At the firm level, a body of work based on the research of Mueller (1977, 1986), which has collectively become known as the 'persistence of profits' literature, examines the process of competition via the following model:

$$\Pi_{it} = \alpha_i + \lambda_i \Pi_{it-1} + u_{it}$$

where the dependent variable Π_{it} is a measure of an individual firm's profits in a given period. The extent to which long-run profits are positive or negative is dependent on the intercept term, α_i. The extent to which profits persist from one period to the next is dependent on λ_i. A value of $\lambda_i = 0$ implies there is no association between profit in successive years, or zero persistence. The closer λ_i is to unity, the greater the persistence of profits. The closer λ_i is to zero, the greater the degree of competition. If $\lambda_i = 1$, profits in successive periods are perfectly correlated, and profits persist indefinitely. This means that profits may at some point return to average values, but the time to do so is infinite. The long-run equilibrium profit (at $t = p$) can be defined as the point at which profits in successive periods are equal. This can be found by taking an estimate of average profits over the period sampled by adopting the following formula:

$$\Pi_{ip} = \frac{\alpha_i}{1 - \lambda_i}$$

Table 6.2 ● **Summary of persistence of profits studies**

Study	Country	Sample period	No. of firms	Mean $\hat{\lambda}_i$
Geroski and Jacquemin (1988)	UK	1949–77	51	0.488
	France	1965–82	55	0.412
	West Germany	1961–81	28	0.410
Schwalbach et al. (1989)	West Germany	1961–82	299	0.485
Mueller (1990)	US	1950–72	551	0.183
Cubbin and Geroski (1990)	UK	1950–72	243	0.482
Jenny and Weber (1990)	France	1965–82	450	0.363
Odagiri and Yamawaki (1990)	Japan	1964–82	376	0.465
Schohl (1990)	West Germany	1961–81	283	0.509
Khemani and Shapiro (1990)	Canada	1964–82	129	0.425
Goddard and Wilson (1996)	UK	1972–91	335	0.458

The hypothesis tested in these studies is that (potential and actual) entry into and exit from any market are sufficiently free to bring any abnormal profits quickly into line with the competitive rate of return. In other words, competitive forces are sufficiently powerful to ensure that no firm can persistently earn profits above the norm. However, industries never reach equilibrium in the conventional sense, because each period brings new random shocks. This means that profits are never the same for all firms. If the market is responsive to excess profits and losses, returns tend to gravitate towards some competitive level. If firm profits do not gravitate to some average value, this means that some firms possess special knowledge or other advantages. These advantages enable them to react to competitive pressures such as the entry of new firms, and thus earn profits above the norm, which persist from one period to the next. Substantial evidence now exists for the United States, UK, Germany, France, Japan and Canada that firm-level profits do persist but eventually gravitate towards competitive levels. We now briefly discuss a selection of the more important studies. A summary of these studies is shown in Table 6.2.

Geroski and Jacquemin (1988) applied the partial adjustment model to a sample of 134 large European firms (51 British, 28 West German and 55 French). Profits were measured as net profit before tax divided by total assets. In a bid to examine profits relative to average values, returns were normalised. This was done by taking an individual firm's profit from the average profit of the sample in the firm's country of origin in a particular year. The authors found that the profits of UK firms are more persistent (i.e. average λ_i is higher) than those of their French and German counterparts. The results are indicative of stronger levels of competition in France and Germany than in the UK.

Schwalbach et al. (1989) used the partial adjustment model to examine the behaviour of firm profits over an extended period for 299 firms over the period 1961 to 1982. Profits were measured in two ways:

● net profit after tax plus interest payments divided by total assets; and
● the market valuation ratio, defined as the market value of shares divided by the book value of assets.

The use of two profit measures checks whether the results observed were sensitive to the performance measure used. Although an adjustment of firm profits towards the average level is found, there are permanent differences in profitability across firms. An interesting finding is that the average speed of adjustment of profits towards average levels (denoted by λ_i) was lower when the model was estimated using the accounting profit rate than when the market valuation ratio was used. Schwalbach *et al.* argued that this is because capital markets value the stream of future profits differently from accounting rates of profit.

After finding persistent profitability differences across firms, Schwalbach *et al.* attempted to find whether firm-specific or industry-wide effects were more important in determining long-run differences in profitability. Firms were grouped into industries based on the three-digit industrial level and long-run profit rates and their standard deviations were calculated for all firms within each industrial group. A wide variation in long-run profit rates indicates that firm effects are relatively important. However, if there is a low variation in profits for firms within each industrial group, then industry effects are more important in explaining long-run differences. For example, for the beer industry, Schwalbach *et al.* found a high long-run profit rate and a low dispersion of returns. This suggested that the industry was protected by entry barriers, and that low mobility barriers cause a fairly equal distribution of profits throughout the industry. However, overall they concluded that firm effects were more important in explaining long-run profitability differences across firms.

Mueller (1990) used a sample of 551 US firms covering the period 1950 to 1972 to test for persistence of profits. The sample of firms was divided into six equal-sized groups based on initial profitability, and he estimated the model for each firm to yield estimates of the speed at which short-run profits adjust to long-run values. Long-run profitability differences were found, and there are differences in the speeds at which short-run excess profits were competed away. The average profitability of the six groups remains stable over time. For example, in the initial period the top group of firms in the sample were earning 5.49 per cent above the norm, while the least profitable firms were earning 4.66 per cent below the norm. Over the entire sample period, the most profitable group was earning 4.68 per cent above the norm, and the least profitable firms were earning 2.83 per cent below the norm.

Although Mueller found differences in long-run profitability differences between firms, there was some movement towards the average. The speed at which entry caused short-run profits to be competed away and adjust towards long-run equilibrium also differed. In the top group this speed of adjustment is at its quickest, with an average $\hat{\lambda}_i$ of 0.121, indicating that these firms are relatively unsuccessful in insulating themselves against entry. Overall, the average $\hat{\lambda}_i$ is 0.167, which implied a relatively rapid convergence of short-run profits to long-run equilibrium.

Drawing on the work of Mueller, Odagiri and Yamawaki (1990) tested for persistence of profits in Japanese manufacturing using a sample of 376 firms for the period 1964 to 1982. The estimation results indicated some movement of profit rates of firms above and below the norm towards long-run equilibrium levels. The average reported $\hat{\lambda}_i$ was 0.47. However, the authors found evidence of differences between firms in the long-run equilibrium rate of profit.

Cubbin and Geroski (1990) tested for the persistence of profits for a sample of 243 UK companies over the period 1951 to 1977. The sample was split into six groups based on initial profitability, and it is found that the groups are ranked in the same order by average profitability over the entire sample period. UK firms' profit rates showed some tendency to converge over the sample period. For the first three years of the sample period the difference in profitability between the top and bottom groups was 13.3 per cent, but for the sample period as a whole this gap was narrowed to 2.58 per cent. However, there was a relatively high average value of $\hat{\lambda}_i$ of 0.491. The authors argued that this was indicative of barriers to entry that prevented short-run excess returns adjusting to long-run values.

Jenny and Weber (1990) applied the persistence of profits methodology to a sample of 450 firms between 1965 and 1982. They found that rankings of firms by profits were stable over time, and that the speed at which short-run profits were competed away varied from group to group. There were quite large differences in long-run profitability across firms, with a gap between the average profitability of the most and least profitable of the six subgroups of 9.69 percentage points. Jenny and Weber also found that the speed of adjustment to long-run values was slowest in the top group of firms. They also split the firms into their respective industrial groups, and found pharmaceuticals, petroleum refining and cement, stone ceramics and glass to be the most successful industries in terms of average profits, while textiles, clothing and rubber products were the least successful.

Khemani and Shapiro (1990) adopted a similar methodology to Mueller (1990) for a study using Canadian data. Long-run profits and the speed of adjustments were calculated for 129 firms using data collected over the period 1962 to 1982. Profits were measured as net profit after tax plus interest payments divided by total assets. The estimations were also carried out using pre-tax profits. The authors found that firms in the most profitable group initially earning 14.4 percentage points above the average were still projected to be earning 7.9 percentage points above the norm in the long run. The authors also found that the speed of adjustment to long-run values was faster than in any of the previous studies except Mueller.

Khemani and Shapiro split the companies into industry groups and calculated the long-run profit rate. The most persistently successful firms were found predominately in the chemicals (also pharmaceuticals), pulp and paper, food and petroleum refining industries, while the least successful firms were predominately in textiles, coal and petroleum exploration.

Khemani and Shapiro also carried out an analysis to investigate the factors which are most important in determining long-run profits. Independent variables included: (1) industrial classification; (2) the firm's diversification strategy (i.e. whether the firm is single-product or multi-product); (3) whether the firm is a multinational, and if so, its country of origin; (4) a sales measure of the firm's size. In general, they found that the industrial classification and firm size variable are important, while diversification strategy and the firm's status as a multinational or otherwise are insignificant.

Schohl (1990) took a critical view of a number of previous studies, presented his own findings and compared them with the findings from earlier studies.[21] He argued that although previous studies had usually found that rankings of firms by long-run average profitability are similar to the rankings by initial profitability (a result which is usually obtained by splitting the sample into six groups according to the rankings by initial profitability and calculating the long-run average for firms with each group), previous studies had failed to test for statistically significant differences between the group averages.

---

[21] Goddard and Wilson (1999) provide a comprehensive econometric critique of the literature.

He tested for differences in group averages using analysis of variance to compare the within-group variance in long-run average profitability with the between-group variance. He found that there were significant differences across the six groups using his data. He then tested the significance of differences in long-run profits between all possible combinations of paired groups. Schohl found significant differences in long-run profitability at the top and bottom end of the profitability rankings, but failed to find evidence of long-run profitability differences in the middle groups. He argued that these results were indicative of stronger convergence of short-run profits to long-run values than previous studies have suggested. He concluded by arguing that profit rate differences only persisted in the top and bottom groups, while differences in profitability between firms in the middle groups were dissolved by the competitive process.

Goddard and Wilson (1996) presented evidence on the persistence of profits for 335 UK manufacturing and 90 service firms for the period 1972 to 1991. They found an average value for the speed of adjustment parameter ($\hat{\lambda}_i$) of 0.45 for manufacturing, and an average of 0.46 for services. Some variation was found around these averages. For example, 22.7 per cent of manufacturing and 25.6 per cent of service firms, $\hat{\lambda}_i$ was found to be less than 0.3. This implied that these firms were subject to strong competitive pressures. On the other hand, for 17.1 per cent of manufacturing and 17.7 per cent of service firms $\hat{\lambda}_i$ was found to exceed 0.7, implying that these firms possessed advantages which insulated them to some degree from competitive pressure. The authors found little difference between the samples of manufacturing and service firms.

Overall, the persistence of profits literature has found evidence that there are differences in the long-run equilibrium rates of profit, and varying degrees of year-to-year persistence, and so differences in the rate at which firms' profits are eroded through the process of entry. These results were thought to reflect differences in efficiency across firms. The smallest estimated λ_i were found for the United States and the highest estimated λ_i for the UK. Whatever the reason for international differences, a general conclusion was that competitive pressure did not appear to be sufficiently strong to completely eliminate differences between firms in profitability, even in the long run.

6.6 Conclusions

This chapter has considered the problem of defining empirical measures of profitability. Measures discussed are those based on stock market valuations, price–cost margins, and accounting rates of return. As we have seen all have limitations as approximations to the theoretical concept of economic profitability. Nevertheless, a number of empirical studies have suggested that accounting profits do correlate significantly with economic profits, and do therefore contain information which can be used in the analysis of firms and industries. This chapter has also examined the role of market structure, in particular market concentration in determining the ways in which firms and industries behave and ultimately perform. The general view that emerged is that firms in highly concentrated industries outperform those in industries that are less concentrated. Empirical evidence as to whether this is due to collusion between established firms or differential efficiencies tends to be somewhat inconclusive. The theory of strategic groups offers an intermediate alternative.

Dynamic views of competition have also been examined which place emphasis on the evolution of profits rather than taking a snapshot of an industry at a moment in time. The general finding that emerged is that the competitive process does not always work instantaneously to erode positions of excess profitability. Instead, many firms often earn profits significantly different from the norm.

Key terms

Accounting rate of profit

Strategic group

Internal rate of return

Tobin's q ratio

Lerner index

Questions for discussion

1. Outline the difficulties that economists have faced in using profitability as a measure of performance.
2. Discuss whether the industry or firm is the appropriate unit of analysis when examining the performance of firms and industries.
3. Assess the extent to which profits in highly concentrated industries are the result of firms exercising market power advantages.
4. Using an industry of your choice, attempt to identify strategic groupings.
5. Compare and contrast the static SCP approach with dynamic views of competition.
6. Examine the proposition that profits persist indefinitely.

Further reading

Britton, L.C., Clark, T.A.R. and Ball, D.F. (1992) Modify or extend? The application of the structure conduct performance approach to service industries, *The Service Industries Journal*, **12**, 34–43.

Caves, R.E. (1986) *American Industry: Structure, Conduct and Performance*, 6th edn. New Jersey: Prentice Hall.

Economist (1998) The economics of antitrust, *The Economist*, May.

Martin, S. (1993) *Advanced Industrial Economics*. Cambridge, MA: Blackwell, chapter 17.

McGee, J. and Thomas, H. (1986) Strategic groups: theory, research and taxonomy, *Strategic Management Journal*, **7**, 141–60.

Mueller D.C. (ed.) (1990) *The Dynamics of Company Profits: An International Comparison*. Cambridge: Cambridge University Press.

Neuberger, D. (1998) Industrial organization of banking: a review, *International Journal of the Economics of Business*, **5**, 97–118.

Scherer, F.M. and Ross, D. (1990) *Industrial Market Structure and Economic Performance*, 3rd edn. Boston: Houghton Mifflin, chapter 11.

Schmalensee, R.C. (1989) Inter-industry studies of structure and performance, in Schmalensee, R.C. and Willig, R.D. (eds) *Handbook of Industrial Organization*, vol. 2. Amsterdam: North-Holland, chapter 16.

Weiss, L.W. (1974) The concentration–profits relationship and antitrust, in Goldschmid, H., Mann, H.M. and Weston, J.F. (eds) *Industrial Concentration: The New Learning*. Boston: Little Brown, pp. 183–233.

Weiss, L.W. (1989) *Concentration and Price*. Cambridge, MA: MIT Press.

CHAPTER 7

Advertising

Learning objectives

After reading this chapter the student should be able to:

- Discuss the various types of product differentiation

- Explain the determinants of advertising expenditures

- Calculate advertising intensity and discuss the various problems associated with such measures

- Appreciate the differences between informative and persuasive advertising

- Discuss the effects of advertising on welfare

- Explain how advertising can raise barriers to entry

- Understand the relationships between advertising and industry concentration and profitability

- Explain the relationship between advertising and prices charged

7.1 Introduction

Advertising is a form of product differentiation whereby firms communicate to consumers what goods and services they have to sell. This chapter discusses the importance of advertising for the analysis of the behaviour and performance of firms and industries. The main emphasis is on analysing the role of advertising in the economy. The level of advertising varies across countries and industries. Indeed, in many industries, advertising is the predominant mode of inter-firm competition. The intensity of this type of competition depends on many factors including the objectives of established firms, market concentration, the age of the industry and the types of product and service produced. In section 7.2, we present some descriptive statistics of advertising across various countries and industries. We also identify some of the most important advertisers at the firm and product level. Much of the analysis of advertising can be traced back to the theory of **monopolistic competition**.

Section 7.3 discusses the theory of monopolistic competition and forwards a general analysis of the various forms of product differentiation which exist in different industries. The section aims to illustrate the ways in which firms can differentiate products to gain a competitive advantage.

Section 7.4 highlights the importance of information in determining the quality and prices of goods and services traded in a given market. One of the main roles of advertising in the economy is to provide consumers with information on the prices and quality of goods and services on offer. The overall aim of this section is to show how a lack of information can crucially affect the quality and prices of goods and services offered for sale in a given industry. Section 7.5 examines the controversy surrounding whether advertising can be regarded as informative or persuasive. Some economists have argued that advertising leads to a misallocation of resources as consumers' preferences are distorted. Others have contended that advertising improves consumer information with regard to product and service attributes and leads to a more efficient allocation of resources in the economy.

Section 7.6 examines advertising and the competitive environment. The level of advertising in a given industry has implications for the structure, conduct and performance of firms in that industry. This type of analysis is made difficult because the level of advertising can be used as a measure of industry structure or as a measure of firm conduct. We examine the relationships between advertising and market concentration and between advertising and firm performance. We highlight the role of advertising as an entry barrier, which may lead to established firms achieving advantages over potential entrants. Given that advertising affects the structural and performance characteristics of many industries, it is likely to affect the prices that consumers pay for goods and services that are advertised.

Drawing on the discussion in previous sections, section 7.7 examines whether advertising leads to lower or higher prices for consumers. Evidence is presented for a number of industries, and examines how prices changed in these industries when advertising increased.

7.2 Determinants of advertising expenditures and intensity

Advertising is a huge global business. In many industries it is the main strategic weapon used by firms to gain a competitive advantage in the market. In the UK, advertising expenditures have increased from £121 million in 1948 to £13.1 billion in 1997. Advertising as a percentage of national income varies across countries (Table 7.1): for example, in 1996 advertising accounted for 1.3 per cent of gross domestic product in the United States, and 1.2 per cent in the UK. In France, Germany, Italy and Japan the corresponding figures were 0.66 per cent, 0.91 per cent, 0.5 per cent and 0.79 per cent respectively (Advertising Association, 1998).

Table 7.1 ● Advertising as a percentage of gross domestic product (at market prices)

Country	1990	1992	1994	1996
Austria	0.75	0.76	0.73	0.73
Belgium	0.57	0.60	0.59	0.64
Denmark	0.84	0.81	0.81	0.86
Finland	1.02	0.86	0.86	0.88
France	0.78	0.69	0.66	0.66
Germany	0.91	0.89	0.89	0.91
Greece	0.63	0.94	1.00	0.79
Ireland	0.95	0.93	0.86	0.87
Italy	0.58	0.59	0.49	0.50
Japan	0.90	0.80	0.73	0.79
Netherlands	0.83	0.82	0.84	0.89
Norway	0.68	0.67	0.69	0.73
Portugal	0.79	0.84	0.96	1.17
Spain	0.90	1.12	0.88	0.82
Sweden	0.80	0.71	0.80	0.77
Switzerland	1.05	0.92	0.91	0.92
UK	1.21	1.10	1.13	1.20
United States	1.35	1.25	1.27	1.35

Data are net of discounts. They include agency commission and press classified advertising expenditure, but exclude production costs.

Sources: *The European Advertising and Media Forecast, National Data Sources,* NTC Publications Ltd. Reproduced from the *Advertising Statistics Yearbook 1998,* table 24.3. Reprinted with permission.

Many factors are thought to affect the overall aggregate expenditures on advertising goods and services. They include the following:

● *National income.* There is likely to be a positive relationship between national income and expenditures on advertising. When national income is high or increasing, consumers tend to have more disposable income to spend on goods and services. This encourages firms to spend heavily on advertising to gain market share.
● *Employment levels.* If unemployment is low then advertising tends to increase. Howard (1998) forwarded two reasons for this phenomenon. Firstly, when unemployment is low, consumers have more income which encourages firms to advertise more (see above point). Secondly, high employment levels lead to firms having difficulty in hiring workers to fill vacant positions. This leads to increased advertising by recruitment agencies.
● *Government regulation.* In recent years many governments have removed restrictions on advertising in many industries. This has often led to increased advertising as firms have attempted to establish brand awareness and ensure customer loyalty. Howard (1998) cited the example of the commercial television market in Sweden where advertising expenditures increased by 250 per cent in one year after the introduction of commercial television. We examine the role of advertising on competition later in the chapter.

- *To launch a product or service.* Firms may use advertising to provide consumers with information regarding a new product or service. New products often involve informative advertisements aimed at educating a consumer as to the attributes of a new product or service. For example, the UK government and financial service firms had to spend heavily on advertising to provide consumers with detailed information before and after the launch of Individual Savings Accounts (ISAs) in 1999.
- *To provide information on price and quality.* Firms may use advertising to provide consumers with information regarding the price and quality attributes of products and services. This is particularly important if prices and quality of products are changing over time as a consequence of increased competition or technological changes. For example, mobile phone providers in the UK have spent heavily on promoting quality and price attributes of various goods and services offered. Advertising can also be used to provide consumers with information on the location of the firm's sales outlets.
- *To increase or protect market share.* Firms may use advertising to gain a competitive advantage by capturing larger shares of the market. Here advertising is used either to inform or to persuade consumers that the firm's products and services are superior to those of their rivals. In a market that is growing, there is likely to be less of a need for advertising as there is a large pool of potential customers; in a declining market firms may advertise heavily to protect dwindling market share.
- *To increase consumer awareness and increase profitability.* Firms may use advertising to increase consumer's awareness of the goods and services the firm has to sell. Over time this advertising is likely to lead to the firm's building up goodwill and reputation advantages over its rivals, which can act as entry barriers to new firms. Consequently, the firm's profitability is increased. For example, in 1997 McDonald's spent over £35 million promoting its brand image (Advertising Association, 1998). *The Economist* (1991) noted that:

> Brands are insubstantial things, mere signals, names, associations. Sometimes they signal real differences between products. Sometimes they are pure illusion. Either way, brands are akin to a product's or company's reputation, and they influence consumers' perceptions. The wearer of a Rolex watch is concerned with more than keeping time; the BMW driver with more than getting from place to place.

In many oligopolistic industries, the predominant type of competition is carried out on a non-price basis. One possible measure of the extent to which advertising predominates as a form of competition (**advertising intensity**) is to examine the proportion of industry sales devoted to advertising. This can give us an indirect method of assessing the type of competition that takes place in particular industries. The Advertising Association (1998) found the advertising to sales ratios of selected product groups varied considerably (Table 7.2). For example, in industries such as vitamins, shampoos, cereals and washing powders, advertising to sales ratios were found to be high, at approximately 24 per cent, 20 per cent, 8.5 per cent and 8 per cent, respectively. In other industries these ratios were found to be low. For example, in cars, carbonated drinks, hairdressing and video recorders, the advertising to sales ratios were 2.5 per cent, 1.5 per cent, 0.03 per cent and 0.02 per cent, respectively.

In many industries, for example vitamins and shampoos, advertising intensity is high, while in others such as soft drinks and cars the intensity is much lower. However, using these ratios as an indicator of the intensity of non-price competition may be misleading. Firstly, the ratios mask the fact that, in many industries (for example, cars), although absolute

Table 7.2 ● Advertising to sales ratios of selected UK product groups, 1996

Product group	Advertising to sales ratio
Vitamins	23.71
Shampoos	19.89
Toilet soaps	17.70
Cinema	13.69
Cereals	8.43
Washing liquids and powders	7.68
Deodorants	7.51
Air fresheners	6.79
Electric razors	6.65
Hairdryers	3.53
Coffee	3.90
Video games	3.16
Tea	3.06
Cars	2.47
Carbonated soft drinks	1.54
Trainers	1.45
Cheese	1.26
Rail travel	0.77
Beer	0.66
Cigarettes	0.43
Televisions	0.37
Carpets, floor coverings and tiles	0.22
Domestic lighting	0.12
Hairdressing	0.03
Video recorders	0.02

Source: adapted from *Advertising Statistics Yearbook 1998*, table 20.1, pp.218–22. Reprinted with permission.

expenditures on advertising are huge, the sales are so large that the proportion of advertising to sales appears small. Secondly, advertising is only one form of product differentiation: other modes of product differentiation being utilised by firms will not be captured by this measure. We examine other forms of product differentiation later in the chapter.

The extent of advertising intensity in any given industry depends on many factors, including the following:[1]

● *Firm objectives.* The level of advertising intensity in any given industry may depend on the overall business objectives of established firms in that industry. If firms are maximising profits, they may have little scope to spend heavily on promoting products and services. On the other hand, if firms are aiming to maximise sales or market share then expenditures on advertising are likely to be much higher. Of course, firms in the same industry may follow different business objectives, so it may be difficult to build up a detailed picture of the competition in any given industry using an advertising intensity measure.

[1] This discussion draws on Albion and Farris (1981).

- *Market concentration.* Many authors have argued that advertising can aid in the growth of large firms, leading to increases in the observed levels of market concentration.[2] Other authors have argued that as concentration increases and industries evolve to form oligopolistic structures comprising a few large firms, the firms in these industries may choose to compete on a non-price basis by spending excessively on advertising, promotion, and research and development. These expenditures are likely to lead to the appropriation of certain advantages to these firms (such as goodwill and brand loyalty), allowing them to increase market share. The overall effect is increased concentration. We examine the relationship between concentration and advertising expenditures later in the chapter.

- *The age of the industry.* In new industries, firms must spend heavily on advertising in order to increase consumer awareness and establish a market presence. Over time this may convey market share advantages to firms that advertise, as consumers become aware of the products and services produced and become loyal to the product.

- *The extent of product differentiation.* If the industry is characterised by a high degree of product differentiation, then consumers will perceive that no close substitute exists for the goods and services they consume. As a consequence, firms will have to spend heavily on advertising in order to capture market share from rivals.

- *Number of brands.* If products are differentiated through branding by established firms, then consumers are likely to be loyal to particular products. If this is the case then firms must spend even more heavily to persuade consumers to switch from one firm's product to another. This argument has been confirmed by Cable (1972) who found a positive relationship between advertising intensity and the number of brands. Schmalensee (1978) argued that the proliferation of brands can lead to the creation of entry barriers to particular industries, thus insulating established firms from competition.

- *Type of product or service produced.* The level of advertising intensity often varies by the type of product or service produced in a given industry (see Table 7.2). Evidence suggests that advertising intensity is generally lower in industries where durable goods are produced. Given the high price of durable products, consumers often undertake more detailed investigations as to the attributes of the products on offer. For example, when purchasing a hi fi system, consumers will tend to consult specialist consumer information publications such as *What Hi-Fi?*, *Hi-Fi World* and *Hi-Fi Choice*, instead of relying solely on the informative and persuasive messages forwarded by advertisers.

- *Frequency of consumer purchase.* Consumers who buy a product or service regularly are unlikely to need either detailed information or to be persuaded by firms as to the desirable attributes of the goods and services they are buying. On the other hand, where goods are bought less frequently, consumers may need the help of advertisements to guide them to optimal consumption decisions.

7.3 Theory of monopolistic competition

Advertising is one of the main strategies of competition in industry. In theoretical terms, we might expect the importance of advertising to vary according to the type of industry

---

[2] The role of advertising and product differentiation in determining industry concentration is discussed in Chapter 4.

under consideration. Under perfect competition there is no real role for advertising because the firm faces a perfectly elastic demand curve and so can sell all the output it produces at the market-determined price. In the long run, the firm will make normal profits. Normal profits are unlikely to be large enough to invest in advertising campaigns even if the firm wanted to do this. Under monopoly, there is also little role for advertising, given that the monopolist already faces an inelastic demand curve and so has substantial control over the prices it charges. Given that the monopolist is insulated from increased competition by barriers to entry, there is no incentive to spend heavily on advertising. Under oligopoly, firms recognise interdependence, may choose to avoid price competition, and instead engage in non-price competition through advertising and innovation.

Much of the literature concerning the economic analysis of advertising can be traced back to the 1930s, when Edward Chamberlin wrote *The Theory of Monopolistic Competition* (1933) which combined the previously separate theories of monopoly and perfect competition. The aim was to fill the gap between the two extremes of competition.

Chamberlin outlined an industry structure where competitive conditions are neither purely competitive nor completely monopolistic. He observed that few monopolies exist because close substitutes exist for most goods and services. Likewise, there are very few types of goods and services which can be regarded as homogeneous, and, as such, perfect competition can rarely exist. However, in many industries, goods and services are produced which are very similar, and as a consequence, prices are determined by both competitive and monopolistic elements. This is best illustrated when he asserted that: 'Monopolistic competition is a challenge to the traditional viewpoint of economics that competition and monopoly are alternatives and that individual prices are to be explained in terms of one or the other.'[3]

Under conditions of monopolistic competition, a firm can earn abnormal profits in the short run. However, these are dissipated over the longer term by the entry of new firms.

Equilibrium conditions

The short- and long-run equilibrium conditions under monopolistic competition are illustrated in Figures 7.1 and 7.2.

In the short run, the firm maximises profits where marginal revenues equal marginal costs, producing at output level Q_0 and charging a price equal to P_0. The average cost of production at this output level is at C_0. At this output level, the firm earns abnormal profits, where average revenues (AR_0) exceed average costs (AC_0). This is shown in Figure 7.1 as the shaded area. When potential rivals see the profits that can be realised in this industry, they begin to enter. As more and more firms enter, the market share of each firm declines. In other words, at a given price each firm will expect to sell less than it did before the entry of new firms. The effect of entry is to shift the demand curve to the left. The demand curve will continue to shift to the left so long as there are abnormal profits being earned by established firms. Long-run equilibrium (or tangency solution) is achieved when average revenue (AR_1) equals average cost (AC_1). The firm produces at Q_1 and charges a price equal to P_1. At this point all firms earn normal profits.

[3] Chamberlin (1933), p.204.

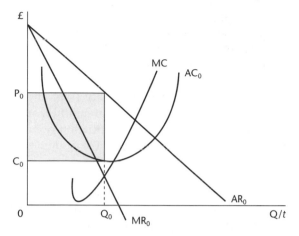

Figure 7.1 Short-run equilibrium under monopolistic competition

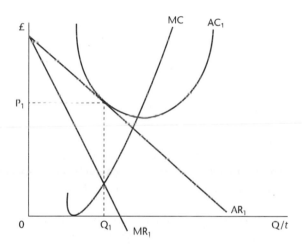

Figure 7.2 Long-run equilibrium under monopolistic competition

Under monopolistic competition, if the firm increases prices, it will lose some, but not all, of its business to rival firms. Some customers will remain loyal in the belief that the product is sufficiently different even at higher prices. This contrasts with perfect competition, where the firm would have been left with no customers following a price rise.

Caves and Williamson (1985, p.128) examined the conditions that would lend themselves to an industry characterised by monopolistic competition. These conditions were related to the complexity of products produced and the ease with which consumers can collect and process information. They argued that:

> We find two sets of conditions that are theoretically sufficient to produce this market pattern. One rests on the complexity of the product's attribute structure and a fixed cost of assembly given any combination of attributes. The other stems from the costliness to buyers of information to guide their choice among competing brands.

Most modern industries are typified by some degree of **product differentiation**. There is no one homogeneous type of car, soap, television station or hotel. Product differentiation can be viewed as the ability of producers to differentiate (in a physical or psychological sense) close substitutes so that customers no longer regard them as similar products. Products and services can be subject to vertical or horizontal differentiation. Vertical differentiation occurs when a product or service differs in quality from another. For example, one brand of beer may have a higher alcohol content than another, and as such be deemed a higher-quality product. In contrast, horizontal differentiation occurs when products are of the same quality but have slightly different attributes. For example, different colours of the same model of car.

Product differentiation can be due to many causes. We can divide these into natural and strategic causes. Natural product differentiation occurs when products become different through a natural process not developed by producers, although exploited by them. Strategic product differentiation is directly controlled by producers through the pursuit of strategies such as advertising and promotion. Natural causes of product differentiation include the following:

- *Geographical variations*. In this case, the location of a seller automatically differentiates a product in the mind of consumers, for example, the ease with which a shop or factory can be reached by consumers, as is the case of when consumers have to make choices between the corner shop and the out-of-town superstore. It is also often the case where identical houses are differentiated by which part of the country they are located in.
- *New technology*. New technology can be used to differentiate a product, for example, the addition of internet and e-mail features on a mobile telephone. *The Economist* (1999) noted that Procter & Gamble had been successful in differentiating many of its products through new technological features. Examples of this included the *Swiffer* mop that captured dust, and the *Nutri-Delight* orange drink which had a special formula to allow iodine to co-exist with certain vitamins and minerals, and allowed children to gain weight.
- *Brands and trademarks*. Brands and trademarks can be exploited to differentiate similar products. Trademarks are normally words or symbols used by producers to denote particular brands. In many cases, firms that own these trademarks have obtained exclusive property rights to exploit them. Examples could include a crocodile or a polo player on horseback as is the case for Lacoste and Ralph Lauren clothing. This gives the firm some degree of monopoly power. However, brands and trademarks can become synonymous with the products they are associated with (for example, Hoover/vacuum cleaner). Bryson (1994) noted that if this is the case the firm may lose its trademark protection.
- *Community or national differences*. Here the country or community of origin is the defining factor that differentiates goods and services. In other words, products and services from different parts of the world are deemed to be different and of higher quality: for example, custard made in Devon, vodka made in Russia, whisky made in Scotland, watches made in Switzerland, curry made in India and clothes made in Italy.
- *Customer wants*. Consumers have different characteristics, tastes and preferences. As a consequence, the type of product demanded varies from consumer to consumer. Differentiation by producers to meet these varied wants is often on a horizontal basis, for example colour of cars and style of clothes.

● *Ignorance.* Ignorance on the part of consumers can allow firms to exaggerate the degree of differentiation of their products and services. Scitovsky (1950, 1971) argued that this allowed firms to suggest that high prices reflect higher quality. This may even lead to these goods and services inheriting Veblenesque characteristics.[4]

Causes of product differentiation over which producers have a more direct control could include the following:

● *Factor variations.* Factor inputs such as labour and capital are rarely homogeneous. As a consequence, the final output arising from these factors of production may well be marketed as being different from that of other firms. Firms may stress that their employees are better skilled, better trained and less likely to make errors, or that their raw material inputs are superior to those of rival firms. This gives the firms some control over the prices they charge.

● *Additional services.* Additional services offered by firms can often be used to differentiate products. Even if products are identical, the conditions surrounding a sale may be different. For example, by offering superior credit facilities, quicker delivery or a more comprehensive after-sales service, producers can effectively differentiate their products. By offering certain after-sales guarantees or warranties the firm is sending signals to consumers that it has confidence in the quality of the products it is selling.

● *Rate of change of product differentiation.* Firms may be able to affect the size and importance of this variable. Products with a short lifespan and taking up a small proportion of a consumer's budget can be subject to the planned obsolescence of desirability. Consumers will be urged to adopt new styles and models. This is particularly prevalent in products such as video games and home computers.

● *Advertising.* This is arguably the most common method of differentiating products and services. By using advertisements to provide information and convey persuasive messages, producers can create or exaggerate differences between goods and services. Over the longer term this can be used to build up brand image and ensure consumer loyalty. Before any real regulation of advertising took place, firms often made outrageous claims to promote their products. Bryson (1994) noted of advertising in 1930s America that many products were portrayed as having miraculous properties. For example, one company boasted that its brand of cigarettes could cure a smoker's cough.

The consequence of successful differentiation through advertising is to provide the individual firm with some degree of monopoly power. The demand curve that faces the individual firm is therefore downward sloping to the right. Further successful differentiation may shift the firm's demand curve to the right. This implies that the firm has some scope to set prices. The degree of product differentiation determines the magnitude of the price elasticity of demand. A product with a high degree of differentiation will generate an inelastic demand curve. The effects of advertising on a firm's profitability are shown in Figure 7.3.

We begin by assuming that the firm operates in an industry where no advertising takes place. The firm faces a downward sloping demand curve (AR_0) and a corresponding marginal revenue curve (MR_0). Before advertising, the firm maximises profits where MR_0 equals MC,

---

[4] Veblenseque goods are often luxury goods such as designer clothes or fine wines. Consumers tend to demand more of these goods as their price increases.

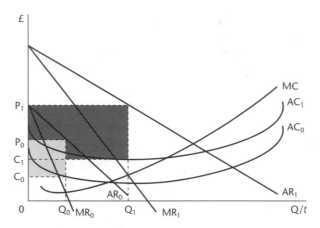

Figure 7.3 Effects of advertising on a firm's profitability

producing at output level Q_0 and charging price P_0. The firm's profit is shown by the pale shaded area. If advertising now takes place, the firm's average costs increase from AC_0 to AC_1. However, the increased advertising has the effect of increasing demand, from AR_0 to AR_1. Because advertising is a fixed cost, marginal costs are unaffected. The firm now maximises profits where the new marginal curve (MR_1) equals marginal cost (MC), producing at output level Q_1 and charging price P_1. The firm's profit is now shown by the dark shaded area. The firm now makes higher profits after advertising than it did before. The extent to which firms make extra profits from advertising will depend on the extent to which advertising promotes increased demand and on the price elasticity of demand.[5]

The theoretical work of Chamberlin and others has stimulated a large body of empirical research. Much of this research has examined the role of advertising in the competitive process. The following sections discuss selected aspects of this research.

7.4 Information and quality

The provision of information plays a crucial role in the competitive process. Under conditions of perfect competition information is perfect. In other words, buyers and sellers have perfect knowledge of market conditions. As a consequence, one price prevails leading to all firms making normal levels of profits. However, if information is imperfect, there may be asymmetric information between producers and consumers. In many situations the seller has more information about the characteristics of the product than the buyer. Consumers therefore do not have enough information to make an informed choice about the products and services they are buying, and this will sometimes have implications for quality and price.

Akerlof (1970) argued that if consumers do not have enough information to distinguish between low and high quality goods and services, a situation can arise where both types of product are sold at similar prices. Akerlof discusses the case of secondhand cars. In this case the sellers have much more information than the potential buyers about the quality of

---

[5] If demand is very inelastic then increases in price lead to large increases in total revenue.

the cars. Some cars will be of a high quality, some will be low: only the seller knows. The prices charged will be somewhere below the price normally charged for a high quality car but above the price for low quality cars. In this case, sellers of good cars will be unwilling to sell their cars for less than they are worth and will withdraw from the market. This results in a market where low quality cars are traded.

Imperfect information with regard to prices of goods and services may give producers some element of monopoly power. In other words, consumers may be unaware that different prices for similar products do not reflect quality differences. Therefore, if information is increased through advertising, consumers are more likely to shop around. As a consequence of increased competition, producers will charge similar prices for similar products and services.[6]

Overall, advertising and other forms of product differentiation may help to improve information with regard to the prices and qualities of products.[7] Firms that advertise products frequently may send a signal to consumers about quality. Davis *et al.* (1991, p.7) argued that advertising provides consumers with useful information on product quality. They asserted that: 'producers only advertise if they have a product they think will sell in the long term. Consumers will only try advertised products as long as there is a tendency for advertised products to be of higher quality than unadvertised ones.' Therefore, there would only be an incentive for a firm to advertise its products if it expected to capture and keep market share. Firms selling low quality products would be unwilling to spend heavily on advertising as they would be unlikely to receive any repeat purchases from consumers. If consumers have access to good information, they would only be willing to pay high prices for high quality goods and services.

7.5 Informative and persuasive advertising

Advertising can be categorised as either informative or persuasive. If advertising is informative, it is useful in providing consumers with enough information to make informed choices with regard to the goods and services they demand. If advertising is persuasive, it distorts the information that consumers receive, making it difficult for them to make informed choices. Information is a prerequisite for effective competition and ensures that resources are used efficiently to produce the goods and services that consumers demand. Persuasive advertising simply changes the preference functions of consumers and can often lead to less competition as firms who enjoy brand loyalty exploit market power by charging higher prices and earning higher profits.

The traditional view of advertising embodied in the writings of Kaldor (1950), Bain (1956), Galbraith (1958, 1967) and Comanor and Wilson (1974) tends to take a negative view of its usefulness. The general argument is that advertising plays a role in distorting consumer preferences, whereby consumers are persuaded to buy products that are heavily

---

[6] Moraga-Gonzalez (2000) makes a useful contribution in this area by presenting a model of informative advertising that reduces problems which consumers face when attempting to collect information on potential purchases.

[7] Other forms of differentiation that may provide information about product quality include: firms with good reputations and who are willing to provide warranties and guarantees for their goods and services; public information announcements by governments; the imposition of standards and licences when producing certain goods and services; and publications produced by consumer associations.

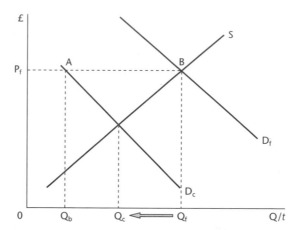

Figure 7.4 Advertising and welfare

promoted. This results in the appropriation of reputation and brand loyalty advantages to advertising firms and allows the potential for the exploitation of market power by charging higher prices for branded products. Nawaz (1997, p.3) sums up this assertion in the following manner:

> The goal of persuasive advertising is to change customers' perceptions of a product. If persuasive advertising works, it means that a branded product is considered in some non-tangible way to be 'different' to its rivals. If successful, therefore, persuasive advertising may generate brand loyalty – customers may be unwilling to switch to competitors' products if they are convinced that their preferred brand offers something that no other product would be able to provide.

Shepherd (1997, p.111) noted that persuasive advertising: 'interferes with the exercise of innate preferences, it alters choices away from the efficient lines that "consumer sovereignty" would yield. Thus persuasive image instilling advertising is largely a form of economic waste.'

One of the most famous of critiques of advertising came from Kaldor (1950). Kaldor argued that advertising is supplied jointly with goods and services and hence consumers are forced to pay more for advertising than they want, and are thus 'unwilling accomplices in a waste of resources'. The amount of advertising supplied exceeds that demanded because it is generally provided as a 'free' service to potential buyers, but also to consumers who will never buy the good or service under consideration. Advertisers do not charge a positive price for advertising since any charge would lead to an amount being demanded which is less than that required for advertisers to successfully achieve profit maximisation. The consequence is that there is an oversupply of advertising and a waste of resources which is financed by consumers who are forced to pay a higher price for the advertised goods. This can be shown by considering Figure 7.4.

The supply curve (S) relates the quantity of advertising to the price of advertising (P). The price can be regarded as the price paid to the advertising media by sellers, or as the advertising component of the price paid by consumers of the advertised goods. D_c refers to consumer demand and D_f to seller demand for advertising respectively. Thus Q_c is the quantity that consumers will be willing to pay for. This is at the intersection of D_c and S. However, the actual amount of advertising supplied is Q_f, where $D_f = S$. This is the amount that advertisers regard as necessary to maximise their profits. The excess advertising and consequent waste of resources is the difference between Q_f and Q_c. The price charged at advertising level Q_f is P_f. At this price level consumers are only willing to pay an amount equal to the area OP_fAQ_b, given that they would only demand Q_b at that price level of advertising. Firms will pay for the remainder of the advertising between Q_b and Q_f. This is equal to the area ABQ_fQ_b.

Shepherd (1997, p.324) noted of advertising in the US cereal industry:

> The advertising of cereals absorbs from 10 to 15 per cent of sales and is almost exclusively of the persuasive type. If that spending is regarded as a welfare loss, then this oligopoly causes a waste of many hundreds of millions of dollars per year.

The main criticisms of Kaldor's argument are as follows:

● Consumers have a choice between advertised and non-advertised goods (Telser, 1966b). If consumers did not buy advertised products, there would be no market for advertising.
● By supplying advertising with goods and services, savings may be made. Nelson (1978) argued that to collect fees for the provision of information would be more expensive than direct advertising by firms.
● Kaldor based his views on the underlying assumptions of standard microeconomic theory, where a consumer with given tastes possesses perfect knowledge. Here Kaldor assumed that the consumer knows how to use information efficiently (Koutsoyannis, 1982). In reality, consumers inhabit societies and markets that are by nature dynamic. Assumptions of static equilibrium can be misleading.[8]

The alternative view of advertising forwarded by writers such as Stigler (1961), Telser (1964), Nelson (1974a,b, 1975, 1978) and Littlechild (1982) argued that advertising provides consumers with valuable information which allows them to make rational choices. Under this view, advertising therefore played a crucial role in ensuring the efficient allocation of resources in the economy. Furthermore, the extent to which consumers are able to make informed choices depends on the knowledge and certainty they have about the attributes of a product or service. In a world of uncertainty the variability of possible choices that a consumer makes is likely to be dispersed widely. The more information consumers have, the less dispersed the number of choices a consumer faces. Overall, this means that consumers are unlikely to pay higher prices for one good or service unless 'real' product differences exist. We now turn to a brief discussion of the views forwarded by some of the economists subscribing to the view that advertising is information.

Stigler (1961) argued that if consumers have perfect information as to prices charged for goods and services, then firms would have to charge similar if not identical prices. He argued that consumers conduct a search process in the pursuit of knowledge to make decisions. In doing so the consumer incurs costs in the form of wages or leisure time forgone. However, although each hour of search involves costs, it also brings benefits in the form of increased knowledge as consumers discover the firms offering products at low prices.[9] We can examine the search process within the context of a cost/benefit analysis. This is shown in Figure 7.5.

---

[8] Nichols (1985) and Hoschman and Luski (1988) provide useful extensions to this early work.
[9] Paton (1998), p.59, contended that 'the benefits of consumer search will be positively related to the importance of price in that market'.

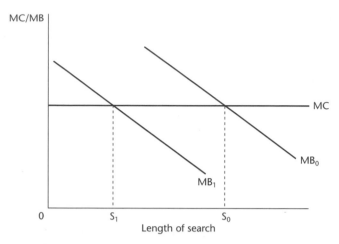

Figure 7.5 The optimal time spent on consumer search

In Figure 7.5, the cost of each additional hour of search is assumed to be constant, and is summarised by the marginal cost function (MC). The benefit to the consumers from each successive hour of search is characterised by a downward sloping marginal benefit function (MB). In other words, the benefits of gathering information on prices decline as the consumer discovers more and more firms selling goods and services at low prices. The process of consumer search is likely to continue for as long as the marginal benefits of the search exceed the marginal costs. In other words, a consumer will continue to collect information as long as the increased knowledge obtained from the search is not outweighed by the costs (in terms of time or resources) used to collect this information. In Figure 7.5, the optimal amount of search is where $MC = MB_0$, at time S_0.

Stigler contended that advertising reduces the costs of obtaining information. In other words, it is easier for the consumer to obtain information on the price and quality of products through advertisements than to engage in a lengthy search process to collect this information independently. He argued (p.182) that:

> Advertising is among other things, a method of providing potential buyers with knowledge of the identity of sellers. It is clearly an immensely powerful instrument for the elimination of ignorance – comparable in force to the use of the book instead of the oral discourse to communicate knowledge.

The more informed consumers are, the more certainty they have when making choices amongst competing products. The provision of information through advertising would have the effect of shifting the marginal benefit function to the left (MB_1), so reducing the optimal length of search time from S_0 to S_1. Given that advertising reduces the search costs of the consumer, the overall prices paid by consumers for products are likely to be lower in industries where advertising is prevalent.

Telser (1964) argued that informative advertising performed the following functions:

- Advertising identifies the existence of sellers. This is particularly important for the development of new products.
- Advertising identifies the key characteristics and attributes of various products and services available to consumers.

● Advertising links the quality of a product to its brand. In other words, only high quality brands will be advertised heavily. This leads the buyer to 'reward' the producer with repeat purchases.[10]

● Advertising plays a useful role in bringing buyers and sellers together by reducing the amount of time and costs that buyers incur searching for available goods and services. This aids in the efficient distribution of resources and leads to higher levels of welfare for the economy.

Overall, Telser argued that in the absence of informative advertising, the rational consumer would have insufficient information to make consumption choices.

Nelson (1974a, p.47) criticised the view that advertising distorts consumer preferences. He contended that: 'consumers are not completely helpless pawns in the hands of greedy businessmen. Though they have far less than perfect information, consumers have far more than zero information'.

Nelson argued that the extent to which advertising provides information crucially depends on whether the goods in question can be classified as search or experience goods.[11] **Search goods** are products which can be inspected by either touch or sight prior to purchase. Common examples include clothes, carpets, household and office furniture. **Experience goods** are generally classified as products which must be consumed in order for an assessment to be made. Common examples include food, mini-discs, CD-ROMs and university courses. Nelson argued that advertising is likely to be informative for search goods given that consumers can easily assess quality and product provider claims prior to purchase. As a consequence, advertising expenditure will be lower for search than for experience goods. Nelson (1974b) found that advertising expenditures on experience goods are likely to be three times those on search goods. However, consumers do have some control over their consumption of experience goods. Nelson (1974a, p.48) argued that:

> Repeat purchases of the brands they like is the major source of control that consumers have over the market for experience goods. However, experimenting with unknown brands is a fairly expensive way for consumers to learn about the qualities of goods. Whenever possible, consumers seek to make their experiments less costly. One of the ways they do this is to choose their experiments guided by the recommendations of relatives and friends or of consumer magazines.

Darby and Karni (1973) introduced the concept of the **credence good**. This is a good whose quality cannot be assessed before or after consumption. They argued that this is likely to be the case when a judgement about quality requires the consumer to have specialised knowledge of the product or service. Common examples would be dental services, medical care and car repair services. Mixon (1995) provided a schematic discussion of search, experience and credence goods.

Some attempts have been made by researchers to assess the informative content of advertising. Resnick and Stern (1977) developed a number of criteria (or cues) to assess

---

[10] Caves and Greene (1996) tested this argument empirically and found that advertising increased with quality for experience goods or new innovative products sold. However, the authors found that this was not the case for convenience products.

[11] Milgrom and Roberts (1986) provide an informative discussion of Nelson's work and some useful extensions.

whether advertising informs consumers. These cues included information on price, quality, performance, component parts or contents, availability, special offers, taste, packaging or shape, guarantees or warranties, safety, nutrition, independent research, company-sponsored research and new ideas. The authors argued that advertisements can be thought of as informative if they included one or more of the aforementioned cues. To test this, the authors assessed 378 advertisements. Of these, only 49.2 per cent were regarded as informative. However, these results are sensitive to any changes in assumptions. They noted (p.52) that: 'If the criterion would have been the communication of three different information cues, only four commercials, or 1% of the total sample, would have been classed as informative.' This conclusion generated a substantial body of research, most of which confirmed the findings of the Resnick and Stern study.

Using data from 60 previous studies, Abernethy and Franke (1996) attempted to synthesise this literature. Analysing a sample of 91,438 advertisements, they find an average number of cues equal to 2.04. The percentage of advertisements found to provide one, two or three information cues were 84, 58 and 33 per cent respectively. Splitting the sample into durable and non-durable goods, the authors found that advertisements for durable goods provided on average 35 per cent more cues than those for non-durable goods. By advertising media, outdoor advertising and TV advertising contained the least amount of information, while magazine and radio provided more information.

In reality, it appears difficult to make a clear distinction between advertising that informs and advertising that persuades. Demsetz (1974a) noted that advertising both informs and persuades consumers as to the desirable aspects of goods and services. Kirzner (1997b, p.57) adds to this when he argued that:

> [T]o interpret advertising effort as primarily designed to persuade consumers to buy what they really do not want, raises an obvious difficulty. It assumes that producers find it more profitable to produce what consumers do not want, and then to persuade them to buy it, with expensive selling campaigns, rather than to produce what consumers do already in fact want (without need for selling effort).

7.6 Advertising and the competitive environment

We have argued that there is a limited role for advertising under conditions of perfect competition. Under monopoly this may also be the case given that the monopolist already faces an inelastic demand curve and so has substantial control over the prices it charges. However, under conditions of oligopoly and monopolistic competition firms may choose to engage in non-price competition through advertising. There is a substantial empirical literature devoted to testing the effects of advertising on the structure (measured by concentration) and performance (measured by profits) of firms and industries. The general hypotheses tested in the literature are that:

● *High levels of advertising lead to increased concentration.* In this case, advertising leads to increased concentration through the operation of economies of scale. In other words, advertising increases the costs of production and the minimum efficient scale of production. This means that firms must be large to reach the minimum efficient scale and to realise economies of scale in production and advertising. This has the effect of increasing industrial concentration in advertising-intensive industries.

- *Advertising increases entry barriers.* Advertising leads to the creation of entry barriers that will affect the profitability of existing firms independently of the level of concentration. In this case, advertising increases advantages to established firms in the form of brand loyalty advantages. These advantages make it difficult for new firms to enter the industry and capture market share.

These two hypotheses imply that there is a positive relationship between advertising and profitability, but only the first implies there is a positive relationship between advertising and concentration. One of the major problems in the empirical analysis of advertising and competition is that expenditures on advertising not only define the structure of the industry but also help explain how firms make strategic decisions.

The traditional view of advertising (subscribed to by writers including Kaldor, 1950; Bain, 1956; Comanor and Wilson, 1967, 1974, 1979) contends that advertising increases the market power and profitability of established firms. This is because advertising increases product differentiation through persuasive messages leading the decreases in the price elasticity of demand. This can often be accompanied by established firms proliferating brands (Monopolies and Mergers Commission, 1966; Schmalensee, 1978).[12] As a consequence, higher levels of industry concentration are likely to ensue, where established firms make high level of profit.

The alternative view (subscribed to by Stigler, 1961; Telser, 1964; Nelson, 1974a,b; Littlechild, 1982; Mixon, 1994) contended that advertising increases competition by providing consumers with more information. This is because advertising has little or no effect on product differentiation, and so leads to increases in the price elasticity of demand. Entry barriers are reduced, leading to declining levels of concentration and profitability.

Most empirical research in this area has examined the relationship between advertising intensity (normally measured by the industry advertising to sales ratio) and the level of concentration, or the correlation between advertising expenditures and profit rates. One of the arguments in favour of advertising is that, unlike other costs, it can stimulate demand and ultimately leads to lower prices by achieving economies of large scale production and distribution. These arguments would have to be examined within the following qualifications:

- Are there methods of stimulating demand other than by advertising? For example, by reducing prices, can firms stimulate demand and benefit from economies of scale?
- Does advertising take place in an industry characterised by potential economies of scale? If no potential economies of scale exist then excessive expenditures on advertising may lead to a misallocation of scarce resources.
- Will any cost savings benefit consumers in the form of lower prices, or will firms exploit their market power by raising prices?

In the analysis of the effects of advertising on competition, entry barriers play a crucial role. It is a common argument that advertising simply increases the barriers to entry by increasing the minimum efficient scale of production for firms operating in an industry. Therefore, any gain in realising economies from increased demand emanating from increased advertising may be offset by the raising of entry barriers. Advertising can act as a barrier to entry in several ways:

---

[12] This is discussed in more detail in Case study 7.2 at the end of this chapter.

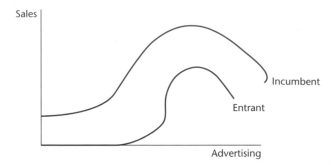

Figure 7.6 Sales response to advertising

- *Advertising increases the costs of production.* Entrants have to spend heavily on advertising and other promotions to gain a foothold in the market. As a consequence, entrants face additional costs to entering the industry. Furthermore, entrants may find it difficult to raise the necessary funds for entry, given that the returns to advertising outlays are likely to be uncertain (Weiss, 1963).
- *High levels of advertising build up the reputation.* Advertising leads to goodwill advantages and brand loyalty for established firms. This is often difficult for entrants to overcome, especially if established firms follow a strategy of proliferating brands (Schmalensee, 1972). Empirical evidence suggests that if the established firm was the first firm to pioneer a product in the market, brand loyalty will be high and any new entrant will find it difficult to capture market share.[13]
- *Advertising increases demand.* Advertising leads to increased demand for an individual firm's product. This in turn may lead to economies of scale for established firms. Scherer and Ross (1990) argued that economies of scale in advertising arise for two reasons. Firstly, firms must advertise a large number of times before the signals from advertising reach consumers and feed back into higher sales and profits for the firms. Secondly, as the firm's messages are passed throughout the economy either by increased advertising or by word of mouth, consumers will respond to these messages by increasing demand. As a consequence, economies of scale arise because increased numbers of advertising messages become more effective as they increase in frequency. In addition, large advertisers pay less per unit of sales than the small-scale advertiser. The responsiveness of a firm's sales to advertising can be illustrated via Figure 7.6.

The effectiveness of advertising may be greater the larger the firm. This could be because larger firms are better known than smaller firms, and their brands may already be familiar to consumers. Therefore, only relatively small amounts of advertising are required to maintain consumer awareness. Evidence suggests that the response of a firm's sales to advertising follows a sigmoid curve (as shown in Figure 7.6). At zero levels of advertising an established

---

[13] Robinson *et al.* (1994) provide an extensive survey covering the advantages of being the first firm to pioneer a product or brand. They noted that the evidence suggests that pioneering firms shape consumer tastes towards pioneering products or brands. To ensure brand loyalty, pioneering firms often adopt strategies of brand proliferation. As a consequence, entrants are unlikely to gain substantial market share at the expense of the pioneering firm. For further discussion, see Glazer (1985).

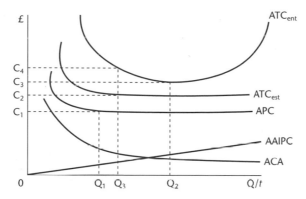

Figure 7.7 Advertising as an entry barrier

firm will have some level of sales. These sales are the result of brand loyalty advantages that have been built up by the firm in the past. As the firm increases its advertising expenditures, the responsiveness of sales increases slowly at first, but then speeds up as more consumers become aware of the product. After a point, the sales response slows down as the number of consumers that have yet to buy the product declines. Eventually, the expenditures on advertising a product will reach a saturation point, beyond which further advertising leads to falling sales. The experience of an entrant to the market is similar, except that in the absence of advertising the entrant has no sales. This is because consumers are unaware of the new product and the firm has not built up any loyalty or reputation advantages over time. As a consequence, an entrant may have to spend a large amount on promoting the product before any sales take place. After this point the entrant's response function will follow a similar path to that of the established firm. Stigler (1968, p.187) noted: '"Reputation" is a word which denotes the persistence of quality, and reputation commands a price (or exacts a penalty) because it economizes on search.'

Furthermore, firms making substantial investment in advertising are likely to be able to spread advertising over larger and larger ranges of output. Any firm wishing to enter the industry will have to spend proportionately more on advertising to overcome brand loyalty and penetrate the market. Any entrant not wanting to face a substantial cost disadvantage (assuming that average cost curves are not flat) from entering at a suboptimal scale will be deterred from entry (Comanor and Wilson, 1967, 1974).[14] Advertising as an entry barrier is shown in Figure 7.7.

The figure shows the costs of production for established firms and entrants. Average costs of production in the absence of advertising for established and entrant firms are shown by the curve APC. In the absence of advertising the minimum efficient scale of production is at Q_1. Average cost of production at this output is equal to C_1. However, if advertising takes place (shown by ACA), the cost of production increases from APC to ATC. The average cost for established firms, ATC_{est} (= APC + ACA), is lower than that of entrants whose average costs are equal to ATC_{ent} (= APC + ACA + AAIPC). The difference between the established firms' and entrants' costs is AAIPC which represents the extra costs entrants incur in trying

---

[14] This is discussed more fully in Chapter 5 on barriers to entry.

to penetrate the market. The minimum efficient scale in an industry where advertising is prevalent is Q_2. As a consequence the average costs are C_2 for established firms and C_3 for entrants. The entrant therefore suffers a cost disadvantage. This cost disadvantage will be even higher if the entrant chooses to enter at a suboptimal scale such as output level Q_3, where average costs of production would increase to C_4. The cost advantages enjoyed by established firms may even allow them to set a limit price to make entry unprofitable to any potential entrant.[15]

Overall, advertising can increase economies of scale and entry barriers and provide established firms with some degree of market power. The importance of advertising as a barrier to entry is disputed by King (1983). King used the specific example of the processed cheese industry to illustrate his argument. In this market, cheese slices produced by Kraft Foods Limited held the dominant position from 1971 to 1975. However, during this time, expenditures on advertising were low. In 1976, Kraft doubled expenditures on advertising, yet several new brands successfully entered the market. King argued that costs of plant and machinery are much more likely to present a substantial barrier to entry than is advertising *per se*.

The theoretical and empirical evidence underlying the relationship between advertising and market structure and performance can now be examined bearing in mind the importance of advertising as a barrier to entry.

Advertising and concentration

Theory
Needham (1978) proposed two alternative and conflicting hypotheses to explain possible relationships between advertising intensity and concentration. These were:

● Increased concentration among sellers leads to a greater recognition of their interdependence. Consequently firms may decide to tacitly co-operate by eliminating competitive advertising. Therefore increased concentration leads to a reduction in advertising.
● Increased concentration and recognition of interdependence also leads to recognition of the damaging nature of price competition. This encourages sellers to substitute non-price forms of competition (including advertising) for price competition. Therefore increased concentration leads to a reduction in advertising.

To develop a framework for these hypotheses, Needham made use of the following expressions:

$$\frac{A}{S} = \frac{E_a}{E_d} \tag{1}$$

$$E_a = E_A + E_{CONJ.} \times E_{AR} \tag{2}$$

$$E_d = \left(\frac{E_m}{S_f}\right)\left(\frac{E_s S_r}{S_f}\right) \tag{3}$$

[15] Strategies involving limit pricing are discussed in Chapter 5.

where A/S is the advertising to sales ratio for the profit maximising firms, and

$$E_a = \frac{\text{proportionate change in quantity demanded}}{\text{proportionate change in advertising}}$$

$$E_A = \frac{\text{proportionate change in demand for a firm's product}}{\text{proportionate change in a firm's advertising}}$$

$$E_{CONJ.} = \frac{\text{proportionate change in rival's advertising}}{\text{proportionate change in firm's own advertising}}$$

$$E_{AR} = \frac{\text{proportionate change in demand for a firm's product}}{\text{proportionate change in rival's advertising}}$$

Equation (1) is known as the Dorfman–Steiner condition.[16] The Dorfman–Steiner condition shows that the advertising to sales ratio of a profit maximising firm depends on the ratio of advertising elasticity of demand to price elasticity of demand (E_a/E_d). Intuitively, the optimal A/S is positively related to E_a, because if E_a is high advertising is highly effective, so it pays the firm to advertise. But A/S is negatively related to E_d, because if E_d is high the firm can easily increase its sales revenue simply by cutting price, rather than by spending heavily on advertising.

In Equations (2) and (3) F_a and E_d are decomposed in order to examine the effects of rivals' actions on the advertising and demand elasticities, and therefore on the optimal A/S.

Equation (2) shows that the profit maximising advertising to sales ratio depends on consumer buyer behaviour and on the behaviour of rival firms. If rivals do not change the level of their advertising when firm i increases its advertising expenditure ($E_{CONJ.} - 0$) the effect on demand for the firm's product depends only on E_A. If rivals respond by increasing advertising ($E_{CONJ.} > 0$), the impact of the second term on the right hand side of (2) on the firm's demand is negative (because E_{AR} is negative). In an extreme case, the second term on the right hand side of (2) could outweigh the first term, in which case an increase in the firm's advertising expenditure could reduce its demand as a result of rivals also increasing their advertising expenditure.

In Equation (3), E_d is the price elasticity of demand for the firm's product, E_m is the price elasticity of total market demand, E_s is the elasticity of supply of rival's output with respect to a change in the firm's price, i.e.

$$E_s = \frac{\text{proportionate change in rival's output}}{\text{proportionate change in firm's price}}$$

S_f and S_r are the market shares of the firm and its rivals. Thus advertising depends not only on rivals' reactions to changes in advertising, but also changes in price. Thus if rivals react not by changing the level of advertising, but by changing their product prices, this action may also affect the level of advertising for the profit maximising firm.

Equation (2) illustrates the first hypothesis, that as concentration rises, firms will recognise their mutual interdependence and thus reduce competitive advertising. In other words, as

---

[16] Developed by Dorfman and Steiner (1954).

concentration increases, $E_{CONJ.}$ will change, thus leading to a fall in the A/S ratio. This will occur if $E_{CONJ.}$ is positive at low levels of concentration, but at some higher, critical level of concentration $E_{CONJ.}$ becomes negative, i.e. rivals will start to reduce their level of advertising. Needham argues that some degree of collusion would be necessary for this outcome to occur.

Equation (3) serves to explain the second hypothesis, that firms will substitute non-price competition (advertising) for price competition at higher levels of concentration. Here one would assume E_s to be negative, and to increase as concentration increases (ceteris paribus). This would lead to a decrease in E_d and therefore to an increase in the optimal A/S ratio as concentration increases. It is assumed that E_a remains constant.[17]

Empirical evidence

Most analysis of advertising and concentration has examined the association between advertising intensity and some measure of concentration.

Telser (1964) stated that if advertising leads to firms exercising market power, then advertising and concentration should be positively related. He took a sample of 42 three-digit consumer goods industries for the years 1947, 1954 and 1958 and calculated advertising to sales ratios for each industry. These ratios were correlated with concentration ratios for each industry. He found a positive but insignificant relationship between advertising expenditures and concentration.

Mann *et al.* (1967) carried out a similar analysis using four-digit industry-level data. This was done because the four-digit industry definition was closer to the theoretical concept of the market. The study used 42 firms, divided into fourteen, four-digit industries. The average advertising to sales ratio for the various firms (the dominant firms in the industry) was calculated for the three periods, 1952 to 1956, 1957 to 1961 and 1962 to 1965. The data were assumed to represent the industry at the four-digit level. These were used to examine whether advertising to sales ratios were correlated with the concentration ratios. A significant positive association was found in all three periods. These findings refuted Telser's conclusions, and instead suggested that advertising intensity is positively related to concentration.

Many later studies of advertising and concentration tested for non-linear relationships. Here it is assumed that there is an inverted U-shaped relationship between advertising and concentration as is shown in Figure 7.8.

The assumption in Figure 7.8 is that firms operating under oligopoly will tend to compete on a non-price basis, and so spend proportionately more on advertising than do monopolists or firms operating under conditions perfect competition. The general equation tested is of the form:

$$\frac{A}{S_i} = \alpha_0 + \beta_1 CR_i + \beta_2 CR_i^2 + u_i$$

where the dependent variable A/S_i is the industry advertising expenditure to sales ratio. The independent variables include CR_i and CR_i^2. CR_i is the concentration ratio in a particular industry, while CR_i^2 is the square of CR_i and is included to capture any non-linear

---

[17] It is possible to analyse the model in terms of changes in both E_d and E_a. If both varied proportionately, there would be no effect on the A/S ratio. Needham (1978), p.140 discusses several possibilities.

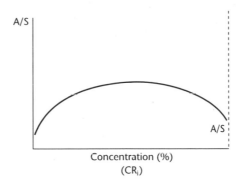

Figure 7.8 Advertising and concentration

relationship between concentration (CR_i) and advertising intensity (A/S_i). Finally, u_i is an error term to capture any determinants of advertising intensity not captured by the independent variables included in the equation.

In the UK, Sutton (1974) used data on 25 consumer goods industries and found a significant positive relationship between A/S_i and CR_i^2, implying an inverted U-shaped relationship between advertising intensities and concentration. Research carried out by Cable (1972) and Buxton *et al.* (1984) found a similar relationship between advertising and concentration. Taken together, these findings lend some support to the view that advertising will be higher under oligopolies than any other type of market structure. However, Reekie (1975) and Rees (1975) used similar data of UK industries and found no significant relationship between A/S_i and CR_i^2.

In the United States, research by Ornstein (1978) found a positive linear relationship between CR_i and A/S_i. In other words, advertising intensity rose with industry concentration. However, no relationship was found between A/S_i and CR_i^2. Later research by Weiss *et al.* (1983) and Uri (1987) did find strong evidence of an inverted U-shaped relationship between advertising and concentration.

Lambin (1976) examined the relationship between advertising intensity and a number of variables including price elasticity of demand and concentration for a sample of 16 product groups covering over 100 brands across eight countries over the period 1960 to 1970. He found (p.147) that: 'no systematic association is observed between market concentration and advertising intensity'. However, he does find (also p.147) that 'Advertising increases the capacity of the firm to charge higher prices to the consumer.'

Overall, the empirical evidence examined suggests that advertising intensity is much higher under oligopolies than perfect competition and monopoly.

Advertising and profitability

As discussed previously, many authors contend that advertising creates a barrier to entry. As a consequence of such barriers, established firms can exercise market power to increase profits. Comanor and Wilson (1967) used US data on 42 consumer goods industries covering the period 1954 to 1957 and found a positive relationship between the advertising to sales ratio and profitability. Similar findings using different data sets were made by Miller (1969) and Weiss (1969).

Using firm-level profits, Vernon and Nourse (1973) tested whether there was any relationship between profits and advertising to sales ratio measured at the firm and industry levels. The authors found a positive significant relationship between profit rates and industry-level advertising to sales ratios. They claimed that these results showed that advertising can be regarded as an entry barrier.

Bloch (1974) argued that the above studies are flawed as they treat advertising expenditures as a current expense. He suggested that advertising should be treated as a capital expenditure and depreciated accordingly. Using data adjusted to reflect advertising as a capital expense, he found for a sample of 97 US industries that there was no longer a relationship between advertising and profits.[18]

Ravenscraft (1983) used US 'line of business data' for 3,186 lines of business drawn from 258 industry categories. He found no relationship between advertising expenditures and profitability. More recently, Paton and Vaughan Williams (1999) found a positive relationship between advertising expenditures and current and future profitability.

Overall, the relationship between advertising and profitability is somewhat inconclusive. The precise relationship found appears to depend on the sample used or how the dependent and independent variables are measured. We discuss these issues in more detail below.

More recently, researchers have examined the link between market share and advertising. The main hypothesis tested is that if advertising promotes competition then the market shares of the top firms should be unstable, while if advertising restricts competition then the opposite applies. A good example of this research is by Eckard (1987), who examined the relationship between advertising intensity and the combined market shares of the four largest firms in 228 manufacturing industries in 1963, 1967, 1972, 1977 and 1982. He found that, as advertising increases, the market shares of the top firms became unstable. In other words, the ranking of firms by market share tends to change over time. He argued that this implies support for the view that advertising promotes competition. Das *et al.* (1993) found similar results for a sample of 163 US industries for the period 1978 to 1988. They concluded (p.1412) that:

> While our results cannot be interpreted to mean that advertising is not ever used anti-competitively, the empirical findings suggest that advertising and promotional activities on balance work to increase the competitiveness of markets across a large set of industries over an extended period of time.

Several problems arise when attempting to interpret the results of studies which test the links between advertising intensity and market share and profitability:

● *Measurement of the advertising to sales ratio.* The advertising to sales ratios used in most empirical studies are likely to be prone to measurement error. Lambin (1976) noted the following two problems. Firstly, if a firm actively pursued a strategy of promotional techniques other than advertising, the correlation between concentration, profitability and advertising may be biased. Lambin (p.13) noted that: 'Advertising sales ratios do not take into consideration the differences that may exist among firms in other marketing variables such as price differentials, frequent changes in design, high rate of new products, size of sales force etc.'

---

[18] Paton (1998) and Paton and Vaughan Williams (1999) provide an extended discussion of this point.

Secondly, if a firm is diversified it is often difficult to assess from company accounts on which parts of the business the firm is spending heavily on advertising. Lambin (1976, p.13) noted that: 'Advertising sales ratios are totals for each enterprise and do not consider whether a firm advertised different products with different intensity or advertised one product with different intensity in different segments of its market.' A study by Ravenscraft (1983) overcame this problem by using data at the line of business level.

- *Advertising and profits: the direction of correlation.* It is often difficult to determine the direction of correlation between advertising and profits. Two points are important here. Firstly, does advertising lead to greater profitability, or do profitable firms advertise more (Vernon and Nourse, 1973)? Secondly, advertising may be a useful way for firms to affect their reported profit levels. In some cases, high profits can be dissipated by spending heavily on advertising. By following such a strategy a firm can increase the awareness of its product while reducing its tax liability. If this is the case, then any results derived from the (non) correlation of advertising intensity with profitability are likely to be biased.
- *Statistical problems.* Miller (1969) argued that, in large industries, various measures of size such as sales, assets and employment are often correlated strongly. These measures are used in the denominator of the advertising, concentration and profits measures. Therefore, to carry out regression analysis of profit rates on advertising to sales ratios may cause some bias.

From the theoretical and empirical evidence reviewed above, it is unclear whether advertising reduces competition by increasing the barriers to entering an industry or leads to economies of scale advantages which are passed on to consumers in the form of lower prices. This has led some researchers to examine explicitly the relationship between advertising and prices charged for goods and services.

7.7 Advertising and prices

We saw in section 7.4 that the extent of information available to consumers can affect the quality and prices of goods and services in a given market. One view of the effect of advertising on prices is based on the notion of informative advertising, and has its roots in the writings of Stigler (1961). An informed consumer is better able to select products at a lower price for given levels of quality. Advertising reduces consumer ignorance and increases the price elasticity of demand. The traditional view is that prices of advertised goods will be higher than those of non-advertised goods owing to the higher selling costs. It is also argued that advertising will *decrease* the price elasticity of demand which will lead to price rises.

The defence of higher prices of advertised goods can be mounted along three fronts:

- The higher-priced advertised good reflects a better quality product with a much smaller variability in that quality (Davis *et al.*, 1991). For example, Coca-Cola versus Tesco Cola.
- High prices reflect part of the search costs saved by the consumer (Nelson, 1975).
- Producers/retailers who market generic or own-brand products at a lower price are simply exploiting the information spread by the advertised goods. They are in essence free-riders (Porter, 1976).

Using evidence from manufacturing, service and distribution industries, this section examines the relationship between advertising and price. The majority of research compares the level and dispersion of prices between industries or market segments where advertising restrictions are imposed and those where there is no restriction. Some selected studies based at a general level are first discussed. This is followed by examples of studies carried out in particular industries.

General studies

Kaul and Wittink (1995) surveyed eighteen studies covering a twenty-year period that had examined the relationship between the extent of advertising and price in producer and consumer goods industries. From these studies the authors formulated three empirical generalisations: (1) an increase in price advertising increased consumer sensitivity (i.e. price elasticity of demand) to price changes; (2) an increase in price advertising leads to intensified competition and results in firms charging lower prices; and (3) an increase in non-price advertising decreased consumer sensitivity to price changes.

Paton (1998) using a sample of UK manufacturing, service and distribution firms assessed the extent to which advertisements incorporate information on product and service prices. Paton surveyed over 1,000 firms to obtain a usable sample of 325 firms. Taking the entire sample, Paton found that 70 per cent of firms included no price information in their advertisements. By sector, he further found that advertising price information is much more common for distribution firms than for their counterparts in manufacturing and services. This price advertising was much more common when consumers were the end-users of a product or service.

Spectacles and optometry services

Benham (1972) examined the differences in the prices paid by consumers for spectacles (eyeglasses) in US states where advertising restrictions exist and those where they do not. Using data based on a national sample of 634 consumers, he compared the prices of glasses in various states. The estimated model is:

$$P_i = \alpha + \beta_1 x_{li} + \sum_{j=2}^{5} \beta_j x_{ji} + u_i$$

where the dependent variable is the price of glasses to an individual consumer, P_i. The independent variables included are x_{li} which is a variable based on whether glasses were purchased in a state with prohibitive advertising or not, and x_{ji} which is a group of variables to control for differences in income, age, sex and family size across states.

In Benham's model the main parameter of interest is β_1, which denotes the difference in price paid between states which prohibit advertising and those which do not. Benham found that spectacles were more expensive in states where advertising is restricted, the difference in the average price being US$6.70. However, the difference in price between the most and least restrictive states was found to be US$19.50. Benham (p.349) contended that:

> The results presented above are consistent with the hypothesis that in the market examined, advertising improves consumer knowledge and that the benefits derived from this knowledge outweigh the price-increasing effects of advertising.

Mackintosh and Frey (1978) examined the dispersion of prices for spectacles in New Orleans and Louisiana where advertising restrictions were prevalent. Using a sample of fifteen dispensers of glasses, the authors examined the differences in price for three types of lens (based on three types of sight deficiency) and two types of frame. Three volunteers visited each of the fifteen dispensers.

Overall, the authors found significant differences in prices due to a lack of price transparency. In other words, consumers did not have enough knowledge to know whether they were receiving a good deal or not. They argued that if advertising restrictions were removed then these price differences would decline.

Maurizi *et al.* (1981) examined the effects of the removal of advertising restrictions in the spectacles market of California. They found no difference in the prices of glasses from opticians who advertised and those who did not. However, those opticians who advertised contact lenses were on average 17 per cent cheaper than their counterparts who did not advertise.

Legal services

Cox (1982) examined the relationship between advertising and the price of legal services in six US states in 1978. He grouped these states as to whether advertising regulations are restrictive (Alabama and Mississippi), moderate (Arizona and Indiana) or permissive (California and Wisconsin). The sample consisted of 250 lawyers drawn from each of the six states. Cox found that lawyers operating in states with permissive advertising regulation were eleven times more likely to advertise than their counterparts operating under restrictive regimes.

Cox tested the following model:

$$P_{ijk} = \alpha + \beta_1 \text{ADVINT}_j + \beta_2 \text{RYCAP}_j + \beta_3 \log(\text{SIZE})_{ij} + \beta_4 \log(\text{YRSEXP})_{ij} + \beta_5 \log(\text{HRS})_{ijk} + e_{ijk}$$

where the dependent variable P_{ijk} denotes the price of an individual lawyer in a certain geographical area who will perform a particular type of service. The independent variable ADVINT_j is the extent to which a lawyer uses advertising in a geographical area; RYCAP_j denotes real income per person in a geographical area (this variable was used to proxy for differences in demand conditions across markets); $\log(\text{SIZE})_{ij}$ is the number of lawyers in the law firm located in a geographical area; $\log(\text{YRSEXP})_{ij}$ measures the years of experience that an individual lawyer has in a geographical area (this variable was included to capture reputation effects and goodwill which may have been built up over time); $\log(\text{HRS})_{ijk}$ is the number of hours an individual lawyer in a particular geographical area would take to perform a certain service (this variable was included to control for efficiency differences across legal practices); and e_{ijk} is an error term to capture any variables which affect prices of legal services but which are not included in the model.

Cox found a negative relationship between P_{ijk} and ADVINT_j, lending some support to the 'advertising as information' view. In other words, higher advertising leads to lower prices. Uncontested bankruptcies were found to be on average US$47 more expensive where advertising restrictions were in force, while divorces were on average US$16 cheaper. Prices were found to be higher where legal firms were large, reputation was deemed important and firms were less efficient.

Cox *et al.* (1982) examined the prices of homogeneous legal services after lawyers were allowed to advertise information on services offered. Approximately two hundred lawyers were surveyed either by mail or in person, and asked for prices charged for certain services. Questions were asked to ascertain whether the lawyer performed the service, how long it would take to carry out the service, whether or not this service involved a flat fee, and the amount of the fee or hourly rate.

The authors found a large variation in the prices charged for certain types of legal service, which they argued implies a high degree of consumer ignorance in the market for legal services. However, they did find that the level and dispersion of price was much lower in cases where lawyers advertise their legal services, thus providing some support for the view that advertising helps consumers to make more informed choices.

Schroeter *et al.* (1987), using data on fees and advertising practices of lawyers from seventeen US states, examined the effects of advertising on individual legal firm demand elasticities. The authors assessed whether advertising provides information (in which case demand should become more elastic) or alters consumers' preference functions (in which case demand should become more inelastic). They tested the following model:

$$\varepsilon_{ij} = f(\text{OWNAD}_{ij}, \text{MARAD}_j, Z_{ij})$$

where the dependent variable ε_{ij} is the price elasticity of demand for an individual lawyer in a specific market. The independent variable OWNAD_{ij} is the level of advertising intensity of an individual lawyer in a specific market, MARAD_j is industry-level advertising expenditure in a specific market, and, Z_{ij} is a group of variables that control for other differences between the location of and income levels in particular markets. The authors found that increased levels of advertising expenditure led to legal firms experiencing more elastic demand curves. They argued (p.59) that: 'the trend over the past decade toward fewer restrictions on seller advertising in professional services markets would appear to be a very favourable one, at least as far as consumers are concerned.'

Drawing on the findings of Cox and others, Stephen (1994) estimated the following model for a sample of 275 legal firms in Scotland:

$$P_{ij} = \alpha + \beta_1 \log(\text{SIZE})_j + \beta_2 \log(\text{BRANCH})_j + \beta_3 \log(\text{UNEMP})_i + \beta_4 \log(\text{HERF})_i + \beta_5 \text{ADV} + e_{ij}$$

where the dependent variable P_{ij} is the price elasticity of demand in a specific market for an individual firm. Log(SIZE)$_j$ measures the size of an individual firm; log(BRANCH)$_j$ is the number of offices operated by an individual firm; log(UNEMP)$_i$ is the unemployment rate in a particular geographical area; log(HERF)$_i$ is the concentration of firms in a geographical area; ADV is a variable which captures whether the firm advertises or not; and e_{ij} is the error term to capture any determinants of price elasticity of demand not included amongst the independent variables.

Stephen found a negative relationship between ADV and P_{ij}, implying that firms that advertise face more elastic demand curves than those who do not. This provided some support for the advertising as information view. Log(SIZE)$_j$ and log(HERF)$_i$ are positive and significant, while log(BRANCH)$_j$ and log(UNEMP)$_i$ are found to be significantly negative.

Medicines

Cady (1976) examined the impact of restrictions on advertising on prices in the retail drug market. Cady contended that prices are likely not only to be higher in markets where advertising is restricted, but also to be more dispersed.

The sample comprised data compiled on ten common products from a national survey of 1,900 US retail pharmacies. Cady found a greater variation in prices where advertising was restricted. To examine the relationship between the price level and the extent of advertising, the following model was estimated:

$$P_{ij} = f(E_j, S_j, O_j, R_j)$$

where the dependent variable P_{ij} denotes the price of an individual drug from a particular pharmacy. The independent variable E_j captures the environmental aspects (such as location, population, average income levels) of the area where a particular pharmacy is located, S_j the structural characteristics of an individual pharmacy, O_j the organisational characteristics of an individual pharmacy, and R_j whether restrictions on advertising exist or not in the area in which an individual pharmacy is located.

Cady found that pharmacies located in states where advertising restrictions were prevalent charged between 2 per cent and 9 per cent more for prescription medicines than their counterparts operating in unrestricted states. Cady estimated that consumers could have saved a total of US $150 million on prescription drugs if no advertising restrictions existed. He concluded (p.29) that:

> advertising can act as a significant stimulus to market competition through the provision of salient, useful information. To ignore this effect and to view all advertising as abusive, deceptive, and contributing to imperfect market conditions is potentially detrimental to consumer welfare.

Physician services

Rizzo and Zeckhauser (1992) examined the impact of advertising on the price of physician services using data from the American Medical Association between 1987 and 1988. They estimated the following equation:

$$\ln P_i = \alpha_1 + \beta_1 X_i + \beta_2 \ln(DOCPOP_i) + \beta_3 ADVERT + \varepsilon_i$$

where the dependent variable $\ln P_i$ is the price charged by an individual physician (expressed as a natural log). Variable $\ln(DOCPOP_i)$ denotes the number of physicians in a geographical area, and $ADVERT_i$ captures whether an individual physician advertises or not.

Initial estimations revealed that advertising appeared to lower the price of physician services. However, the authors found that after controlling for sample selection bias and measurement errors in the advertising variable, the price of physician services increased.

On balance the evidence suggests that advertising appears to reduce the variability and level of prices across several service industries. The empirical evidence examined for several service industries tends to suggest that advertising aids consumer search, and enables consumers to make more informed choices.[19] However, some evidence suggests that the price information contained in advertisements produced by service sector firms is often low (Paton, 1998; Paton and Vaughan Williams, 1999).

---

[19] Love and Stephen (1996) provide a useful survey that examines the relationships between advertising, prices and quality.

7.8 Conclusions

This chapter has examined the role of advertising in the economy. Advertising can provide useful information on product attributes allowing consumers to make more informed choices. However, it can also lead to a waste of resources and a subsequent loss in consumer welfare if it is excessive and aimed at altering consumer preferences. The competitive process is crucially affected by levels of advertising. Many studies have found that the intensity of advertising is often determined by the type of industry structure examined. Some evidence has suggested that the relationship between advertising and concentration is a positive one, while others have argued that the relationship follows an inverted U-shape, where advertising is typically found to be higher in oligopolistic market structures.

The relationship between advertising and profitability is somewhat unclear owing to problems in measurement and treatment of advertising. More recent evidence suggests that increased advertising leads to increased competition which causes instability in firm market shares.

The effects of advertising on competition were also examined with reference to price levels and advertising. The general view in many of the industries examined is that advertising leads to increased price elasticity of demand through more informed consumers and entry of new firms which causes the price of advertised goods to be lower than that of identical non-advertised goods. This lends some support to the view that advertising provides information. However, this support is by no means universal (Paton, 1998).

Key terms

Advertising intensity
Credence goods
Experience goods

Monopolistic competition
Product differentiation
Search goods

Case study 7.1
Responsiveness of sales to advertising for a new product

The responsiveness of sales to advertising expenditures has stimulated much research over the years. For example, a study by Palda (1964) examined the relationship between advertising and sales revenue over the period 1908 to 1960 for a US medicine company. He found a positive non-linear relationship. Lambin (1976) presented similar findings for a product produced by a Belgian food company. More recently, Holstius (1990) used Finnish data for the 1980s for a 'frequently purchased low priced product' and found a positive correlation coefficient equal to 0.44 between advertising expenditures and increased sales.[1]

An interesting study of the responsiveness of sales to changes in advertising was carried out by Croome and Horsfall (1983) of Leo Burnett Limited. The authors examined the role of advertising expenditures in the successful launch of the *Super Noodles* product by Kellogg's.

[1] Other important research on this topic can be found in Borden (1942), Vidale and Wolfe (1957) and Krugman (1965).

The product at the time was unique, which meant that it had no close substitutes. However, the product was marketed as an alternative to rice, potatoes and pasta. The only branded rival was an instant potato mixture *Smash* produced by Cadbury.

Croome and Horsfall examined the effectiveness of various types of advertising on the sales of *Super Noodles*. Over the period 1979 to 1982, the authors estimated the following econometric model:

$$s_t = \beta_1 ADV + \beta_2 DIST + \beta_3 PRICE + D$$

In the model the sales of Kellogg's *Super Noodles*, s_t, depends on advertising expenditures ADV, level of distribution support DIST, price, and a rate of sales decay variable, D which captures the extent to which sales decay in the absence of advertising.

Expenditure on advertising explained over 80 per cent of the variation in *Super Noodle* sales. Price and distribution support were found to be relatively unimportant. The authors found, however, that any increased sales arising from advertising were relatively short-lived and were dissipated after five weeks. Overall, the expenditures on advertising established Kellogg's *Super Noodles* as a brand name.

Case study 7.2
Advertising and competition in household detergents

The extent to which advertising promotes or inhibits competition has sometimes been of interest to the competition authorities. In 1966, in one of the first cases of its kind, the Monopolies and Mergers Commission investigated competition in the household detergents market. The investigation was prompted when it was found that the two leading suppliers (Unilever and Procter & Gamble) accounted for 98 per cent of the sales in the market. The Commission was particularly interested in claims that the excessive expenditures on advertising and promotion, and the large numbers of brands offered by the leading firms were inhibiting competition.

The Commission criticised the nature of competition in the industry on several counts. These were that:

● Advertising of detergent products appeared to be concerned only with building brand image, and did not inform consumers about the factual attributes of the products.
● Excessive advertising was taking place for many similar products under different brand names. This was a waste of resources. As a consequence, consumers were paying indirectly for this excessive advertising without receiving any real benefit. In other words, prices were higher than they would have been in the absence of advertising.
● So-called new, improved products which were introduced by both firms did not alter substantially the quality of the products.
● The large numbers of similar brands offered and expenditures on advertising by the established firms raised the capital requirements to entering the industry. This made it difficult for new firms to raise finance to enter the industry and overcome the reputation advantages held by the established firms. The large number of similar products offered also made it difficult for new firms to find a market niche in which to sell their products.

The two firms argued that high levels of advertising were necessary to inform consumers of the factual attributes of products, promote brand image, and to stimulate demand to realise economies of scale in production which would ultimately lead to greater efficiency. This they argued would lead to benefits for consumers and retailers. The leading firms further argued that if the expenditures on advertising were excessive, then this would have left these established firms at a cost disadvantage to potential entry of new firms.

The Commission rejected the arguments of the two firms, given that advertising and promotion expenditures were excessive, but entry of new firms was still not taking place. The investigation recommended that both firms should reduce the prices of their products and that the two companies should reduce their expenditures on advertising and promotion by 40 per cent.

Case study 7.3
Advertising and prices: the case of UK opticians

In the early 1980s, significant advertising restrictions existed in the market for spectacles in the UK. Only limited advertising took place, confined mainly to yellow pages and reference sections of libraries. In 1982, the Office of Fair Trading conducted a survey of prices charged by opticians in the Greater London area. Researchers visited a substantial number of opticians between June and August 1982 to gain quotes on six types of prescription.

The study found a substantial variation in the prices charged for the same prescriptions. The survey contended that: 'substantial cost savings in the price of spectacles would be possible if consumers were to shop around for them.'[1]

The investigation compared these findings with prices charged for cameras where advertising was permitted. The OFT study found that the results obtained for cameras:

> show a much narrower range of prices than in the case of spectacles, supporting the contention that in a market where advertising is allowed, the better information available to consumers will increase the effectiveness of competition and bring about greater similarity in prices.[2]

Overall, the investigation recommended fewer restrictions on advertising and other forms of promotional activity for opticians.[3] In 1985, many restrictions on advertising were removed, leading to an average fall of 20 per cent in the price of spectacles.

Case study 7.4
Information and consumer welfare

Much of the discussion relating to the economics of advertising focuses on the role of advertising in providing information to consumers to enable them to make informed choices. In 1997, the Office of Fair Trading commissioned London Economics to examine the effects of imperfect information on consumer welfare.

[1] Office of Fair Trading (1982), p.119.
[2] Ibid.
[3] Studies by Benham and Benham (1975) and Kwoka (1984) produced similar findings for investigations of opticians in the United States.

Three measures were constructed to denote the level of information. They were R, A, and T:

- R denotes a set of rational beliefs the consumer has prior to making a purchase of a good or service. This is arrived at through a search process which involves the consumer making comparisons with previous purchases, conducting conversations with peer groups, and receiving and evaluating advertising messages from firms.
- A denotes the set of beliefs the consumer has at the time of purchasing the good or service. In a world of perfect information, R = A. In reality, consumers may not have perfect information even after consuming goods (as is often the case with credence goods).
- T denotes all possible available information about goods and services. It is likely that suppliers of products will have more information than buyers, and could even give false information to keep it that way. False information is more likely to arise when consumers cannot assess products prior to purchase (experience goods) or after purchase (credence goods). The study argued that losses to consumer welfare may occur if R ≠ T and A ≠ R.

Using this as a theoretical base, the study identified six indicators to assess markets where imperfect information is a problem. These were as follows:

- Where prices are dispersed for identical products. This would imply that the search procedures used by consumers are not sufficient to identify lowest priced goods and services.
- Where focal points of competition exist such as similar price or non-price strategies. For example, in 1994 the OFT had found that, in the photocopying industry, price per copy was the focal point for competition between firms.[1] These practices provide indirect evidence of tacit collusion between firms.[2]
- Where goods and services are combined or involve primary and secondary purchases. This would be prevalent in industries where warranties and after-sales services were part of a bundle of goods. Markets where goods may involve secondary purchases include contact lenses and solutions, and photocopiers and toner.
- Where commission payments are paid by firms to retailers. This may result in retailers selling inappropriate products. As a consequence, consumers pay more than is necessary for goods and services, or buy poor quality goods and services.
- Where goods and services are complex. This type of good or service requires the consumer to have specialised knowledge. Examples include health services, financial services and electronic products.
- Where goods can be characterised as credence goods (for example dental services) or are purchased infrequently (for example funeral services).

Table 1 shows the extent to which each of these indicators applies to selected markets.

The study found that every market sampled satisfied at least three of the indicators constructed. Of the sixteen product groups sampled, fourteen were regarded as having some credence qualities, and ten as requiring consumers to have complex knowledge. Price dispersion was also indicated in nine of the sixteen product groups.

---

[1] For a full discussion, see Office of Fair Trading (1994b).
[2] Chapter 3 presents a detailed discussion of the various forms of tacit collusion.

Table 1 ● Markets where information problems appear frequently

Market	Price dispersion	Focal points	Secondary purchases	Commissions	Complex products	Infrequent or credence purchases
Life insurance	X	–	–	X (+ ties)	X	X
Pensions	–	–	–	X (+ ties)	X	X
Mortgages	–	X	X	X (+ ties)	X	X
Extended warranties	X	–	X	–	–	X
New cars	–	X	X	Ties	X	X
Secondhand cars	X	X	–	–	X	X
Building services	X	–	–	–	X	X
Plumbers	X	–	–	–	X	X
Mobile phones	–	X	–	X	X	X
Appliance repairs	X	–	–	–	X	X
Photocopiers	X	X	X	X	X	X
Package holidays	–	X	X	X (+ ties)	–	–
Domestic appliances	–	–	X	–	–	X
Funerals	X	X	X	–	–	X
Contact lens solutions	X	–	X	–	–	X

X denotes that the indicator is valid for that particular market. Ties denote that in these markets the selling of one product is tied to another.

Source: Office of Fair Trading (1997a), table 1, p.109.

Table 2 ● Consumer complaints based on selling techniques, 1995

Market	Number of complaints	Rank
Other household goods and services	40,864	1
Secondhand cars	22,034	2
Food and drink	21,077	3
Electrical goods hire	11,305	4
Clothing and fabrics	10,859	5
Home maintenance and repairs	10,090	6
Major appliances	5,821	7
Double glazing	5,662	8
Packaged holidays	5,325	9
Non life insurance	4,229	10

Source: Office of Fair Trading (1997a), table 2, p.110.

Given that information may be a problem in the markets analysed, the OFT attempted to measure consumer satisfaction in these markets. As an indirect measure of consumer satisfaction, the study examined the number of complaints received regarding producer/supplier selling techniques in selected markets. The results are shown in Table 2.

The report found that many of the industries where information provision was a problem are characterised by high levels of complaints, and as a consequence are likely to be damaging to consumer welfare. However, the report did acknowledge (p.111) possible shortcomings of the methodology adopted, arguing that:

> We have tried to identify factors and indicators that are sufficiently operational to assist the OFT in its assessment of 'problem markets'. It should come as no surprise, however, that the process of identifying problem markets and assessing the extent to which consumer detriment occurs is too complex for an easy, mechanical solution. It is impossible to develop a comprehensive checklist that would lead to unambiguous results. We hope, however, that the factors and indicators identified in the chapter will provide guidance for an initial screening of markets and industries in which the consumer detriment is likely to arise.

Questions for discussion

1. With reference to examples, discuss the various ways in which products can be differentiated.
2. Using a diagram, demonstrate Kaldor's view that consumers are 'unwilling accomplices in a waste of resources'.
3. Discuss the relationship between advertising and concentration.
4. With reference to the empirical evidence, discuss whether advertising can be regarded as informative or persuasive.
5. Using Case study 7.4, discuss the implications for consumer welfare when information is imperfect.

Further reading

Albion, M.S. and Farris, P. (1981) *The Advertising Controversy*. Boston: Auburn House.

Bearne, A. (1996) The economics of advertising: a re-appraisal, *Economic Issues*, **1**, 23–38.

Comanor, W.S. and Wilson, T. (1979) Advertising and competition: a survey, *Journal of Economic Literature*, **17**, 453–76.

Kaul, A. and Wittink, D.R. (1995) Empirical generalisations about the impact of advertising on price sensitivity and price, *Marketing Science*, **14**, 151–60.

Love, J.H. and Stephen, F.H. (1996) Advertising, price and quality in self regulating professions: a survey, *International Journal of the Economics of Business*, **3**, 227–47.

Luik, J. and Waterson, M.J. (1996) *Advertising and Markets: A Collection of Seminal Papers*. Oxford: NTC Publications.

Innovation

8.1 Introduction

Technical change can be thought of as the introduction of superior qualities to products or technical processes that eventually render the existing range of products and processes obsolete. In studies of industrial organisation, research and development undertaken by firms is assigned a high level of importance. Not only does it confer market advantages on successful innovators but it can also be seen as a strategy that is fundamental to the economy. At a general level, changes in technology will affect the growth in economic welfare, and at a specific level, technology affects output, product quality, levels of employment, trade, wages and profits. Thus the rate at which industries develop new ideas, launch new products and introduce new processes will be of interest not only to firms but also to governments.

In this chapter we examine firstly how we define innovation by identifying the various stages of the research and development process. This leads us to discuss the final stage, the diffusion of innovative effort. The quicker a new technology can be adopted and adapted to various uses, the greater the benefits to industries and society. One possible cause for the slow rate of diffusion is the existence of patents; but patents are critical in many cases to stimulate the incentive to innovate. These issues are examined in section 8.3. In section 8.4 we examine the general payoffs from industrial research and development and this is followed in section 8.5 by an analysis of the issues that confront a firm when faced with such investment decisions. Section 8.6 develops theoretical models that attempt to link structure, firm size and the level of research effort; and this is followed in section 8.7 by an examination of some of the empirical work on the deduced hypotheses. To relate some of the theoretical and empirical arguments to the context of modern economies, the last section analyses some of the problems facing European firms in their attempts to improve research and development performance.

Much of the analysis of industrial research and development is based on ideas developed by Joseph Schumpeter (1928), who viewed technical change as exerting a disruptive force on market equilibria. Schumpeter saw the performance of capitalistic markets as inevitably linked to the introduction of new technology and a consequent short-run destabilising effects on the market system. He referred to this as a system of 'creative destruction', whereby innovation would not only lead to new goods, services and more efficient processes, but also challenge the power of the existing firms who were wedded to the older, less efficient technologies. In turn, the successful innovators, while enjoying (temporary) market power would also have continually to guard against any encroachment of their market by further advances in technology. This they would attempt to do by focusing on new sources of supply, new types of organisation and new technology, rather than simply relying on price competition.[1] However, Schumpeter recognised that this technology also generated long-run growth in productivity. Thus, short-run disruption in the market was inexorably linked to long-run growth in productivity.

Stages of research and development

Research and development can be regarded as a process that entails many different stages. There is no general agreement as to the number of stages that can be identified: different economists and management scientists have developed their own particular taxonomies. Probably the best-known of these was the Schumpeterian trichotomy which identified three stages: **invention**, **innovation** and **diffusion**.[2] Perhaps these three stages seem an

[1] Schumpeter (1942), p.84.
[2] Stoneman (1995), pp.2–8.

oversimplification, as the process of research and development involves other important issues. We suggest the following five-stage classification:

- *Basic research.* This refers to what may be termed as 'inventive activity'. An invention is the creation of an idea and its first reduction to practice. At its extreme, such activity is carried out regardless of any practical application in view. Hence basic research in molecular physics was carried out without any foreknowledge of the development of the valve to be used in broadcasting and communications. This type of research is unattractive to industrial firms owing to the uncertainty of outcome and is normally the province of government agencies and universities.[3]

- *Applied research.* Unlike basic research, applied research has a stated objective. Following an investigation of potential economic returns, research will be undertaken to determine the technological feasibility of the proposed application.

- *Development work.* Generally this can be considered as the bringing of an idea or invention to the stage of commercial production and, together with stage two, can be referred to as 'innovatory activity'. It is at this stage that resources are heavily committed as pilot plants or prototypes may have to be built. Although it is clear that at every stage of research and development the firm must review its progress, it is here that the selection process for the next stage is at its most important. A new product failure at the next stage would be very costly to the organisation.

- *Commercial production.* This stage refers to the full-scale production of the new product or application of a new process. Notwithstanding the level of research and development carried out into the technical characteristics of the new ideas and the amount of market research undertaken, there will still be a large element of uncertainty. We can thus define the difference between invention and innovation as the level of risk. Typically, the innovating firm must bear a high degree of risk in the development and launch of a new product. The 'pure' inventor, on the other hand, will not be interested in any commercial application, as his interest is in the generation of ideas and not the production of goods and services. Risks will thus be appreciably lower.

- *Diffusion.* The final stage refers to the spread of the new idea through the firm as well as the copying and adoption of the techniques and products by other firms in the industry and other industries in the economy. One can also identify spatial diffusion, whereby ideas spread to other countries through transfers such as foreign direct investment, licensing agreements and joint ventures. We examine diffusion in greater detail in section 8.2.

The five stages should not be seen as a linear process, whereby inventions, via innovation lead to commercial production and eventual diffusion. There may also be extensive feedback from stages that can lead to the abandonment of existing projects and which can set into motion newer ideas and projects. Diffusion may be slow at first and then accelerate.

A distinction is sometimes made between product innovation and process innovation. This distinction is a little less clear when one considers that new products will often require new methods of production and, likewise, new production techniques may well alter the

---

[3] In a study of the petroleum and chemical industries, Mansfield (1969) found that only some 9 per cent of firms' total R&D expenditure was spent on basic research, whilst 45 per cent was spent on applied research and 46 per cent on development.

nature of the final product. One could also argue that one firm's product innovation may become another firm's process innovation. Thus from the point of view of a producer, a new machine would be classed as product innovation; whereas from the point of view of the buyer (user), the machine would be seen as part of process innovation. Nonetheless, a distinction can be made. Blaug (1963) suggested that process innovation could refer to any technique that leads to a reduction in average costs, keeping input prices constant. Product innovation could then be regarded as the development of a new product without altering the production process. One could also add to the above twofold distinction by introducing changes in, for example, the structure of the management of the organisation, the procurement of inputs and the market (i.e. selling an existing product to a new market). All these could be described as innovatory.

It is important to note that the stages of research and development outlined above are not the only source of technological change for a firm. Technology can be acquired by copying the techniques of other firms and industries, by entering into collaborative and licensing agreements with other firms, or by acquiring the technology from suppliers of capital goods.

8.2 Diffusion

The speed at which inventions are transformed into commercial goods will vary from product to product and from industry to industry. The greatest obstacle to the speed of technical change in an economy is the rate of diffusion. Some technologies seem to languish in oblivion and then suddenly take off, others may never get to challenge the existing technological process or products, while others still are rapidly adopted and spread quickly through the firm and the industry. It is important therefore to discuss the factors that help or hinder the spread of ideas. We first identify the general factors that retard the rate of diffusion to other firms ('inter-firm diffusion') and then we focus on the specific factors that affect diffusion within a firm ('intra-firm diffusion'). We conclude by examining the theoretical and empirical work in the area of diffusion.

General factors

Labour fears

There is evidence that organised labour will at times resist the adoption of a new technology if they see it as a threat to their employment. In the UK, print unions were reluctant to accept 'direct-inputting' technology in the 1970s (Storey, 1979). This technology allowed journalists to electronically transfer their copy direct to the photosetting department, thereby bypassing the composing rooms. The three unions that represented workers in the composing rooms refused to accept this and other innovations for a number of years and as a result Fleet Street was slow to adapt to technical changes that were being adopted elsewhere in newspaper publishing. There is evidence, however, that in some major industrial sectors, trade unions were not an impediment to the adoption of a new technology (Linter et al., 1987).

Poor communications

Government reports have in the past highlighted the lack of co-operation between inventors and innovators and the business community.[4] The development of science parks and other initiatives has been an attempt to bring universities, the producers of new knowledge, and the immediate users, closer together. A summary of what these science parks aim to achieve is provided by the United Kingdom Science Parks Association (1999):

> A science park is a business support and technology transfer initiative the aims of which are:
>
> ● To encourage and support the start up and incubation of innovation led, high growth, knowledge based businesses.
> ● To provide an environment where larger and international businesses can develop specific close interactions with a particular centre of knowledge creation for their mutual benefit.
>
> Science parks deliver these aims through the provision of:
>
> ● Intellectual and physical infrastructure and support services that include collaborative links with local and regional economic development agencies.
> ● Formal and operational links with centres of knowledge creation such as universities, higher education institutes and research organisations.
> ● Management support activity engaged in the transfer of both technology and for their SME [small and medium sized enterprises] clients, business skills (UK Science Parks Association, 1999).

Management inertia

An important reason why some firms may adopt new products or new processes more quickly than other firms is that such firms are controlled by technically trained managers, attuned to the characteristics of the new technology. Managers with a poor technical background may fail to recognise the superiority of a new technology and adopt it only when existing capital needs replacing. It is also possible that firms could be run by a lethargic and over-bureaucratic cadre of managers who may simply move too slowly in seizing technical opportunities. Patel and Pavitt (1987) found that the rate of diffusion of four engineering innovations was much lower in Britain than in Germany. This was blamed on a lack of commitment to develop and commercialise new products and processes, as well as a lack of engineering expertise on the part of British management. Blair (1972) quoted the following case in the UK where managers were happy to stick with their existing technology. In 1959, Pilkington Brothers Limited, a glass manufacturer, developed a new 'float glass' process that revolutionised the production of flat glass. When attempting to patent the process in the United States, Pilkington's management was astonished to discover that although an identical patent had been in existence in the United States since 1907, no American or foreign firm had developed the idea. Blair (1972, p.236) concluded:

> The most charitable explanations are ignorance of the US patents, which would hardly be a tribute to their technical awareness, or satisfaction with the existing technology and a consequent disinclination to embark on the development work ultimately and successfully pursued by a smaller British firm.

[4] See, for example, National Economic Development Council (1983).

Protecting an older technology

There is some evidence to suggest that dominant firms may protect their existing market shares and status quo by either keeping new ideas secret or denying entry to firms with a newer technology. Maclaurin (1950)[5] detailed how major communications firms in the United States (Western Union, Postal Telegraph and American Telephone and Telegraph) resisted the development of radio, preferring instead to buy up competitors and to enter into restrictive agreements. They also attempted to prevent the Marconi Company from getting a franchise in Newfoundland. The UK Post Office also attempted to frustrate Marconi's new technology by refusing to connect its overseas service to Post Office telegraph lines. Blair (1972, pp.230–2) added other similar cases in the rubber, shoe-making machinery and golf clubs industries.[6]

Government or local regulations

Where an industry is faced with a cumbersome regulatory framework regarding standards for materials, design, and safety, the adoption of a new technology may be sluggish, as amendments in regulations may be slow and bureaucratic. Oster and Quigley (1977) found that local building codes significantly reduced the diffusion of technical progress in the building industry. Evidence of an opposite effect, whereby regulations stimulate the rapid diffusion of a technology was provided by Hannan and McDowell (1984) who examined the adoption of automated telling machines (ATMs) by banks across the United States. Some states had restricted the number of branches allowed to a bank, and the adoption of ATMs was seen as a way of circumventing these restrictions.

Patents

In a free market, new knowledge is a free resource, available to all firms. The consequence of this is that there would be too little, or no research and development, as innovating firms would be reluctant to see their rivals enjoy a 'free ride' from their costly and risky investments. To shield innovators from too rapid a diffusion, governments offer patents as protection. In the UK, a successful patent will grant a firm a twenty-year monopoly of the product or process. The problem facing society is that too effective a patent system may result in the slow diffusion of knowledge through the economy.

There is little evidence that the patent system in the UK does result in slow diffusion, as most firms will enter into patent-sharing or licensing agreements. Taylor and Silberston (1973) found that large firms in the UK were fairly liberal about granting licences, especially to foreign firms operating in non-competing markets. Patents are discussed in detail in Section 8.3.

Specific factors

Age of existing capital

The speed at which new technology replaces older technology will be related to the age profile of a firm's capital stock. Faced with a new process, firms with a profile of older

---

[5] Quoted in Blair (1972), p.229.
[6] See Case study 8.3 for a discussion of this topic.

machines will adopt the innovation at a faster rate than those which have only recently installed machines using the older process.

Degree of risk

A technology may be only slowly adopted if there is a substantial risk associated with its introduction. For example, the technology may require inputs that either are not readily available or may be unfamiliar to the firm. This may increase the costs of production and squeeze the estimated profit margins to such an extent that the firm is reluctant to apply the technology. Risks may also stem from uncertainties over the level of market demand. Oster and Quigley (1977) found that the effective demand for housing fluctuated widely, based on changes in the market for credit. These fluctuations inhibited the adoption of new technologies in the housebuilding industry. An application of capital-intensive methods of production could make firms more vulnerable to changes in demand.

Liquidity

It may be argued that the more profitable a firm, the better able it will be to generate internal funds for the application of a new technology. It is implicit that investment in new technology is risky, and firms may have difficulty in raising external finance to fund such projects, though the evidence for this is limited.[7]

Degree of competition

There is some debate as to the effects of market structure and the rate of diffusion. This mirrors the market structure and level of research and development debate discussed further in the chapter. There are two arguments. Will more competition in the industry spur firms to adopt new ideas faster as a means of gaining an advantage over rivals; or will diffusion be faster where we have imperfectly competitive industries who enjoy the high profits and the protection of entry barriers to invest in new technology? The empirical evidence is inconclusive.[8]

Size of firm

The introduction of an innovation may well require large inputs of capital and technical expertise, which would tend to favour the larger firm. Oster and Quigley (1977) found that in the housebuilding industry many of the innovations were in organisation, systems design and integration of housing components. This would have required a large scale of production and one not commonly found amongst the majority of housebuilding firms.

Theory and empirical evidence of diffusion

One of the first models that was developed to explain the rate of diffusion was that of Mansfield (1961). The rate of diffusion is expressed as $dx(t)/dt$, where $x(t)$ is the proportion of firms adopting the innovation at time t. Mansfield argued that the rate would be proportional to both the number of firms using the innovation $x(t)$ and the number of firms without the innovation, in other words the potential innovators, i.e. $1 - x(t)$. Thus the

---

[7] See, for example, Hannan and McDowell (1984), p.332.
[8] See, for example, Kamien and Schwartz (1982), chapters 4 and 5.

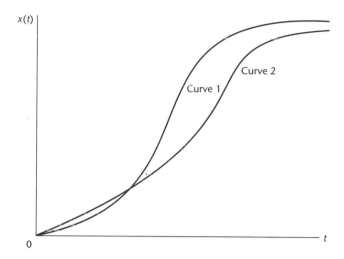

Figure 8.1 Growth over time of the proportion of firms using an innovation

probability of a potential innovator adopting a new idea will depend on the numbers of existing firms that use the technology. The fewer the number of firms involved with the new idea, the more the new technology is viewed as experimental and risky by the rest of the firms. This is expressed in the following function:

$$\frac{dx(t)}{dt} = bx(t) \cdot [1 - x(t)]$$

Over time, as the number of innovating firms increases, so the number of potential innovators decreases and the rate of diffusion diminishes. This model has been described as 'epidemic', in other words the innovation can be likened to a contagious disease or even a 'meme'.[9] The relationship is represented in Figure 8.1. The S-shaped (or sigmoid) curve reflects the process of growth and maturity. When the technology is first adopted, the proportion of firms imitating the technology will grow only slowly, but after a while the proportion will grow at an increasing rate. At a point of inflection, the rate of growth begins to diminish until some maximum is reached (less than or equal to unity, in which case *all* firms would have adopted the technology). The formula for the S-curve is

$$x(t) = \frac{1}{1 + e^{-(A+B_t)}}$$

where A and B are parameters that will vary with different technologies in different industries. On the basis of research into innovations in coal mining, brewing, iron and steel, and railroads, Mansfield (1968, chapter 7) found that the shape of the curve, whether diffusion is quick as in curve 1 or slow as in curve 2, depended on factors such as profitability of the technology, size of investment, degree of risk, degree of competition and attitude of workers.

[9] Dawkins (1998), p.304, defined the meme as 'good ideas, good tunes, good poems, as well as drivelling mantras. Anything that spreads by imitation'.

Mansfield (1968, chapter 8) also found that the size of firm was an important determinant of the rate of diffusion.[15] The argument rested on the notion that larger firms were in a better position to meet the conditions of innovation. They had the expertise and the capital resources to exploit new ideas more quickly than the smaller firms.

Mansfield (1969) illustrated some of the above conclusions by examining the adoption of numerical control (a process of operating machine tools via numerical instructions on cards or tape) in the US tool and die industry in the 1960s.[16] The industry was made up of many small firms with a low concentration and simple decision-making processes. He then analysed the characteristics of the early users. He found that the following were significant:

- *Size of firms.* It was expected that the larger firms would have the financial resources and the technical know-how to adopt new ideas quickly. This was supported by the evidence. The median firm size in 1968 was 70 employees, while the median employment for non-users was 25.
- *Age and educational level of firms' chief executives.* He argued that better-educated managers are better informed about the possibilities of a new technology. He also posited that younger managers will be less set in their ways and more likely to take on the risks of new ideas. Mansfield did find that the majority of the users were college graduates with a median age of 48, while the majority of non-users only finished high school or less and the group's median age was 55. Mansfield also found that some 10 per cent of firm owners who were close to retirement had decided to stay with the existing technology. He concluded: 'Judging by the interviews and other evidence, the diffusion process seems to have been slowed perceptibly by misunderstanding of the innovation and resistance to change.'[10]

Romeo (1975) applied Mansfield's methodology to the machine tools industry in the United States and examined the effects differences in concentration, scale, and research and development expenditure might have on the shape of the S-curve. He found that innovation tended to spread more rapidly in the less concentrated industries; and that industries operating on a larger scale experienced a slower rate of diffusion as they had to do *more* in an absolute sense if they wished to achieve the same rate of diffusion as that enjoyed by smaller scale industries. Finally, Romeo found evidence that the greater the level of research and development expenditures by firms, the greater the probability that they would be more receptive to new technologies.

Karshenas and Stoneman (1995) raised three points as regards the epidemic models popularised by Mansfield. Their first criticism was aimed at the assumption that all imitators were homogeneous and that their number, the technology and profitability of the investment were all constant over time. In addition it was assumed that the adopters were 'passive recipients rather than active seekers of information'.[11] More sophisticated models have included variables that recognise search costs faced by the adopters as well as the information effects of networking.[12] Secondly, they argued that the epidemic models were fundamentally demand-based models and ignored supply-side factors. Once the supply-

---

[10] Mansfield (1969), p.71.
[11] Karshenas and Stoneman (1995), p.273.
[12] *See* Midgley *et al.* (1992).

side was taken into account, the path of diffusion would be influenced by such things as the suppliers' cost functions, their market structure, and any improvements in technology passed down by the supplying industry.[13] Finally, the costs faced by the adopting firms were never properly analysed. They argued that the actual costs will be greater than just the cost of acquiring new capital goods. The technology may have to be adapted to the particular circumstances of the firm and there may be additional training and organisational costs accompanying the new technology. They conclude that: 'In the limit, technology may be purpose built for a firm in which case the study of diffusion becomes a study of customer supplier relationships.'[14]

8.3 Patents

As mentioned in the previous section, the problem facing governments eager to promote technical change is how best to encourage investment in new technology. A problem arises in that once a new idea has been created and developed, under free market conditions it is virtually costless to share this idea with other firms. Knowledge is a free good. However, such sharing of ideas would be a disincentive to undertake innovatory activity as the returns to such an investment would be greatly diminished. The granting of a **patent** to an innovator confers a property right over that new knowledge. The innovator will own an economic asset which can be sold, licensed or exploited by the firm itself. Its use is subject to the authorisation of the patent holder. However, granting such rights to an innovator will also create temporary monopoly power, which may compromise allocative efficiency. Governments must therefore attempt to find a balance between the encouragement of research and development on the one hand and preventing the abuse of market power on the other.

In most countries, if an invention or innovation is to be 'patentable' it must meet three criteria:

● *It must be new*, in the sense that it has not been previously used, published or demonstrated in the public domain. There are certain ideas that cannot be patented, such as scientific discovery, mathematical formulae, mental processes and artistic creations.
● *It should non-obvious* in so far as it would not have occurred to reasonably well informed people in the field. In other words, it requires an 'inventive step' to have been taken.
● *It should be capable of industrial application*, so that it can, in theory, be usable in some form as a piece of equipment or as a process.

Applying for patents can be costly to medium- and small-sized firms. When filing a complicated patent application, consultants (patent agents) may be required to ensure that the patent is correctly drawn up so as to avoid possible imitations 'around the patent' and potential future litigation. Application fees, annual renewal fees (from the fourth year) and foreign patent applications will add to the expense. Small firms must therefore weigh up the advantages of using a new technology with or without the protection of a patent. If a firm feels that it is too weak to defend and enforce its patent it may choose to open its ideas to the whole market which, will at least prevent larger firms from 'stealing' the idea

[13] See Stoneman (1989) for a fuller discussion.
[14] Karshenas and Stoneman (1995), p.279.

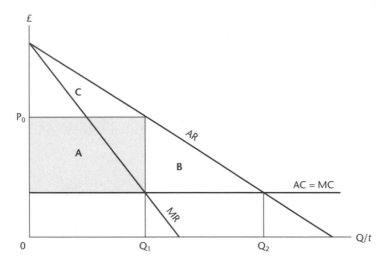

Figure 8.2 Gains to society from innovation

and patenting it themselves. Even larger firms may consider that the costs of policing and enforcing intellectual property rights (transaction costs) are too high in their particular industry, and thus the incentive to patent is low.

If we apply standard microeconomic analysis to the question of patents, we can begin with the theory of monopoly. Patents create monopoly rights and a successful patentee will enjoy monopoly profits. Let us consider the production of a new patented product under conditions of constant long-run costs; we can further assume that the costs of developing the new product are not included in the average cost curve. This cost curve is shown as AC in Figure 8.2.

The diagram shows that optimal production will be at Q_2 where MC equals price. Should the firm produce at Q_2 it will make no monopoly profits as price is equal to average cost. The firm will in fact equate its marginal cost with its marginal revenue, reduce production to Q_1, charge price P_0 and enjoy abnormal profits equal to the shaded area A. This would then imply a waste of resources as shown by the loss of consumer surplus equal to triangle B.

Despite the potential waste, consumers are better off than before. Had the innovation not occurred there would be no consumer surplus equal to triangle C. Thus with the introduction of the new product the net gain to society is area A + C, the monopoly profit added to consumer surplus. It may not be the maximum gain, but a gain nonetheless. The model simply shows that patenting is not an optimal solution but a 'second-best' solution.

The length and breadth of patents

The above analysis requires us to ask for how long patents should be issued and how wide their coverage should be. Since patents have a finite life (a maximum of twenty years in the UK) there will come a time when diffusion and competition increase output of the new product to Q_2 (Figure 8.2). As a consequence, the monopoly profits and the waste will have disappeared. The question is, for how long should governments protect firms with regard

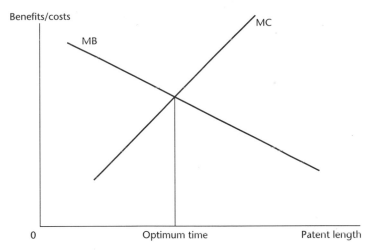

Figure 8.3 Marginal costs and marginal benefits of patent length

to innovation? In theory, the **length** of a patent should be long enough to ensure that the research and development investment is sufficiently profitable. If it is too short, the returns may not justify the innovation and society will be denied a new product. On the other hand, if the patent is too long then firms will enjoy abnormal profits and consumers suffer high prices for a longer time. Since different innovations, different firms and different industries incur different costs of innovation, it is difficult for governments to determine a patent length suitable for all situations.

In theory, the answer can be provided by marginal cost (MC) and marginal benefit (MB) analysis. If we define the cost to society of all patents as a summation of triangles B in Figure 8.2, then the marginal cost is the increase in cost if one were to extend the patent life by one year. Figure 8.3 shows the marginal cost curve as a rising function since, as the patent length grows there is a greater and greater number of firms reaping monopoly rewards *above* those necessary to stimulate investment in research and development.

Benefits refer to areas A and C (Figure 8.2) for all new products. Thus marginal benefit is the increase to this amount as the patent life is extended by one year. Marginal benefit falls as the patent length increases since, as the longer the patent life expands, it will encourage the introduction of less and less profitable innovations. The optimum time is thus determined at the intersection of the MC and MB functions.[15]

Determining the optimal **breadth** of a patent is more difficult since it entails a concept difficult to measure, unlike length which can be measured reasonably easily. One suggestion is to determine the exact amount by which a new idea should differ from an existing idea to encourage an innovation.[16] The difference should be large enough to prevent other firms 'inventing around' and reducing the patentee's profits. When linked to the question of length, the issue becomes complex and the empirical work appears inconclusive.[17] An interesting analysis is provided by O'Donoghue *et al.* (1998) who define the 'effective

[15] For a formal analysis see Nordhaus (1969).
[16] See Pepall *et al.* (1999), p.606.
[17] See, for example, Denicolò (1996).

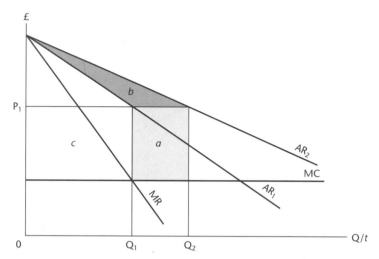

Figure 8.4 Too much spending on innovation

patent life' as a patent which either expires or is superseded by a newer innovation. They showed that the effective patent life depends on the breadth of the patent. Two types of patent breadths are defined: a 'lagging breadth', which protects the firm from imitation, and a 'leading breadth' which protects the firm from new products.

Patent races

The above discussion focused on the problem that not enough research may be undertaken if the patents are too restrictive. It is possible to analyse situations where firms may produce *too much* research.[18] This could arise where firms enter into a strategy of competing innovations where the first firm successfully to introduce a new technology is rewarded with a patent and reaps all the rewards. This can be referred to as a 'winner takes all' situation. Assume a market dominated by a monopoly as a result of a patented product and that the only entry strategy for a potential competitor is to develop a superior product. Once accomplished, this would not only allow the competitor to enter but also force the existing firm out of the market. Consider Figure 8.4. Assuming a linear marginal costs function, the existing firm is selling OQ_1 at price OP_1. If the potential competitor successfully launches a better product, we can assume that at the market price of OP_1 all existing consumers will switch to the new product and some new consumers will be attracted into the market. The new demand function will now be AR_2. If we assume that development costs of the superior product are equal to X, we are in a position to determine the efficiency of entry. From society's point of view, entry will be efficient if the increased profits (*a*) and consumer surplus (*b*) (shaded areas) are greater than X. From the entrant's point of view, entry will be undertaken if total profits (rectangle *c* + *a*) are greater than X. In Figure 8.4, areas *a* + *b* (benefits to society) appear smaller than areas *c* + *a* (the profits accruing to the entrant). If the costs of development (X) are greater than area *a* + *b*, but smaller than area

---

[18] For example, Hirschliefer (1971) and Cockburn and Henderson (1994).

$c + a$, then entry (and research) will be undertaken. In this 'winner takes all' market, the successful firm, keen to wrest control of the market from the incumbent, will have spent too much on research *from society's point of view*.

Patents and the incentive to innovate

A fundamental point in any discussion on patents is whether patents do encourage industrial innovation. A number of issues can be identified:[19]

- Does the patent system encourage investment in research and development or does it focus attention on patentable activity? There seems no reason to assume that patented work is necessarily that which is of greatest economic benefit.
- Patents may increase the risks of failure, by encouraging patent races. The cost of research and development will be greater as firms realise no returns for their investments. This could be referred to as the risk of 'gambler's ruin'.
- By granting monopoly status, patents tend to protect innovating firms rather than inventing firms, and some firms may use a strategy of pre-emptive patenting to limit competition. It could be argued that greater competition is needed at the innovation stage to help the diffusion process.
- It is also important to determine the market structure that would be best served by the patent system. In other words, a market structure that lacks any other incentive for investment in research and development. At a general level, one could argue that monopolies would not view patents as an incentive to innovate as they already enjoy the security of not facing rivals. Instead, patents could be seen as buttressing their market dominance by adding barriers to entry. On the other hand, in theoretical models of perfect competition, patents would provide incentives to innovate. Without such protection their new knowledge would be immediately shared by rivals.

The latter point is based on a simplistic view of market structure, where only the two extremes are considered. If we open up the analysis to include the wide variety of forms that characterise more realistic (oligopolistic) structures, it is often argued that innovation is one of the main vehicles for competitive activity in such markets. This could still be the case even in the absence of patents, since competing firms may be slow, through various market imperfections, to imitate and adapt to new ideas, products and processes. This delay could be caused by the lag effects of introducing a new technology, such as the need to acquire new skills, retrain labour, the risks of investing in new capital, buying unfamiliar inputs and accurately gauging the level of demand.

The above points are echoed by much of the research into the incentive effects of patents. Taylor and Silberston (1973) found that in their sample of UK research-intensive firms, the vast majority would still have carried out research even in the absence of patent protection. Research by Schankerman (1998) into patent renewals in France for four technology fields, of pharmaceuticals, chemicals, mechanical engineering and electronics, showed that patents provided a substantial incentive to research and development effort, but that they did not constitute the major source for the incentives. He also found that there were differences in the importance of patent protection in the various technology fields. The

---

[19] The following is based on arguments outlined by George *et al.* (1991), pp.255–7.

least important seemed to be in the pharmaceutical field, which he argued could be owing to the strong level of price regulation in that industry:

> The finding that patent rights are surprisingly less valuable in pharmaceuticals, where there is stringent price regulation in France, highlights the important point that R&D incentives are shaped not only by patent law but also other institutional constraints that effect the appropriability environment.[20]

8.4 The returns to industrial research and development

Beath *et al.* (1994) identified two fundamental reasons why firms undertake research and development. Firstly, the activity is profitable and secondly, successful research and development confers strategic advantages. We examine these two issues in this section.

Profitability

The effect of successful research and development is to lower the average cost function, via process innovation, or to shift the demand curve to the right, via product innovation. Both these outcomes will lead to increased profitability, assuming that competitors are unable to imitate the ideas either through institutional arrangements or through high market transaction costs. Empirical research that considers the relationship between innovation and profitability was carried out by Geroski *et al.* (1993).

The model below was used to test the level of profitability of innovating firms and was based on a sample of 721 UK manufacturing firms observed between 1972 and 1983 with a subset of 117 'innovating firms'. The regression model was:

$$\text{ROR}_{it} = f_i + \alpha_0\text{MS}_{it} + \alpha_1\text{CON}_{it} + \alpha_2\text{IMP}_{it} + \alpha_3(\text{MS}_{it}\text{CON}_{it}) + \alpha_4\text{UN}_{it} + \alpha_5\text{ROR}_{it-1} + \alpha_6\text{IPI}_{it}$$
$$+ \alpha_7\text{IUI}_{it} + \alpha_8 T_i + \sum_{j=0}^{6} \lambda_j\text{INN}_{it-j} + \mu_{it}$$

Profit margins (ROR) were determined by market shares (MS), industry concentration (CON), import intensity (IMP), and the interaction between market shares and concentration (MS · CON). Since profits can be 'siphoned off' by labour, a variable for unionisation (UN) was added. The lagged profit margins variable ROR_{t-1} detected firm-specific effects regarding technological opportunity and conditions of appropriability across firms as well as the time effects that are associated with departures from, or movements to equilibrium. The data on innovations was based on a data set collected by the Science Policy Research Unit which identified important innovations over the period 1945 to 1983 as well as the ownership of the new knowledge. INN referred to the number of innovations produced by any one firm in a year, and its effects on profitability over the subsequent six years were examined. IPI referred to the number of innovations produced within a two-digit industry definition and IUI was the number of innovations used by other firms within the same industry classification. These two variables thus attempt to capture possible spillovers of innovation. The subscripts i and t refer to firms and time. The intercept f_i is a firm-specific effect; T_i is a time dummy, and λ_0 is the impact of innovations on profit margins in the short run. The impact of innovations in the long run is measured as $\sum_j \lambda_j/(1 - \alpha_5)$.

[20] Schankerman (1998), p.104.

The overall conclusion reached by Geroski *et al.* was that the number of innovations produced by a firm did have a positive effect on profitability although the effects were modest. Furthermore, the spillover effects were meagre in comparison with research carried out in the United States, though this could have been due to different definitions of innovatory output.

Geroski *et al.* attempted not only to measure the size of the correlation between innovation and profitability but also to find answers to two other questions. Their first question was to determine whether the relationship between profit and innovative *output* was similar to profit and research *input*. This is discussed further in section 8.7 when we analyse the issues surrounding the measurement of innovatory activity.

The second question that they posed was: 'Does the correlation between innovative output and profitability reflect transitory or permanent performance differences between innovating and non-innovating firms?'[21] The importance of the question rests on two different views as to why innovations may improve performance. Firstly, performance may be enhanced owing to the *innovative process*, which refers to the creation of new products and processes which help to strengthen the market position of a firm, until such time as rivals come up with better ideas. This would seem to reflect the more common argument. The second reason is that performance may be enhanced through the *process of innovation*, which means that the firm's culture is transformed, making it more flexible, more adaptable and possibly better able to survive than non-innovating firms. The question can be answered by a statistical analysis that identifies whether innovatory returns are transitory (consistent with the first hypothesis) or permanent (consistent with the second hypothesis). The approach taken to answer the question was to examine whether the profit differences between innovating firms and non-innovating firms were due to specific new products or processes (transitory observations) or whether the differences were fixed and permanent, which would support the second hypothesis. Geroski *et al.* found that large fixed differences occurred only in times of recessions. Innovating firms were thus able to withstand cyclical downturns better than non-innovating firms.

Strategy

In an economic environment where uncertainty characterises most decision-making, it is unrealistic to assume that firms view policies such as innovatory effort as a means of contributing to the maximisation of profits alone. We can achieve a greater appreciation of why firms invest in research and development by examining a wide variety of business strategies which such activity can open up. The discussion below is not meant to be exhaustive as it would be impossible to cover the full texture of real-life strategies. We aim instead to provide an indication of how innovatory activity can be used by firms to achieve various objectives, by focusing on just a few examples.[22]

Offensive strategy

An offensive strategy is one designed to give a firm dominance in the market through the introduction of technological change. The main focus of activity in the firm is to generate

[21] Geroski *et al.* (1993), p.199.
[22] The discussion that follows is based on Freeman and Soete (1997).

new ideas and to protect these ideas and associated spin-offs by patent application with a view to achieving monopoly status. The firm will have to invest heavily in scientific resources of both labour and capital. Examples of such a heavy resource commitment to research were DuPont's development of nylon and lycra, IG Farben's development of PVC, and RCA's development of colour television. It is claimed that these types of firm may even invest in highly speculative basic research, though certainly not of the purest type. To be ahead of any other possible rival does imply that firms who wish to pursue an offensive strategy must concentrate on experimental development work, requiring the capacity to design, build and test prototypes and pilot plants. To be good at research and development also requires that the firm 'educates' the market as well as its own personnel to ensure that the technology is firmly rooted in the marketplace. This will require the production of training manuals, seminars, videos and other related support services. One can appreciate how Microsoft partly achieved its success by ensuring that its software was accompanied by an investment in market education.

Defensive strategy

Not all firms will wish to take the commitments and risks entailed by an offensive strategy, but in most industries some form of research and development is inevitable if only to guarantee survival of the firm. Changes in technology and continual product improvement force many firms to attempt to keep pace with such changes. In the absence of any other marketing strategy, to do nothing will see market share collapse, as rivals introduce processes and products that marginalise the laggards. The defensive strategy does not imply no research, but rather the timing of the research. The defensive strategist simply follows the technology leads of the offensive firms. The defensive firm either may lack the large technical resources needed to become an offensive firm or may wish to avoid the risks associated with a heavy commitment to such speculative investments, preferring instead to invest in proven processes and products. It may also be possible that the defensive firm wishes to improve on the technology by attempting to produce 'second generation' ideas, permissible within the constraints of the patent breadth. Research does confirm that in most oligopolistic industries, defensive innovation is not only typical but also a rational reaction to new technology.[23] This implies that these defensive firms must also invest in technical resources in order to be able to react quickly to new ideas if they are to retain their market shares or even possibly to 'leapfrog' over the offensive firms.

Imitative strategy

Unlike the defensive firm, the imitator does not wish to produce a better product by differentiating it from that launched by the offensive firm. Instead it is happy to produce an identical product, either by a licence in the short run or exploiting free knowledge in the long run. Investment in technical resources will be low as the firm need not attempt any product adaptation or improvement and will not need to meet the costs of educating the market. In the latter case it will have benefited from the information generated by the offensive and defensive firms. Nonetheless, for the strategy to be profitable, the imitator must possess certain advantages such as low costs or a captive market. One reason why DuPont left the rayon market was its inability to compete with the low-cost producers.

[23] Freeman and Soete (1977), p.273.

Imitating firms may also apply the new ideas where they benefit most from a captive market, for example demand from their own subsidiaries or markets protected by political patronage or tariff walls. These are markets from which the offensive firm is excluded. Indeed, government and capital market support can be harnessed in various countries to exploit such a strategy of imitation to diffuse technological change quickly and efficiently.[24]

Dependent strategy

A dependent strategy implies a subservient role with regard to the stronger offensive or defensive firms. These firms can be regarded as satellites or subcontractors of stronger firms and they initiate no investment in research and development. They will accept the new technology handed down, often as a condition of continuing supply relations with customers or suppliers. The new technology will often be accompanied by technical assistance, the loaning of skilled labour and help with ancillary investments. The Japanese electronics and automotive industries can be cited as an example of this type of subcontracting and dependency strategy. This strategy may, under certain circumstances, suggest a move towards vertical integration as the dominant firm may wish to protect its technology and investments.[25]

Traditional strategies

The output of the traditional firm is not responsive to changes in technology. This is because of the nature of the market demand: consumers either do not seek frequent technical changes in the products, or they may be ignorant of the new technology. Competition from rivals may be less potent or, at the other extreme, competition may be so strong as to erode any abnormal profits that could be diverted to exploring the introduction of new ideas. Differentiation, if important, would be focused on design changes which are non-technical. These industries may be likened to craft industries, and would include hairdressing, restaurants and building contractors.

8.5 Investment in innovation

In many cases it is fairly clear how a firm should allocate research and development expenditures. In small firms the direction of investment will follow the aspirations and hunches of the owner or technical director. In some industries where technology is changing rapidly it is clear the direction that such expenditures should take. There are firms, however, that may have large research and development budgets and a degree of discretion as to the allocation of such funds. Most of the issues discussed below fall into standard models of investment appraisal, which attempt to estimate the profitability of research and development by estimating the future level of customer demand and the level of development costs. As Griliches (1958, p.431) commented:

> Conceptually, the decisions made by an administrator of research funds are among the most difficult economic decisions to make and to evaluate, but basically they are not very different from any other type of entrepreneurial decision.

[24] For example, the South Korean steel industry; ibid., p.280.
[25] See Chapter 9 for a discussion of vertical integration.

The major difference between the decision to invest in the replacement of capital goods and research and development lies in the level of uncertainty attached to the latter type of investment. Risks attached to innovative effort differ from other risks in that they cannot be regarded as insurable, i.e. risks that are repetitive and measurable. Risks will naturally decrease as decisions focus more on the application and modification of established technology than on basic research and radical product or process development.

With the risk constraint defined, let us now consider what factors may influence the discretionary use of research and development funds.[26]

Market issues

The first issue that firms may consider is whether the new idea meets an unsatisfied market demand. This may not be as difficult a problem as it first appears, since in many cases it is the customers that alert the firms to a gap in the market. Research has shown that a large proportion of research and development is as a result of requests for product or process improvement from the users.[27]

Secondly, firms will have to consider the growth potential of the new market. This may involve some form of long-term forecasting, which is of course highly speculative. Firms with a high commitment to innovation as an offensive strategy may attempt the **Delphi technique** to determine the future level of demand. The Delphi technique was developed by the RAND Corporation in the late 1960s as a forecasting methodology. It works by asking a group of experts drawn from many different fields to present opinions as to the future of a market. These opinions are reached individually and then circulated to the other members of the group, who are then asked to revise their opinions in the light of what they have read. Through this process of iteration, a consensus is reached. According to Madu *et al.* (1991), Taiwan used this method to prioritise its entire information technology industry. They concluded that:

> Finally, these decisions reflect the experts' world views, life experiences, cognitive feelings and perceptions. Thus, these results are based on the participants' subjective assessments which may also be influenced by data. Decision-making in itself is subjective. However, the use of experts in a systematic manner will yield a satisfactory solution to sociotechnical problems.[28]

The problem with the Delphi technique is that it assumes that a collective consensus will always be better than the views of one individual. An alternative approach to technological forecasting is trend extrapolation, whereby firms examine the history of products using time series data and then attempt to forecast developments. The problem with this approach is that one has to assume that all the parameters will remain constant into the future, which over a ten- or twenty-year period would be highly unlikely.

The difficulty of attempting to determine future technological developments can best be illustrated when one considers that some of the most dramatic innovations have been the least expected:

---

[26] The discussion loosely follows the structure suggested by Livesey (1987).
[27] See, for example, Minkes and Foxall (1982).
[28] Madu *et al.* (1991), quoted in Cline (1998).

Almost every major innovation in these two industries [electronics and synthetic materials] was hopelessly underestimated in its early stages, including polyethylene, PVC and synthetic rubber in the material field, and the computer, the transistor, the robot and numerical control in electronics.[29]

A third important issue is to consider the strength of rivals and the likelihood of their entry into a new product market. An example of a firm unable to withstand the entry of powerful firms was Lestoil, a small American company which developed and launched liquid household cleaners. The success of the product attracted the attention of major manufacturers such as Lever Brothers, Procter & Gamble, and Colgate Palmolive, whose entry Lestoil was unable to prevent.[30]

Costs

If firms wish to determine the profitability of research and development investments, they must also attempt to estimate the level of development costs. Given that these costs will be incurred well into the future and that they are the costs that accompany an inherently uncertain and risky project, the chance of correctly estimating their level is not high. Firms can reduce these costs by concentrating on less speculative innovations, but even then the estimating errors can be large:

> Those firms who speak of keeping development cost estimating errors within a band of plus or minus 20 per cent are usually referring to a type of project in which technical uncertainty is minimal, for example, adapting electronic circuit designs to novel applications, but well within the boundaries of existing technology . . .[31]

The implication is that innovation which is anything other than a simple application of an existing technology will incur a much higher variance in the estimated costs. A further point that can be identified is that there appears to be a tendency to underestimate the costs in such projects and much more so than other forms of investment. The estimation of such costs is quite possibly dependent on sociopolitical in-fighting amongst the interest groups within the organisation. Some evidence exists that corporate engineers in one particular firm had deliberately made low estimates to ensure that projects were adopted.[32]

Marketing

There are many issues that need to be considered when firms are faced with the marketing of a new product. Firstly, can the firm exploit its existing reputation to help the development of a new market? New firms with new products may be at a disadvantage from suspicious and conservative consumers. Secondly, the firm may have to consider whether the new product has clear and distinctive 'promotable' features. If, for example, the new product or idea is too complex for the average consumer to understand or if it appears unattractive, then the market may never fully develop. Distribution is another key element in the marketing strategy. If firms have well developed distribution channels and dealer

[29] Freeman and Soete (1997), p.249.
[30] Sutton (1980) quoted in Livesey (1987), p.233.
[31] Freeman and Soete (1997), p.246.
[32] Ibid., p.247.

networks, then the new product can be promoted through these existing structures, accompanied by the correct amount of promotional activity. The alternative is to rely on independent distributors who may have to be persuaded to adopt the new product or prised away from existing suppliers. Finally, firms will have to consider the price at which the new product is sold. It may be possible to overcome consumer inertia or resistance to a new product by a pricing strategy. For example, if a new product is subject to a taboo effect,[33] whereby consumers will not pay a positive price for the product until they believe sufficient other consumers are already in the market, then the firm may be forced to charge a zero price to break the taboo and stimulate market demand. In the UK in the late 1980s there was much resistance to the new subscription satellite TV and the purchase of satellite dishes, which prompted Sky TV to give the dishes away free for a six-month period in order to establish a market for its service.

Production

A firm will need to evaluate the demands placed on its production capabilities when considering an investment in innovation. Questions that will have to be considered focus on whether the firm has the capacity, capital, and the trained staff and the technical expertise necessary to see the project through. In addition, a new technology may require new inputs which will involve the firm in new and unfamiliar supply relationships. As regards the issue of spare capacity, it may well be the case that the firm is prompted into developing new products simply to exploit its spare capacity.

Finance

It is clear that investment in innovation is speculative as the cash flows are difficult to estimate. Firms hoping to attract external funds may be faced with a reluctance on the part of lenders and may be forced to rely on internally generated funds. One problem that may frustrate the flow of funds is that the managers undertaking the research have much better information as to the likely success of the project than the financier, who is less able to monitor and control the use of such funds. Owing to such possible information asymmetries, the projects may not be financed efficiently. The type of support that might be forthcoming would only be short term, since the risks of fluctuations in revenue and costs will be much lower from projects with a short timespan. Financiers may also be more able to monitor managers in the short run. It is therefore not surprising that many small and medium-sized firms turn to their own internal funds to finance innovation. This is well illustrated by Table 8.1, which compares sources of finance for small firms in the south-east of England, Scotland and California in two time periods.

Timescale

A final consideration to be made by a firm will be to determine the speed at which the research and development should take place. The reason for considering the rate of

---

[33] The taboo effect exists when some consumers will not purchase a (new) good because insufficient numbers of other consumers are buying the good. See Leibenstein (1950).

Table 8.1 ● Sources of investment finance for small high technology firms (%)

Source of finance	SE England		Scotland		California	
	1981/82	1985/86	1981/82	1985/86	1981/82	1985/86
Local bank	8	20	24	2	10	5
Profits	82	63	65	76	75	81
Venture capital	3	0	2	5	15	0
Other	7	17	9	17	0	14
Number of firms	60	46	54	41	60	43

Source: Oakey *et al.* (1988).

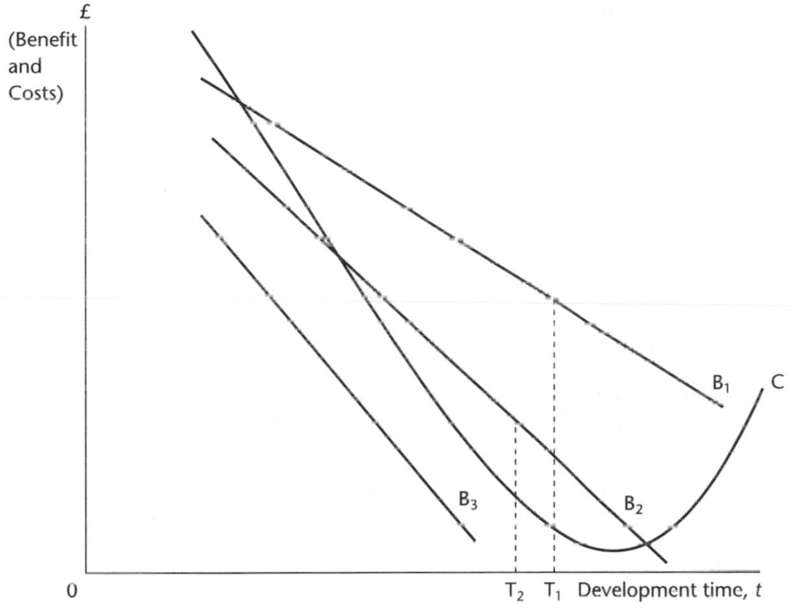

Figure 8.5 Optimum development time in oligopolistic markets

development will be the presence or absence of rivals. A tight oligopolistic market structure, characterised by powerful rivals will encourage rapid innovation, and as pressure from rivals declines the less pressing will be the need to gain strategic advantages. Scherer (1967a) developed a model that helps to explain the time choices that face firms. This is illustrated by Figure 8.5.

The model is based on the following assumptions:

● Research and development is carried out to maximise profits.
● Patent barriers do not exist.
● Rivalry is expressed through qualitative changes in the product.
● Each firm is responsible for its own research.

In Figure 8.5, C is the time/cost trade-off function. A firm can innovate at a slow, leisurely pace or at a very fast pace (a crash programme), or at various speeds in between. If it wishes to speed up the pace of innovation, the firm must accept that costs are likely to rise for three reasons:

● Errors being made when the firm does not wait for a full analysis of various tests.
● The need to maintain parallel research as a hedge.
● The potential of diminishing returns in the short run.

B_1 is a benefits function, which represents the benefits to an innovator of proceeding at various speeds. It is negatively sloped for two reasons: early completion of the project allows the firm to exploit the market over a longer period of time, and it indicates the firm's improved market power over its rivals.

Being a profit-maximising firm, the firm will select the optimum time, where there is a maximum surplus over costs, i.e. where the slope of the benefits function equals the slope of the cost function. Development time OT_1 is thus chosen. The shape of the C function is largely determined by the level of technology. The slope of the B function is determined by market structure. Will the slope get steeper (B_2) and thus reduce the optimum development time if there are more or fewer firms? Will the slope be affected by the relative size of the firms? These questions can only be answered by applying and analysing various oligopolistic scenarios. As Scherer concluded, there is no general, unambiguous answer. It is possible that entry of rival firms may shift the benefits function so far to the left (B_3) that the profit potential is so low and the potential number of imitators so high that no development will be undertaken.

8.6 Schumpeter, industrial structure and innovation

One of the most traditional of arguments against monopoly is that without the spur of competition the monopolist is content with its existing production techniques, which are generating monopoly profits. Thus, there is no incentive to invest in research and development to improve these methods. However, it has been shown, and claimed implicitly by Schumpeter (1942), that highly concentrated industries are often sources of great inventive and innovative activity.[34] The reasons for this, according to Yamey (1972a) and other so-called neo-Schumpeterians, are not generally found in formal models of price theory. Yamey summarises some general reasons why monopolists may be attracted to innovatory activity:

● Highly concentrated industries enjoy greater profits which can be invested in 'risky' innovatory activity. Fragmented industries earn only normal profits and have no 'uncommitted' resources. The higher profits earned by monopolies can also secure better input resources with which to exploit technological investments.
● The absence of competition allows the firm an environment of security in which to carry out the risky projects. There are fewer potential imitators and the firm is free to consider speculative innovation, knowing that failure will not be exploited by a rivalrous fringe. The firm has room to develop and grow.

---

[34] See also Scherer (1992) for an excellent review of the **Schumpeterian hypothesis**.

- Competition at high levels of concentration can still exist in the guise of near-monopolies and highly concentrated oligopolies. Innovation may be an important source of non-price competition in these market structures.
- Monopolies are typically large and they face a large market in which it may prove easier to exploit a variety of new ideas.
- There exists a potential for economies of large-scale research and development production for the large firms operating under conditions of oligopoly and monopoly.

An argument contrary to the Schumpeterian hypothesis can be made, which highlights possible negative effects that a monopoly has on innovative activity:

- In the absence of competitive forces, management may become lazy, and over-bureaucratic structures may lead to loss of control and other x-inefficiencies.[35]
- Since there are so few potential rivals to a monopolist there will be fewer firms doing innovatory work. Assuming that successful innovation is more likely the more firms there are, since the *intensity of research* as well as the *probability of success* is greater, it follows that monopolistic structures will have a lower level of innovative output.
- Monopolies that owe their market power to past successful innovations will view new innovations as displacing their current technology with the effect that *net returns* will be less than those enjoyed by entrants who will be unencumbered with an existing technology. In addition, the monopoly firm may be so tied to an existing technology that to switch resources to a newer product or process would be considered too costly.

Incentive to innovate: the theoretical arguments

When considering the question as to which market structure best favours investment in innovation, we shall turn first to the traditional theoretical arguments of Arrow (1962). These arguments were based on the following problem. Would an innovator be more interested in innovating for a perfectly competitive firm or for a monopolist? (In the latter case we will assume that the innovator is the monopolist.) In which of the two polar market structures are the returns higher? (We assume all other things are equal and that there are no contractual problems.)

Consider Figure 8.6. Arrow assumed that the innovation brings about a cost reduction. Thus the per-unit cost of production falls from C to C*. The competitive price after the invention is P_c^*, i.e. C* plus a royalty per unit. Naturally, this cannot be higher than C, since in that case the firm would revert to its older production technique. The royalty per-unit is set at P_c^* so as to maximise rectangle B, which is the total royalty revenue. This is achieved where quantity Q will equate MR to C* (MC). Rectangle B is the *incentive to innovate*. Under a monopoly model the incentive to innovate is the increase in profits, a sort of lump-sum royalty, i.e. rectangle B less rectangle A (profits prior to innovation). Arrow concluded that an innovator will sell to a competitive firm so long as development costs are less than rectangle B. The inventor as a monopolist will only invent if development costs are less than B – A. Since the area B – A is always less than B, Arrow concluded that there is less

---

[35] X-inefficiency is considered to be the difference between the lowest level of costs that can be realised by the firm and the level of costs that are in fact being incurred. The difference can be due to such things as lack of technical know-how on the part of management, and managers pursuing objectives other than strict profit maximisation.

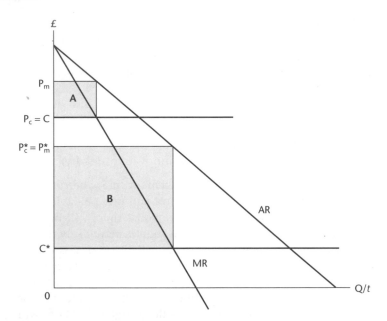

Figure 8.6 Arrow's incentive to innovate

incentive to invent under monopoly. The argument is based primarily on the replacement effect that the innovation has on the existing technology. The monopolist will see the market for existing products greatly reduced, whereas the competitive firm will enjoy increased market share at the expense of rivals.

Demsetz (1969) claimed that Arrow compared a small monopolist with a large competitive firm. In order to isolate the pure effects of research and development, Demsetz assumed that the pre-innovation output is the same for both firms, i.e. both the competitive firm and the monopolist are of the same size. To obtain such an effect he assumed that the marginal revenue curve of the monopolist is also the average revenue curve of the firm in perfect competition. In Figure 8.7, the pre-innovation output for both firms will be at CX. Costs fall to C' as a result of the innovation. The monopoly profit before the innovation was equal to rectangle A, while after the innovation it rose to rectangle B + C. Thus the incentive to innovate, or the lump-sum royalty, is (B + C) − A. If the monopolist innovator sold the innovation to a competitive firm, the expected total royalties payments are equal to rectangle B (the output level at which total royalties are maximised). In this case the incentive to innovate is obviously on the side of the monopolist.

Kamien and Schwartz (1970) widened the scope of the analysis by assuming that elasticities of demand as well as outputs are equal. Figure 8.8 shows the pre-innovation outputs for both firms to be at Q* and that elasticities of demand at that point are also equal. (When two demand curves are drawn from the same point on the x-axis, the elasticities of demand will be equal at any level of output.)

The pre-innovation costs are at C and the monopoly price is P_m, whereas the competitive price is P_c. As before, innovation reduces the average costs to C' and as a consequence, following the reasoning in the previous models, monopoly price is set at P'_m and the competitive price at P'_c (royalty per unit is C'P'$_c$). The incentive to innovate under a monopoly

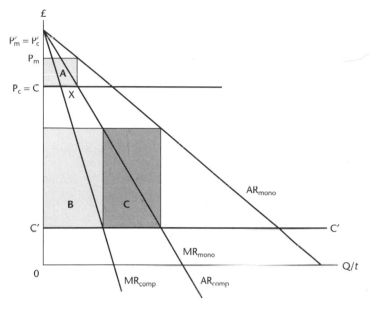

Figure 8.7 Demsetz's incentive to innovate

is the difference between rectangle C'XBP$'_m$ and CYAP$_m$, whereas under competition the incentive is equal to rectangle C'ZDP$'_c$. Kamien and Schwartz concluded that the incentive to innovate in this case is greater with a monopolist.

Yamey (1970) also contributed to the Arrow–Demsetz debate. He made the observation that the arguments had all centred around costs reducing innovative activity. If one considered new product innovation or if costs were too high previously to justify any output at all, then the pre-innovation output will have been the same, zero. In this case Yamey claimed that the incentive to innovate is the same for both market structures. In Figure 8.9 total royalties in the competitive case or the increase in profits in the monopoly case are identical.

What is clear from the above theoretical analysis is that there is no clear and unequivocal conclusion as to which market structure best favours research and development. As we saw earlier, Schumpeter argued that it was the monopolies and large firms that were best suited to provide the necessary impetus for technical advance. They had the resources, the prospect of additional profits in the future as well as the security of monopoly power to undertake the risks of innovation. Schumpeter suggested that high concentration and high innovatory effort went hand in hand but never tested this hypothesis himself. This did not deter many others who did, as we see in the next section. Markham (1965) criticised attempts to test such a simple, continuous and increasing function for three reasons:

- Industry concentration ratios are poor indicators of monopoly power. The same level of concentration may often generate totally different levels of profitability.
- Schumpeter defined innovation very broadly, to include mergers, new organisations, new advertising campaigns as well as new products and new processes. Schumpeter implied that 'uncommitted balances' (surplus profits) were necessary to engage in highly uncertain

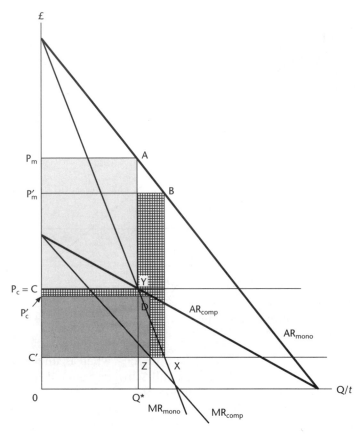

Figure 8.8 Kamien and Schwartz's incentive to innovate

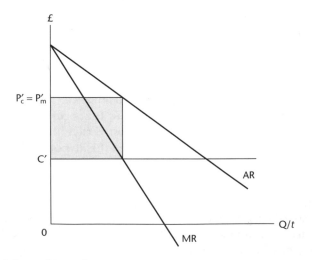

Figure 8.9 Yamey's incentive to innovate

commercial ventures. Therefore to explain research and development expenditures by concentration ratios is to test only a fraction of Schumpeter's hypothesis.

- To imply that research and development and concentration vary continuously and systematically is questionable. Between 1930 and 1963, outlays on research and development rose by around 4,310 per cent; concentration did not rise so dramatically. Markham claimed that the increase in science and scientific personnel seemed independent of increases in concentration. Science does exhibit a sort of natural growth rate. (It is claimed that 80 per cent of all scientists of the past three hundred years are alive today.)

Markham concluded that we should expect a rather weak association between monopoly power and innovation. Much of the research undertaken by firms is imitative and competitive, and not strictly innovative as in the Schumpeterian context.

Oligopolies

Some economists have interpreted Schumpeter to have suggested that at both extremes (perfect competition and monopoly) firms are adverse to large amounts of research and development. In this case we would be testing for an inverted U-shaped function when regressing research and development expenditures and levels of concentration. Scherer confirmed this sort of relationship when he found that research and development employment as a share of total employment increased with industry concentration up to around 50 per cent, after which point it declined (1967b). These findings suggest the classic argument that it is oligopolies that have the most incentive to innovate to free themselves from the tyranny of rivalrous markets.[36]

Given the lack of clear and consistent oligopoly theory, much of the theorising is complex and speculative. As Scherer (1992, p.149) comments: '[T]he results of this theoretical research are sensitive to the assumptions made, and with the appropriate constellation of assumptions, virtually anything can be shown to happen.' This did not, however, preclude attempts at such theorising and research. Let us examine two possible scenarios suggested by Scherer (1992). Increased rivalry, whether by an increase in the number of firms or a greater research and development effort by a major rival, will stimulate an innovatory response from the remaining firms. However, this is only true if the total industry profits to be made are sufficiently large to cover the initial development costs to these firms. Should the number of firms in the industry increase, or if total industry profits fall due to price competition, then firms may fear that profits will not cover their development costs and consequently reduce or abandon further investment in innovation. Thus as rivalry intensifies, so innovative output increases up to a point, beyond which further rivalry acts to discourage further investment and we have an inverted-U relationship. A second line of theorising is to suggest that Schumpeterian monopolies are capable of innovating at an early date, but choose instead to achieve profit maximisation via slower, risk-free research and development investments. If, however, they are faced with the irritant of smaller rivals or entrants investing in new technology they will have an incentive to accelerate their research and development investments to reduce the threat.

---

[36] See, for example, Galbraith (1952), chapter 7.

In view of the tendency of oligopolists to seek co-operative solutions to reduce market uncertainty, we may ask why it is that oligopolists rarely succeed in limiting this form of non-price competition. Price competition reduces industry profits and the same could be said of non-price competition such as advertising and technical innovation. One would thus expect rational oligopolists to attempt to cover non-price aspects of competition.

For an oligopolistic structure of just a few firms it would be relatively easy to agree and decide on a common price. However, to determine what should be the optimal level of research and development expenditure for the group may prove impossible. Price-fixing agreements make it relatively easy to calculate the consequences for the returns over a period of time. Fixing research and development effort will not lead to any easy predictions as to the likely output of research in the industry. If one firm were to be selected to do all the research for the industry, there is the risk that the other firms may be excluded from the ownership of that research. If research were to be shared it would be difficult to co-ordinate the effort across the industry. Given the inherent uncertainty of research and with many firms involved, there may be a temptation to cheat by taking a free ride. This would be compounded by the difficulty of enforcing and policing such agreements.

An additional problem that could frustrate any such agreement is the concern with what would occur if the agreement were to break down. The breakdown of a price agreement implies only minor consequences in the short run. A breakdown of research agreements, on the other hand, would most probably have differential effects on the firms, as those that invested large amounts suffer more than those with a smaller commitment.

The above discussion outlined the difficulties of entering into co-operative research agreements. This should not imply that these types of venture are never undertaken. Research agreements do exist and are usually of two types: firstly, where the focus is on the 'pre-competitive stage', where firms share knowledge at the research and development stages but remain rivals in the product market; secondly, where firms extend their co-operation to include the product market. The aim is to enjoy greater security and higher returns, and to recoup research and development outlays with more certainty. D'Aspremont and Jacquemin (1988) argued that these types of agreement might lead to a reduction in research and development so as to avoid wasteful duplication as well as to a reduction in output as collusive action creates monopoly structures. However, they found little evidence that this was the case, and concluded that the liberal attitudes of governments to joint research and development ventures were justified.

8.7 Empirical work

The Schumpeterian analysis poses two distinct hypotheses. Firstly, that market structure will affect the quantity of research output, and secondly that large firms are more likely to carry out research owing to the benefits of economies of scale in staff, equipment, risk-bearing and financial economies. In this section we briefly examine some of the evidence for these two hypotheses. However, before we start it is important to draw attention to a number of problems that have dogged the research in this area. There are three main problems:

● The direction of causation
● The different innovatory opportunities
● The measurement of innovation

Direction of causation

Research and development can affect concentration levels. Assume an industry of twenty equal-sized firms, which generates a four-firm concentration ratio (CR4) of 20 per cent. Through changes in technology, innovatory opportunities will increase and some firms will benefit while others will be slow to adapt. In twenty years the CR4 statistic will have risen. Thus the existence of innovative opportunities has led to a greater level of concentration. It was Phillips (1966) who first suggested that innovation can affect market structure in that success breeds success and the dominance of certain firms would become more entrenched. This was counter to the Schumpeterian view that any success from innovation would in time be eroded by the imitative strategies of rivals. The latter view was supported by Geroski (1994) who did not believe that innovation could have such a large impact on the rise in post-war industrial concentration. He felt that increased product differentiation, the financial benefits of size as well as stochastic effects exerted far greater influences on the observed increases in concentration. He tested Blair's (1972) hypothesis that technology over the past century (specifically the advent of new materials and electronics) had in fact reduced the minimum efficient size of plants and was thus a force for deconcentration.[37] Geroski (1994, p.40) concluded: 'our results suggest that innovative activity does affect the evolution of market structure in particular industries, and that innovation plays a deconcentrating role wholly consistent with Blair's hypothesis'.

It is often difficult to unravel the direction of causation and it may be safer to conclude that causation moves in both directions.

Different innovative opportunities

Early research and development and concentration correlations were criticised as unsound because it was considered unrealistic to assume that different industries faced the same opportunities for research and development. The opportunities for invention and innovation in the cotton textile industry would appear to be less than those in the pharmaceutical industry. Technical opportunity could be considered as the existence of an industry tradition in creating a vigorous scientific culture. This culture would then generate technical advances to achieve a state termed 'technology-push' as opposed to 'demand-pull', a state where firms were slow to respond to the inevitable change in technology.

Methods used to deal with this problem have been largely impressionistic, for example dividing one's sample into high/low innovatory-opportunities industries. Scherer (1965) excluded firms with low innovatory opportunities and introduced dummy variables for the high innovatory-opportunities firms. Comanor (1967a) made similar impressionistic choices. Jaffe (1986) attempted to classify firms according to twenty 'technological opportunity clusters' by examining the distribution of patents in various patent categories. Levin *et al.* (1987) defined technological opportunities on the basis of interviews conducted with research and development executives, which were intended to discover the extent to which firms were receptive to the advances in science, in terms of information flows from government, universities, suppliers and clients.[38]

---

[37] Minimum efficient size refers to the minimum output which generates constant returns to scale, i.e. lowest long-run average costs. This is further discussed in Chapter 4.

[38] For further discussion on this topic, see Cohen and Levin (1989), pp.1083–90.

Measurement of research and development

Research and development is generally measured in three ways:

- By inputs, i.e. by research and development expenditure (the hiring of scientific personnel and spending on research equipment).
- By outputs of research and development, usually by the numbers of patents issued.
- By lists of inventions or innovation.

The use of research and development expenditure as a measure can be of only limited use for a number of reasons. Firstly, all research and development expenditure in a firm may be allocated to that firm's principal activity, whereas in reality the effort may be directed at a subsidiary activity. Secondly, some innovatory work in a firm may be located outside the research and development departments, for example in design offices. Thirdly, official statistics may not be able to detect the level of research being undertaken by small and medium-sized firms if those firms do not have separate accounting procedures for their research and development activities. Finally, one can simply say that the measure is focused on inputs; it is thus a measure of effort rather than one of technical output.

Patents measure that part of the process between research and development expenditure and the diffusion of the new ideas. The use of patent statistics does have the implicit advantage that, in most cases, firms apply for patents with a view to future commercial exploitation. The problems of using patents, however, are firstly that the propensity to patent tends to vary from industry to industry. For example, firms in defence industries, working on government contracts, seldom patent their inventions since the government will enjoy exclusive rights to all their research output. In other industries, such as organic chemicals and petrochemicals, market advantages can be gained by making small changes to the molecular structure of compounds. This leads to profuse 'manipulated molecule' patenting in such industries. Other reasons to account for different propensities to patent by industries and countries could be the use of patents as entry barriers, and the institutional difficulties in different countries of securing a patent. A second problem with patent statistics is that patents lead to very different outcomes, ranging from the commercially exploitable to the useless. As Geroski (1994, p.7) pointed out, to be meaningful measurements, one must compare like with like. Thus a count of two would imply that two patents are the worth of one patent when measuring technical output. Finally, patents do not always fall into neat categories that can be conveniently correlated with industry sectors.[39]

Some economists have suggested a better measure might be to produce lists of major (or even minor) inventions and innovations over a particular timespan.[40] This has the benefit of hindsight in examining the economic contribution of the major technological advances. The major drawbacks of this approach to measuring innovative activity are that it is expensive to draw up such lists and also highly selective. Judgements have to be made as to what constitutes a major innovation and what may be regarded as only a minor one. One particular approach which Scherer (1992, p.1423) found impressive was to identify relevant technological innovations as those that were 'important enough to warrant annotation in the vast array of trade journals covering particular industries'.

[39] See Patel and Pavitt (1995), p.23, for a rejection of the last two problems.
[40] See ibid., pp.26–33, for details of such measurements and other measures.

A slightly different approach was attempted by Allen (1969) who used the rate of change of labour productivity as his measure of innovatory activity which he regressed against the level of concentration. However, he found no significant relationship. Unfortunately, the methodology of his approach meant that he ignored new product innovation which did not contribute to increased labour productivity. It is also possible that some firms enjoy labour-saving innovations as a result of innovations spilling over from other industries.

Regardless which of the methods is used (input or output), both are highly correlated. It appears that there is a close relationship between the effort put into research and the output of that research. Comanor and Scherer (1969) found in their study that the simple correlation coefficient between the average number of total research employees in 1955 and 1960 and the number of patents issued between those two dates was an impressive 0.821.

Empirical research

Most of the empirical research in the field of industrial innovation has tended to focus on the twin Schumpeterian hypotheses that highly concentrated industries and large firms were more likely to invest in research and development than industries with low concentration measures and small firms. Since a thorough coverage of the literature can be found in surveys conducted by Kamien and Schwartz (1982), Cohen and Levin (1989), Scherer (1992) and Cohen (1995), we focus here on just a few pieces of research in varying detail, to present a flavour of some of the methodologies employed.

Scherer (1965) made use of inputs (scientists employed) and outputs (patents) for 448 of the *Fortune 500* list of companies in the United States in 1955. He found that inventive output increased with firms' sales, but at a less than proportionate rate. Secondly, that differences in technological opportunity were responsible for inter-industry differences in research output, and lastly that research output did not appear to be systematically related to variations in market power, prior profitability, liquidity or product line diversification. A dip in innovative output at high levels of concentration is specifically addressed by Scherer (p.1122) in his conclusion:

> These findings among other things raise doubts whether the big, monopolistic, conglomerate corporation is as efficient an engine of technological change as disciples of Schumpeter (including myself) have supposed it to be. Perhaps a bevy of fact-mechanics can still rescue the Schumpeterian engine from disgrace, but at present the outlook seems pessimistic.

Comanor (1967a) subdivided his sample of industries, somewhat subjectively, into two groups: industries where product and design differences were an important feature of market structure, for example consumer durables, and industries where the above features were unimportant, for example cement and aluminium. The implication was that the first group required greater inputs of research to alter the existing products than did the second group. Comanor found that research levels were in fact greater in the first group.

He then examined the effect that concentration may have in the two groups. Each group was further subdivided into high concentration (a CR8 greater than 70 per cent) and low concentration. He found that in industries where product differentiation was an important factor, concentration was not a significant determinant of innovatory activity. However, in those industries where product differentiation was less important, concentration did seem to play an important role. He interpreted the result by suggesting that, in the latter group, research would be focused on process innovation which is less likely to create 'competitive consequences', i.e. stimulate reactions from rivals. Thus the Schumpeterian hypothesis may well apply to this type of industry. As regards those industries where research is closely linked to competitive strategies, Comanor found that increased concentration did not lead to greater levels of research and thus supported the earlier conclusions of Scherer. He did, however, warn against reading too much into these results as he believed that these differences could completely disappear if innovatory opportunity was taken into account.

Comanor also examined the role that research might play in industries in helping to erect entry barriers. He divided his sample into high and low entry barriers, measured by calculating minimum efficient size of plants (average size of the top 50 per cent of plants by industry output) divided by total industry shipments. He found that where barriers to entry were high, there was no association between concentration and research and development. This he explained by suggesting that high entry barriers were so protective that research and development was an unnecessary form of non-price competition. On the other hand, where barriers to entry were low then concentration was associated with research and development.

Geroski (1994) tested the Schumpeterian hypothesis to discover whether monopolistic structures were more conducive to innovation than competition. Using a data set of 4,378 innovations produced and used between 1945 and 1983 in the UK, Geroski developed the following regression model:

$$I_i = f_i + \lambda_1 \log \pi_i^e + \lambda_2 CON_i + \lambda_3 ENTRY_i + \lambda_4 IMPORT_i + \lambda_5 SFIRM_i + \lambda_6 EXIT_i + \lambda_7 DCON_i \\ + \lambda_8 SIZE_i + \lambda_9 GROW_i + \lambda_{10} KAYO_i + \lambda_{11} EXPORT_i + \lambda_{12} UNION_i + \eta_i$$

where I referred to the level of innovative output; $\log \pi^e$ was the expected price–cost margins following the innovation in natural logs; CON the five-firm concentration ratio; ENTRY, the extent of market penetration by entrants; IMPORT, the market share of imports; SFIRM, small firms with fewer than ninety-nine employees; EXIT, the market share of exiting firms; DCON, the percentage change in the level of concentration during the observed period; SIZE, the industry size; GROW, the growth of the industry; KAYO, the capital intensity; EXPORT, the level of export intensity; UNION, a measure for industry unionisation; and finally η, a measure that captured all other factors that may have influenced innovative output. The subscripts i referred to the firms.

Geroski was reluctant to rely solely on CON as a measure of the degree of monopoly or market power and decided to use ENTRY, IMPORT, SFIRM, DCON and EXIT as well as CON, as more flexible measures of rivalry. Thus an industry with high levels of entry, many small firms, a low and falling concentration ratio and low exit rates could be seen as being competitive. On the other hand, an industry with low entry, few small firms, and high and rising concentration ratios could be seen as experiencing little rivalry and close to the model of monopoly. Thus positive coefficients on ENTRY, IMPORT and SFIRM and negative ones on DCON, EXIT and CON would be consistent with a negative effect on innovation. The remaining six variables referred to all the other factors that might have influenced the speed with which industries responded to expected post-innovation returns.

The estimates calculated by Geroski found strong evidence that there was little effect of monopoly power on the level of innovation. Other than λ_4 (which was insignificant), λ_2 and λ_7 were negative and significant, λ_6 was negative, and λ_3 and λ_5 were both positive.

On the basis of the research it would seem that those industries that were highly concentrated, and becoming more so, were less innovative than the competitive industries. The expectations of monopoly profit as measured by $\log \pi^e$ did have a positive effect on innovation, though Geroski was worried about the difficulty of estimating such a variable. Industry size, export intensity and unionisation appeared to be unrelated to innovatory activity, whilst growth and capital intensity were, though in the case of the latter two, only weakly. With further evidence presented in his analysis of the results, Geroski was able to make a fairly robust conclusion: 'There is, in short, almost no support in the data for popular Schumpeterian assertions about the role of actual monopoly in stimulating progressiveness.'[41]

Alexander *et al.* (1995) re-examined the question of the relationship between research and development productivity and the size of firms, as well as their performance in the global market. For their model they used cross-sectional data from twenty-six international pharmaceutical firms over a three-year period, 1987 to 1989. Their measure of research output was the number of new compounds that any one firm had in its 'R&D pipeline' (OUTPUT); as well as the more traditional R&D output per R&D employee (OUTPUTEMP). Size of firms was measured by employment (TOTALEMP) rather than sales, since the latter could fluctuate with changes in market demand. Additional variables that might affect the level of R&D output, were the levels of R&D investments per employee (RDEXEMP). A squared variant of the latter was used to measure the possible diminishing returns from additional R&D spending $(RDEXEMP)^2$. A measure of past R&D expenditures (PASTRDEMP) was also added to capture the effects of past successes with the expectation that the coefficient would be positive. Finally a dummy variable (FOREIGN) was included to control for differences in regulatory climates between the United States-based firms (0) and those located elsewhere (1). The results showed that the independent variables did have their expected signs and that most were statistically significant. Alexander *et al.* concluded that firm size did matter in the pharmaceutical industry in respect of R&D productivity. In addition they found that greater R&D expenditures did lead to greater levels of R&D output, up to a point after which diminishing returns set in. Finally, the sign on FOREIGN was negative, which suggested that firms outside the United States were less R&D productive, owing possibly to different regulatory climates.

Interpretations of the empirical research

Examining the literature on firm size and innovative activity, Scherer (1992) drew the following conclusions:

- Large firms were more likely to invest in formal research and development and to receive patents, but there was evidence that most manufacturing firms, even those of a modest size, were involved in some innovatory work.
- Using traditional measures of research and development spending ignored a large amount of informal innovatory activity by the smaller firms.
- Within subsets of firms that performed research and development and received patents, there seemed to be evidence that research and development and patenting did, on average, rise linearly with size, as measured by sales.

[41] Geroski (1994), p.59.

- Company research and development to sales ratios did vary more from industry to industry, than within an industry.
- Large size achieved through diversification did not lead to higher research and development to sales ratios, though where the diversification strategy was pursued specifically to develop research and development synergies, the ratio may have been higher.

Cohen (1995) concluded that most of the studies of research and development and firm size showed that there was evidence that size and research and development spending did seem to be related linearly but that research output increased less than proportionately with firm size and could even decline. In effect, this meant that small firms were achieving more innovations per unit of research and development expenditure than the larger firms. This could be interpreted to suggest that large firms were simply concentrating on fewer innovations, but that they followed them more intensively. Thus the average innovation of the large firm could be of a better quality than that of a smaller firm.

When considering the effect that market concentration may have on the level of research and development the results seem to generate a small positive relationship that becomes more fragile as other effects such as technological opportunity and appropriability conditions are considered. Four possible basic interpretations have been made in the literature:

- The positive association between research and development and concentration is compatible with the hypothesis put forward by Schumpeter or the neo-Schumpeterian analysis.
- It may be possible that the medium-sized firms in concentrated industries do a disproportionate amount of research and development. If, for example, an industry consists of eight firms, the high research and development may be due to the bottom four firms. This would imply a conclusion opposite to that of Schumpeter. Williamson (1975) supported this hypothesis. He used data from an earlier study by Mansfield and showed that the medium-sized firms conducted a disproportionate amount of research and development. Medium-sized firms were more marginal to the industry and thus they faced greater risks of survival, whereas the top (four) firms could enjoy a degree of security. A condition of survival in certain industries could then be the ability to come up with innovative ideas. Rosenberg (1976) extended the analysis by examining the coefficient on market share as it affected research and development. He found a negative and significant coefficient at the 5 per cent level, i.e. the largest firm in the industry produced proportionately less research than the next largest, and so on. He interpreted this to mean that the larger the firm, the less it had to gain from generating inventions and innovations. At the extreme, large firms are as much at risk of being put out of business by investing in speculative research and development as the small firms.
- A further possible interpretation is that research and development causes concentration to rise since successful research and development could expand the markets of the firms undertaking it.
- If research and development tended to increase the minimum efficient size of firm, then high research and development expenditures would act as entry barriers which would then create greater concentration.

Thus, the empirical work has not generated clear and unambiguous conclusions. Many of the findings are based on weak data sets, and at times even weaker methodologies. What does seem to permeate the literature is that a simplistic interpretation of the Schumpeterian hypothesis cannot be supported.

8.8 European innovation

Most economic observers would agree that competitiveness of business enterprises and public institutions is an important ingredient of economic growth, development and long-term employment, which are key objectives of public policy. Competitiveness in turn depends on the ability of firms to innovate, to introduce new processes and new products. Whether we consider this process at an enterprise or at a country level, it can either be imported from outside or generated internally. In so far as public policy is involved, the emphasis in the past was to focus on supply-side policies, by developing the necessary infrastructure for 'research-centre' based outputs to provide the country with basic research. In recent times the emphasis has shifted somewhat by attempting to invest in innovation, education and training so as to develop an innovation culture at all levels of business enterprise. Furthermore, policies have also aimed at developing networks, or clusters, not only to stimulate innovation but also to help disseminate innovative output more efficiently.

Nonetheless, in the context of a European policy, a worrying trend was identified by the European Commission (1995a), which it termed 'the European paradox'. This paradox was the fact that, compared with Europe's principal competitors – the United States and Japan – Europe's scientific performance in a number of key areas, such as electronics and information technology, has deteriorated. One of the major weaknesses identified by the Commission was Europe's inferiority in translating research output into an innovative output and consequently losing competitive advantage. In addition, this weakness was further exacerbated by the fact that the two main rivals to Europe were spending proportionally more on global research than was Europe (Table 8.2), and that the gap was not closing.

The Green Paper illustrated the European paradox with the graphs shown in Figure 8.10. In terms of scientific performance, the EU's output, measured by publications per million Ecus (1987 US prices) was above that of its rivals. However, the European technological performance, measured by patents per million Ecus, lagged behind that of the United States and Japan.

The paper went on to identify the reasons why the United States and Japan may have this advantage in their ability to transform inventive output into innovatory output so much more efficiently than Europe (Table 8.3).

By implication, Europe falls short in meeting many of the factors discussed in Table 8.3. The paper proceeds to identify and discuss all the problems that directly hamper the realisation of the sort of innovative culture enjoyed in the United States and Japan. Four main causes were identified.

Table 8.2 ● Total research expenditure as a percentage of GDP, 1993

	%
Europe	2.0
Japan	2.8
United States	2.7

Source: European Commission (1995a).

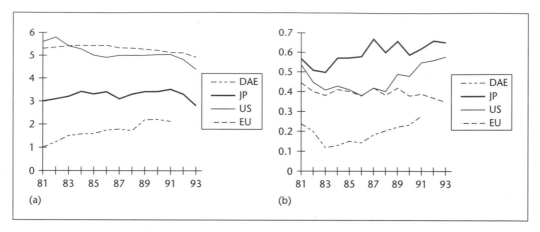

Figure 8.10 Propensity of the EU, Japan, United States and the Dynamic Asian
Economies (Korea, Taiwan and Singapore) to produce technology, 1981–93.
(a) Scientific performance (number of publications per million ecus,
at 1987 US prices, non-BERD); (b) technological performance
(number of patents per million ecus, at 1987 US prices, BERD)

Source: *First European Report on Science and Technology Indicators: Summary*, EUR 15929 (1994).

Table 8.3 ● Some of the factors explaining the American and Japanese successes

United States	Japan
● A more important research effort	● Idem
● A larger proportion of engineers and scientists in the active population	● Idem
● Research efforts better co-ordinated, in particular with regard to civilian and defence research (in particular in the aeronautic, electronic and space sectors)	● A strong ability to adapt technological information, wherever it comes from. A strong tradition of co-operation between firms in the field of R&D
● A close university–industry relationship allowing the blossoming of a large number of high-technology firms	● An improving co-operation between university and industry, especially via the secondment of industrial researchers in universities
● A capital risk industry better developed which invests in high technology. NASDAQ, a stock exchange for dynamic SMEs	● Stable and strong relationships between finance and industry fostering long-term benefits and strategies
● A cultural tradition favourable to risk-taking and to enterprise spirit, a strong social acceptation of innovation	● A culture favourable to the application of techniques and ongoing improvement
● A lower cost for filing licences, a single legal protection system favourable to the commercial exploitation of innovations	● A current practice of concerted strategies between companies, universities and public authorities
● Reduced leadtime for firm's creation and limited red tape	● A strong mobility of staff within companies

Source: European Commission (1995a) p.6.

Weak research base

- *Inadequate inputs.* As shown in Table 8.2, Europe devotes less to research and development than does the United States and Japan. This gap is now three times what it was in the early 1980s.
- *Fragmented efforts.* The paper suggested that Europe has its finger in too many pies. Whereas the United States and Japan concentrate on a limited number of strategic areas, Europe is attempting to cover too many fields of research.
- *Too little industrial research.* European industrial research carried out by enterprises tends to be on a small scale, in contrast to that undertaken in the United States and Japan. The European figure in 1992 was 1.3 per cent of European gross domestic product compared with more than 1.9 per cent in both the competitor countries. Of these amounts, state funding accounted for 12 per cent of the total in Europe, 20 per cent in the United States, but only 1.2 per cent in Japan.
- *Lack of anticipation.* The paper claimed that Europe has failed to anticipate trends and techniques as well as potential constraints on innovative activity. However, the paper was happy to note that Germany and the UK have set up long-term forecasting agencies to help predict future technologies and their potential applications.

Human resources

- *Poor education and training.* European education structures were considered to be too rigid to meet the challenges of new technologies. Educational establishments had placed too much stress on academic knowledge and had shied away from attempting to integrate courses. The concept of lifelong learning had still not been fully accepted and developed by many institutions. More specifically, the paper identified the poor level of technical education in Europe. It argued that technical disciplines are still viewed as non-academic and that science teaching avoids technology, personal experimentation, and key skills such as project work, teamwork, communications, appreciation of markets, entrepreneurship and quality research.
- *Too little mobility.* It was suggested that innovation is a function of exchanges and cross-fertilisation of ideas between firms and universities. In Europe this integration lacks levels achieved in the other two nations. As the paper noted, goods, capital and services move more easily than people and know-how. This lack of mobility was blamed on the reluctance of individual countries to recognise qualifications from other member states; the rigidities in the mortgage market that frustrate people from moving (in contrast to the United States) as well as a whole plethora of taxes and social security payments. One could add the very real problem of communication problems. Both Japan and the United States are far more culturally homogeneous (though the United States less so) than the countries of Europe.

Finance

- *The financial system.* Effective innovation depends on an efficient financial market. Although the major part of risk investment is usually covered by self-finance, enterprises will rely on institutions to help with funding development and commercial production of new products. This market may not work efficiently from the firms' point of view if the lenders view risks as excessive requiring greater guarantees and greater returns. Because of increased globalisation and deregulation of financial markets, lenders now have more opportunities to invest their funds in short-term, low-risk ventures instead of domestic long-term and speculative innovations. The paper reports that between 1987 and 1994, the quantity of venture capital raised in Europe quadrupled to Ecu40 billion, but that the share devoted to high-technology investment fell from 37 per cent in 1985 to just 10 per cent in 1994. Additional evidence identified the over-cautious attitude of banks and fund managers, as well as their reluctance to consider firms not listed on stock exchanges. There was also a lack of an electronics sector stock market specialising in high-tech firms, such as NASDAQ in the United States. (This has changed with the recent introduction of exchanges such as Easdaq in Brussels and TechMARK in London.)

● *Public financing.* Public funding of innovation is both direct (grants to research agencies and firms) and indirect (education, vocational training, infrastructure, and so on). Firms in the United States receive on average twice the amount that European firms do from such state funding. Most of this funding is concentrated on specific, strategic sectors such as defence, aerospace and electronics.

● *Unfavourable tax environment.* As far as personal taxation is concerned, European tax systems do not seem to encourage individuals to invest in unlisted firms pursuing innovatory strategies. As regards company taxation, the regimes tend to vary across Europe, though there were some common factors. Firstly, tax systems tended to favour financing by borrowings rather than from own reserves, and since a large part of innovatory investment is self-financed this places many firms at a disadvantage. Secondly, the tax treatment of intangible investments, for example training, is less advantageous than the taxation of tangible investments. Finally, the range of risk-capital tax systems in Europe is large and this leads to institutional complexity which may frustrate the transnational movement of such investment.

Legal and regulatory environment

● *Too little use made of patents.* In comparison with the United States and Japan, the number of patent applications in Europe has been declining. It was argued that this is due to: the cost of applying for and maintaining the patents; expensive litigation in the case of disputes; and the lack of awareness of the revenues that can be earned from licensing patents.

● *Standards, certification and quality systems.* Innovations are developed under various systems that govern standards, certifications and quality. These can either encourage or hamper innovation. The design of new products may well be constrained by having to meet what firms may consider to be unrealistic performance standards, for example safety requirements. In the case of process innovation, firms may have to conform to employee safety rules, environmental rules and export regulations.

● *Cumbersome administrative formalities.* The paper claimed that the amount of administrative red tape that exists in Europe can frustrate the setting up of businesses and their expansion in line with a new technology. It was considered in excess of what American firms had to face.

In view of the problems hampering investment in research and development as well as the diffusion of that research within Europe, the European Commission suggested thirteen courses of action that could be pursued to correct the problems identified. These initiatives appear fairly obvious in the light of the above arguments. For example, the suggestions cover actions such as attempting to forecast future technologies, placing a greater focus on strategic research, developing better education and training, improving the mobility of labour, and better financing of innovatory investment. Whether these strategies are implemented and followed and whether European enterprises manage to close the gap on their American and Japanese rivals, only time will tell.

8.9 Conclusions

In this chapter we have examined the role of innovation in industrial markets. We have also examined innovation as a strategy, and its usefulness in determining industrial performance. We defined the stages of research and development to understand the long and often highly uncertain progress by which an idea is transformed to wide commercial exploitation. The obstacles to the efficient spread of technical advances were considered at inter- and intra-firm levels, which implicitly suggested a role for public policy in attempting to ameliorate some of the bigger obstacles. Our discussion led us to assess the issue of patents and to determine their usefulness in creating the conditions that can stimulate new technologies for the benefit of industry and society.

In sections 8.4 and 8.5 we considered the returns to industrial research and development to determine how such investments can help profitability and achieve other defined corporate objectives. The parameters defining the investment choices in research are many and complex, but to ignore them is to court failure of the strategy which can have far-reaching consequences for the individual firm. The high risks of failure may be sufficient to dampen the ardour of all but the largest or the most committed of firms to be the first in the field with a new idea.

We also examined the empirical evidence for the Schumpeterian hypotheses regarding industry structure and firm size. What was evident is that the clarity and precision of the hypotheses is not matched by the empirical work. When faced with the complexity of real industrial structures, the wide variety of possible strategies, the different technical opportunities and the difficulties in measuring the variables, the results appear fragile and often qualified to the point of irrelevance. Nonetheless, a general consensus does seem to have emerged, though it is not as robust as one could wish. It seems to suggest that large size and high levels of concentration are not *particularly* important to the realisation of technological change.

In the final section, we focused on the performance of European industry in comparison with the achievements of American and Japanese industry and identified possible reasons why Europe seemed to be lagging behind.

Key terms

Delphi technique
Diffusion
Innovation
Invention

Patent
Patent length and breadth
Schumpeterian hypothesis

Case study 8.1
Getting a grip on innovation

Innovation is the key, says Hugh Facey as he shows off the headquarters of Gripple, his metal engineering business, which is expanding at a time when many other engineering companies are struggling. He has pursued innovation and creativity, whether in new products and processes, devising the right physical working environment, or beating the rise of sterling. Gripple, which makes wire fencing products, operates from a converted Victorian gun works in Sheffield. It is a bright, airy building that mixes factory floor space with open plan offices. The restoration award the site won in 1995 sits among many awards, for exports and innovation, that line the office shelves. 'This was given to us by President Mitterrand,' says Mr Facey, pointing out a Sevres vase, awarded by the French president in 1990 for the Grand Prix inventor's prize. That invention, a wire joining mechanism, has since been refined and developed to produce three core products that now sell in more than 40 countries. Exports, mainly to Europe and the US, account for about 80 per cent of output.

Gripple's core product, the wire joiner, is a single-cast piece of metal containing springs and toothed wedges that grip metal rope when pressure is applied. It is used by farmers and fruit growers to join and tighten fencing and trelliswork. Vineyards in France and South Africa are among Gripple's biggest customers. BHP of Australia is its largest single customer, primarily for wire fencing on agricultural land. 'In the agricultural sector, we are replacing something that used to be done by hand, and by that I mean tying knots,' says Mr Facey. 'Vineyards have to retension their wire trellises after every harvest. In trials in South Africa, we were able to retension 30 rows in the time it took a guy to do one.' Gripple's two other main products, the rope grip and hang-fast systems, are used in the building and electricals industries to suspend ventilation, heating and wire ducts. Gripple fasteners are used to fix signs suspended by wires in supermarkets, hospitals and airports. From a slow start in the early 1990s, when Gripple was developing its products, profits are starting to grow and sales are rising fast, says Mr Facey. The company is aiming for turnover of £8.5m this year, up from £6m last year. Staff numbers have risen from 50 to 75 in the past 18 months and the company has opened offices in Johannesburg, Chicago, Montevideo and Strasbourg.

'Driving innovation' is the company's watchword. Mr Facey recently commissioned a black cab bearing that slogan to help raise Gripple's profile in Sheffield, particularly among graduates from the city's two universities. The company has close links with both Sheffield Hallam and the University of Sheffield, whose research graduates have helped develop new, harder materials and other aspects of product design. The need to innovate means a constant search for high-quality staff. 'About 25 per cent of our staff are qualified engineers and we also bring in graduates for research and development.' Mr Facey started his first company, Estate Wire, in the 1980s when he set up in competition with a former employer, making wire fencing. He sold the company for about £1m in 1993 to concentrate on wire gripping mechanisms. However, 'we were not making the inroads we had hoped for', he says. 'So we went back to fencing and packaged the rope grips with it.' With the rope grips included as part of a kit, the product took off.

3i, the venture capitalist, took a 10 per cent stake in the business three years ago, investing £900,000. Ken Beaty, 3i investment director, says: 'The upside for us is that the product is protected by patents and it is so demonstrably better than anything else that joins bits of wire.' Gripple has spent about £500,000 on patents and a further £50,000–£60,000 a year maintaining them. When a producer in China tried to copy a Gripple mechanism, the company slapped an injunction on it. 'Patents work,' says Mr Facey. Striving for innovation does not mean taking wild risks. Mr Facey maintains an unusual balance between creativity and conservatism. When the value of sterling began to climb against other European currencies, Mr Facey converted the company's £400,000 mortgage into a D-Mark account, and later into a euro account. 'We have effectively reduced our currency risk with back-to-back cover,' he says. Ways to drive down costs is another preoccupation. 'We are constantly automating to get down labour costs,' he says, adding that the company spent £1.25m on new machinery last year. 'He is highly creative and full of energy and entrepreneurialism,' says Mr Beaty. 'But he also has a conservative approach to running the business. He is risk-averse which makes for a good combination. Most entrepreneurs need another manager to sweep up after them.'

© The Financial Times Limited, 15 June 2000. Reprinted with permission.

Case study 8.2
Strategy for creativity

Corporate leaders and government ministers are forever exhorting UK business to do more to develop new ideas. But what are the qualities that mark out the most innovative companies? Some of the answers can be found by going to the pub. At Bass, the brewing group, new brands such as All Bar One and O'Neill's represent a novel partnership between corporate might and individual spark. Bass's traditional market on the housing estates in the Midlands and the north of England was flagging in the early 1990s. 'We needed a radical "break-out" strategy of new product development and concept innovation,' says Tim Clarke, chief executive of Bass Leisure Retail. Senior executives went talent-spotting in the pub business and persuaded two young entrepreneurs, Amanda Wilmott and David Lee, to come and work with the group for a fixed period in exchange for a share of profits if the venture succeeded.

Ms Wilmott developed All Bar One, the upmarket, female-friendly chain that has opened 50 outlets in city centres in the past five years. Mr Lee was responsible for It's a Scream, a 75-strong chain of student venues. 'They've had the personal satisfaction of expressing their creativity, which is very important to them,' says Mr Clarke. 'We take ownership of the brand and the intellectual property, but they have corporate cashflow behind them and an extremely attractive earn-out.' Other brands, including Vintage Inns and Hollywood Bowl, were conceived in-house by aspiring entrepreneurs who were taken off regular duties and encouraged to put their ideas into practice in a kind of 'fit-out studio'. The retail brands Bass has developed over the past five to six years are now contributing a third of turnover, he says. Top-level backing in the company is crucial. 'Senior management spends two or three nights a week out and about in the business, understanding where the creative ideas are and tying them back in with the formal process of consumer market research.'

Bass's experience accords with new research from PA Consulting, the management consultancy group, that emphasises the importance of creativity and leadership for stimulating innovation. PA questioned chief executives, marketing directors and technical directors at 150 companies, identifying nine elements of innovative companies. 'There's no silver bullet to making innovation happen,' says John Buckley, PA's head of technology. 'You have to have all the jigsaw in place, the infrastructure, the technology and so on. But the surprise for me was that without this vision and committed leadership from the top, it's not going to happen.' PA finds that high R&D expenditure does not necessarily lead to greater innovation or bigger turnover from new products. Indeed, companies spending most on R&D are getting the least return, says Mr Buckley. Larger, more mature companies are often under considerable pressure to improve existing products rather than develop new ones, he says. They often have a greater aversion to risk than smaller or younger companies. 'Although they have much larger R&D budgets in absolute terms, they spend much less of them on really innovative products,' he says. 'The leaders of smaller companies are showing more vision and leadership and fostering a creative culture.' Both he and Mr Clarke at Bass argue that companies need to pursue both risky new projects and straightforward product improvements if they are to increase total shareholder return. 'For every All Bar One that emerges, there has to be a willingness to take the failures,' says Mr Clarke. 'The investment in pilots would be anything from £1m to £3m per outlet, and you never know whether they're going to be successful or not.' From nothing, Bass put £25m to £30m of revenue investment a year over three years into new brand development. 'The payback can be quite dramatic. If you do a concept trial on five outlets and write that off, it's completely dwarfed by the results from 75 It's a Scream pubs.'

How do companies make the necessary shift to a more creative environment? They may only be forced into it by finding themselves in a strategic cul de sac, as Bass was. This was the case with Kenwood, the appliance maker that is undergoing a painful restructuring and switching the bulk of its production from Hampshire to China. 'We took the decision to encourage innovation as part of our turnround strategy,' says Colin Gordon, chief executive. Last year, Kenwood launched 28 products ranging from dishwasher-safe deep fat fryers to a bathroom steam-cleaner for the Italian market. This was more than double the number of new products two years ago, he says. The changes have included recruiting more 'creative' people, improving the timing of launches, learning from mistakes, ensuring successes are widely broadcast in the company, and introducing multi-disciplinary development teams. Designers can get the chance to see their product through to the manufacturing stage and ensure it is made to the right specifications. Innovation is now part of a broader strategy, not something locked away in the R&D department, he says. 'People can push their ideas forward and have them listened to. This was missing before.'

The most profitable companies put far more emphasis than less profitable ones on innovation in the marketplace, the research finds. Yet there are serious disagreements between technical directors on one side and chief executives and marketeers on the other about whether innovation is primarily a technological issue or a customer issue. 'Far too many companies are trying to focus on the product,' says Mr Buckley. 'If I'm a shareholder in a food company, do I want them spending my investment on basic research or getting a better product on to the market faster? I think it should be the latter. Innovation is a chief executive issue, not an R&D issue.'

Case study 8.3
Shedding light on the limits to innovation

Last weekend, I bought some light bulbs for less than £2 each. The manufacturer claims they use one-quarter of the electricity of a conventional light bulb and that they last 10 times longer. The story of the everlasting light bulb is among the hoariest myths in business economics. According to legend, inventors have frequently come up with designs for an everlasting light bulb which would cost no more to make than ordinary bulbs. But a conspiracy of light bulb manufacturers has always ensured that these innovations are suppressed, so that the continuing market for disposable light bulbs is not spoiled. As with all urban myths, there are numerous variations. The product is not always a light bulb. The same claims are made for tights: what woman would not rush to purchase a pair of long-lasting tights? And why don't batteries go on for ever? It must surely be possible to build automobiles that would never wear out. But not only do Ford and General Motors choose not to do this, they constantly introduce superficial redesigns to their products to induce us to buy unnecessary replacements. We are all led to believe that built-in obsolescence is endemic to contemporary capitalism.

But the myth is indeed a myth. There is no need to appeal to the better nature, or environmental conscience, of light bulb manufacturers: they will not suppress the everlasting light bulb because it does not pay them to do so. The clearest demonstration of the issues was provided 30 years ago by Peter Swan, an Australian economist. Suppose there are several competing producers of light bulbs. Our hypothetical inventor approaches one of them. The company will indeed recognise that ultimately, when all the world's bulbs have been replaced by the new discovery, its sales will fall. But until then, it can expect a 100 per cent market share. Most of the lost sales will be the lost sales of its competitors. Innovation has always been the mainstay of competition and no competitive company would pass up such an opportunity. Now give the story a more sinister turn; the myth relies on conspiracy. Even if an individual company was prepared to seize the opportunity created by the everlasting light bulb, the manufacturers would establish a cartel to see that our inventor was assassinated or otherwise removed from the scene. But would they? Visualise yourself as the light bulb king, a John D. Rockefeller or Bill Gates dominating the world market. It is easiest to see how you would respond to the inventor if you imagine yourself renting rather than selling your bulbs. And it is very likely that if you were a light bulb monopolist, that is what you would do. Renting these prized objects would allow you to discriminate according to the ultimate use, charging more for office and public lighting than for domestic illumination.

That is what utilities generally did when they had a monopoly. It is how Xerox behaved, for example, so long as its patents upon photocopiers remained effective. Rental gives you control; only once the photocopying market became competitive did sales take over from rental as the principal means of supply. In such a world, the incentives of the light bulb monopoly are to charge whatever rental the market will bear, and to provide that service as cheaply as possible. The monopoly will grasp the benefits of the everlasting bulb for itself, and thank the inventor for adding to its profits. The rental structure makes the issue particularly clear, but there is no real difference if you monopolise the sale of light bulbs rather than the provision of light bulb services. You recoup the benefits of the new technology in the price of the bulb. A competitive company would wish to introduce the everlasting light bulb as soon as possible, and so would a cartel or monopoly. It is a little harder, but still relatively straightforward, to deal with imaginary cases between perfect competition and true monopoly, and to show that the same arguments hold. Built-in obsolescence arises mainly because consumers genuinely want new things. Trivially new brands of washing powder, or restyled automobile designs, or new season's fashions, are all the results of competition: they arise from rivalry, not monopoly. And this account fits reasonably well with what has happened in the light bulb market. It has always been possible to manufacture light bulbs that would last for many years.

But the higher cost and lower efficiency of these bulbs meant that they were not an attractive proposition for consumers. Only recently did new technology enable long-life, low-energy bulbs to be produced at costs reasonably comparable to those of conventional bulbs. While the number of manufacturers of these new bulbs was relatively small, and production limited, their high prices took full account of their value to consumers. But as competition in the market increased, so price fell towards the cost of supply. That is why I was able to buy my bulbs for £1.90. And the reason there are no eternal automobiles or indestructible tights is that at the price and in the quality at which these goods can be manufactured, they are not products which many people wish to buy.

© John Kay, 1999.

Questions for discussion

1. 'Economists believe that new knowledge is more important to growth than the accumulation of physical capital' (Schmookler, 1952). Explain. Are all high-growth economies technically advanced?

2. Suggest how one may calculate the profitability of new product innovation, assuming that it is intended to replace an existing product. (Use net present value method.)

3. Explain how research and innovation can benefit society.

4. It is sometimes argued that research and development may not be subject to diminishing returns. Why? Is there no limit to what man can invent?

5. Do you believe that car manufacturers have an incentive to develop a safer vehicle, other than for a relatively narrow niche market?

6. With reference to Case study 8.1, discuss the factors that have helped Gripple's innovation strategy.

7. Case study 8.2 has the following sentence:

   Yet there are serious disagreements between technical directors on one side and chief executives and marketeers on the other about whether innovation is primarily a technological issue or a customer issue.

   Discuss the reasons why such a tension may exist in modern organisations.

Further reading

Cohen, W.M. and Levin, R.C. (1989) Empirical studies of innovation and market structure, in Schmalensee, R. and Willig, R. (eds) *Handbook of Industrial Organisation*, vol. 2. Amsterdam: North-Holland, pp.1059–107.

European Commission (1995) *Green Paper on Innovation*, COM(95)688.

Freeman, C. and Soete, L. (1997) *The Economics of Industrial Innovation*, 3rd edn. London: Pinter.

Geroski, P. (1994) *Market Structure, Corporate Performance and Innovative Acitivity*. Oxford: Clarendon Press.

Karshenas, M. and Stoneman, P. (1995) Technological diffusion, in Stoneman, P. (ed.) *Handbook of the Economics of Innovation and Technical Change*. Oxford: Blackwell, chapter 7.

Mansfield, E. (1969) Industrial research and development: characteristics, costs and diffusion results, *American Economic Review, Papers and Proceedings*, **59**, 65–79.

Patel, P. and Pavitt, K. (1995) Patterns of technological activity: their measurement and interpretation, in Stoneman, P. (ed.) *Handbook of the Economics of Innovation and Technical Change*. Oxford: Blackwell, Chapter 2.

Scherer, F.M. (1992) Schumpeter and plausible capitalism, *Journal of Economic Literature*, **30**, 1416–33.

Schumpeter, J. (1942) *Capitalism, Socialism, and Democracy*. New York: Harper.

Stoneman, P. (1995) *Handbook of the Economics of Innovation and Technical Change*. Oxford: Blackwell.

CHAPTER *9*

Vertical relationships

Learning objectives

After reading this chapter the student should be able to:

- Understand the benefits that vertical integration can confer on firms

- Evaluate the conflicting arguments regarding monopoly and the incentive to vertical integrate

- Evaluate the problems of measuring vertical integration and appreciate some of the empirical evidence for vertical integration

- Appreciate other forms of vertical relationships such as franchising and networks

- Identify various vertical restraints imposed by firms, and evaluate their contribution to allocative efficiency and competition

9.1 Introduction

Vertical relationships refer to a variety of issues that cover relations between firms involved at successive stages of the production process. These issues refer to such things as **vertical integration**, **agency** theory and bilateral monopoly. We can regard the production process as a flow, starting from the extraction or acquisition of raw materials which are then processed into intermediate goods. These are eventually transformed into the finished product. We refer to activities located at the initial stages of production as 'upstream' activities and those which are closer to the market for the final product as 'downstream' activities. Thus upstream (or **backward**) vertical integration refers to firms undertaking the production of inputs necessary for their production process, whilst downstream (or **forward**) vertical integration refers to firms moving into activities that utilise their outputs. Since capacity may differ at different stages of production, firms may also have to rely on external market transactions to make up their required capacity. Balanced vertical integration would occur if capacities at successive stages were equal. Firms may decide to integrate vertically for a wide variety of reasons. Alternatively they may decide not to integrate, but to develop vertical relationships by relying on 'vertical controls'. Vertical controls arise from contracts between firms at successive stages of production and these limit the freedom of the 'agents' *vis-à-vis* their principal firms. An example of such contracts is franchising, which is discussed in section 9.5.

Why do firms develop vertical relationships? Fundamentally, these relationships allow firms to improve the co-ordination of their production activities. Firms merge or enter into contractual obligations so as to increase joint upstream and downstream profits. Should firms exploit their increased market power, the effects of such action may result in welfare loss to the consumer and decreased economic efficiency. However, vertical relationships may just as equally increase welfare and economic efficiency if co-ordinated activity leads to lower costs of production.

9.2 Vertical integration

Vertical integration can be defined as the ownership of the production of an input used in the production of a firm's output, or the ownership of a production unit that uses the firm's outputs. Firms will be attracted to vertical integration if it leads either to an increase in their revenue or to a reduction of their costs. Thus if profits of non-integrated firms can be improved through such a strategy then firms will consider vertical integration. When one considers cost reductions, one may have to bear in mind that the strategy of vertical integration can generate additional costs to the organisation. Carlton and Perloff (1999) identified three possible costs. Firstly the firm may find that using its own resources to produce inputs or to distribute its output may not be as efficient as using specialised firms in the market. Secondly, as a firm integrates, management may face increasing costs of managing a larger organisation. Finally, vertical mergers may attract the attention of anti-monopoly agencies and consequently the firm may be faced with expensive legal fees.

The reasons for vertical integration are varied and do not lend themselves well to neat categorisations. Nonetheless some broad classifications have been identified and analysed. The earliest explanations for vertical integration tended to focus on issues such as the technological advantages of linking successive stages of production, the risk and uncertainty attached to the supply of upstream products or the distribution of firms' finished products, the avoidance of government taxation and price controls, and finally the desire to secure market power. Williamson (1971) developed an alternative rationale to the classical paradigm. The 'transaction costs' approach did not deny the earlier explanations, but managed to place most of these reasons into a more logically coherent methodology. This section explores reasons put forward by economists to explain why firms integrate vertically:

● *Transaction costs*. Transaction costs differ from production costs in that they are associated with market transactions between buyers and sellers. Vertical integration may reduce or eliminate such costs.

- *Technological conditions*. Vertical integration may lead to the reduction of production costs. This may occur where there are complementary processes that need to be carried out quickly so as to save intermediate costs of delivery.
- *Uncertainty*. The relationship between firms in successive stages of production is subject to many uncertainties. One of the major causes of such uncertainty is the lack of complete information. Vertical integration can help to correct such incompleteness and thus reduce uncertainty.
- *Assured supply*. Firms may be concerned about the risks of being let down by a supplier. To ensure a steady supply of inputs, firms will consider backward vertical integration.
- *Externalities*. Externalities will arise when a vertical relationship leads to a situation where a firm is unable to avoid incurring additional costs brought about by the actions of its supplier or distributor.
- *Complexity*. Vertical relationships may be characterised by complex technical and legal relations that may prove too costly to arrange between two 'separate' firms.
- *Moral hazard*. The lack of moral hazard simply implies that a firm may have no incentive to maximise revenue or minimise costs when it is contracted by another firm at a different stage of production.
- *Specificity*. Specificity arises when a firm invests in the production or distribution of custom-made products for specific clients. This may leave the firm vulnerable to threats from clients in the event of disputes.
- *Government action*. Through vertical integration firms will be able to avoid various government taxes, restrictions and regulations when imposed on one stage of production and not on another.
- *To increase market power*. Firms may be attracted to vertical integration as a means of restricting competition. If a firm were to acquire the source of a raw material input it could then squeeze the profit margins of its rivals by setting a high price and even force them out of the industry. The role that monopolists can play in vertically integrating backwards or forwards is discussed in section 9.3. Market power as exercised through various vertical restraints is discussed in section 9.6.

Transaction costs

Williamson (1971, p.112)[1] argued that vertical integration could reduce market transaction costs. He wrote: '[T]he firm is not a simple efficiency instrument . . . but possesses coordinating potential that sometimes transcends that of the market'. This idea was based on Coase's (1937) seminal article on the nature of the firm. Coase had asked the basic question of why firms exist. If the price mechanism that operates in the market allocates goods and co-ordinates economic activity, why do we have firms? Coase argued that there were costs involved in the use of the price mechanism owing to poor information and contractual problems. These costs were well summarised by Joskow (1985) as the costs involved in negotiating contracts, monitoring performance, enforcing contractual promises and pursuing litigation in the event of breach of promises. In addition, firms relying on market transaction would have to acquire, handle and process information to ensure correct decisions were being taken. Within a firm, co-ordination is achieved via management direction and not

[1] See also Williamson (1975, 1989) for further discussion.

through prices. It was the 'supersession' of this price mechanism that defined the nature of the firm. Williamson took the basic Coasian ideas and fleshed out a convincing argument as to why firms integrate. He argued that where the market *fails* to work well, i.e. proves costly, the firm will 'internalise' that particular market transaction. Thus the definition of market failure is any transaction which involves costs which can be reduced by substituting internal organisation for external market exchange. Whenever there is a large differential between external (market) co-ordination and internal organisation, there will be a tendency towards vertical integration. The market failures identified by Williamson are discussed below.

Why is it that the firm is able to organise and coordinate production at less cost than the market? According to Williamson, the firm will benefit from internal organisation in three ways: incentives, controls and 'inherent structural advantages'. Incentives cover the advantages of being able to avoid costly and time-consuming bargaining with other producers at different stages of production. Controls imply that the firm can benefit from stronger controls over intra-firm activity as opposed to inter-firm activity. Controls will also imply that through a process of organisational rewards and penalties, the firm will have the ability to access more wide-ranging and more accurate information flows. Williamson also noted that the firm has more efficient 'conflict resolution machinery'. Should conflict arise within a firm, this can normally be resolved by fiat rather than rely on expensive arbitration or litigation. Finally, structural advantages may increase the economies of communication exchange. Thus staff within the organisation will share common training, experiences and codes of practice which will ensure that the quality of the communications is improved.

The benefits outlined above need not apply universally to all firms. Different firms have different strengths and weaknesses. Some firms may be good at exploiting the market by possessing good bargaining skills and clever lawyers and not so good at internalising market transactions. Let us now move to the specific arguments for vertical integration. Most of these can be accommodated within the Williamson paradigm.

Technological conditions

A familiar argument for vertical integration is that technical conditions may dictate that production processes should be integrated under one co-ordinating unit. A traditional example is the steel industry. Blast furnaces that make steel and the strip mills that shape and cut the steel are not only controlled by the same firm but will also be located within the same plant so as to conserve heat (thermal economies). Another example is the production of timber pulp and papermaking. Since the stage involves weight-loss production processes, vertical integration can save high transport costs. Generally speaking, where there are close, technologically complementary processes, vertical integration can achieve better planning and co-ordination, longer production runs, and better use of capacity. In most cases, however, such a justification for vertical integration does not lead to vertical mergers, since where such advantages exist, integrated plants are built from the outset and one could argue that the two successive stages of production have evolved into just the one stage. Nonetheless should technologies change then opportunities may arise for integration. Pickering (1974, p.57) quoted the example of ICI in the man-made fibre industry, which, in the early 1970s found that when the bulking process had become closely associated with the new texturising process, decided to integrate vertically so as to be better able to co-ordinate the new process with its existing output.[2] However Williamson (1989) argued that the production economies realised by common ownership is greatly exaggerated. The real reason why closely related technical processes are integrated is that the alternative of using a market transaction is too expensive. The costs of drawing up and monitoring a contract between an owner of a blast furnace and an owner of steel mill would be prohibitively high if not impossible: an example of an 'incomplete contract'.

Uncertainty

Uncertainty creates a number of problems for firms in the organisation of production. The co-ordination of production involves many complex event variables, some that can be predicted others that cannot. This is what Simon (1959) termed 'bounded rationality'; the limited ability of economic agents to absorb and process information to make correct decisions. Success will depend on how well firms can react and adapt to unanticipated events. Helfat and Teece (1987) discussed two types of uncertainty. The first can be referred to as primary uncertainty which is determined by factors external to the firm and the industry. These factors would include such things as changes in technology, changes in consumer demand and changes in government direction. Secondary uncertainty arises because of the lack of information facing decision-makers. This information may be difficult to secure as vertically related firms may fail to disclose it, or worse, attempt to distort the information so as to deliberately increase the costs to their rivals. Choi (1998) argued that vertical integration could be used as a means of concealing information. When a vertically integrated firm produces goods for its own consumption it avoids making publicly observable market transactions. In certain cases the absence of such 'transaction signals' creates uncertainty in the minds of rivals. Choi argued that Japanese software companies developed most of their output for specific firms, never selling the goods on the open market. This was in sharp contrast to the practices in the American market. This then made it difficult to assess the costs and true profitability of the software used by Japanese firms.

Transactions between firms at different stages of production can be subject to many additional uncertainties. Raw material supplies can be subject to political and climatic factors which may interfere in the smooth flow of inputs. Demand for the finished products may also be subject to unexpected disturbances. If the supply of inputs is out of equilibrium with the demand for the finished products, firms will lose revenue. Carlton (1979) noted that most market prices do not adjust automatically to ensure a balance between supply and demand. In fact, for prices to be an 'effective' signal, they must remain unchanged for a period of time, to allow for decision-making to take place. As a consequence, a firm will never quite know the level of demand for its product in the short term. Production, in response to demand changes, is never instantaneous and decisions have to be taken prior to any clear price signals. Thus firms face the risk of over- or under-production. Some of these uncertainties can be reduced by vertical integration. Arrow (1975) discussed the possibility that integrated firms may secure information about supply and demand conditions earlier than non-integrated firms.

[2] Pickering (1974), p.57.

Another possible cause of uncertainty is the quality of the inputs. Without directly observing a supplier's production process a firm will be faced with the risk that it may be in receipt of substandard inputs that have a short life expectancy. Thus the desire to monitor the production process may encourage a firm to integrate vertically. This is echoed by Hennessy (1997) who found that in the food industry one of the transaction costs involved in the marketing of intermediate goods was the cost of determining quality.

Uncertainty, however, need not always lead to vertical integration. In an industry characterised by rapid technological change, a firm will be able to reduce uncertainty by buying in its required inputs. Jacobson and Andréosso-O'Callaghan (1996) used the example of major software firms such as Microsoft and Lotus who did not publish their own users' manuals, preferring instead to use specialised firms. All the uncertainty surrounding the continuing demand for such manuals was thus borne by the specialist firms. In the event, demand did fall as online manuals and online help functions largely superseded the manual. Carlton (1979) concluded that an equilibrium strategy would occur where a firm integrates to meet high probability demand and leaves low probability demand to other firms in the market. Carlton referred to this strategy as the concept of 'partial integration'. In a further development, Emons (1996) considered the case of downstream firms faced with a stochastic demand for inputs, which required 'less in bad times than in good times'. These downstream firms can either produce their own inputs or buy them through the market. Two assumptions were made. Firstly, firms invest in the required capacity to meet demand in good times, and secondly, firms will not sell their inputs. Given the two assumptions, he concluded that vertical integration can lead to additional costs when firms face idle capacity in bad times. However, Emons argued that when downstream firms produce their own inputs, aggregate demand for the inputs falls, which leads to a fall in input prices. This price effect will outweigh any possible costs of excess capacity.

Assured supply

Adelman (1955) reasoned that shortages in the supply of goods typically arise through lags in the growth of supply of those goods while demand is growing strongly. Firms in the market for final goods are better able to judge the level of demand than firms producing the inputs. Under normal market conditions, price rations the availability of goods to buyers. However, in the short run, the prices of most standard goods will not adjust instantaneously to perceived shortages and instead manufacturers ration the available supply. Therefore, there is a danger that buyers will not be supplied with sufficient inputs to complete their planned output. This may even occur when firms have agreed contracts to ensure supply but where enforcement of such contracts is difficult.[3] In the long run, as supply shortages become apparent, prices increase and this in turn increases the costs of production. If this becomes a frequent scenario, firms may consider vertical integration to supply their own product. One must be careful to distinguish the causes of the supply shortages. If the shortage is due to factors beyond the control of supplying firms, such as climatic effects on output, then vertical integration will not protect the firm.

[3] See Gow and Swinnen (1998) for an example of difficulties in enforcing contracts in the agricultural industry in eastern Europe.

Assuring the level of supply or indeed the most efficient method of distribution led some economists to argue that the level of vertical integration in an industry can be linked to a lifecycle of an industry.[4] In the early stages of an industry, firms must vertically integrate backwards to develop their own specific components and integrate forwards to ensure efficient marketing of the final product. As the industry matures, supply industries and independent distribution channels evolve, allowing firms to divest themselves of upstream and downstream activities. Eventually, as the industry reaches full maturity, vertical integration may be considered for strategic reasons as a means of achieving market power.

Externalities

An externality exists when property rights are poorly specified, which means that a resource is not subject to effective ownership and control by its producer. A few examples will help to explain the problem.

Firm A discovers an advantageous process that only firm B can develop and produce. A will ask B to keep the idea a secret from A's rivals and to sell the finished product to no one but A. However, incentives exist for B to cheat, in which case A will have lost any benefit. A has a clear incentive to integrate with B to ensure 'effective ownership' of the new process. Another example is the case of the US automobile and petrol industries in the 1920s. Their development and profitability were retarded by the slow pace of innovation of petrol retailing: petrol was still being sold in small corner shops. To speed up the development of petrol retailing, the petrol industry integrated forwards. Had it invested in petrol stations *and* allowed them to stay independent, the new stations could have sold other firms' petrol. Similar cases can be found in the UK, in, for example, brewing, tailoring and airlines. Some manufacturers argue that forward integration into distribution is necessary to protect their investments. Final demand may be too important to be left in the hands of inexperienced or inefficient retailers.

Complexity

When two successive stages of production are linked by potentially complex legal relations it may be more efficient to integrate vertically. To guarantee a more certain supply of goods or distribution outlets, a firm may attempt to negotiate a long-term contract with its supplier or buyer. However, if the product is non-standardised and surrounded with a great deal of uncertainty, such as frequent changes in product design or technology, the contract must be exhaustively specified to avoid all possible contractual ambiguities which could result in expensive litigation. An alternative might be to negotiate only a short-term contract. In some cases, though, vertical relations may require a commitment by a firm to long-term investments, and thus only a long-term contract will be considered to ensure a guaranteed return on the investment. In these cases neither long-term nor short-term contracts are efficient solutions. This was referred to by Williamson (1971, p.115) as **contractual incompleteness**. The resolution of the problem is for the firm to integrate vertically.

[4] For example, Adelman (1955) and Langlois and Robertson (1989).

A slightly different argument for complexity was provided by Monteverde and Teece (1982). They found that the higher the level of investment undertaken by engineering firms in the production of component parts, the greater the tendency towards integration. They suggested that the buyers of technologically complex and strategically important inputs could find themselves at the mercy of their suppliers. To avoid any possible threats of foreclosure, downstream firms would be attracted to upstream integration.

A good example of complexity is the film industry in its manufacturing and retailing stages. Each film is unique and patterns of distribution of one film will never quite coincide with those of another. Issues of pairing, regional exposure, repeat showings, television sales, and degree of promotional effort determine a unique distribution strategy for each film. In effect this implies complex contractual relations between the film-maker, the distributor and the exhibitor. Contractual agreements would also have to be monitored with a sophisticated, and costly, inspectorate. It may be simpler for film-makers to integrate vertically forwards with distributors and cinema chains or vice versa.[5]

Moral hazard

Moral hazard occurs when an agent lacks the incentive to work in the best interests of the principal and the principal cannot observe the actions of the agent. In our context, moral hazard implies that a firm has no incentive to maximise revenue or minimise costs when contracted by other firms at a different stage of production.

Assume a situation where a buying firm arranges a contract under conditions of uncertainty.[6] It is possible for the supplier to bear the risks, but this means adding a premium to the normal cost of production. In consequence, a much higher price is charged. The buying firm may regard this premium as excessive and may decide to bear the risk itself by offering a 'cost-plus contract'. The buyer will remunerate the supplier for all costs and add a mark-up for profit. This is typical of government contracts. However, there is now no incentive for the supplier to cut costs.[7] The buyer might have to insist on monitoring the supplier's work. If this proves too difficult and costly, it may propel the firm to integrate vertically. A common example is where one firm hires another to carry out some research and development. The resultant contract not only involves the issue of moral hazard, but may also include the issue of complexity.

Specificity

Asset specificity occurs when two firms are 'tied', or are dependent on one another, by investments in specific physical capital, human capital, sites or brands. The consequence of the specialised asset is that a bilateral monopoly will arise. There will be one firm buying and one firm supplying the input. For example, a shipper of antique furniture may have a limited demand for specialised padded wagons for long-distance rail transport. Given the

---

[5] A similar example, regarding the broadcasting industry and the relationship between networks and producers can be found in OECD (1993a), chapter 7.

[6] Based on Williamson (1975), p.84.

[7] In engineering companies in Yorkshire in the 1960s, the term 'govy work' meant the opportunity to do your own work, for example servicing your car or bicycle. This term originated from the relaxed attitude that management and staff took when working on government (cost-plus) contracts.

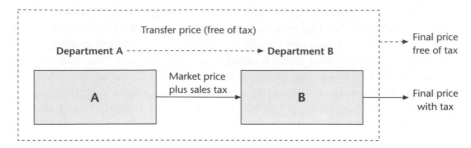

Figure 9.1 Vertical integration to avoid sales tax

level of demand, only one firm will specialise in the production of such wagons. The two firms are now 'locked in' by the specific asset. Both can undertake opportunistic behaviour to extract a higher price. The supplier may demand a higher price, threatening a refusal to supply, knowing that the buyer has no alternative source of supply. The buyer may demand a lower price with the threat of refusing to buy the supplier's output, knowing that the supplier will be unable to find an alternative market. Put more formally: 'Because non-redeployable specific assets make it costly to switch to a new relationship, the market safeguard against opportunism is no longer effective.'[8] As a result the market transaction is characterised by expensive haggling and high contractual costs which may propel the firms to integrate vertically.

Krickx (1995) tested the argument that increased vertical integration is expected when asset specificity is high. Relying on data from ten large computer companies between 1950 and 1970, Krickx analysed the three major components used over the twenty-year period, namely receiving tubes, transistors and integrated circuits. Each subsequent input was regarded as more specific to the needs of the computer industry. He showed that as the specificity of the components increased so did the tendency towards vertical integration. By the late 1960s all of the top six firms had vertically integrated backwards into the integrated circuit industry. John and Weitz (1988) measured specificity via the extent of staff training and experience required to sell a product for a sample of industrial firms. They found that the coefficient on specific skills explaining the level of vertical integration was positive and significant. Section 9.6 discusses this latter study in more detail.

Government action

Vertical integration between downstream and upstream firms as well as across national boundaries can also be used to avoid government taxes and price controls. A market transaction which is subject to a sales tax or price controls can be replaced by an internal transaction and thus escape the restriction. A few examples will help to explain some possible strategies:

● Government may impose a sales tax on A but not on B (the next stage of production). There is now a clear incentive for A to integrate with B to escape the tax (see Figure 9.1). An example was the German iron and steel industries before the Second World War.

[8] John and Weitz (1988), p.340.

- Government may impose a minimum price on A, for example a minimum price on margarine so as to encourage a higher demand in the butter industry. There is now an incentive for the margarine industry to vertically integrate forwards with the margarine-using industry to protect its output.
- Government may impose a maximum price on A, say flour producers. This maximum price may not correspond to the profit-maximising price. Thus the flour producers have an incentive to vertically integrate forwards with the bakers to recoup lost profits.

Williamson (1989) suggested that there was a clear incentive for firms, regulated by government and thus earning only 'fair profits', to vertically integrate backwards into the input supply industry to increase their profits. This would only be profitable if the input supply industry was free of government regulation. Williamson noted that such regulatory agencies were aware of these possibilities and applied regulation to upstream firms as well. An example of firms switching profits from highly taxed stages of production to lower-taxed stages had been discussed earlier by Scherer.[9] Scherer noted that there was evidence to show that in the United States and Europe, integrated petroleum firms showed low accounting profits in the refining and marketing stages of production, while enjoying much higher profits at the crude oil extracting stage, a stage that attracted a much lower rate of tax on profits. Jacobson and Andréosso-O'Callaghan (1996) also observed that in European Union countries, rates of tax on profit were very different and this encouraged firms to locate their subsidiaries in low-tax areas such as Ireland, to exploit such differences.

9.3 Vertical integration and monopoly power

A major debate in the area of industrial organisation has been the role and power of monopolies when contemplating vertical integration. Below we discuss a number of monopoly-related incentives for firms to vertically integrate.

Forward vertical integration

If a monopolist A supplies a competitive downstream industry B, it is clear that it could enter the downstream industry and become the dominant firm. But is it worthwhile? The traditional answer is that the monopolist will have no incentive to integrate into the industry if B is competitive and efficient.[10] The monopolist cannot do B's job any cheaper. This was known as the Adelman–Spengler hypothesis.[11] This argument is based on the assumption of fixed factor proportions. If the B firms can vary the proportions of A's output and A increases price then the B firms will substitute for A's inputs, for example use their labour more efficiently. A may try to force the B firms to use fixed factor proportions contractually, although enforcement costs may be high. In the end, A may decide to integrate vertically with B so as to escape any possible reductions in demand for its output. Vernon and Graham (1971) illustrated the argument as shown in Figure 9.2, which was slightly modified by Scherer and Ross (1990, pp.522–3).

---

[9] See Scherer (1980), p.305 for further discussion.
[10] If the industry is inefficient, then cost savings could be achieved via vertical integration, for example by reducing sales promotion and stock levels.
[11] Adelman (1949) and Spengler (1950).

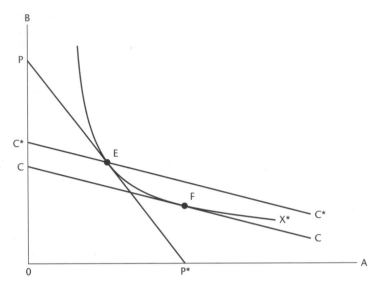

Figure 9.2 Vertical integration and variable input proportions

Figure 9.2 shows an isoquant for output X*, with two inputs A and B. The producer of the A input is a monopoly supplier and the B inputs are produced under competitive conditions. Prior to vertical integration the isocost line is PP*, its relatively steep slope reflecting the monopoly price charged by the monopolist. Least-cost production occurs at point E. As the monopolist integrates into the B industry, then as a user of A it will view the cost of A not as a monopoly price but as its marginal cost. The isocost line will thus be less steep, at CC, and this will prompt the firm to select production at point F, in effect leading to a more intensive use of the A input. The input combination prior to integration lies on a higher, parallel isocost curve C*C*. Thus the integrated firm will make a cost saving equal to distance CC*. Scherer and Ross (1990) suggested that this would be a fact in favour of the monopoly if the cost saving were to be passed on to final consumers in the form of lower prices. However, the firm will now control all inputs in the production process, both A and B. The restrictions it may place on the use of the B inputs may reduce the final output of X* and increase its price.

An alternative analysis was presented by Sibley and Weisman (1998) who considered the incentives facing an upstream, regulated monopolist. Traditional analysis would suggest that the ambition of the upstream firm would be to raise rivals' prices in the downstream industry. Even if the price of inputs were regulated, the monopolist could provide a poor service to its rivals or attempt to refuse to supply the input at strategically important times. However, Sibley and Weisman argued that there was a second effect at work in the opposite direction. Raising downstream prices would reduce demand and thus lower profits from that market. The net outcome would be determined by the structure of the firm. They concluded that in certain cases it would benefit the monopolist to reduce costs in the downstream market, rather than increase them. Another alternative theory was provided by Hardt (1995), who argued that market dominance by an upstream monopolist in the downstream market need not be achieved by vertical integration alone. Reliance on future

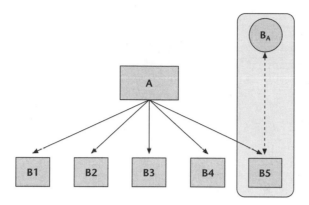

Figure 9.3 Backward vertical integration 1

trade, switching costs and the monopolist's reputation may be sufficient to create the required market discipline.

Backward vertical integration 1

An incentive to vertically integrate backwards is provided by the following example. Assume that an industry is monopolised by firm A. Thus firm A imposes a 'tax' on the users of A's output in the form of higher prices. Any of the B firms that can do their own A activity will now have an incentive to vertically integrate backwards. This is shown in Figure 9.3. Firm B5 is assumed to be able to use an alternative input (D_A) and will do so if it considers the prices and conditions demanded by firm A excessive. The incentive will only exist if the B firm can undertake A's activity at a cost lower than it pays A. If a monopolist feels that some of its customers are actively pursuing a policy of vertical integration to escape the 'tax', it may be willing to accommodate them or 'buy them off' with special price concessions, to frustrate such a move.

An example of this type of behaviour was News International's reluctance to use British Rail to distribute its newspapers to wholesalers around the country. News International turned instead to its own subsidiary TNT, a road haulage company as an alternative method of distribution. A formal approach was suggested by Oi and Hunter (1965) in their analysis of why firms might be tempted to develop their own private motor transportation systems rather than contract carriers in the market. They suggested that it was the presence of non-competitive prices (as well as specificity) that encouraged firms into vertical integration. What is a little puzzling in this analysis is the monopoly control exercised by the A firm. If firms find it relatively easy to vertically integrate backwards, what is there to stop other specialist firms from entering the A industry and competing prices down?

Backward vertical integration 2

Another example of a situation where a firm considers backward vertical integration is illustrated by Figure 9.4.

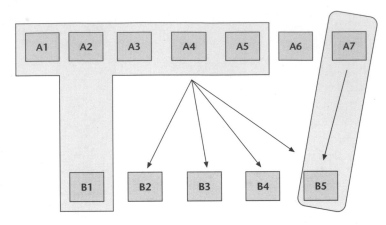

Figure 9.4 Backward vertical integration 2

In this case, a firm in the downstream market (B5) integrates backwards to avoid fore-closure by a rival firm (B1) which is attempting to monopolise the A industry.[12] While, in the long run, rival suppliers may emerge to challenge the emerging monopoly, in the short run, refusals to supply may be extremely damaging. A full analysis of foreclosure is considered in section 9.6.

Bilateral monopoly

In a bilateral monopoly a single supplier is faced with a single buyer. The problem facing the two firms is illustrated in Figure 9.5.

In Figure 9.5, subscripts S and B refer to the supplier's and buyer's functions. The seller's demand is AR_S. The supplier's marginal revenue is shown by MR_S and marginal cost by MC_S. If the monopoly supplier was in a dominant position it would equate its marginal cost with its marginal revenue and sell OQ_S and price OP_S. However, if the buying firm was equally dominant it would seek a different outcome. To the buyer, the supplier's marginal cost curve MC_S can represent its own supply curve. If the buyer were to be dominant in the market, then the position of the supplier could be equated to a supplier in a perfectly competitive industry, in which case the marginal costs will be equal to the supply curve. If the buyer views the MC_S function as its supply curve, this curve will also equal its average cost curve. However, if the buyer is faced with a rising supply curve, the function marginal to MC_S, shown as MC_B, represents the cost of buying an additional unit. The buyer will buy additional units as long as they add more to revenue than to cost. Thus the buyer will demand units up to the point where its marginal cost MC_B is equal to its marginal revenue MR_B. Quantity OQ_B will thus be demanded from the supplier at the purchase price of OP_B. Both the selling and the buying prices were determined on the assumption that one of the firms was dominant. This is highly unlikely and we have a model where the outcome is indeterminate and

---

[12] An interesting alternative for vertical integration was provided by Colangelo (1995) who examined the possibility that a firm may consider vertical integration, forwards or backwards, as a means of avoiding horizontal mergers or takeovers.

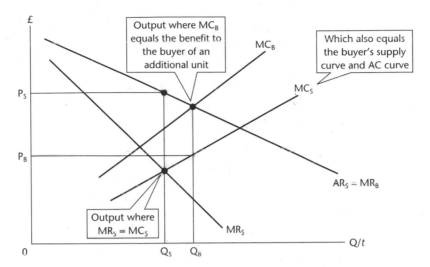

Figure 9.5 Bilateral monopoly

economic theory asserts that the outcome will be determined by bargaining between the two parties.

Faced with expensive 'haggling' costs, the optimal solution may be to integrate vertically and to set prices and outputs at a level that extracts the maximum possible surplus. Machlup and Taber (1960), nonetheless, argued that an optimal outcome, without recourse to vertical integration, could be achieved if both firms bargained on both price and output, though they recognised that the division of profits between the two firms would still be subject to 'bargaining skills'.

Price discrimination

For successful price discrimination to occur, three conditions must be present. Firstly the supplier must have monopoly control in the market. Secondly, the price elasticities of demand will be different for different classes of buyer. Finally, the supplier must ensure that no resale or seepage occurs, whereby customers charged a lower price sell surplus stock to those customers faced with a higher price. In Figure 9.6 we assume a monopoly supplier of aluminium.[13]

Aluminium is sold to the aircraft industry and to the household industry (for pots and pans). Since there are many substitutes for the production of pots and pans, the price elasticity of demand will be high and the price-discriminating supplier will set a low price. In the aircraft industry, there are fewer substitutes for aluminium and consequently the price elasticity of demand is low and the price set is high. Given no other changes in the market, the pots and pans industry has an incentive to resell surplus aluminium ingots to the aircraft industry. By forward vertical integration with the pots and pans industries the aluminium supplier can prevent such seepages. Price discrimination is thus

---

[13] The example is based on the Alcoa case in the United States, see Perry (1980).

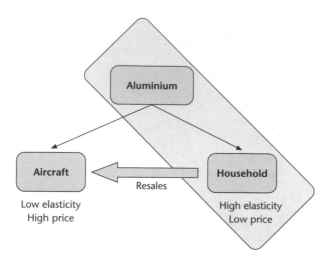

Figure 9.6 Forward vertical integration to effect price discrimination

concealed. It was argued in the Monopolies and Mergers Commission (1968) that Courtaulds supplied cellulose fibres on more favourable terms to its own subsidiaries than to its competitors.

9.4 Empirical evidence on vertical integration

In this section we explore the different methodologies used in measuring vertical integration. We then examine a few studies that have attempted to determine the main causes for vertical integration.

Measurement

Method 1
The first approach used to measure the extent of vertical integration is a simple count of the stages of production a firm is involved in. The greater the number of stages, the greater is the degree of vertical integration. A major difficulty is to decide what constitutes a stage of production. How does one define the boundaries of such stages? The measure will also be irrelevant across various different industries. In some industries, one hundred per cent integration may involve just a few stages, whereas in others it may involve many more stages.

Method 2
The second approach, suggested by Adelman (1955) is the value-added to sales approach. The ratio of value-added (VA) to sales measures the degree of 'self-sufficiency'. The less self-sufficient a firm is, the smaller the statistic. As an illustration consider the following example. We assume that firm A sells crude oil and firm B refines the crude oil.

Firm A		Firm B	
Purchases	50	Purchases from A	100
Value-added	50	Value-added	50
Sales	100	Sales	150
VA/Sales	0.5	VA/Sales	0.33

If A and B were to integrate, then value-added would rise to 0.66 as shown:

Firm A + B	
Purchases	50
Value-added	100
Sales	150
VA/Sales	0.66

A perfectly integrated firm would have a value-added to sales ratio equal to unity. In other words, value-added is exactly equal to final sales. However, a number of problems are associated with this measure:

● Value-added represents factor payments such as payroll, rents and profits. Any of these may change by a lesser or greater proportion than the change in the price of the inputs. This will distort the measure.
● If the industry evolves from competition to oligopoly, profits will increasingly include an element of rent. A change in the level of industrial concentration will affect the value-added to sales statistic that is wholly unconnected with the level of vertical integration.
● If a firm introduces labour-saving innovations or better organisation, its purchases will fall and the ratio will again be affected.
● The final problem is one of directional bias. Consider Figure 9.7, showing three firms each at a different stage of production. Each firm contributes 40 in value-added and we assume that firm A has no purchases as it is totally self-sufficient. Consider a vertical integration strategy undertaken by firm B. B's original value-added to sales is 0.5 (40/80). If it wishes to vertically integrate backwards then value-added to sales will be unity (80/80). Vertical integration forwards will result in value-added to sales being 0.67 (80/120). Thus an upstream merger has increased the statistic more than a downstream merger. The measure is thus distorted by the nearness of the integration to primary production.

Method 3
To overcome some of the above problems, Adelman (1955) suggested an alternative measure: the inventory to sales measure. This is based on the view that the longer the production process in an integrated firm, the greater will be the stocks of work-in-progress. Needham

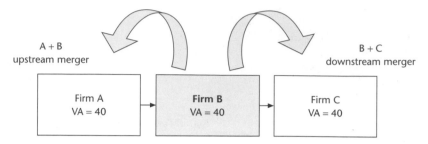

Figure 9.7 Directional bias of value-added to sales statistic

(1978), however, argued that this measure would be invalid if firms integrated vertically to economise on stockholdings.

Method 4

Gort (1962) suggested that vertical integration could be measured by a ratio of the percentage employed in a company's auxiliary activities (as opposed to its primary activity) to its total company employment. The greater the ratio, the greater is the level of vertical integration. Testing for a sample of industries, Gort found that the range ran from 9.7 per cent for transportation to 67.3 per cent for the petroleum industry. One major difficulty with this type of measure is what constitutes primary and auxiliary activities of any given company. As a consequence the statistic is highly subjective.

Method 5

A good measure of vertical integration according to Davies and Morris (1995) should possess the following characteristics. It should be based on firm theory; it should avoid subjective assessments and instead be based on objective census data; and finally it should be general so that it can be applied to both firms and industries with the ability to aggregate data from firms to industries. They suggested a measure based on the Coase–Williamson paradigm, which defined vertical integration on the basis of substituting internal firm co-ordination for external market co-ordination. Since data on intra-firm transactions are difficult to collect, Davies and Morris imputed such flows indirectly from input/output tables and market shares of firms across industries.

Selected empirical research

In contrast to the quantity of theoretical material published on vertical integration over the past thirty years, the amount of empirical evidence has been poor. This seems to be due largely to the difficulty of measuring vertical integration efficiently, as discussed above. The following three empirical studies have attempted to tackle vertical integration issues.

Spiller (1985) attempted to determine which of two competing hypotheses best explained the rationale for vertical integration. The first hypothesis was the neoclassical rationale based on economies of scope, risk reduction, tax evasion and price control arguments. The alternative hypothesis was described as the 'specific assets' approach which broadly covered the Williamson transaction costs arguments. By examining a number of vertical mergers

Spiller tested which of the two rationales was dominant. For his database he used the Federal Trade Commission's classification of vertical mergers, which he further refined by examining the exact details of the vertical links and by excluding data prior to 1970. Twenty-nine mergers were identified for the purposes of the analysis. Specificity of the invested assets was inferred by the location of vertically related plants and the extent of correlation between firm-specific shocks. The gains from mergers and the systematic risks in the market were determined by using the capital asset pricing model. Spiller concluded that the evidence seemed to favour the 'specific assets' argument.

John and Weitz (1988) attempted to test the 'transaction cost analysis' of forward vertical integration. They began their study by identifying direct channels of distribution present in an organisation as opposed to indirect channels. The former covers the practice of a firm retaining ownership of the product until it reaches the end-user, in other words vertical integration. The indirect channel, in their words 'comprises a bewildering array of institutional structures', as we have seen in this chapter. Fundamentally, these indirect channels cover the use that firms make of independent resellers. John and Weitz identified four independent variables that may increase the use of direct channels: greater asset specificity, greater environmental and behavioural uncertainty, and greater production costs. Environmental uncertainty covered market volatility, and behavioural uncertainty referred to opportunistic behaviour of one of the contracting parties in a vertical relationship. The production cost argument was based on the notion that larger firms would integrate more readily when economies of scale and scope were present.

By interviewing sales managers in a sample of industrial firms a measure for the variables was computed. Direct channels were computed on the basis of what percentage of company sales were sold to end-users (per cent DIRECT). Specific assets were measured on the basis of the time spent training newly hired, but experienced, salespeople to become familiar with the product (SPSKILLS). Environmental uncertainty was computed on the basis of responses to various business contingencies such as the ability to predict sales (ENVUNCT). Behavioural uncertainty was proxied by measuring the lag between the initial contact with a buyer and the eventual order, the assumption being that where time lags were very short or instantaneous, performance of either party is more easily monitored (BEHUNCT). Two scale variables were calculated. The first was sales (SALES) and the second the density of customers. If customers were sparse, it was difficult to assign sales staff to the territory and to use their time efficiently. Sales managers were thus asked questions about the efficient use of a salesperson's time, for example time spent travelling (SPARSE). The estimated equation was:

$$LN\frac{\%DIRECT}{1 - \%DIRECT} = -1.061CONSTANT + 0.147SPSKILLS + 0.773ENVUNCT$$
$$+ 0.218BEHUNCT - 0.057LNSALES - 0.059SPARSE$$

The model explained 28 per cent of the variation in sales through direct channels. The coefficients on the independent variables measuring specific assets and uncertainty were significant. The coefficient on the scale effect as measured by sales was not significant, though when measured by sparse territories, it was significant. John and Weitz claimed that this result provided considerable support for the transaction cost analysis.

Using historical rather than empirical analysis, Krickx (1995) examined the transaction cost analysis in the computer mainframe industry by observing changes in 'vertical governance patterns' for a number of components over a twenty-year period. The institutional analysis focused on ten firms and Krickx identified three separate vertical states, or governances: vertically integrated, intermediate exchange and market exchange. He concluded that, in the mainframe industry, vertical integration was consistent with the transaction cost and production cost arguments. In addition, variables such as technology, appropriability (the ease with which a new technology can be copied) and industry maturity also played an important role in determining whether a firm in this industry would vertically integrate.

9.5   Agency and vertical relationships

In section 9.3 we examined the reasons why firms may be attracted to a strategy of vertical integration. However, vertical integration is only one of many possible vertical structures. In this section we examine the reasons why firms may prefer to enter into different vertical relationships. These alternative relationships are often referred to as 'principal–agent relationships'. Thus a manufacturing firm (acting as the principal) will contract a supplying firm (the agent) to produce its inputs. Contracts imply restrictions, and these restrictions are examined in section 9.6. It is clear that the fundamental reason why firms develop contractually specific vertical ties is to harmonise production, processing and distribution activities. But the main question is, why should firms choose this approach rather than rely on the advantages of vertical integration? Generalising, we can argue that firms prefer to enter into such agreements for two reasons: firstly, to maintain some degree of independence, and secondly, to avoid the costs of entry into upstream or downstream operations. If we assume that firms wish to remain in their familiar stage of production and maintain their independence then vertical relationships can be used primarily to reduce uncertainty in the market.[14] However, other factors may play also play a part. Bonanno and Vickers (1988) suggested that 'vertical separation' as opposed to vertical integration could create 'friendly relations' and facilitate collusion amongst the principals.

Harrigan (1983) suggested three alternatives to vertical integration:

- *Tapered integration* exists when vertically integrated firms rely on independent suppliers or distributors for part of their operations. Using such channels will allow firms to fully exploit their capacity, ensuring that it is the 'outside' firms which bear the risk of market uncertainties. Furthermore, developing contacts with upstream and downstream firms may provide useful intelligence regarding new product and market development. Harrigan believed that tapered integration was best applied in situations where technological interdependencies were absent and raw material inputs were plentiful.
- *Quasi-integration* refers to a situation where a firm may not own the adjacent business unit but will be able to control all or part of the operation through franchises or other joint ventures. The strategy may appear attractive to those firms facing high risks of new technology and demand uncertainty.
- *Contracts* can specify the exact relationship between an agent and principal and can thus take a multitude of forms to reflect the minutiae of the different risks in the market as well as the market power of the firms involved. Harrigan claimed that the greater the

---

[14] See, for example, Gal-Or (1991, 1999) and Aust (1997).

level of monopoly power, the greater the possibility that firms would integrate. Where a market was characterised by 'competitive volatility' and principal firms possessed enough market power to monitor and enforce contracts, then contracting was seen as an appropriate solution.[15] Such contracts mean that firms can gain advantages in vertical relationships without having to commit excessive financial resources.

We now examine two common institutional developments in the field of vertical relationships: **franchising** and **networks**.

Franchising

Franchising refers to a vertical relationship between two independent firms: a franchisor and a franchisee.[16] The franchisor sells a proven product, process or brand to a franchisee subject to a specific contractual relationship in return for set-up fees, licence fees, royalties or other payments. The contracts will cover issues such as prices to be charged, services offered, location and marketing effort. The most common types of franchise agreement involve retail franchising, whereby a manufacturer of a product develops a vertical relationship with a retailer. A number of different franchise agreements can be identified within the very large continuum of such contractual arrangements. The best known is the 'business format franchise' which covers not only the sale of a product or brand, but also the entire business format, comprising a marketing strategy, staff training, manuals, quality control processes, store layout and close communications between the franchisor and franchisee. Kentucky Fried Chicken, Dynorod and Prontoprint are examples of these types of franchise. The alternative is the 'product or trademark' franchise, which implies less control by the franchisor. For example, a relationship between a car manufacturer and a car dealer may allow the dealer a large degree of independence in the selling of the brand. Car dealers of similar brands do manage to differentiate their service, whereas Kentucky Fried Chicken outlets are characterised by their homogeneity. However, Klein (1995) believed that the difference has been overstated. Both types of franchise can include more or fewer controls and large 'grey' areas exist. To complete our list of various franchise agreements we could also add 'manufacturer to wholesaler' franchises, such as Coca-Cola, and 'wholesaler to retailer' franchises such as the grocery chains of Spar and Mace.

We may wish to ask why is the relationship between the franchisor and franchisee subject to contractual control? Decisions on price, quality, service offered, quality of factor inputs taken by one of the parties will affect the profits and performance of the other. It is also possible that the decisions of one franchisee may impact on rival franchisees. Thus while individual decisions may maximise the profits of one of the parties, the resulting externality effects may reduce *aggregate* profits for the whole vertical operation. Contractual control is thus aimed fundamentally at reducing possible externalities. This was summed up by Klein (1995, p.12) as: 'The crucial economic fact that underlies franchising contracts is that the incentives of the transacting parties do not always coincide.'

---

[15] Lafontaine and Slade (1996) found evidence to suggest that where firms found the costs of monitoring such agreements too high or too complex, they would prefer to integrate vertically.

[16] Much of the following discussion is based on OECD (1993b).

Klein identified four possible areas where such conflict may occur:

- When franchisees jointly use a common brand a free-rider incentive is created. Each franchisee is faced with the opportunity of reducing the quality of the product (to save costs) since the firm does not bear the full consequence of its action. The consequence of a reduction in the perceived quality of the product is borne by all franchisees using the brand. The reduction in future demand is spread across the whole market and does not fall directly on the free-rider.

- A potential conflict could also arise when a franchisee is expected to provide a pre-sales service. Free-riding franchisees might be able to avoid providing such a service by relying on other firms to offer the initial service. Klein (1995) used the example of American car distributors (book dealers) in the 1960s who could charge a lower price by selling cars out of catalogues and avoid having to provide showrooms, test drives and sales staff to answer queries. These dealers relied on the franchised outlets to provide such a service for interested buyers.

- A franchisee may have some degree of market power in the setting of a price for the final product. This may come about by the franchisor granting exclusive distribution rights. In this case, a 'successive monopoly' or 'double marginalisation' has been created and the higher price may not be in the interests of the franchisor.

- Finally, Klein identified two major causes for what he termed the 'malincentive problem'. Firstly, the franchisees may control some inputs into the production and distribution of the final product in such a way that demand for the franchisor's product is affected. Secondly, the price at which the franchisor sells its product to the franchisees is greater than its marginal cost. Given these circumstances, there is an incentive for the franchisor to increase the output of its product, which would then imply that the franchisee should also increase the supply of its complementary input, for example, additional marketing. However, the amount of marketing that a franchisee supplies will not be dependent on the level of output and profits of the franchisor. A simple example will explain the argument (see below).

Consider Figure 9.8. We assume that a franchisor sells its product at a wholesale price of £4.50 and that the competitive retail price is £5.00. The 50p represents the average cost of distribution to the franchisee[17]. We now assume that a particular buyer has a reserve price of £4.00, but that if the buyer were to be exposed to marketing services costing £3.00, the reserve price would rise by £1.00 to £5.00. It is clear that the franchisee cannot afford to spend £3.00 on marketing services since its margin is too low. However, if the franchisor's marginal cost were below £1.50, then it would benefit the franchisor to spend the £3.00 to attract a revenue of £5.00. Naturally if the producer were vertically integrated with the distributor, the additional marketing service would be funded. In a franchise agreement, the franchisor may have to subsidise the franchisee's marketing effort, because on the basis of the above argument the franchisee has no incentive to supply such additional services.

The consequence of the four issues raised above is that franchise agreements must be accompanied by contractual obligations that reduce the externality and malincentive problems. Three basic contractual controls, or vertical restraints, can be identified:

---

[17] The average cost includes a provision for normal profit.

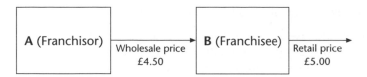

Figure 9.8 The malincentive problem

- Relationships can be co-ordinated by giving the franchisor direct control over the franchisee's decisions, such as price-setting, quality and marketing effort.
- A process of incentives can be determined to ensure that the objectives of both parties coincide. Thus the contract could specify a franchise fee plus buying the variable inputs at marginal cost so that the franchisee is committed to the maximisation of aggregate profits.
- Contracts may be used to reduce potential externalities. Thus, to reduce competition between the franchisees (intra-brand competition) a franchisor may wish to offer exclusive territorial contracts or fix a minimum retail price.

Contracts may include aspects of all three of the above to deal with the specific nature of the market problem and can thus be varied. Macho Stadler and Pérez-Castrillo (1998) viewed franchise contracts as a mix of centralised (characteristics closer to vertical integration) and decentralised decision-making. Thus some decisions in the fast-food industry, such as menu selection and building designs, are centralised by the franchisor, while employee recruitment and local advertising are decentralised out to the franchisees. In certain cases a franchisor may also decide to run some of the outlets itself. Macho-Stadler and Pérez-Castrillo claimed that one factor that led to decentralised franchise contracts was the geographical location of the outlets. Outlets far from the franchisor's headquarters, outlets in rural areas and those close to motorways were found to have more decentralised contracts. Gal-Or (1999) focused on the nature of contracts in oligopolistic markets. She suggested that the reactions of rival firms to changing economic parameters may dictate the contract terms.[18]

A frequent issue regarding franchise agreements is to decide whether the agreements aid allocative efficiency or whether they reduce competition and increase market power. The efficiency arguments focuses on the following:

- Franchise agreements can reduce 'double price mark-ups' (see p.299) which leads to reduced retail prices and increase profits. Thus both producer and consumer surplus increases.
- If franchise agreements can reduce the externalities inherent in vertical relationships, then this may encourage the provision of more and better services to consumers.
- Provisions in the agreements that encourage a greater productivity of downstream or upstream investments will result in a more efficient use of resources.
- Franchise operations can also be used as a vehicle for entry, by allowing firms access to products, retail outlets and technical know-how.

---

[18] For an empirical analysis of contractual arrangements in agency theory see Lafontaine (1992).

However, franchising could also lead to greater market power through the following:

● A franchisor could use agreements to enhance market power and maximise profits. Thus the choice of quality of the product or the service offered may reflect the desire to maximise the franchisor's profit rather than consumer surplus.
● There may be an added risk of cartelisation in the market by reducing competition between the suppliers.
● Franchise agreements may also create entry barriers.

There is no clear, unambiguous conclusion that might state that a particular restraint or contractual condition will result in greater efficiency or greater market power. It is clear that government agencies investigating such relationships must analyse each case on its merits to determine whether the efficiency arguments outweigh the anti-competitive arguments. They may also analyse whether alternative vertical relationships might not achieve the same objective.

Networks

Networks refer to groups of firms linked vertically by regular contact and relationships that in time develop into formal relations. Thus, supplying firms may train staff in downstream firms, provide technical know-how and customise their outputs to meet specific requirements of buyers. The relationship is non-exclusive and both parties sell to and buy from other firms. This is in contrast to independent firms who rely solely on market transactions for standardised products and develop no 'relationships' with upstream or downstream firms. Kranton and Minehart (1999) cited the garment industry in New York and the Japanese electronics industry as examples of such networks. In the face of uncertain demand, it was argued that networks can lead to a better solution than simple vertical integration. Kranton and Minehart offered three possible explanations. Firstly, buyers who rely on multiple sourcing arrangements may be able to reduce the bargaining power of sellers. Secondly, firms in networks can make specific investments, to meet the needs of buyers or sellers. This is in contrast to the traditional approach that would regard vertical integration as the sole solution to specificity problems. Finally, the aggregate level of investment in specific assets by the network may be less than the inefficiently high levels undertaken by some vertically integrated firms.[19]

Robertson and Langlois (1995) argued that networks could be defined within the familiar Coasian and Williamson spectrum: of independent, market-based firms at one extreme to firms that have managed to internalise transactions through common ownership or contractual agreements at the other. However, they suggested that networks could be analysed within a second dimension. This approach focused on two definitions of the firm. The first is the 'nexus of contract' view, developed by Cheung (1983). This view holds that the firm is characterised by internal contracts, as much as those for market transactions. However, the nature of the contracts is different: those within a firm are less formal, are subject to revision and are often implicit. These contracts need to be administratively co-ordinated and the essence of a firm is its ability to manage such contracts efficiently. The alternative approach is the 'property rights' definition of the firm. In this case, the crucial variable is

---

[19] See Bolton and Whinstone (1993) for a further discussion.

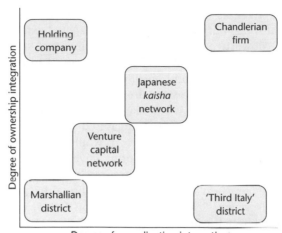

Figure 9.9 Robertson and Langlois' two dimensions of integration

ownership of assets. Thus vertical integration is seen as *ownership* of two successive stages of production. Robertson and Langlois argue that in order to understand vertical relationships both definitions are useful and both can be applied separately. Thus it may be possible to have two independent firms that are linked by close administrative co-ordination, or an integrated firm that deals with its subsidiary through the market. The two defining characteristics – the degree of ownership integration and the degree of co-ordination integration – can be plotted on two axes and various organisational forms can then be identified within this 'integration space' (see Figure 9.9).

Robertson and Langlois suggested six such organisational forms, drawn from history and literature, that could be placed within the integration space:

● *Marshallian district.* This refers to the loosest of all networks, based on Alfred Marshall's analysis of nineteenth-century British manufacturing firms. These firms were found clustered in geographical areas, which themselves were often highly specialised. These firms were small and produced a homogeneous product, concentrating on a small part of the overall production process. Being vertically separated they relied purely on local market transactions. The network (or district) did, however, allow for the realisation of potential external economies, such as the recruitment of specialised labour and the spread of new technologies.

● *Third Italy district.* This refers to a system developed in north-east Italy, where small firms, located in small towns, tended to specialise in the production of standardised products, such as ceramics or textiles. The major difference from the Marshallian district is the level of co-operation undertaken by the firms, often in the form of government-sponsored co-operatives. Co-operation may take the form of sharing accounting services, domestic and international marketing initiatives and investment in infrastructure.

● *Venture capital network.* This can also be referred to as an innovative network and an example of such a network is Silicon Valley in America or the Cambridge Science Park in the UK. Co-ordination integration is low, though higher than in the Marshallian district since some co-ordination is provided by a network of venture capitalists who inject the initial funds. These investors will protect their investments by ensuring that the new firms have at their disposal entrepreneurial and managerial expertise as well as contacts with upstream and downstream firms. The involvement of such venture capital also implies that the small innovating firms cede some control to the investors and thus a movement towards centralisation and outside control can be detected.

● *Japanese kaisha network.* Where industries are characterised by large economies of scale, the existence of industrial districts is less likely. Instead we may expect 'core networks', which refer to many small satellite firms organised around one large firm, often an assembler. An example of this type of network would be American and Japanese car manufacturers. American (and British) car firms have tended to rely on suppliers via short-term contracts, ensuring discipline by an exercise of monopsony power. If supply firms do not meet the large firm's specification regarding price, quality and timing, then the firm will shop elsewhere. Robertson and Langlois (1995) claim that this detached attitude by the large buyer towards the upstream firms creates little loyalty and little incentive to act in any other way than to stick closely to the terms of the contract. The Japanese car firms behave differently. The large assemblers will typically offer long-term contracts to their suppliers, and these contracts include the sharing of many technical and design inputs. As regards the ownership dimension, the Japanese firms will often own a substantial part of the supplying firms. Owing to such close financial connections, both upstream and downstream firms will share the same business and financial goals. The Japanese system is thus based on the strategy of developing an efficient supporting network of supplying firms rather than attempting to develop inputs in-house.

● *Chandlerian firm.* This represents the traditional vertically integrated firm, where the successive stages of production are centrally owned and market transactions have been internalised.[20]

● *Holding company.* This will reflect ownership integration, but not any co-ordination integration, allowing subsidiaries to behave in an independent, market-orientated manner. Robertson and Langlois (1995) argue that the development of multi-divisional structures was a form of decentralisation. Although vertically integrated, the core firm retained only very narrow strategic functions and the sub-units acted almost as autonomous firms.

What is clear from the above is that vertical relationships are far more varied and far more complex than a simple discussion concerning whether two firms should integrate or remain independent. Identifying different vertical structures can allow us to analyse their effects on various performance variables such as profitability, technical change and product quality.[21] The Robertson and Langlois (1995) network classification was developed to attempt an understanding of the incentive to innovate under different vertical forms. Unfortunately the results were somewhat inconclusive.

9.6 Vertical restraints

An alternative to vertical integration, which some firms may find too costly to monitor and organise, is to rely on an armoury of vertical restraints.[22] Vertical restraints refer to

---

[20] Named after Chandler (1977).
[21] See, for example, Economides (1996).
[22] See, for example, Mathewson and Winter (1984).

the various restrictions imposed by firms linked by vertical relationships. Thus, if a manufacturer makes it a condition of supply that the retailer should charge a minimum price, then a vertical restraint or restriction is said to exist. Unfortunately, the word 'restraint' or 'restriction' has a negative implication of wrongdoing. Such conditions surrounding the sale of goods may have beneficial as well as harmful effects on economic welfare. If we consider book publishing in the UK we can identify at least three different types of vertical restraint.[23]

- No part of a published book can be copied and distributed without the permission of the copyright owner.
- Books cannot be sold below a certain minimum price determined by the publisher. In the UK this was known as the Net Book Agreement, a legal agreement that had satisfied the Restrictive Trade Practices Court. In recent years, however, the agreement has all but disappeared as the large retail booksellers have begun to discount prices.[24]
- No paperback can be rebound by a buyer into a hardback edition.

Each of the above restraints is anti-competitive. The first ensures that no other firm or individual is able to sell the same book. It thus serves as an entry barrier. The second ensured that there was no price competition between booksellers. The last is a form of price discrimination. Since the cost of hard-binding a book is much less than the price differential, the publisher is in effect differentiating the product. Publishers believe that the demand for hardback books is less elastic than the demand for paperback books; thus, by segmenting the market they can charge different prices.

However, the agreement also generates positive benefits. Firstly, if books could be copied and sold by rival firms, publishers would see a drop in revenue and an inability to cover the full costs of publishing a book. The rival firms would be enjoying a free ride, having escaped the costs of contracting an author, typesetting and marketing. To protect firms from such piracy, the government defines strict property rights covering the written word and other media. Resale price maintenance was argued to be in favour of protecting small booksellers who, it was claimed, provided useful services such as information and local availability of books. Being small, these booksellers were faced with high costs and consequently would be unable to cover these costs if book prices were lower. It is also argued that price discrimination allows non-economic books (such as academic textbooks) to be published at a reasonable price, cross-subsidised by the popular books.

The Chicago school

As we have seen above, vertical restraints may be viewed potentially as a force for economic efficiency, as anti-competitive, or possibly as having a neutral effect. The debate in Europe and the United States has tended to revolve around the views of the Chicago school.[25] The traditional thinking prior to the Chicago school arguments was that restrictions, by their very nature, reduced the independence of distributors by controlling their ability to supply final consumers. Resale price maintenance was seen as little different from horizontal

[23] Example used by Kay (1990b).
[24] The agreement was formally abandoned in 1995.
[25] See, for example, Telser (1960), Bork (1978) and Posner (1981).

price-fixing and was banned in most countries. The Chicago school was a body of academic lawyers and economists who, in the 1960s and 1970s, developed a line of research stressing a strict neoclassical approach to markets. Fundamentally, their approach was an attempt to separate vertical restraints from horizontal restraints, arguing that competition is defined within a market and therefore only horizontal and not vertical restraints can affect competition. Specifically, it was argued that manufacturers would not impose restrictions downstream as this would in turn reduce demand for their products. If restrictions are imposed it is because a potential efficiency can be realised. These efficiencies were the elimination of externalities and moral hazard problems discussed earlier in the chapter. Thus some perfume manufacturers may believe that selling their perfume at high prices, by attractive assistants and only in upmarket stores will maximise their sales. To reduce price and allow downmarket chain-stores to stock the perfume may in fact reduce total market demand. The approach attracted a lot of criticism and in more recent years the tide has turned away from the Chicago analysis and the focus is now based on a case by case approach.[26] Restraints may be viewed as having possible entry barrier and collusive effects which lead to a distortion of the retail market especially where there is little competition at the retail or manufacturing stage. Thus resale price maintenance can be used as an alternative to horizontal price-fixing, the latter being more obvious as well as illegal.[27] Comanor (1985) also argued that the provision of expensive services and marketing may be inappropriate for established products where consumers are familiar with the product and do not place a high value on additional services, the implication being that these additional services can serve as an additional barrier to entry.

We now turn to a more comprehensive examination of the reasons why firms impose vertical restraints followed by a listing of the major restraints in vertical relationships.

Reasons for vertical restraints

As we saw above, vertical restraints may serve two purposes: to correct distribution inefficiencies and to exploit market power. Whether a restriction is anti-competitive or whether it generates efficient allocation is often a source of much academic debate and ultimately for competition agencies to decide.[28] We examine the reasons under those two headings.

Anti-competitive effects

● *Foreclosure.* In the context of vertical restraints, foreclosure is to deny buyers access to one's goods or to prevent your rivals from supplying goods to your buyers. As we will see later, this type of behaviour has many variants. There are two effects on competition. Firstly, groups of buyers are prevented from acquiring and distributing goods, and secondly there is a consequent reduction of intra-brand competition. Consumers are forced to buy their goods from a smaller subset of distributors.

---

[26] See, for example, Comanor (1985) and Rey and Tirole (1986).
[27] Why upstream firms should wish to co-operate in the creation of downstream market power is a little unclear. Kay (1990b) suggested that a downstream cartel may implicitly threaten a boycott of the upstream firm's output if resale price maintenance was not imposed.
[28] See, for example, Dobson and Waterson (1996) and European Commission (1997d).

Table 9.1 • Price squeezing

	Integrated Dominant firm		Other firms Non-integrated	
	A	B	A	B
First level				
Aluminium ingots				
Cost	800	800		
Price	1,000	1,490		
Profit	200	690		
Second level				
Aluminium products				
Cost (ingot price and manufacturing)	1,500	1,990	1,500	1,990
Price	2,000	2,000	2,000	2,000
Profit	500	10	500	10
Total profit	700	700	500	10

- *Increase in final prices and deterioration of service.* Any restraints that result in buyers being forced to concentrate their orders on a narrow range of suppliers results in customers being denied access to alternative (more efficient) sources of supply of the same product as well as access to alternative products. This can lead to a reduction of not only intra-brand competition but also inter-brand competition. Unable to exploit alternative sources, consumers may face higher prices and poorer conditions of supply.
- *Increased opportunities for collusion.* The practice of 'forcing' buyers to resell the product at a minimum price reduces intra-brand price competition and presents opportunities for effective horizontal price-fixing.
- *Extending monopoly.* Monopoly power at one stage of production or distribution can be extended to the next stage by the use of vertical restraints. Thus government regulation of privatised utility monopolies ensures that the utilities' power is not extended downstream. Banks can identify suitable customers to their financial services subsidiaries by denying rivals in the financial services sector similar access to this type of information. Another example of the extension of such monopoly power is through a 'price squeeze'. An integrated monopolist can narrow the margin between the price of the raw material input and the price of the finished product. Consider the following example illustrated by Table 9.1.[29]

The dominant firm sells aluminium ingots to its own manufacturing division and to other firms at a price of 1,000 per ton in the first instance, shown by column A. After processing, at a cost of 500, aluminium products are sold to final consumers for 2,000 per ton. The 1,000 price that the dominant firm charges its division is a 'shadow' or 'transfer' price. If the firm were to raise ingot prices to 1,490 (column B) the 'accounting'

[29] Based on Shepherd's (1997), p.276, example of the famous Alcoa case. See also Singer (1968), pp.215–20, for further comments on the Alcoa case and other examples of vertical squeezing.

costs to its manufacturing division would rise to 1,990, but this is offset by the extra 490 profit on ingot production. Total profits remain unchanged at 700. However, the non-integrated firms and customers of the dominant firm will see their profits squeezed from 500 to 10.

● *Raising rivals' costs*. Restraints discourage entry by raising sunk costs. Exclusive distribution agreements may deny outlets to entrants who are then forced to develop their own distribution networks. The existence of tie-in sales (discussed later in the chapter) also forces entrants to carry a wider range of goods. Both these restraints give rise to a capital requirements entry barrier. If potential rivals are denied access to cheap or high-quality inputs by an integrated firm then they will face an absolute cost disadvantages type of barrier. Finally, it may also be argued that potential entrants could be fearful about the level of supply. An upstream firm could deny sufficient inputs to a downstream firm which would frustrate its attempts to produce at the minimum efficient size. This would be regarded as an economy of scale entry barrier.[30]

Efficiency effects

Efficiency effects will exist when arm's length dealing between manufacturers and distributors focusing on simple price/quantity contracts leads to a suboptimal level of sales and investment in the market. They may be caused by the following:

● *The free-rider or externality problem*. This will occur when a manufacturer or seller makes special efforts to market the goods but is unable to exploit the full benefits of these actions. A retailer may invest in a large retail space, where customers can browse at their leisure, examining a wide range of products. The retailer may also invest in staff training to ensure that staff can provide useful information to potential customers. A rival 'discount' retailer who offers no such services relies on customers accessing the services provided by other retailers. As a free-rider, the rival can undercut the price of those retailers providing additional services. To prevent such an externality, manufacturers may refuse supplies to discount shops or impose resale price maintenance.

The European Commission (1998a) suggested three tests to ascertain whether the free-rider problem is a valid reason for imposing restraints: firstly, that the free-riding issue refers to pre-sales service rather than after-sales service; secondly, that the goods on sale are new or technically complex so that the consumer has to receive information to make rational choices; finally, that the good in question is a relatively high priced good, so that it would pay a consumer to receive information from one retailer but to shop at another.

There are other issues relating to the free-rider problem. One is the question of 'certification'. This occurs where retailers with a high reputation 'certify' the quality of a good by stocking it. This may apply to new products that need such a recognition. If the product were to be stocked at downmarket stores it may lack credibility and fail to establish itself in the market. Restrictions may help to protect the product from price discounters in the early stages of its development. Another issue is the 'hold-up' problem. This may occur when either a buyer or a supplier is committed to making

---

[30] For a critique of these arguments see Bork (1954). See also Williamson (1975), pp.110–13.

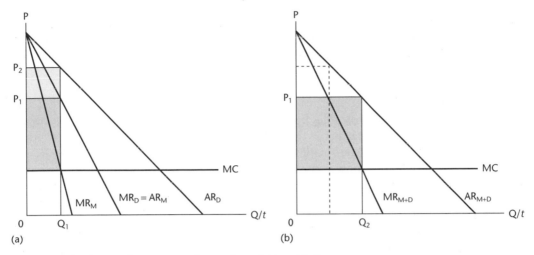

Figure 9.10 Successive monopolies and vertical restrictions

specific investments to help with the distribution of goods. Once an investment has been made, the firm is 'tied' to its supplier or buyer. The fear of being so dependent on other parties, allowing them a 'free ride' may 'hold up' such investments until specific market arrangements are agreed.

● *Double marginalisation.* The problem of **double marginalisation** or a double mark-up exists when both stages of production and distribution are monopolised and each firm adds its own monopoly mark-up. The net effect is to force prices higher than would be the case under just one monopoly. It is argued that restraints such as resale price maintenance could bring price down to a monopoly level. Consider Figure 9.10.

Figure 9.10(a) illustrates two monopolies at successive stages of production and distribution. The monopoly distributor is facing a demand and marginal revenue curve shown by AR_D and MR_D, respectively. The monopoly manufacturer's demand curve, equal to the distributor's marginal revenue curve, is shown as AR_M and its marginal revenue curve as MR_M. To maximise profits, the manufacturer equates marginal revenue with marginal costs of manufacturing to produce OQ_1 at price OP_1. The wholesale price OP_1 becomes the marginal cost facing the distributor. To maximise its profits the distributor will equate this marginal cost with its marginal revenue curve, MR_D, to then sell OQ_1 units at price OP_2. We assume zero costs of distribution. The final price has been subject to two monopoly mark-ups. Figure 9.10(b) shows the vertically integrated solution or what might be achieved through vertical restrictions. As an integrated operation the manufacturer-cum-distributor equates its marginal revenue curve with the marginal cost curve to charge a final price of OP_1 and the lower price generates a greater demand of OQ_2. The problem facing the non-integrated manufacturer is that the mark-up imposed by the distributor acts against the interests of the manufacturer. Solutions to this problem, other than vertical integration, would be the imposition of a maximum resale price or quantity forcing, the latter being used to force prices down.[31]

---

[31] For a classic analysis of successive monopoly, see Machlup and Taber (1960).

Types of vertical restraint

We now consider some of the principal vertical restraints that are employed by firms to realise the objectives discussed above. It must be noted that many of these restrictions are at times similar and can easily be substituted for one another.

Resale price maintenance

Resale price maintenance (RPM) has been defined as: 'any contract in which an upstream firm (e.g., a manufacturer) retains the right to control the price at which a product is sold downstream, usually in the retail market'.[32]

Resale price maintenance most commonly refers to the fixing of a minimum price or a 'price floor', though maximum prices or 'price ceilings' are also possible as we saw in the case of double marginalisation. The practice is viewed with suspicion in most countries and has consequently been deemed to be illegal in many countries. This suspicion originates from two directions, one legal and the other economic. From a legal viewpoint such price restrictions are seen to be contrary to the legal principle of alienation which implies that as an individual relinquishes ownership of goods he or she should have no further rights over the use and disposal of such goods. The economic viewpoint is that such price restrictions result in a loss of competition. The anti-competitive argument focuses on the following issues:

● *Dealer cartel hypothesis*. Retailers or dealers often group together for benign trade purposes but this can then develop into collusive agreements. Such cartels, like all cartels, are subject to potential instability brought about by independent action.[33] Price discipline and thus greater stability can be injected into the collusive arrangements by resale price maintenance imposed by the suppliers. In addition, resale price maintenance can protect the dealer cartel from the entry of discount dealers. This view was attacked by the Chicago school, which claimed that dealer cartels are rare owing to relatively low entry barriers, the existence of large discount stores and the opportunity for dealers to differentiate their services.[34] Secondly, there is little evidence that manufacturers should wish to support a dealer cartel that might work against the interests of the manufacturer.

● *Manufacturer cartel hypothesis*. Normally one would expect that manufacturers wishing to collude on prices will decide to fix the wholesale price. This may work if the cost and demand conditions faced by the individual downstream firms are constant. However, if these conditions vary, then the downstream firms will be setting different prices and the upstream colluders will have no way of knowing whether the price differentials are due to efficiency gains or because of cheating by cartel members. Resale price maintenance can eliminate such price variations, since downstream firms cannot pass on their lower wholesale price by charging a lower retail price. This view was attacked by the Chicago economists as unrealistic. Price-fixing is complex to organise and many variables affect the ultimate efficiency of the outcome. To suggest that resale price maintenance is the one solution that can guarantee cartel stability is far-fetched. For example, there seems no

---

[32] Mathewson and Winter (1998), p.58.
[33] See Chapter 3 for a further discussion of cartel stability.
[34] See, for example, Bork (1978), Posner (1981) and Ornstein (1985).

reason to suggest that manufacturers would desist from secret price reductions. Offering such reductions would increase the profit margins of a downstream firm who might use the profit to invest in greater non-price competiton, which would in time gain greater market share for itself and the upstream firm.

Support for resale price maintenance also comes from a legal and an economic direction. A legal argument could be built on the notion that the owner of a good has the 'right' to offer any contract associated with the sale of that good that he or she wishes, and that this 'right' supersedes the right of the buyer. The economic argument revolves around transactional hypotheses which identify distribution inefficiencies. Thus success in the production and marketing of a product depends on the actions of both manufacturers and dealers. It is possible for individually rational behaviour to lead to suboptimal outcomes for both the manufacturer and the dealer. Resale price maintenance may be used to correct these potential market failures. Two of these issues are discussed below.

- *Service hypothesis.* Demand for a good depends not only on price but also on the associated pre-sales services.[35] These services will include convenient locations, availability of parking space, waiting time, displays and demonstrations, and information provided by staff. The fact that we have retail outlets implies that retailers or dealers do supply such value-added, otherwise consumers would buy direct from the manufacturers. To increase the final demand for their products, manufacturers have an incentive to ensure that retailers are providing such services. Resale price maintenance increases the retail price and thus the retail margin, which allows retailers to invest in the provision of such services. We may ask why certain retail outlets are unable to produce the necessary 'services' under normal conditions. The traditional answer is that the incentive for a retailer to supply such pre-sales services is diminished if customers 'informed' at one shop were then able to buy the goods at a discount store, which offered no services but a lower price. This is an example of a free-riding externality.[36]

  One problem with the above argument is that the service hypothesis can only be applied to a narrow range of products, normally high priced, new or technically complex products, such as consumer electronics. Since resale price maintenance has historically been applied to a much larger range of goods, such as confectionery, tobacco, books and clothing, an additional argument has been suggested.[37] This was the 'certification' argument discussed earlier, which argued that retailer services could also include the expectation that a reputable store has invested in searches and inspections to certify that a particular good is of high quality. In the mind of consumers the linking of the retailer's brand name to the product is a sufficient guarantee of its quality. Discount stores can simply observe the products stocked and decide what is worth stocking, without having to incur any of their own search or inspection costs.

---

[35] The discussion follows the arguments suggested by Mathewson and Winter (1998).

[36] As an example, Raleigh (UK bicycle manufacturer) argued at the Monopolies and Mergers Commission (1981) that demand for bicycles depended on pre-delivery services, such as pre-sales inspection, final assembly and adjustments, as well as post-delivery services such as advice, repairs and stock of spare parts. They argued that the discount stores, such as Halfords, could not offer these services and sell at a lower price. See also Hardt (1995) for an application of the Raleigh case to the case of market foreclosure without vertical integration.

[37] See Marvel and McCafferty (1984).

While on the topic of the service hypothesis, one may wish to consider the nature of the information that is provided to consumers. The arguments for advertising as presented in Chapter 7 focused on the issue of whether advertising or any promotional effort was informative or persuasive. This dichotomy will also influence our discussion as to the efficiency argument for the provision of services. Thus if the services provided seek to persuade consumers by distorting the nature of the product, consumer welfare may be negatively affected by a higher price and lower output.[38]

● *Contract enforcement.* The pre-sales and certification services argument assumes that manufacturers are unable to directly contract for these services. The problem with such contracts would be the difficulty to manufacturers of monitoring contractual obligations. It has been suggested that resale price maintenance can act as a potential discipline for the efficient provision of these services.[39] If the manufacturer is happy with the level of service provided, the retailers will earn an abnormal profit, assuming the costs of providing services is within their margin. If, however, the manufacturer was unhappy with the services offered, then the dealer's quasi-rents would be lost as the manufacturer terminates the contract. Had the retailer been earning only a normal profit, then the termination of the contract would not have led to any further penalty, other than that of losing business.

Gilligan (1986) attempted to test the importance of resale price maintenance as a means of both achieving allocative efficiency and pursuing anti-competitive strategies. He examined the effect on manufacturers' profits of anti-trust complaints against the use of resale price maintenance. Using changes in share prices as a proxy for changes in future profits, Gilligan found that share prices were significantly affected by anti-trust challenges. This led him to conclude that resale price maintenance was an important determinant of the profits of manufacturers using this strategy. He also concluded that the share price changes were related to structural characteristics of the firms and industries, a relationship which was consistent with the existence of the dealer/manufacturer cartel hypothesis. His conclusions were strongly anti-Chicago:

> Finally, the findings of this study do not support the recent recommendations that RPM should enjoy benign treatment under contemporary antitrust policy . . . The results from our study of a sample of firms that were the object of antitrust adjudication clearly suggest that RPM sometimes causes allocative distortions in manufacturing and distribution. When RPM appears to promote efficiencies in the distribution process, its use is outlived and persists only because of marketing inertia. Calls for *per se* legality of RPM must, given the findings of this study, be based on grounds other than economic efficiency.[40]

Using a slightly different methodology, Hersch (1994) examined the share prices of high-volume retailers and industries associated with high resale price maintenance usage, after the 1951 'Schwegmann' decision.[41] He found little effect on the share prices, though he did find significant differences in the 'efficacy' of resale price maintenance based on firm and market characteristics. This conclusion lent support for the dealer cartel hypothesis.

---

[38] For a fuller discussion, see Katz (1989).
[39] Klein and Murphy (1988) and Blair and Lewis (1994) provide a further discussion of this issue.
[40] Gilligan (1986), pp.554–5.
[41] A decision by the American Supreme Court that severely limited the enforcement of resale price maintenance.

Foreclosure

Market **foreclosure** refers to the practice of firms refusing to supply downstream firms or to purchase from upstream firms. Complete or absolute foreclosure occurs when either a supplier obtains all the downstream outlets, or a buyer obtains all the supplying outlets, to deny non-integrated rivals a share in the relevant market. Foreclosure need not be total and one can compute a degree of foreclosure.[42] Thus if an upstream firm A controls 50 per cent of the input market, merges with a downstream firm B which controls 10 per cent of the final product market, we can conclude that rivals of B are foreclosed from 50 per cent the supplying market, while rivals of A are foreclosed from 10 per cent of the final market. The situation may deteriorate for A's rivals as firm A may, in time, control 50 per cent of the final market as well. Whether considering exclusive distribution or exclusive purchasing agreements, Dobson (1997) argued that the effectiveness of any potential fore-closures will depend on three conditions being met:

- That a sufficient proportion of upstream or downstream firms are covered by the exclusive agreement.
- That there are substantial barriers to entry or an inability to expand output internally at the upstream or downstream stage.
- That the agreements are relatively long term.

Let us now consider whether such exclusionary practices will harm competition. Bork (1978) argued that the anti-competitive effects of foreclosure were exaggerated. He argued, for example, that benefits to an acquiring firm might be offset by the losses of the acquired firm. If a firm acquires a downstream firm and then forces it to buy only from itself this would increase the profitability of the acquiring firm. However, the downstream firm may see a loss of sales and profits if it can no longer sell other, possibly better quality brands. In essence, Bork felt that foreclosure was an irrelevancy and what mattered was the degree of concentration in upstream and downstream markets. Vertical mergers and foreclosure were of little consequence in competitive horizontal markets. This view was challenged by Ordover *et al.* (1990)[43] who suggested that vertical mergers will reduce competition in the input markets. As a firm vertically integrates downstream it will have less incentive to compete with other upstream firms in terms of price to attract downstream customers. As a consequence the upstream firms can increase their prices and hence costs to the downstream firms. These higher costs will result in higher prices to final consumers. More recently, examining the markets for hardware and software systems, Church and Gandal (2000) found that foreclosure could lead to monopolisation of the hardware market.

Krattenmaker and Salop (1986) suggested the following conditions could be applied to test whether market competition was harmed:

- *The ability of the excluded rivals to compete is reduced.* This will be achieved if rivals' costs are increased as a consequence of foreclosure. Foreclosure itself need not increase the costs to the rivals, if there are abundant and comparable supplies from alternative sources. However, exclusion might lead to an increase in costs in the following situations. Firstly, if a firm manages to control the entire supply of a low-cost or high-quality input, this

---

[42] Comanor (1967b) provides a discussion of this issue.
[43] See also Comanor and Frech (1985) and Bolton and Whinston (1991).

will force rivals to acquire inputs which are more costly or of a lower quality. Secondly, if exclusion reduces the supply of inputs on the open market, then rivals will be forced to bid up the price of the remaining inputs. A final possibility is that exclusion may reduce the number of independent suppliers, which may grant the remainder a degree of market power, and higher input prices may be determined.

● *Increased market power after exclusion.* It may be that the ability to foreclose does not increase a firm's market power owing to the existence of powerful rivals or the entry of new firms. In the latter case, one could argue that exclusion harms competitors but not competition.

● *Do rivals have counterstrategies?* It may be possible that rivals are able to protect themselves from the foreclosure. The most obvious counterstrategy is to have access to alternative sources of supply. If rivals have no immediate access to such supplies, they may attempt to take over an input supplier or to encourage the entry of a new firm into the supplying market by agreeing long-term contracts for the purchase of inputs. A further possibility is for the rival to consider 'self-entry', i.e. to set up the supply operation itself. Naturally, all these strategies depend on the opportunity costs of the foreclosure. If the potential costs of the foreclosure are estimated to be lower than the costs of the counterstrategy, then rivals will be forced to absorb such costs.

● *Exclusion must be profitable.* To exclude rivals from supplies implies lost revenue to the supplier. Thus the firm that implements a policy of foreclosure has to ensure that the increased profits of such a policy outweigh the profits forgone through lower sales.

Having identified and discussed the anti-competitive effects, we now turn to a consideration of other factors that may determine the extent to which firms pursue the strategy of exclusive dealing. Heide *et al.* (1998) identified the following additional issues:

● *Free-riding.* As discussed earlier, suppliers or manufacturers may attempt to capture and control the full benefits of services that are provided to final customers. Exclusive contracts prevent other firms benefiting from specialised services associated with a particular brand. This encourages manufacturers to increase the level of such services.

● *Transaction costs.* The costs of monitoring and policing violations of exclusivity agreements may in some circumstances be too high. It may be very costly for a supplier to assess accurately whether a distributor is or is not stocking rivals' products. For example, firms would have to recruit an inspectorate to monitor compliance with contractual obligations. In such cases where costs are high, one would expect less reliance on exclusive dealing.

● *End-customer costs.* Exclusive dealing from the point of view of the final customer means that he or she cannot make a full comparison of different brands at one location. To save on such search costs, customers may prefer to shop at outlets that carry a larger selection of brands. The implication to distributors is that they may lose custom if they restrict their supply to a narrow range of brands. This may reduce the desire of such distributors to enter into such agreements.

● *Firm size.* Firm size may also influence the level of exclusive dealing, the suggestion being that larger firms can benefit from economies of scale and scope in distribution by developing exclusive dealerships.[44] In addition, large firms are able to benefit from promotional economies that enhance the reputation of their brands. This increases final demand for their brands and places large firms in a strong position as regards exclusive dealing.

---

[44] Heide *et al.* (1998), pp.392–3.

Exclusive territories

Manufacturers can restrict their dealers territorially by allowing dealers to operate in specified locations. This can take two forms. The dealers are restricted to operating in a particular territory, but can serve any customer who approaches them. Alternatively, dealers may be forced to serve only customers from a specified location.[45] Katz (1989, p.700) suggested that such territorial agreements affect the search costs to final consumers. If consumers wish to 'comparison shop' they may have to visit a range of outlets in different locations. The effect is to increase search costs and Katz concluded that consumers will be unwilling to 'shop around' and this will reduce inter-brand competition and increase industry profits. This is a different conclusion from the one discussed above under 'end-customer costs' when we considered exclusive dealing. Implicit in Katz's argument is that spatial distances between dealers significantly influence consumer search costs. In addition, Katz argued that territorial agreements can help to develop and maintain dealer collusion by limiting the number of dealers in a given area. Rey and Stiglitz (1988) also suggested that such agreements would lessen competition amongst the upstream firms. If retailers exercised their market power as quasi-monopolists they would charge a higher price for their goods. This price change affects the demand for the output of the upstream firms, in effect reducing their price elasticity of demand.

Quantity-dependent pricing

Quantity-dependent pricing as defined by Katz (1989) refers to the practice whereby the price that a buyer pays for an intermediate good will depend on the quantity bought. Broadly, there are three types of vertical restraint that fall under this heading. 'Quantity forcing' occurs when a buyer is obliged to buy more than he or she would wish to under normal circumstances. This practice can be accomplished by forcing the buyer to make a minimum payment for purchases up to a certain level. A second restraint is 'non-linear pricing', or a 'two-part tariff', which takes place when a buyer pays a fixed fee (a franchise fee) plus a price per unit. As more is bought so the average total cost will fall. Finally, 'tie-in' selling and 'bundling', again describes a situation where buyers are forced to buy more than they wish. Ties occur when a buyer wishes to acquire a product but is forced, as a condition of supply, to accept additional products or services. The first good is referred to as the tying good and the second as the tied good. 'Full-line forcing' is said to exist if a dealer is forced to stock a full range of products. A camera retailer may be interested in selling only one particular type of camera, but to do so it may be required to stock the full range of cameras manufactured by the supplier. **Bundling** refers to the practice of selling two or more goods as a single package. We briefly examine these three practices.

Quantity forcing

Forcing buyers to stock and sell more than they may wish to will have the effect of improving the service to ensure such sales are made as well as helping to reduce prices to final consumers. This latter effect may overcome the problem of double marginalisation discussed above.

---

[45] Waterson (1988) doubted whether restrictions on dealing with consumers from different locations could ever be enforced.

Non-linear pricing

The policy of charging a fixed 'franchise' fee for the opportunity of stocking and selling the manufacturer's product on top of a constant per-unit charge can also be used to solve the double marginalisation problem. Figure 9.10 illustrated a solution to the problem via vertical integration. Non-linear pricing can solve the problem without the need for vertical integration. If, in Figure 9.10(a), the manufacturer charges, not OP_1 but the marginal cost, the distributor will equate its marginal revenue to its marginal cost and sell OQ_2, the same outcome as for the vertical integration solution shown in Figure 9.10(b). However, by charging its marginal cost the manufacturer makes no profit whereas the distributor appropriates the full monopoly profit. By using franchise fees the manufacturer can increase its revenue and profits. In the case of a perfectly competitive distribution industry, dealers compete for the right to supply the goods by bidding up the franchise fee to the extent that the manufacturer earns the same profits as it would have done had it integrated vertically.

Dobson (1997) argued that where the average cost to the buyer falls as purchases from a seller increase, we have a situation similar to 'exclusive purchasing'. Buying firms will wish to restrict the number of supplying firms they deal with, to protect their *de facto* quantity discounts. This may facilitate upstream inter-brand collusion in so far as firms will be reluctant to cheat by increasing sales to their dealers as this will reduce the average wholesale price.

Kay (1990b) suggested two reasons why suppliers may impose a non-linear pricing strategy. As remuneration increases more than proportionately with the total amount of business done with a particular supplier it may help to 'bias' retailers. Thus an insurance company may wish independent brokers to recommend its policies above others, or a breakfast cereal company may wish a supermarket to display its brand prominently on the shelves. Non-linear pricing can act as an incentive for dealers to promote the product. Secondly, if dealers stock only one product, to capitalise on increasing their revenues, this will then increase the switching and search costs to consumers. Consumers are less likely to search out and switch to alternatives if outlets carry a narrow range of products. This will increase the market power of the suppliers.

Tying

Tying is usually defined as the selling of two or more 'distinct' products, where the sale of one good is conditioned on the purchase of another.[46] Whether products are distinct can be determined if in the absence of tying arrangements the products are purchased in two separate markets. For example, the supply of shoes with laces would not generally be considered as the supply of two distinct products. However, the case of a buyer who buys a machine from a supplier and is then faced with a contractual obligation to have the machine serviced by engineers from the supplying firm is an example of two distinct supply markets, one for the machine and the other for machine servicing. Singer (1968) proposed five reasons why suppliers might be interested in tying:

- *Price evasion.* If suppliers were facing government restrictions on the price of the products, they could then force their buyers to stock an unregulated product at a high price so as to regain some of their lost profits on the regulated item.

---

[46] European Commission (1999a).

- *Protection of goodwill*. A supplier may wish to protect the quality of its product by insisting that repairs and spare parts to, say, a machine are supplied only by the firm. The argument may focus on the technical complexity of the machine and to have the machine serviced by non-approved engineers may harm the machine and damage the firm's reputation. Whether the argument is justified depends on whether efficient alternatives to the tying arrangement exist.
- *Economies of distribution*. Firms may tie two or more products if they are strong complements to benefit from distributional economies. In theory, all assembled products such as cars, are in effect, a tying arrangement of many separate products such as engines, crankshaft, axles, wheels and other parts.
- *Price discrimination*. Price discrimination can also be achieved in the following way. Assume a monopolist supplier sells colour printers (the tying product) and ink cartridges (the tied product). The firm charges a competitive price for its printers but a 'high' price for the cartridges. Large customers (those with a low elasticity of demand) are forced to pay a higher overall price for 'printing services' since they use proportionately more of the expensive cartridges than the low-intensity users. Resale is ruled out since the price of cartridges is the same for all customers. Thus price discrimination is achieved indirectly. Another example of this type of covert price discrimination covers the common practice of selling machines and expensive service contracts. The more machines that are bought the higher the overall 'price' paid.
- *Leverage*. Tying arrangements can extend the power of a monopolist into related markets. The arrangement can create market power in the market for the tied products and prices can be increased. The amount of leverage that a monopolist can exert will depend on the extent to which tying arrangements can account for the whole tied market.[47]

Bundling

Bundling, as briefly described above, refers to the practice of a seller offering several goods as one package. Thus hotels will offer rooms bundled with the use of other hotel facilities such as in-house gyms and swimming pools. The prices of all these additional services are included in the price of the room, whether one uses them or not. Adams and Yellen (1976) showed that such bundling was profitable since customers can be sorted into different groups with different reserve prices and their consumer surplus appropriated accordingly. In other words, bundling can be used as a form of price discrimination. The following example (based on Stigler's (1963b) example of block-booking in the film industry[48]) helps to explain the strategy.

Block-booking refers to the practice of offering an exhibitor only a package of films rather than the films individually. This policy increases revenue to the sellers. Assume that a London film distributor knows the reserve prices of two exhibitors. One exhibitor owns an 'art house' in Hampstead and the other a West End cinema showing popular films.

---

[47] See also Whinston (1990) and Chen and Ross (1999) for a discussion of tying arrangements and anti-competitive effects.
[48] This was undoubtedly based on the famous *US Supreme Court v. Paramount Pictures Inc.* 334 US 131 (1948).

The reserve prices that each exhibitor is willing to pay for the two films, *Jean de Florette* and the latest *Star Wars*, are:

Exhibitor	Star Wars	Jean de Florette
Hampstead	7,000	3,000
West End	8,000	2,500

If each film were to be sold separately and the distributor could prevent resales, we would achieve perfect price discrimination and the total rental would be £20,500 (7,000 + 3,000 + 8,000 + 2,500). However, under normal market conditions, perfect price discrimination is impossible and the best the distributor could earn would be to charge £7,000 for the *Star Wars* film and £2,500 for *Jean de Florette*. This would generate an income of only £19,000 (7,000 × 2 + 2,500 × 2). If the distributor practised block-booking non-discriminatingly, he would sell the two-film package at £10,000 to both exhibitors. The total rental would rise to £20,000.

In conclusion, we can draw a few strands together. The Chicago approach to vertical restraints, arguing that such restraints are commercially legitimate, is plausible under a number of circumstances. However, one should not ignore the obvious strategic advantages that such a policy can present to firms. Vertical restraints can be used to change an industry structure or to preserve an uncompetitive status quo. In view of this dichotomy the most obvious conclusion is to treat each restraint on an ad hoc basis by examining the consequences of such actions. Thus if prices are considered to be fair and entry is not retarded, the presence of vertical restrictions may be tolerated.

9.7 Conclusions

In this chapter we have examined a range of vertical relationships, from vertical integration to much looser relationships determined by a vast array of contractual obligations. The choice of which vertical strategy to follow can only be resolved by an analysis of the potential costs and benefits present in any given market structure. What was clear was that there was no one unequivocal answer as to what constituted an equilibrium condition for most firms. To understand why firms develop complex vertical relationships one must appreciate the risks, the level of investment, the extent of co-ordination and bargaining present in such relationships. One can then also understand why firms undertake vertical integration if market contracts are a less efficient method of organising production and distribution.

The chapter also discussed the wider issues of vertical relationships to assess the benefits to society. Clearly such relationships are beneficial to society if they result in lower costs, greater output and a control on the power of monopolies. However, vertical restraints can reinforce market power and frustrate greater competition and economic welfare. What is clear is that one cannot support or condemn such practices in any general sense. Only a case by case analysis can determine useful and practical solutions.

Key terms

Agency
Backward vertical integration
Bundling
Contractual incompleteness
Double marginalisation
Foreclosure
Forward vertical integration

Franchising
Networks
Quantity forcing
Resale price maintenance
Tying
Vertical integration

Case study 9.1
Business and the law: in search of a remedy

When the Net Book Agreement collapsed in late 1995, Asda, the supermarket group, immediately turned its attention to toppling the UK's last legal price-fixing arrangement – resale price maintenance (RPM) for non-prescription medicines. The group, which by discounting popular titles had hastened the end of the arrangement that allowed publishers to set minimum prices, felt equally strongly that the public was paying too much for over-the-counter (OTC) medicines. Announcing that resale price maintenance on basic health products amounted to a hidden tax of £280m a year on the British public, it cut prices on 82 vitamin and mineral products by 20 per cent. Legal action by manufacturers forced it to back down, but last summer it halved the price of Anadin. When legal action again followed, it took the drug off its shelves rather than restore prices to the manufacturer's recommended minimum. Asda argues that for every £1 spent on a typical branded painkiller, such as Anadin, there is an 80p profit – 55p to the manufacturer and 25p to the retailer.

By this stage resale price maintenance for OTC medicines was under review by the Office of Fair Trading. Encouraged by its success with the Net Book Agreement, the OFT had decided a re-examination was merited because of the changes in retailing since the issue was looked at by the Restrictive Practices Court in 1970. At the time the court decided it was in the public interest that manufacturers should set and enforce minimum resale prices for OTC medicines. If RPM were not allowed, significant numbers of community pharmacies would close. This would reduce access for the elderly and sick and for young mothers. In October last year, Mr John Bridgeman, director-general of fair trading, announced that he intended to refer the issue back to the court. The first stage in that process is for the director-general to make an application to the court for leave or permission for a hearing. Under the Resale Prices Act 1976 the court can grant leave only on prima facie evidence that there has been a material change in relevant circumstances since its last decision. To date, no application for leave has been made. The OFT's original intention was to make the application in the spring. Now it can say only that it expects to apply to the court 'sometime in the summer'. In his announcement, however, Mr Bridgeman made clear he felt there had been a material change. He noted that pharmacy numbers have been relatively stable in recent years; pharmacies derive a higher proportion of their income from dispensing than they did; OTC medicine sales make up a smaller percentage of turnover; consumers visit pharmacies more often to have a prescription dispensed than to buy an OTC medicine; and pharmacies are more secure than in 1970, partly because of the proportion of income they now receive from the National Health Service. The pharmacy profession was very disappointed with these conclusions. The National Pharmaceutical Association, the Royal Pharmaceutical Society and the Proprietary Association had joined together under the umbrella of the Community Pharmacy Action Group to put the case for the defence of RPM. In the months leading up to Mr Bridgeman's October announcement, the group had worked hard to gather the best possible data and information for the OFT review, but the director-general appeared to have ignored or discounted it in deciding to refer the issue to the court.

The group's case is broadly that RPM is essential so that small independent pharmacies can compete with large retailers and supermarkets and thus stay in business to provide essential healthcare services. Without RPM, it argues, edge of town supermarkets would use all their marketing muscle to cut the price of key medicines, forcing small pharmacies out of business. Supermarkets cannot provide localised specialist healthcare services and because they sell large quantities they can charge less and still make a profit. Small pharmacies cannot compete against the buying power of supermarkets and supermarkets would not offer the same full range of products or services. According to Mrs Sue Sharpe, head of the legal department at the Royal Pharmaceutical Society: 'All our research suggests ending RPM will have a significant adverse effect on the viability of community pharmacies.'

The group commissioned research last year from the Deloitte & Touche Consulting Group into the costs and benefits of abolishing RPM. The consultants found that up to 3,055 pharmacies out of the 12,000 in the UK would be at risk of closure. Between 1,153 and 2,232 pharmacies are estimated to be already at risk of closing even before the removal of RPM. Between 3.2m and 6.5m people have their prescriptions dispensed by pharmacies already at risk. A further 500,000 to 1.7m people would be affected if RPM goes. Additional travel costs of between 4.4m and 15.9m would be incurred by people affected by the closure of their local pharmacies. And a significant proportion of the population would have reduced access to pharmacists' professional and free advice. That could lead to additional burdens on local GPs.

By contrast the benefits of removing RPM are estimated by Deloitte & Touche at savings of about £180m a year if prices were cut across the board, which is the equivalent of £3 per year per person, or 6p a week. The £100,000 annual costs of enforcing RPM would also be saved. The group believes there is no economic case for abolishing RPM. About 70 per cent of small pharmacies' turnover comes from NHS dispensing compared with only 7 per cent in 1970 with only 10 per cent to 20 per cent coming from OTC medicines. But the problem is that income from dispensing medicines has been squeezed badly. Many pharmacies rely on income from non-prescription medicines to survive. The group also disputes the case that manufacturers and pharmacies make huge profits from RPM. Of the 33p of every pound spent on OTC medicines that goes to retailers, just 6p is net profit, it says. Nor does it accept the British public are paying too much for OTC medicines. Mrs Sharpe says it will not be the big retailers such as Boots which suffer from the abolition of RPM, nor the small multiples, but the local community and rural pharmacies. An accelerating trend towards convenience shopping through superstores would also fly in the face of planning policy guidance issued by the Department of Environment last summer, she says. The message from the professional group is that the OFT needs to think again. If the OFT pursues the case to the court it will meet a very determined industry.

Case study 9.2
Vertical integration sets building materials debate

Across the UK building materials sector consolidation continues apace as a continental style of vertical integration gets under way. The shift threatens to upset traditional relationships in the industry and could put pressure on margins. According to some observers, the most sensitive of the recent deals is RMC's £900m bid for Rugby, the cement maker, which is due to be completed within the next three to four weeks. This breaks the industry mould, which previously has kept cement manufacturers separate from the producers of aggregates and ready mix concrete.

Vertical integration – the ownership of cement-making capacity by aggregates and ready mix concrete companies – is the pattern in continental Europe and appears poised to cross the Channel. The debate about vertical integration may appear the stuff of business school studies but the building materials industry is concerned that long-established relationships could be under threat. The RMC bid for Rugby may be the first but others could be in the offing with Lafarge, the French building materials group, reported to be interested in bidding for Blue Circle Industries, the UK's largest cement maker. Cement represents the main cost item in the production of ready mix concrete, so there are powerful incentives for ready mix suppliers to secure access to supplies of cement to add to their existing supplies of aggregates.

But many in the industry say there are equally strong reasons for the UK building materials industry to stay the way it is. Cement is a very different industry to the quarrying of aggregates and the mixing and supply of concrete. 'Cement is a manufacturing process whereas concrete is a distribution skill,' said one analyst. 'Just like food manufacturing and retailing, the skill sets are different.'

Cement manufacturing also involves high levels of capital investment and maintenance costs compared with quarrying stone and producing ready mix concrete. A cement factory can cost £100m to build while a ready mix batching plant can be set up for £1.5m. But the main argument against acquiring a cement producer are the economics of distributing cement compared with aggregates and ready mix. Because of their weight and bulk, aggregates cannot be moved far by road. Ready mix concrete, which carries the additional problem of setting as it is transported, can only travel 10–15 miles. Cement is worth 10 times a tonne more than aggregates, so can be shipped 10 times further by truck. But RMC, whose bid for Rugby was cleared by the European competition authorities on Wednesday, has no plans to ship cement long distances once it has acquired Rugby. 'The maximum economic radius for moving cement by lorry is 100 miles,' says Bob Lambourne, RMC finance director. 'There would be little advantage in us replacing, say, Blue Circle with supplies from Rugby.'

In Germany, where the building materials market is integrated and RMC has a 17 per cent market share, it still buys only 20 per cent of its cement from its own plants because of the cost of haulage. The decision to acquire Rugby was not motivated by a desire to increase direct supplies of cement to RMC's ready mix plants but to build a stronger position in cement internationally, says Mr Lambourne. Mr Lambourne says he is puzzled by the fuss that has been made over the issue of vertical integration. 'The UK is virtually the only market in Europe which is not vertically integrated. We don't see why [acquiring Rugby] should have such an effect on the market.' But other industry observers believe that integration across the three product areas may persuade companies that have access to cement to subsidise their own operations and put up the price to rivals. At present, aggregates and ready mix companies benefit from strong competition between their cement suppliers.

'One reason for buying a cement company is the perception that the quality of earnings are higher because of the barriers to entry,' said one analyst. 'But RMC's quality of earnings will only be better if it does not destabilise the market – and if other people behave themselves.' Even those who do not fear damage from vertical integration say high transport costs mean there are no benefits from putting cement together with aggregates and ready mix concrete. 'We decided we didn't want to lead the industry into vertical integration because we don't believe it creates value,' says Rick Haythornthwaite, chief executive of Blue Circle. Access to aggregates is a more important determinant of success, according to Andrew Dougal, chief executive of Hanson. 'Concrete is competitive and it is difficult to raise your price but that doesn't matter as long as you are strong in aggregates.'

Case study 9.3
UK retail group seeks review of PC pricing

John Lewis Partnership, the retail group, has threatened legal action unless the Office of Fair Trading reopens an investigation into alleged price fixing in the home computer market. The OFT cleared Dixons, the electrical retailer, in October 1999 of allegations that it abused its market position to overcharge for PCs. But John Lewis and rival group Comet – part of the Kingfisher chain – claim the 10-month investigation improperly measured Dixon's market share and that exclusive supply agreements with Compaq Computers and Packard Bell had further increased its market power. Dixons dismissed the claims that it was fixing the market as 'utter nonsense'.

An executive close to the affair said on Sunday: 'The OFT has made a mistake in law and unless it takes another look at this, John Lewis will seek a judicial review.' The group claims Compaq and Packard Bell computers accounted for 60 per cent of its PC sales last year. It has warned Kim Howells, minister for consumer affairs, that other big name brands may enter into similar exclusive supply deals, threatening the government's aim of putting a PC into every home. 'Even the loss of these two [brands] would severely limit our ability, and that of other high street retailers, to present a competitive range of products,' it said.

The OFT investigation concluded that no retailer or manufacturer was in a position of market power because equivalent computers were available through mail order and internet suppliers. However, Nick Palmer, Labour MP for Broxtowe and secretary of the Commons cross-party internet working group, rejected this and will call on Stephen Byers, trade and industry secretary, on Tuesday to re-examine the home computer market. 'The average first time buyer still prefers to deal with traditional high street shops, which are dominated by Dixons and its subsidiaries Currys and PC World,' he said. The OFT said it had not received an official complaint from John Lewis or Comet, but that the exclusivity agreements could be prohibited under the Competition Act if there was evidence of them leading to higher prices. Dixons said: 'Our objective is to secure the lowest prices and the widest range of products for our customers, and that is all we are doing'.

Questions for discussion

1. Give examples of firms forced to vertically integrate backwards to guarantee their sources of supply and those that have had to integrate forwards to safeguard their distribution outlets.

2. Are oligopolists more or less likely to be attracted to vertical integration?

3. Some economists claim that vertical integration could be related to the age of the product or industry. Explain how.

4. Explain how vertical integration may help some firms to reduce their tax exposure.

5. What measures can be employed to measure the extent of vertical integration?

6. Discuss the strategy of 'recommended retail prices' as opposed to resale price maintenance.

7. Examine the three case studies and identify the nature of the vertical relationships. On the basis of the evidence presented as well as any other relevant evidence you may discover, discuss the extent to which the vertical relationships could be regarded as anti-competitive.

Further reading

Bork, R. (1978) *The Antitrust Paradox: A Policy at War with Itself*. New York: Basic Books.

Dobson, P.W. and Waterson, M. (1996) *Vertical Restraints and Competition Policy*, Office of Fair Trading Research Paper No. 12. London: OFT.

Jensen, M.C. (2000) *Foundations of Organisational Strategy*. Cambridge, MA: Harvard University Press.

Katz, M.L. (1989) Vertical contractual relations, in Schmalensee, R. and Willig, R.D. (eds) *Handbook of Industrial Organisation*, Vol. 1. Amsterdam: North-Holland, chapter 11.

OECD (1993) *Competition Policy and Vertical Restraints: Franchising Agreements*. Paris: OECD.

Phlips, L. (ed.) (1998) *Applied Industrial Economics*. Cambridge: Cambridge University Press, chapters 9, 15 and 21.

Pickering, J.F. (1999) Competition policy and vertical integration relationships: the approach of the UK Monopolies and Mergers Commission, *European Competition Law Review*, **40**, 225–39.

Scherer, F.M. and Ross, D. (1990) *Industrial Market Structure and Economic Performance*. Boston: Houghton Mifflin, chapters 14 and 15.

Williamson, O.E. (1971) The vertical integration of production: market failure considerations, *American Economic Review*, **61**, 112–27.

Williamson, O.E. (1989) Transaction cost economics, in Schmalensee, R. and Willig, R.D. (eds) *Handbook of Industrial Organisation*, Vol. 1. Amsterdam: North-Holland.

Diversification

10.1 Introduction

A diversified firm, as opposed to a 'specialised' firm, is involved in the production of a number of different goods and services. We can thus also refer to a diversified firm as a 'multi-product' firm.

Diversification can be of three types:

- *Product extension.* Firms can diversify by moving into a related activity and adding to their product line. This type of diversification can be relatively close to or distant from the core product. Thus a sweet manufacturer who sells a milk chocolate bar may decide to produce and sell a dark chocolate bar as a product extension. The firm may diversify further afield by marketing related products such as ice-cream or snack foods. Product extension will usually occur when there are potentials for 'economies of scope'. Such economies are realised when two related goods can be produced jointly at a cost lower than if they were produced independently.

Diversification by product diversification, however, should not be viewed as a discrete series of easily identifiable steps, but rather as part of a continuous process. Since almost all firms produce more than one type of product or offer more than one particular service, it could be true to say that all firms are to some extent diversified, multi-product firms. A steel manufacturer can produce different qualities of steel in various shapes and sizes; and even the sandwich shop can extend its product range by adding new ingredients to its sandwiches and offering a greater range of drinks. Theoretically, the steel manufacturer (and the shop) will develop and add more products as long as the marginal benefits outweigh the marginal costs of doing so.

● *Market extension.* As a firm develops a specialisation in a given technology and product base, it may wish to exploit different markets. Markets refer to different groups of buyers, as discussed in Chapter 4. Such markets can be defined by different industries, different social groups as well as different geographical areas.[1] Thus a chemical company may decide to sell its chemicals not only to industrial users but also to the agricultural sector of the economy. The challenge of selling an existing product to a new market is the ability of a firm to ensure that it has the resources, knowledge and ability to exploit such new marketing opportunities.

● *'Pure' diversification.* This type of diversification exists when firms move into unrelated fields of activity. Firms that are involved in different industries are often referred to as **conglomerates**. Gribben (1976, p.19) offered the following Office of Fair Trading definition of conglomerates:

> [C]onglomerate mergers are mergers between companies that do not produce similar products and where neither is an actual or potential supplier of the other; . . . it would follow from this that a conglomerate (the firm) is composed of a series of parts which are not horizontally or vertically related.

An example of such pure diversification is the British firm Virgin Plc which began as a record store, but is currently involved in aeroplanes, trains, financial products, soft drinks, mobile phones, holidays, cars, wines, publishing and bridal wear. The diversification discussed in the first two points above referred to a strategy which is based on some basic core product specialisation. Conglomerates or purely diversified firms will rely less and less on such a common base. As we shall see, very few firms engage in 'pure' diversification. Most firms tend to enter adjacent markets rather than move into totally new areas of production and distribution. At times it may appear that a firm is involved in pure diversification but on closer examination there is a logical explanation why a firm has decided on a particular direction. For example, Mars UK, the confectionery firm, developed marine radar, aimed at the small boat market. At first glance this would seem to be an example of pure diversification. In fact the company had developed a successful electronics business on the basis of technical expertise accumulated through their vending machine operations. Having spotted a gap in the market for a cheap and reliable radar, the company, Mars Electronic, invested in this new 'niche' market.

---

[1] For a discussion and empirical work on the benefits of international diversification see Heston and Rouwenhorst (1994), Aw and Batra (1998) and Griffen and Karolyi (1998).

The **direction** that any diversification takes depends on the market opportunities, the nature of the technology facing the firms and the ability of management to exploit such opportunities. A further issue that may be considered is the manner in which firms can diversify since diversification can be achieved either through internal expansion or by acquisition and merger. Penrose (1995, p.143) pointed out that internal expansion would require a consideration of the expansion of the existing plant, equipment, raw materials and application of skills and technical and managerial know-how. These factors are very much less important if a firm considers diversification through acquisition. The only require-ment for the latter strategy is to select an appropriate firm and to manage the integration efficiently.

Jacobson and Andréosso-O'Callaghan (1996, p.169) noted that diversification in Europe after the Second World War tended to be characterised by internal expansion, whereas American diversification was achieved through acquisitions. One explanation for this observed difference was suggested by de Jong (1993) who claimed that diversification stra-tegy might depend on the industry lifecycle. New industries have opportunities to extend their product lines as the market grows and rivalry is less pronounced. This will encourage internal expansion. However, as an industry moves into a maturity stage, further market growth and new product development are constrained and firms will look towards the acquisition of new firms to maintain a diversification strategy. An alternative explanation was offered by Chandler (1990), who suggested that European firms' ability to raise finance for acquisitions and mergers was constrained by the small European capital market, com-pared with its American counterpart.

We consider reasons for diversification in section 10.2. These reasons cover issues such as the desire by firms to secure more market power, to achieve greater growth, to lower costs and to exploit their specific assets in different industries. Section 10.3 discusses the reasons for diversification as viewed from a newer perspective of the firm, developed by Teece *et al.* (1994) and referred to as the 'coherent corporation'. It is clear from the discussion in sections 10.2 and 10.3 that diversification does not generate unlimited advantages and that at some point costs of diversification force firms to consider strategies of divestment or deconglomeration to refocus their attention on core activities. This is discussed in section 10.4. Finally, section 10.5 provides some empirical evidence of the diversification experience in the UK and Europe in the latter half of the twentieth century.

10.2 Reasons for diversification

There are many reasons why firms pursue a diversification strategy, and how one classifies these explanations is largely a matter of choice. Montgomery (1994) offered one convenient classification by suggesting three basic reasons for diversification. These are outlined below.

Market-power view
Through access to conglomerate power, diversified firms might be able to exploit a new strand of anti-competitive behaviour. Montgomery suggested three examples of such behaviour. Firstly, **cross-subsidisation** or 'deep pocket' (sometimes referred to as 'long purse') strate-gies. These occur when a firm relies on profits from its various operations to finance predatory practices in other markets. Secondly, 'reciprocal buying' (**reciprocity**) which in-volves an agreement that, for example, firm A will purchase its inputs from firm B on the

condition that firm B then purchases its inputs from firm A. Clearly, conglomerate firms are in a stronger reciprocal position than specialised firms, who may find that they have no need for the output of the buying firm. Thus specialised firms may be foreclosed from certain markets. A third anti-competitive consequence is 'mutual forbearance', whereby large conglomerates will recognise each other's power and decide to co-exist or accommodate one another in various shared markets.

Agency view

Due to a separation of ownership from control in the modern corporation, managers (the agents) may pursue growth through diversification strategies in excess of that necessary to benefit their shareholders (the principals). Managers may be tempted to do this for three reasons. Firstly, their power, status and remuneration may be related to the growth of the organisation. Secondly, diversification in other activities may complement the talents and skills of the managers, thus making them indispensable to the organisation. Lastly, unlike shareholders, who are able to reduce business risks by diversifying their portfolios, managers will be exposed to employment risks should the firm fail. Diversification of a firm might then be seen as a means of reducing the potential risks of failure faced by the firm and its managers.

Resource view

Firms will possess a range of resources and assets which can be exploited in other markets. If such resources could be sold in the market, to other firms, then the rationale for diversification would disappear. However, in cases where transaction costs are high, firms may be forced to exploit these assets themselves. Such assets have been given various names, such as 'specific assets',[2] 'core competences'[3] and 'core capabilities'.[4] Montgomery and Wernerfelt (1988) saw diversification as a way in which 'rents' could be extracted in related activities.[5] They assumed that potential diversifiers have excess capacity in their factor inputs which can be exploited beyond their current scope. As a firm diversifies it will transfer these excess factors to its 'closest' market, which is defined as the market which yields the highest rents. Should excess capacity remain, the firm will diversify into markets further afield until the marginal rents have disappeared. The rents that can be extracted in this way will depend on the 'specificity' (or applicability) of the factors and the degree of 'closeness' of the market.

The following section considers and expands the above reasons.

Market power

There is a belief that the diversified firm, relying on many different geographical and product markets, has a competitive advantage over the specialised firm and that it can draw on resources from its many different operations to fight rivals in specific markets. It

---

[2] Gorecki (1975).
[3] Prahalad and Hamel (1990).
[4] Stalk et al. (1992).
[5] 'Rents', or more specifically 'Ricardian rents', were defined as the returns to owners of unique factors, such as an innovation.

may also be the case that large near-monopolies and oligopolies seeking yet more market power may be reluctant to expand in one market as this would alert the anti-monopoly authorities. An alternative may be to cross to related markets to escape the attention of the competition regulators. We consider four possible anti-competitive consequences of diversification.

Cross-subsidisation and predation

The diversified firm can outbid, outspend and outdo the specialised firm since it can rely on profits and cash flows from many sources. In essence it is a better fighter. However, care must be taken when analysing such strategies, as cross-subsidisation can be rational conduct for the specialised firm as well as the diversified firm. Specialised firms often face a number of submarkets and they may wish to subsidise the less profitable segments by income earned in the more profitable segments, so as to develop a broader market appeal over time, or to ride out seasonal fluctuations. A typical strategy for a diversified firm might be to undercut the prices of a specialised firm and force it out of the market. In order for this strategy to succeed the predator must have a 'deeper pocket' than its prey. Once the firm has left the market, prices are reset at the original or a higher level. Such behaviour is referred to a predatory pricing. The Office of Fair Trading defined predatory behaviour as:

> the acceptance of losses in a particular market which are deliberately incurred in order to eliminate a specific competitor, so that supra-normal profits can be earned in the future, either in the same or in other markets.[6]

Predation is, however, not as straightforward a strategy as one would first believe. Firstly, predatory pricing will only be profitable where entry barriers exist, otherwise the sacrifice of lower prices and lower revenues will have been in vain. As Adelman (1959, p.369) noted: 'Predatory competition is an expensive pastime, undertaken only if monopoly and its fruits can be obtained and *held*' (emphasis added).

It could be argued that the act of predation signals to future potential entrants that the incumbent is a 'fighter' and is willing to sacrifice short-term profits to maintain or increase market share.[7] This 'reputation effect' may act as an entry barrier.

Predatory practices imply that resources from one operation are being diverted to fight elsewhere. In a specialised firm, alternatives do not compete. Thus, whilst the diversified firm may have the capability to carry out such a strategy, it may refrain from predatory practices since it would place its alternatives at risk. One of Rockefeller's associates echoed the above argument when he remarked that Standard (Oil) 'gained or lost on a titan's scale while our opponents did so on a pygmy's'.[8] Aron (1993) referred to this strategy as 'cannibalisation', whereby a firm entering a submarket may draw resources and demand away from its original market. It could be argued that the specialised firm might be the better fighter as it would be fighting for survival. Finally, some economists have argued that if firms wish to eliminate rivalry there may be alternative, less costly strategies than predation, such as collusive pricing or acquisition.[9,10]

---

[6] Myers (1994), p.9.
[7] See, for example, Milgrom and Roberts (1982) and Chen (1997).
[8] See Nevins (1953), p.65 for a detmied discussion.
[9] See McGee (1958) and Telser (1966a).
[10] For a fuller discussion of predatory pricing, see OECD (1989) and Scherer and Ross (1990).

Reciprocity

Reciprocity can be defined as: 'the practice of basing purchases upon the recognition of sales to the other party, rather than on the basis of prices and product quality'.[11] Thus sellers realise that a buyer may shift purchases if reciprocal transactions are not made. It can be argued that in effect all economic transactions involve an element of reciprocity and in the extreme case of bartering, transactions are based solely on reciprocal arrangements. The anti-competitive aspect of reciprocity might be inferred if some firms were *forced* into such transactions. Utton (1979, pp.91–2) noted that the Federal Trade Commission in the United States argued that reciprocal trade would increase existing entry barriers and possibly create a new one if potential entrants were foreclosed from a market by the existence of reciprocal trade. To overcome such a barrier, the entrant would have to be diversified. A specialised firm will have only a limited range of input demands whereas a diversified firm will have a much wider spread of purchasing requirements. Thus the diversified firm is in a better reciprocal position. Much of the evidence of anti-competitive effects of such strategies tends to be based on anecdotal evidence of cases that were brought before the courts. The three cases below will help to explain the possible advantages of reciprocal dealing.

General Dynamic produced many goods for the US government and as a large and powerful conglomerate it also acted as a monopsonist as regards many of its input needs. The government, aware of General Dynamic's market power, insisted on cost-plus contracts so that any reduction in input costs would be passed on to government and not retained by the firm to boost its profits. To get round this loss of monopsony profits, General Dynamic paid a (higher) market price for its inputs but made it a condition of purchase that the suppliers buy goods from one of its subsidiaries, Liquid Carbonic, a supplier of liquid and solid carbon dioxide. Liquid Carbonic saw its sales rise dramatically, undoubtedly aided by this 'special sales program', the euphemism used for these reciprocal arrangements.[12]

Scherer (1980, p.343) quotes the example of two officials in the Armour Meat Packing Corporation who had decided to diversify into engineering by buying stock in a small company specialising in the manufacture of gears used by the rail industry. A condition of shipping their meat with a given railroad was that the railroad company should buy its gears from its subsidiary. The railroad companies, fearing that they might lose an important customer such as Armour to the alternative road haulage business, agreed. In only six years the engineering company moved from seventh place in the industry, with just 1 per cent market share to become a dominant firm with a 35 per cent share.

A further example provided by Scherer (1980, p.345) showed how reciprocal action can be used as a form of leverage. Consolidated Foods, a food manufacturer, owned seven supermarkets in the Chicago area. In 1965, it launched an aggressive price-cutting and advertising campaign to boost its market share. This strategy hit National Tea, a national supermarket chain with 237 stores. In retaliation, National stopped its purchases of baked products from Consolidated's subsidiary Sara Lee for just one week. Not long after, Consolidated abandoned not only its price-cuts, but also its entire supermarket operations. Such leverage through reciprocity was possible only because National Tea was a large diversified firm and was a buyer of Consolidated's outputs.

[11] Weston (1970), p.314.
[12] Blackstone (1972), p.459.

Considering the anecdotal evidence presented above, Needham (1978) argued that the consensus among economists was that reciprocity was just one method by which a firm could exploit its existing market power, rather than a strategy of extending that power. Consequently the practice itself could not be viewed as particularly harmful to competition.

Tie-in sales

In Chapter 9 on vertical relationships we discussed the nature and effects of tie-in sales. We defined **tie-in sales** or **tying** as the sale of two distinct products, where the sale of one good is conditional on the purchase of another. Thus a conglomerate supplies a buyer with good X on the condition that the buyer also purchases good Y from the conglomerate. In this way the diversified firm is able to increase revenues. The advantages of tying discussed in Chapter 9 can equally be applied to the case of diversified firms.

Entry barriers

It may be argued that conglomerate mergers increase the height of entry barriers through economies of scale, absolute cost and capital requirement type barriers.[13] Tremblay and Tremblay (1996) noted that in the United States brewing industry, large national firms attempted to fill all possible niches and market segments, through brand and product proliferation, to maintain their market power and deny market space to potential entrants, though it could also be argued that conglomerates may realise scale and scope economies which could lead to greater efficiency in various markets. Furthermore, Berry (1974) argued that diversification was a means by which large firms could enter highly concentrated markets and infuse greater competition.[14]

Growth of the firm

A reason frequently put forward for diversification is to achieve growth, and some commentators have suggested that diversification is the chief method of growth for medium-sized firms.[15] Mueller (1969) offered the argument that conglomerate mergers are a strategy which might be pursued by managers who are more concerned with the maximisation of the growth rate of the firm rather than the maximisation of shareholder wealth. To managers who are keen to maximise the growth rate of the firm, the opportunity cost of investments in the firm will be equated with the returns on the marginal projects in the organisation, rather than on returns on investment projects outside the organisation. The latter is the opportunity cost of shareholders' investments in the organisation. As a consequence, the discount rate of managers for investment projects will be much lower than that of their shareholders and this will lead to higher investments by the managers. Such investments can be directed towards horizontal, vertical and diversification opportunities. If the regulatory authorities make it difficult for firms to expand into horizontal or vertical markets, Mueller argued that managers will consider conglomerate mergers as an alternative strategy.

---

[13] See Weston (1970), p.314.
[14] This argument was in response to an earlier theory by Shepherd (1970) which had suggested that diversification was associated with higher industrial concentration and strengthened market power.
[15] See, for example, Marris (1964) and Mueller (1969).

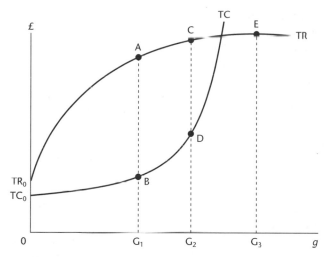

Figure 10.1 Growth equilibrium and diversification

A model which explains the issues facing firms who pursue growth through diversification was suggested by Baumol (1967, Chapter 10). Baumol considered the effects of diversification on the firm's total costs. The first effect was the increase in fixed and variable costs due to increased production, which he termed the output costs. The second group of costs which had to be considered were the costs of diversification concerned exclusively with the strategy of diversification. Assuming constant returns to scale, output costs can be regarded as growing proportionately with the firm's output. However, diversification costs rise proportionately faster as the rate of diversification increases. The explanation for these increasing costs is as follows. Diversification through mergers results in increasing business mistakes as the firm moves into new and unfamiliar areas of operations. These mistakes will increase costs as 'poor' acquisitions are made. Secondly, acquisitions may have to be funded by a greater reliance on the capital market (as opposed to retained profits), which may result in higher interest rates as the firm accumulates more debt. Thirdly, as a firm develops new operations at a rapid pace it has to purchase more resources and apply these resources in an unfamiliar environment. Again, mistakes will be made and costs will rise. Thus, as a firm diversifies it will experience an increasing cost schedule shown by TC in Figure 10.1, which shows the different growth rates of the firm (g) and the relevant total cost, total revenue, and profits.

Total revenue (TR) will rise as acquisitions and products are increased. There is, however, a limit to the increase in revenue. As the firm expands operations so sales begin to increase at a diminishing rate and eventually possibly to decline as returns to the marketing effort of ever newer products begin to diminish. The difference between total revenue and total cost (TC) is the profitability of the firm. At a zero rate of growth, the firm relies on its current products and earns a low profit ($TR_0 - TC_0$). As the rate of growth increases, so profitability increases and then eventually declines. The maximum profit is at the point of the greatest distance between total revenue and total cost (AB) and this corresponds to growth rate G_1. We can thus see that firms will wish to grow through diversification to achieve higher profitability. However, managers may have other, equally important objectives, such as higher sales achieved through higher growth. This may be the case if their remuneration is tied to sales and the power of shareholders is weak. It can then be argued that managers will pursue a strategy of growth maximisation, subject to a minimum profit constraint. Maximum growth of sales would occur at point E, but that level of growth results in a loss and managers would no longer be able to fund some of their future investments. If we assume that the minimum profit required to satisfy the capital market and shareholders is CD, then managers aim to achieve a growth rate of G_2. The conclusion drawn from the above model is that if we assume managers are growth-maximisers, then the firm follows a more robust diversification strategy than if the firm attempted to maximise profits. The above argument is consistent with Montgomery's (1994) 'agency view' outlined earlier.

Rose and Shepard (1997) tested for a relationship between top managers' salaries and the extent of diversification. They found that in their sample of US firms, managers' salaries were 13 per cent higher in diversified firms than those in similar specialised firms. However, the reason given for this was that diversified firms were more complex to manage and required managers with greater ability. Incumbent managers who pursued diversification strategies were not rewarded with higher salaries, but newly appointed managers of diversified firms were paid more than managers in non-diversified firms.

Any firm which wishes to maintain growth will face two possible constraints. Firstly, the existing market may be declining or not expanding quickly enough. The latter case implies that the firm is faced with opportunities for investments and acquisitions in new markets which can achieve better growth prospects than those in the existing product markets. Penrose (1995, p.105) noted that these opportunities may reflect not just the changes in prices, tastes and other market conditions, but also the development of know-how and skills within the firm. Secondly the firm may find that further expansion in its existing market may meet increasing rivalry from its competitors as it tries to encroach on their market share. Three historical examples illustrate these two constraints.

The brewer Guinness felt, by the 1960s, that it had reached saturation point in the stout market. Brewed and sold all over the world, the company's proud boast had been that six million pints were drunk every day. To achieve greater growth, new products had to be developed and marketed. Guinness decided to diversify into the lager market by launching a new brand, Harp. It was then forced to integrate vertically into pubs to guarantee outlets for the new drink. It also moved into microbiology, biochemistry and confectionery.

In the 1960s, Cadbury also faced limited growth prospects for its confectionery products. It was felt that chocolate consumption in the UK (already the highest per capita consumption in the world) could not grow any further. The firm also faced a powerful rival, Rowentree–Macintosh. Cadbury diversified into a range of foods such as instant milk, instant mashed potato, tea, jams, and most importantly of all, soft drinks, by acquiring Schweppes in 1969. By the 1980s, Cadbury–Schweppes concentrated further expansion on its core business of confectionery and soft drinks.

At the turn of the century, Hoover's existing business was the manufacture of harnesses. Worried by the decline in the horse-drawn carriage industry due to the advance of the motor car industry, W.H. Hoover was keen to diversify out of harness-making. In 1907, he acquired the rights to J.M. Spangler's 'vacuum cleaner' and, by applying the company's technical skills, was able to market a superior product with great success.

Examples can also be found of diversification strategies intended to generate growth and profitability which have failed. British Match, a monopolist producer of matchsticks in the UK, faced a decline in the demand for matches by the mid-1960s. It diversified into wood, chipboard and fireworks. During an investigation by the Monopolies and Mergers Commission of its acquisition of the razor producer Wilkinson Sword, British Match claimed that its past diversification had not been particularly successful.[16] In 1973, its non-match activities accounted for 47 per cent of total group sales, but only 26 per cent of group profits. The group blamed this on the poor growth of the acquired companies and problems in managing the new firms.

Cost reductions

Let us now turn to the consideration of the argument that diversification can bring about cost reductions. This can be achieved in two ways: firstly, through economies of scale and scope and, secondly, through the reduction of risk and uncertainty. We also examine the argument that diversification can reduce a firm's tax exposure.

Economics of scale
Economies of scale can be realised if a firm can spread its indivisible inputs over a variety of outputs so as to reduce costs. This is often referred to as **economies of scope**, whereby the costs associated with the production of two different goods are lower than if the two goods were produced separately. A frequently quoted example is that of fruit and sheep.[17] A fruit-grower will have to leave enough space between the trees to allow access for labour and farm equipment. The land between the trees can be exploited by grazing sheep. Thus the fruit-grower can use one input, namely land, in the production of two products. In manufacturing, the cause of such cost savings would be the existence of technological interdependencies of the two goods.

The existence of such economies, however, does not necessarily imply that the fruit-grower must diversify. The alternative for the grower is to rent the land to a sheep farmer. This market transaction will produce the same outcome as the diversification strategy. If, however, the market transaction costs were too high, the grower may be forced to exploit the asset through diversification. We consider the problem of such market failure under 'Specific assets'.

Needham (1978, p.206) was sceptical about the economies of scale argument and he identified three objections. Firstly, economies due to the spreading of indivisible inputs over a greater output can also be realised by a specialised firm. Secondly, the argument assumes that the inputs are non-specific, i.e. that they can be spread over different activities. He suggested that the sorts of indivisible input that might work best would be managerial, marketing and financial functions. Finally, the inputs must be such that only diversification can lead to cost reductions, i.e. expansion by a specialised firm would somehow be insufficient to spread the cost of these inputs. Needham believed that circumstances in which these conditions could be fulfilled were very limited.

[16] The Monopolies and Mergers Commission (1973), para. 74.
[17] See, for example, Douma and Schreuder (1998), p.173.

Reduction of risk and uncertainty

All firms are vulnerable to adverse changes in demand and increased competition for their individual products. The more products that a firm develops, the lower is this vulnerability. Penrose (1995, p.140) further suggested that it was the difficulty of predicting such fluctuations in demand that led to uncertainty which in turn motivated the firm to seeking product diversification:

> Except for seasonal variations, it is rarely possible accurately to predict fluctuations in demand. The less accurate the firm feels its predictions are, the more uncertain are profit expectations; consequently the firm will give more weight to the possibilities of obtaining a more complete utilisation of its resources and a more stable income stream and less weight to the possible restriction on its ability to meet fully the peak demand for its existing product.

Gillette UK is one historical example of a firm that was keen to reduce the risks of relying on one product. Gillette's management had been worried that the firm was too heavily committed in just the one razor market. It faced strong competition from one rival, Wilkinson Sword. When, in the early 1960s, sales fell dramatically as a result of product innovation by Wilkinson, Gillette decided to diversify into the related field of male toiletries, so as to reduce its risks. One minimises the risk of 'gambler's ruin' by investing in 'offsetting activities'. Stable cash flows can be achieved when firms develop products or services with different seasonal peaks. Examples of such offsetting activities are Wall's ice cream and meat products, Valor Gas's combination of heating and gardening equipment, and W.H. Smith's entry into the travel agency business. However, such activities are not always easy to identify and, in the absence of any obvious activity, the best approach might be to select an activity at random. However, bearing in mind the potential advantages of exploiting familiar assets and technologies, firms will rarely stray into random activities.[18]

If the risks to various branches of a firm's activity are randomly distributed, or follow 'offsetting cycles', then their combined risks are lower.[19] The conglomerate can thus enjoy more stable profits. Consequently, this ability to reduce risk via diversification can help firms to secure investment funds at a lower cost. From the point of view of the lender, however, it is not immediately obvious why a diversified firm should receive such advantageous treatment in comparison to the specialised firm. A lender in the capital market can reduce risk by diversifying its portfolio by making investments among a number of specialised firms. Possibly, if the lender is a small investor, then the attraction of holding shares in one diversified firm are clearer, though in practice the existence of financial securities such as unit trusts can channel such small-scale funds into managed diversified portfolios and reduce an investor's exposure to risk equally well.

One obvious advantage of risk reduction is the benefit to management, who are concerned with survival. Diversified operations are more likely to save a firm from 'gambler's ruin' should the firm invest in just one set of specialised operations. This reason for diversification is part of the 'agency view' suggested by Montgomery (1994). Amihud and Lev (1981) attempted to test the hypothesis that conglomerate mergers might be motivated by managers' own preferences. They noted that a large part of managers' reward is their income from employment and that this income is closely correlated with the firm's performance. Thus

[18] This point is explored when we consider the specific assets argument later in the chapter.
[19] For a fuller explanation see, for example, Koutsoyannis (1982), pp.239–41.

risks to managers' income will be closely related to risks faced by the firm; and in the extreme case of bankruptcy, managers would lose their employment. Since such employment risk cannot be easily reduced by diversifying personal portfolios, managers will diversify their employment risk by supporting conglomerate mergers. Amihud and Lev (1981) found that manager-controlled firms tended to pursue more conglomerate mergers than owner-managed firms.

A further advantage of conglomerate mergers from the point of view of managers is their ability to manage internal operations efficiently. Traditional analysis would argue that the capital market will reward efficient management by increasing the market value of the firm and punish inefficiency by decreasing the market value. In practice, investors in the capital market may be unable to secure correct information to judge the performance of management. This is even more the case if investors rely on managers for information flows. It would require a great deal of altruism for managers to pass on information that might reflect badly on their efficiency as managers. Bad performances might be explained with distorted facts or what these days is referred to as 'spin'. This 'information impactedness'[20] leads to a market transaction cost that will frustrate efficient allocation of investment funds. These transaction costs can be reduced by conglomerate merger and an organisational structure[21] where senior managers have access to correct information. The headquarters of the conglomerate will in essence perform the task of the capital market by allocating funds for investments. But unlike the capital market, the headquarters will have two advantages. Firstly, the managers of the various divisions are subordinates to senior managers and can be ordered to provide good and accurate information. Accurate information will flow since middle managers are under an implicit threat of discipline should they fail to provide such information, and rewards if they do.[22] The divisional managers will also share confidential information with senior staff which they would not do with external investors. Secondly, the headquarters of the conglomerate will be able to carry out internal audits to guard against possible mismanagement by the divisional managers. As a consequence the conglomerate acts as a miniature capital market but enjoys better access to information and is more able to monitor the efficiency of the various divisions. One qualification to the above argument is that managing many divisions may require that senior managers understand a far greater diversity of business environments. As managers become overloaded with information they may be unable to take focused, objective decisions.

Tax reductions

Diversification can, under various tax regimes, reduce a firm's tax liability. Firms can offset losses in one activity with profits in another. A specialised firm that makes a loss obviously pays no tax on profits; but the tax payable by other profitable specialised companies is not reduced. Needham (1978) suggested further advantages that might make shares in diversified companies attractive to shareholders since diversified activities will result in lower taxes being paid on gross earnings, thereby increasing after-tax earnings.[23] This can be achieved in so far as interest payments on loans are tax deductible. Thus a greater reliance on debt,

---

[20] A term developed by Williamson (1971), p.119.
[21] For example, the M-form as suggested by Williamson (1975).
[22] See for example Harris and Raviv (1996).
[23] Needham (1978), pp.208–9.

as opposed to equity finance, will reduce a firm's taxable profits. Needham claimed that in diversified firms there was a greater reliance on debt than in the specialised firm.[24] These arguments were tested by Berger and Ofek (1995) and were largely dismissed as marginal in any firm's decision whether to diversify or to divest itself of various operations:

> Two potential benefits of diversification are increased interest tax shields resulting from higher debt capacity and the ability of multi-segment firms to immediately realise tax savings by offsetting losses in some segments against profits in others. Our estimate of tax saving, however, is only 0.1 per cent of sales, far too small to offset the documented value loss.[25]

Specific assets

Gorecki (1975) noted that some, if not all, firms possess **specific assets** that can be of value if exploited in other industries.[26] These assets would include such things as a new technology, trade secrets, brand loyalty, managerial experience and expertise. If a firm wishes to capitalise on these assets, it faces a choice. It can either sell the assets in the market or diversify into the relevant industry to exploit the asset itself. The decision whether to sell or diversify depends on the extent of market imperfections surrounding such transactions. These imperfections increase the transaction costs. Gorecki identified the following imperfections:

● No market may exist due to the non-exclusion principle and thus no price can be set. Basic knowledge, which is non-patentable, is an example of this type of specific asset.
● It may be too difficult to transfer a specific asset independently of its owner. Gorecki suggests that a team of managers or skilled labour may be uniquely loyal to an owner and thus be unwilling to work for another organisation.
● The transaction cost of transferring the asset may be too high. An example might be if the nature of the technology is complex and no buyer has the necessary skills and facilities to fully exploit such an asset. In addition, the sale of technical know-how might include not only the blueprints and recipes for a new process or product but also 'learning by doing' skills. The latter would imply the training of technical staff in the buying company, which may be difficult if the staff have a different technical background.
● Market transactions are also subject to many potential externalities. For example, if B purchases A's brand or trademark, this may affect A's profits if B is unable to maintain a complementary standard of quality as consumers link B's poor product and service with the brand. As a consequence, A's sales and profits may fall. Another example might occur if negotiations between a seller and a buyer reveal production methods and strategies sufficient for the buyer to contemplate entry into the seller's industry. To guard against such externalities or 'spillovers', strict and complex contractual relations would have to be specified. These would involve expensive monitoring and policing costs.

[24] It was reported in the *Financial Times* in 1985 that Britoil bought a stake in Amax Petroleum primarily to cover its tax exposure in its US operations.
[25] Berger and Ofek (1995), p.60.
[26] A similar argument is put forward in a later paper by Teece (1982). See also Markides and Williamson (1994) for a discussion of strategic assets and core competences, written from the perspective of a strategic management approach.

In view of these market imperfections, and high transaction costs, firms might feel it to be more advantageous to diversify An example of the exploitation of specific assets would be Gillette's acquisition of Duracell, the battery manufacturer. At first glance there seemed no obvious economies of scope between the two products. Capital equipment and technical know-how are very different in both markets. It was suggested that Gillette wished to exploit its established marketing and sales operations in countries such as Brazil, China and India by selling batteries to those countries as well as razors.[27]

Sutton (1980) expanded the above argument to suggest that a firm in a dynamic context is facing continual changes in the economic environment. These changes will affect the firm's specific assets which over time generate fresh opportunities and incentives. The value of any asset depends not only on its technical applicability in alternative industries, but also on the profits that can be earned from its use in the existing industry and in the alternative industries. Thus market price changes as well as changes in costs affect the relative attractiveness of such assets in their alternative uses. Major and sustained changes in market conditions thus present diversification opportunities to firms.

10.3 Corporate coherence

An interesting approach to the question of why firms diversify, or why they do not, was provided by Teece *et al.* (1994).[28] They argued firstly that firms are 'coherent' in that they do not diversify at random as that would imply an 'incoherent' strategy. Secondly, they claimed that this corporate coherence is stable over time. Companies such as Shell Oil, ICI and Boeing have tended to focus on a relatively narrow range of activities for close to a century. They ask, why has Shell not diversified into jewellery, Boeing into buses or ICI into supermarkets? If coherence implies that a firm's different products are related, Teece *et al.* attempt to develop a theory that explains why firms diversify *coherently*.

As mentioned in the Introduction to this chapter, few firms are truly specialised by producing just one product. In most cases, owing to a natural variation in market demand, firms will be forced to offer products in more than one size, colour, flavour, or some other characteristic. In contrast, diversification refers to product extension, which is far more 'variegated' than the above examples. Firms add new products over time which enjoy technical and market similarities with the existing product lines. Since a firm is considered coherent if its products are related, a measure of this coherence is then suggested.

Measure of coherence

To determine a measure of coherence, Teece *et al.* first constructed a measure of relatedness. This is computed on the basis that frequently observed combinations of activities within firms in the same industry will be related. In other words, if firms in a given industry almost always involve themselves in two or more activities, then the activities are related. A measure of relatedness was computed on the basis of a sample of over 18,000 United States manufacturing firms, active in 958 different four-digit SIC industries and with close to 67,000 activities.[29] The highest relatedness was between SIC 5181 and SIC 5182, which

[27] Douma and Schreuder (1998), p.177.
[28] This section follows the arguments presented in Teece *et al.* (1994).
[29] See Chapter 4 for an explanation of SIC.

referred to beer wholesalers and spirits wholesalers. The measure of coherence is then presented as the weighted-average relatedness of one activity to all other activities in the firm. Teece *et al.*'s finding suggested that as diversification increases, firms add activities that relate to part of their existing activities and that the strength of this relatedness does not change as the firms grow through further diversification. Teece *et al.* concluded that coherence is a major characteristic of diversified business operations.

A theory of corporate coherence

In an attempt to develop a theory that might explain corporate coherence, Teece *et al.* have attempted to redefine the firm in terms of enterprise learning, path dependencies, and selection. We consider each of these in turn.

Enterprise learning

Learning is an important aspect of any economic and business activity. It is through learning that improvements to processes are made and new opportunities identified. Such learning takes place not only through the traditional trainer and trainee interaction, but also through group interaction. The successful outcome of such learning will be found in organisational 'routines'. There are two types of organisational routine: static and dynamic. Static routines cover activity that can be copied or replicated, though in time repetition may lead to refinement and modification and the development of new routines. Dynamic routines refer to activity by which the organisation learns and develops new processes, an obvious example being its research and development strategy. These routines are often difficult to classify formally and may thus also be difficult to apply to other situations and environments. Thus these routines can be thought of as a specific characteristic or asset of a particular firm, as well as ways in which firms can be differentiated from one another.

Path dependencies

The value of enterprise learning will depend largely on what the firm has achieved in the past. Its past investments and routines will shape its future because learning tends to be 'local'. Local learning implies that firms will develop opportunities that lie close to their existing knowledge and skills. The two most important aspects of the learning process for new products are the technology used and market into which the new product will be launched. To enter a new market with a new product may over-extend a firm's learning range and the strategy may fail. As a consequence of the above discussion, firms will follow (or, depend on) well defined paths as regards investments in new products. Teece *et al.* identified three aspects of these path dependencies:

● *Complementary assets.* These help to construct paths for future growth. In many cases, assets used by firms will have alternative uses that can be exploited vertically and horizontally.[30]
● *Technological opportunities.* These will determine how far and how fast a firm will move down a certain path. Research and development undertaken by the firm will identify the technological opportunities present for the existing products as well as potential alternatives.

---

[30] Teece *et al.* (1994) illustrate this point with the example of Singer sewing machines diversifying into the furniture business as a result of its ability to build wooden cabinets to house its machines.

- *Convergence of paths*. This will occur when there are major shifts in basic knowledge. As the technological bases of industries change, paths may converge or diverge. For example, the development of digital electronics is creating a convergence between computer and telecommunications firms. Products once aimed at different markets and based on different technologies are now sharing the same core technology.

Selection

Selection implies that firms survive and prosper if they are efficient and that they decay if they are inefficient.[31] The rate at which this selection takes place depends on the level of competition, public policy, technology and the amount of exposure to external debt. The more debt the firm accumulates, the greater the threat of discipline from the capital market. Teece *et al.* argued that the 'tighter' the selection process, the greater the reliance the firm will place on its core competences or specific assets.

In view of the above theory, Teece *et al.* advanced the following hypotheses that could explain the existence of the three different types of firms:[32]

- *The specialist firm*. Characterised by rapid learning, many technological opportunities and narrow path dependencies. This type of firm tends to be young, as the probability that technological opportunities remain promising declines over time.
- *The coherent diversifier*. Characterised by quick learning, a broad path dependency based on generic technologies and 'tight' selection. As opposed to the specialist firms, these firms tend to be much older and to have weathered periods of recession.
- *The conglomerate*. Defined by its slow learning, low path dependencies and a weak selection. Should selection become stronger then some of the more extreme cases might be weeded out of the market.

What is clear in the above analysis is that Teece *et al.* do not view conglomerates in any positive way, viewing them as largely temporary phenomena. In response to the question as to why some conglomerates seem to have prospered, the authors offer two arguments. The first is that conglomerates may serve as **internalised capital markets** as suggested by Williamson (1975) and discussed earlier in the chapter. Teece *et al.* recognise that this may be a reason for their existence, but suggest that this existence could hamper the efficient allocation of capital if investors are denied information as to the efficiency of the individual business units. In their second argument, Teece *et al.* refer to such conglomerates as 'hopeful monsters' which have evolved through some form of organisational mutation. Some of these monsters will have a number of characteristics that allow them to survive for a period of time, but eventually selection will eliminate all but a few.

In view of the Teece *et al.* arguments for coherent diversification and incoherent conglomerates, we now examine whether there is any evidence for the failure of diversified firms and conglomerates, which would then lead to a process of deconglomeration. The term implies a firm wishing to divest itself of unrelated activities and to focus on its core activities.

---

[31] This is clearly related to Stigler's (1968) concept of the 'survivability' as a test of efficiency.

[32] Three other types are discussed: the vertically integrated firm, network firms, and the 'hollow corporations'.

10.4 Focus and deconglomeration

In a study of 33 large and prestigious US firms over the period 1950 to 1986, Porter (1987) noted that most of them had divested more acquisitions than those they had kept. Of the 33 firms, each had entered an average of 80 new industries and 27 new fields. Of these, 70 per cent were acquisitions, 22 per cent were through internal expansion and the remaining 8 per cent were through joint ventures. On average, the firms divested themselves of over 50 per cent of acquisitions in new industries and 60 per cent in new fields. Fourteen companies had abandoned more than 70 per cent of their acquisitions in new fields. The most 'startling' finding was that 74 per cent of the acquisitions in unrelated fields were relinquished. Similar conclusions were made by Scharfstein (1998) who analysed a 1979 sample of 165 conglomerates, firms which had diversified into at least one other unrelated activity. By 1994, 55 (33 per cent) of these firms became 'focused' on their core activity; 57 (35 per cent) of firms that did not become more focused were acquired by other firms, and only 53 firms (32 per cent) survived as conglomerates by 1994.[33]

We now consider the reasons that have been put forward to explain why large conglomerates became more focused in the 1980s and 1990s. The fundamental reason is that as firms became more diversified they became less profitable,[34] but as they became more focused so their profitability increased. Daley *et al.* (1997) noted that prior research had shown that stock market prices of parent firms that sold off some of their activities had risen. They found that these price rises were higher in firms that sold off unrelated activities as opposed to related activities. This would then imply that the capital market viewed increased focus as a profitable strategy. Lang and Stulz (1994) had also found that Tobin's q for specialised firms was greater than the Tobin's q for diversified firms, which again reinforced the view that the capital market favoured the specialised firm.[35] If stock prices of diversified firms were consistently lower than those of specialised firms, it would suggest that shareholders have tended to penalise such firms. One could thus conclude that unrelated diversification as a strategy was (and is) intended to benefit managers and not shareholders. Analysing the profitability of the parent firms who had divested themselves of their acquisitions as well as the units that had been divested, Daley *et al.* (1997) found that profitability increased for both organisations, which lent support to capital market optimism for firms which had become more focused.

On the basis of the above and similar empirical work, Berger and Ofek (1995) attempted to test for the existence of a 'diversification discount'. This they calculated by comparing the individual business units of a conglomerate with specialised firms in the same industry. They then calculated a hypothetical 'stand alone' market value of each of the constituent units of the conglomerate and compared it to the actual market value. The 'diversification discount' is thus the difference. The excess of the 'stand alone' value over the market value averaged some 15 per cent. With such a large discount it was no surprise that shareholders pushed managers towards a strategy of **deconglomeration**. The question remains, however,

---

[33] Similar evidence can be found in Ravencraft and Scherer (1987a,b), Kaplan and Weisbach (1992) and Comment and Jarrell (1995).

[34] See, for example, a note by Rhoades (1974).

[35] Tobin's q is the ratio of the market value of a firm to its replacement cost of assets. This is discussed in Chapter 6.

what is the cause of such a diversification discount? Berlin (1999) suggested two possible reasons:

● *Management inefficiencies.* Berlin argued that managers in conglomerates may be viewed as 'jack of all trades and masters of none', and that a frequent exhortation to managers is to 'stick to what you know'. It may also become more and more difficult to provide sufficient incentives for managers as the number of activities increases.
● *Internal capital market inefficiencies.* A previous argument for an advantage of diversification was that managers will have better access to information and thus be in a position to allocate capital more efficiently than the capital market. The opposing view is that managers in the large diversified firm will be *less* efficient in the allocation of funds to their various divisions. Some evidence shows that firms will prop up ailing divisions at the expense of the profitable ones.[36] This behaviour was termed 'socialism in capital budgeting' by Scharfstein (1998). Berlin (1999) suggested that one cause for such behaviour is that divisions in a conglomerate bargain for funds and that the bargaining power of a division may be enhanced by investments that may not benefit the organisation as a whole. It may also be possible that head office 'buys' the co-operation of divisions by diverting investment funds in their direction.

Porter (1990) presents a similar sort of conclusion, though he adds a further reason for poor performance. This is the neglect of innovation in the various divisions of the conglomerate. He argued that innovation stems from a focus, commitment and sustained investment in a specific activity, and it is this which creates a competitive advantage for firms. On the other hand he noted that:

> Unrelated diversification, particularly through acquisition, makes no contribution to innovation. Unrelated diversification almost inevitably detracts from focus, commitment and sustained investment in the core industries, no matter how well-intentioned management is at the outset. Acquired companies, where there is no link to existing businesses, often face short-term financial pressures to justify their purchase price. It is also difficult for corporate managers of a diversified firm to be forward-looking in industries they do not know.[37]

In view of the above arguments one may ask why companies in the past diversified into unrelated activities and why some still exist. A possible reason is that the 'diversification discount' may not have been as high in the past.[38] Another reason could be changes in the economy. One such change could be the more relaxed attitude in the 1980s towards horizontal mergers and increased concentration, allowing firms to become more focused in their markets. Another possibility might be that the increasing efficiency in the capital market has reduced the importance of the internal capital market. The refocusing of companies in the 1980s and 1990s was made possible in the United States and the UK by many 'leveraged buyouts'. Investors could obtain finance by unsecured (junk) bonds and loans and buy out large diversified firms. The large conglomerate would then have parts of the business sold off and be left with its profitable core activities. Such increased profits and revenue from

---

[36] For example, Berger and Ofek (1995) and Scharfstein (1998).
[37] Porter (1990), p.605.
[38] See, for example, Servaes (1996) who noted that the diversification discount in the early 1970s was almost zero. See also Matsusaka (1993) who examined stock market responses to the conglomerate merger wave in the United States in the 1960s.

the sale of unrelated activities would pay for the large interests on the unsecured loans. An example of this type of buy out was Hoylake's (in essence a consortium led by three high-profile financiers, James Goldsmith, Jacob Rothschild and Kerry Packer) attempt to buy British and American Tobacco, at the time the ninth largest company in Europe.[39] In another case, Hanson bought a 2.8 per cent share in ICI, which the market interpreted as a prelude to a full takeover bid. The market reasoned that to finance the takeover, Hanson would be forced to sell off some of the ICI divisions and refocus the remaining activities. ICI fought back by announcing a restructuring of the company. By 1993, ICI had split into two independent companies, one (ICI) concentrating on chemicals and the other (Zeneca) on pharmaceuticals and agriculture. As a result of this activity share prices and profits rose.

A good conclusion to this section is provided by John Bridgeman, director-general of Fair Trading, who said:

> I will continue to hold the view that management too often underestimates the problems in carrying through mergers, especially of companies in unrelated fields. It has indeed been one of the more welcome developments of recent years that companies have been increasingly concentrating on their core activities, divesting themselves of some of the enterprises they have acquired in earlier diversifications. It is the very pressures of competition I referred to earlier that have forced so many companies to re-examine their structure.[40]

10.5 Empirical evidence

In this section we examine some empirical evidence for the reasons for diversification and its direction. Some of the research carried out for diversification in the UK in 1970s is presented in some depth so as to illustrate the methodologies used and difficulties encountered in attempting research in such a complicated area of industrial organisation. The section begins by examining how one can measure the level of diversification.

Measurement

Measures of diversification are in effect similar to measures of concentration. Where concentration measures the number and relative size of firms in an industry, diversification measures relate to the numbers and relative size of industries or activities in which one firm is involved. The following measures have been used:

● *A simple count of activities.* By using Standard Industrial Classifications (SIC) at three- or four-digit levels, one can compute how many activities can be found in a given firm. This is perhaps too simple for most purposes. One would naturally discount activities where the firm's commitment is very small.
● *Ratio of primary activity to all other activities.* In other words $B/(A + B)$, where A is the primary activity and B all other activities. A fully specialised firm would have a value of zero and the greater the degree of diversification the closer is the value to unity. Thus a firm with two activities would have a value of 0.5 and one with twenty, 0.95. However, the index does not tell us the degree of importance of the 'other' activities.

---

[39] Examples taken from Griffiths and Wall (1995), pp.111–12.
[40] Speech to the European Policy Forum, 30 January 1996.

● *Herfindahl index of specialisation, H(S).* This index identifies the number of activities and weights the degree of involvement. The index is calculated as the sum of the squares of the 'share' of the activities (x_i), which means a higher weight will be given to the principal activities:

$$H(S) = \sum_{i=1}^{n} x_i^2$$

The index is influenced by both the number of activities and their relative importance. The more specialised a firm is the greater the H(S) will be. Berry (1971) transformed the above measure into an index of diversification:

$$H(D) = 1 - H(S)$$

Thus 100 per cent specialisation will imply an H(S) of unity or an H(D) of zero. A variant of the Herfindhal index of diversification is:

$$H(D) = \frac{1}{\sum_{j-1}^{n} x_{ij}^2}$$

Where x_{ij} is a fraction of firm i's sales in its j activity. If a firm operates in one activity then H(D) equals unity. If the firm has ten equal activities then x_{ij} will equal 0.1 and H(D) will equal 10. As a higher proportion of a firm's activities are concentrated in fewer activities so the index approaches unity.[41]

Empirical evidence

Gorecki (1975) attempted, firstly, to test for the direction of diversification in UK manufacturing industries in 1963 and, secondly, to ascertain the determinants of diversification. The first of these tests was an attempt to answer whether firms diversified outside their broad two-digit industry definitions or whether they tended to diversify within their industry grouping. Diversification outside the group could then be interpreted as evidence lending support to a risk-reduction hypothesis. Diversification within the group could be seen as supporting the view that firms wish to reduce the transaction costs of selling specific assets as well as wishing to exploit a similar technology in related activities. To test for this direction, Gorecki used a T value, which measured the extent of participation of diversified firms in other industries, within a broad industry grouping, referred to as an order.[42] He formally defined the T value as follows:

> T is the summation of the total number of enterprises which own establishments in each of the other industries within the same Order divided by the summation of the total number of enterprises which own establishments in each of the other industries within the manufacturing sector.[43]

[41] For a full discussion of suggested properties of an index of diversification and a survey of the various indices, see Gollop and Monahan (1991).
[42] This reflects the older method of industry classification used in the UK prior to 1980. An order broadly corresponds to an industry at the two-digit level.
[43] Gorecki (1975), p.134.

Table 10.1 ● Calculation of Gorecki's T measure

Order X	Total number of firms	Number of firms diversifying within Order X	Firms diversifying into all Orders, including X
Industry A	30	13 (i.e. in B, C or D)	16
Industry B	20	9 (i.e. in A, C or D)	17
Industry C	80	53 (i.e. in A, B or D)	61
Industry D	20	11 (i.e. in A, B or C)	18
		$\Sigma = 86$	$\Sigma = 112$

A simple example will help to explain the above methodology. Assume that order X is composed of four industry subsets, A, B, C and D, and that the direction of diversification is as shown in Table 10.1.

The T value is then a simple ratio 86/112, which is 0.76. The measure will take any value between zero (all diversification takes place outside the broad industry definition) and one (all diversification is within the broad industry definition). Gorecki's data comprised 14 orders and 51 industries.

Gorecki then compared the actual T value with the expected T value. The expected value was based on the assumption that firms in a given industry diversified at random into any one of the other 50 industries. Thus if a firm in the cereal and foodstuffs industry were to diversify at random (to reduce risk), the chances that it would diversify into the four other industries in its own order (food, drink and tobacco) would be 4/50, i.e. 0.08. A table of results showed that in the majority of cases the actual T value was greater than the expected T value and that in only a handful of cases was the actual value less than the expected. In those few instances such as building materials, footwear and furniture, the diversification was largely outside the broad industry group and Gorecki suggested this was due, in part, to a desire to integrate vertically. The overall conclusion was unequivocal, the direction of diversification in UK manufacturing industry in 1963 was not random.

Gorecki also tested for the determinants of diversification. Two categories of variables explaining diversification were suggested. The first was related to enterprise activities, such as advertising and research and development. The argument was that these produced specific assets, such as brands, trademarks and innovations which could then be exploited through diversification. An advertising to sales ratio was computed, with dummy variables to take into account consumer and non-consumer goods industries. Research and development was measured by the number of research employees in the various industries, again with dummy variables to take into account the differences for consumer and non-consumer goods industries. The second category of variables related to environmental factors such as industry growth and level of industrial concentration. The growth hypothesis was that industries that were experiencing low growth and possibly low profitability would be tempted to exploit their specific assets in industries that were thriving. The expectation was that there would be a negative relationship between growth rates and the extent of diversification, though Gorecki recognised that this negativity might be offset by the fact that firms in declining industries may be short of funds to invest in a diversification strategy. Industry growth was measured by the rate of change of sales over the period 1958 to 1963. The concentration argument implied that firms in highly concentrated industries faced higher costs of expansion in those industries, as the only way of expansion was through mergers and takeovers. It was thus expected that the relationship would be positive. A four-firm concentration index for 1958 was used. Finally, the dependent variable, diversification, was calculated as a ratio of employment in non-primary activities to total employment.

The results of the linear regression were patchy. The results on research and development were consistent with the hypothesis that research expenditure was positively related to diversification, and that the effect was greater for consumer goods industries. The coefficient on advertising to sales was negative, instead of the expected positive value. Gorecki rather tentatively offered the following explanation. Firms in consumer goods industries characterised by heavy advertising might vertically integrate forwards to protect their brands and that this integration might be at the cost of diversification. The coefficients on growth and concentration were statistically insignificant. The growth result was explained by referring to the earlier argument that lack of growth may deny a firm access to investment funds for diversification. Gorecki argued that the concentration result might imply that highly concentrated industries such as oligopolies might prefer horizontal integration to diversification as a growth strategy.

In a more detailed analysis, Utton (1977) examined the extent of large firm diversification in the UK for 1974. Using a sample of 200 of the largest manufacturing firms, Utton attempted to examine the level of specialisation and the extent and characteristics of large firm diversification. The 200 firms were arranged into 14 orders and their activities into 121 three-digit industries. The degree of involvement at these stages was calculated by the level of employment. The first test was to see the extent of specialisation of these 200 firms. This was achieved by first calculating the percentage employment in each firm's primary three-digit activity and then calculating the average for the order. The lowest level of specialisation was 38 per cent for textiles; the highest, 75 per cent, in shipbuilding. The average across all 200 firms was 57 per cent. Taking into account the level of employment in the next most important activities, the percentage share dropped dramatically to produce a highly skewed distribution of activities. This result seemed at variance with the perceived wisdom at the time, that large firms are almost by definition eager diversifiers. Utton concluded: 'the picture that emerges is of enterprises that, on the whole, are still rather more highly specialised than some recent comment would suggest.'[44]

To measure the extent of diversification Utton developed the following measure:

$$W = 2\sum_{i=1}^{n} ip_i - 1$$

where i refers to the ranking of the industries in which an enterprise has some involvement, p_i is the proportion of the firm's employment in the ith industry, and W is a numbers equivalent index of diversification. The index will have a value between 1 (total specialisation) and infinity. A number 4 will imply that the firm is diversified to an equivalent of one firm operating equally in four industries. Thus the higher the value of W the greater the extent of diversification. A weighted average was calculated for each order. For the fourteen orders the range ran from 9 (coal, petroleum, chemicals and allied products) to 1.7 (instrument

[44] Utton (1977), p.100.

engineering), with a total weighted average of 4.4. Again, Utton concluded that this seemed to run counter to common perceptions:

> [T]he data ... on the whole run counter to the popular view of a small number of very large conglomerates with tentacles stretching into every corner of industry and able to strangle existing competitors should the need arise. Where the largest enterprises are diversified to the equivalent extent of operating equally in only about four fairly narrowly defined industries, inclusive of vertical integration, we may question whether they are likely to have much scope for practices such as cross subsidisation, predatory reciprocal purchases and avoidance of competition which some authorities have envisaged.[45]

Utton also compared the rate of diversification with the different sizes of firms. In the sample of 200 firms, the size of the largest firms was some twelve times greater than that of the smallest. The index of diversification (W) averaged 3.85 for the fifty largest firms and just 2.63 for the fifty smallest firms. There was a consistent increase in the index as size increased, but the overall differences were much smaller than those between the orders. Utton tentatively suggested that perhaps once a certain size is reached then further benefits of diversification may no longer be realised owing possibly to management limitations.

Finally, Utton, like Gorecki (1975), tested for the direction of the diversification. He decided to examine whether diversification followed a 'narrow spectrum', which meant firms moved into related activities, or whether diversification followed a 'broad spectrum' which referred to a movement into unrelated activities. Diversification into three-digit industries within the same order as a firm's primary activity was considered as narrow spectrum diversification. Movement into three-digit industries outside the order in which the firm's primary activity was located was then defined as broad spectrum diversification. The results are shown in Table 10.2.

Table 10.2 shows, for example, that in food, drink and tobacco, 73 per cent of firms' secondary activities were concentrated within that order. In metal goods, the figure was only 15 per cent, which meant that 85 per cent of secondary activities were found outside that order. Excluding shipbuilding and instrument engineering as special cases, seven of the remaining twelve orders had a broad spectrum diversification of over 60 per cent. For the total sample, 55 per cent of all secondary activity, measured by employment, was outside the order of the firms' primary activities. Although at first sight this result appears to be at odds with Gorecki's (1975) earlier findings, one must bear in mind that the sample populations were very different. Furthermore, Utton made two important observations. Firstly, he found that there was no correlation between the index of diversification (W) and broad spectrum diversification. In other words, prolific diversifiers were equally likely to diversify narrowly as broadly. Secondly, the destination of much of the secondary activities was in orders that were fairly closely related technologically. If one were to treat mechanical engineering, electrical engineering, vehicles and metal goods as just one order, then 73 per cent of secondary activity in that order could be classed as narrow and the overall narrow spectrum diversification for the 200 firms increased from 44 per cent to 58 per cent. Utton's general conclusion was that UK firms' diversification strategies were, on the whole, 'fairly cautious'.[46]

---

[45] Ibid., p.106.
[46] For some more empirical work on the UK diversification experience in the period 1949 to 1973, see Goudie and Meeks (1982).

Table 10.2 ● Direction of diversification in UK top 200 manufacturing enterprises, 1974

Enterprises (SIC Order)	No. of enterprises	Narrow spectrum diversification	Broad spectrum diversification
Food, drink and tobacco	31	0.729	0.271
Coal, petroleum, chemicals, etc.	18	0.378	0.622
Metal manufacture	10	0.210	0.790
Mechanical engineering	31	0.318	0.682
Instrument engineering	3	0.000	1.000
Electrical engineering	22	0.556	0.445
Shipbuilding and marine engineering	6	0.000	1.000
Vehicles	17	0.065	0.935
Metal goods	6	0.149	0.851
Textiles	13	0.605	0.395
Clothing and footwear	6	0.452	0.548
Bricks, pottery, glass, cement, timber	14	0.141	0.859
Paper, printing and publishing	13	0.731	0.269
Other Manufacturing	10	0.254	0.746
Total	**200**	**0.446**	**0.554**

Source: adapted from Utton (1977), p.109. Used with permission.

Luffman and Reed (1984) provide a further analysis of diversification in the UK in the 1970s, written from a strategic management perspective and using the four-category methodology developed by Rumelt (1974).[47] The categorisation begins with the 'single business', where more than 95 per cent of the company business is accounted for by one product. The next stage is termed a 'dominant' firm, where somewhere between 70 and 95 per cent of turnover is accounted for by one product. Thirdly, we have the 'related' firm, in which no one product accounts for more than 70 per cent of turnover but all the products are related. Finally, there is the 'unrelated' firm in which no one product accounts for more than 70 per cent of turnover and the products are unrelated. The approach would appear somewhat subjective as no real justification is given for the 70 per cent critical measure, other than: 'The 70 per cent cut-off was chosen because it seemed to match fairly well the judgements expressed by informed observers.'[48] Besanko et al. (1996, p.220) were also troubled by the Rumelt methodology: 'Rumelt's classification scheme is somewhat hard to follow, owing to the lack of a precise definition of relatedness.'

Luffman and Reed (1984) attempted to assess the strategic changes that were occurring in British industry between 1970 and 1980. They concluded on the basis of their research that there was a strong movement towards greater diversification, though not as strong as

[47] Luffman and Reed (1984), chapter 4.
[48] Rumelt (1974), p.16.

Table 10.3 ● Measures of diversification, EU largest manufacturing enterprises

	Number of industries, N		Production outside primary industry, DR		Berry index, D	
	3-digit	2-digit	3-digit %	2-digit %	3-digit %	2-digit %
Mean	4.9	2.9	28.3	17.1	0.37	0.23

Source: adapted from Rondi *et al.* (1996), p.171.

in the decades immediately after the Second World War. Movement into unrelated (conglomerate) activities provided the greatest percentage increase.

Rondi *et al.* (1996) attempted to provide an analysis of the extent of diversification within the European Union's major firms and to identify the major determinants of such diversification.[49] The sample was based on the five leading EU firms in a given industry. The sample focused on the manufacturing sector as the authors felt that non-manufacturing firms might move into other industries as a strategy of vertical integration rather than diversification. The sample included only those production activities carried out in the EU. Thus EU and non-EU firms were considered but any production activity outside the EU was ignored.

The indices of diversification used in the study were the three mentioned at the beginning of this section, namely a simple count of different industry involvement (N); a ratio of secondary production to total production (DR); and the Berry index (D), which is 1 minus the Herfindhal index of specialisation. All three measures were calculated at two-digit and three-digit levels to allow a distinction to be made between related and unrelated or conglomerate diversification.[50] Table 10.3 summarises the results.

The average firm was involved in almost five three-digit industries and in three two-digit industries. Over 28 per cent of the output was produced outside the primary three-digit industry and 17 per cent was produced outside the primary two-digit industry. Rondi *et al.* found that the greatest level of diversification at the three-digit level occurred in the UK and the Netherlands, with the lowest found in Italy and Germany. At the two-digit level, the greatest level of diversification was found in Belgium and Italy. A possible explanation mooted was that the organisational structure of enterprises was affected by the different capital market in those two countries.

To test for the determinants of diversification, Rondi *et al.* focused on three major strands of firm diversification. The first was referred to as the Marris–Penrose argument which suggests that managers are concerned with the growth of the firm, and that the exploitation of specific assets such as marketing skills and technology in other industries provides a convenient vehicle for such an objective. The second is the Bain argument, which explores conditions which make entry sufficiently attractive. Issues such as profitability, growth and concentration levels and entry barriers would be included for consideration. The third strand refers to Rumelt–Williamson relationships or relatedness between various

[49] Davies and Lyons (1996), chapter 10.
[50] Production outside the two-digit level would imply unrelated diversification.

industries that can make diversification attractive. Relationships exist where there are possibilities of using similar markets, similar technologies as well as similar production and organisational methods.

The diversified firm in the context of the specified model was a firm that was involved in more than one three-digit industry. The model was presented as:

$$P(F,P,S) = f\{W(F), X(P), Y(S), Z(P,S)\}$$

The dependent variable $P(F,P,S)$ was the probability that firm F, with a primary activity in P, diversified into some secondary activity, S. $W(F)$ was a vector of characteristics of the firm F; $X(P)$ was a vector of the firm's primary activity characteristics; $Y(S)$ was a vector of characteristics of a potential secondary activity; and $Z(P,S)$ was a vector that measured the relationship or relatedness between P and S.

The vector $W(F)$ reflected the Marris–Penrose arguments and included three variables. Firstly, size of the firm to reflect the ease with which a firm can acquire resources. Secondly, a measure of the size of the domestic market, which reflected the growth and opportunities in the different countries, and finally a dummy variable was used for those countries that were characterised by a capital market strong enough to reduce the power of managers over the shareholders. Vector $X(P)$ included advertising, research and development, productive skills and level of capital intensity. These measured a firm's potential specific assets. Vector $Y(S)$ attempted to measure the attractiveness of the secondary industries by their growth, profitability, research and development, advertising, productive skills and level of capital intensity. The latter was viewed as a potential entry barrier. The final vector was made up of four variables which measured the *closeness* of a secondary industry to the primary industry, in terms of advertising, research and development, skills and capital intensity. Closeness was measured as the difference between the variables. Thus a small difference would imply a greater degree of closeness. The coefficients in the econometric results were almost all significant and had the expected signs. The authors drew the following conclusions.

Firstly, size mattered, as larger firms tended to be more diversified than smaller firms. Secondly, firms originating from countries where there was a separation of ownership from control, as proxied by strength of the capital market, did experience higher rates of diversification. The size of the domestic market had no effect on the probability of diversification. Rondi *et al.* argued that this tended to support the notion that domestic markets matter less once the size of a firm is taken into account.

The effect of research and development, advertising and skills was positive in both primary and secondary activities, but negative in the case of their closeness. The complex and detailed interpretation focused on the net effects. In general it was argued that specific assets play an important role in determining diversification as does the degree of relatedness, since as firms diversify they tend to enter secondary industries with characteristics similar to their primary industry. The significant coefficients on capital intensity were negative and supported the view that this acted as an entry barrier.

What we have seen in the above studies into the direction and determinants of diversification in the UK and Europe is that firms tend to be cautious in their diversification strategies, preferring for the most part to stay close to their technological and market bases. The single most important factor that encouraged firms to diversify was the opportunity to exploit specific assets within their broad industry definitions.

10.6 Conclusions

In this chapter we have considered what is generally meant by diversification. Although it is popularly assumed that diversification is a strategy that moves a firm into unrelated businesses and activities, we saw that in practice diversification has a much wider definition, which includes product and market extension. The vast majority of diversification strategies fall into this large set. In section 10.2 we examined the reasons why firms wish to diversify, and these fell into a number of categories such as market power, growth, cost reductions and specific assets. As an adjunct to an economic analysis of diversification, section 10.3 developed the notion of corporate coherence, which attempts to explain the attractiveness of diversification as seen from a strategic management viewpoint.

Section 10.4 explained the reasons why some firms may decide to divest themselves of a variety of businesses to focus, once again, on their core activities. If diversification resulted only in advantages then one could reasonably expect to see just a few large conglomerates in our economies. That this has not happened goes some way to show that there are limits to the ability of firms to manage ever-increasing commitments. In the final section we discussed some of the evidence for the direction and determinants of diversification in the UK and Europe since 1970.

Key terms

Conglomerate

Corporate coherence

Cross-subsidisation

Deconglomeration

Direction of diversification

Economies of scope

Internal capital market

Predation

Reciprocity

Specific asset

Tie-in sales (tying)

Case study 10.1
Larger British and German companies are using mergers and acquisitions to specialise and internationalise as the conglomerate model loses its appeal

How far is global competition eroding national differences in the way companies are organised and managed? Is 'Rhineland' capitalism transmuting itself into something closer to the Anglo-American model? A partial answer to these questions is provided by a survey that examines structural change in large British and German companies over the past five years. The survey, based on questionnaires sent to the chief executives of the 250 largest non-financial companies in the two countries, shows that Britain and Germany are indeed converging in some areas – most strikingly in the accelerating trend towards de-conglomeration – but that there are still important differences between them in the pace and character of change. A recurring theme in responses was the need for specialisation and internationalisation. Several German companies spoke of 'concentrating on core competences', and this was linked with strenuous efforts to strengthen their global market position.

Mergers and acquisitions are the most important tool for implementing this strategy. An overwhelming 84 per cent of British and 71 per cent of German respondents said the structure of their business had been significantly altered by mergers and acquisitions over the past five years. Many companies were also active in divesting or demerging their 'non-core' operations, although just over one third of the German respondents had engaged in demergers and divestments, compared with 52 per cent of the British companies. The bulk of the merger activity in both countries has been 'horizontal', involving companies in the same line of business. About 90 per cent of respondents made at least one horizontal acquisition during the five-year period; only 15 per cent integrated vertically – buying suppliers or customers.

Diversifying mergers, by contrast, have gone out of fashion. Back in 1996, when the last survey of this kind was undertaken, about a third of the German respondents were expanding into unrelated lines of business, compared with 16 per cent in Britain; now the figure in both countries is less than 10 per cent. To the extent that some companies are still diversifying, a common motivation is the desire to provide their customers with a more comprehensive service. In automotive components, for example, manufacturers are under pressure to deliver whole systems rather than single components. This, in turn, is tending to reduce the number of suppliers – 'you either have to consolidate or be consolidated', as one respondent put it. Companies were asked whether the structural changes that they had initiated were prompted mainly by competition in product markets or by pressure from the capital markets. Perhaps surprisingly, a majority of the respondents put most weight on the former, and there was no clear difference on this issue between British and German companies. 'Price pressure from our customer base has been and still is extreme,' one engineering company reported. Another said: 'The real driver is the need to focus on customer needs fast.' A large oil company spoke of 'intensified competition due to market liberalisation and new entrants'. One British company noted that the strength of the pound had reinforced the case for a narrower focus, and for getting out of sectors where little product differentiation was possible. Another spoke of shifting from low-growth 'old economy' businesses to high-growth activities.

The influence of the capital market, however, was important in both countries. Several German companies referred to 'shareholder value' as a factor in their decision-making. One commented that the capital market had to be taken seriously, but 'we should not surrender unconditionally'. On the other hand, German companies are more sceptical than their British counterparts about the effect of mergers and demergers on their share price. Asked if their M&A activity had had a positive impact on their shares, 60 per cent of the British said it did, but only 40 per cent of the German respondents agreed. Similar results were obtained for divestments and demergers.

'Globalisation' figured prominently in the responses; smaller businesses with a purely national orientation were the most likely candidates for divestment. One company, the number two in its industry, had recently merged with the number three in order to 'close the gap with the market leader, achieve economies of scale, reduce overheads, widen our brand portfolio and improve our geographic balance'. Interestingly, it was the British companies that emphasised acquisitions outside their home base. This may be because de-conglomeration is less advanced in Germany, especially among the largest companies, leaving more scope for asset swaps. Joint ventures and strategic alliances were widely practised in both countries, with 40 per cent of all respondents saying that they had engaged in such activities over the past five years. Management buy-outs appear to have been declining in importance, although this technique is still used more extensively in Britain than in Germany; nearly 40 per cent of British companies said that they had been involved in at least one management buy-out. The pattern of the future, in both countries, is tighter central control of a narrower portfolio of businesses.

© The Financial Times Limited, 9 May 2000. Reprinted with permission.

Case study 10.2
Life sciences and pharmaceuticals: the end of the affair

After a brief affair with pharmaceuticals, agribusiness is going back home to the chemicals industry. As investors come to the conclusion that a pure-play pharmaceuticals company is a more profitable business model, chemicals companies are fighting to boost their presence in agribusiness.

Back in 1996, when Novartis was formed from the high-value businesses of the Swiss chemicals companies Ciba and Sandoz, a combination of pharmaceuticals and agrochemicals seemed like a good bet. After all, the world was poised on the verge of a new millennium in which biology – whether applied to plants, animals or humans – would rule supreme. With escalating research costs and long development times, putting drugs and agrochemicals on the same production line looked like a good way of squeezing the most from invested capital. Champions of the concept such as Alex Krauer, then the chairman of Novartis, and Sir David Barnes, who was head of Zeneca, said the life science model provided synergy. But just as competition to acquire seed companies pushed valuations up to unaffordable heights, the global farming economy slipped into recession. To be fair, even the supposed advocates of the life science model, such as Sir David, can justifiably claim they were merely being pragmatic. After all, he was in charge of a company that had both human medicines and agrochemicals in its portfolio. What was he supposed to say?

But as the 1990s wore on, the model became less defensible. It was partly cyclical, determined as much by the Asian and Brazilian economic crises as by weather patterns in the US and elsewhere. It was also political. By late 1999, as consumer hostility in Europe to genetically modified crops reached its peak, Novartis saw agribusiness revenues collapse by 41 per cent as sales stalled and margins contracted. Pharmaceuticals is a $350bn industry, growing at double digits and with margins of up to 35 per cent. Crop protection, on the other hand, has stagnated at around $32bn. Margins are well below 20 per cent and falling (though an upturn in the cycle could change that).

And so the companies that had used the life science model as a temporary stop – between a chemicals conglomerate and a focused pharmaceutical company – began to dismantle themselves. Novartis and Astra Zeneca are spinning out their agrochemicals interests to form Syngenta. American Home Products has sold Cyanamid to BASF of Germany. And Fred Hassan at Pharmacia, a product of the merger between P&U with Monsanto, is clearly not committed to the concept of life sciences. Even Jurgen Dormann, chairman of Aventis, a life science company formed only last year through the merger of Hoechst of Germany with Rhône–Poulenc of France, is sounding more pragmatic every day. 'If I look at our R&D budget, I would say less than 10 per cent of the joint group budget covers topics of interest for both activities [pharmaceuticals and agriculture],' he said. 'This, long term, will not be sufficient to justify anything.' But as Mr Dormann points out, it depends on how you define life sciences. Aventis is 75 per cent pharmaceuticals, 25 per cent agrichemicals. Monsanto is just the reverse.

To the more traditional, diversified chemicals companies, agrochemicals look more appealing. Dealing with cyclical businesses has been a way of life for companies such as Dow Chemicals and DuPont of the US and BASF and Bayer of Germany. Ironically, it is their determination to move towards more predictable and higher-margin businesses that attracts them to agrochemicals. From the perspective of bulk chemicals, agribusiness can look like a moneyspinner. That is why BASF was prepared to pay $3.9bn, a seemingly extravagant 2.4 times 1999 revenues, for Cyanamid, the crop protection business of American Home Products, and why AHP was so desperate to sell it. It is also why Bayer, which is number 15 in pharmaceuticals and fifth in pesticides, has invested $600m in biotechnology that can be applied to both agriculture and human medicine.

DuPont, which until fairly recently was considering a separate stock to track its life science activities, is busily coining a new term: 'integrated science'. The company now stresses that all its activities, from Lycra to Teflon, and from pharmaceuticals to genetically modified soya, draw on a knowledge of science – chemistry, physics, mathematics and, crucially, biology. Charles Holliday, DuPont's chairman and chief executive, says the successful companies of the future will be those that best master the art of 'knowledge intensity'. DuPont, which has not grown for four years, must prove that it can turn this twist on the life science concept into sustained profitability. If it can, its way of doing business could become all the rage. If it cannot, investment bankers will have one more business model to dismantle.

Case study 10.3
Mogul in a slicker mould: profile Marco Tronchetti Provera – the flamboyant head of the Italian tyre group believes its future lies with a strategy of high-technology, diversification and revolutionary production systems

Tyremakers are an obsessively secretive lot. And none more so than Michelin. The French company once went so far as to refuse even General de Gaulle access to its plant in Clermont Ferrand, the company town in central France. But ever since Marco Tronchetti Provera has run Pirelli, the Italian tyre group has broken industry conventions. The company has been far more relaxed than Michelin, its historic rival, in letting strangers visit its facilities. Now Mr Tronchetti Provera is going a step further. In July, he will invite the world to visit what he believes will set the standard in tyre production: an automated tyre manufacturing system called MIRS (Modular Integrated Robotised System) that will slash costs and provide greater flexibility in an area only one-fifth the floor space of a conventional factory.

Pirelli's main competitors are all working on similar projects. But the Italian company, which trailed Michelin in the development of the revolutionary radial tyre, has this time taken the lead. At its Bicocca facility in Milan, the first MIRS production line is ready. It will produce a complete tyre, with no direct labour input, in 72 minutes, instead of the six days a conventional plant takes. If customers so wish, they will be able to place an order via the internet and collect a customised tyre from the factory the same day.

Sun-tanned after a weekend sailing in Portofino for a Pirelli trophy, snappily dressed as always, softly spoken and concise as ever, the 52-year-old Pirelli chairman explains his open-door policy as a natural evolution of modern business. 'The development of internet and e-commerce is turning transparency into a priority,' he says. 'It changes the way we work with consumers and suppliers and simplifies our business relations. Everything that is mysterious these days is now suspect.' Coming from the head of a grand old Italian company this is something of a novelty. Yet the transparency and technology is in keeping both with Mr Tronchetti Provera's own management style and his company's revival. He also believes that it is the secret of Pirelli's future as a diversified industrial group in an era of industrial specialisation.

Since he took over nine years ago and successfully restructured and relaunched the 128-year-old company, there has been repeated speculation that he would sell the tyre operations to concentrate on his expanding cables and advanced fibre-optics businesses. These account for 60 per cent of the group's €6.5bn (£3.9bn) of annual sales. The company strengthened its high-technology strategy two months ago by launching, with great fanfare, a €1bn e-Pirelli programme to transform the entire company into what Mr Tronchetti Provera called at the time 'a leader in the world of high-tech and the new e-conomy'.

The company has moved fast. It recently forged an alliance with Cisco Systems of the US. A new optical-component company has just been incorporated in the US, with American management, to exploit Pirelli's numerous patents. Pirelli is also launching a series of investments with strategic partners in micro-components. The Pirelli & Co. holding company, which controls the Pirelli SpA, industrial company, has launched a fund, called EuroCube, to finance European start-ups. The holding company is also participating in a consortium that is bidding for one of Italy's new-generation mobile telephone licences.

Such diversification has merely encouraged speculation about a sale of an ill-fitting business like tyres. But Mr Tronchetti Provera insists 'there is no need to move out of tyres, they are starting to deliver results; we want to remain in the tyre sector'. Showing off the company's new tyre-manufacturing processes and technologies, Pirelli is also working on an 'intelligent' tyre that will provide drivers with real-time information on the wear and tear of their tyres, is another way of confirming the company's commitment to this business.

Mr Tronchetti Provera disputes the idea that the high-tech expansion makes Pirelli unwieldy. The company's all-out push to transform itself into a champion of the new economy – both by expanding its internet-related activities and re-engineering its old economy core businesses by introducing them to online technology – is an evolution, he says. 'What we are doing is simply keeping a window open on high technology and the future, while maintaining and enhancing the competitiveness of our traditional businesses in a deflationary world. And the internet is deflationary,' he explains. 'The real challenge as a manufacturer is that without breaking our relationship with our intermediaries we are now able to improve our service to our end-users and respond to their demands faster,' he says.

As for the internal management of a complex multinational group – Italy now accounts for only 10 per cent of Pirelli's annual turnover – the new technologies are enabling it to be run like a small corner-shop. 'At the end of the day, we can open the cash till and see exactly what has happened, how much we have made and where our problems lie.' Yet Pirelli is held together by management as well as technology. Here, Mr Tronchetti Provera's success, his friends and associates say, is his ability to command loyalty. This is matched by his own deep sense of loyalty in a country where it is often in short supply.

Only by delegating could he hope to run the range of the company's businesses. Along with its intelligent tyres and automated manufacturing plants, its cables and new optical-communication technologies, the company has growing property investments that were developed through the conversion of its old Milanese plant. A huge area of nearly 1m sq m, this was once said to be the biggest factory in Europe. And Mr Tronchetti Provera's diversification is not finished yet. He is also about to launch a new Pirelli line of stylish shoes, luggage and watches. High-tech with high fashion.

© The Financial Times Limited, 22 May 2000. Reprinted with permission.

Questions for discussion

1. Why might some large firms be attracted to conglomerate mergers rather than horizontal or vertical mergers?

2. The argument that diversification benefits a firm through the realisation of economies of scale by the spreading of indivisible inputs over a greater output is of limited appeal according to some economists. Explain why.

3. Williamson argued that one reason for conglomerate mergers is the opportunity to take over inefficiently managed and undervalued firms. He argued that owing to information impactedness, capital markets and shareholders were unable to efficiently 'discipline' poor management. Can you suggest why an efficient cadre of corporate managers is better able exact control within the organisation?

4. Give examples of firms that fall into Teece et al.'s definition of the specialist firm, the coherent diversifier and the conglomerate.

5. Discuss the measures that can be employed to determine the extent of diversification in an industry.

6. With reference to the three case studies in this chapter, explain why firms in the first two cases have divested themselves of their past acquisitions whilst Pirelli is attracted to new and unrelated activities. Discuss the extent to which Pirelli's other activities are unrelated to tyre production.

Further reading

Berger, P.G. and Ofek, E. (1995) Diversification's effect on firm value, *Journal of Financial Economics*, **37**, 39–65.

Blackstone, E.A. (1972) Monopsony power, reciprocal buying, and government contracts: the General Dynamic case, *Antitrust Bulletin*, **17**, 445–66.

Comment, R. and Jarrell, G. (1995) Corporate focus and stock returns, *Journal of Financial Economics*, **37**, 67–87.

Gorecki, P. (1975) An inter-industry analysis of diversification in the UK manufacturing sector, *The Journal of Industrial Economics*, **24**, 131–46.

Luffman, G.A. and Reed, R. (1984) *The Strategy and Performance of British Industry, 1970–80*. London: Macmillan.

Montgomery, C. (1994) Corporate diversification, *Journal of Economic Perspectives*, **8**, 163–78.

Penrose, E. (1995) *The Theory of the Growth of the Firm*, 3rd edn. Oxford: Oxford University Press.

Rondi, L., Sembenelli, A. and Ragazzi, E. (1996) Determinants of diversification patterns, in Davies, S. and Lyons, B. (eds) *Industrial Organisation in the European Union*. Oxford: Oxford University Press, chapter 10.

Teece, D., Rumelt, R., Dosi, G. and Winter, S. (1994) Understanding corporate coherence, theory and evidence, *Journal of Economic Behaviour and Organisation*, **23**, 1–30.

Utton, M.A. (1977) Large firm diversification in British manufacturing industry, *The Economic Journal*, **87**, 96–113.

Utton, M.A. (1979) *Diversification and Competition*. Cambridge: Cambridge University Press.

CHAPTER 11

Competition policy

Learning objectives

After reading this chapter the student should be able to:

- Understand the theoretical arguments underlying competition policy

- Analyse the advantages and disadvantages of monopolistic market structures

- Discuss the goals of policy aimed at monopoly, mergers and restrictive practices

- Explain how market power can be measured

- Use case study evidence to compare and contrast competition policy in the EU, UK and United States

- Assess the success or otherwise of UK legislation towards monopoly, mergers and restrictive practices

---

11.1 Introduction

Competition encourages efficiency by allowing the most efficient firms to survive and grow at the expense of their inefficient counterparts. Furthermore, competition is often seen as a spur to economic efficiency as firms pursue and adopt innovations in order to gain a competitive advantage. To this end, some economists have argued that competitive market structures will increase consumer choice and welfare, while monopoly tends to lead to the opposite. As a consequence, competition policy is necessary to ensure that efficiency is rewarded and consumer welfare is maximised. However, some economists have argued that monopoly can be conducive to economies of scale and innovation. This chapter examines

347

competition policy in the United States, UK and the European Union. Section 11.2 examines the arguments for and against monopoly structures. The arguments forwarded in favour of monopoly are economies of scale in production, technical progress and the reduction of wasteful competition. Arguments against monopoly include that monopoly leads firms to lower output, raise prices and encourage restrictive practices towards consumers that may ultimately lead to welfare losses in the economy. Section 11.3 provides a rationale for competition policy, while section 11.4 examines the evolution of competition policy in the United States, UK and EU, respectively. Here we adopt a historical approach to examine the various legislative measures passed by the US, UK and EU policy-makers. We highlight several cases to illustrate competition policies in action. Recent developments in competition policy are also highlighted, and the overall contribution of policy in promoting competition is assessed.

11.2 A critique of monopolies

Under the Structure–Conduct–Performance (SCP) approach, a good structure was defined in terms of perfect competition. Some authors, including Clark (1940) and Sosnick (1958), argued that, in reality, perfect competition was unlikely to prevail in most industries. Therefore, the goal of competition policy was to make competition 'workable'. As a consequence, the SCP approach was expanded to encompass what has become known as the 'workable competition' approach. This approach focused on the performance of industries, and suggested aspects of structure and conduct that could be adjusted to bring about desirable performance outcomes. In other words, workable competition defines good performance, and then finds the appropriate industry structure to ensure such performance. Once the appropriate performance is defined, competition policy can be used to achieve the desired structure. This means that each industry would have a number of criteria for workable competition (for example the number of firms required in an industry to exploit available scale economies, the informative content of advertising, and so on).

The workable competition approach has been criticised. Firstly, the approach does not specify how much weight should be given to each dimension of performance. Secondly, the subjective aspects of this approach have led to disagreement as to what constitutes a uniform set of structural, conduct and performance indicators for any industry type. In fact, Stigler (1968) criticised the approach for its 'serious ambiguity'.[1] Overall, the SCP/workable competition approach towards competition policy implicitly assumed that monopolies are against the interests of consumers and the economy in general. This section examines disadvantages and advantages of monopoly.

Although there are many reasons to criticise monopoly, various economists have argued that monopolies are not necessarily a bad thing. The Austrian school argued that competition is a dynamic process; Kirzner (1997b, p.59) noted that: 'departures from the optimality conditions of perfectly competitive equilibrium are not a threat to any relevant notion of economic efficiency. Equilibrium is not an attainable ideal, nor are perfect or "near perfect" competition attainable.'

Any monopoly profits earned are the reward for innovative behaviour and superior management by creating new products and processes. These new products and processes generate increased demand, and encourage entry of new firms, ultimately leading to increases

---

[1] Reid (1987) provides a comprehensive discussion of workable competition.

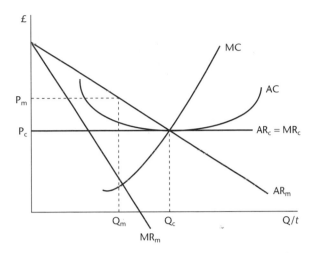

Figure 11.1 Profits and costs under perfect competition and monopoly

in economic welfare. As a consequence, an analysis of welfare losses arising from monopoly positions is uncalled for. A related Chicago view argued that competition generally prevails in all industries. Impediments to competition persist only if instituted and supported by governments (Demsetz, 1982). As a consequence, any monopoly profits observed are the reward for more efficient firms (Demsetz, 1973; Posner, 1979). Some authors argued that monopolies are not necessarily bad if industries are contestable. If monopoly markets are contestable the threat of entry and competition constrains monopolists' pricing behaviour so that only normal profits are earned (Baumol *et al.*, 1982). Bearing the above points in mind, we can examine the disadvantages and advantages of monopoly.

Disadvantages of monopoly

Higher prices and lower output
Monopolies often mean that prices will be higher, and output lower than is the case for an industry where competition prevails. Consider Figure 11.1, in which two firms face similar costs. Firms in one industry are producing under conditions of perfect competition, while the other firm is operating under conditions of monopoly. The costs of production are the same for each industry and are constant (AC = MC). In the diagram, firms in the perfectly competitive industry will produce where price (P_c) is equal to marginal costs (MC) and produce a competitive output equal to Q_c. The monopolist produces where marginal revenue is equal to marginal cost and produces output Q_m and charges a price equal to P_m. As we can see from Figure 11.1, prices are higher and output lower under monopoly than is the case for perfect competition (i.e. $P_m > P_c$ and $Q_m < Q_c$).

Excess capacity
Following from Figure 11.1, if the monopolist is restricting output in order to keep prices high, then excess capacity may be assumed to exist within the industry. There is a consequent waste of resources equal to $Q_m - Q_c$.

Excess profits

High profits made by the monopolist are not necessarily an indication of efficient methods of production (Demsetz, 1973). The monopolist may in fact be using its market power to raise prices above marginal costs in order to increase its revenues (Shepherd, 1997).[2]

Price discrimination

Monopolists as sole suppliers can discriminate between different groups of customers located in different market areas. They can achieve this as long as markets can be separated by either geography, consumer ignorance or tariffs. The monopolist must separate these markets in such a way that no resale or seepage can occur, and for price discrimination to be profitable, elasticities between the markets must differ.[3] The European Commission (1995b) contended that car manufacturers based in Europe have pursued successful price discrimination strategies that have caused large disparies in the prices paid by consumers in various countries.

Restrictive practices

Monopolists often use unfair practices (such as limit pricing) to keep potential rivals out of the market.[4] Even if rivals are successful in entering the market, the monopolists may choose to eliminate these firms by various restrictive price and non-price strategies such as predatory pricing and vertical restraints. For example, Myers (1994) argued that predatory pricing practices in the deregulated bus industry led to a decline in the number of bus operators. Dobson and Waterson (1996) found that vertical restraints in many industries led to some firms prospering at the expense of others.[5]

Limited technical progress

Some evidence suggests that technical progress is often slow when a single or group of firms dominates an industry. Monopolists are under no real pressure to spend any abnormal profits on research and development of product and processes as they face no real competition. As a consequence, technical progress in these industries is likely to be slow.[6]

Welfare losses

As we have seen, monopolistic market structures can often lead to higher prices and lower output than is the case under perfect competition. These high prices and low outputs can lead to a loss in an economy's welfare. We can examine this process in Figure 11.2.

In Figure 11.2, we assume a constant average cost curve, which is also equal to the marginal cost curve. Under conditions of perfect competition (AR = AC), output is QC, and price is at P_c. The consumer surplus is equal to the area AP_cB. If this industry were now

---

[2] Chapter 6 examines whether the high profits made by firms in concentrated industries are the result of firm-specific efficiency differences or market power.

[3] A monopolist can practise price discrimination in several ways. Under first-degree (perfect) price discrimination, the monopolist charges each customer what they are willing to pay. Under second-degree price discrimination, the monopolist charges customers different prices based on usage. Third-degree price discrimination separates customers into markets based on different demand elasticities. Customers with inelastic demand are charged higher prices than those with elastic demand.

[4] Entry deterrence by monopolists is discussed in Chapter 5.

[5] Predatory pricing and vertical restraints are examined in Chapters 5 and 9, respectively.

[6] The relationships between market structure and innovation are discussed in Chapter 8.

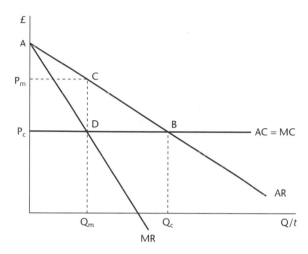

Figure 11.2 Welfare loss under monopoly

monopolised, output would fall to Q_m. This is because the monopolist will maximise profits where marginal revenues equal marginal costs and price would increase to P_m. Consequently, consumer surplus is now AP_mC, and monopoly profit is equal to rectangle P_mCDP_c. The monopolist has eaten its way into the consumer surplus that previously existed under conditions of perfect competition. However, the criticism is not that consumer surplus is reduced from AP_cB to AP_mC, as this is merely a simple redistribution of welfare from the consumer to the producer, but the triangle BCD is lost to both consumers and producers. This area is referred to as **deadweight loss**, the true welfare loss of monopolisation.

The welfare loss in Figure 11.2 can be calculated from the area of the triangle (BCD) as $-\frac{1}{2}\Delta P \Delta Q$, where ΔP and ΔQ represent the difference in prices and quantities produced under perfect competition and monopoly respectively. Harberger (1954) found that in the United States over the period 1921 to 1928, the welfare loss from monopolisation accounted for 0.1 per cent of gross national product. In a subsequent study using US data, Kamerschen (1966) found that over the period 1956 to 1961, welfare losses on average accounted for almost 6 per cent of national income in any given year. Cowling and Mueller (1978) adopted several measures of welfare loss for the United States (1963–1966) and the UK (1968–1969). They found that in the former case, welfare losses arising from monopoly range from 4 to 13.1 per cent of national income, while in the latter they range from 3.9 to 7.2 per cent. Jenny and Weber (1983) found welfare losses for France ranging between 0.14 and 8.9 per cent for the period 1967 to 1974. Hay and Morris (1991) argued that many of these studies were carried out at a national level, and so give little information as to welfare losses at the industry level. Littlechild (1981) contended that monopoly profits are a temporary phenomenon, and that, consequently, an analysis of short-run welfare losses is uncalled for.[7]

Leibenstein (1966) and Comanor and Leibenstein (1969) argued that owing to an absence of competition under monopoly, monopolists have no incentive to minimise costs. This means that under conditions of monopoly and in the absence of competition, a firm may operate above its average cost curve at the point corresponding to the level of output it

[7] Sawyer (1985) provides a comprehensive discussion of welfare losses arising from monopoly.

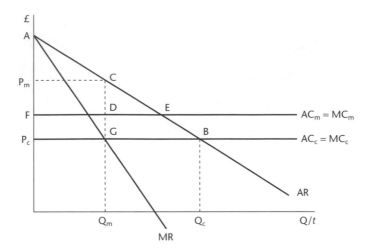

Figure 11.3 Welfare implications of increased production costs after monopolisation

chooses to produce. This would in turn mean that firms with monopoly power may not choose to pursue profit-maximisation policies. They may instead engage in high levels of discretionary spending aimed at maximising utility (Williamson, 1963). As a consequence, costs of production will be higher under monopoly than under competition (Figure 11.3). This argument is often used against mergers which may lead to a monopoly position.

In Figure 11.3, under conditions of perfect competition firms set prices equal to marginal costs (i.e. $P_c = MC_c$) and produce at output level Q_c. Initial welfare is identified as the consumer surplus as area AP_cB. After monopoly the consumer surplus falls by the area P_mCBP_c and is now represented by area AP_mC. Part of the loss in consumer surplus is transferred to the monopolist, and is shown by the area P_mCDF. The remaining area, CDE is the welfare loss. However, Comanor and Leibenstein (1969) argued that monopoly leads to higher costs. Under monopoly, average costs are higher than under perfect competition (i.e. $AC_m > AC_p$). This means that at production level Q_m additional costs of production are represented by area $FDGP_c$. Overall, the welfare losses attributable to monopoly are equal to the areas $CDE + FDGP_c$.

Advantages of monopoly

Monopolies do not always lead to increased prices, lower outputs and welfare losses. In fact monopolies can often lead to increases in society's welfare as large monopolists benefit from economies of scale in production and distribution. These falls in costs can often be passed on to consumers in the form of lower prices.

Lower production costs and increased welfare

Under monopoly, greater output and standardisation can lead to lower costs. This can lead to economies of scale and scope which can be passed on to consumers in the form of lower prices. This is examined in Figure 11.4. The arguments relating to Figure 11.4 follow closely those of Williamson (1968a,b) and are often used in favour of two large firms merging to a gain a dominant position within a given industry.

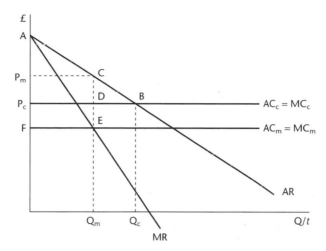

Figure 11.4 Welfare implications of a reduction in costs after monopolisation

Figure 11.4 considers prices, costs and output under conditions of monopoly and perfect competition. The main difference between Figures 11.2 and 11.4 is that the monopolist and firms operating under conditions of perfect competition do not have the same costs. Under conditions of perfect competition, firms face constant costs of production ($AC_c - MC_c$). Prices are set equal to marginal costs (P_c) and firms in the industry produce Q_c units of output. The welfare is measured by the consumer surplus and is equal to area AP_cB. After the industry becomes monopolised, the monopolist maximises profits where marginal costs equal marginal revenue, and produces output at Q_m. The price increases from P_c to P_m. Under monopoly the consumer surplus is the area AP_mC, a loss equal to P_mCBP_c. Of the area P_mCBP_c, P_mCDP_c is transferred to the monopolist in the form of monopoly profits.[8] The deadweight welfare loss arising from the monopoly is equal to the area BCD. However, if, as Williamson (1968a,b) argued, monopoly leads to economies of scale and consequently lower average costs (AC_m under monopoly versus AC_c under perfect competition), then a welfare gain may occur from the lower costs of production. In Figure 11.4, the lower costs of production mean that there is additional welfare equal to the area P_cDEF. Therefore if this gain in welfare outweighs the welfare loss associated with monopoly, then it is possible that monopoly may lead to overall welfare gains.

Natural monopolies

It could be argued that some industries are more efficiently organised as monopolies. Industries such as water, gas, electricity and communications are often referred to as 'natural monopolies'. A natural monopoly arises when the ratio of the minimum efficient scale to industry size is so large that industry can support only one efficient firm. In natural monopolies, fixed costs form a large part of total costs. This means that competition would therefore lead to wasteful duplication (and competition) of systems. Historically, many natural monopolies were placed in public ownership. However, throughout the 1980s and

---

[8] Although this is a transfer of welfare from the consumer to the producer, many authors, including Posner (1976), argue that this represents an additional (social) cost of monopoly.

1990s, these publicly owned monopolies have been privatised (George *et al.*, 1991). We examine the regulation of natural monopolies in Chapter 12.

Technical progress

Large monopoly profits may be used to finance research and development programmes (Schumpeter, 1950). Littlechild (1981) argued that welfare losses from monopoly do not really exist. He argued that monopoly profits are the reward for successful innovations. These innovations bring welfare gains to society in the form of new products and processes. Furthermore, these monopoly profits will not persist as there will eventually be entry by imitators, or patents will lapse which will eventually dissipate these profits. The competition authorities in the UK have tended in the past to look favorably upon firms that devote large amounts of resources to research and development.[9]

Avoidance of wasteful forms of competition

Monopolies may avoid wasteful forms of competition such as advertising, which are prevalent features of many oligopolistic market structures (Kaldor, 1950).[10] Given that monopolists to some extent have a captive market, there is little incentive for them to advertise. In addition, monopolists may also generate a degree of price stability. They may be expert in gauging the level of demand and supply. A monopolist may also be better placed to endure any downturn in the business cycle.

Monopolies can be regarded as detrimental to the economy if they arise from the exercise of market power by dominant firms, leading to reduced outputs, higher prices for consumers and higher profits for the monopolist. However, the empirical evidence which has examined the welfare losses arising from monopoly vary in their estimates of the severity of this problem. Monopolies are likely to benefit the economy if they arise as a consequence of efficiency differences between firms. If this is the case, a firm will acquire a monopoly position only if it employs lower-cost production techniques than its rivals, enabling that firm to increase its market share and profitability. The increased efficiency of the monopolist may lead to lower prices for consumers. Other evidence suggests that firms will enjoy monopoly positions by successful innovation. Therefore, the monopoly profits are merely the appropriation of advantages gained by investing in research and development. If this is the case, then this is likely to lead to greater choice for consumers. The empirical evidence suggests that these monopoly positions will not persist as rival firms replicate the innovation.

Overall, the evidence as to whether monopolies lead to a reduction in efficiency and consumer welfare or otherwise is unclear. As a consequence, monopolistic market structures must be analysed on a case by case basis. To assist in this process, most industrialised countries have developed legal frameworks based on economic principles to examine the relative merits of monopoly and associated restrictive practices. Utton (1986, p.135) contended that regulating monopolies is a complex process, when he concluded that:

> The regulatory problems posed by dominant positions in the private sector can be brought into focus by considering the distinction between technical efficiency and allocative efficiency. In many markets the need of technical efficiency may threaten allocative efficiency by allowing

---

[9] Chapter 8 examines these issues.
[10] The relationships between advertising and market structure are examined in Chapter 7.

firms to attain dominance due to economies of large size to bolster their position by restrictive or exclusionary practices. Success in this respect may then also create x-inefficiency and thus reduce welfare still further.

11.3 Competition policy: theoretical framework

This section discusses competition policy from a theoretical and empirical perspective. Competition policy is generally designed to promote competition and to control abuses of market power by firms. Competition policy aims to increase efficiency, improve consumer choice through more transparent information, and encourage innovation. A report by the Organization for Economic Co-operation and Development (1984) noted that:

> Competition policy has its central economic goal as the preservation and promotion of the competitive process, a process which encourages efficiency in the production and allocation of goods and services over time, through its effects on innovation and adjustment to technological change, a dynamic process of sustained economic growth.[11]

Competition policy can be classified under three main headings: **monopoly**, **restrictive practices** and **merger**:

● *Monopoly policy.* If a firm has a large market share, it may have a dominant position that allows it to pursue policies to the detriment of consumers. Monopoly policy will attempt to prevent the abuse of market power. The approach taken in the UK is to weigh the advantages and disadvantages to the public interest (defined below) of allowing firms to follow certain types of strategy which may reduce competition in a given market.

● *Restrictive trade practices policy.* This type of policy examines cases where a firm or groups of firms are engaging in practices which may prove detrimental to consumers. Such practices may include price-fixing agreements, predatory pricing and vertical restraints (Pickering, 1982).[12] George and Joll (1981) identified four main types of restrictive practice: horizontal agreements, vertical agreements, tacit collusion and industrial property rights. **Horizontal agreements** are between firms in the same industry, and are primarily aimed at decreasing competition with respect to pricing, output or the entry of new firms. Such agreements relate to common pricing policies, production quotas, market allocation, or sharing of information on prices, output and quality. **Vertical agreements** are between firms in successive stages of production or distribution, such as exclusive dealing contracts and resale price maintenance. Tacit collusion occurs when firms collude in an implicit manner. This may involve dominant firm, barometric or effective price leadership.[13] Industrial property rights include patents, copyright and trademarks. The ownership of any of these instruments guarantees the firm some degree of monopoly power. The availability of property rights of this kind may encourage research, development and innovation.[14] However, if the rights last for an excessively long time, they may tend to stifle competition. In some cases, firms may adopt a strategy of pre-emptive patenting to prevent competition.

[11] OECD (1984), para 232.
[12] Price fixing and predatory pricing are discussed in Chapter 3, while vertical restraints are examined in Chapter 9.
[13] Tacit collusion is examined in Chapter 3.
[14] These issues are discussed in Chapter 8.

● *Merger policy.* Government intervention may become important if two or more firms propose a merger which may lead to a dominant position in the market for the newly formed firm. Merger policy considers whether any growth of market power arising from a merger is in the public interest. For example, the regulator has to judge the benefits of rationalisation against the growth of concentration that a merger may bring. However, merger policy must not be so restrictive as to protect inefficient management from take-over. Mergers can be viewed in many cases as a spur to managerial efficiency (Marris, 1964). Policies aimed at controlling mergers are normally based on the likely market share enjoyed by the new, merged entity.

Competition policy is normally aimed at promoting efficiency, innovation, price reductions and consumer choice. In other words, this type of policy aims to control firm behaviour (such as pricing and non-price strategies, and merger activity) which will lead to the pursuit and exercise of market power. If industries are competitive there is efficiency in the production of products and the allocation of resources. Production is efficient if firms utilise all available resources to operate where production costs are at a minimum (i.e. the minimum efficient scale). At this point, all economies of scale and scope are exhausted (Caves, 1992). Competitive pressures will lead to the elimination of firms that are unable to produce at this scale. Nickell *et al.* (1992) have tested these arguments empirically, and have found that firms are less efficient (productive) in industries where concentration is high. In other words, competitive pressures in these industries do not provide sufficient incentive for firms to achieve efficiency.

Consumption is efficient under competition, as consumers pay a price equal to the firm's marginal cost of production for a given good or service. This means that the economy's resources are allocated to the production of goods and services demanded by the consumer leading to allocative efficiency.

Dynamic efficiency may also be related to the intensity of competition. Dynamic efficiency refers to technology improvements that lead to increases in the efficiency and welfare of the economy. Two views are important here:

● The first, generally referred to as the Schumpeterian hypothesis, argued that firms must make high levels of profits and enjoy some monopoly power in order to invest the funds necessary for successful innovation (Kamien and Schwartz, 1975).
● A second view argues that competition leads to increased incentives for firms to gain a competitive advantage. One way of doing this is to invest in research and development projects (Nickell, 1996).[15]

Competition policy has to weigh up the efficiency gains that may result as firms grow in size (either by internal growth or by acquisition and merger) against the potential for large firms to exercise market power. Competition authorities often have a more complex task in assessing the benefits of monopoly power than was illustrated in Figure 11.2, where we assumed that costs remained unchanged following the monopolisation of an industry. In reality, monopoly positions (arising, for example, from merger) will lead to changes in the cost structure of an industry. On the one hand, the growth of large firms may lead to economies of scale advantages and lower production costs (Figure 11.4). On the other

---

[15] These issues are discussed in Chapter 8.

hand, the increased size of a firm may insulate it against competition and thereby diminish the necessity to reduce costs (Figure 11.3).

If no gains are made from increased concentration of industries, competition authorities must then assess if abuses of market power are taking place. One way of measuring the extent of market power in a given industry is to employ the Lerner index of monopoly power, where the index, L, is given by:

$$L = \frac{P - MC}{P}$$

where P is price charged and MC is marginal cost. The index reflects a firm's ability to raise prices above marginal costs (Lerner, 1934).[16] If P > MC this would indicate a deviation from perfect competition and the exercise of market power by the firm in question.

Using the Lerner index to examine market power has two associated problems. Firstly, estimates of marginal costs are not included in firms' annual reports. We saw that, in some cases, average costs can be used as a proxy if the firm is assumed to operate under constant cost conditions. Secondly, perfect competition does not exist in reality so all firms can potentially raise prices above marginal costs and enjoy some element of market power.

Bain (1959) argued that if a firm earns excess profits it has a monopoly position. Bain measured excess profits via the following formula:

Economic profit = R − C − D − i × V

where R denotes total revenue, C current costs, D depreciation, V the value of the owners' investment in the firm, and i the prevailing market interest rate on investments of a similar type. Bain argued that if the firm's revenue (R) equals its total costs (C + D + i × V) then normal profits are earned. However, if revenue exceeds costs, the firm is exercising monopoly power, given that it is earning revenue over and above what could be regarded as consistent with a similar investment.

A more practical measure of market power potential is market share. Shepherd (1997) argued that market share and concentration measures are useful in determining the structure, and so the likely conduct of firms, in any given industry. Under Shepherd's classification, abuses of market power are more likely to take place in industries with four-firm concentration ratios (CR4) exceeding 60 per cent (tight oligopoly). As a consequence, competition policy should look at the behaviour in these industries. However, Baumol et al. (1982) argued that concentration of market share in the hands of a few firms does not necessarily lead to the abuse of market power. Questions must be asked as to the likelihood of entry, industry traditions and the objectives of firms operating in the industry.

Before assessing whether market power abuses are taking place, regulators must first define the relevant market for the analysis of competition. If a narrow definition of a market is used, the extent of market power held by any firm may be overstated. In contrast, if a wide definition of the market is used, abuses of market power may be overlooked. Markets can be defined in terms of product groups or geographical area.[17] Product markets

---

[16] Other measures forwarded to measure the degree of monopoly power include the Rothschild index and the Papandreou index. A discussion of these measures is outside the scope of this chapter but many be found in Rothschild (1942) and Papandreou (1949), respectively.

[17] The issue of defining markets is discussed in Chapter 4.

should include all products that are close (demand or supply) substitutes of the product in question. This often faces economists with the problem of which products to include within this definition. For example, Fosters lager would be included in the same market as Tenants lager. However, would other types of beer (such as bitter and real ale) belong in the same product market? Do we include other types of beverage such as soft drinks, tea, coffee, wines and spirits in the market definition? Obviously the market definition will vary depending on the problem in question. However, so will any market share calculations. Defining markets by geographical areas presents economists with similar problems. Is the relevant geographical market defined at a local, regional, national or international level? Any market definition must capture the true competitive environment. If a definition fails to do this, then any policy decisions will be biased. In practice, the competition authorities in the UK and elsewhere tend to use a range of market definitions.[18]

The Office of Fair Trading (1999) argued that policy-makers should examine several aspects of competition to assess whether abuses of market power are taking place. These include an examination of:

- How market shares of established firms have changed over time.
- How potential entrants could affect the level of competition in a given market, if they made decisions to enter.
- The extent to which the power of buyers in the industry may offset the market power of sellers.

11.4 Competition policy: legal framework

Here we discuss briefly the development of competition policy in the United States, UK and the European Union. The emphasis is on the development of policy in the UK, but this is contrasted with the experiences in the United States and European Union.

United States

Competition law began in the United States in the late nineteenth century in response to the growth in corporate trusts. The trust was an arrangement whereby shareholders of different companies signed over the ownership of their shares to a single group of trustees. As a consequence, many competing independent firms were consolidated into large entities which quickly became dominant firms within many industries. This led to a substantial increase in concentration in many US industries. These new firms carried out various types of practice, including price-fixing and price discrimination, which had the effect of eliminating smaller competitors and led to less choice for consumers and higher prices. In response to this, a series of **anti-trust** laws was passed which aimed at lessening the impact on competition of the growth in corporate trusts. Enforcement of these laws (discussed below) is carried out either by the Antitrust Division within the US Department of Justice or by the Federal Trade Commission. The Antitrust Division's traditional role was that of prosecutor rather than as a strategic policy-making body. In contrast, the Federal Trade Commission is an independent body charged with providing economic analysis of various

---

[18] National Economic Research Associates (1992) provides a full discussion of the methodology for finding the relevant market for analysis in UK competition policy.

competition issues along with conducting formal investigations and prosecutions. It is also possible for private parties to bring prosecutions for violations of anti-trust laws.[19] The main Acts that have defined US anti-trust policy are now discussed briefly.

Sherman Act

The Sherman Act was passed in 1890. It comprised two main sections. The first section made it illegal for firms to pursue strategies aimed at reducing trade between competitors and reducing competition within the industry. These activities included price-fixing, quotas and market allocation. Section 2 of the Act made it illegal for firms to monopolise an industry. The Act empowered the courts to impose fines of up to US$5,000 for each violation of the Act. By 1992 this had increased to a maximum of US$10 million. However, it was unclear from the content of the Act as to what constituted an illegal monopoly position. As a consequence, what constituted a monopoly position has been left for the courts to interpret.

The first major prosecution under the terms of the Sherman Act was against the Standard Oil Company of New Jersey in 1911 for monopolisation of the crude and refined oil and petroleum goods industries. Standard Oil had a market share exceeding 80 per cent in the market for refined oil. The firm was accused of pursuing strategies of price discrimination in selected markets in an attempt to eliminate rival firms. The company had also used its market power to gain preferential transport rates from railway operators. The court found that Standard Oil had abused its monopoly position through the use of anti-competitive strategies, and ordered the break-up of the firm into 34 separate companies.

The finding in the Standard Oil case was an example of courts referring to the **rule of reason** doctrine. Under this doctrine, any investigation is more interested in the practices carried out by a firm, and the consequences of such behaviour on competition and welfare within any given market, than in the firm's size or structure of the market *per se*. Two types of market definition are important to regulators wishing to assess abuses of monopoly power: **anti-competitive practices** and the competitive effects of mergers. The relevant geographical market defines the geographical bounds of a market which the firm's activities are likely to affect. A wide definition would relate to a national or international market, while narrow definitions may be more interested in regional and local markets. The relevant product market attempts to define the product market in terms of close substitutes and complements. The effect of any activities or proposed merger would be judged against their likely impact on competition for these products.

The courts reversed the rule of reason doctrine in 1945 for a more straightforward assessment of monopoly. In this case Alcoa (Aluminum Company of America) was found guilty of operating a monopoly position in the virgin ingot production market where it held a market share exceeding 90 per cent. Under an earlier decision, the courts had ruled that Alcoa had not held a monopoly position. However, this decision was based on a wide definition of the market (which included other types of aluminium product). When a narrower definition of the market was used, Alcoa was found to have a monopoly position. Although the courts found no evidence that the firm was abusing its monopoly position, it was found to have acted illegally because it was a monopoly. To increase competition in

---

[19] Shepherd (1997), p.394, described a case involving Archer–Daniels–Midland which was sued by over seventy of its customers after being found guilty of price-fixing in the supply of fructose and citric acid. He noted that under private prosecutions the plaintiffs are entitled to three times the value of the economic damages caused by the defendant.

the industry the government banned Alcoa from purchasing any government aluminium production facilities that were on sale at the time.

In 1956, an action was brought against DuPont for monopolising the cellophane market where it had a market share exceeding 75 per cent. DuPont argued that the relevant market was much wider, and should include other substitutes which could be used to wrap products. The courts acquitted DuPont of the charges.

In 1974, in one of the largest anti-trust cases ever filed, the world's largest company, American Telephone and Telegraph Company (AT&T) was accused of carrying out various practices aimed at monopolising the markets for telephone equipment, and local and long distance calls. AT&T was accused of using its position as a large, vertically integrated firm to restrict competition and eliminate rivals in those markets. In the telephone equipment markets, AT&T had restricted competition by purchasing equipment only from its own manufacturing divisions. The firm was also accused of restricting access to its telephone networks by independent providers of telephone equipment and services. In 1982, AT&T agreed to divest itself of its 22 local telephone companies. This divestiture amounted to approximately two-thirds of the firm's assets, and had the effect of changing the competitive environment in the US telecommunications industry. However, the firm was allowed to keep its manufacturing divisions and its interests in providing long distance telephone services. It was also allowed to diversify into the cable television and computing industries.[20] At the time this was one of the biggest ever anti-trust cases. However, even this has been overshadowed by a recent case.[21]

An early example of prosecution for collusive behaviour under the Sherman Act can be found in the American Tobacco case of 1946. The industry was dominated at the time by three firms: American Tobacco, Reynolds, and Ligget and Myers. It was found that for a period of twenty years the firms had charged almost identical prices for their retail products. It was also found that the firms contrived to bid identical prices for their tobacco at auctions. Although, the courts found no evidence of a collusive agreement to fix prices, the observed behaviour of the firms suggested that collusion was taking place. The courts imposed a total fine of US$255,000, but did not impose any remedies to change the structure or behaviour of the firms in the industry.

Clayton Act

The passing of the Clayton Act in 1914 augmented the Sherman Act. The Act outlined specific instances of abuses of monopoly power in the case of price discrimination and out-lawed the practice of price discrimination whereby firms would charge different customers different prices. This would only be allowed in cases where there were:

● differences in the quantities purchased;
● differences in the quality of the products bought by consumers;
● substantial differences in transportation and distribution costs which meant that different prices had to be charged.

[20] Shepherd (1997), chapter 16, provides a comprehensive discussion of the AT&T case, and its impact on the evolution of competition in the US telecommunications industry.
[21] This case involves one of the world's most valuable firms, Microsoft, which was prosecuted by the Department of Justice for operating a monopoly in the personal computer operating systems industry. This ongoing case, and a recent enquiry launched by the European Commission, are examined in Case studies 11.6 and 11.7 at the end of the chapter.

The Act also deemed illegal any types of contract based on exclusive supply of products or any form of tied arrangement.

Regulations were also passed under this Act which prevented substantial cross-shareholdings between firms, and mergers which created monopoly positions through share acquisition between firms operating in the same industry. The provisions of this Act were extended in 1950 with the passing of the Celler–Kefauver Act which prevented mergers between firms involved at different stages of the production process (vertical mergers) or firms in unrelated activities (conglomerate mergers) which would create monopoly positions and thus prevent competition.

An example of the application of the Clayton Act was the DuPont–General Motors case in 1957. In this case, DuPont which at the time held a dominant position in the supply of fabrics, paints and other chemicals, acquired 23 per cent of shares in the General Motors Company. The anti-trust authorities argued that this reduced competition in the supply of paint and fabrics to automobile manufacturers, and placed other suppliers of paint at a competitive disadvantage. As a consequence, the courts ruled that DuPont was guilty of violating the provisions of the Clayton Act and should divest itself of any shareholdings.

Robinson Paton Act

The Robinson Paton Act was passed in 1936 to extend the provisions of the 1914 Clayton Act to cover cases where monopoly buyers exploited their position through strategies of price discrimination. This made price discrimination illegal on the demand side of the market as well as on the supply side.

Federal Trade Commission Act

This Act, passed in 1914, set up the Federal Trade Commission, which was entrusted with investigating alleged abuses of monopoly power and other forms of anti-competitive practice. The Act was augmented in 1938 by the Wheeler–Lea Act which extended the investigative powers of the Federal Trade Commission to cover not only anti-trust protection but also consumer protection.

Antitrust Improvements Act

The Antitrust Improvements Act was passed in 1976 with the specific aim of improving merger regulation. This Act required firms with assets exceeding US$100 million that wished to merge with firms with assets exceeding US$10 million to notify the appropriate regulatory authority 30 days before the merger was due to take place. This Act made it much easier for regulators to investigate and take action against proposed mergers.

The Antitrust Improvements Act has been augmented by merger guidelines introduced in 1982 and augmented in 1992. The 1982 guidelines made it much easier for mergers to be investigated with simple reference to concentration measures (for example the Herfindahl–Hirschman index). Amendments to these guidelines in 1992 resulted in less emphasis being placed on concentration measures, but also took account of changes in firm efficiency and product prices after the merger.

The penalties imposed for abuses of monopoly power and restrictive practices have varied considerably in the United States. Remedies have ranged from breaking up large firms into smaller components (Standard Oil), limiting expansion (Alcoa), to large fines (American Tobacco). The extent to which anti-trust policy has been active has depended very much on the period under consideration. Generally, this policy was quite harsh towards monopoly from the 1900s to 1920s, 1930s to 1950s, and in the 1970s and 1990s. The policy towards restrictive practices (in particular price-fixing) has been strict. In other words, any form of price-fixing has been deemed illegal. However, regulators have found it difficult to prove instances of tacit collusion. Overall, the United States was the first country to develop a full set of competition laws to deal with abuses of monopoly power and restrictive practices. However, varying interpretations of the clauses of different laws have made it difficult for courts to come to decisions.

United Kingdom

Until recently, competition policy in the UK was the remit of the Office of Fair Trading (OFT) and the Monopolies and Mergers Commission (MMC). The Office of Fair Trading investigated complaints of anti-competitive practices, and if these complaints are found to be justified, refers the findings to the Monopolies and Mergers Commission. The president of the Department of Trade and Industry or the Restrictive Practices Court takes final decisions as to the validity of any findings.

The framework underlying the UK's competition policy embodies a number of Acts. In the main this legislation has sought to regulate monopolies, mergers and anti-competitive practices. The Office of Fair Trading (1995, p.7) stated that: 'an anti-competitive practice is defined as any practice that has or is intended to have or is likely to have the effect of restricting, distorting or preventing competition in some market in the United Kingdom.'

Competition policy in the UK has evolved through a series of legislations. The main legislative measures include the Monopolies and Restrictive Practices Act 1948, Restrictive Trade Practices Act 1956, Resale Prices Act 1964, Monopolies and Mergers Act 1965, Restrictive Trade Practices Act 1968, Fair Trading Act 1973, Restrictive Trade Practices Act 1976, Competition Act 1980, Companies Act 1989 and the Competition Act 1998. In the EU, the legislation that deals with competition policy is embodied in Articles 81 and 82 of the Treaty of Amsterdam and the European Merger Control Regulation 1989.

Monopolies and Restrictive Practices Act 1948

The Monopolies and Restrictive Practices Act was the first major piece of UK legislation towards monopolies and restrictive practices. The Act defined monopoly in terms of a firm or a cartel controlling one-third or more of industry supply. The Act also founded the Monopolies and Restrictive Practices Commission. The Board of Trade (now the Department of Trade and Industry) could, if a monopoly position was found to exist, refer the case to the Monopolies and Restrictive Practices Commission for investigation.

The Act also defined the public interest, and argued that if a monopoly was in the public interest then it should be allowed to continue to operate. A monopoly would be deemed to be in the public interest if the firm(s) in question were:

- efficient;
- making full use of scarce resources, in other words no excess capacity exists;
- meeting the wishes of the public in terms of price, quantity and quality;
- developing new technologies; and
- expanding the market.

The Monopolies and Restrictive Practices Act suggested that each instance of monopoly had different defining characteristics, and suggested a case by case approach to determining outcomes. However, many authors have argued that the pragmatic approach adopted by the UK competition authorities has led them to make many inconsistent decisions (Clarke *et al.*, 1999).

The Monopolies and Restrictive Practices Commission had to examine whether or not a monopoly position was in the public interest. This was likely to be the case if the monopoly position led to more efficient production techniques, higher-quality goods and lower prices for consumers than would be the case under conditions of competition. On balance, the reports produced concluded that monopoly power on its own was not evidence of anti-competitive behaviour; rather it depended on how the power was being exercised. However, the reports found that restrictive practices were widespread and were not in the public interest. As a consequence, the government sought to tackle the problem of restrictive practices.

Restrictive Trade Practices Act 1956

This Restrictive Trade Practices Act aimed to ban all restrictive practices in UK industry. The Act set up the Restrictive Trade Practices Court to deal with collusive agreements between firms. The Act required that trade association agreements with respect to prices charged, production processes employed, and conditions surrounding the sales of goods be registered. These agreements were kept in a Register of Restrictive Trading Agreements. The newly appointed Registrar had to bring these registered agreements before the Restrictive Practices Court. This court would then decide whether the agreement in question was against the public interest. If so, the court could declare an agreement void and issue orders that the parties involved in the agreement should cease such practices. The Restrictive Practices Court assumed that registered agreements were against the public interest. Firms could decide to end any agreement voluntarily or defend the argument in the Restrictive Practices Court. However, the onus on proof was on the firms.

A series of defences or gateways was introduced, and firms could argue that their agreements were exempt under these. The gateways stipulated by the Act meant that an agreement was admissible if its outcome were to:

● protect the public against injury;
● provide specific benefit to the public;
● help prevent other restrictive practices;
● help secure fair terms from suppliers or purchasers;
● help protect jobs;
● promote exports; or
● support another agreement acceptable to the court.

Even if firms could prove the agreement was valid through one or more of the aforementioned gateways, it did not necessarily mean that the court would grant the agreement an exemption. The Act had a clause that argued that if the agreement did not on balance serve the **public interest**, although satisfying one of the gateways, it could be terminated. This was referred to as the tailpiece. For example, in the Yarn Spinners agreement of 1959, it was argued that ending the agreement would result in unemployment. This was successfully proved, but the Restrictive Practices Court ordered the agreement should cease, given that on balance the costs associated with increased unemployment did not outweigh the detriment to competition.[22]

The Restrictive Practices Court was extremely strict. Most of the agreements were terminated voluntarily once firms saw that expensive litigation was proving fruitless. Over the period 1956 to 1965, of the 4,500 or so agreements that were registered, no more than fifty cases were argued in the court; of those, twelve were successful, but have now all disappeared. An amended version of the Act was instituted in 1968, where information agreements among firms with respect to quantities produced and prices charged had to be registered (discussed below). This amended Act also introduced substantial fines for failure to register agreements. This Act was later augmented by the Restrictive Trade Practices Act 1976 (discussed below), Restrictive Trade Practices Court Act 1976 and the Resale Prices Act 1976.

Resale Prices Act (1964)

This Resale Prices Act generally defined price maintenance as against the public interest. The Act extended the power of the Restrictive Practices Court to include cases where resale prices were thought to be a problem.[23] Consequently, firms wishing to impose resale price maintenance had to obtain permission from the Restrictive Practices Court. Firms involved in price maintenance were assumed to be guilty unless proved otherwise. Gateways were introduced where price maintenance would be allowed if the abolition of such practices would:

● reduce the quality and choice of goods produced;
● lead to a decline in retail outlets;
● lead to injury to the public;
● lead to increased prices; or
● reduce the quality or level of service provision.

In most cases, resale price maintenance was abolished. Notable exceptions were medicines and books.[24] Overall, the Act abolished all forms of resale price maintenance. Walker (1997, p.2) argued that it is not that resale prices are fixed which is potentially anti-competitive and of interest to policy-makers, but it is when the fixing of resale prices is accompanied by 'an explicit or implicit threat by a manufacturer, to refuse to supply or to offer unfavourable terms to any retailer that undercuts its "recommended prices"'.

Monopolies and Mergers Act 1965

One of the main outcomes of the Restrictive Practices Act 1956 was to combat collusive practices in UK industry. The success of the Restrictive Practices Court in breaking up anti-competitive agreements led to a merger boom or a switch to more tacit forms of collusion (as firms pursued other forms of strategies aimed at reducing competition). The 1960s saw a merger boom in the UK, and the Monopolies and Mergers Act 1965 was passed to deal

---

[22] An extended discussion of the Restrictive Practices Act and the conduct of the court can be found in Stevens and Yamey (1965).

[23] Resale prices and other forms of vertical restraints are discussed in Chapter 9.

[24] In the case of books, there had been the Net Book Agreement. Under this agreement between publishers and booksellers, the publisher set a resale price for the book (net price), and booksellers had to sell the book at that price. The agreement was designed to allow publishers a reasonable return on books which had a limited print run. The agreement was also designed to protect small retailers from price competition emanating from larger rivals. The Net Book Agreement was abolished in 1995.

with the rising concentration which resulted. This Act gave the Monopolies Commission power to regulate prices charged and to break up monopolies. The Monopolies Commission now became the Monopolies and Mergers Commission. The Board of Trade could refer a merger to the Commission if the merger would create a monopoly position. A monopoly position would exist if the new firm controlled one-third of the market or had annual turnover exceeding £5 million. This threshold was increased to £30 million in 1984. The Commission would finally present findings to the secretary of state of the Board of Trade, who made a final decision as to whether the merger was in the public interest.

One problem with government policies towards monopolies and mergers during this period was that another strand of policy was aimed at promoting mergers. In 1966, the government passed the Industrial Reorganisation Act. This Act led to the creation of the Industrial Reorganisation Corporation (IRC) which was charged with promoting efficiency and profitability in the UK economy. In particular, the IRC sought to find opportunities for rationalisation and consolidation across industries that would lead to increased efficiency and productivity, and ultimately lead to welfare benefits for the UK economy. One of the areas where the IRC was most active was in the area of mergers. The IRC support ranged from general advice to more active support by suggesting potential areas for mergers and help in carrying these out. Any IRC-sponsored merger was automatically exempt from reference to the Monopolies and Mergers Commission. The IRC was criticised by many economists for focusing on already concentrated industries and for helping to increase monopoly power in many of these industries. The IRC was disbanded in 1971.

Restrictive Trade Practices Act 1968
After the 1956 Act, many firms had entered into agreements to share information regarding prices, quality and costs of production. The Restrictive Trade Practices Act 1968 made the registration of these agreements compulsory, and subject to the supervision of the Restrictive Practices Court. An information agreement could be exempted from the legislation if the agreement was of substantial importance to the well being of the UK economy or where its main aim was to improve production and promote efficiency.

Fair Trading Act 1973
The Fair Trading Act led to the creation of the Office of Fair Trading and the appointment of a Director-General of Fair Trading to oversee competition policy relating to monopolies, mergers and restrictive practices. Section 84 of the Act defined the public interest. In particular, a merger was thought to operate in the public interest if:

● it promoted or maintained competition;
● it was in the overall interest of consumers and other market participants;
● it led to a reduction of costs through economies of scale;
● it stimulated innovatory activity and led to technical progress.

A reference to the Monopolies and Mergers Commission could be made if a scale or complex monopoly position existed. A scale monopoly was where one firm had a market share of 25 per cent of the relevant industry.[25] A complex monopoly position referral could even

[25] A scale monopoly had previously been defined under the Monopolies and Mergers Act 1965 as when one firm had a market share exceeding one-third of the relevant industry.

be made if two or more firms had a combined market share of 25 per cent of the relevant market and engaged in concerted practices to affect competition. A reference could also be made if the worldwide assets being taken over by an acquisition exceeded £70 million.

The Office of Fair Trading advised the president of the Department of Trade and Industry on whether a merger should be referred to the Monopolies and Mergers Commission. If investigated, the Commission's role was to assess whether the proposed merger operated against the public interest. The Commission then reported to the president of the Department of Trade and Industry who decided whether the merger should proceed.

The Act was extended in 1980 to cover restrictive practices in the service industries (such as banks, travel agents and estate agents), nationalised industries and local monopolies. Overall, the Fair Trading Act covers monopoly pricing, mergers, restrictive agreements, predation, price discrimination and vertical restraints, and led to major changes in the way that monopoly and restrictive practices were investigated.

Restrictive Trade Practices Act 1976

The Restrictive Trade Practices Act 1976 brought together previous legislation relating to restrictive practices. The Act required registration of all verbal and written agreements to the director-general of fair trading. The details of these agreements were entered in a public register.

In theory, the director-general of fair trading should refer all agreements to the Restrictive Practices Court. However, if the agreements did not fundamentally affect competition, this was not done. At the end of 1999, over 15,000 agreements were disclosed on the public register. However, only about 1 per cent of these agreements went to court.

Competition Act 1980

The Competition Act 1980 replaced much of the previous legislation that had aimed to deal with anti-competitive practices. In particular, the Act extended the provision of the Fair Trading Act 1973. The Act defined clearly what constituted restrictive and anti-competitive practices. These were defined to include price-fixing, price discrimination, predatory pricing, vertical squeezes, exclusive dealing and tie-in sales. It also outlined how complaints of anti-competitive practices should be handled and the process of investigation if the Office of Fair Trading received a complaint from the Secretary of State of the Department of Trade and Industry or a member of the public. The Act allowed firms to comply voluntarily with Office of Fair Trading recommendations prior to reference to the Monopolies and Mergers Commission, and made it easier for nationalised industries to be investigated. The aim was to promote efficiency in nationalised industries. Overall, the Competition Act covered predatory pricing, price discrimination and vertical restraints. Until recently the Restrictive Practices Act dealt with collusion, The Fair Trading Act dealt with mergers, while monopoly power was dealt with by the Fair Trading and Competition Acts.

Companies Act 1989

The Companies Act forwarded several procedures aimed at improving the investigation and administration of mergers. The Act required firms to notify the Office of Fair Trading of details of a proposed merger before it took place. The Director-General of Fair Trading then decided whether a reference to the Monopolies and Mergers Commission was required. If no reference was made within 21 days of the notification, the merger was allowed to proceed. If an investigation ensued, firms could not acquire shareholdings in the other firm during the investigation.

Most of the UK legislation reviewed above was repealed in March 2000 with the introduction of a 'new' Competition Act 1998. The Competition Act brought the UK's approach into line with that of the European Commission. We now discuss briefly the European Commission's approach to competition policy, and then examine the current developments in the UK.

European Union

Competition policy in the European Union is aimed at achieving a single internal market through the promotion of competition. In general, competition policy is aimed at preventing the development of dominant positions of firms by preventing mergers or strategies that may result in a lessening of competition. The cornerstones of EU competition policy are Articles 81 and 82 of the Treaty of Amsterdam. Previously, Articles 85 and 86 of the Treaty of Rome were concerned with competition policy; however, after the ratification of the Treaty of Amsterdam, these Articles were renumbered Articles 81 and 82, respectively, in May 1999.

Article 81 of the Treaty of Amsterdam deals with the regulation of restrictive practices within the European Union. This Article prohibits restrictive practice agreements between firms from member states which have the effect of preventing and restricting competition. These agreements can be horizontal or vertical (see above). For example, agreements to fix prices, production quotas and share markets are deemed illegal.

One of the underlying aims of Article 81 is to integrate EU markets by removing distortions to competition. It is therefore not concerned with monopolies or oligopolies within member states. Any restrictive practice agreements were deemed illegal if they had the effect of distorting competition. Exemptions of agreements from Article 81 may occur if the benefits of the agreement outweigh the costs to the consumer, for example if an agreement led to increased production, economies of scale and more efficient distribution processes, or to technical progress, and where consumers were likely to receive lower-priced or higher-quality products.[26]

Overall, Article 81 covers restrictive agreements, collusion and vertical restraints within the European Union. Historically, the policy towards restrictive practices within the Union has been much stricter than that of the UK. In a recent case the European Commission fined Volkswagen and Audi Ecu102 million for various restrictive practices which distorted competition within the European car market (see Case study 11.4).

Article 82 regulates against abuses of dominant position through monopoly. A dominant position exists if an individual firm can prevent competition and behave independently of the competitive pressures facing its rivals, and exercise control over production and prices. An investigation takes place if a single firm has a dominant position in the relevant market, which is defined as 40 per cent of market share. A firm is abusing its dominant position if it is fixing prices, refusing to deal with certain customers, and so on. Overall, Article 82 covers monopoly pricing, mergers, predatory pricing and price discrimination. In contrast to Article 81, Article 82 does not offer any exemptions from activities that could be regarded as abuses of market power.

---

[26] In essence, this is an application of the rule of reason.

Both Articles 81 and 82 are confined to EU firms trading with other EU countries. These Articles do not apply to domestic competition. Cases are investigated and Articles enforced by the Competition Directorate-General IV, which has the power to fine companies up to 10 per cent of their annual worldwide turnover.

Mergers have traditionally been regulated by Article 82 and Regulation 4064/89, 'European Council Merger Regulation (ECMR), The Control of Concentrations'. The ECMR was passed in 1990, and subsequently amended by Council Regulation 13/10/97 which has been in force since March 1998. The ECMR covers mergers, acquisitions and joint mergers. Mergers qualify for investigation if they have a European dimension. In other words, if a merger has a fundamental effect on competition within the European Union. The ECMR outlines a number of circumstances under which a merger investigation may take place. These are as follows:

● If the firms involved in the merger or acquisition have worldwide sales exceeding Ecu 5 billion or have sales in the European Union exceeding Ecu 250 million.
● If the Europe-wide sales of each of the firms concerned exceeds Ecu 100 million.
● If the combined sales of the firms concerned exceeds Ecu 100 million in at least three EU member states.
● If two or more firms involved in any deal have sales exceeding Ecu 25 million in each of the same three EU member states.
● Where one of these firms has two-thirds of its market share in a single EU state.

Notification of any such mergers should be made to Competition Directorate-General IV not more than one week after a bid has been made or a deal has been announced. Failure to do so may result in fines for the parties concerned. The Directorate examines the effect of a merger based on the effects on competition within the European Union. Most investigations assess whether a merger will lead to a dominant position for the newly formed firm in any product or geographical markets. Any investigation would weigh the effects on competition against the potential benefits (which may include scale economies or technological advances). Directorate-General IV decides whether an investigation should take place or if a merger may proceed. Overall, it is unlikely that a merger would be allowed to take place if it leads to or augments a dominant position, as this is likely to have detrimental effects on competition.

Recent developments in UK competition policy

The UK's approach to competition policy has recently undergone major change. The (new) Competition Act was ratified by Parliament on 9 November 1998 and came into force on 1 March 2000, when most of the existing legislation relating to monopolies, mergers and restrictive practices was repealed. The Act aimed to rationalise the UK's competition policy and to bring it into line with the competition policy adopted by the European Union (Bloom, 1999). In other words the Act is concerned with the effects on competition of firm behaviour rather than the form of any practice or agreement (Maitland-Walker, 1999). The Act also increased the powers of investigation and intervention of the Director-General of Fair Trading. The Competition Act set up a new Competition Commission to take over the role of the Monopolies and Mergers Commission and to hear appeals arising from any decisions made under the Competition Act 1998. The Competition Commission came into being on 1 March 1999.

The Competition Act is composed of two main components known as chapter prohibitions, referred to as **Chapter I** and **Chapter II** respectively. The Chapter I prohibition deals with anti-competitive (restrictive) practices, while Chapter II prohibition deals with abuses of dominant (or monopoly) positions. The chapters are concerned only with promoting competition within the UK. Section 60 of the new Act makes provision that any investigations and enforcement of the Act should be consistent with existing EU policy. The following gives a brief discussion of Chapter I and II prohibitions.

The Chapter I prohibition applies to agreements between firms which prevent, distort or otherwise affect trade within the UK. These agreements can range from oral agreements to formal written agreements. Types of agreements which fall under the remit of the Act include:

- agreements to fix buying or selling prices;
- agreements to share markets;
- agreements to limit production;
- agreements relating to collusive tendering;
- agreements involving the sharing of information.

Exemptions can be granted if the agreement leads to an improvement in the production and distribution of goods and services or promotes technical progress that leads to substantial benefits for consumers.

Section 36 of the Act discusses the penalties that firms face if violating either of the chapter prohibitions. The maximum penalty is 10 per cent of annual turnover for each year that the violation takes place, up to a maximum period of three years.

The Chapter I prohibition is closely related to Article 81 of EU legislation. However, if there is an overlap between Chapter I prohibition and Article 81 in any investigation, the Competition Directorate-General IV will take charge of the investigation. If an exemption is granted under Article 81, then the firms concerned will automatically receive a parallel exemption from the Chapter I prohibition. However, an exemption from the Chapter I prohibition does not automatically lead to an exemption from Article 81.

The Chapter II prohibition is based on Article 82 of the Treaty of Amsterdam and deals with abuse of a dominant position. This is covered in section 18 of the Competition Act. The investigation of a dominant position involves conducting a two-stage test, which assesses (i) whether the firm is dominant in the relevant product or service market, and (ii) whether, if dominant, the firm is abusing this position. Practices that constitute abuse of a dominant position include situations where there are excessive prices being charged, price discrimination, predatory behaviour, vertical restraints and refusals to supply.

Since the Competition Act came into force in March 2000, the competition policy towards monopoly and restrictive practices has become much stricter. Nazerali and Cowan (1999) argued that this may lead to the reopening of previously investigated cases, and may impose a strain on the limited resources of the competition authorities.

Assessment of competition policy

Some attempts have been made to analyse the effectiveness of UK monopoly and mergers policy. In particular, studies by Shaw and Simpson (1986) and Davies *et al.* (1999) are of note.

Shaw and Simpson (1986) assessed the effectiveness of UK monopoly policy, and found that firms investigated by the Monopolies and Mergers Commission tended to lose market share. The authors examined cases brought before the Monopolies and Mergers Commission over the period 1959 to 1973. In particular, the authors investigated whether the market shares of dominant firms declined after Commission report recommendations had been made. A sample of 28 markets were identified which had been investigated by the Commission. This sample was matched with a sample of 19 similarly structured markets that had not been investigated by the Commission. The authors then examined what happened to the leading firms' market shares for a period of ten years after reports had been published. The Monopolies and Mergers Commission sample and the matched sample produced similar results.

Davies *et al.* (1999) examined the determinants of Monopolies and Mergers Commission finds against a monopoly position. The authors mainly investigated the decisions made under the Fair Trading Act 1973. In general they found that there is a 66 per cent chance of the Commission finding against the firm.

Of a sample of 73 cases, the Commission found against 48. Of these 48 cases, the recommendations were either a termination of a practice (34 cases), price controls (9 cases) and divestment of assets (9 cases). Of these 73 cases, 36 examined pricing problems (monopoly pricing, collusion and predatory pricing), while 37 examined vertical restraints (vertical integration, resale price maintenance, tie-in sales, exclusivity in distribution and purchasing).

The authors used a model to predict the probability of finding against a firm or group of firms:

$$P_{it} = f(S_{it}, C_{it}, R_{it}, t)$$

where the dependent variable P_{it} is the probability of the Commission finding against firm i in time period t. The independent variable S_{it} was designed to capture the structural characteristics (such as concentration, rate of entry and market shares of leading firms) of the industry being investigated. C_{it} captured the conduct of firms which had prompted the investigation. This conduct can take many forms and included vertical integration, exclusive purchasing, exclusive distribution, monopoly, predatory pricing, price discrimination and collusive practices. R_{it} denotes whether the investigation being undertaken is a repeat referral. Finally, t examined whether the Commission's decisions change over time.

The authors estimated the model and found that the Monopolies and Mergers Commission was more likely to find against the public interest the larger the market share of the biggest firm in the industry and where exclusive dealing was taking place. The Commission has been less inclined to find against the public interest where vertical restraints were prevalent. The authors also found that the Commission was more likely to find against the public interest in the 1970s and 1980s than in the 1990s.

It is easier to prevent the development of concentrated industries by thwarting mergers than to try to break up firms once they are in existence. However, as we have seen already, the UK government encouraged mergers in the 1960s when it formed the IRC. Weir (1992) noted that the extent to which competition was affected was instrumental in many of the Monopolies and Mergers Commission's decisions to disallow mergers. Weir (1993) extended this work to analyse Commission decisions on referred mergers using a sample of 73 published reports on such mergers covering the period 1974 to 1990. Weir split the sample into two groups comprising cases where the Commission thought a merger would decrease competition and those where the Commission thought the merger would increase or decrease competition.

Weir adopted regression analysis to examine the variables which would aid the Commission in taking a decision as to whether a merger is in the public interest or not. The variables included in this analysis captured the effects of the merger on market shares, efficiency, prices, balance of payments, research and development, profits and quality. The author allowed these decisions to differ by merger type (whether horizontal, vertical or conglomerate).

In the cases where the Monopolies and Mergers Commission thought competition would increase, it was much more likely to allow the merger to take place. Significant variables in reaching this decision were lower prices, increased efficiencies, increased expenditures on research and development or improvements to the UK's balance of payments. In contrast, in cases where competition was thought to decrease, mergers were much more likely to be disallowed. In such cases, increases in market shares of leading firms and increased prices were likely to take place.

Empirical evidence suggests that competition policy aimed towards restrictive practices led to an improvement in performance of many firms who had previously operated agreements.[27] However, problems of tacit collusion appear to still exist (Rees, 1993b). However, this is very difficult for investigators to uncover. Historically, the disincentives to firms to collude in the UK are seen as low, with small fines imposed on firms caught colluding. Prior to the Competition Act 1998, there were no fines for first offences under the existing restrictive practices legislation. However, the new competition Act passed in the UK along with the high fines imposed by the European courts are likely to deter such behaviour in the future. As a consequence of UK and EU legislation, firms can be fined up to 10 per cent of their annual turnover for abuses of monopoly position of restrictive practices.

The policy regarding monopoly has been much more cautious. Policy has proceeded on a case by case basis. The question posed by regulators is not whether there is monopoly power, but how it is used.

What is the public interest? This term has always been ambiguous, although the definition has been tightened up as competition policy legislation has progressed. However, many authors feel that the results of investigations often seem inconsistent as the public interest is assumed afresh for each case. Therefore there has been no case law to bind the Monopolies and Mergers Commission to precedent. The Department of Trade and Industry could previously ignore the Commission's recommendations. This may change under the Competition Act 1998. In recent years there has been a shift in policy away from private firms (which, it is argued, face a number of constraints imposed by the competitive conditions in any particular industry) to publicly owned firms. We examine these issues in Chapter 12.

11.5 Conclusions

In this chapter we have argued that it is often necessary for government to intervene in concentrated industries to ensure competitive outcomes. We have examined the arguments in favour of monopoly and those against. The arguments against monopoly generally centre on the assumption that monopoly leads to higher prices and welfare losses for the

---

[27] O'Brien *et al.* (1979) provides an excellent discussion of the effects of UK competition policy on firm and industry performance.

economy. The extent of these welfare losses has been the subject of some controversy. Arguments for monopoly have contended that large firms are more likely to benefit from economies of scale, and thus to be able to pass on such cost savings to consumers in the form of lower prices. Others have argued that the lure of monopoly profits is the spur to the competitive process and leads to technological progress. All of these arguments have some merit, which has led policy-makers to examine each case based on its merits.

Government policies towards assessing and regulating against abuses of market power have evolved in the United States and the UK since the passing of the Sherman Act 1890 and the Monopolies and Restrictive Practices Act 1948. In the European Union, policy has evolved since the adoption of Articles 85 and 86 of the Treaty of Rome (1957). These changes have been necessary as the strategies which firms carry out to distort competition have become more sophisticated over time. Most recently, the UK Parliament has passed a new Competition Act which came into force on 1 March 2000. This Act harmonised the UK's competition policies with those of the European Union. Overall, the challenges facing policy-makers are likely to increase as changes in technologies used to produce products and services, and the goods produced themselves, affect the ways in which firms compete.

Key terms

Anti-competitive practice	Horizontal agreement
Anti-trust	Merger policy
Article 81	Monopoly policy
Article 82	Public interest
Chapter I prohibition	Restrictive practices policy
Chapter II prohibition	Rule of reason
Deadweight loss	Vertical agreement

Case study 11.1
The British Sugar case

This case involved the supply of sugar in the UK.[1] Under Article 85 of the Treaty of Rome, several firms were accused of engaging in restrictive practices to raise sugar prices in the industrial and retail sugar markets. The firms involved in the case comprised two sugar producers (British Sugar and Tate & Lyle) and two sugar merchants (Napier Brown Limited and James Budgett Sugars Limited). Collectively these producers accounted for 90 per cent of the white granulated sugar market in the UK. The investigation covered the period 1986 to 1990. Prior to this, British Sugar had waged a price war against its competitors.

The European Commission found evidence of nineteen meetings between the four afore-mentioned firms with reference to the industrial sugar market, and eight meetings for the retail market between Tate & Lyle and British Sugar only. Overall, the Commission argued that a cartel was operating.

[1] A full discussion of this case can be found in European Commission (1999b).

All parties were found guilty of co-ordinating pricing of sugar in industrial white granulated sugar markets, while British Sugar and Tate & Lyle were found guilty of price co-ordination in the retail white granulated sugar market. British Sugar and Tate & Lyle were fined Ecu 39,000,000 and Ecu 7,000,000 respectively, while Napier Brown Limited and James Budgett Sugars Limited were each fined a total of Ecu 1,800,000. Given the marker leadership of British Sugar, and its role in instigating the meetings and activities with regard to pricing, the company was fined substantially more than the others.

Case study 11.2
Not so sweet: abuse of dominant position of Irish Sugar

In 1997, the European Commission concluded an investigation into the abuse of a dominant position in the Irish sugar market at various times over the period 1985 to 1995.[1] Under Article 86, the company investigated was Irish Sugar Plc. Irish Sugar is the main sugar supplier in Ireland, with a market share exceeding 90 per cent. It is the only sugar company in Ireland with an extensive distribution network. Distribution of Irish Sugar's sugar is carried out by Sugar Distributors Limited (a wholly-owned subsidiary of Irish Sugar since 1990). Most retail and industrial customers in Ireland bought supplies of granulated sugars from Irish Sugar. A smaller number of customers purchased sugar from importers, in particular ASI International Foods Limited. Imports of sugar came from Northern Ireland, France, Germany and Belgium. The market for granulated sugar comprised the retail and industrial markets. In markets where sugar is purchased for industrial use, competition has come from imported sugar from France, through a company called ASI International Foods Limited. Retail competition came from Round Tower Foods and ASI International Foods Limited. However, ASI withdrew from the retail market in 1994. Overall, the prices of sugar in Ireland are amongst the highest in the European Union.

Irish Sugar, in conjunction with Sugar Distributors Limited, was accused by the European Commission of abusing its monopoly position via a series of practices that had the effect of reducing competition and distorting trade within the European Union. These practices included transport restrictions, selective pricing and product swapping, export rebates and fidelity rebates.

● *Transport restrictions*. Irish Sugar stopped competition from imported French sugar by threatening to withdraw all Irish Sugar business from The British and Irish shipping line company if it continued to import French sugar on behalf of ASI International Foods Limited.

● *Selective pricing and potential customers*. The Commission uncovered evidence that Irish Sugar offered low prices of sugar to potential customers of ASI International Foods Limited. Evidence was also found that suggested that customers on the border of Northern Ireland and Ireland were offered Irish Sugar at a 5.5 per cent discount in an attempt to restrict imports from across the border (known as the border rebates).

● *Selective pricing and target rebates*. Irish Sugar offered customers discounts on sugar if they increased their purchases of Irish Sugar products. This had the effect of tying customers to Irish Sugar supplies to the detriment of other competitors.

[1] A full discussion of this case can be found in European Commission (1997e).

- *Selective pricing and export rebates*. Irish Sugar offered discounts to customers who would be exporting sugar out of Ireland. This offer was not made to firms buying sugar for resale within Ireland. The Commission suspected some cross-subsidisation to be taking place here.
- *Product swapping*. When ASI International Foods Limited introduced *Eurolax* sugar, comprising French imported sugar, Irish Sugar arranged to swap wholesalers and retailers their products for *Eurolax*, as a consequence eliminating any significant competition in the retail market. This practice also distorted trade between EU member states.

Irish Sugar argued that it had only engaged in these practices to meet the challenges of increased competition. As a consequence it argued that they had not infringed Article 86.

Overall, Irish Sugar was found guilty of abusing its dominant position in the Irish sugar market. This had the effect of discouraging imports of sugar, and caused difficulties for Irish Sugar rivals. The firm was fined Ecu 8,800,000.

Case study 11.3
All bets are off: the merger of Ladbrokes and Coral

This case involved the merger of Ladbroke Group Plc and the Coral Betting Company (owned by Bass Plc) the first and third largest betting establishments in the UK, respectively.[1] Before the merger took place, Ladbroke had 21 per cent of all betting establishments and 26 per cent of market sales. After the merger took place, these figures rose to 30 per cent and 38 per cent, respectively.

Ladbroke argued that the merger would not affect national competition as betting was based at a local level. However, the firm was willing to sell 134 of the acquired betting shops to a rival (Tote Bookmakers Limited).

The Monopolies and Mergers Commission rejected this solution and argued that the merger would lead to fewer betting shops at a local, regional and national level and subsequently a fall in consumer choice as competition declined. It would also increase substantially the market dominance of Ladbroke over its main rival William Hill Organisation Limited. There would also be a reduction in innovation.

According to the Monopolies and Mergers Commission investigation, the costs of the merger exceeded benefits. As a consequence, Labroke was ordered to sell off Coral's UK betting business.

Case study 11.4
Market partitioning and price discrimination in European car markets

Consumers had noted price differentials in various countries for Audi and Volkswagen cars.[2] Some consumers had attempted to take advantage of this by attempting to purchase cars from Italy where the price of Audi and VW cars was much lower. However, they found

---

[1] A full discussion of this case can be found in Monopolies and Mergers Commission (1999a).
[2] A full discussion of this case can be found in European Commission (1998b).

it difficult to do this and many complained to the European Commission, which in turn launched an investigation.

During inspections of the premises of Audi, Volkswagen and Autogerma (an Italian subsidiary of VW-Audi), the Commission found evidence that the three companies had actively partitioned the European market. These offences had taken place over a period of ten years. To enforce this partitioning Volkswagen, Audi and Autogerma had threatened that any dealers found selling cars to foreign customers would have bonuses reduced and could ultimately lose their dealership. By successfully partitioning European markets Audi and Volkswagen had managed to charge consumers in different countries different prices.

The firms had argued that the Commission's evidence was over-reliant on internal documents which represented internal discussions and therefore did not qualify for investigation. The Commission rejected this and found Volkswagen guilty of infringing Article 85 of the Treaty of Rome and consequently imposed fines of Ecu 102 million for instructing Italian dealers not to sell to foreign buyers.

Case study 11.5
Manchester United and BSkyB merger

Following an investigation by the Office of Fair Trading, the proposed merger between Manchester United and BSkyB was referred to the Monopolies and Mergers Commission in October 1998.[1,2] It was thought that this merger would lead to a lessening of competition in the premium sports channels television market and the football industry. BSkyB is a broadcasting company that buys rights to televise sporting events. The firm is also involved in producing and distributing its own programmes through a subscription system. At the time of the investigation BSkyB operated three premium sports channels, and its portfolio of offerings included the exclusive right to show live English Premiership football until 2001. Manchester United products and services included competing in Premier League, FA Cup, Worthington Cup and UEFA competitions. The club was also involved in merchandising its products and selling (in conjunction with other English Premier League clubs) television rights to broadcasters to televise live Premier League games. One of the main concerns arising from the merger was that, through its ownership of Manchester United, BSkyB would have an unfair advantage over rival broadcasters when bidding for television rights.

Representatives of Manchester United and BSkyB argued that the merger would not restrict competition given that the two companies operated in different markets. BSkyB argued that the merger would allow it to grow and add a strong brand to the firm's existing portfolio of products. The Monopolies and Mergers Commission rejected these arguments and concluded that the merger would lead to a lessening in competition for broadcasting rights to English Premier League games. In addition, if the merger were to take place, BSkyB would obtain increased market power in negotiating live televised football matches, leading to a reduction in competition in the premium sports channels market. This decline in competition could lead to a stifling of innovatory activity. In football, the Commission

---

[1] A detailed report of the entire investigation and subsequent conclusions can be found in Monopolies and Mergers Commission (1999b).

[2] The Office of Fair Trading Investigation took place under the terms of the Fair Trading Act 1973 – see above.

argued that the merger would harm competition within the industry by increasing the gap between rich and poor clubs. It was also thought that it would give BSkyB undue influence over decisions being made on the future of the Premier League. Overall, the Commission (p.5) contended that:

> We considered whether the adverse effects we have identified could be remedied by undertakings by BSkyB. We did not find any that we regarded as effective. We think that the adverse effects are sufficiently serious that prohibiting the merger is both an appropriate and a proportionate remedy. Accordingly, we recommend that the acquisition of Manchester United by BSkyB should be prohibited.

Case study 11.6
The Microsoft case

In 1997, the US Department of Justice launched an investigation that accused Microsoft Corporation of operating a monopoly position in the computer industry.[1] Specifically, Microsoft was accused of:

● operating a monopoly in operating systems in the personal computer industry;
● using its market power to prevent firms from offering applications that would run on the Microsoft Windows operating system;
● preventing rival firms from developing alternative operating systems;
● bundling software products (such as internet browsing applications) with operating systems.

Microsoft was able to pursue these activities because of its power as a vertically integrated firm that offered not only operating system provisions, but also thousands of applications which ran on these operating systems. Any firms wishing to compete with Microsoft would have to produce a huge number of applications to go with any new operating system. On the supply side, then, firms faced barriers to entry with respect to cost of capital, while on the demand side firms faced disadvantages in persuading consumers to switch from the numerous established Microsoft products to alternatives.

Microsoft argued that the pace of change in the computing industry meant that its dominance in the industry had arisen through the natural forces of competition. It pointed to the development and success of other companies in developing rival software systems.

The court found Microsoft guilty of operating a monopoly and of using this position to reduce competition. However, the court did not at the time decide what the punishment was to be. The proposed remedies could be either structural or conduct. Structural remedies would affect the future structure of the computing industry, whilst conduct remedies would place limits on the strategies which Microsoft could pursue. Possible remedies could include the following:

● Breaking the company into two parts comprising an operating software company to run the Windows system and a software applications company. However, this would still leave Microsoft with a monopoly in the operating software market.

---

[1] Various issues of *The Economist* throughout 1999 and 2000 give a detailed discussion of the Microsoft case, as does the US Department of Justice website at www.usdoj.com (last accessed July 2000).

- Breaking Microsoft into several smaller vertically integrated companies that would still provide operating systems and software applications. Whether these companies would compete is questionable. There may be incentive for collusion. There may also be a loss in efficiency if the break-up is accompanied by wasteful competition as the smaller firms duplicate efforts. Technical and learning economies of scale and scope may be lost.
- Force Microsoft to publish details of the code underlying the Windows operating system to firms who want to develop applications to run on this system.
- Force Microsoft to license the Windows operating system to any company who wishes to buy it and let these companies alter or improve the software as they see fit. However, this may lead to a fall in standards and a fragmentation of operating systems.
- Place limits on the ways in which Microsoft conducted its business, for example by preventing the expansion of its monopoly into other areas of the computing business. However, this could prove costly to enforce, as extensive monitoring would be required.

After talks between a mediator (Judge Richard Posner) and Microsoft regarding a suitable remedy broke down in April 2000, the court came to a final decision. Judge Jackson ruled that Microsoft should split its Windows operating systems from its software application arm. Microsoft appealed against the decision, arguing that it would stifle future innovation in the industry.

Case study 11.7
Brussels launches Microsoft probe: rivals say Windows 2000 could extend market dominance

The European Commission has started an antitrust investigation into Microsoft's latest computer operating system, Windows 2000, due to be launched worldwide on February 17. Mario Monti, EU competition commissioner, yesterday said the Commission had received complaints from rivals and end-users that Microsoft had designed its new product to allow it to extend its dominance in PC operating systems into markets for servers, and ultimately e-commerce.

Servers are pieces of hardware that connect PCs to the internet, and Mr Monti said that if Microsoft were to extend its market dominance, it could affect e-commerce. 'Whoever is dominant in server software is likely to control e-commerce too.' He said the EU's competition watchdog sent a formal request for information to Microsoft last week giving it four weeks to reply. If the Commission finds Microsoft has broken competition law, it can force the company to alter Windows 2000 or prohibit it from sale in the EU. It can also impose fines of up to 10 per cent of Microsoft's worldwide turnover.

The EU investigation comes as Microsoft is preparing for oral hearings in a Washington court on February 22 in the US antitrust case against it. Microsoft could face being broken up if it loses the US case, in which it is accused of abuse of its dominant position.

'It is important to differentiate between the trial in the US and our first step in a preliminary examination,' Mr Monti said. But he added that the EU had a good co-operative relationship with the US Justice Department and the Federal Trade Commission, antitrust regulators in the US.

According to the allegations made to the Commission, Mr Monti said, 'Microsoft had bundled its PC operating system with its own server software and other Microsoft products in a way that permits only Microsoft products to be fully inter-operable'.

He said if this were found to be true, it would prove a significant competitive disadvantage for rivals and allow Microsoft to extend its dominance of PC operating systems.

Microsoft said the allegations – which it blamed on rivals that could not compete with it on price – were fundamentally flawed.

'We've worked very hard and are very committed to high quality inter-operability for Windows 2000,' said John Frank, European director of law and corporate affairs at Microsoft Europe, Middle East and Africa. He said that the investigation would not delay the launch of Windows 2000. The current investigation is one of four pending by the Commission into Microsoft.

Questions for discussion

1. Assess the view that monopolies are an economic evil.

2. Discuss the usefulness of the Lerner index in measuring market power. Are there other, more useful methods?

3. Compare and contrast the traditional, Chicago and Austrian views as to the usefulness of competition policy.

4. Outline the UK government's approach to the regulation of monopolies and restrictive practices. How does this differ from that of the European Commission?

5. Using empirical evidence, discuss the effectiveness of the UK government's policy toward monopolies, mergers and restrictive practices.

Further reading

Davies, S.W. (1996) Competition and competition policy in the UK, *OECD Economic Surveys: United Kingdom*. Paris: OECD.

Neven, D., Nuttall, R. and Seabright (1993) *Merger in Daylight: The Economics and Politics of European Merger Control*. London: Centre for Economic Policy Research.

Neven, D., Papandropoulos, P. and Seabright, P. (1998) *Trawling for Minnows: European Competition Policy and Agreements Between Firms*. London: Centre for Economic Policy Research.

Pickering, J.F. (1982) The economics of anti-competitive practices, *European Competition Law Review*, **3**, 253–74.

Pickering, J.F. (1999) Competition policy and vertical relationships: the approach of the UK Monopolies and Mergers Commission, *European Competition Law Review*, **20**, 225–39.

Shepherd, W.G. (1997) *The Economics of Industrial Organization*. Englewood Cliffs, NJ: Prentice Hall.

Whish, R. (1993) *Competition Law*, 3rd edn. London: Butterworths.

CHAPTER 12

Privatisation and regulation

Learning objectives

After reading this chapter the student should be able to:

- Discuss why regulation is needed

- Analyse the implications for resource allocation under conditions of natural monopoly

- Discuss the arguments for and against public ownership and privatisation

- Assess the success of the UK privatisation programme by examining the performance of privatised firms

- Compare and contrast price cap and rate of return regulation

- Discuss the uses and relative merits of franchising and competitive tendering

---

12.1 Introduction

For resources to be allocated efficiently in an economy they should be distributed in a manner where it is impossible to make any one individual better off without imposing a reduction in welfare on someone else.[1] Regulation of industry is required when resource allocation inefficiencies take place. Stewart (1997) argued that these inefficiencies arise where there is asymmetric information, monopoly power, externalities and public goods. These are now discussed briefly.

---

[1] This is referred to in standard microeconomic textbooks as allocative efficiency or Pareto optimality.

- *Asymmetric information.* Asymmetric information can arise when buyers and sellers have access to varying degrees of information. Akerlof (1970) argued that when buyers have less information than sellers in the secondhand car market, a situation may arise when only lower-quality products will be traded. To protect consumers, regulations can be passed which require various forms of licensing and certification whereby car sellers offer guarantees and warranties on cars sold. This sends an important signal to prospective buyers as to the quality of products they are about to purchase. Stigler (1961) argued that prices are likely to be more dispersed if consumers do not have access to information regarding the quality and prices of products available to them. In this case, there could be a role for government intervention to encourage information flows about product prices. For example, the removal of restrictions on advertising may give consumers more information in making optimal resource choices.[2]

- *Monopoly power.* As we saw in Chapter 11, under perfect competition firms set prices equal to marginal costs, and output is at a level where all resources are fully utilised. At this level of output no individual can be made better off by increasing output without making someone else worse off. If all industries operate under conditions of perfect competition then there is allocative efficiency. At the other end of the competitive spectrum, the monopolist restricts output and prices products above marginal costs, thus leading to a waste of resources. This distortion in resource allocation may lead to consumer welfare losses. Regulation is therefore required to stop or curb monopoly power.

- *Externalities.* Regulation is often required when externalities in production and consumption exist. An externality exists when additional benefits or costs are incurred by society outside those incurred by the buyer or seller of a product. The consequence is that the true costs of production are not realised. For example, the sale of petrol may impose an externality in the form of pollution on society. However, this would not be a cost which would be borne directly by the producer or consumer of the petrol. If externalities are negative, this is likely to lead to firms producing more of these products than would be the case if the true costs were realised for the product. On the other hand, if externalities are positive (such as the benefits accruing to society from expenditures on research and development and training), firms would produce less than if the true benefits were realised. This then leads to a misallocation of resources in the economy. There is, therefore, a role for governments to impose taxes and other forms of penalty on producers of goods and services that result in negative externalities and reward producers of goods and services that lead to positive externalities. Overall, allocative efficiency exists only if resources are allocated to take into account any externalities.

- *Public goods.* Some goods have characteristics that make it difficult for a direct price to be charged for them, since no consumer can be excluded from the benefit. Such goods are known as public goods. These types of good can be consumed by many consumers without excluding other consumers. Examples of public goods include police and fire protection and streetlighting. To charge a direct price for these services may lead to a free-rider effect, whereby some consumers can receive the benefits of public good provision without paying for them. As a consequence, private firms would generally be unwilling to provide these goods. Governments are often left to intervene in the markets for these types of product and service markets.

---

[2] This is discussed in Chapter 7.

In this chapter we focus on the ways in which regulation is carried out by government in response to various market failures. In particular, the chapter examines the relative merits of organising production in the private and public sectors when industries are characterised by natural monopoly. The advantages of public sector production include the elimination of wasteful competition and the subsequent achievement of economies of scale and scope. However, under public sector production, firms often lack competitive pressure, which may lead to inefficiencies of management and poor performance. By organising production in the private sector, firms are subject to competitive pressure from product and capital markets leading to increases in efficiency and improvements in performance. However, this may lead to problems as monopolies are transferred form public to private control. If competition is introduced there may be a loss of economies of scale and scope. This means that, in these industries, regulation must be provided to increase competition. Alternatively, competition can be created prior to the transfer of monopoly from public to private hands by encouraging firms to compete for franchises, which give these firms the monopoly rights.

The chapter is organised as follows. Section 12.2 examines natural monopolies and discusses the arguments for public ownership, proposing that nationalisation eliminates wasteful competition and achieves economies of scale and scope, and in many cases provides services which would otherwise be deemed uneconomic in the private sector. Section 12.3 examines the disadvantages of nationalisation. These disadvantages relate to the structure of ownership, control and performance of these industries caused by excessive interference by governments. Section 12.3 also examines the process of privatisation in the UK and the performance of these industries. Section 12.4 examines the type of regulation used to control natural monopolies. The approaches to regulation in the United States and UK are examined. We also discuss briefly the record of regulation since the privatisation of the telecommunications, electricity, gas and water industries in the UK. Section 12.5 examines franchising. This is a policy whereby services carried out by the public sector are franchised to private contractors. In the UK, this policy is aimed at increasing competition in certain industries by encouraging firms to bid for contracts and licences.

12.2 Natural monopoly and public ownership

One of the arguments for public control of industry revolves around the assertion that some industries are natural monopolies. A **natural monopoly** exists when efficient production can exist only if the industry production is concentrated in the hands of one firm. In this case the minimum efficient scale of production is almost equal to, or equals, the market size. Under natural monopoly, economies of scale are available over a wide range of output (Waterson, 1987). Natural monopolies involve high levels of fixed (sunk) costs. We can consider natural monopoly via Figure 12.1.

In Figure 12.1, if the monopoly is in private hands, the monopolist maximises profits where marginal costs equal marginal revenues and produces at output level Q_m and charges price P_m. The monopolist makes excess profits equal to the shaded area. If the firm were forced to charge a price that would prevail under competition, it would set price equal to marginal costs and produce at output level Q_c. At this output level the firm would make losses given that AR < AC. This could be solved in two ways. Firstly, the government could pay the firm a subsidy equal to the losses incurred at output level Q_c. This is shown in

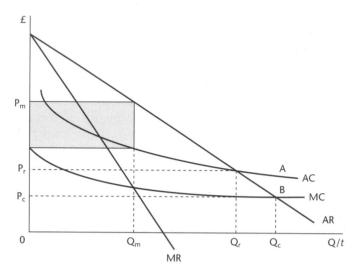

Figure 12.1 Pricing under natural monopoly

Figure 12.1 as the distance between points A (AC) and B (AR). Alternatively, governments could allow the firm to charge a price where normal profits are made. Thus the firm would produce at output level Q_r and charge a price of P_r. P_r is the price that maximises consumer welfare subject to the constraint that the firm must make normal profits. In this case, production is efficient in the hands of a single firm. The entry of new firms could lead to inefficiencies. For example, suppose we have a water company which supplies a certain part of the country through a network of pipes. It would be inefficient for a new firm to enter the market, set up its own system of pipes and then start supplying a segment of the market because the level of output the firm produces would yield insufficient revenue to cover total costs. In essence, natural monopolies may lead to wasteful competition through an unnecessary duplication of services. Ogus (1996, p.265) noted of the UK that: 'a degree of scepticism of the merits of competition developed, particularly in relation to water and gas, as the duplication of facilities funded by major capital outlays and often surplus capacity, was perceived to be wasteful.'

Regulation is important in cases of natural monopoly, as increased competition would lead to a decline in the monopolist's market share and subsequently affect the firm's ability to exploit all available economies of scale (Waterson, 1987). Regulation is also important in ensuring that the monopolist does not abuse its monopoly power.[3] However, under

---

[3] In the case of some natural monopolies that offer many types of good and service, cross-subsidisation takes place, whereby the monopolist subsidises loss-making activities with proceeds from profitable ones. This has been the case in the UK, where many services were provided by utilities at below-cost. As a consequence, any increases in competition will only target the profitable parts of the market. This is known as cream-skimming, whereby new entrants only compete in profitable parts of the market. The established monopolist is then left to service unprofitable parts of the market. Therefore any regulation must take account of these imperfections. The successful introduction of competition may lessen this problem as firms strive to increase their internal efficiency. If this happens, loss-making activities may become profitable.

certain circumstances, competition may be desirable under conditions of natural monopoly. In industries where sunk costs are low and entry and exit from the market is free, the mere threat of competition by rivals is enough to constrain the established firm's pricing behaviour. Baumol *et al.* (1982) argued that natural monopoly markets can often be regarded as perfectly contestable. In such a market, firms will actively set prices equal to average costs and make normal profits. This would deter entry of any rival firms.

There are several solutions to the natural monopoly problem. These include public ownership which normally involves granting statutory rights to a single firm. This ensures that products are priced in a reasonably competitive manner. Another solution is to allow temporary monopoly rights through the granting of a franchise. In this case, competition only takes place prior to the award of the franchise, as firms have to bid for these rights in an auction. A final solution would be to open the industry to competition. This has been done in many countries (particularly the UK) through the privatisation of nationalised industries, whereby state-owned assets are transferred to the private sector. However, this can often lead to monopoly power resting in private hands. As a result, this is often accompanied by increased regulation.

Ogus (1996, p.5) summed up the merits of these three approaches when he argued:

> First, the firm can be publicly owned . . . , the expectation being that the mechanics of political direction and accountability will be sufficient to meet public interest goals. Secondly, the firm may remain in, or be transferred to, private ownership but be subjected to external constraints in the form of price and quality regulation . . . Thirdly, firms desiring to obtain a monopoly right may be forced to compete for it . . . As part of their competitive bid, they are required to stipulate proposed conditions of supply, relating especially to prices and quality; and those conditions then become terms of the licence or franchise under which they exercise the monopoly right.

We examine each of these solutions to the natural monopoly problem. The rest of this section examines nationalisation.

Nationalisation normally means that an industry is a statutory monopoly owned and controlled by the government. This means that competition is prohibited. New firms cannot enter the market and compete with the established monopolist. Domberger and Piggot (1986) argued that public ownership is necessary in the case of natural monopoly. In this case the government instructs firms to follow certain objectives with the overall aim of correcting market failures associated with monopoly power, externalities and asymmetric information, thereby satisfying the necessary conditions for allocative efficiency. In reality, it is difficult to achieve allocative efficiency given that the natural monopolist will make losses when prices are set equal to marginal costs. As a consequence, 'second best' policies are pursued where firms either set prices equal to average costs or receive government subsidies.[4] Overall, nationalisation eliminates wasteful competition and achieves economies of scale. Nationalised industries also meet 'social' obligations by providing services which would otherwise be deemed uneconomic in the private sector, for example, telephone services to rural areas. Morrison (1933) argued that nationalised industries should not have commercial objectives, and should only pursue strategies that operate in the public interest.

---

[4] For a full discussion of second-best policies see Lipsey and Lancaster (1956).

Inherent problems exist in the public provision of goods and services. Nationalised industries are protected from competition. This means there is little threat of bankruptcy as any losses will be offset by government subsidy. Therefore, there is little incentive to be efficient given that managers' pay is not linked to performance. Nationalised industries are also protected from takeover. Traditionally, there has been conflict between political and economic objectives. Nationalised industries may be instructed to follow non-commercial objectives to aid government policies of employment, procurement and trade. Foster (1992) noted that the political objectives of nationalised industries far outweighed any object-ives designed to achieve economic efficiency, while Rees (1984) argued that nationalised industries' attempts to pursue commercial objectives were stifled by the power of trade unions.

Nationalised industries' performance has been criticised extensively by Bos (1991), who suggested that poor performance was caused by imperfections in the structure of owner-ship, control and performance of these industries, for example the financial constraints on borrowing and investment, the incentives for efficient performance for nationalised indus-tries, the lack of clarity in the objectives, excessive interference by governments and the imposition of inappropriate objectives. These problems had led authors to contend that the performance of nationalised industries was poor, though the empirical evidence has been mixed. A selection of these studies is now discussed briefly.

Pryke (1981) examined the performance of nationalised industries and concluded that they were third rate. He examined trends in productivity performance for a sample of nine nationalised industries over the period 1968 to 1978. In industries subject to technological change such as airlines and telecoms, productivity (measured as percentage change in labour or total factor productivity) increased. Smaller increases were found for gas and electricity. However, performance of steel, coal, postal services and bus and rail declined over this period. Pryke (1982) carried out a similar study examining the productivity and profitability per-formance of selected nationalised industries. He (p.81) concluded that:

> What public ownership does is to eliminate the threat of takeover and ultimately of bankruptcy and the need which all private undertakings have from time to time, to raise money from the market. Public ownership provides a comfortable life and destroys commercial ethic . . .

Molyneux and Thompson (1987) updated the Pryke studies for the period 1978 to 1985 and found an increase in productivity for all nine nationalised industries. They attributed these improvements to greater flexibility in the workforce, tighter controls over subsidy to industry which had encouraged more efficiency across industry, increased investment, technology improvements, rationalisation and learning economies of scale. Millward (1990) compared the productivity of nationalised firms with private counterparts in the gas, electricity, water and transport industries. Over the period 1950 to 1986, he found that publicly owned firms increased their productivity faster than their private counterparts in many cases. Finally, Lynk (1993) examined differences in the efficiency of private and state-owned water companies before privatisation in 1989. He found that publicly owned water companies were more efficient than their private counterparts. Overall, the empirical evidence reviewed above provides a mixed view of the efficiency and performance of nationalised industries.

12.3 Privatisation

In this section, we discuss **privatisation**: in particular, the process of privatisation within the UK, and the subsequent performance of these enterprises. We can split privatisation into three types of policy: denationalisation, deregulation and franchising.

- *Denationalisation.* This involves the transfer and sale of assets from the public to the private sector (Wright, 2000). Examples have been telecoms, water, gas and electricity. This transfer of assets from the public to private sector may or may not be accompanied by a process of deregulation (or liberalisation).
- *Deregulation.* The process of deregulation (often referred to as liberalisation) comprises government policies aimed at increasing competition in any given industry (Winston, 1993). This often involves policies aimed at altering the structure of the industry by encouraging the entry of new firms. However, this is often accompanied by a process of reregulation of the industry which is aimed at controlling how these new entrants behave. Advantages of deregulation are that inefficient organisations that were previously protected from entry would be eliminated and successful groups, which had benefited from regulation, would no longer hold these advantages in a competitive market.
- *Franchising.* This is a policy whereby services carried out by the public sector are franchised to private contractors (often referred to as contracting out). This policy has been used in industries where direct competition has been deemed impossible or undesirable. In the UK, examples of this are local bus services and operators of commercial train passenger services. The overall aim is to increase competition indirectly by encouraging firms to bid for contracts and licences to offer certain goods and services.

A process of denationalisation has taken place in the UK since 1980, as successive Conservative governments of 1979 to 1997 embarked on a process of privatisation. Politically, these governments argued that by pursuing a policy of denationalisation they could increase share ownership,[5] finance tax cuts and promote economic policies aimed at the supply side of the economy. These policies were aimed at curbing trade union power and increasing flexibility in the labour market. Generally under any process of privatisation the government tended to break up industries into component parts. Industries where competition is not feasible (such as rail networks) have been heavily regulated by government. In contrast, a process of deregulation has taken place in areas where competition was prevalent (for example the provision of mobile phone services). These are now discussed briefly. Table 12.1 shows a selection of UK privatisations.

In this section, we examine the arguments for and against privatisation. We also examine the performance of firms prior to and since privatisation. The rationale for privatisation generally centres around the positive effects which competition exerts on the behaviour and performance of firms. In other words, by introducing competition, firms are more likely to follow strategies aimed at minimising costs and maximising profits. Many authors argued that privatisation leads to productive efficiency. Several arguments have been forwarded in favour of privatisation. These are now discussed in turn.

---

[5] Fraser (1988) noted that between 1979 and 1988, the proportion of adults in the UK owning shares increased from 7 per cent to 21 per cent.

Table 12.1 ● Selected UK privatisation by industry and year of first sale

Enterprise	Industry	Year privatised
British Aerospace	Aerospace	1981
Cable & Wireless	Telecommunications	1981
Britoil	Oil	1982
National Freight Corporation	Transport	1982
Associated British Ports	Ports	1983
British Telecom	Telecommunications	1984
British Leyland (Austin–Rover)	Cars	1984
Jaguar	Cars	1984
British Gas	Gas	1986
National Bus Company	Buses	1986
British Airports Authority	Airports	1987
British Airways	Airlines	1987
British Steel	Steel	1988
Water authorities (10 companies)	Water	1989
Electricity distribution (12 companies)	Electricity	1990
Electricity generation	Electricity	1991
British Rail (Railtrack)	Railways	1995
British Energy	Nuclear energy	1996

Arguments in favour of privatisation

Increased competition in product and service markets

The privatisation of industries has often been accompanied by increased competition. The introduction of market forces leads companies to pursue strategies aimed at improving efficiency (Moore, 1983). For example, firms are more likely to search for efficient sources of supply and to utilise existing factors of production more effectively. The competitive pressures also lead to the elimination of x-inefficiencies. Firms that are successful in the new competitive environment grow quickly and find it easier to raise finance from capital markets. Overall, the increased competition is likely to lead to a reduction in prices and a wider choice of products and services available to consumers.

Increased discipline of capital markets

Under privatisation, management is likely to become more efficient and search for more profitable opportunities. Privatisation by invoking market forces will lead to less bureaucracy, waste and inefficiency (see above). It also leads to an increase in capital market incentives for managers and firms to perform well. These incentives can be examined with reference to principal–agent theory, and from this theoretical framework, the implications of the separation of ownership from control for the efficiency and performance of privatised industries.

In the case of privatised industries, the principal is the shareholder whilst the manager is the agent. Incentives exist for managers to perform well given that they are likely to be rewarded for success, but punished for failure. In contrast, in the nationalised industry, the principal is the government, while the agent is the manager. However, this time the relationship is facilitated through a complex hierarchy. This hierarchy often makes communication difficult between agent and principal, and distortions can take place in the transmission of information. Given that the manager of the firm is protected from competition and takeover by other firms, there is little incentive for the manager to perform well. Therefore, if competition accompanies privatisation, then the performance of privately owned enterprises is likely to exceed that of their public counterparts. If privatised firms are owned by private individuals there is greater accountability of management to shareholders. Evidence also suggests that there is a strong correlation between managers' salaries and firm performance. There is thus an incentive for managers to perform well. The performance of privatised firms will ultimately affect the share price of these firms. If share prices fall, then takeover may take place. For example, by the end of 1997, ten of twelve privatised regional electricity distribution firms had been acquired by domestic or foreign rivals (Helm and Jenkinson, 1997). Therefore, the takeover threat acts as a spur to the managers of privatised firms to be efficient. In fact, it is possible that privatised firms can go bankrupt.

Reduction in government borrowing
The policy of privatisation in the UK had the effect of reducing the economy's debt. Over the 1980s, the UK government, in contrast to many other developed countries, reduced its borrowings and repaid a portion of the national debt. Foster (1992) noted that the borrowing requirements of nationalised industries declined from £1.1 billion in 1984 to a surplus of £1.35 billion in 1987. This reduced the public sector borrowing requirement (PSBR) by decreasing the reliance of industry on government funding. Successive UK governments cut subsidies to what were once loss-making industries, while at the same time reducing the PSBR. Helm and Jenkinson (1997) noted that assets exceeding £100 billion had been transferred from public to private ownership through the UK government's policy of privatisation.

Reduction in government controls
Privatisation leads to a reduction in the control which governments exercise over the strategies of nationalised industries (Moore, 1983). Firms are freed from the constraints imposed by government controls and pursue policies aimed at maximising profits. These firms are more likely to have clearly defined profit objectives. For example, managers are freer to pursue market strategies instead of carrying out directives, and privatised firms can access sources of finance (via capital markets) that were previously closed to them. However, firms may not follow strategies aimed at maximising profits: they may instead pursue objectives aimed at maximising size, growth or managerial satisfaction.

Domberger and Piggott (1986, p.150) argued that:

> Efficiency gains from privatisation arise essentially out of the interaction of product and capital market pressures. Competition in product markets means that the persistent underperformance will ultimately lead to bankruptcy. Competitive capital markets mean that if management is not successful in averting a downward performance trend, it will be displaced through takeover well before the company has reached the point of no return.

There are however several arguments against privatisation. These are now discussed briefly.

Arguments against privatisation

Natural monopolies versus private monopolies

The process of privatisation may lead to the transfer of monopoly from public to private ownership. This may leave the privatised firms free to exploit monopoly power. This creates the problem of how best to regulate against private monopoly.[6]

Short-termism

The policy of selling public enterprises has been seen as a short-term measure to lessen the financial burden of government involvement in industry. However, in many cases these short-term gains in lower subsidies and increased revenues from selling these industries may be offset in the longer term by losing the profit-making potential of these enterprises.

Economies of scale and scope may be lost

If privatisation is accompanied by the break-up of monopolies into smaller components, then there may be a reduction in the extent to which firms can achieve the economies of scale and scope under monopoly. This means that costs may increase after privatisation.

Difficulties in introducing competition

By privatising industries, competition should increase, thereby making industries more contestable. However, the extent to which privatised industries can be regarded as contestable is questionable. Competition is only desirable if the costs of natural monopoly eventually increase over some range of output. If this is not the case, then competition may be wasteful. For example, the introduction of competition when there is monopoly control of a network, as is the case for railways, may be difficult.

The success or otherwise of privatisation can be assessed by examining the efficiency and performance of privatised firms. A substantial literature now exists which examines this issue. Yarrow (1986, 1989), using a sample of seven privatised firms, examined changes in performance and productivity. The sample comprised Cable & Wireless, National Freight Corporation, Associated British Ports, Britoil, Jaguar and British Airways. He found that productivity and profitability increased in only three of the seven cases sampled (Associated British Ports, Cable & Wireless, and the National Freight Corporation). However, Estrin and Perotin (1991) observed that in France and the UK, there was no substantial difference in the performance of firms in public and private hands.

Parker (1991) examined the performance of five privatised firms over the period 1987 to 1990. The sample consisted of British Gas, British Telecom, Rolls-Royce, Associated British Ports, Jaguar and Enterprise Oil. The performance measures used were profitability (calculated as a return on capital) and productivity (calculated as sales per employee and the number of workers employed). Parker found that profitability increased for British Gas, British Telecom and Rolls-Royce, but declined for Associated British Ports, Jaguar and Enterprise Oil. Productivity was found to increase for British Gas, British Telecom, Associated British Ports and Jaguar, but declined for Rolls-Royce and Enterprise Oil. The number

---

[6] Chapter 11 provides a detailed discussion of the UK, US and European approaches to monopoly policy.

of employees fell for British Gas and Associated British Ports, but increased for British Telecom, Rolls-Royce, Jaguar and Enterprise Oil.

Bishop and Thompson (1992) used a sample of nine industries to examine changes in productivity and profitability over the period 1970 to 1990.[7] They found that productivity and profitability improved over the period 1970 to 1990, and that this growth was strongest in the 1980s. However, the authors found no substantial evidence that privatisation had any effect on firm efficiency and profitability.

Price and Weyman-Jones (1993) examined differences in efficiency of British Gas over the periods 1977 to 1978 and 1990 to 1991. The data were split into twelve geographical areas covered by British Gas's distribution network. The authors found that the company's productivity improved after privatisation.

Parker (1994) examined the effects of privatisation on the performance of BT (formerly British Telecom) over the period 1984 to 1994. The author employed a number of performance indicators to examine the changes in prices charged, quality of services offered, employment levels, research and development activity, and productivity. He found that prices charged fell on average by 11 per cent over the period examined, but that there was a wide dispersion in these averages. The reliability of network equipment and quality of installation improved. Employment increased during the latter part of the 1980s in an attempt to improve service quality, but had since declined in an attempt to realise efficiencies. Profits measured (as percentage return on capital) increased from 18.3 per cent to 20.7 per cent post-privatisation. Research and development was found to decline, which was a result of short-term competitive pressures on BT to maximise profits. Labour productivity improved, but the productivity of other factors of production was found to decline. Parker (p.108) concluded that:

> [N]oteworthy gains have been achieved by BT in terms of service, overall prices, profitability and labour productivity since privatisation. However, it is important to treat these results with some caution. In reviewing BT's restructuring and performance over the past ten years, it is not possible to say with certainty that the same changes would not have occurred had BT remained state owned.

Parker and Martin (1995) analysed the change in productivity performance of eleven privatised firms by comparing productivity changes over time. The authors measured performance by changes in labour and total factor productivity. Labour productivity was measured by changes in an individual firm's output in response to changes in labour inputs. Total factor productivity was measured by changes in an individual firm's output in response to changes in various inputs, including capital, raw materials, energy and labour. The authors split the periods under investigation into several stages which captured the firm's performance during nationalisation, the period directly before privatisation, a period post-privatisation and a period of recession. They argued that these stages should capture any trends in performance and reduce the influence of performance in any year, which could be regarded as unrepresentative. In general, the authors found that there was a substantial improvement in the performance of most of the firms considered in the lead-up to privatisation. However, performance did not always improve. This was especially true if a

---

[7] The industries and firms sampled comprised British Airports Authority, British Airways, British Telecom, British Coal, electricity supply, British Gas, Post Office, British Rail and British Steel.

recession took place, where competition was intense or where there was under investment in the firm's capital assets.

Parker and Wu (1998) used data covering the period 1979 to 1994 to assess the performance of British Steel before and after privatisation in 1988. The performance measures used were labour and total factor productivity and profits. The authors found an improvement in all performance measures before privatisation, but that these improvements slowed considerably after 1988.

Parker and Wu also examined the efficiency of British Steel against the steel industries of Australia, Canada, France, Germany, Japan and the United States over the sample period. They found that, prior to privatisation, British Steel was more efficient than its French, German and US counterparts, but this was reversed by the early 1990s. The authors concluded that:

> [T]he results suggest that British Steel achieved considerable efficiency gains in the years immediately before privatisation. One interpretation is that the prospect of privatisation spurred management to improve performance. An alternative interpretation is that major efficiency gains can occur under state ownership, given a government and management determined to bring about change.[8]

Borcherding *et al.* (1982) examined the results of studies, which compared the performance of public and privatised industries.[9] The survey analysed the results of 52 studies on the efficiency of public and private enterprises in the United States, Germany, France, Canada and Australia. The industries studied included airlines, banks, bus services, cleaning services, debt collection, electricity, fire protection, forestry, hospitals, housing, insurance sales and claims, railroads, refuse collection, water and weather forecasting. Borcherding *et al.* found that private enterprises outperformed their public counterparts in 43 of the 52 studies sampled. These findings were confirmed in a separate study by Megginson *et al.* (1994) which used data from eighteen countries to examine the performance of privatised firms. In most cases the authors found that privatisation led to increased investment expenditures, lower costs and higher profitability than was the case under public ownership.

Overall, the empirical evidence reviewed suggests that the efficiency and profitability of firms improved after privatisation. However, it is unclear whether these improvements would have taken place anyway without the transfer of assets from the public to the private sector.

12.4 Regulation of utilities

Privatisation is likely to lead to incentives for firms to pursue productive efficiency. However, this will not ensure allocative efficiency unless regulation is introduced to ensure that competition takes place. Another policy would be to pursue a policy of deregulation, for example by removing entry barriers to encourage increased competition. Once an industry is privatised, government no longer has direct control over the objectives and strategies of these firms. As a consequence there is a need for regulation.

---

[8] Parker and Wu (1998), p.45.
[9] Boardman and Vining (1989) provide additional evidence.

In the United States, there has been a long tradition of utility regulation as these types of industry have been in private hands for long periods of time. In the UK, the regulation of utilities is a much more recent phenomenon. Helm (1994) noted that the state has moved from being primarily concerned with production to being primarily concerned with regulation. He argued that intervention by the government is only efficient if the benefits derived from intervention exceed the costs of market failures in any given industry.

Kay and Vickers (1990) characterised the regulatory process in the context of principal–agent theory. In this case, regulators can be regarded as the principal who has a given set of objectives which it wants to achieve. The firm in this case is the agent who should carry out the principal's instructions to meet the required objectives. However, two problems occur here:

● The agent is likely to have different objectives from those of the principal. In addition, the agent has more information about the industry than the regulator. If this is the case the principal will find it difficult to construct a framework to ensure that its objectives are met.
● Over time, the regulator's objectives are influenced and altered by the actions of the firms, which ultimately may lead to the regulator representing the interests of the industry and not the consumer. Stigler (1971) and Peltzman (1976) argued that regulation actually created market inefficiencies rather than solved them. The regulated firms are more organised than the consumers that the regulators represent. As a consequence they have the power to lobby the regulator more effectively. This may lead in the longer term to **regulatory capture**.

Two types of regulation are open to policy-makers: structural and conduct regulation. Structural regulation seeks to alter or maintain the structure of a given industry. Measures include the functional separation of firms into different activities (electricity generators and distributors), entry restrictions and rules regarding the operation of foreign firms. Structural regulation is likely to make entry into industries difficult. This type of regulation may protect established firms from competitive pressures. In contrast, conduct regulation attempts to alter the behaviour of firms by controlling the extent of individual firm strategies. These controls can restrict the levels of prices charged, regulate fees and commissions charged, the extent of advertising and research and development expenditures, and restrict the rate at which firms can expand their distribution networks. Kay and Vickers (1990, p.233) argued of structural and conduct regulation that: 'The former aims to create a situation in which the incentives or opportunities for undesirable behaviour are removed, while the latter addresses not the underlying incentives, but the behaviour that they would otherwise induce.'

For effective regulation, the regulator needs information on future changes in costs and market conditions. In a stable market this task is relatively straightforward. In a dynamic market, where market conditions are changing constantly, it may be difficult to build up a detailed picture. Regulators attempt to balance the need to promote competition by encouraging new entry, while at the same time regulating prices to ensure that shareholders receive a reasonable return on capital invested. The main types of regulation carried out in the United States and UK can be characterised as **rate of return** and **price cap regulation**, respectively. We now briefly discuss regulation in these two countries.

Rate of return (or cost-plus regulation)

In the United States, the main type of regulation that has taken place is commonly known as rate of return regulation. In this case the regulator fixes a required rate of return on capital (R*) which can be expressed as:

$$R^* = \frac{\text{Total revenues} - \text{Total costs}}{\text{Capital employed}}$$

Firms operating under this type of regime are guaranteed the required rate of return. The regulator allows the utility to set a price which covers costs and allows the firm a mark-up to give the firm a 'fair' rate of return. This return is an amount that allows the firm to cover costs, attract new investment from shareholders and to replace and update capital equipment. Under this type of regulation, price reviews can be frequent. Therefore, it is more likely that a relationship between regulator and firms can build over time. As a consequence, there is a danger of regulatory capture.

One of the main problems with this type of regulation is that there is no incentive for firms to minimise costs, given that the rate of return on assets is fixed. As a consequence, managers of firms may seek to maxmise their own utility by excessive spending on pet projects. If costs were to rise, the firm's return on capital employed will fall below the target set by the regulator. If this is the case, the firm must apply to the regulator to increase prices so that it once again makes the required rate of return. US regulators have sought to address this problem by imposing a lag between when firms request a change in price and when the change actually takes place. In this case if costs increase, firms will make returns less than the required rate for the period until the application to increase prices has taken place. In contrast, if costs were to decline, then firms will make a rate of return exceeding the required rate for a period until the next price review. If a regulatory lag is imposed there is then an indirect incentive for firms to minimise costs.

A second problem with this type of regulation is that if the required rate of return is set at a wrong level it can encourage firms to either over- or underinvest in assets. This has become known as the Averch–Johnson effect (Averch and Johnson, 1962). For example, if the rate of return is set too high it encourages firms to overinvest in capital assets or to use capital-intensive methods. In this case the greater the firm's investment in capital assets the greater the profits must be in order to meet the required rate of return, given that the capital base is now increased. If firms then overinvest in capital assets they are unlikely to record profits in excess of the required rate of return. Klevonich (1966) argued that this problem of overinvestment can be overcome by reducing the rate of return in cases where the firm's capital base was increased dramatically. However, Sherman (1985) contended that this would merely introduce other distortions into the way in which firms employ their factors of production. In contrast, if rates are set too low, firms seek to make savings (by reducing the quality of their inputs or outputs), in order to meet the required rate of return.

A third problem is that regulators find it difficult to calculate capital. Valuing capital is often problematic. Should the firms' capital be valued on a historical cost basis or should it be calculated as the replacement cost of assets? As a consequence the required rate of return is likely to vary depending on which approach is used.

Price cap regulation

In the UK, the main type of regulation used is price cap regulation. This regulation places a limit on the prices that firms can charge. In the UK, this has generally been of the form 'RPI minus an X factor', where RPI denotes the retail price index and is a measure of inflation, whilst X is the amount by which the regulators feel that productivity gains can be made and thus costs reduced. In this case, the regulator would fix the X factor based on the expected productivity gains in an industry over a given period. The formula would work in the following way. Suppose that inflation in a given period was expected to be 5 per cent, and that the industry was expected to make productivity gains of 3 per cent over this period. This would mean that firms in the industry could only increase prices by 2 per cent. This type of regulation is, therefore, designed to make sure that any cost savings are passed on to consumers in the form of lower prices. There is an incentive for the firm to seek to minimise costs still further as it will be allowed to keep any additional cost savings, this boosting profitability. However, the regulator may increase the X factor in response to public pressure when privatised industries make higher than expected profits. In the UK, price caps are generally reviewed every four or five years.

The value of the X factor depends on several factors, including the cost and structure of a firm's asset base, expected efficiency gains through enhanced productivity and the extent to which industry demand is expected to increase or decrease, future investment plans and the likely effects that any regulation is likely to have on competition within the industry. If a natural monopoly is broken up into smaller components, competition will increase. The increased competition can be used as a yardstick and makes it easier for regulators to set price cap legislation.[10] Future caps can be based on RPI – X, which is calculated by examining trends in costs general to the economy (employing estimation techniques), costs of capital and valuing assets. Key components of any price cap include operating and capital expenditure valuation, cost of capital valuation and asset valuation.

The X factor is the perceived scope for the firm to lower costs over the period of the price cap. If the price is set too high (i.e. X is low), firms make excess profits. However, if prices are set at too low a level this is likely to lead to firms facing difficulties in breaking even. Any increase or decrease in a firm's costs caused by changes in the general economic conditions is offset by linking these costs to the level of inflation. If the firm makes cost savings greater than the imposed X factor, it is allowed to keep these savings for the length of time the price cap is imposed. This type of regulation has several associated advantages, including that it is less vulnerable to cost inefficiency (as firms are allowed to keep any cost savings). It also allows multi-product firms to alter prices for individual products as long as the price charged corresponds to the average allowable price increase under regulation. However, there are associated problems in setting X.

The initial value of X is set at the time of privatisation when the government still owns the firm. In this case X is likely to be set in the interests of consumers, given that governments are generally assumed to have the objective of maximising consumer welfare. After privatisation, the regulator must balance the interests of consumers (by encouraging firms to charge low prices) with those of investors (by allowing shareholders in the newly privatised firm to make a reasonable rate of return).

[10] Shleifer (1985) provides a full discussion of the theory of yardstick competition.

Beesley and Littlechild (1997) argued that there are several differences between RPI – X and the US-style rate of return regulation. These are:

● If X is set for a defined period then the firms face some degree of risk over that period. In contrast, under rate of return regulation the firm can apply for a price review if its rate of return falls below that of the required rate.

● Calculations for rate of return regulations are based on historic costs, revenues and capital valuations. The RPI – X formula takes account of the firm's future trading conditions by building in potential efficiency gains to the pricing formula. This means that it is possible for firms to make efficiency gains that exceed the X factor, which they can appropriate over the length of the price cap.

● Given that the RPI – X formula is based on expected efficiency, the firm's cost of capital and future investment plans, it gives the regulator some discretion in adjusting any of the variables thought to affect X.

● In some cases, the levels of RPI – X tend to be set without widespread consultation. This contrasts with the US approach where legalistic and economic reasons must always justify the reasons for any given level of price.

● Prices can change for individual products under the RPI – X approach as long as the average price of the firm's portfolio of products meets the price cap. This contrasts with the US rate of return regulation where the price of each individual product would have to be approved.

Beesley and Littlechild (1997) argued that industries where technology is changing quickly are more suited to the application of the RPI – X formula. This is because there is scope for more productivity improvements in these industries.

The rationale for this type of regulation arose from the work of Littlechild (1983) on the UK telecommunications industry. Littlechild analysed five possible types of regulation for the industry. These were: to have no interference, rate of return regulation (as in the United States), impositions of profit ceilings, an output related profit levy[11] and the RPI – X formula. Each of these possibilities was analysed as to its effectiveness against the following criteria:

● To protect consumers against monopoly
● Encourage competition and efficiency
● Ease of regulation
● Ability to promote competition

The study compared the five types of regulatory regime and found that the RPI – X regime was the most effective. As a consequence, this type of regulation was extended to other UK industries as they were privatised.

The advantage of this system is that it allows firms that produce many products some discretion over the prices they charge for individual products as long as the average price

[11] The output related profits levy was based on an inverse relationship between tax and output. If firms produced at low output levels they were unlikely to be operating at the industry minimum efficient scale and would thus be inefficient. In such cases the level of tax on profits was to be high. However, if firms expanded output to achieve efficiency gains, taxes would be charged on profits at a lower rate.

of these products does not exceed the price cap. Littlechild (1983) argued that this has cut down many of the administration costs of regulation which would otherwise have been incurred if all product prices were regulated individually.

There are several associated advantages of price cap regulation. These are:

- It is less open to x-inefficiency than rate of return regulation. This is because firms that make productivity gains can keep these savings and boost profitability.
- Firms do not overinvest in capital assets.
- Multi-product firms can vary prices within their portfolio of products as long as the average price corresponds with the price cap.
- The formula is relatively simple to operate and is transparent to consumers.

The disadvantages of the system are that:

- If the X factor is set too low, firms make supernormal profits.
- There may be a danger of regulatory capture. However, this is less likely than under rate of return regulation, as the information requirements of regulators are less onerous.
- Regulation is often complicated in industries where market conditions are changing quickly. This could lead to uncertainties in firms' planning of future investment programmes and non-price strategies.

Price caps vary from industry to industry depending on the structure and behaviour of firms in that industry. In industries such as telecommunications, firms can vary the price of individual services as long as their overall service provision meets the price cap. Armstrong *et al.* (1994, p.168) note that: 'The price cap applies to an average of prices if the firm sells multiple products, and the firm is usually allowed some freedom to alter relative prices within the overall constraint.'

If the costs were to rise substantially firms would be unable to meet the price cap. If this were the case, regulators could allow some of these costs to be passed through to prices charged to consumers. Alternatively they could reduce the number of years between price review (regulatory lag).

Regulatory lag tends to be much larger under RPI – X regulation than under rate of return regulation. This provides an incentive to firms to drive for efficiency gains. However, this may have negative effects on consumer welfare as efficiency gains are not passed on to consumers in the form of lower-priced products. The regulation has to balance the interests of firms with those of consumers.

In addition to price cap regulation, there has been an increased need for regulation of product quality. This is because quality may suffer as firms strive for efficiency gains. Some attempt was made to introduce quality regulation by the Competition and Service Utilities Act 1992.

In the UK, separate Acts of Parliament have created a number of agencies to regulate privatised industries. There now exist offices for regulation of telecommunications, gas, electricity, water and railways.[12]

The President of the Department of Trade and Industry and the secretary of state for the environment grants firms operating licences (for electricity, gas, telecommunications

---

[12] OFTEL for telecommunications, OFGAS for gas, OFFER for electricity, OFWAT for water, ORR for railways. In 1998, OFGAS and OFFER were subsumed under a new office known as OFGEM.

and water) which outline general guidelines to which firms must adhere. The regulators have varying degrees of power. In general they are responsible for collecting and publishing information on competitive conditions in a given industry, advising the Office of Fair Trading and the Competition Commission of any abuses of market power or the existence of anti-competitive practices, and enforcing competition law. The regulators are also responsible for setting price and quality levels and investigating complaints. They also have the right to alter conditions of licences granted to certain companies. The Competition Commission and various parliamentary select committees reporting to parliament oversee the overall activities of each regulator. These bodies can make rulings in cases where disputes arise between the regulator and a privatised firm.[13]

Helm and Jenkinson (1997) described the UK approach to regulation as one of contracts and discretion. Contracts exist as utilities are given licences and instructed to operate within price and quality guidelines imposed by the regulator. Discretion exists as regulators have the power to intervene in these markets to ensure that competition prevails.

Under competition, entry and exit of firms ensure that firm profits tend towards normal levels over the longer term (Mueller, 1986). In privatised industries this process does not happen freely. It is therefore the regulators' job to ensure that these industries conform not necessarily to the process, but to the consequences of competition. Helm (1994, p.25) argued that: 'in principle, the regulator can intervene to lower prices or increase costs to keep the actual rate of return at or around the normal level – to mop up excess returns.'

In the UK, regulators have attempted to increase competition, which should in the longer term lessen the need for regulation. However, Helm and Jenkinson (1997) noted that this need for regulation has not lessened.

Regulation of privatised utilities

Telecommunications was the first industry in the UK to be privatised. The incumbent monopolist, BT, was privatised in 1984 as a fully integrated company. The industry was initially a duopoly comprising BT and Mercury Communications. By 1998, over two hundred operators existed within the industry. Regulation has been most active in the areas of national and international calls and rental of fixed lines. Regulation was introduced after BT was privatised in 1984 under the Telecommunications Act. This act set up the Office of Telecommunications (OFTEL) to regulate the industry. The RPI – X formula was set at –3 per cent of any increase in the retail price index over the period 1984 to 1989. This was subsequently increased in the periods 1989–91 ($-4\frac{1}{2}$ per cent), 1991–93 ($-6\frac{1}{4}$ per cent) and in 1993–98 ($-7\frac{1}{2}$ per cent). The price cap was subsequently reduced again over the period 1997–2000 ($-4\frac{1}{2}$ per cent). Since privatisation the telecommunications industry has become much more competitive (Caves and Williamson, 1996). This is partly as a response to changes in technology and the entry of new firms, particularly in the area of mobile phones. Armstrong (1997) noted that regulation now applies only to approximately one-quarter of BT revenues.

Under the Gas Act 1986, British Gas was privatised as an integrated firm which explored, produced and supplied gas. The Office of Gas Supply (OFGAS) undertook regulation. In the

---

[13] Green (1999) provided an extensive discussion of the role of the competition commission and parliamentary select committees in the regulatory process.

supply of gas, the RPI − X + Y formula is used. In this case, Y represents the costs (i.e. gas supplies) which firms are allowed to pass on to consumers as they increase. As competition has increased and productivity gains have been achieved, the RPI − X + Y formula has been altered. For the periods 1987–92, 1992–97 and 1997–2000, the formulas were RPI − 2% + Y, RPI − 5% + Y, and RPI − 4% + Y, respectively. In 1992, competition was introduced when new rivals were allowed to use British Gas's networks if supplying large customers (measured as greater than 2,500 therms per year). As a consequence, British Gas's market share has fallen to 35 per cent in this market. The Gas Act 1995 encouraged competition in the market where customers used less than 2,500 therms. Use was also allowed of pipeline systems for the shipping and supply of gas. The charges for use of British Gas's pipeline were set at RPI − 5% for the period 1995–97, and increased to RPI − 6^1/$_2$% for the period 1997–2001. By 1998 there were 70 new suppliers who had captured over 70 per cent of the industrial and commercial markets. In response to a Monopolies and Mergers investigation,[14] in 1996, British Gas split its operations into a gas supply company (British Gas Trading) and an exploration and production company (Centrica).[15] Regulation of the industry is now undertaken by the Office of Gas and Electricity Markets.

Under the provision of the Electricity Act 1989, the electricity industry (in England and Wales) was privatised in 1989 into three main activities: generation, transmission and regional distribution.[16] In Scotland the two electricity providers were privatised as fully integrated firms. The industry was regulated by the Office of Electricity Regulation (OFFER), now known as the Office of Gas and Electricity Markets (OFGEM). After privatisation, twelve suppliers were given local monopolies (in corresponding geographical locations). However, since 1998, competition has been permitted between regional suppliers. Given the complexity of the industry, there have been many changes in regulation. In electricity transmission, regulators have adopted the simple RPI − X formula. This X factor was increased over the period 1990 to 1997, but has since been reduced.[17] A similar process has occurred in the transmission and distribution parts of the industry. However, in these segments a Y factor has also been introduced which allows firms to pass on any unforeseen cost increases involved in the generation and distribution of electricity (Green and Newbery, 1997).

The Water industry Act 1991, Water Resources Act 1991 and the Competition and Service Utilities Act 1992 were instrumental in privatising and determining future competition in the water industry. After privatisation the industry comprised ten regional companies, which were responsible for water supplies and sewerage. The Water Industry Act 1991 set up the Office of Water Services (OFWAT) to oversee regulation in the industry. To formulate price regulation, OFWAT has compared the performance of regional water providers (known as yardstick competition).[18] The Competition and Service Utilities Act 1992 allowed rival firms to supply 'new' domestic customers, and competition was extended to large corporate customers (Cowan, 1997). Regulation in the water industry has been carried out using the formula RPI + Y + K, where K represents an amount required to improve networks to meet

[14] Monopolies and Mergers Commission (1993) provides a full discussion of this issue.
[15] Waddams-Price (1997) contains a detailed discussion of these issues.
[16] Armstrong *et al.* (1994) provide a full discussion of the privatisation process.
[17] Over the periods 1990–92, 1992–96, 1996–97 and 1997–2000, the X factors were −0%, −3%, −20% and −4%, respectively.
[18] Van den Berg (1997) provides a detailed discussion of this process.

environmental and efficiency standards.[19] Van den Berg (1997) noted that water privatisation had led to increased investment of £17 billion in the six years after privatisation. However, this had led to price increases of 28 per cent over the same period, and excess profits for many of the privatised water firms (Van den Berg, 1997).

In the UK, regulation has developed and increased in complexity since the privatisation of British Telecom in 1984. The UK operates regulation that gives the regulator some degree of discretion over price regulation. This means that the system is flexible. There is a much greater incentive to make efficiency savings. This is in contrast to the system of rate of return regulation imposed in the United States, where there is little incentive to minimise costs. Under the UK policy of price cap regulation, the main problem of fixed pricing intervals is that demand and supply conditions change. Helm (1994) argued that as the period of the price cap increases, the divergence between the regulated and the prices that would prevail under competition is likely to widen. As a consequence, regulators can intervene to make interim price reductions, require enhancements of product or process quality or increased investments to update networks and processes. However, Helm (1994, p.37) argued that: 'The central problem of the British system is excessive discretion. However, Dnes (1995b), in a study examining the effects of regulation on the telecommunications industry, found that intervention by regulators favoured neither the interests of the dominant firm (BT) nor the interests of consumers.

Current developments in UK regulation

In 2000, the Utilities Bill is proceeding through the Houses of Parliament. This Bill is intended to cover regulation in the gas, electricity, telecommunications and water sectors, and aims to represent the interests of consumers and shareholders of privatised utilities by adjusting the regulatory structure and powers of regulators. The Utilities Bill initially proposed to establish independent consumer councils for each utility sector. However, in March 2000, the president of the Department of Trade and Industry announced that the Bill would now apply only to the regulation of the gas and electricity industries. The Department of Environment would undertake water regulation, while plans to continue to actively regulate in the telecommunications industries have been scrapped. This was because it was thought that, given changes in technology, previous deregulation and globalisation of markets meant that competition was likely to be intense in this industry, and so negated the need for any updated regulatory framework. The Utilities Bill gives much more weight to the interests of consumers; in particular, by imposing new objectives on regulators to promote competition where appropriate, and through the establishment of independent consumer councils. The consumer councils will address and seek to solve complaints by consumers. These councils will also have the power to publish information regarding utilities when this can be regarded as useful to the consumer. The Bill also alters the structure and functioning of regulation. For example, in the gas and electricity sectors, individual regulators will be replaced by regulatory authorities, while for water an advisory panel is to be appointed to assist the regulator. Regulation is to be made much more transparent and requirements for regulators to publish explanations of major decisions and plans for future regulation.

[19] Case study 12.2 at the end of the chapter explores some of the recent competitive trends in the UK water industry.

12.5 Franchising and competitive tendering

Franchising can be thought of as the allocation of exclusive rights to provide certain types of goods and services.[20] This right or licence protects businesses from competition over the period of time that the contract runs. The aim of governments when granting franchises is to have an efficient industry that provides services which are available at competitive prices to consumers. Franchising is useful when restrictions on entry are required to ensure that firms have access to all available economies of scale and scope to achieve productive efficiency. This has been used in the UK, where companies have been granted licences to operate specific product and service areas, for example in the provision of train passenger services.

Under franchising, there is no competition within the industry, but competition takes place when firms are bidding for a contract for the right to control part or all of the industry (Demsetz, 1968). This means that franchisers are subject to the competitive pressure that if they do not operate the franchise agreement to the satisfaction of the government, they will not have their licence renewed. In contrast to RPI – X regulation where the firm is guaranteed some certainty of revenues and costs defined in the formula, in franchising the extent to which the franchise is profitable depends on the cost and revenue efficiency of the franchisee.

A related policy is known as **competitive tendering**. In this case, existing local authority (in-house) providers and private contractors are invited to tender for contracts to provide services for local government. This has been used for many services that were previously supplied by local or central government, including refuse collection, school catering, street cleaning and tax collection.[21] In this case the risks tend to be borne by the government because, by the nature of the contract, the firm is guaranteed a fee for services rendered. However, in such a case it is much easier for the government to monitor performance given that it maintains effective ownership of the service.

Franchising

Franchises can be characterised as 'ownership' or 'operating'. Ownership franchises encourage investment as the firm is insulated from competition. For example, in the UK, the government granted Railtrack the right to operate the rail network. Operating franchises encourage competition but discourage investment in that there is a danger of the loss of contract at the end of the franchise agreement. This is the situation faced by passenger train operators of certain networks.

Many authors have argued that franchising leads to increased contestability (Winston, 1993). In other words, conventional entry barriers are eliminated. To win a contract the future monopoly provider has had to price contracts competitively. Any government-imposed barrier can be overcome by successfully bidding for and obtaining a contract.[22]

---

[20] Chapter 9 provides an extended discussion of franchising contracts and vertical relationships.
[21] Lavery (1997), table 12.1, p.183, outlined the services included under competitive tendering.
[22] A full discussion of entry barriers is provided in Chapter 5.

The award of a franchise contract is normally determined by auction. There are many ways of bidding for a franchise contract (McAfee and McMillan, 1987; Milgrom, 1989). These include bidding by cost or price per unit of output, by lump sum payment or subsidy. Auctions provide the regulator with information about the future efficiency and performance of the potential operators of the franchise. Regulators have control over performance by the right of termination of the franchise, in cases where an awarded contract is not being fulfilled.

We now discuss briefly three types of bidding contests which can be used to allocate a franchise.

- *Cost per unit.* This method was first suggested by Demsetz (1968). In this case information is public. Competition is based on which firm can perform the service at lowest average cost. If competition in the auction exists it is likely that prices will be bid to a level where average costs equal average revenues. This means that the winner of the contract who is awarded a franchise will earn normal profits. This type of bidding process ensures that competition takes place prior to the awarding of the franchise contract and ensures that no excess profits are made. As a consequence, the most efficient firm is granted the franchise to carry out a particular service. Certain problems arise under this method of bidding. Firstly, if market conditions change through technological advances, which lead to the firm's making productivity gains, these gains will not necessarily be passed on to consumers in the form of lower prices. Secondly, if the franchise comprises several types of product or service, there may be some difficulties in allocating the contract, as it may be difficult to determine which firm is making the lowest overall bid. Thirdly, firms make bids which are less than average costs. After the franchise has been awarded they may claim that costs have risen and attempt to renegotiate the franchise agreement.

- *Bidding by lump-sum payment.* In this case, firms bid a fixed-sum payment to provide a good or service over a period of time. This method of franchise allocation is often used in cases of natural monopoly, where breaking an industry into many parts is not feasible. In the short term, the lump-sum payment provides funds for the government. A potential drawback of this form of franchise allocation is that the successful firm can exploit any prevailing monopoly power over the period of the franchise contract. This problem could be overcome by some form of price regulation such as RPI − X or rate of return regulation.

- *Bidding by the lowest fixed level of subsidy.* Here, in markets where prices have been kept artificially low by the government (possibly for some social reasons), any operation of the market will lead to firms' sustaining losses (for example through the provision of bus or train services to rural areas). However, if the government is willing to pay a subsidy equal to any shortfall that a firm may make running a market then there is an incentive for firms to bid for the franchise contract. The firm which can carry out the service while making the smallest loss (i.e. requiring the lowest subsidy) will win the contract. It may be written into the franchise agreement that this subsidy will be reduced over time as the firm's productivity improves. The overall effect, if successful, is to reduce government expenditures in that particular industry.

There are associated problems with operating bidding to determine the award or otherwise of a franchise. These are now discussed:

- *Setting the length of the contract.* This factor is important in determining the extent of competition at the bidding stage. If the length of the contract is for too short a period, bidding is discouraged, as the franchisee would realise profits over only a short period of time. These short-term profits may not offer a large enough incentive to bidders given the risks undertaken. Short-term contracts offer the government more control over what the franchiser is doing. If the length of contract awarded is for a long period, there will be a large number of bidders. Long-term contracts will encourage investment, but there is a danger that the franchisee would abuse its monopoly position or perform below expectation.
- *Bidding firms adopting collusive behaviour.* Bidding firms may decide to collude to ensure that the contract goes to a particular firm. Any gains from this collusion can be split between the colluding firms. This type of collusion is much more likely when the duration of a contract is short and in cases of sealed bidding.[23]
- *The level of fixed investment.* If the level of fixed investment which the franchisee would have to make over the duration of the contract is high, bidding is likely to be discouraged. This is because the franchisee may lose this investment if the franchise is not renewed. To solve this problem, governments would have to institute some scheme of transferring asset ownership at the end of the contract. However, this may prove difficult in cases where assets are firm-specific and non-transferable. Operating franchises may be optimal where levels of sunk costs are low, or zero, given that little or no exit costs are incurred if the franchisee is replaced.
- *Information asymmetries.* If bidding for franchise renewal, information asymmetries may give established firms unfair advantages in the bidding process. This is because established firms have access to specialised knowledge that has accrued over the time they have run the franchise

In allocating franchises the government must ensure that enough competition takes place prior to the awarding of the contract. It is therefore important to ensure there are enough bidders, that no collusion takes place, and that established firms do not have an unfair advantage. It may be possible to have auctions where firms bid on the basis of price and quality combinations. However, how do we measure quality? Baldwin and Cave (1998) argued that the price cap formula could be altered to reflect changes in quality as follows: RPI $- X + \Delta Q$, where ΔQ reflects the change in product or service quality over time.

Baldwin and Cave argued that those firms that meet the desired level of prices and improve product quality should be entitled to increase price. How do we assess different combinations of price and quality? This is not as clear-cut as a price auction.[24] Franchising has been used to increase competition in the UK rail industry. The Railways Act 1993 laid the foundation for the future regulation of the industry (Dnes, 1995a, 1997). This Act privatised the rail industry, and involved dividing railways into separate components. The first component involved a single firm (Railtrack) which owned and operated the rail network (specifically responsible for the track, stations and compiling train timetables). The Office of the Rail Regulator (ORR), which aims to promote and protect the public interest, regulates Railtrack. Railtrack charges individual operators for use of its network. The charges

[23] A full discussion of factors favouring collusion can be found in Chapter 3. For an extended discussion of the application of sealed bidding in utilities industries, see Schmalensee (1979).
[24] Rovizzi and Thompson (1995) provide a full discussion of these issues.

are based on the RPI − X formula. Since privatisation in 1995, these charges have been set at RPI − 8% and RPI − 2% for the periods 1995–96 and 1996–2001, respectively. Three firms now control the rolling stock provision of the previously nationalised British Rail. To increase competition in the industry, the government offered firms the opportunity to bid for exclusive franchises to operate certain train routes. To encourage bidding the government offered the successful franchisees protection from outside competition. The nature of bidding for a franchise depends on the route under consideration. In cases where the franchise involves operating services on parts of the train network that are profitable, potential franchisees offer fixed payments to run the network. The firm bidding the highest fixed payment wins the franchise. In contrast, for loss-making services of the rail network, firms bid for a lump-sum subsidy to run the service. In this case, the firm bidding for the lowest subsidy wins the contract. Charges are set by individual rail companies with reference to the subsidy set at the beginning of the franchise agreement. Regulation of these operating franchises is the responsibility of the Office of Passenger Rail Franchising (OPRAF).[25] OPRAF monitors the performance of franchise operators and has the power to fine them if they do not meet the terms of their franchise contracts.

Competitive tendering

Domberger and Rimmer (1994) argued that any organisation (whether government-controlled or privately owned) has to decide whether to produce products and services within the organisation or use the market as the source. Compulsory competitive tendering was introduced in the UK under the terms of the Local Government Act 1988, which came into force in 1989.[26] The Act covered service provision in areas such as catering (schools, hospitals, residential care centres), cleaning (of local authority buildings, hospitals, schools) and refuse collection. The aim of the Act was to increase efficiency in the provision of local services. Under competitive tendering the local authority invites tenders for certain local services which were previously provided in-house. The tenders can come from in-house (teams comprising existing employees) or from private contractors. After the tenders have been submitted, the local authority can decide whether to allow the in-house labour force to continue to provide the service or whether to award the contract to private contractors. Domberger and Rimmer (1994, p.441) argued that competitive tendering: 'offered a convenient half-way house between public production and private ownership. By retaining public sector control over the activity whilst simultaneously introducing commercial discipline through a formal contracting process'.

Most researchers have argued that by introducing competitive tendering, cost savings arise whether or not the service is contracted out or remains in-house. The tendering process leads in-house providers and private contractors to strive to offer services at low cost.

[25] Case study 12.3 at the end of the chapter discusses some of the current issues relating to the franchising of rail services.

[26] This Act has been augmented by various initiatives such as the Private Finance Initiative (1992), the Next Steps Initiative (1991), Continuity and Change White Paper (1994) and the Competing for Quality White Paper (1991). A full discussion of these initiatives and White Papers is outside the scope of this chapter. However, UK Cabinet Office (1996), chapter 2, provides a discussion of these issues.

There are several arguments that have been forwarded in favour of competitive tendering:

● In-house teams or private contractors who are awarded contracts are forced to strive for improvements in productivity and service provision lest they be replaced in the longer term.
● Competitive tendering also offers some degree of control on local government expenditure and as a consequence may in the longer term lead to reduction in the government's public sector borrowing requirement. By the end of 1995, over £2 billion of local government expenditures were subject to competitive tendering (Domberger and Jenson, 1997).
● Competitive tendering can lead to flexible working practices such as part-time work, job sharing, casualisation. However, this can often lead to the deterioration in working conditions facing many employees (Ascher, 1987).

Substantial costs are involved in specifying the nature of the contract to be carried out, the method of bidding and then monitoring the contract after it has been awarded. These are in essence the transaction costs of the process. Domberger and Hall (1995) argued that if the potential savings from contracting out a service exceed the transaction costs of formulating, awarding and monitoring the contract, then the service should be contracted out. Prager (1994) contended that monitoring costs would be higher if a contract were awarded to a private contractor. This was because private contractors would be more motivated by profit consideration than their in-house counterparts and as a consequence seek to minimise costs often at the expense of quality.

Prior to the Local Government Act 1988 many UK local authorities operated competitive tendering systems (Wilson, 1994). However, Domberger (1999, p 162) noted that 'most of the services that were put up for contracting in the UK in the 1980s for the first time had no prior specifications.'

Several attempts were made to see whether the services that had been subject to competitive tender were more efficiently provided than those that were still provided by local authorities. As an example of empirical work in this area, the following discusses briefly the success or otherwise of competitive tendering in the provision of refuse collecting services.[27]

In a seminal UK study, Domberger *et al.* (1986) examined the efficiency of refuse collection services that had been subject to competitive tendering over the period 1984 to 1985. Using a sample of local authorities derived from Chartered Institute of Public Finance Accounting surveys, the authors constructed a data set comprising sixteen variables describing the volume, type and quality of refuse services carried out within respective local authorities. The authors used regression analysis to examine the relative importance of the sixteen variables in determining the cost performance of local authorities. The authors constructed variables that attempted to capture efficiency differences between local authorities who had followed policies of competitive tendering and those who did not. The authors found that refuse collection services that had been contracted out to private sector contractors were 20 per cent less costly to run than those where local authorities had not employed competitive tendering. The authors also found that in cases where in-house labour had submitted successful tenders and operated refuse services, costs had been reduced by almost the same amount (17 per cent). This result implied that it was the operation of

---

[27] For examples of studies that have examined the effects of competitive tendering in the National Health Service, see Milne and McGee (1992).

competitive tendering that led to increased efficiency whether private or in-house con-tractors were used.[28]

Szymanski and Wilkins (1993) examined the efficiency of competitive tendering of refuse collection services over the period 1984 to 1988. Adopting a similar but more sophisticated analytical approach to Domberger *et al.* (1986), the authors found similar results. Szymanski and Wilkins (1993, p.128) argued that: 'most of the cost savings associated with contract-ing out can be identified with productivity improvements'. Drawing on previous work, Szymanski (1996) found that privately owned firms were more efficient at providing refuse services than their publicly owned counterparts.

Domberger and Rimmer (1994) presented a survey of the literature that had attempted to assess whether productivity improved when local and national governments adopted competitive tendering policies. By synthesising the findings of 23 studies drawn from countries including Australia, Canada, Switzerland, the UK and United States, the authors concluded that in almost all cases competitive tendering led to substantial cost savings in the provision of many different types of service. In the UK, for example, the introduction of competitive tendering policies had led to savings in costs ranging from 20 to 30 per cent for hospital services and 20 per cent in refuse collection.[29] The authors contended however, that these results must be treated with caution, given that cost reductions could be achieved through means other than productivity improvements. They argued that changes in demand, technology and costs of raw materials could substantially affect any estimates of productivity changes. Jackson (1997, p.230) noted that:

> It is difficult to place a monetary value on the results of competitive tendering. How, for example, does one assess how much any budgetary change should be attributed to competitive tendering rather than restraints upon public sector expenditure and wages, or the use of new management techniques?

The extent to which competitive tendering improves the quality of product and service provision is less clear. Problems arise when trying to directly measure quality. Having measured quality, how does one assess if quality is of a high or low standard? Hall and Rimmer (1994) found that contracts were normally awarded to firms offering the lowest bid. They further argued that these low-cost suppliers offered lower-quality services than many higher-cost firms. Several studies have examined the effects on the quality of goods and services of competitive tendering. For example, Hartley and Huby (1986) assessed the costs and benefits of competitive tendering policies in the UK over the period 1984 to 1985.[30] The authors used a sample drawn from local authorities, districts of the National Health Service and private firms. Of the 410 local authorities that were sent a questionnaire, only 75 had operated competitive tendering policies (areas covered included cleaning con-tracts, refuse collection, pest control, security and management services). Of these, 57 went to in-house contractors. In many cases, however, the authors found that the contract was not awarded to the lowest-cost bidder.

---

[28] Ganley and Grahl (1988) argued that these results were biased because the sample contained some local authorities that were not representative of the sample in general. Acknowledging this criticism, Domberger *et al.* re-estimated their empirical model, but found little difference in the results.

[29] These findings for hospital services and refuse collections are discussed in full in Domberger *et al.* (1987) and Domberger *et al.* (1986), respectively.

[30] Other studies include Ascher (1987), Walsh (1991,1992), Walsh and Davis (1993), McMaster (1995), and Domberger *et al.* (1995).

A sample of 192 districts of the National Health Service was also used to examine the prevalence of competitive tendering policies. Of the 119 completed questionnaires, only 10 offered full data. Of these authorities, the estimates of costs ranged from an increase of 68 per cent to reductions of 28 per cent.

Hartley and Huby also sent 81 questionnaires to private firms. Only 19 offered completed data. Some cost reductions were identified for private versus in-house teams. However, many of these savings were thought to relate to firms' using fewer but lower-paid workers.

The authors argued that in cases where there is competitive tendering there are high monitoring costs associated with specifying and monitoring contractual arrangements. They argued that private contractors would often offer extremely low bids in order to eliminate in-house competition. By doing this, the private contractor has more power in future bids. The authors also argued that private contractors would often reduce quality of products and services to meet productivity improvements. They argued (p.289) that: 'Cost savings, if any, are short lived and offset by reductions in the quality of services supplied'.

A report by the UK Cabinet Unit Office (1996) assessed the impact of the 1991 Competing for Quality White Paper on competition in areas where competitive tendering had been used. The sample period was 1992 to 1995 and the data consisted of information supplied by various government departments, completed questionnaires from consumers and interviews with staff involved in providing these goods and services. The study found substantial evidence of cost savings where competitive tendering had been used; these savings on average equalled 18 per cent.

The main aim of the study, however, was to examine the impact on quality of the 1991 Competing for Quality Initiative. The analysis considered quality prior to implementation, during implementation and after the Competing for Quality Initiative. Prior to the 1991 White Paper, 83 per cent of users surveyed were satisfied with the quality of the services provided. During the period when the White Paper was being implemented (tendering was taking place), quality was found to decline. Of the staff surveyed, four out of five acknowledged a decline in quality standards. In a survey of consumers, 32 per cent thought that standards had declined, while 17 per cent thought they had improved. After the tendering process had been completed, 34 per cent of consumers thought that quality had improved, 32 per cent thought that it had stayed the same, 29 per cent thought it had got worse, whilst 5 per cent did not know. The results of the study provided strong support for the view that competitive tendering results in substantial cost savings. However, the extent to which it leads to increased quality through achieving high quality services provision along with greater choice and diversity is limited.

Although the evidence shows cost savings, there are also some suggestions that quality suffers. However, some authors, such as Stevens (1984) and Albin (1992), found little impact on product and service quality of competitive tendering in the United States and Australia, respectively.

Overall, to ensure efficiency and quality under a process of competitive tendering, the following factors must be present:

● The contract should clearly outline the type and standard of service or product to be provided.
● Potential providers should only be allowed to tender if they have a good reputation for quality.
● An integrated system of measuring and monitoring performance should be in place.[31]

---

[31] Hall and Rimmer (1994) provide a full discussion of these points.

12.6 Conclusions

This chapter has examined regulation, in particular the regulation of natural monopolies. We have seen that as a consequence of natural monopoly, governments have felt the need to intervene in industry. One way is to place the natural monopoly under public ownership. In this case the government will instruct the firms to follow certain objectives with the overall aim of correcting market failures associated with monopoly power, externalities and asymmetric information. As we have seen, governments often pursue 'second best' policies. Public ownership of industry eliminates wasteful competition and achieves economies of scale. However, some empirical evidence contends that the performance of nationalised industries was poor, as the absence of competition meant that firms did not strive to make efficiency gains. As a consequence, many governments (particularly the UK) have pursued policies aimed at transferring assets from public to private ownership. In many industries this has been accompanied by liberalisation in order to encourage increased competition. However, this has also been accompanied by regulations to ensure that competition prevails in these industries. In other industries, governments have offered franchise contracts or pursued policies such as competitive tendering as a means of encouraging competition and promoting efficiency.

Key terms

Competitive tendering	Privatisation
Franchising	Rate of return regulation
Natural monopoly	Regulatory capture
Price cap regulation	

Case study 12.1
Welcome to the ways of the market: Sweden is learning private sector ways, but resisting wholesale privatisation

On a bright November morning in central Stockholm, 100 analysts and journalists trooped through the city's streets to attend the capital markets day of Vasakronan, a Swedish real estate company.

There would be nothing unusual in this if Vasakronan were a quoted company sharing its ideas on strategy, markets and prospects with its investors. But Vasakronan is 100 per cent state-owned and yesterday's capital markets day was just the sort of market-friendly behaviour the Swedish government wants to encourage. The aim is to promote transparency and comparisons with listed companies in its sector, and help make the company itself more efficient.

'Any marginal improvement in the performance of state-owned companies will have an effect on the whole Swedish economy,' says Dag Detter, an investment banker-turned-civil servant who is leading the efficiency drive within the ministry of industry.

For years, state ownership and Swedish politics were mixed up and there was little attempt to manage companies professionally. Today the emphasis is firmly on active management. Private sector disciplines are being brought to bear on state-owned companies, irrespective of whether they are eventually privatised. Sweden has fully or partially privatised some state-owned companies, such as Nordbanken, the banking group, and AssiDomän, the forestry group, and is likely to continue the process, but its approach is pragmatic and it has ruled out privatising companies with natural monopolies.

According to a senior official in the UK Treasury, countries such as the UK and Italy are also seeking to manage their state assets more professionally, and the issue is receiving close attention from the Organisation for Economic Co-operation and Development.

What differentiates Sweden is the scale and diversity of its holdings, and the cohesive approach it is trying to bring to the 60 companies it owns or part owns. They range from Telia, the former telecoms monopoly being merged with Telia of Norway and Vattenfall, the country's biggest utility, to the Royal Opera and Royal Dramatic Theatre. The companies have a combined turnover of SKr286bn (£21.2bn) and are worth about SKr500bn, about a quarter of the whole of Swedish-owned industry.

James Sassoon, head of privatisation at Warburg Dillon Read in London, says: 'Many countries think about how do we privatise companies, rather than how do we look after the companies we have and manage them actively. The Swedish initiative is particularly interesting, because it is the first European government to revisit this area, and because of the size and diversity of the government holdings.'

Too often with privatisation and asset management programmes different state companies remain under the control of different ministries and a coherent approach becomes impossible to implement because of power struggles between them. Sweden feels it has largely got around this problem by bringing 80 per cent of its state-owned assets under the wing of the Ministry of Industry and giving one minister overall responsibility for state-owned companies.

The attempt to inject market discipline has led the ministry to recruit people with backgrounds in capital markets to head the civil service unit responsible for state enterprises. Preparatory work has also included deregulating a number of industries to promote competition in areas such as telecoms and power.

According to Mr Detter, the words 'economic value-added' – the attempt to create, and measure the creation of, shareholder value – are very much part of his team's lexicon. He says the efficiency drive aims to achieve five things. First, to make companies more transparent and benchmark them against their competitors. Companies are expected to publish detailed financial information and annual reports, and host capital markets days, as if they were listed companies. Some have been assessed by independent analysts.

The second aim is to increase focus. One company that has come under particular scrutiny is SJ, the state railway operator. The government is encouraging it to divest its non-core activities such as ferries, hotels and restaurants so that it can concentrate on its passenger and cargo activities. Daniel Johannesson, SJ chief executive, says: 'Our goals are purely of a financial and service quality nature. SJ is no longer an instrument for transport policy but seen by government as a commercial transport operator.'

Next, the drive aims to get people with private sector experience on to the boards of state-owned companies. In the last year, about 40 per cent of the board members have been replaced in the eight largest state-controlled companies.

Fourth, it intends to make the capital structure of state-owned groups more efficient. There are plans to take up to SKr15bn in surplus capital out of their balance sheets and increase the amount paid in annual dividends by around SKr4bn a year to SKr12bn.

The ministry is also looking at privatising the debt of some companies – as an alternative to privatising the equity – as a way to get them a credit rating. Mr Detter accepts this could increase borrowing costs, but argues the dynamic effects of the move on companies should outweigh that. Two companies where this is being considered are the national grid and the civil aviation authority.

Last, it aims to implement incentive programmes. This is a controversial area because it could be seen as going against the public sector ethos. But it is also a way of recruiting and retaining talent that might otherwise be lost to the private sector.

Vasakronan is piloting an incentive scheme that rewards employees for meeting targets over a three-year cycle. Hakan Bryngelson, chief executive, says the company's salary structure is competitive with rivals in the private sector, but he admits it is hard for state-owned companies to replicate the share option programmes that are increasingly a feature of Swedish corporate life.

It is too early to judge the success of the Swedish programme. However, it is clear that it marks a distinctive approach to managing state-owned companies. This is as relevant to countries that have already sold off big chunks of their assets, but still have some more difficult cases on their books, as it is to those just starting out on the privatisation process. As one observer of the Swedish programme says: 'This is the opposite of what Mrs Thatcher was doing in Britain in the 1980s. She took the view that state companies would only become efficient once they were in the private sector, and she didn't mind selling companies cheaply to achieve her aims. The Swedish way should ensure that taxpayers get reasonable returns, if and when the companies that it owns are eventually privatised.'

© The Financial Times Limited, 12 November 1999. Reprinted with permission.

Case study 12.2
Pressure rises in least competitive utility: competition in the UK water industry

Britain's water industry is facing its biggest challenge since it was privatised just over a decade ago. The introduction of full-blooded competition and the overturning of local water and sewerage companies' regional monopolies is taxing the imaginations of politicians, regulators and industry executives. Water has lagged behind electricity, gas and telecommunications in introducing full competition because of concerns over safety and water quality, and the difficulty of developing national water trading.

An indication of government thinking on the problem should emerge in the next few weeks when it publishes the findings of a review of ways of increasing competition in the sector.

Just before Christmas, the Institute for Public Policy Research [IPPR], a think tank with strong links to New Labour, proposed, among several options, the enforced separation of ownership of local pipe networks from provision of water supply and sewage treatment.

The separation of ownership of infrastructure and supply of services has been central to development of competition in electricity and gas sectors. All household gas customers have been free to choose another supplier since 1998 and electricity customers since last year. Even the rail industry has uncoupled the ownership of track and stations from the provision of train services.

Under the IPPR proposals, water companies, removed from owning pipe networks, would be expected to bid against each other for franchises to supply local water and sewerage services. Companies wishing to continue to supply a local area would have to ensure that prices and service remained competitive or risk losing their franchise when it came up for re-bidding.

Ownership of pipe networks would remain a regulated monopoly in the same way that Transco operates the national gas pipe network and National Grid high voltage electricity power transmission lines in England and Wales. At the moment, operating licences of regional suppliers, which also own pipe networks, run until 2014. Other options considered by IPPR include trading in water abstraction licences. Companies might even be forced to sell unused rights to extract water, says the report. The government could set a deadline for voluntary opening up of the market using the potential threat of mandatory measures to encourage the industry to meet targets. Some measures are already in train. Under the Competition Act, which becomes law in March, water companies must allow rivals access to their pipes.

Ian Byatt, water industry regulator, has asked companies to provide details of how they intend to set charges to ensure they do not price potential competitors out of the market. Under the Act, he can fine companies up to 10 per cent of their annual turnover. The new rules, however, will not resolve the problem of where competitors may get their water supplies.

Trading between regions is restricted by the lack of a national pipe network. Gas and electricity, by comparison, can be traded nationally and even internationally through a cross-Channel connector linking Britain and France. Nonetheless, there is already some limited competition in water markets. About 500 of the largest customers, using more than 250m litres a year, have the right to move to another supplier if they can find sufficient local supplies. So far, only six customers have deserted their local utility to pursue these so-called 'inset' appointments. A seventh scheme, allowing Hartlepool Water to supply water to Kodak in Harrow in place of Three Valleys, has also been approved recently by the regulator.

The prospect of increased competition has prompted some industry concerns that safety and investment could suffer in a more fragmented market. There is also the problem of how to compensate existing suppliers that have invested heavily to meet the long-term needs of the public. Spreading the load of future investment among a larger number of competing suppliers could also create difficulties. The industry faces a continuing large bill – £15bn over the next five years – to satisfy national and European Union standards on water quality and the environment.

Supporters of competition say none of these problems is insurmountable. Mr Byatt finishes his stint as regulator this year. His replacement has much to consider.

Case study 12.3
Current developments in rail franchising:
the wait for re-franchising process to get back on track

Uncertainty characterises every aspect of the rail re-franchising process: the carving up of networks; who will win and lose franchises; which companies are vulnerable to takeovers. One thing is almost certain, however. The decisions made over the next couple of years will determine who controls the railways for at least the next two decades.

'We are at an absolutely crucial moment for the railways in this country for this century,' says Anthony Smith, director of the Central Rail Users' Consultative Committee.

The shadow Strategic Rail Authority [SRA] has thrown 25 existing franchises in the air and asked operators to design new systems. Everybody agrees that reliability, overcrowding and service must improve. The prevailing logic is that big changes need big investment by big companies with big balance sheets, and wider and longer franchises to reward them.

As few as 14 'super-franchises' could emerge this time, lasting 20 years instead of the previously common seven years, and run by maybe eight of the existing 11 operators.

In the long-term the SRA and government envisage four or five main players running the network, with possibly a handful of special 'micro franchises', such as Isle of Wight or the Pennines.

Details of the SRA's proposals in the Invitation to Contenders have been kept under wraps, but published guidelines point the way. Its priorities are to extend and improve services in and out of and around London, relieve bottlenecks at Birmingham and Manchester, and do better in Wales and the northwest.

These are being interpreted as an opportunity to create single franchises in Wales, the northeast and maybe even the Midlands and in and out of main London terminals such as Waterloo, Liverpool Street and Paddington. More generally they are a signal that larger regional monopolies will be not just tolerated, but encouraged – with stricter regulation of performance and fares. However, it is causing upheaval among operators.

Recent speculation has centred on takeover bids for Prism Rail's West Anglian Great Northern, Wales and West and Cardiff railways, and MTL's Merseyrail and Northern Spirit lines. Meanwhile, shares in GB Railways, which has the Anglia franchise, rose in expectation that it will not survive long alone. With bigger rail empire-builders less interested in small, often poor performing and sometimes almost bankrupt lines, Arriva – the bus operator keen to get into rail – has been linked to at least two. The company also pre-qualified to bid for Laing Group's Chiltern franchise, but some in the industry are sceptical. 'You may be good at buses, but it doesn't necessarily follow you'd be good at rail,' said one senior industry figure.

The SRA says willingness to take financial risk is as important as big balance sheets, and this week Sir Alastair Morton, the chairman, urged bidders to get City finance and international project management companies to support them.

Recent strike action by Connex drivers even led to speculation that if companies were too big it would be difficult to regulate them. 'You could fine Connex millions and it would be like a grain of sand to Vivendi,' said one commentator.

But the size of investment and a simpler timetable are likely to make winners out of bigger players. Virgin Rail, which runs West Coast Mainline and Cross Country routes and is bidding for the East Coast Mainline route, has expressed interest in rebuilding the old British Rail intercity network out of these three plus Great Western. It has two long-term franchises under its belt, and Chris Green, the former InterCity boss, as chief executive. But Great Western operator FirstGroup, and East Coast's US owner Sea Containers are powerful rivals, and many think it is more likely to be taken over by Stagecoach, which owns 49 per cent of the company. That leaves six big players fighting for four or five controlling places: FirstGroup, which already has three franchises, National Express, the biggest with five, and Stagecoach, with two and its stake in Virgin. These three bus rivals are followed by GoAhead, a smaller bus operator with two franchises, Sea Containers, and Vivendi, the French multi-utility, which runs the two Connex networks.

With mixed performance records, unknown bids, and wider considerations of group strategies, it is too early to predict what Sir Alastair or the companies will decide.

© The Financial Times Limited, 20 January 2000. Reprinted with permission.

Questions for discussion

1. Discuss the implications for firm efficiency arising from natural monopoly.
2. Assess the arguments for public ownership of industry.
3. Does privatisation lead to increased efficiency and performance of firms?
4. Compare and contrast the rate of return and price cap systems of utility regulation.
5. Discuss the effectiveness of contracting out and franchising in the UK.

Further reading

Beesley, M.E. (ed.) (1997) *Privatization, regulation and de-regulation*, 2nd edn. London: Routledge.

Domberger, S. and Hall, C. (1995) *The Contracting Casebook: Competitive Tendering in Action*. Canberra: Australian Government Publishing Service.

Helm, D. and Jenkinson, T. (1997) The assessment: introducing competition into regulated industries, *Oxford Review of Economic Policy*, **13**, 1–14.

Kay, J., Mayer, C. and Thompson, D. (eds) (1986) *Privatization and Regulation: The UK Experience*. Oxford: Clarendon Press.

Parker, D. (1991) Privatisation ten years on, *Economics*, **27**, 155–63.

Vickers, J. and Yarrow, G. (1988) *Privatization: An Economic Analysis*. Cambridge, MA: MIT Press.

Wilson, J. (1994) Competitive tendering and UK public services, *The Economic Review*, April.

Winston, C. (1993) Economic deregulation: days of reckoning for microeconomists, *Journal of Economic Literature*, **31**, 1263–89.

Wright, V. (2000) *Privatization and Public Policy*. Aldershort: Edward Elgar.

Regression analysis

A.1 Introduction

Various chapters in the book refer to empirical evidence which supports or refutes particular hypotheses and economic models. In most cases this evidence is presented in the form of estimated linear regressions, and in this appendix we attempt to cover a brief introduction into the advantages and limitations of this analysis. It will be sufficient to allow the reader to understand the basics of regression but will in no way provide a substitute for a course in introductory econometrics. Readers are strongly advised to consult formal textbooks to gain a deeper and fuller appreciation of regression analysis.

Industrial economists have access to vast quantities of economic data, collected by government agencies as well as the private sector, which are of two basic types: time series and cross-sectional data. Time series data refer to observations over time, such as days, months or years. Cross-sectional data are records of values of variables at a fixed point in time, for example government census data on UK industry collects information from a cross-section of firms over a specified period of time. Time series and cross-sectional data can be combined so long as the data are compatible. Industrial economists can use these data to describe the structure, behaviour and performance of industries and firms in the economy. Primarily, data can be tabulated, graphed and grouped in convenient ways and used to produce summary statistics, such as frequency distributions, measures of averages, and measures of dispersion. All such work, which can be loosely referred to as 'descriptive statistics', will help economists to gain a broad understanding of industries and firms.

The accumulation of vast quantities of data may, however, be only the first step in the analysis of firms and industries. The data collected may represent only a sample drawn from a much wider population. It might be interesting to see what can be deduced about the characteristics of a population (an industry) on the basis of a sample of firms. There are also more interesting questions that such data collection can answer, more specifically whether there are relationships between various variables. Thus if we have information on the level of advertising expenditures by firms as well as their sales we may wish to find out if there is any evidence of a relationship between the two variables. Economic theory may suggest the existence of such a relationship and the data may not only confirm the relationship but also measure the strength of the relationship. This second approach to the use of data is referred to as 'statistical inference'.

One of the main problems of statistical inference is the reliance on samples drawn from a population. Since samples do not include all the data in a population they are in effect a piece of incomplete data. The consequence of using such samples will be the presence of an element of uncertainty in one's conclusions. This means that for any conclusions to be taken seriously, in other words be to 'statistically significant', the potential uncertainty must be very low. Formally stated, the statistical significance of a result is the probability that the observed relationship may have occurred by chance and that no such relationship exists in the population from which the sample was drawn.

A.2 Simple regression

The most common method of estimating economic models is by the use of regression analysis. Regression analysis attempts to explain relationships between one or more independent variables and a dependent variable. Thus if we wish to examine the effect that advertising has on sales, the dependent variable is sales and the independent, or explanatory variable, is advertising. Consider Table A.1 which, for a given firm, records levels of advertising expenditure for nine time periods.

The data can be plotted on a graph as shown in Figure A.1.

Regression analysis assumes that the mean value of the dependent variable is a linear function of the mean value of the independent variable. The equation for this linear function is then written as:

$$\hat{Y} = \alpha + \beta X$$

The dependent variable, sales, is represented by Y and the independent variable, advertising expenditures, by X.[1] α is the intercept of the function, i.e. the predicted value of sales

---

[1] We write the dependent variable with a ˆ ('hat') to show that we are attempting to find the *predicted* value of advertising expenditures, rather than the actual value.

Table A.1 ● Firm's advertising and sales data

Advertising expenditure £m	Sales m
1	4
2	6
4	8
8	14
6	12
5	10
8	16
9	16
7	12

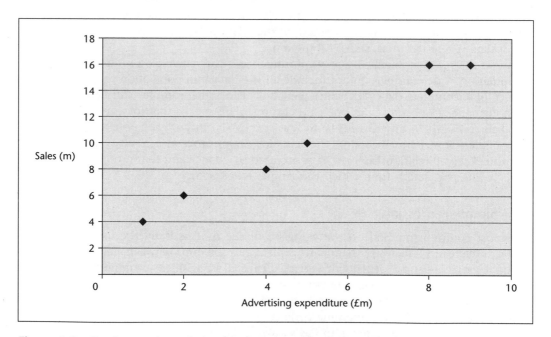

Figure A.1 Graph mapping relationship between advertising and sales

if advertising were to be zero. β is the slope of the function, which measures the changes in the predicted value of sales for a one unit (£1m) change in advertising expenditure. Although we assume a linear relationship between advertising and sales we would not expect the data to fit a linear curve exactly as there are other variables that affect sales as well as the possibility of random fluctuations.

In its simplest form, linear regression can consist of no more that using a ruler to fit a straight line through the middle of the plotted points and then reading off a forecast

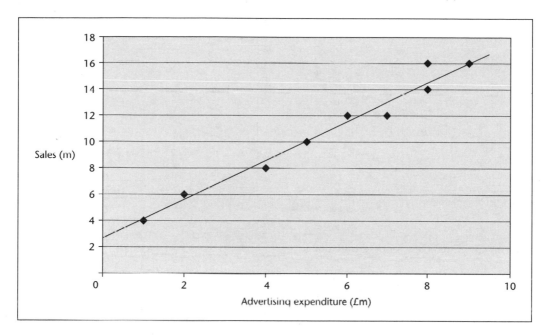

Figure A.2   The regression line

Table A.2 ● Regression statistics for Table A.1

	Coefficients	Standard error	*t* statistic
Intercept	2.54	0.61	4.19
X Variable 1	1.50	0.10	15.27
SEE	0.78		
R^2	0.97		

of sales for a given level of advertising expenditure. A more accurate forecast is to fit the line mathematically by a process known as *least squares regression*. This has been done in Figure A.2.

The method of least squares is to find values for the estimates of α and β which will minimise the sum of the squared errors. The error is measured by the difference between the observed value Y and its predicted value $\hat{Y}$.[2] Using computer software we can easily calculate the equation for the regression line in Figure A.2. Table A.2 shows the results (rounded to two decimal places).

The equation for the regression line is thus:

$$\hat{Y} = 2.54 + 1.50X$$

[2] A full discussion of least squares can be found in Gujarati (1995), chapters 2 to 5, and Maddala (1992), chapter 3.

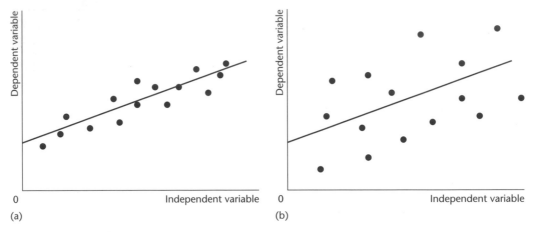

Figure A.3 Coefficient of determination

It is important to note the difference between Y and Ŷ. Y refers to the actual level of sales, whereas Ŷ is the predicted level of sales. When advertising expenditures were £4m, sales equalled 8 million units. If we apply our estimated regression line, forecast sales for an outlay of £4m on advertising are 8.54 million units (2.54 + 1.5 × 4). The intercept is equal to 2.54 million units, which implies that if our company did not undertake any advertising expenditure it would expect sales of 2.54 million units.

The regression equation cannot tell us the degree of confidence we can place in our forecasts. We have to rely on other statistics that are produced alongside the estimated equation. We shall discuss the coefficient of determination (R^2), the standard error of the estimate (SEE) and the standard error of the coefficients (SE).

Coefficient of determination, R^2

The coefficient of determination measures the proportion of the total variation in the dependent variable that is explained by the independent variable or variables included in the model. Consider Figures A.3(a) and (b).

In both figures the same regression line has been fitted. Both lines have the same intercept and the same slope. It is clear, however, that in Figure A.3(a) the equation is a 'better fit' than in Figure A.3(b). The data in Figure A.3(b) are more dispersed around the line and we would be less confident about making predictions about the size of the dependent variable. Regression statistics will almost always compute a coefficient of determination or R^2, which indicates how well the model explains the changes in the dependent variable. R^2 can take any value between zero and unity. Should R^2 equal zero, we would conclude that the model provides no explanation of changes in the dependent variable. If, on the other hand, R^2 equals one, we would conclude that all variation in the dependent variable is explained by the independent variable. The higher the level of R^2 the more confidence we can have in our model. The coefficient of determination is sometimes referred to as the 'goodness of fit'. In Table A.2 the value for R^2 is 0.97; thus 97 per cent of the variation in sales can be explained by the level of advertising expenditure.

Standard error of estimate, SEE

The standard error of estimate allows us to predict a range within which we can predict the dependent variable with varying degrees of statistical confidence. For all normal distributions there is a 68 per cent probability that the predicted dependent variable will lie within ±1 SEE. There is a 95 per cent probability that the predicted dependent variable will lie within ±2 SEEs, and a 99 per cent probability that the dependent variable will lie within ±3 SEEs. For a level of advertising of £4m we predicted that the firm's sales would be 8.54 million units. We can now say that there is a 95 per cent chance that actual sales will lie between two SEEs of that forecast, i.e. between 6.98 million units and 10.1 million units (8.54 − 2 × 0.78 and 8.54 + 2 × 0.78, respectively).

Standard error of the coefficient (SE)

The standard error of the coefficient tells us the degree of confidence we can place on the value of the coefficient. If we consider the slope coefficient in our estimated regression line we can say that there is a 68 per cent probability that the true value of β lies within 1 SE of the estimated value and that there is a 95 per cent probability that β lies within 2 SEs of the estimated value ($\hat{\beta}$). Thus there is a 95 per cent probability that β lies between 1.3 and 1.7 (1.50 − 2 × 0.1 and 1.50 + 2 × 0.1, respectively). The smaller the SE the greater the confidence we can place on the value of the coefficient.

An additional statistic is the t statistic, which is computed in the following way:

$$t \text{ statistic} = \frac{\text{Value of the coefficient}}{\text{Standard error of the coefficient}}$$

In our example the t statistic is 15 (1.50/0.1).[3] The higher the t statistic, the greater our confidence in the coefficient. As a rule of thumb, if the t statistic is greater than 2 we can place a reasonable confidence on the value of the estimated coefficient. The 'null hypothesis' is that β is equal to zero, which would mean there is no relationship between advertising and sales. In other words, we are asking ourselves: what is the chance that the slope really does equal 1.50, rather than equalling it by chance? If the standard error is small, or the t statistic is large, the chance that β is equal to zero is very small. If the t statistic is greater than 2 then β is unlikely to equal zero. On the other hand, if the t statistic were less than 2 then β could be equal to zero and there would be a high likelihood that advertising and sales were not related.

A.3 Multiple regression

The simple regression method discussed above can be extended to include more than one independent variable. Thus we may wish to expand our model that explains the variation in sales by adding more independent variables. We may believe that, for a particular firm or for an industry, sales will depend on price, advertising, rivals' advertising, wage levels in the economy and interest rates. Thus the equation we estimate is as follows.

Sales = $\alpha + \beta_1$PRICE + β_2ADV + β_3RIVADV + β_4WAGE + β_5INT

[3] Table A.2 shows a value of 15.27, which was based on figures prior to rounding up.

Such an equation cannot be illustrated graphically, but computer software can easily estimate the values of the coefficients and the statistics R^2, SEE and SE. In multiple regression it is important to note that the β coefficients represent the *independent* contributions of each of the independent variables to the prediction of the dependent variable. Thus, using the example above we can say that the price variable is correlated with sales, holding all other independent variables constant. This is often referred to as 'partial correlation'.[4]

A.4 Problems of regression analysis

There are a number of problems that can limit the effectiveness of regression analysis.

The direction of causation

Although regression may be able to confirm the existence of significant relationships it may be unable to determine the causality. For example, one could find that there is a positive relationship between research and development and the level of industrial concentration. However, it may be difficult to decide if high concentration leads to high levels of research and development or whether high levels of research and development create concentrated industries.

Multicollinearity

Multicollinearity is said to exist when the independent variables are highly correlated with one another. Thus we may find that the coefficient of determination, R^2 is high, but that the standard error of the coefficient is also high. The independent variables explain the variation in the dependent variable en masse, but we are unable to separate the specific relationships. For example, demand for a firm's product will depend on its own price and also on a rival's price (as well as other variables). If the price of the rival's product is perfectly correlated with the firm's price, the two variables are said to be 'perfectly collinear' and an estimate of the coefficients will not be possible. An estimate will be possible, however, if there is only a small difference between the two prices. This is referred to as 'near collinearity'. The rival may be reacting to the firm's price changes in only a slightly different way. Interpretation of the effect of a coefficient on a variable, while holding all other variables constant, is compromised by the fact that not all other variables can be constant. An attempt to analyse the effect of a firm's price change on its customers, by holding the prices of the rival firm constant, will not be possible. In the case of perfect collinearity one can simply exclude one of the variables as it adds nothing to the estimated function. However, in the case of near collinearity it might be risky to exclude one of the variables as the equation would omit a possibly important explanatory variable.

Multicollinearity can be detected by computing a simple correlation between pairs of explanatory variables. If the correlation is close to unity we have near collinearity. It is, however, more difficult to detect collinearity between subsets of explanatory variables, rather than pairs. The presence of such multicollinearity is best confirmed by the presence of a high R^2 and high SEs as mentioned above.

[4] For a full discussion of multiple regression, see Gujarati (1995), chapter 7 and Maddala (1992), chapter 4.

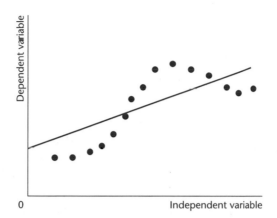

Figure A.4 The presence of autocorrelation

It may be possible to remodel or respecify the equation to reduce the possibility of collinearity. For example, demand for a product may be explained by price and the money wage. Since the two variables, prices and money wages, are highly correlated, it would be better to measure the income effect on demand by relying on real wages, where the effect of prices has been filtered out. If no alternative variables can be found, then the only other alternative is to try to find alternative data.[5]

Autocorrelation

Autocorrelation or serial correlation problems exist when errors in our observations are not random but correlated with errors of other observations.[6] This can be restated as, in the absence of autocorrelation the random error in any given period affects the dependent variable in that period only, and then disappears completely. However, this may be an unlikely assumption in certain cases. Demand for a good may be affected by many factors that change only slowly through time and are omitted from an estimated equation, such as lifestyle, tastes, customs, habits and quality. Consequently the deviations of observations from the regression line, the error terms, will also move slowly as the value of each error term is dependent on the value of the error term in the preceding time period. Thus if the error term were to be negative (or positive) in one time period, it would also be negative (or positive) in the next periods as well, as illustrated by Figure A.4. What is clear from the above discussion is that this problem usually affects time series data.

The effect of autocorrelation is to distort the various regression statistics such as R^2 and the SE which will then exaggerate the precision of the estimates in the regression. The most common method of detecting the presence of autocorrelation is the Durbin–Watson test.[7]

[5] See Maddala (1992), chapter 7.
[6] Ibid., chapter 6.
[7] See Gujarati (1995), chapter 12.

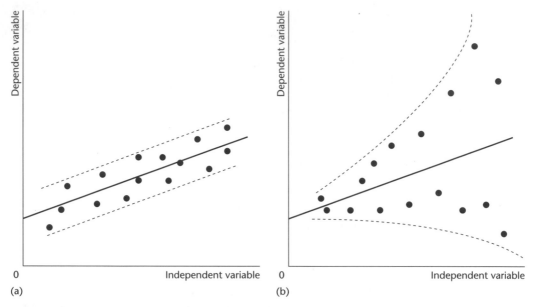

Figure A.5   (a) Homoskedasticity; (b) heteroskedasticity

Heteroskedasticity

If we observe that the variance[8] of the error changes as the dependent variable changes, we are faced with the problem of heteroskedasticity. Figure A.5(a) shows homoskedasticity, where the variance of the error term is constant, whereas Figure A.5(b) illustrates heteroskedasticity.

   Heteroskedasticity can occur with cross-sectional data when the size of the independent variable increases. Thus for a cross-section of firms in a given industry, one might expect that sales for the larger firms are subject to greater variation than those for smaller firms. The consequences of such heteroskedasticity are that the standard error of the parameter estimates is biased and the hypothesis tests are invalid. The simplest way to detect for the presence of heteroskedasticity is by plotting the errors around a regression line as shown in Figures A.5(a) and (b). Standard textbooks suggest more formal tests and solutions to this problem.

Misspecification

Misspecification errors will arise when independent variables have no contributory effect on the dependent variable or when important independent variables have been omitted.[9] Another potential error is the selection of an incorrect functional form of the estimated equation. If one were to suspect that the effect of advertising in a given industry is quadratic rather than linear, then to ignore such a squared term would bias the result. In

---

[8] Variance is a measure of dispersion which tells us how individual observations are distributed around a mean.
[9] See Gujarati (1995), chapter 6.

practice, accurate specification of a model is difficult and can be likened more to an art than a science. The fact that there are many hundreds of economic variables, each dependent on one another, as well as a lack of sufficient theoretical precision, requires researchers to take great care over specifying their model. Several model specifications may be required, with different independent variable combinations, before a final model is accepted.

Although the last few pages have concentrated on the problems of regression analysis one should bear in mind that these are offset by the advantages that such analyses produce. Economic theory gives largely qualitative answers and it is the role of regression as well as the wider study of econometrics to ensure that managers and other decision-makers have the quantitative answers as well.

Glossary

Absolute cost advantages Refers to an entry barrier where the long run average costs of the potential entrant lie above those of the incumbent firm.

Accounting rate of profit A measure of profit that utilises data compiled in companies' annual reports. Normally calculated by deflating profits by assets (return on capital), equity (return on equity), or turnover (return on sales).

Advertising intensity Refers to the extent to which advertising is an important variable in any market structure. Normally measured as the proportion of industry sales devoted to advertising.

Agency Refers to the study of relationships between principal firms and agent firms. For example, a manufacturing firm, acting as principal will contract a supplying firm, the agent, to produce its inputs.

Aggregate concentration This is the broadest measure of industry concentration. Any measure of aggregate concentration attempts to quantify the size distribution of the largest n (where n is normally 100) firms in an economy.

Anti-competitive practice An anti-competitive (restrictive) practice can be defined as any strategy, which distorts, restricts or prevents competition. Strategies such as predatory and limit pricing, and various vertical restraints such as refusals to deals and tie-in sales would fall into this category.

Anti-trust An American term to describe a series of laws aimed at promoting competition and lessening the impact on competition of the growth in corporate trusts. In the United States the Antitrust Division and the Federal Trade Commission enforce these laws.

Article 81 This Article forms part of the Treaty of Amsterdam and deals with the regulation of restrictive practices of firms located within the boundaries of the European Union. This Article covers restrictive agreements, collusion and vertical restraints within the European Union. Article 81 is enforced by the Competition Directorate-General IV.

Article 82 This Article forms part of the Treaty of Amsterdam and regulates against abuses of a monopoly position. A monopoly position is said to exist if a single firm has a 40 per cent market share in a given market. The Article deals with monopoly pricing, predatory pricing and price discrimination. Article 82 is enforced by the Competition Directorate-General IV.

Austrian school The collective term to describe a school of thought emanating from researchers based at the University of Vienna in Austria. The school sees competition as a dynamic process driven by the introduction of new products and processes, along with the destruction of existing methods of production and goods and services. High profits are the result of successful innovation. The school tends to be against government intervention in the form of competition policies to industry.

Backward vertical integration This involves a firm moving ('upstream') into stages of production closer to sources of supply.

Basing-point pricing Also known as delivered pricing. It is the practice of setting a price which includes the cost of transport which is not dependent on the location of the seller. The transport cost is calculated on the basis that all sellers are located at one, predetermined 'basing point'. Customers close to a seller are charged for 'phantom freight' whereas customers further away enjoy a subsidy. The practice is intended to facilitate collusion as all firms quote the same price, irrespective of their location.

Bundling Refers to the practice of sellers offering several goods as one package and thus being able to price discriminate and reduce consumer surplus.

Cartels These are formal organisations of independent firms that act collectively to improve their economic return by attempting to monopolise the market.

Chapter I prohibition This prohibition forms part of the Competition Act (1998) and deals with anti-competitive (restrictive) practices. The Chapter I prohibition applies to agreements between firms which prevent, distort or restrict competition within UK industries. The Chapter I prohibition is closely related to Article 81 of EU legislation.

Chapter II prohibition This prohibition forms part of the UK Competition Act 1998. The prohibition regulates abuses of monopoly positions. Practices that constitute abuses include charging excessive prices, price discrimination, predatory behaviour, vertical restraints and refusals to supply.

Chicago school The collective term used to describe a group of economists emanating from the University of Chicago. Although more famous for their contributions to monetary economics through the developments in the quantity theory of money, the school was also active in the area of industrial organisation. The school, represented by prominent academics such as George Stigler (1968) and Harold Demsetz (1973), argued that government intervention in industry leads to less competition rather than more. This school of thought argues that high profits are the reward for superior efficiency.

Competitive tendering A policy whereby existing providers and private contractors are invited to tender for contracts to provide specific services for local government. Such services may include refuse collection, school catering, street cleaning and tax collection.

Concentration indices Concentration indices quantify the number and size distribution of firms in various industries. The size of firms is assessed with reference to data on sales, assets, employees or output. Various measures of concentration can be utilised. The more common measures include the Concentration Ratio, Herfindahl–Hirschman index, Hannah and Kay index, Gini and entropy coefficients.

Conglomerate A firm that is involved in many unrelated activities.

Conjectural variation Refers to the extent to which a firm reacts or adjusts to changes in rivals' strategies in an oligopolistic market.

Contestable market This is a market where potential entrants and established firms face similar costs. The approach was developed by William Baumol and colleagues (1982). In this type of market entry and exit conditions are free which means that new entrants can withdraw and cover their costs upon exit. This type of market structure implies that the behaviour of established firms is constrained not only by actual competition, but also by potential competition.

Contractual incompleteness This occurs when firms are unable to conclude efficient contractual agreements due to the presence of transaction costs.

Co-operative games Those games (*see* Game theory) that result in some form of a binding agreement.

Corporate coherence A term developed by Teece *et al.* (1994) to refer to companies that do not diversify at random.

Credence goods Goods whose quality cannot be assessed before or after consumption. Prevalent where the consumer must have specialist information or knowledge to assess the quality attributes of goods and services. Medical care is an example.

Cross-subsidisation Occurs when revenue from one activity can be used to support (subsidise) other activities.

Deadweight loss Describes the loss in welfare attributable to the reduced output and increased prices after the monopolisation of an industry.

Deconglomeration The practice whereby conglomerates divest themselves of unrelated activities so as to focus more on their core activities.

Degrees of collusion Refers to the strength and effectiveness of agreements.

Delphi technique A method of making long-term demand and supply forecasts for product markets. The technique involves a process of iteration by which experts working independently eventually reach a consensus.

Diffusion Refers to the rate at which new products and processes are adopted, within the firm (intra-firm diffusion), by other firms (inter-firm diffusion), by other industries and eventually by other countries.

Direction of diversification An attempt to identify whether firms diversify within their industry or technological groupings, or whether they diversify into less related fields of activity.

Double marginalisation This occurs when two linked stages of production are both monopolised and each firm adds its own monopoly mark-up.

Economies of scale barriers These entry barriers exist when entrants are forced to enter at a scale which puts them at a disadvantage to the incumbent firms.

Economies of scope These economies are realised when the average cost of producing two or more goods is lower than if they were produced separately.

Experience goods Goods and services that must be consumed for an assessment as to quality to be made.

Explicit collusion Covers collusive practices that require some formal communication to take place.

Foreclosure The practice of firms refusing to supply downstream firms or to purchase from upstream firms.

Forms of collusion Refers to the custom and practice as well as the organisational structures that characterise various collusive agreements.

Forward vertical integration Involves a firm moving ('downstream') into stages of production closer to the final market.

Franchising The allocation of exclusive rights to provide certain types of goods and services. This protects the holder of such rights from competition over the period of the franchise. Franchising is prevalent in industries where limited firm numbers are required to achieve efficiency.

Game theory This approach plays an important role in a segment of industrial organisation theory (the 'new industrial organisation'). The approach looks at particular competitive issues in the context of a game which examines the strategic behaviour, and outcomes of decisions made by firms with respect to price and non-price variables.

Geographical barriers Those entry barriers that affect foreign firms attempting entry into a domestic market. These involve factors such as tariffs, quotas, frontier controls, national standards, regulations and exchange controls.

Horizontal agreement An agreement between firms in the same industry which leads to decreased competition. Such agreements take a variety of forms and can relate to common pricing policies, production quotas, market allocation, or sharing of information on prices, output and quality.

Industry An industry is a group of firms producing and selling similar goods and services, using the same technology and competing for factors of production. Standard Industrial Classifications (SICs) can group firms by broad division, product class, group or activity.

Innovation Defines a stage of research and development, between invention and commercial production. It covers the stages of applied research, and development work.

Interdependence This is the chief characteristic of oligopolistic markets. Firms in an oligopoly are interdependent in so far as success for one firm will depend on actions taken by its rival and, equally, the actions of the firms will affect the success of the rival.

Internal capital market Refers to the allocation of investment funds within the organisation. It is argued that managers allocate these funds more efficiently than investors in the external capital market since managers have access to better information flows.

Internal rate of return Commonly used in investment appraisal. The measure finds a cost of capital to the firm (the discount rate) at which the net present value of the project under consideration equates to zero.

Invention The first stage of research and development and refers to the creation of new ideas, regardless of any practical economic application.

Joint ventures Organisations of independent firms that co-operate for a specific project.

Law of proportionate effect Describes the implications for industry concentration if the growth rate of each firm in an industry is unrelated to its current size; in other words, what happens to industry structure if firm sizes are subject to a sequence of random shocks. This phenomenon was first examined by the French economist Robert Gibrat (1931). The law of proportionate effect predicts that if firm sizes are subject to a multiplicative growth process of this kind, the distribution of firm sizes tends to become skewed with a few large firms, several medium-sized firms and numerous small firms, and industry concentration increases over time.

Legal barriers Entry barriers that prevent or delay entry due to government legislation, for example franchised monopolies, registration and patents.

Lerner index A measure of market (monopoly) power that examines the extent to which an individual firm can raise prices above marginal costs. The resultant value of the index varies between zero (under conditions of perfect competition) and one (under conditions of monopoly).

Limit pricing A pricing strategy by an incumbent firm to deter or retard the rate of entry. The implication is that the incumbent will forgo some profits in order to set a lower price, sufficient to make entry uneconomical for a higher-cost entrant.

Market A market is where firms produce similar goods and services from the buyer's perspective. Close substitutes and complements exist on the demand side of the industry.

Merger policy This policy assesses whether growth of market power arising from a merger is in the public interest. For example, the regulator has to judge the benefits of rationalisation against the growth of concentration that a merger may bring.

Monopolistic competition An industry structure which is a hybrid of monopoly and perfect competition. Applies to industries comprising large numbers of firms, where goods and services are produced which are very similar, but not identical.

Monopoly A market structure comprising one supplier and numerous buyers; a market that is normally characterised by high levels of fixed costs and substantial barriers to entry.

Monopoly policy This type of policy is applied in cases where a firm or group or firms has a large share of a market. This type of policy aims to prevent dominant firms abusing market power.

Natural monopoly This type of industry exists when the minimum efficient scale of production is almost equal to, or equals, the market size. Natural monopolies involve high levels of fixed costs. In such industries, production is efficient in the hands of a single firm, as it can access all available economies of scale and scope.

Networks Groups of firms linked vertically by regular contact and relationships.

Non-cooperative games Those games (*see* Game theory) where players are unable to reach a binding agreement.

Passive and committed incumbents A distinction is made between firms that do not prepare to resist entry and those that do.

Patent A patent is the deliberate creation of a property right over new knowledge. A patentee becomes the legal owner of a new product or process and no other firm or individual will be allowed to copy the idea without the patentee's permission. Patents grant monopoly status and thus provide the incentive for individuals and firms to invest in innovation.

Patent length and breadth These terms cover issues facing regulatory authorities in their ability to grant sole ownership of new knowledge. The first issue is how long should the patent last and the second issue is how wide should the coverage be as regards possible spin-offs. Long and broad patents will encourage innovation but slow down the rate of diffusion.

Perfect competition A market structure where a long-run competitive equilibrium exists where all firms make normal profits. Firms are price-takers in an environment where there are many buyers and sellers, economic agents have perfect knowledge and where there are no geographical (or other) barriers to the mobility of resources or to entry and exit from the market.

Predation/predatory pricing Occurs when a dominant firm attempts to force a weaker firm out of the market. The usual strategy is to undercut the prices of the rival, even if this means selling at below marginal cost.

Price cap regulation This regulation places a limit on the prices that firms can charge. It has been used extensively in the UK in the regulation of utilities.

Price leadership This refers to an informal or 'tacit' agreement that price changes set by a leader will be followed by most of the other firms in the industry. Can also be termed 'parallel pricing'.

Price rigidity Refers to the observed phenomenon in oligopolistic markets that firms do not change prices frequently, preferring instead to concentrate on non-price competition.

Privatisation A process that involves the transfer and sale of assets from the public to the private sector. Industries that have been privatised in the UK include telecommunications, water, gas and electricity. Privatisation is often used to describe a number of policies including denationlisation, deregulation and franchising.

Product differentiation Refers to the ability of firms to make close substitutes different, so that customers no longer regard them as similar products; for example, different colours of the same model of car.

Product differentiation barriers Barriers to entry due to the brands and reputation of the incumbents, which generate a high level of loyalty. An entrant will then find it difficult to attract customers to its products.

Public interest A term used to describe whether certain activities carried out by established firms have desirable or undesirable implications for competition, efficiency and consumer welfare. A strategy undertaken by a firm is likely to be in the public interest if it increases competition, firm efficiency or improves consumer welfare.

Quantity forcing The practice of forcing buyers to stock more goods than they would wish under normal conditions.

Rate of return regulation This type of regulation fixes a required rate of return on capital, which allows the firm to set a price which covers costs and to earn enough profits to attract new investors and to replace and update capital equipment.

Reaction function This measures the response of one firm to price or output changes set by another firm. Reaction functions are the basis for much analytical work in oligopolistic markets.

Reciprocity The practice of firm A buying from firm B on the basis that firm B will have bought goods from firm A. Large conglomerates are thus in a better reciprocal position.

Regulatory capture This phenomenon occurs when regulated firms are more organised than the consumers that the regulator represents. As a consequence the firms have the power to lobby the regulator more effectively. Such lobbying may influence the regulator's objectives and lead to the regulator's representing the interests of the industry and not the consumer.

Resale price maintenance The practice of upstream firms who fix a minimum (or possibly maximum) price to be charged in the downstream (usually retail) market.

Restrictive practices policy This type of policy is applied in cases where a firm or group of firms is engaging in practices which may prove detrimental to consumers. Examples may include price-fixing agreements, predatory pricing and vertical restraints. May also include **horizontal agreements** and **vertical agreements**.

Rule of reason Relates to US anti-trust laws and dictates that any investigation into distortions of competition should be more interested in the consequences of various types of firm strategy on competition and welfare within any given market, rather than on the structural attributes of the market under investigation.

Schumpeterian hypothesis This argues that monopolies and near-monopolies are far from being lazy innovators as traditional microeconomic theory would suggest. They enjoy conditions that allow them to invest in speculative research and development.

Sealed bidding A process by which firms bid for contracts independently and secretly. Sealed bids are sent to a buyer, who will select the best bid, normally, the lowest price.

Search goods Goods and services that can be inspected by either touch or visual inspection prior to purchase.

Semi-collusion Occurs in markets where collusion covers only some parts of strategic decision-making, for example pricing. Other activities such as marketing and innovation are not covered by collusive agreements.

Specific asset Refers to assets that most firms possess which can be exploited in other activities and industries, for example innovation, labour skills, and brands.

Strategic group A group of firms which are similar in structure or follow similar behaviour. Members of a strategic group act interdependently. The extent of entry barriers differs between these groups (mobility barriers), resulting in some groups of firms earning higher profits than others within the same industry.

Structure–Conduct–Performance paradigm A framework developed primarily by Joe Bain (1956) which is used to examine the behaviour of firms and industries. In its simplest form, structural characteristics of industries influence or dictate the conduct and ultimately the performance of firms. More complex forms of the model attempt to explain the structural evolution of industry by examining the feedback effects of firm performance and behaviour on the future structure of the industry. High profits are assumed to arise from firms' exercising market power advantages. The approach advocates active government involvement in industry to ensure that competition prevails.

Tacit collusion Refers to collusive practices that arise out of industry 'understandings' and that have not been agreed via direct communication. A common form of tacit collusion is price leadership.

Tie-in sales *See* Tying.

Tobin's *q* ratio A measure of profitability defined as the ratio of the market value to the replacement cost of capital to the firm. In an industry where competition prevails, the q value should be close to one. However, if the firm grows larger, the value of q becomes larger and is likely to exceed one under conditions of monopoly.

Trade association An organisation that represents the interests of firms in a given industry. It differs from a cartel in that it has no monopolistic intentions.

Transaction cost analysis This approach asks the question 'Why do firms exist?' Instituted by Ronald Coase (1937) and subsequently developed by Oliver Williamson (1985), this approach assumed that information is imperfect, and trade within the market takes place in a world of uncertainty. As a consequence of uncertainty, economic agents behave with only bounded (limited) rationality. This leads to costs in carrying out market transactions. These include time spent collecting information about product attributes and prices. Transaction costs may also be involved in drawing up, monitoring and enforcing contracts.

Tying Occurs when purchases of one distinct product force buyers to buy another distinct product.

Type 1 and Type 2 industries This approach to classifying industries was developed in a seminal work by John Sutton (1991). Type 1 industries exist where products and services tend to be homogeneous. The primary mode of competition is based on price, and prevailing cost and technological conditions drive subsequent competition and industry structure. Examples of Type 1 industries are household textiles, leather products, footwear, clothing, printing and publishing. Type 2 industries are industries where product differentiation is prevalent. In this type of industry firms spend heavily on discretionary investments such as advertising and research and development. Examples of Type 2 industries are motor vehicles and pharmaceuticals.

Vertical agreements These occur when firms at successive stages in the production process engage in activities aimed at distorting competition to gain increased market power; for example, by imposing exclusive dealing contracts on customers.

Vertical integration The ownership of two or more stages of production.

Workable competition An approach to competition analysis that lists a number of criteria for industry structure and firm conduct that would result in bringing about desirable performance.

Bibliography

Aaronovitch, S. and Sawyer, M.C. (1975) Mergers, growth and concentration, *Oxford Economic Papers*, **27**, 136–55.

Abernethy, A. and Franke, G.R. (1996) The information content of advertising: a meta-analysis, *Journal of Advertising*, **25**, 1–17.

Acs, Z.J. and Audretsch, D.B. (1990) *Innovation and Small Firms*. Cambridge: Cambridge University Press.

Adams, W.J. (1981) The automobile industry, in De Jong, H.W. (ed.) *The Structure of European Industry*. Amsterdam: Martinus Nijhoff, reading VII.

Adams, W.J. and Yellen, J. (1976) Commodity bundling and the burden of monopoly, *Quarterly Journal of Economics*, **90**, 475–98.

Adelman, M.A. (1949) Integration and antitrust policy, *Harvard Law Review*, **63**, 27–77.

Adelman, M.A. (1955) Concept and statistical measurement of vertical integration, in Stigler, G.J. (ed.) *Business Concentration and Price Policy*. Princeton, NJ: Princeton University Press.

Adelman, M.A. (1959) *A&P: A Study in Price–Cost Behaviour and Public Policy*. Cambridge, MA: Harvard University Press.

Advertising Association (1998) *Advertising Statistics Yearbook 1998*. Oxon: NTC Publications.

Aitchison, J. and Brown, J.A.C. (1966) *The Lognormal Distribution*. Cambridge: Cambridge University Press.

Akerlof, G.A. (1970) The market for lemons: quality uncertainty and the market mechanisms, *Quarterly Journal of Economics*, **39**, 489–500.

Albaek, S., Møllgaard, P. and Overgaard, P.B. (1997) Government-assisted oligopoly co-ordination? A concrete case, *The Journal of Industrial Economics*, **45**, 429–43.

Albin, S. (1992) Bureau shaping and contracting out: the case of Australian Local Government, *Public Policy Program Discussion Paper*, No. 29. Canberra: Australian National University.

Albion, M.S. and Farris, P. (1981) *The Advertising Controversy*. Boston: Auburn House.

Alchian, A. and Allen, W.R. (1969) *Exchange and Production Theory In Use*. Belmont, CA: Wadsworth.

Alexander, D.L., Flynn, J. and Linkins, L. (1995) Innovation, and global market share in the pharmaceutical industry, *Review of Industrial Organisation*, **10**, 197–207.

Allen, B.T. (1969) Concentration and economic progress: note, *American Economic Review*, **59**, 600–4.

Amato, L. and Wilder, R.P. (1990) Firm and industry effects in industrial economics, *Southern Economic Journal*, **57**, 93–105.

Amihud, Y. and Lev, B. (1981) Risk reduction as a managerial motive for conglomerate mergers, *The Bell Journal of Economics*, **12**, 605–17.

Andrews, P.W.S. (1951) Industrial analysis in economics, in Wilson, T. and Andrews, P.W.S. (eds) *Oxford Studies in the Price Mechanism*. Oxford: Clarendon Press.

Armentano, D.T. (1975) Price fixing in theory and practice, in Brozen, Y. (ed.) *The Competitive Economy*. Morristown, NJ: General Learning Press, reading 30.

Armstrong, M. (1997) Competition in telecommunications, *Oxford Review of Economic Policy*, **13**, 64–82.

Armstrong, M., Cowan, S. and Vickers, J. (1994) *Regulatory Reform: Economic Analysis and British Experience*. Oxford: Oxford University Press.

Aron, D.J. (1993) Diversification as a strategic preemptive weapon, *Journal of Economics and Management*, **2**, 41–70.

Arrow, K.J. (1962) Economic welfare and the allocation of resources for invention, in *The Rate and Direction of Inventive Activity*, National Bureau of Economic Research Conference Report, Princeton: Princeton University Press, pp.609–25.

Arrow, K. (1975) Vertical integration and communication, *Rand Journal of Economics*, **6**, 173–83.

Asch, P. (1969) Collusive oligopoly: an antitrust quandary, *Antitrust Law and Economic Review*, **2**, 53–68.

Asch, P. and Seneca, J. (1975) Characteristics of collusive firms, *Journal of Industrial Economics*, **23**, 223–37.

Asch, P. and Seneca, J. (1976) Is collusion profitable? *Review of Economics and Statistics*, **58**, 1–10.

Ascher, K. (1987) *The Politics of Privatisation: Contracting Out Public Services*. London: Macmillan.

Aust, P. (1997) An institutional analysis of vertical coordination versus vertical integration: the case of the US broiler industry, Department of Agricultural Economics, Michigan State University Staff Paper, 97–24.

Averch, H. and Johnson, L.L. (1962) Behaviour of the firm under regulatory constraint, *American Economic Review*, **52**, 1052–69.

Aw, B. and Batra, G. (1998) Firm size and the pattern of diversification, *International Journal of Industrial Organisation*, **16**, 313–31.

Axelrod, R. (1984) *The Evolution of Cooperation*. New York: Basic Books.

Bagwell, K. and Staiger, R.W. (1997) Collusion over the business cycle, *Rand Journal of Economics*, **28**, 82–106.

Bailey, D. and Boyle, S.E. (1971) The optimal measure of concentration, *Journal of the American Statistical Association*, **66**, 702–6.

Bain, J.S. (1948) Output quotas in imperfect cartels, *Quarterly Journal of Economics*, **62**, 617–22.

Bain, J.S. (1951) Relation of profit rate to industry concentration: American manufacturing, 1936–1940, *Quarterly Journal of Economics*, **65**, 293–324.

Bain, J.S. (1954) Economies of scale, concentration and the condition of entry in twenty manufacturing industries, *American Economic Review*, **64**, 15–39.

Bain, J.S. (1956) *Barriers to New Competition*. Cambridge, MA: Harvard University Press.

Bain, J.S. (1959) *Industrial Organisation*. New York: John Wiley.

Bain, J.S. (1960) Price leaders, barometers, and kinks, *Journal of Business of the University of Chicago*, **33**, 193–203.

Baldwin, J.R. and Gorecki, P.K. (1987) Plant creation versus plant acquisition: the entry process in Canadian manufacturing, *International Journal of Industrial Organisation*, **5**, 27–41.

Baldwin, R. and Cave, M. (1998) *Understanding Regulation*. Oxford: Oxford University Press.

Barney, J.B. and Hoskisson, R.E. (1990) Strategic groups: untested assertions and research proposals, *Managerial and Decision Making Economics*, **11**, 187–98.

Baumol, W.J. (1967) *Business Behaviour, Value and Growth*. New York: Harcourt Brace Jovanovich.

Baumol, W.J. (1982) Contestable markets: an uprising in the theory of industry structure, *American Economic Review*, **72**, 1–15.

Baumol, W.J. and Willig, R.D. (1986) Contestability: developments since the book. *Oxford Economic Papers* (Special Supplement), **38**, 9–36.

Baumol, W.J., Panzer, J. and Willig, R.D. (1982) *Contestable Markets and the Theory of Industry Structure*. New York: Harcourt Brace Jovanovich.

Beath, J., Katsoulacos, Y. and Ulph, D. (1994) Strategic R&D and innovation, in Cable, J. (ed.) *Current Issues in Industrial Economics*. London: Macmillan, chapter 8.

Beesley, M.E. and Littlechild, S.C. (1997) The regulation of privatised monopolies in the United Kingdom, in Beesley M.E. (ed.) *Privatisation, Regulation and Deregulation*, 2nd edn. London: Routledge.

Benham, L. (1972) The effect of advertising on the price of eyeglasses, *Journal of Law and Economics*, 15, 337–52.

Benham, L. and Benham, A. (1975) Regulating through the professions, *Journal of Law and Economics*, 18, 421–48.

Benton, W. (1943) *Cartels and Peace*, No. 277, University of Chicago Round Table.

Benz, G. and Wolkomir, S. (1964) A decision-making framework within an oligopolistic group structure, *American Journal of Economics and Sociology*, **24**, 291–99.

Berger, A.N. (1995) The profit–structure relationship in banking: tests of market power and efficient structure hypotheses, *Journal of Money Credit and Banking*, **27**, 404–31.

Berger, A.N. and Hannan, T.H. (1998) The efficiency cost of market power in the banking industry: a test of the quiet life and related hypotheses, *Review of Economics and Statistics*, **80**, 454–65.

Berger, P.G. and Ofek, E. (1995) Diversification's effect on firm value, *Journal of Financial Economics*, **37**, 39–65.

Berlin, M. (1999) Jack of all trades? Product diversification in nonfinancial firms, *Federal Reserve Bank of Philadelphia Business Review*, May, 15–29.

Berry, C.H. (1971) Corporate growth and diversification, *Journal of Law and Economics*, 14, 371–83. Reading 24 in Yamey, B.S. (1973) *Economics of Industrial Structure*. Harmondsworth: Penguin.

Berry, C.H. (1974) Corporate diversification and market structure, *Rand Journal of Economics* (formerly the *Bell Journal of Economics and Management Science*), 5, 196–204.

Bertrand, J. (1883) Théorie mathématique de la richesse sociale, *Journal des Savants*, 499–508.

Besanko, D., Dranove, D. and Shanley, M. (1996) *The Economics of Strategy*. New York: John Wiley.

Bishop, M. and Thompson, D. (1992) Regulatory reform and productivity growth in the UK's public utilities, *Applied Economics*, **24**, 1181–90.

Blackstone, E.A. (1972) Monopsony power, reciprocal buying, and government contracts: the General Dynamic case, *Antitrust Bulletin*, 17, 445–66.

Blair, B.F. and Lewis, T.R. (1994) Optimal retail contracts with asymmetric information and moral hazard, *Rand Journal of Economics*, **25**, 284–96.

Blair, J.M. (1972) *Economic Concentration*. New York: Harcourt Brace Jovanovich

Blaug, M. (1963) A survey of the theory of process-innovations, *Economica*, 30, 13–22.

Bloch, H. (1974) Advertising and profitability: a reappraisal, *Journal of Political Economy*, **82**, 267–86.

Bloom, M. (1999) A UK perspective on the Europeanisation of national competition law. Paper presented at the Centre for the Law of the European Union, University College of London, 17 September 1999.

Board of Trade (1944) *Survey of Internal Cartels*. Public Records Office.

Boardman, A.E. and Vining, A.R. (1989) Ownership and performance in competitive environments: a comparison of performance of private, mixed and state owned enterprises, *Journal of Law and Economics*, **32**, 1–33.

Bolton, P. and Whinston, M. (1991) The 'foreclosure' effects of vertical mergers, *Journal of Institutional and Theoretical Economics*, **147**, 207–26.

Bolton, P. and Whinston, M. (1993) Incomplete contracts, vertical integration, and supply assurances, *Review of Economic Studies*, **60**, 121–48.

Bonanno, G. and Vickers, J. (1988) Vertical separation, *Journal of Industrial Economics*, **36**, 257–65.

Borcherding, T.E., Burnaby, T., Pommerehne, W.W. and Schneider, F. (1982) Comparing the efficiency of private and public production: evidence from five countries, *Zeitschrift für Nationalokonomie* (Supplement 2), 127–56.

Borden, N. (1942) *The Economic Effects of Advertising*. Chicago: Irwin.

Bork, R.H. (1954) Vertical integration and the Sherman Act: the legal history of an economic misconception, *University of Chicago Law Review*, **22**, 157–201.

Bork, R. (1978) *The Antitrust Paradox: A Policy at War with Itself*. New York: Basic Books.

Bos, D. (1991) *Privatisation: A Theoretical Treatment*. Oxford: Clarendon Press.

Bosch, J.C. (1989) Alternative measures of rates of return: some empirical evidence, *Managerial and Decision Making Economics*, **10**, 229–339.

Brealey, R. and Myers, R. (1999) *Principles of Corporate Finance*, 6th edn. New York: McGraw-Hill.

Brems, H. (1951) Cartels and competition, *Weltwirtschaftliches Archiv*, **66**, 51–67.

Bresnahan, T. (1992) Sutton's sunk costs and market structure: price competition, advertising and the evolution of concentration. Review article, *Rand Journal of Economics*, **23**, 137–52.

Bresnahan, T.F. and Schmalensee, R.C. (1987) The empirical renaissance in industrial economics: an overview, *Journal of Industrial Economics*, **35**, 371–8.

Briggs, H. (1996) Optimal cartel trigger strategies and the number of firms, *Review of Industrial Organisation*, **11**, 551–61.

Britton, L.C., Clark, T.A.R. and Ball, D.F. (1992) Modify or extend? The application of the structure conduct performance approach to service industries, *The Service Industries Journal*, **12**, 34–43.

Brod, A. and Shivakumar, R. (1999) Advantageous semi-collusion, *The Journal of Industrial Economics*, **47**, 221–30.

Brofenbrenner, M. (1940) Applications of the discontinuous oligopoly demand, *Journal of Political Economy*, **48**, 420–7.

Brozen, Y. (1971) Bain's concentration and rates of return revisited, *Journal of Law and Economics*, **13**, 279–92.

Brozen, Y. (1975) *The Competitive Economy*. Morristown, NJ: General Learning Press.

Bryson, B. (1994) *Made in America*. London: Minerva.

Burke, T. (1991) *Competition in Theory and Practice*. London: Routledge.

Buxton, A.J., Davies, S.W. and Lyons, S.R. (1984) Concentration and advertising in consumer and producer markets, *Journal of Industrial Economics*, **32**, 451–64.

Byers, J.D. and Peel, D.A. (1994) Linear and non-linear models of economic time series: an introduction with applications to industrial economics, in Cable J. (ed.) *Current Issues in Industrial Economics*. London: Macmillan.

Cable, J. (1972) Market structure, advertising policy and intermarket differences in advertising intensity, in Cowling, K. (ed.) *Market Structure and Corporate Behaviour: Theory and Empirical Analysis of the Firm*. London: Gray Mills.

Cable, J. and Schwalbach, J. (1991) International comparisons of entry and exit, in Geroski, P.A. and Schwalbach, J. (eds) *Entry and Market Contestability: An International Comparison*. Oxford: Blackwell.

Cady, J. (1976) An estimate of the price effects of restrictions on drug price advertising, *Economic Inquiry*, **14**, 493–510.

Call, G.D. and Keeler, T.E. (1985) Airline deregulation, fares and market behaviour: some empirical evidence, in Daugherty, A.H. (ed.) *Analytical Studies in Transport Economics*. Cambridge: Cambridge University Press.

Carlton, D. (1979) Vertical integration in competitive markets under uncertainty, *Journal of Industrial Economics*, **27**, 189–209.

Carlton, D. and Perloff, J.M. (1999) *Modern Industrial Organisation*. Harlow: Addison-Wesley.

Cave, M. and Williamson, P. (1996) Entry, competition and regulation in UK telecommunications, *Oxford Review of Economic Policy*, **12**, 100–21.

Caves, R.E. (1980) Corporate strategy and structure, *Journal of Economic Literature*, **28**, 64–92.

Caves, R.E. (1992) Productivity dynamics in manufacturing plants: comments and discussion, *Brookings Papers on Economic Activity*, 187–267.

Caves, R.E. (1998) Industrial organization and new findings on the turnover and mobility of firms, *Journal of Economic Literature*, **36**, 1947–82.

Caves, R.E. and Greene, D.P. (1996) Brands, quality levels, prices, and advertising outlays: empirical evidence on signals and information costs, *International Journal of Industrial Organisation*, **14**, 29–52.

Caves, R.E. and Porter, M.E. (1977) From entry barriers to mobility barriers: conjectural decisions and contrived deterrence to new competition, *Quarterly Journal of Economics*, **91**, 241–62.

Caves, R.E. and Porter, M.E. (1980) The dynamics of changing seller concentration, *Journal of Industrial Economics*, **29**, 1–15.

Caves, R.E. and Williamson, P.J. (1985) What is product differentiation really? *Journal of Industrial Economics*, **34**, 113–32.

Chamberlin, E. (1933) *The Theory of Monopolistic Competition*. Cambridge, MA: Harvard University Press.

Chamberlin, E. (1957) On the origin of oligopoly, *Journal of Economics*, **67**, 211–18.

Chandler, A.D., Jr (1977) *The Visible Hand: The Managerial Revolution in American Business*. Cambridge, MA: Harvard University Press.

Chandler, A.D. (1990) *Scale and Scope: The Dynamics of Industrial Capitalism*. Cambridge, MA: Harvard University Press.

Chen, Y. (1997) Multidimensional signalling and diversification, *Rand Journal of Economics*, **28**, 168–87.

Chen, Z. and Ross, T.W. (1999) Refusals to deal and orders to supply in competitive markets, *International Journal of Industrial Organisation*, **17**, 399–418.

Chesher, A. (1979) Testing the law of proportionate effect, *Journal of Industrial Economics*, **27**, 403–11.

Cheung, S.N. (1983) The contractual nature of the firm, *Journal of Law and Economics*, **26**, 386–405.

Choi, J.P. (1998) Information concealment in the theory of vertical integration, *Journal of Economic Behaviour and Organisation*, **35**, 117–31.

Church, J. and Gandal, N. (2000) Systems competiton, vertical merger and foreclosure, *Journal of Economics and Management Strategy*, **9**, 25–51.

Clanton, D.A. (1977) Trade associations and the FTC, *Antitrust Bulletin*, **22**, 307.

Clark, J.B. (1899) *The Distribution of Wealth*. London: Macmillan.

Clark, J.M. (1940) Towards a concept of workable competition, *American Economic Review*, **30**, 241–56.

Clarke, R. (1979) On the lognormality of firm and plant size distribution: some UK evidence, *Applied Economics*, **11**, 415–33.

Clarke, R. (1985) *Industrial Economics*. Oxford: Blackwell.

Clarke, R. (1993) Trends in concentration in UK manufacturing, 1980–9, in Casson, M. and Creedy, J. (eds) *Industrial Concentration and Economic Inequality*. Aldershot: Edward Elgar.

Clarke, R., Davies, S. and Waterson, M. (1984) The profitability–concentration relation: market power or efficiency? *Journal of Industrial Economics*, **32**, 435–50.

Clarke, R., Davies, S. and Driffield, N.L. (1999) *Monopoly Policy in the UK: Assessing the Evidence*. Cheltenham: Edward Elgar.

Coase, R.H. (1937) The nature of the firm, *Economica*, **4**, 386–405.

Coate, M.B. (1989) The dynamics of price–cost margins in concentrated industries, *Applied Economics*, **21**, 261–72.

Cockburn, I. and Henderson, R. (1994) Racing to invest? The dynamics of competition in the ethical drugs market, *Journal of Economics and Management Strategy*, **3**, 481–519.

Cohen, K.J. and Cyert, R.M. (1965) *Theory of the Firm*. New Jersey: Prentice Hall.

Cohen, W.M. (1995) Empirical studies of innovative activity, in Stoneman, P. (ed.) *Handbook of the Economics of Innovation and Technical Change*. Oxford: Blackwell, chapter 8.

Cohen, W.M. and Levin, R.C. (1989) Empirical studies of innovation and market structure, in Schmalensee, R. and Willig, R. (eds) *Handbook of Industrial Organisation*, Vol. 2. Amsterdam: North-Holland, pp.1059–107.

Colangelo, G. (1995) Vertical vs horizontal integration: pre-emptive merging, *Journal of Industrial Economics*, **43**, 323–37.

Collins, N.R. and Preston, L.E. (1966) Concentration and price–cost margins in food manufacturing industries, *Journal of Industrial Economics*, **15**, 271–86.

Comanor, W.S. (1967a) Market structure, product differentiation and industrial research, *Quarterly Journal of Economics*, **18**, 639–57.

Comanor, W.S. (1967b) Vertical mergers, market power and the antitrust laws, *American Economic Review, Papers and Proceedings*, **57**, 254–65.

Comanor, W.S. (1985) Vertical price-fixing, vertical market restrictions, and the new antitrust policy, *Harvard Law Review*, **98**, 983–1002.

Comanor, W.S. and Frech III, H.E. (1985) The competitive effects of vertical agreements, *American Economic Review*, **75**, 539–46.

Comanor, W. and Leibenstein, H. (1969) Allocative efficiency, X-efficiency and the measurement of welfare losses, *Economica*, **36**, 304–9.

Comanor, W.S. and Scherer, F.M. (1969) Patent statistics as a measure of technical change, *Journal of Political Economy*, **77**, 392–8.

Comanor, W.S. and Wilson, T. (1967) Advertising, market structure and performance, *Review of Economics and Statistics*, **49**, 423–40.

Comanor, W.S. and Wilson, T. (1974) *Advertising and Market Power*. Cambridge, MA: Harvard University Press.

Comanor, W.S. and Wilson, T. (1979) Advertising and competition: a survey, *Journal of Economic Literature*, **17**, 453–76.

Comment, R. and Jarrell, G. (1995) Corporate focus and stock returns, *Journal of Financial Economics*, **37**, 67–87.

Connor, J.M., Rogers, R. and Bhagavan, V. (1996) Concentration and countervailing power in the US food manufacturing industries, *Review of Industrial Organisation*, **11**, 473–92.

Contini, B. and Revelli, R. (1989) The relationship between firm growth and labour demand, *Small Business Economics*, **1**, 309–14.

Cook, M. and Farquharson, C. (1998) *Business Economics*. London: Pitman.

Cournot, A. (1838) Recherches sur le Principes Mathématiques de la Théorie des Richesses. Reprinted as *Researches into the Mathematical Principles of the Theory of Wealth*. London: Macmillan, 1897.

Coursey, D., Isaac, M.R. and Smith, V.L. (1984) Market contestability in the presence of sunk costs, *Rand Journal of Economics*, **15**, 69–84.

Cowan, S. (1997) Competition in the water industry, *Oxford Review of Economic Policy*, **13**, 83–92.

Cowan, T. and Sutter, D. (1999) The costs of cooperation, *Review of Austrian Economics*, **12**, 161–73.

Cowling, K. and Mueller, D.C. (1978) The social costs of monopoly power, *Economic Journal*, **88**, 727–48.

Cox, S.R. (1982) Some evidence on the early price effects of attorney advertising in the USA, *Journal of Advertising*, **1**, 321–31.

Cox, S.R., De Serpa, A. and Smith, S. (1982) Attorney advertising and the pricing of legal services, *Journal of Industrial Economics*, **30**, 305–18.

Croome, P. and Horsfall, P. (1983) Advertising: key to the success of Kellogg's Super Noodles, in Bullmore, J.J.D. and Waterson, M.J. (eds) *The Advertising Association Handbook*. London: Holt, Rinehart & Winston.

Cubbin, J.S. and Geroski, P.A. (1990) The persistence of profits in the United Kingdom, in Mueller D.C. (ed.) *The Dynamics of Company Profits: An International Comparison*. Cambridge: Cambridge University Press.

Curry, B. and George, K. (1983) Industrial concentration: a survey, *Journal of Industrial Economics*, **31**, 203–55.

Cuthbert, N. and Black, W. (1959) Restrictive practices in the food trades, *Journal of Industrial Economics*, **8**, 33–57.

Cyert, R. (1955) Oligopoly behaviour and the business cycle, *Journal of Political Economy*, **63**, 41–51.

Cyert, R. and March, J.G. (1964) *A Behavioural Theory of the Firm*. Englewood Cliffs, NJ: Prentice Hall.

Daley, L., Mahotra, V. and Sivakumar, R. (1997) Corporate focus and value creation: evidence from spinoffs, *Journal of Financial Economics*, **45**, 257–81.

Dalton, J.A. and Rhoades, S.A. (1974) Growth and product differentiation as factors influencing changes in concentration, *Journal of Industrial Economics*, **22**, 235–40.

Darby, M. and Karni, E. (1973) Free competition and optimal amount of fraud, *Journal of Law and Economics*, **16**, 67–88.

Das, B.J., Chappell, W. and Shughart, W. (1993) Advertising, competition and market share instability, *Applied Economics*, **25**, 1409–12.

d'Aspremont, C. and Jacquemin, A. (1988) Joint R&D ventures, cooperative and non-cooperative R&D in duopoly with spillovers, *American Economic Review*, **78**, 1133–7.

d'Aspremont, C., Jacquemin, A., Gabszowiez, J. and Weymark, J. (1983) On the stability of collusive price-leadership, *Canadian Journal of Economics*, **16**, 17–25.

Davidson, K. (1983) The competitive significance of segmented markets, *California Law Review*, **71**, 445–63.

Davies, S.W. (1979) Choosing between concentration indices: the iso-concentration curve, *Economica*, **46**, 67–75.

Davies, S.W. (1989) Concentration, in Davies, S. and Lyons, B. (eds) *The Economics of Industrial Organisation*. London: Longman.

Davies, S.W. (1996) Competition and competition policy in the UK, *OECD Economic Surveys: United Kingdom*. Paris: OECD.

Davies, S.W. and Lyons, B.R. (1982) Seller concentration: the technological explanation and demand uncertainty, *Economic Journal*, **92**, 903–19.

Davies, S.W. and Lyons, B.R. (1996) *Industrial Organisation in the European Union*. Oxford: Clarendon Press.

Davies, S.W. and Morris, C. (1995) A new index of vertical integration: some estimates for UK manufacturing, *International Journal of Industrial Organisation*, **13**, 151–77.

Davies, S.W., Driffield, N.L. and Clarke, R. (1999) Monopoly in the UK: what determines whether the MMC finds against the investigated firms, *Journal of Industrial Economics*, **47**, 263–83.

Davis, E.H., Kay, J.A. and Star, J. (1991) Is advertising rational? *Business Strategy Review*, **2**, 1–23.

Davis, L.E. (1974) Self-regulation in baseball 1909–71, in Noll, R.G. (ed.) *Government and the Sports Business*. Washington, DC: Brookings Institute.

Dawkins, R. (1998) *Unweaving the Rainbow, Science, Delusion and the Appetite for Wonder*. London: Penguin.

de Jong, H.W. (ed.) (1993) *The Structure of European Industry*. Dordrecht: Kluwer.

Demsetz, H. (1968) Why regulate utilities? *Journal of Law and Economics*, **11**, 55–65.

Demsetz, H. (1969) Information and efficiency: another viewpoint, *Journal of Law and Economics*, **12**, 1–22.

Demsetz, H. (1973) Industry structure, market rivalry and public policy, *Journal of Law and Economics*, **16**, 1–9.

Demsetz, H. (1974a) Advertising in the affluent society, in Brozen, Y. (ed.) *Advertising and Society*. New York: New York University Press.

Demsetz, H. (1974b) Two systems of belief about monopoly, in Goldschmid, H.J., Mann, H.M. and Weston, J.F. (eds) *Industrial Concentration: The New Learning*. Boston, MA: Little Brown.

Demsetz, H. (1982) Barriers to entry, *American Economic Review*, **72**, 47–57.

Denicolò, V. (1996) Patent races and optimal patent breadth and length, *Journal of Industrial Economics*, **44**, 249–65.

Dennis, P.T. (1992) Practical approaches: an insider's look at the new horizontal merger guidelines, *Antitrust*, **6**(6), 6–11.

Dixit, A. (1982) Recent developments in oligopoly theory, *American Economic Review, Papers and Proceedings*, **72**, 12–17.

Dnes, A. (1995a) Franchising and privatization, *Public Policy for the Private Sector*, March. World Bank.

Dnes, A. (1995b) Post-privatization performance – regulating telecommunications in the UK: testing for regulatory capture, *Public Policy for the Private Sector*, October. World Bank.

Dnes, A. (1997) The privatization of British Rail: a track record, *Economic Review*, September, 4–6.

Dobson, P. (1997) The EC green paper on vertical restraints: an economic comment, Competition and Regulation Bulletin, London Economics, edition 7.

Dobson, P. and Waterson, M. (1996) *Vertical Restraints and Competition Policy*, Office of Fair Trading Research Paper No. 12. London: OFT.

Dobson, P. and Waterson, M. (1997) Countervailing power and consumer prices, *Southern Economic Journal*, **64**, 617–25.

Dobson, P. and Waterson, M. (1999) Retailer power: how regulators should respond to greater concentration in retailing, *Economic Policy*, **28**, 135–64.

Dolan, R.J. (1977) How an association is investigated and what the government is looking for – a Federal Trade Commission perspective, *Antitrust Bulletin*, **22**, 273–86.

Dolbear, F.T., Lave, L.B., Bowman, G., Lieberman, A., Prescott, E., Reuter, F. and Sherman, R. (1968) Collusion in oligopoly an experiment on the effect of numbers and information, *Quarterly Journal of Economics*, **82**, 240–59.

Domberger, S. (1986) Economic regulation through franchise contracts, in Kay, J., Mayer, C. and Thompson, D. (eds) *Privatisation and Regulation: The UK Experience*. Oxford: Clarendon Press.

Domberger, S. (1999) *The Contracting Organization: A Strategic Guide to Outsourcing*. Oxford: Oxford University Press.

Domberger, S. and Fiebig, D.G. (1993) The distribution of price changes in oligopoly, *The Journal of Industrial Economics*, **41**, 295–313.

Domberger, S. and Hall, C. (1995) *The Contracting Casebook: Competitive Tendering in Action*. Canberra: Australian Government Publishing Service.

Domberger, S. and Jenson, P. (1997) Contracting out by the public sector: theory, evidence, prospects, *Oxford Review of Economic Policy*, **13**, 67–78.

Domberger, S. and Piggott, S. (1986) Privatisation policies and public enterprise: a survey, *Economic Record*, **62**, 145–62.

Domberger, S. and Rimmer, S. (1994) Competitive tendering and contracting in the public sector: a survey, *International Journal of the Economics of Business*, **1**, 439–53.

Domberger, S., Meadowcroft, S. and Thompson, D. (1986) Competitive tendering and efficiency: the case of refuse collection, *Fiscal Studies*, **7**, 69–87.

Domberger, S., Meadowcroft, S. and Thompson, D. (1987) The impact of competitive tendering on the costs of hospital domestic services, *Fiscal Studies*, **8**, 39–54.

Domberger, S., Hall, C. and Li, E. (1995) The determinants of price and quality in competitively tendered contracts, *Economic Journal*, **105**, 1545–70.

Donsimoni, M.P., Economides N.S. and Polemarchakis, H.M. (1986) Stable cartels, *International Economic Review*, **27**, 317–27.

Dorfman, R. and Steiner, P.O. (1954) Optimal advertising and optimal quality, *American Economic Review*, **44**, 826–36.

Douma, S. and Schreuder, H. (1998) *Economic Approaches to Organisations*, 2nd edn. Hemel Hempstead: Prentice Hall.

Droucopoulos, V. and Lianos, T. (1993) The persistence of profits in the Greek manufacturing industry, 1963–1988, *International Review of Applied Economics*, **7**, 163–76.

Duetsch, L. (1984) An examination of industry exit patterns, *Review of Industrial Organisation*, **1**, 60–8.

Dunne, P. and Hughes, A. (1994) Age, size, growth and survival: UK companies in the 1980's, *Journal of Industrial Economics*, **42**, 115–40.

Dunne, T., Roberts, M.J. and Samuelson, L. (1988) Patterns of firms entry and exit in US manufacturing industries, *Rand Journal of Economics*, **19**, 495–515.

Dunne, T., Roberts, M.J. and Samuelson, L. (1989) The growth and failure of US manufacturing plants, *Quarterly Journal of Economics*, **104**, 671–98.

Eckard, E.W. (1987) Advertising, competition and market share instability, *Journal of Business*, **60**, 539–52.

Eckard, E.W. (1995) A note on the profit–concentration relation, *Applied Economics*, **27**, 219–23.

Economides, N. (1996) The economics of networks, *International Journal of Industrial Organisation*, **14**, 673–99.

Economist (1991) The purest treasure, *The Economist*, 7 September.

Economist (1998) The economics of antitrust, *The Economist*, May.

Economist (1999) Procter and Gamble: Jager's gamble, *The Economist*, 5 November.

Economist (2000) The future of economics, *The Economist*, 4 March.

Edgeworth, F. (1897) La teoria pura del monopolio, *Giornale degli Economisti*, **15**, 13–31. Reprinted as The pure theory of monopoly, in *Papers Relating To Political Economy*. London: Macmillan, 1925.

Edgeworth, F.Y. (1932) *Mathematical Psychics*. London: Kegan Paul [originally published 1881].

Edwards, J., Kay, J.A. and Mayer, C.P. (1987) *The Economic Analysis of Accounting Profitability*. Oxford: Clarendon Press.

Efroymson, C.W. (1955) The kinked demand curve reconsidered, *Quarterly Journal of Economics*, **69**, 119–36.

Ellison, G. (1994) Theories of cartel stability and the Joint Executive Committee, *Rand Journal of Economics*, **25**, 37–57.

Elzinga, K.G. and Hogarty, T.F. (1973) The problem of geographic delineation in anti-merger suits, *Antitrust Bulletin*, **18**, 45–81.

Elzinga, K.G. and Hogarty, T.F. (1978) The problem of geographic delineation revisited: the case of coal, *Antitrust Bulletin*, **23**, 1–18.

Emerson, M., Aujean, M., Catinat, M., Goybet, P. and Jacquemin, A. (1988) *The Economics of 1992: The EC Commission's Assessment of the Economic Effects of Completing the Single Market*. Oxford: Oxford University Press.

Emons, W. (1996) Good times, bad times, and vertical upstream integration, *International Journal of Industrial Organisation*, **14**, 465–84.

Erickson, W.B. (1969) Economics of price fixing, *Antitrust Law and Economic Review*, **2**, 83–122.

Esposito, L. and Esposito, F.F. (1971) Foreign competition and domestic industry profitability, *Review of Economics and Statistics*, **53**, 343–53.

Estrin, S. and Periton, V. (1991) Does ownership always matter? *International Journal of Industrial Organization*, **9**, 55–72.

European Commission (1985) *Completing the Internal Market*, White Paper.

European Commission (1994) Evolution of mergers in the community, *European Economy*, **4**, 13–40.

European Commission (1995a) *Green Paper on Innovation*, COM(95)688.

European Commission (1995b) Car price differentials in the European Union on 1 May 1995, IP/95/768. Brussels: European Commission.

European Commission (1997a) Competition issues, *The Single Market Review*, Subseries V, vol. 3.

European Commission (1997b) Economies of scale, *The Single Market Review*, Subseries V, vol. 4. London: Kogan Page.

European Commission (1997c) *Panorama of EU Industry: The Key to European Industry*, vols 1 and 2. Luxemburg: Office for Official Publications of the European Communities.

European Commission (1997d) *Green Paper on Vertical Restraints in EU Competition Policy*, COM(96)721.

European Commission (1997e) Irish sugar, *Official Journal of the European Communities*, L258, 22 September.

European Commission (1998a) *Communication from the Commission on the application of the Community Competition Rules to Vertical Restraints*, COM(98)544.

European Commission (1998b) Audi-VW, *Official Journal of the European Communities*, L124, 25 April.

European Commission (1999a) *Draft Guidelines on Vertical Restraints*, at http://europa.eu.int/comm/dg04/antitrust/others/vertical_restraints/reform/consultation/draft_guidelines_en.pdf (last accessed October 1999).

European Commission (1999b) British sugar, *Official Journal of the European Communities*, L76, 22 March.

Eurostat (1997) *Retailing in the European Economic Area*. Brussels: European Commission.

Evans, D.S. (1987a) Tests of alternative theories of firm growth, *Journal of Political Economy*, **95**, 657–74.

Evans, D.S. (1987b) The relationship between firm growth, size and age: estimates for 100 manufacturing industries, *Journal of Industrial Economics*, **35**, 567–81.

Evely, R. and Little, I.M.D. (1960) *Concentration in British Industry*. Cambridge: Cambridge University Press.

Fellner, W. (1949) *Competition Among the Few*. New York: Alfred Knopf.

Fellner, W. (1965) *Competition Among the Few*. London: Frank Cass.

Fisher, F.M. and McGowan, J.J. (1983) On the misuse of accounting rates of return to infer monopoly profits, *American Economic Review*, **73**, 82–97.

Fisher, I. (1898) Cournot and mathematical economics, *Quarterly Journal of Economics*, **12**.

Fog, B. (1956) How are cartel prices determined? *Journal of Industrial Economics*, **5**, 16–23.

Fortune (1969) How judgement came to the plumbing conspirators, *Fortune*, December.

Foster, C.D. (1992) Privatisation, public ownership and the regulation of natural monopoly. Cambridge: Cambridge University Press.

Fraas, A.G. and Greer, D.F. (1977) Market structure and price collusion: an empirical analysis, *Journal of Industrial Economics*, **26**, 21–44.

Fraser, R. (ed.) (1988) *Privatisation: The UK Experience and International Trends*. Cambridge: Cambridge University Press.

Freeman, C. and Soete, L. (1997) *The Economics of Industrial Innovation*, 3rd edn. London: Pinter.

Friedman, M. (1962) *Capitalism and Freedom*. Chicago: Chicago University Press.

Fudenberg, D. and Tirole, J. (1989) Noncooperative game theory for industrial organization: an introduction and overview, in Schmalensee, R.C. and Willig, R. (eds) *Handbook of Industrial Organization*. Amsterdam: North-Holland.

Galbraith, J.K. (1952) *American Capitalism: The Concept of Countervailing Power*. Boston: Houghton-Mifflin.

Galbraith, J.K. (1958) *The Affluent Society*. Boston: Houghton Mifflin.

Galbraith, J.K. (1967) *The New Industrial Estate*. Boston: Houghton Mifflin.

Gal-Or, E. (1991) Optimal franchising in oligopolistic markets with uncertain demand, *International Journal of Industrial Organisation*, **9**, 343–64.

Gal-Or, E. (1999) Vertical integration or separation of the sales function as implied by competitive forces, *International Journal of Industrial Organisation*, **17**, 641–62.

Ganley, J. and Grahl, J. (1988) Competitive tendering and efficiency in refuse collection: a critical comment, *Fiscal Studies*, **9**, 81–5.

George, K.D. and Joll, C. (1981) *Industrial Organisation*. London: Allen & Unwin.

George, K.D., Joll, C. and Lynk, E.L. (1991) *Industrial Organisation: Competition, Growth and Structural Change*. London: Routledge.

Geroski, P.A. (1990) Modelling persistent profitability, in Mueller, D.C. (ed.) *The Dynamics of Company Profits: An International Comparison*. Cambridge: Cambridge University Press.

Geroski, P.A. (1991a) *Market Dynamics and Entry*. Oxford: Blackwell.

Geroski, P.A. (1991b) Domestic and foreign entry in the United Kingdom, in Geroski, P.A. and Schwalbach, J. (eds) *Entry and Market Contestability: An International Comparison*. Oxford: Blackwell.

Geroski, P.A. (1994) *Market Structure, Corporate Performance and Innovative Acitivity*. Oxford: Clarendon Press.

Geroski, P.A. (1995) What do we know about entry? *International Journal of Industrial Organization*, **13**, 421–40.

Geroski, P.A. (1999) *The Growth of Firms in Theory and Practice*, Centre of Economic Policy Research Discussion Paper Series, No. 2092.

Geroski, P.A. and Jacquemin, A. (1988) The persistence of profits: a European comparison, *Economic Journal*, **98**, 375–89.

Geroski, P.A. and Toker, S. (1996) The turnover of market leaders in UK manufacturing industry, 1979–1986, *International Journal of Industrial Organization*, **14**(2), 141–58.

Geroski, P., Machin, S. and Van Reenen, J. (1993) The profitability of innovating firms, *Rand Journal of Economics*, **24**, 198–211.

Gibrat, R. (1931) *Les Inegalities Economiques*. Paris: Sirey.

Gilligan, T.W. (1986) The competitive effects of resale price maintenance, *Rand Journal of Economics*, **17**, 544–56.

Gini, C. (1912) *Variabilità e Mutabilità*. Bologna.

Glazer, A. (1985) The advantages of being first, *American Economic Review*, **75**, 473–80.

Glover, F.J. (1977) Government contracting, competition and growth in the heavy woolen industry, in Tucker, K.A. (ed.) *Business History Selected Readings*, London. Frank Cass.

Goddard, J.A. and Wilson, J.O.S. (1996) Persistence of profits for UK manufacturing and service sector firms, *The Service Industries Journal*, **16**, 105–17

Goddard, J.A. and Wilson, J.O.S. (1999) Persistence of profit: a new empirical interpretation. *The International Journal of Industrial Organisation*, **17**, 663–87.

Goddard, J.A., Wilson, J.O.S. and Blandon, P. (2000) Panel tests of Gibrat's Law for Japanese manufacturing, *International Journal of Industrial Organisation*, forthcoming.

Goddard, J.A. and Wilson, J.O.S. (2000) Growth and Convergence, *Economics Letters*, forthcoming.

Gollop, F.M. and Monahan, J.L. (1991) A generalised index of diversification: trends in US manufacturing, *Review of Economics and Statistics*, **73**, 318–30.

Goodacre, A. and Tonks, I. (1995) Finance and technological change, in Stoneman, P. (ed.) *Handbook of the Economics of Innovation and Technical Change*. Oxford: Blackwell, chapter 8.

Gorecki, P. (1975) An inter-industry analysis of diversification in the UK manufacturing sector, *The Journal of Industrial Economics*, **24**, 131–46.

Gort, M. (1962) *Diversification and Integration in American Industry*. Princeton, NJ: Princeton University Press.

Goudie, A.W. and Meeks, G. (1982) Diversification by merger, *Economica*, **49**, 447–59.

Gow, R.H. and Swinnen, F.H. (1998) Up- and downstream restructuring, foreign direct investment, and hold-up problems in agricultural transition, *European Review of Agricultural Economics*, **25**, 331–50.

Graham, D.R., Kaplan, D.P. and Sibley, R.S. (1983) Efficiency and competition in the airline industry, *Bell Journal of Economics*, **14**, 118–38.

Green, E.J. and Porter, R.H. (1984) Noncooperative collusion under imperfect price information, *Econometrica*, **52**, 87–100.

Green, R. (1999) Checks and balances in utility regulation: the UK experience, *Public Policy for the Private Sector*, May. World Bank.

Green, R. and Newbery, D.M. (1997) Competition in the electricity industry in England and Wales, *Oxford Review of Economic Policy*, **13**, 27–46.

Gribben, J.D. (1976) The conglomerate merger, *Applied Economics*, **8**, 19–35.

Griffen, J.M. and Karolyi, G.A. (1998) Another look at the role of the industrial structure of markets for international diversification strategies, *Journal of Financial Economics*, **50**, 351–73.

Griffiths, A. and Wall, S. (1995) *Applied Economics*, 6th edn. London: Longman.

Griffiths, A. and Wall, S. (eds) (1999) *Applied Economics: An Introductory Course*. London: Longman.

Griliches, Z. (1958) Research costs and social returns: hybrid corn and related innovations, *Journal of Political Economy*, **66**, 419–31.

Gujarati, D.N. (1995) *Basic Econometrics*, 3rd edn. New York: McGraw-Hill.

Gupta, B. (1995) Collusion in the Indian tea industry in the Great Depression: an analysis of panel data. Unpublished working paper, University of Alicante.

Hall, B. (1987) The relationship between firm size and firm growth in the US manufacturing sector, *Journal of Industrial Economics*, **35**, 583–606.

Hall, C. and Rimmer, S.J. (1994) Performance monitoring and public sector contracting, *Australian Journal of Public Administration*, **53**, 453–61.

Hall, R.L. and Hitch, C.J. (1939) Price theory and business behaviour, *Oxford Economic Papers*, No. 2, pp.12–45.

Hannah, L. (1983) *The Rise of the Corporate Economy*. London: Methuen.

Hannah, L. and Kay, J.A. (1977) *Concentration in Modern Industry*. London: Macmillan.

Hannah, L. and Kay, J.A. (1981) The contribution of mergers to concentration growth: a reply to Professor Hart, *Journal of Industrial Economics*, 29, 305–13.

Hannan, T.H. and McDowell, J.M. (1984) The determinants of technology adoption: the case of the banking firm, *Rand Journal of Economics*, 15, 328–35.

Harberger, A.C. (1954) Monopoly and resource allocation, *American Economic Review, Papers and Proceedings*, 44, 77–87.

Harbord, D. and Hoehn, T. (1994) Barriers to entry and exit in European competition policy, *International Review of Law and Economics*, 14, 411–35.

Hardt, M. (1995) Market foreclosure without vertical integration, *Economic Letters*, 47, 423–9.

Harrigan, K.R. (1983) A framework for looking at vertical integration, *Journal of Business Strategy*, 3, 30–7.

Harris, M. and Raviv, A. (1996) The capital budgeting process: incentives and information, *Journal of Finance*, 51, 1139–74.

Harrod, R. (1952) *Economic Essays*. London: Macmillan.

Hart, P.E. (1962) The size and growth of firms, *Economica*, 29, 29–39.

Hart, P.E. (1971) Entropy and other measures of concentration, *Journal of the Royal Statistical Society, Series A*, 134, 73–86.

Hart, P.E. (1981) The effects of mergers on industrial concentration, *Journal of Industrial Economics*, 29, 315–20.

Hart, P.E. and Clarke, R. (1980) *Concentration in British Industry: 1935–1975*. Cambridge: Cambridge University Press.

Hart, P.E. and Oulton, N. (1996) The size and growth of firms, *Economic Journal*, 106, 1242–52.

Hart, P.E. and Oulton, N. (1999) Gibrat, Galton and job generation, *International Journal of the Economics of Business*, 6, 149–64.

Hart, P.E. and Prais, S.J. (1956) The analysis of business concentration: a statistical approach, *Journal of the Royal Statistical Society, Series A*, 119, 150–91.

Hart, P.E., Utton, M.A. and Walshe, G. (1973) *Mergers and Concentration in British Industry*. Cambridge: Cambridge University Press.

Hartley, K. and Huby, M. (1986) Contracting out policy: theory and evidence, in Kay, J., Mayer, C. and Thompson, D. (eds) *Privatisation and Regulation: The UK Experience*. Oxford: Clarendon Press.

Haskel, J. and Scaramozzino, P. (1997) Do other firms matter in oligopolies? *Journal of Industrial Economics*, 45, 27–45.

Hay, D. and Morris, D. (1991) *Industrial Economics and Organization: Theory and Evidence*, 2nd edn. Oxford: Oxford University Press.

Hay, G.A. and Kelley, D. (1974) An empirical survey of price fixing conspiracies, *Journal of Law and Economics*, 17, 13–38.

Heide, J.B., Dutta, S. and Bergen, M. (1998) Exclusive dealing and business efficiency: evidence from industry practice, *Journal of Law and Economics*, 41, 387–407.

Helfat, C.E. and Teece, D.J. (1987) Vertical integration and risk reduction, *Journal of Law, Economics and Organisation*, 3, 47–68.

Helm, D. (1994) British utility regulation: theory, practice and reform, *Oxford Review of Economic Policy*, 10, 17–39.

Helm, D. and Jenkinson, T. (1997) The assessment: introducing competition into regulated industries, *Oxford Review of Economic Policy*, 13, 1–14.

Hennessy, D.A. (1997) Information asymmetry as a reason for vertical integration, in Caswell, J.A. and Cotterill, R.W. (eds) *Strategy and Policy in the Food System: Emerging Issues. Proceedings of NE-165 Conference, Washington DC*.

Herfindahl, O.C. (1950) Concentration in the US steel industry. Unpublished PhD thesis.

Herling, J. (1962) *The Great Price Conspiracy: The Story of the Antitrust Violations in the Electrical Industry*. Washington: Robert Luce.

Herold, A.L. (1977) How can an association avoid antitrust problems? A private practitioner's perspective, *Antitrust Bulletin*, **22**, 299–306.

Hersch, P.L. (1994) The effects of resale price maintenance on shareholder wealth: the consequences of Schwegmann, *Journal of Industrial Economics*, **42**, 205–16.

Heston, S.L. and Rouwenhorst, K.G. (1994) Does industrial structure explain the benefits of international diversification? *Journal of Financial Economics*, **36**, 3–27.

Hexner, E. (1946) *International Cartels*. Chapel Hill: University of North Carolina Press.

Hirschliefer, J. (1971) The private and social value of information and the reward of inventive activity, *American Economic Review*, **61**, 561–74.

Hirschman, A.O. (1945) *National Power and the Structure of Foreign Trade*. Berkeley: University of California Bureau of Business and Economic Research.

Holstius, K. (1990) Sates response to advertising, *International Journal of Advertising*, **9**, 38–56.

Hoschman, J. and Luski, I. (1988) Advertising and economic welfare: comment, *American Economic Review*, **78**, 290–6.

Howard, J.A. (1954) Collusive behaviour, *Journal of Business*, **27**, 196–204.

Howard, T. (1998) Survey of European advertising expenditure, 1980–1996, *International Journal of Advertising*, **17**(1), 115–24.

Howe, W.S. (1978) *Industrial Economics*. London: Macmillan.

Hunter, A. (1954) The Monopolies Commission and price fixing, *Economic Journal*, **66**, 587–602.

Hurdle, G.J., Johnson, R.L., Joskow, A.S., Werden, G.J. and Williams, M.A. (1989) Concentration, potential entry, and performance in the airline industry, *Journal of Industrial Economics*, **38**, 119–39.

Hurwicz, L. (1945) The theory of economic behaviour, *American Economic Review*, **35**, 909–25.

Hymer, S. and Pashigan, P. (1962) Firm size and rate of growth, *Journal of Political Economy*, **52**, 556–69.

Jackson, P.M. (1997) Planning, control and the contract state, in Corry, D. (ed.) *Public Expenditure: Effective Management and Control*. London: Dryden.

Jacobson, D. and Andréosso-O'Callaghan, B. (1996) *Industrial Economics and Organisation: A European Perspective*. Maidenhead: McGraw-Hill.

Jaffe, A.B. (1986) Technological opportunity and spillovers of R&D, *American Economic Review*, **76**, 984–1001.

James, L.M. (1946) Restrictive agreements and practices in the lumber industry 1880–1939, *Southern Economic Journal*, **13**, 115–25.

Jenny, F. and Weber, A.P. (1983) Aggregate welfare loss due to monopoly power in the French economy: some tentative estimates, *Journal of Industrial Economics*, **32**, 113–30.

Jenny, F. and Weber, A.P. (1990) The persistence of profits in France, in Mueller, D.C. (ed.) *The Dynamics of Company Profits: An International Comparison*. Cambridge: Cambridge University Press.

Jevons, W.S. (1970) *The Theory of Political Economy*. Harmondsworth: Penguin [originally published 1871].

John, G. and Weitz, B.A. (1988) Forward integration into distribution: an empirical test of transaction cost analysis, *Journal of Law, Economics and Organisation*, **4**, 337–356.

Johnston, J. (1960) *Statistical Cost Analysis*. New York: McGraw-Hill.

Joskow, P.L. (1985) Vertical integration and long-term contracts: the case of coal-burning electric generating plants, *Journal of Law, Economics and Organisation*, **1**, 33–80.

Jovanovic, B. (1982) Selection and evolution of industry, *Econometrica*, **50**, 649–70.

Kaldor, N. (1950) The economic aspects of Advertising, *Review of Economic Studies*, **18**, 1–27.

Kalecki, M. (1945) On the Gibrat distribution, *Econometrica*, **13**, 161–70.

Kamerschen, D.R. (1966) An estimation of the 'welfare losses' from monopoly in the

American economy, *Western Economic Journal*, **4**, 221–36.

Kamerschen, D.R. (1968) Market growth and industry concentration, *Journal of the American Statistical Association*, **63**, 228–41.

Kamien, M.I. and Schwartz, N.L. (1970) Market structure, elasticity of demand and incentive to invent, *Journal of Law and Economics*, **13**, 241–52.

Kamien, M.I. and Schwartz, N.L. (1975) Market structure and innovation: a survey, *Journal of Economic Literature*, **13**, 1–38.

Kamien, M. and Schwartz, N. (1982) *Market Structure and Innovation*. Cambridge: Cambridge University Press.

Kantzenbach, E., Kottman, E. and Krüger, R. (1995) *New Industrial Economics and Experiences from European Merger Control – New Lessons about Collective Dominance?* Luxemburg: Office for Official Publications of the European Communities.

Kaplan, S. and Weisbach, M. (1992) The success of acquisitions: evidence from divestitures, *Journal of Finance*, **47**, 107–38.

Karshenas, M. and Stoneman, P. (1995) Technological diffusion, in Stoneman, P. (ed.) *Handbook of the Economics of Innovation and Technical Change*. Oxford: Blackwell, chapter 7.

Kashyap, A. (1995) Sticky prices: new evidence from retail catalogues, *Quarterly Journal of Economics*, **43**, 245–74.

Katz, M.L. (1989) Vertical contractual relations, in Schmalensee, R. and Willig, R.D. (eds) *Handbook of Industrial Organisation*, vol. 1. Amsterdam: North-Holland, chapter 11.

Kaul, A. and Wittink, D.R. (1995) Empirical generalisations about the impact of advertising on price sensitivity and price, *Marketing Science*, **14**, 151–60.

Kay, J.A. (1976) Accountants, too could be happy in a golden age: the accountants' rate of profit and the internal rate of return, *Oxford Economic Papers*, **28**, 447–60.

Kay, J.A. (1990a) Identifying the strategic market, *Business Strategy Review*, **1/2**, 2–24.

Kay, J.A. (1990b) Vertical restraints in European competition policy, *European Economic Review*, **34**, 551–61.

Kay, J.A. (1993) *Foundations of Corporate Success*. Oxford: Oxford University Press.

Kay, J.A. and Mayer, C.P. (1986) On the application of accounting rates of return, *Economic Journal*, **96**, 199–207.

Kay, J.A. and Vickers, J. (1990) Regulatory reform: an appraisal, in Majone, G. (ed.) *Deregulation or Reregulation? Regulatory reform in Europe and the United States*. London: Pinter.

Keating, B. (1991) An update on industries ranked by average rates of return, *Applied Economics*, **23**, 897–902.

Khemani, R.S. and Shapiro, D.M. (1990) The persistence of profitability in Canada, in Mueller, D.C. (ed.) *The Dynamics of Company Profits: An International Comparison*. Cambridge: Cambridge University Press.

King, S. (1983) Advertising and market entry, in Bullmore, J.J.D. and Waterson, M.J. (eds) *The Advertising Association Handbook*. London: Holt, Rinehart & Winston.

Kirzner, I. (1973) *Competition and Entrepreneurship*. Chicago: Chicago University Press.

Kirzner, I. (1997a) Entrepreneurial discovery and the competitive market process: an Austrian approach, *Journal of Economic Literature*, **35**, 60–85.

Kirzner, I. (1997b) *How Markets Work: Disequilibrium, Entrepreneurship and Discovery*, IEA Hobart Paper No. 133. London: Institute of Economic Affairs.

Klein, B. (1995) The economics of franchise contracts, *Journal of Corporate Finance*, **2**, 9–37.

Klein, B. and Murphy, K. (1988) Vertical restraints as contract enforcement mechanisms, *Journal of Law and Economics*, **31**, 265–97.

Kleit, A.N. and Palsson, H.P. (1999) Horizontal concentration and anticompetitive behavior in the central Canadian cement industry: testing arbitrage cost hypothesis, *International Journal of Industrial Organisation*, **17**, 1189–202.

Klepper, S. (1996) Entry, exit, growth, and innovation over the product life cycle, *American Economic Review*, **86**, 562–83.

Klevonich, A.K. (1966) The graduated fair return: a regulatory proposal, *American Economic Review*, **56**, 477–84.

Knight, F.H. (1921) *Risk, Uncertainty and Profit*, Part 2. Boston: Houghton Mifflin.

Koutsoyannis, A. (1979) *Modern Microeconomics*. London: Macmillan.

Koutsoyannis, A. (1982) *Non-price Decisions, The Firm in a Modern Context*. London: Macmillan.

Kranton, R.E. and Minehart, D.F. (1999) *Vertical Integration, Networks and Markets*, Cowles Foundation Discussion Papers No. 1231. New Haven, CT: Yale University.

Krattenmaker, T.G. and Salop, S.C. (1986) Anticompetitive exclusion: raising rivals' cost to achieve power over price, *The Yale Law Journal*, **96**, 209–93.

Kreps, D., Milgrom, P., Roberts, J. and Wilson, R. (1982) Rational cooperation in the finitely repeated prisoners' dilemma, *Journal of Economic Theory*, **27**, 245–52.

Krickx, G.A. (1995) Vertical integration in the computer main frame industry: a transaction cost interpretation, *Journal of Economic Behaviour and Organisation*, **26**, 75–91.

Krugman, H.E. (1965) The impact of television advertising, *Public Opinion Quarterly*, **29**, 349–56.

Kuhlman, J.M. (1969) Nature and significance of price fixing rings, *Antitrust Law and Economic Review*, **2**, 69–82.

Kumar, M.S. (1985) Growth, acquisition activity and firm size: evidence from the United Kingdom, *Journal of Industrial Economics*, **33**, 327–38.

Kwoka, J.E. (1981) Does the choice of concentration measure really matter? *Journal of Industrial Economics*, **29**, 445–53.

Kwoka, J.E. (1984) Advertising, and the price and quality of optometric services, *American Economic Review*, **74**, 211–16.

Lafontaine, F. (1992) Agency theory and franchising: some empirical results, *Rand Journal of Economics*, **23**, 263–83.

Lafontaine, F. and Slade, M.E. (1996) Retail contracting and costly monitoring: theory and evidence, *European Economic Review*, **40**, 923–32.

Lambin, J.J. (1976) *Advertising, Competition and Market Conduct in Oligopoly over Time*. Amsterdam: North-Holland.

Lang, L.H. and Stulz, R.M. (1994) Tobin's q, corporate diversification, and firm performance, *Journal of Political Economy*, **102**, 1248–80.

Langlois, R.N. and Robertson, P.L. (1989) Explaining vertical inegration: lessons from the American automobile industry, *Journal of Economic History*, **49**, 361–75.

Lavery, K. (1997) *Smart Contracting for Local Government Services: Processes and Experience*. Westport: Praeger.

Leibenstein, H. (1950) Bandwagon, snob, and Veblen effects in the theory of consumers' demand, *Quarterly Journal of Economics*, **64**, 183–207.

Leibenstein, H. (1966) Allocative efficiency versus X-efficiency, *American Economic Review*, **56**, 392–415.

Lerner, A.P. (1934) The concept of monopoly and the measurement of monopoly power, *Review of Economic Studies*, **1**, 157–75.

Levenstein, M.C. (1996) Do price wars facilitate collusion? A study of the bromine cartel before World War 1, *Explorations In Economic History*, **33**, 107–37.

Levenstein, M.C. (1997) Price wars and the stability of collusion: a study of the pre-World War I bromine industry, *Journal of Industrial Economics*, **45**, 117–37.

Levin, R.C., Klevorick, A.K., Nelson, R.R. and Winter, S.G. (1987) Appropriating the returns from industrial R&D, *Brookings Papers on Economic Activity*, pp.783–820.

Levy, D. (1987) The speed of the invisible hand, *International Journal of Industrial Organisation*, **5**, 79–92.

Levy, D., Bergen, M., Dutta, S. and Venable, R. (1997) The magnitude of menu costs: direct evidence from large supermarket chains, *Quarterly Journal of Economics*, **112**, 791 825.

Lewis, P. and Thomas, H. (1990) The linkage between strategy, strategic groups, and performance in the UK retail grocery industry, *Strategic Management Journal*, **11**, 385–97.

Liefmann, R. (1932) *Cartels, Concerns and Trusts*. London: Methuen.

Lindenberg, E. and Ross, S. (1981) Tobin's *q* ratio and industrial organisation, *Journal of Business*, **54**, 1–32.

Lintner, V.G., Pokorny, M.J., Woods, M.M. and Blinkhorn, M.R. (1987) Trade unions and technological change in the UK mechanical engineering industry, *British Journal of Industrial Relations*, **25**, 19–29.

Lipsey, R. and Lancaster, K. (1956) The general theory of second best, *Review of Economic Studies*, **24**, 11–32.

Lipczynski, J. (1994) Selected aspects of cartel stability. Unpublished PhD thesis, London School of Economics.

Littlechild, S. (1981) Misleading calculations of the social costs of monopoly power, *Economic Journal*, **91**, 348–63.

Littlechild, S. (1982) *The Relationship between Advertising and Price*. London: Advertising Association.

Littlechild, S. (1983) *Regulation of British Telecommunications' Profitability*. London: HMSO.

Livesey, F. (1987) *Economics for Business Decisions*. London: Pitman.

London Economics (1997) The power of the puppy – does advertising deter entry? *Competition and Regulation Bulletin*, **6**. http://www.londecon.co.uk/pubs/comp/crb6_web.htm. Last accessed December 1999.

Lorenz, M.O. (1905) Methods of measuring the concentration of wealth, *American Statistical Association Journal*, **9**, 209–19.

Love, J.H. and Stephen, F.H. (1996) Advertising, price and quality in self regulating professions: a survey, *International Journal of the Economics of Business*, **3**, 227–47.

Low, R.E. (1970) *Modern Economic Organisation*. Homewood, IL: Irwin.

Luffman, G.A. and Reed, R. (1984) *The Strategy and Performance of British Industry, 1970–80*. London: Macmillan.

Lynk, E. (1993) Privatisation, joint production and the comparative efficiencies of private and public ownership: the UK water case, *Fiscal Studies*, **14**, 98–116.

Lyons, B., Matraves, C. and Moffatt, P. (1997) Industrial concentration and market integration in the European Union, *Wissenschaftszentrum Berlin für Sozialforschung*, Discussion Paper FSIV 97–21.

MacGregor, D.H. (1906) *Industrial Combination*. London: Bell.

Machlup, F. (1952a) *The Economics of Sellers' Competition*. Baltimore: Johns Hopkins University Press.

Machlup, F. (1952b) *The Political Economy of Monopoly*. Baltimore: Johns Hopkins University Press.

Machlup, F. and Taber, M. (1960) Bilateral monopoly, successive monopoly and vertical integration, *Economica*, **27**, 101–19.

Macho-Stadler, I. and Perez-Castrillo, J.D. (1998) Centralised and decentralised contracts in a moral hazard environment, *Journal of Industrial Economics*, **46**, 489–510.

Mackintosh, D.R. and Frey, S. (1978) The prices of prescription eyeglasses under advertising restraints, *Journal of Consumer Affairs*, **12**, 323–32.

Maclaurin, W.R. (1950) The process of technological innovation: the launching of a new scientific industry. *American Economic Review*, **40**, 90–112.

Maddala, G.S. (1992) *Introduction to Econometrics*, 2nd edn. New York: Maxwell Macmillan.

Madu, C., Chu-Hua, K. and Madu, A. (1991) Setting priorities for the IT industry in Taiwan: a Delphi study, *Long Range Planning*, **24**, 105–18, quoted in Cline, A. (1998) *Prioritization Process using Delphi Technique*, in http://www.carolla.com (last accessed December 1999).

Maitland-Walker, J. (1999) The new UK competition law regime, *European Competition Law Review*, **20**, 51–4.

Mann, H., Henning, J. and Meehan, J.W. (1967) Advertising and concentration, *Journal of Industrial Economics*, **16**, 34–45.

Mansfield, E. (1961) Technical change and the rate of imitation, *Econometrica*, **29**, 741–66.

Mansfield, E. (1962) Entry, Gibrat's Law, innovation, and the growth of firms, *American Economic Review*, **52**, 1023–51.

Mansfield, E. (1968) *Industrial Research and Techno-logical Innovation.* New York: W.W. Norton.

Mansfield, E. (1969) Industrial research and development: characteristics, costs and diffusion results, *American Economic Review, Papers and Proceedings,* **59,** 65–79.

Mansfield, E. (1975) *Microeconomics, Theory and Applications,* 2nd edn New York: W.W. Norton.

Marion, B.W., Mueller, W.F., Cotterill, R.W., Geithman, E.E. and Schmelzer, J.R. (1979) *The Food Retailing Industry: Market Structure, Profits and Prices.* New York: Praeger.

Markham, J.W. (1951) The nature and significance of price leadership, *American Economic Review,* **41,** 891–905.

Markham, J.W. (1965) Market structure, business conduct and innovation, *American Economic Review,* **55,** 323–32.

Markides, C. and Williamson, P.J. (1994) Related diversification, core competencies and corporate performance, *Strategic Management Journal,* **15,** 149–65.

Marris, R. (1964) *The Economic Theory of Managerial Capitalism.* London: Macmillan.

Marris, R. (1966) *The Economic Theory of Managerial Capitalism.* London: Macmillan.

Marshall, A. (1961) *The Principles of Economics,* 9th edn, with annotations by C.W. Guillebaud. London: Macmillan [originally published 1890].

Martin, S. (1984) The misuse of accounting rates of return: comment, *American Economic Review,* **74,** 501–6.

Martin, S. (1988) *Industrial Economics.* New York: Macmillan.

Martin, S. (1993) *Advanced Industrial Economics.* Cambridge, MA: Blackwell.

Marvel, H. and McCafferty, K. (1984) Resale price maintenance and quality certification, *Rand Journal of Economics,* **15,** 346–59.

Marx, D. (1953) *International Shipping Cartels.* Princeton, NJ: Princeton University Press.

Mason, E.S. (1939) Price and production policies of large scale enterprise, *American Economic Review,* **29,** 61–74.

Mason, E.S. (1949) The current state of the monopoly problem in the United States, *Harvard Law Review,* **62,** 1265–85.

Mathewson, F. and Winter, R.A. (1984) An economic theory of vertical restraints, *Rand Journal of Economics,* **15,** 27–38.

Mathewson, F. and Winter, R.A. (1998) The law and economics of resale price maintenance, *Review of Industrial Organisation,* **13,** 57–84.

Matsui, A. (1989) Consumer-benefited cartels under strategic capacity investment competition, *International Journal of Industrial Organisation,* **7,** 451–70.

Matsusaka, J.G. (1993) Takeover motives during the conglomerate merger wave, *Rand Journal of Economics,* **24,** 357–79.

Maurizi, A., Moore, R.L. and Shepard, L. (1981) The impact of price advertising: the California eyewear market after one year, *Journal of Consumer Affairs,* **15,** 290–300.

McAfee, R. and McMillan, J. (1987) Auctions and bidding, *Journal of Economic Literature,* **25,** 699–738.

McCloughan, P. (1995) Simulation of industrial concentration, *Journal of Industrial Economics,* **43,** 405–33.

McGahan, A.M. (1999) The performance of US corporations: 1981–1994, *Journal of Industrial Economics,* **47,** 373–98.

McGee, J.S. (1958) Predatory price cutting: the Standard Oil (NJ) case, *Journal of Law and Economics,* **1,** 137–69.

McGee, J. and Thomas, H. (1986) Strategic groups: theory, research and taxonomy, *Strategic Management Journal,* **7,** 141–60.

McMaster, R. (1995) Competitive tendering in the UK health and local authorities. What happens to the quality of service? *Scottish Journal of Political Economy,* **42,** 407–27.

Megginson, W., Nash, R. and von Randenborgh, M. (1994) The financial and operating performance of newly privatized firms: an international empirical analysis, *Journal of Finance,* **49,** 403–52.

Midgley, D.F., Morrison, P.D. and Roberts, J.H. (1992) The effect of network structure in industrial diffusion processes, *Research Policy*, **21**, 533–52.

Milgrom, P. (1989) Auctions and bidding: a primer, *Journal of Economic Perspectives*, **3**, 3–22.

Milgrom, P. and Roberts, J. (1982) Predation, reputation and entry deterrence, *Journal of Economic Theory*, **27**, 280–312.

Milgrom, P. and Roberts, J. (1986) Price and advertising signals of product quality, *Journal of Political Economy*, **94**, 796–821.

Miller, R.A. (1969) Market structure and industrial performance: relation of profit rates to concentration, advertising intensity and diversity, *Journal of Industrial Economics*, **17**, 95–100.

Millward, R. (1990) Productivity in the UK services sector: Historical trends 1956–1985 and comparisons with the USA, *Oxford Bulletin of Economics and Statistics*, **52**, 423–435.

Milne, R.G. and McGee, M. (1992) Competitive tendering in the NHS: a new look at some old estimates, *Fiscal Studies*, **13**, 96–111.

Minehart, D. and Neeman, Z. (1999) Termination and coordination in partnerships, *Journal of Economics and Management Strategy*, **8**, 191–221.

Minkes, A. and Foxall, G. (1982) The bounds of entrepreneurship: inter-organisational relationships in the process of industrial innovation, *Managerial and Decision Economics*, **3**.

Mixon, F.G. (1994) The role of advertising in the market process: a survey, *International Journal of Advertising*, **13**, 15–23.

Mixon, F.G. (1995) Advertising as information: further evidence, *Southern Economic Journal*, **61**, 1213–18.

Molyneux, R. and Thompson, D. (1987) Nationalised Industry performance, *Fiscal Studies*, **8**, 48–82.

Monopolies and Mergers Commission (1966) *Household Detergents: A Report on the Supply of Household Detergents*. London: HMSO.

Monopolies and Mergers Commission (1968) *Supply of Man-made Cellulose Fibres*, HC 130. London: HMSO.

Monopolies and Mergers Commission (1973) *British Match Corporation Ltd and Wilkinson Sword Ltd: A Report on the Proposed Merger*, Cmnd 5442. London: HMSO.

Monopolies and Mergers Commission (1981) *Bicycles: A Report on T.I. Raleigh Industries (1981/2)*, HC 67. London: HMSO.

Monopolies and Mergers Commission (1993) *Gas and British Gas Plc*. London: HMSO.

Monopolies and Mergers Commission (1997a) *London Clubs International and Capital Corporation PLC: A Report on the Merger Situation*. London: HMSO.

Monopolies and Mergers Commission (1997b) *First Bus Plc and S.B. Holdings Ltd: A Report on the Merger Situation*. London: HMSO.

Monopolies and Mergers Commission (1997c) *Domestic Electrical Goods II*. London: HMSO.

Monopolies and Mergers Commission (1998) *Tomkins Plc and Kerry Group Plc: A Report on the Merger Situation*. London: HMSO.

Monopolies and Mergers Commission (1999a) *Ladbroke Group Plc and the Coral Betting Business*. London: HMSO.

Monopolies and Mergers Commission (1999b) *British Broadcasting Group Plc and Manchester United Plc: A Report on the Proposed Merger*. London: HMSO.

Monteverde, K. and Teece, D.J. (1982) Supplier switching costs and vertical integration in the automobile industry, *Bell Journal of Economics*, **13**, 206–13.

Montgomery, C. (1994) Corporate diversification, *Journal of Economic Perspectives*, **8**, 163–78.

Montgomery, C.A. and Wernerfelt, B. (1988) Diversification, Ricardian rents, and Tobin's q, *Rand Journal of Economics*, **19**, 623–32.

Moore, J. (1983) Why privatise? in Kay, J., Mayer, C. and Thompson, D. (eds) *Privatisation and Regulation: The UK Experience*. Oxford: Clarendon Press.

Moore, T.G. (1986) US airline deregulation: its effect on passengers, capital and labour, *Journal of Law and Economics*, **29**, 1–28.

Moraga-Gonzalez, J.L. (2000) Quality, uncertainty and informative advertising, *International Journal of Industrial Organization*, **18**, 615–40.

Morrison, H. (1933) *Socialisation and Transport*. London: Constable.

Morrison, S.A. and Winston, C. (1987) Empirical implications of the contestability hypothesis, *Journal of Law of Economics*, **30**, 53–66.

Mueller, D.C. (1969) A theory of conglomerate mergers, *Quarterly Journal of Economics*, **84**, 643–59.

Mueller, D.C. (1972) A life cycle theory of the firm. *Journal of Industrial Economics*, **20**, 199–219.

Mueller, D.C. (1977) The persistence of profits above the norm, *Economica*, **44**, 369–80.

Mueller, D.C. (1986) *Profits in the Long-run*. Cambridge: Cambridge University Press.

Mueller, D.C. (1990) The persistence of profits in the United States, in Mueller, D.C. (ed.) *The Dynamics of Company Profits: An International Comparison*. Cambridge: Cambridge University Press.

Mueller, W.F. and Hamm, L.G. (1974) Trends in industrial concentration, *Review of Economics and Statistics*, **56**, 511–20.

Mueller, W.F. and Rodgers, R.T. (1980) The role of advertising in changing concentration of manufacturing industries, *Review of Economics and Statistics*, **62**, 89–96.

Mund, V.A. and Wolf, R.H. (1971) *Industrial Organisation and Public Policy*. New York: Appleton-Century-Crofts.

Myers, G. (1994) *Predatory Behaviour in UK Competition Policy*, Office of Fair Trading Research Paper No. 5.

National Economic Development Council (1983) *Innovation in the UK*. London: National Economic Development Office.

National Economic Research Associates (1992) *Market Definition in UK Competition Policy*, Office of Fair Trading Research Paper, No. 1.

Nawaz, M. (1997) The power of the puppy – does advertising deter entry? *London Economics – Competition and Regulation Bulletin*, Edition 6, April, 1–7.

Nazerali and Cowan, M. (1999) Importing the EU model into UK competition law: a blueprint for reform or a step into 'Euroblivion', *European Competition Law Review*, **20**, 55–61.

Needham, D. (1976) Entry barriers and non-price aspects of firms' behaviour, *Journal of Industrial Economics*, **25**, 29–43.

Needham, D. (1978) *The Economics of Industrial Structure Conduct and Performance*, Edinburgh: Holt, Rinehart & Winston.

Nelson, M.N. (1922) *Open Price Associations*. Urbana: University of Illinois.

Nelson, P. (1974a) The economic value of advertising, in Brozen, Y. (ed.) *Advertising and Society*. New York: New York University Press.

Nelson, P. (1974b) Advertising as information, *Journal of Political Economy*, **82**, 729–54.

Nelson, P. (1975) The economic consequences of advertising, *Journal of Business*, **48**, 213–41.

Nelson, P. (1978) Advertising as information once more, in Tuerck, D.C. (ed.) *Issues in Advertising: The Economics of Persuasion*. New York: New York University Press.

Nelson, R.R. and Winter, S. (1982) *An Evolutionary Theory of Economic Change*. Cambridge: Cambridge University Press.

Neuberger, D. (1998) Industrial organization of banking: a review, *International Journal of the Economics of Business*, **5**, 97–118.

Neven, D.J. (1989) Strategic entry deterrence: recent developments in the economics of industry, *Journal of Economic Surveys*, **3**, 213–33.

Nevins, A. (1953) *Study in Power: John D Rockefeller*. New York: Scribner's.

Newman, H.H. (1978) Strategic groups and the structure–performance relationship, *Review of Economics and Statistics*, **60**, 417–27.

Nichols, L. (1985) Advertising and economic welfare, *American Economic Review*, **75**, 213–18.

Nickell, S.J. (1996) Competition and corporate performance, *Journal of Political Economy*, **104**, 724–46.

Nickell, S.J., Wadhwani, S. and Wall, M. (1992) Productivity growth in UK companies, 1975–1986, *European Economic Review*, **36**, 1055–91.

Nightingale, J. (1978) On the definition of industry and market, *Journal of Industrial Economics*, **27**, 1–12.

Noll, R.G. (1977) Major league team sports, in Adams, W. (1977) *The Structure of American Industry.* New York: Macmillan, chapter 11.

Nordhaus, W. (1969) *Invention, Growth and Welfare.* Cambridge, MA: MIT Press.

Oakey, R., Rothwell, R. and Cooper, S. (1988) *Management of Innovation in High Technology Small Firms.* London: Pinter.

O'Brien, D.P. and Swann, D. (1969) *Information Agreements, Competition and Efficiency.* London: Macmillan.

O'Brien, D., Howe, W., Wright, D. and O'Brien, R. (1979) *Competition Policy, Profitability and Growth.* London: Macmillan.

Odagiri, H. and Yamawaki, H. (1990) The persistence of profits in Japan, in Mueller D.C. (ed.) *The Dynamics of Company Profits: An International Comparison.* Cambridge: Cambridge University Press.

O'Donoghue, T., Scotchmer, S. and Thisse, J. (1998) Patent breadth, patent life, and the pace of technological progress, *Journal of Economics and Management Strategy*, **7**, 1–32.

OECD (1965) Glossary of Terms Relating to Restrictive Business Practices, B-2.

OECD (1984) *Competition and Trade Policies.* Paris: OECD.

OECD (1989) *Predation*, http://www.oecd//dat/clp/Publications/PREDA.PDF. Paris: OECD.

OECD (1993a) *Competition Policy and a Changing Broadcasting Industry.* Paris: OECD.

OECD (1993b) *Competition Policy and Vertical Restraints: Franchising Agreements.* Paris: OECD.

OECD (1999) *Oligopoly*, Committee on Competition Law and Policy DAFFE/CLP(99)25. Paris: OECD.

Office of Fair Trading (1982) *Opticians and Competition.* London: HMSO.

Office of Fair Trading (1985) *Competition and Retailing.* London: Office of Fair Trading.

Office of Fair Trading (1994a) *Report on Fife Scottish Omnibuses Limited.* London: Office of Fair Trading.

Office of Fair Trading (1994b) *Photocopier Selling Practices.* London: Office of Fair Trading.

Office of Fair Trading (1994c) *Predatory Behaviour in UK Competition Policy*, Research Paper No. 5. London: Office of Fair Trading.

Office of Fair Trading (1995) *An Outline of United Kingdom Competition Policy.* London: Office of Fair Trading.

Office of Fair Trading (1997a) *Consumer Detriment under Conditions of Imperfect Information*, Research Paper No. 11. London: Office of Fair Trading.

Office of Fair Trading (1997b) *Competition in Retailing*, Research Paper No. 13. London: Office of Fair Trading.

Office of Fair Trading (1999) *The Major Provisions*, OFT 400. *The Chapter I Prohibition*, OFT 401. *The Chapter II Prohibition*, OFT 402. *Market Definition*, OFT 403. *Powers of Investigation*, OFT 404. *Concurrent Application to Regulated Industries*, OFT 405. *Transitional Arrangements*, OFT 406. *Enforcement*, OFT 407. *Trade Associations, Professions and Self-regulating Bodies*, OFT 408. *Director General of Fair Trading's Procedural Rules*, OFT 411. *Assessment of Individual Agreements and Conduct*, OFT 414. *Assessment of Market Power*, OFT 415. *Mergers and Ancillary Constraints*, OFT 416. *The Application of the Competition Act to the Telecommunications Sector*, OFT 417. *Intellectual Property Rights*, OFT 418. *Vertical Agreements and Restraints*, OFT 419. *Land Agreements*, OFT 420. *General Economic Interest*, OFT 421. London: Office of Fair Trading.

Ogus, A.I. (1996) *Regulation: Legal Form and Economic Theory.* Oxford: Oxford University Press.

Oi, W.Y. and Hunter, A.P., Jr (1965) *Economics of Private Truck Transportation*, New York: William C. Brown. Reprinted in Yamey, B.S. (ed.) (1973) *Economics of Industrial Structure.* Harmondsworth: Penguin, reading 16.

Oppenheim, S. and Weston, G. (1968) *Federal Antitrust Laws*, 3rd edn., St Paul, MN: West Publishing Co.

Ordover, J., Saloner, G. and Salop, S. (1990) Equilibrium vertical foreclosure, *American Economic Review*, **80**, 127–42.

Ornstein, S. (1978) *Industrial Concentration and Advertising Intensity*. Washington DC: American Enterprise Institute.

Ornstein, S.I. (1985) Resale price maintenance and cartels, *Antitrust Bulletin*, 30, 401–32.

Ornstein, S., Weston, J.F., Intriligator, M.D. and Shrieves, R.E. (1973) Determinants of market structure, *Southern Economic Journal*, 39, 612–25.

Orr, D. (1974) The determinants of entry: a study of the Canadian manufacturing industries, *The Review of Economics and Statistics*, 56, 58–65.

Orr, D. and MacAvoy, P. (1965) Price strategies to promote cartel stability, *Economica*, 32, 186–97.

Osborne, D.K. (1976) Cartel problems, *American Economic Review*, 66, 835–44.

Oster, S.M. (1999) *Modern Competitive Analysis*, 3rd edn. New York: Oxford University Press.

Oster, S.M. and Quigley, J.M. (1977) Regulatory barriers to the diffusion of innovation: some evidence from building codes. *Bell Journal of Economics*, 8, 361–77.

Palda, K.S. (1964) *The Management of Cumulative Advertising Effects*. Englewood Cliffs, NJ: Prentice Hall.

Palmer, J. (1972) Some economic conditions conducive to collusion, *Journal of Economic Issues*, 6, 29–38.

Papandreou, A.G. (1949) Market structure and monopoly power, *American Economic Review*, 39, 883–97.

Parker, D. (1991) Privatisation ten years on, *Economics*, 27, 155–63.

Parker, D. (1994) A decade of privatisation: the effect of ownership change and competition on British Telecom, *British Review of Economic Issues*, 16, 87–115.

Parker, D. and Martin, S. (1995) The impact of UK privatisation on labour and total factor productivity, *Scottish Journal of Political Economy*, 42, 201–20.

Parker, D. and Wu, H.L. (1998) Privatisation and performance: a study of the British steel industry under public and private ownership, *Economic Issues*, 3, 31–50.

Patel, P. and Pavitt, K. (1987) The elements of British technological competitiveness, *National Institute Economic Review*, 122(4), 72–83.

Patel, P. and Pavitt, K. (1995) Patterns of technological activity: their measurement and interpretation, in Stoneman, P. (ed.) *Handbook of the Economics of Innovation and Technical Change*. Oxford: Blackwell, chapter 2.

Patinkin, D. (1947) Multiple-plant firms, cartels, and imperfect competition, *Quarterly Journal of Economics*, 61, 173–205.

Paton, D. (1998) Who advertises prices? A firm level study based on survey data, *International Journal of the Economics of Business*, 5, 57–75.

Paton, D. and Vaughan Williams, L. (1999) Advertising and firm performance: some evidence from UK firms, *Economic Issues*, 4, 89–105.

Peltzman, S. (1976) Toward a more general theory of regulation, *Journal of Law and Economics*, 2, 211–40.

Peltzman, S. (1977) The gains and losses from industrial concentration, *Journal of Law and Economics*, 20, 229–64.

Penrose, E.T. (1959) *The Theory of the Growth of the Firm*. Oxford: Basil Blackwell.

Penrose, E. (1995) *The Theory of the Growth of the Firm*, 3rd edn. Oxford: Oxford University Press.

Pepall, L., Richards, D.J., Norman, G. (1999) *Industrial Organisation: Contemporary Theory and Practice*. St Paul, MN: South-Western College Publishing.

Perren, R. (1979) Oligopoly and competition: price fixing and market sharing among timber firms in northern Scotland 1890–1939, *Business History*, 213–25.

Perry, M.K. (1980) Forward integration by Alcoa: 1888–1930, *Journal of Industrial Economics*, 29, 37–53.

Phillips, A. (1962) *Market Structure, Organisation and Performance*. Cambridge, MA: Harvard University Press.

Phillips, A. (1966) Patents, potential competition and technical progress, *American Economic Review*, 56, 301–10.

Phillips, A. (1972) An econometric study of price-fixing, market structure and performance in British industry in the early 1950s, in Cowling, K. (ed.) *Market Structures and Corporate Behaviour Theory and Empirical Analysis of the Firm.* London: Gray Mills, pp.177–92.

Phillips, A. (1976) A critique of empirical studies of relations between market structure and profitability, *Journal of Industrial Economics*, **24**, 241–9.

Phimister, I.R. (1996) The Chrome Trust: the creation of an international cartel, 1908–38, *Business History*, **38**, 77–89.

Pickering, J.F. (1974) *Industrial Structure and Market Conduct.* London: Martin Robertson.

Pickering, J.F. (1982) The economics of anti-competitive practices, *European Competition Law Review*, **3**, 253–74.

Pindyck, R.S. (1977) Cartel pricing and the structure of the world bauxite market, *Rand Journal of Economics*, **8**, 343–60.

Pindyck, R.S. and Rubinfeld, D.L. (1992) *Microeconomics*, 2nd edn. New York: Macmillan.

Piotrowski, R. (1932) *Cartels and Trusts.* London: Allen & Unwin.

Podolny, J.M. and Scott Morton, F.M. (1999) Social status, entry and predation: the case of British shipping cartels 1879–1929, *Journal of Industrial Economics*, **47**, 41–67.

Porter, M.E. (1976) Interbrand choice, media mix and market performance, *American Economic Review*, **66**, 398–406.

Porter, M.E. (1979) The structure within industries and companies performance, *Review of Economics and Statistics*, **61**, 214–27.

Porter, M.E. (1980) *Competitive Strategy: Techniques for Analysing Industries and Competitors.* New York: The Free Press.

Porter, M.E. (1987) From competitive advantage to corporate strategy, *Harvard Business Review*, May/June, 43–59.

Porter, M.E. (1990) *The Competitive Advantage of Nations.* London: Macmillan.

Porter, R. (1983) A study of cartel stability: the Joint Executive Committee 1880–1886, *Bell Journal of Economics*, **14**, 301–25.

Posner, R.A. (1976) *Antitrust Law – An Economic Perspective.* Chicago: University of Chicago Press.

Posner, R.A. (1979) The Chicago school of anti-trust analysis, *University of Pennsylvania Law Review*, **127**, 925–48.

Posner, R. (1981) The next step in the antitrust treatment of restricted distribution – per se legality, *University of Chicago Law Review*, **48**, 6–26.

Prager, J. (1994) Contracting out government services: lessons from the private sector, *Public Administration Review*, **54**, 176–84.

Prahalad, C. and Hamel, G. (1990) The core competence of the corporation, *Harvard Business Review*, May/June, 79–91.

Prais, S.J. (1976) *The Evolution of Giant Firms in Great Britain.* Cambridge: Cambridge University Press.

Pratten, C.F. (1971) *Economies of Scale in Manufacturing Industry.* Cambridge: Cambridge University Press.

Price, C. and Weyman-Jones, T.G. (1993) *Malmquist Indices of Productivity Change in the UK Gas Industry Before and After Privatisation*, Department of Economics, Research Paper 93/12, Loughborough University.

Prokop, J. (1999) Process of dominant-cartel formation, *International Journal of Industrial Organisation*, **17**, 241–57.

Proudhon, P. (1888) *The Evolution of Capitalism*, trans. Tucker, B.R. (1972). New York: Arno Press [originally published as *Système des Contradictions Economiques*].

Pryke, R. (1981) *The Privatised Industries: Policies and Performance since 1968.* Oxford: Martin Robertson.

Pryke, R. (1982) The comparative performance of public and private enterprise, *Fiscal Studies*, **3**, 68–81.

Qualls, D. (1974) Stability and persistence of economic profit margins in highly concentrated industries, *Southern Economic Journal*, **40**, 604–12.

Quandt, R.E. (1966) On the size distribution of firms, *American Economic Review*, **56**, 416–32.

Ravenscraft, D.J. (1983) Structure–profit relationships at the line of business and industry level, *Review of Economics and Statistics*, 65, 22–31.

Ravenscraft, D. and Scherer, F. (1987a) *Mergers, Sell Offs and Economic Efficiency*, Washington, DC: The Brookings Institution.

Ravenscraft, D.J. and Scherer, F.M. (1987b) Life after takeover, *Journal of Industrial Economics*, 36, 147–56.

Reder, M.W. (1982) Chicago economics: permanence and change, *Journal of Economic Literature*, 20, 1–38.

Reekie, W.D. (1975) Advertising and market structure: another approach, *Economic Journal*, 85, 156–64.

Rees, R. (1975) Advertising, concentration and competition: a comment and further results, *Economic Journal*, 85, 165–72.

Rees, R. (1984) *Public Enterprise Economics*. London: Weidenfeld & Nicolson.

Rees, R. (1993a) Collusive equilibrium in the great salt duopoly, *Economic Journal*, 103, 833–48.

Rees, R. (1993b) Tacit collusion, *Oxford Review of Economic Policy*, 9, 27–40.

Reid, G.C. (1987) *Theories of Industrial Organization*. Oxford: Blackwell.

Reid, G.C. (1992) *Small Firm Growth and its Determinants*, Department of Economics Discussion Paper No. 9213, University of St Andrews.

Resnick, A. and Stern, B.L. (1977) An analysis of information content in television advertising, *Journal of Marketing*, 41, 50–3.

Rey, P. and Stiglitz, J.E. (1988) Vertical restraints and producers' competition, *European Economic Review*, 32, 561–8.

Rey, P. and Tirole, J. (1986) The logic of vertical restraints, *American Economic Review*, 76, 921–39.

Rhoades, S.A. (1974) A further evaluation of the effect of diversification on industry profit performance, *Review of Economics and Statistics*, 56, 557–9.

Richardson, G.B. (1966) The pricing of heavy electrical equipment: competition or agreement? *Bulletin of the Oxford University Institute of Economics and Statistics*, 28, 73–92.

Rizzo, J. and Zeckhauser, R. (1992) Advertising and the price, quantity and quality of primary care physician services, *Journal of Human Resources*, 27, 381–421.

Robertson, P.L. and Langlois, R.L. (1995) Innovation, networks, and vertical integration, *Research Policy*, 24, 543–62.

Robinson, J. (1933) *The Economics of Imperfect Competition*. London: Macmillan.

Robinson, J. (1969) *The Economics of Imperfect Competition*, 2nd edn. London: Macmillan.

Robinson, W.T. and Chiang, J. (1996) Are Sutton's predictions robust? Empirical insights into advertising, R&D and concentration, *Journal of Industrial Economics*, 44, 389–408.

Robinson, W.T., Kalyanaram, G. and Urban, G.L. (1994) First-mover advantages from pioneering new markets: a survey of empirical evidence, *Review of Industrial Organisation*, 9, 1–23.

Romeo, A.A. (1975) Interindustry and interfirm differences in the rate of diffusion of an invention, *Review of Economics and Statistics*, 57, 311–19.

Rondi, L., Sembenelli, A. and Ragazzi, E. (1996) Determinants of diversification patterns, in Davies, S. and Lyons, B. (1996) *Industrial Organisation in the European Union*. Oxford: Oxford University Press, chapter 10.

Rose, N.L. and Shepard, A. (1997) Firm diversification and CEO compensation: managerial ability or executive entrenchment? *Rand Journal of Economics*, 28, 489–514.

Rosenberg, J.P. (1976) Research and market share: a reappraisal of the Schumpeter hypothesis, *Journal of Industrial Economics*, 25, 133–42.

Ross, T.W. (1992) Cartel stability and product differentiation, *International Journal of Industrial Organisation*, 10, 1–13.

Rotemberg, J.J. and Saloner, G. (1986) A supergame-theoretic model of price wars during booms, *American Economic Review*, 76, 390–407.

Roth, A.E. (1991) Game theory as a part of empirical economics, *Economic Journal*, 101, 107–14.

Rothschild, K.W. (1942) The degree of monopoly, *Economica*, 9, 24–40.

Rothschild, K.W. (1947) Price theory and oligopoly, *Economic Journal*, **57**, 299–302.

Rothschild, R. (1999) Cartel stability when costs are heterogeneous, *International Journal of Industrial Organisation*, **17**, 717–34.

Rothwell, G. (1980) Market coordination by the uranium oxide industry, *Antitrust Bulletin*, **25**, 233–68.

Rovizzi, L. and Thompson, D. (1995) The regulation of product quality in public utilities, in Bishop, M., Kay, J. and Mayer, C. (eds) *The Regulatory Challenge*. Oxford: Oxford University Press.

Rumelt, R.P. (1974) *Strategy, Structure and Economic Performance*. Boston, MA: Harvard Business School.

Samuals, J.M. (1965) Size and growth of firms, *Review of Economic Studies*, **32**, 105–12.

Samuals, J.M. and Chesher, A.D. (1972) Growth, survival, and size of companies, 1960–69, in Cowling, K. (ed.) *Market Structure and Corporate Behaviour*. London: Gray–Mills.

Sawyer, M.C. (1985) *The Economics of Industries and Firms*, 2nd edn. London: Croom-Helm.

Schankerman, M. (1998) How valuable is patent protection? Estimates by technology field, *Rand Journal of Economics*, **29**, 77–107.

Scharfstein, D.S. (1998) The dark side of internal capital markets II, NBER Working Paper No. 6352.

Schary, M.A. (1991) The probability of exit, *Rand Journal of Economics*, **22**, 339–53.

Scherer, F.M. (1965) Firm size, market structure, opportunity, and the output of patented inventions, *American Economic Review*, **55**, 1097–125.

Scherer, F.M. (1967a) Research and development resource allocation under rivalry, *Quarterly Journal of Economics*, **81**, 359–94.

Scherer, F.M. (1967b) Market structure and the employment of scientists and engineers, *American Economic Review*, **57**, 524–31.

Scherer, F.M. (1980) *Industrial Market Structure and Economic Performance*, 2nd edn. Chicago: Rand McNally.

Scherer, F.M. (1992) Schumpeter and plausible capitalism, *Journal of Economic Literature*, **30**, 1416–33.

Scherer, F.M. (2000) Professor Sutton's technology and market structure, *Journal of Industrial Economics*, **48**, 215–23.

Scherer, F.M. and Ross, D. (1990) *Industrial Market Structures and Economic Performance*. Boston: Houghton Mifflin.

Scherer, F.M., Beckenstein, A., Kaufer, E. and Murphy, R.D. (1975) *The Economics of Multiplant Operation: An International Comparisons Study*. Cambridge: Cambridge University Press.

Schick, F. (1997) *Making Choices: A Recasting of Decision Theory*. Cambridge: Cambridge University Press.

Schmalensee, R.C. (1972) *The Economics of Advertising*. Amsterdam: North-Holland.

Schmalensee, R. (1973) A note on the theory of vertical integration, *Journal of Political Economy*, **81**, 442–9.

Schmalensee, R.C. (1978) Entry deterrence in the ready-to-eat cereal industry, *Bell Journal of Economics*, **9**, 305–27.

Schmalensee, R.C. (1979) *The Control of Natural Monopolies*. Lexington: DC Heath.

Schmalensee, R. (1982) The new industrial organisation and the economic analysis of modern markets, in Hildenbrand, H. (ed.) *Advances in Economic Theory*. Cambridge: Cambridge University Press.

Schmalensee, R.C. (1985) Do markets differ much? *American Economic Review*, **74**, 341–51.

Schmalensee, R. (1988) Industrial Economics: an overview, *Economic Journal*, **98**, 643–81.

Schmalensee, R.C. (1989) Inter-industry studies of structure and performance, in Schmalensee, R.C. and Willig, R.D. (eds) *Handbook of Industrial Organization*, vol. 2. Amsterdam: North-Holland, chapter 16.

Schmalensee, R. (1990) Empirical Studies of rivalrous behaviour, in Bonanno, G. and Brandolini, D. (eds) *Industrial Structure in the New Industrial Economics*. Oxford: Clarendon Press.

Schmalensee, R. (1992) Sunk costs and market structure: a review article, *Journal of Industrial Economics*, **40**, 125–34.

Schmitt, N. and Weder, R. (1998) Sunk costs and cartel formation: theory and application to the dyestuff industry, *Journal of Economic Behaviour and Organisation*, **36**, 197–220.

Schmookler, J. (1952) The changing efficiency of the American economy, 1869–1938, *Review of Economics and Statistics*, **34**, 214–31.

Schohl, F. (1990) Persistence of profits in the long-run: a critical extension of some recent findings, *International Journal of Industrial Organisation*, **8**, 385–403.

Schonfield, A. (1965) *Modern Capitalism*, Oxford: Oxford University Press.

Schotter, A. (1994) *Microeconomics: A Modern Approach*. New York: Harper Collins.

Schroeter, J., Smith, S. and Cox, S.R. (1987) Advertising and competition in routine legal service markets: an empirical investigation, *Journal of Industrial Economics*, **36**, 49–60.

Schumpeter, J. (1928) The instability of capitalism, *The Economic Journal*, **38**, 361–86.

Schumpeter, J. (1942) *Capitalism, Socialism, and Democracy*. New York: Harper.

Schumpeter, J.A. (1950) *Capitalism, Socialism and Democracy*, 3rd edn. New York: Harper & Row [originally published 1942].

Schwalbach, J. (1991) Entry, exit, concentration and market contestability, in Geroski, P.A. and Schwalbach, J. (eds) *Entry and Market Contestability: An International Comparison*. Oxford: Blackwell.

Schwalbach, J., Grasshoff, U. and Mahmood, T. (1989) The dynamics of corporate profits, *European Economic Review*, **33**, 1625–39.

Schwartz, M. (1986) The nature and scope of contestability theory, *Oxford Economic Papers* (Special Supplement), **38**, 37–57.

Schwartz, M. and Reynolds, R. (1983) Contestable markets: an uprising in industry structure: comment, *American Economic Review*, **73**, 488–90.

Schwartzman, D. (1963) Uncertainty and the size of the firm, *Economica*, **30**, 287–96.

Schwed, F. (1965) *Where are the Customers' Yachts?* New York: Simon & Schuster.

Schwert, G.W. (1981) Using financial data to measure the effects of regulation, *Journal of Law and Economics*, **24**, 121–58.

Scitovsky, T. (1950) Ignorance as a source of monopoly power, *American Economic Review*, **40**, 48–53.

Scitovsky, T. (1971) *Welfare and Competition*, rev. edn. London: Allen & Unwin.

Scott Morton, F. (1997) Entry and predation: British shipping cartels 1879–1929, *Journal of Economics and Management Strategy*, **6**, 679–724.

Servaes, H. (1996) The value of diversification during the conglomerate merger wave, *Journal of Finance*, **51**, 1201–25.

Shalit, S.S. and Sankar, U. (1977) Measurement of firm size, *Review of Economics and Statistics*, **59**, 290–8.

Shaw, R.W. and Simpson, P. (1986) The persistence of monopoly: an investigation of the effectiveness of the United Kingdom Monopolies Commission, *Journal of Industrial Economics*, **34**, 355–69.

Shepherd, W.G. (1967) What does the survivor technique show about economies of scale? *Southern Economic Journal*, **36**, 113–22.

Shepherd, W.G. (1970) *Market Power and Economic Welfare*. New York: Random House.

Shepherd, W.G. (1972) Structure and behaviour in British industries with US comparisons, *Journal of Industrial Economics*, **20**, 35–54.

Shepherd, W.G. (1984) Contestability v Competition, *American Economic Review*, **74**, 572–87.

Shepherd, W.G. (1986) Tobin's q and the structure–performance relationship: comment, *American Economic Review*, **76**, 1205–10.

Shepherd, W.G. (1997) *The Economics of Industrial Organization*, 4th edn. London: Prentice Hall.

Sherif, M. and Sherif, C.W. (1956) *An Outline of Social Psychology*. New York: Harper.

Sherman, R. (1977) Theory comes to industrial organisation, in Jacquemin, A. and de Jong, H.W. (eds) *Welfare Aspects of Industrial Markets*. Amsterdam: Martinus Nijhoff.

Sherman, R. (1985) The Averch and Johnson analysis of public utility regulation twenty years later, *Review of Industrial Organization*, **1**, 178–191.

Shleifer, A. (1985) A theory of yardstick competition, *Rand Journal of Economics*, **16**, 319–27.

Shubik, M. (1959) *Strategy and Market Structure*. New York: John Wiley.

Sibley, D. and Weisman, D.L. (1998) Raising rivals' costs: the entry of an upstream monopolist into downstream markets, *Information Economics and Policy*, **10**, 451–69.

Siegfried, J. and Evans, L. (1994) Empirical studies of entry and exit: a survey of the evidence, *Review of Industrial Organisation*, **9**, 121–55.

Silberman, I.H. (1967) On lognormality as a summary measure of concentration, *American Economic Review*, **57**, 807–31.

Simon, H. (1959) Theories of decision-making in economics and behavioural science, *American Economic Review*, **49**, 253–83.

Simon, H.A. and Bonnini, C.P. (1958) The size distribution of business firms, *American Economic Review*, **48**, 607–17.

Singer, E.M. (1968) *Antitrust Economics*. Englewood Cliffs, NJ: Prentice Hall.

Singh, A. and Whittington, G. (1968) *Growth, Profitability and Valuation*. Cambridge: Cambridge University Press.

Singh, A. and Whittington, G. (1975) The size and growth of firms, *Review of Economic Studies*, **42**, 15–26.

Singh, S., Utton, M.A. and Waterson, M. (1998) Strategic behaviour of incumbent firms in the UK, *International Journal of Industrial Organization*, **16**, 229–51.

Sleuwaegen, L. and Dehandschutter, W. (1991) Entry and exit in Belgian manufacturing, in Geroski, P.A. and Schwalbach, J. (eds) *Entry and Market Contestability: An International Comparison*. Oxford: Blackwell.

Smiley, R. (1988) Empirical evidence on strategic entry deterrence, *International Journal of Industrial Organisation*, **6**, 167–80.

Smirlock, M., Gilligan, T.W. and Marshall, W. (1984) Tobin's *q* and the structure performance relationship, *American Economic Review*, **74**, 1051–60.

Smith, A. (1937) *An Inquiry into the Nature and Causes of the Wealth of Nations*, Cannan, E. (ed.). New York: Modern Library [originally published 1776].

Smyth, D., Boyes, W. and Pesau, D.E. (1975) Measurement of firm size: theory and evidence for the US and UK, *Review of Economics and Statistics*, **57**, 111–13.

Solberg, E.J. (1992) *Microeconomics for Business Decisions*. Lexington: D.C. Heath.

Sonkondi, L. (1969) *Business and Prices*. London: Routledge & Kegan.

Sosnick, S.H. (1958) A critique of concepts of workable competition, *Quarterly Journal of Economics*, **72**, 380–423.

Spaan, R.M. and Erickson, E.W. (1970) The economics of railroading: the beginning of cartelisation and regulation, *Bell Journal of Economics*, **1**, 227–45.

Spence, A.M. (1981) The learning curve and competition, *Bell Journal of Economics*, **12**, 49–70.

Spence, M.A. (1983) Contestable markets and the theory of industry structure: a review, *Journal of Economic Literature*, **21**, 981–90.

Spengler, J.J. (1950) Vertical integration and antitrust policy, *Journal of Political Economy*, **68**, 347–52.

Spiller, P.T. (1985) On vertical mergers, *Journal of Law, Economics and Organisation*, **1**, 285–312.

Sraffa, P. (1926) The laws of returns under competitive conditions, *Economic Journal*, **36**, 535–50. Reprinted in Boulding, K.E. and Stigler, G.J. (eds) *Readings in Price Theory*. London: Allen & Unwin.

Stackelberg, H. von (1934) *Marktform und Gleichgewicht*, Vienna: Julius Springer. Translated by Peacock, A. (1952) *Theory of the Market Economy*. New York: Oxford University Press.

Stalk, G., Evans, P. and Shulman, L.E. (1992) Competing on capabilities, resources and the concept of strategy, *Harvard Business Review*, March/April, 57–69.

Stanley, M.H.R., Buldyrev, S.V., Havlin, S., Mantegna, R.N., Salinger, M.A. and Stanley, H.E. (1995) Zipf plots and the size distribution of firms, *Economics Letters*, **49**, 453–7.

Stauffer, T.R. (1971) The measurement of corporate rates of return: a generalised formulation, *Bell Journal of Economics*, **2**, 434–69.

Steen, F. and Sørgard, L. (1999) Semicollusion in the Norwegian cement market, *European Economic Review*, **43**, 1775–96.

Stephen, F. (1994) Advertising, consumer search costs and prices in a professional service market, *Applied Economics*, **26**, 1177–88.

Stern, L.W. (1971) Antitrust implications of a sociological interpretation of competition, conflict, and cooperation in the marketplace, *Antitrust Bulletin*, **16**, 509–30.

Stevens, B. (1984) Comparing public and private sector productive efficiency: an analysis of eight activities, *National Productivity Review*, Autumn, 395–406.

Stevens, R.B. and Yamey, B.S. (1965) *The Restrictive Practices Court: A Study of Judicial Process and Economic Policy*. London: Weidenfeld & Nicholson.

Stewart, G. (1997) Why regulate? *The Economic Review*, September.

Stigler, G.J. (1947) The kinky oligopoly demand curve and rigid prices, *Journal of Political Economy*, **55**, 432–47.

Stigler, G.J. (1951) The division of labor is limited by the extent of the market, *Journal of Political Economy*, **59**, 185–93.

Stigler, G.J. (1952) *The Theory of Price*. New York: Macmillan.

Stigler, G.J. (1955) *Business Concentration and Price Policy*. Princeton, NJ: Princeton University Press.

Stigler, G.J. (1957) Perfect competition, historically contemplated, *Journal of Political Economy*, **65**, 1–17.

Stigler, G.J. (1958) The economies of scale, *The Journal of Law and Economics*, **1**, 54–71.

Stigler, G.J. (1961) The economics of information, *Journal of Political Economy*, **69**, 213–25. Reprinted in Stigler, G.J. (1968) *The Organization of Industry*, pp.171–90.

Stigler, G.J. (1963a) *Capital and Rates of Return in Manufacturing*. Princeton, NJ: Princeton University Press.

Stigler, G.J. (1963b) United States v. Loew's Inc.: a note on block booking, *Supreme Court Review*, pp.152–7.

Stigler, G. (1964) A theory of oligopoly, *Journal of Political Economy*, **72**, 44–61.

Stigler, G. (1966) *The Theory of Price*, 2nd edn. New York: Macmillan.

Stigler, G. (1968) *The Organization of Industry*. Holmwood, IL: Irwin.

Stigler, G. (1971) The theory of economic regulation, *Bell Journal of Economics*, **2**, 3–21.

Stigler, G.J. (1978) The literature of economics: the case of the kinked oligopoly demand curve, *Economic Inquiry*, **16**, 185–204. Reprinted in Wagner, L. (ed.) (1981) *Readings in Applied Microeconomics*. Oxford: Oxford University Press, reading 10.

Stocking, W. and Mueller, W. (1957) Business reciprocity and the size of firms, *Journal of Business*, **30**, 73–95.

Stoneman, P. (1989) Technological diffusion, and vertical product differentiation. *Economic Letters*, **31**, 277–80.

Stoneman, P. (1995) *Handbook of the Economics of Innovation and Technical Change*. Oxford: Blackwell.

Storey, Sir R. (1979) Technology and the trade unions, in Henry, H. (ed.) *Behind the Headlines*. London: Associated Business Press, chapter 4.

Strassmann, D.L. (1990) Potential competition in the deregulated airlines, *Review of Economics and Statistics*, **72**, 696–702.

Sultan, R.G.M. (1974) *Pricing in the Electrical Oligopoly*, vol. I. Cambridge, MA: Harvard University Press.

Sutton, J. (1974) Advertising, concentration and competition, *Economic Journal*, **84**, 56–69.

Sutton, C.J. (1980) *Economics and Corporate Strategy*. Cambridge: Cambridge University Press.

Sutton, J. (1991) *Sunk Costs and Market Structure*. London: MIT Press.

Sutton, J. (1998) *Technology and Market Structure: Theory and History*. Cambridge, MA: MIT Press.

Sweezy, P. (1939) Demand under conditions of oligopoly, *Journal of Political Economy*, **47**, 568–73.

Sylos-Labini, P. (1962) *Oligopoly and Technical Progress*. Boston: Harvard University Press.

Symeonidis, G. (1999) Cartel stability in advertising-intensive and R&D-intensive industries, *Economic Letters*, **62**, 121–9.

Szymanski, S. (1996) The impact of compulsory competitive tendering on refuse collection services, *Fiscal Studies*, **17**, 1–19.

Szymanski, S. and Wilkins, S. (1993) Cheap rubbish? Competitive tendering and contracting out in refuse collection – 1981–88, *Fiscal Studies*, **14**, 109–30.

Taylor, C. and Silberston, Z.A. (1973) *The Economic Impact of the Patent System*. Cambridge: Cambridge University Press.

Teece, D. (1982) Toward an economic theory of the multiproduct firm, *Journal of Economic Behaviour and Organisation*, **3**, 39–63.

Teece, D., Rumelt, R., Dosi, G. and Winter, S. (1994) Understanding corporate coherence, theory and evidence, *Journal of Economic Behaviour and Organisation*, **23**, 1–30.

Telser, L. (1960) Why should manufacturers want fair trade?, *Journal of Law and Economics*, **3**, 86–105.

Telser, L. (1964) Advertising and competition, *Journal of Political Economy*, **72**, 537–62.

Telser, L. (1966a) Cut throat competition and the long purse, *Journal of Law and Economics*, **9**, 259–77.

Telser, L. (1966b) Supply and demand for advertising messages, *American Economic Review*, **56**, 457–66.

Thomadakis, S.B. (1977) A value based test of profitability and market structure, *Review of Economics and Statistics*, **59**, 179–85.

Tirole, J. (1988) *Theory of Industrial Organization*. Cambridge: Cambridge University Press.

Tremblay, C.H. and Tremblay, V.J. (1996) Firm success, national status, and product line diversification: and empirical examination, *Review of Industrial Organisation*, **11**, 771–89.

Tremblay, V.J. (1985) Strategic groups and the demand for beer, *Journal of Industrial Economics*, **34**, 183–98.

Turner, P. (1980) Import competition and the profitability of United Kingdom manufacturing industry, *Journal of Industrial Economics*, **29**, 155–66.

UK Cabinet Office (1996) *Competing For Quality Policy Review: An Efficiency Unit Scrutiny*. London: HMSO.

United Kingdom Science Parks Association (1999) http://www.ukspa.org.uk/htmfiles/aboutus.htm (last accessed November 1999).

Uri, N.D. (1987) A re-examination of the advertising and industrial concentration relationship, *Applied Economics*, **19**, 427–35.

Utton, M.A. (1970) *Industrial Concentration*. Harmondsworth: Penguin.

Utton, M.A. (1971) The effect of mergers on concentration: UK manufacturing industry 1954–1965, *Journal of Industrial Economics*, **20**, 42–58.

Utton, M.A. (1972) Mergers and the growth of large firms, *Bulletin of Oxford University Institute of Economics and Statistics*, **34**, 189–97.

Utton, M.A. (1977) Large firm diversification in British manufacturing industry, *Economic Journal*, **87**, 96–113.

Utton, M.A. (1979) *Diversification and Competition*. Cambridge: Cambridge University Press.

Utton, M.A. (1982) Domestic concentration and international trade, *Oxford Economic Papers*, **34**, 479–97.

Utton, M.A. (1986) *Profits and the Stability of Monopoly*. Cambridge: Cambridge University Press.

Van den Berg, C. (1997) Water privatization and regulation in England and Wales, *Public Policy for the Private Sector*, May. World Bank.

Vanlommel, E., de Brabander, B. and Liebaers, D. (1977) Industrial concentration in Belgium: empirical comparison of alternative seller concentration measures, *Journal of Industrial Economics*, **26**, 1–20.

Vernon, J.M. and Graham, D.A. (1971) Profitability of monopolisation in vertical integration, *Journal of Political Economy*, **79**, 924–5.

Vernon, J.M. and Nourse, R.E. (1973) Profit rates and market structure of advertising intensive firms, *Journal of Industrial Economics*, **22**, 1–20.

Vickers, J. (1995) Concepts of competition, *Oxford Economic Papers*, **47**, 1–23.

Vidale, M.L. and Wolfe, H.B. (1957) An operations research study of sales response to advertising, *Operations Research*, **5**, 370–81.

von Neumann, J. and Morgenstern, O. (1944) *The Theory of Games and Economic Behaviour*. Princeton, NJ: Princeton University Press.

Waddams-Price, C. (1997) Competition and regulation in the UK gas industry, *Oxford Review of Economic Policy*, **13**, 47–63.

Wagner, J. (1992) Firm size, firm growth and the persistence of chance, *Small Business Economics*, **4**, 125–31.

Walker, M. (1997) RIP for RRP, *London Economics – Economics in Action*, No. 2.

Walsh, K. (1991) *Competitive Tendering for Local Authority Services: Initial Experiences*. London: Department of Environment.

Walsh, K. (1992) Quality and public services, *Public Administration*, **69**, 503–14.

Walsh, K. and Davis, H. (1993) *Competition and Service: The Impact of the Local Government Act, 1988*. London: Department of the Environment.

Waterson, M. (1987) Recent developments in the theory of natural monopoly, *Journal of Economic Surveys*, **1**, 59–80.

Waterson, M. (1988) On vertical restraints and the law: a note, *Rand Journal of Economics*, **29**, 293–7.

Waterson, M. (1993) Are industrial economists still interested in concentration?, in Casson, M. and Creedy, J. (eds) *Industrial Concentration and Economic Inequality*. Aldershot: Edward Elgar.

Weir, C. (1992) The Monopolies and Mergers Commission merger reports and the public interest: a probit analysis, *Applied Economics*, **24**, 27–34.

Weir, C. (1993) Merger policy and competition: an analysis of the Monopolies and Mergers Commission's decisions, *Applied Economics*, **25**, 57–66.

Weiss, L.W. (1963) Factors in changing concentration, *Review of Economics and Statistics*, **45**, 70–7.

Weiss, L.W. (1965) An evaluation of mergers in six industries, *Review of Economics and Statistics*, **47**, 172–81.

Weiss, L.W. (1969) Advertising, profits and corporate taxes, *Review of Economics and Statistics*, **54**, 421–30.

Weiss, L.W. (1974) The concentration–profits relationship and antitrust, in H. Goldschmid, Mann, H.M. and Weston, J.F. (eds) *Industrial Concentration: The New Learning*. Boston: Little Brown, pp.183–233.

Weiss, L.W. (1989) *Concentration and Price*. Boston, MA: MIT Press.

Weiss, L.W., Pascoe, G. and Martin, S. (1983) The size of selling costs, *Review of Economics and Statistics*, **65**, 668–72.

Weston, J.F. (1970) Conglomerate firms, *St John's Law Review*, **44**, 66–80. Reprinted in Yamey, B.S. (ed.) (1973) *Economics of Industrial Structure*. Harmondsworth: Penguin, pp.305–21.

Whinston, M. (1990) Tying, foreclosure and exclusion, *American Economic Review*, **80**, 837–59.

White, L.J. (1981) What has been happening to aggregate concentration in the United States, *Journal of Industrial Economics*, **29**, 223–30.

Whittlesey, C. (1946) *National Interest and International Cartels*. New York: Macmillan.

Wilcox, C. (1960) *Public Policy Toward Business*. Homewood, IL: Irwin.

Williamson, O.E. (1963) Managerial discretion and business behaviour, *American Economic Review*, **53**, 1032–57.

Williamson, O.E. (1965) A dynamic theory of interfirm behaviour, *Quarterly Journal of Economics*, **79**, 579–607.

Williamson, O.E. (1968a) Economies as an antitrust defence: the welfare trade-offs, *American Economic Review*, **58**, 18–36.

Williamson, O.E. (1968b) Economies as an antitrust defence: correction and reply, *American Economic Review*, **58**, 1372–6.

Williamson, O.E. (1971) The vertical integration of production: market failure considerations, *American Economic Review, Papers and Proceedings*, **61**, 112–23.

Williamson, O. (1975) *Markets and Hierarchies: Analysis and Antitrust Implications*. London: Macmillan.

Williamson, O.E. (1979) Transaction-cost economics: the governance of non-contractual relations, *Journal of Law and Economics*, **22**, 233–61.

Williamson, O.E. (1985) *Economic Institutions of Capitalism*. New York: Free Press.

Williamson, O.E. (1989) Transaction cost economics, in Schmalensee, R. and Willig, R.D. (eds) *Handbook of Industrial Organisation*, vol. 1. Amsterdam: North-Holland, chapter 3.

Wilson, J. (1994) Competitive tendering and UK public services, *The Economic Review*, April.

Wilson, J.O.S. and Morris, J.E. (2000) The size and growth of UK manufacturing and service firms, *The Service Industries Journal*, **20**, 25–38.

Wilson, J.O.S. and Williams, J.M. (2000) The size and growth of banks: evidence from four European countries. *Applied Economics*, **32**, 1101–9.

Winston, C. (1993) Economic deregulation: days of reckoning for microeconomists, *Journal of Economic Literature*, **31**, 1263–89.

Wright, V. (2000) *Privatization and Public Policy*. Aldershot: Edward Elgar.

Yamey, B.S. (1970) Notes on secret price cutting in oligopoly, in Kooy, M. (ed.) *Studies in Economics and Economic History in Honour of Prof. H.M. Robertson*. London: Macmillan, pp.280–300.

Yamey, B.S. (1972a) Do monopoly and near monopoly matter? A survey of the empirical studies, in Peston, M. and Correy, B. (eds) *Essays in Honour of Lord Robbins*. London: Weidenfeld & Nicolson, pp.294–308.

Yamey, B.S. (1972b) Predatory price cutting: notes and comments, *Journal of Law and Economics*, **15**, 137–47.

Yamey, B.S. (1973) Some problems of oligopoly, *Proceedings of the International Conference on International Economy and Competition Policy, Tokyo*.

Yarrow, G. (1986) Privatisation in theory and practice, *Economic Policy*, **2**, 319–78.

Yarrow, G. (1989) Privatisation and economic performance in Britain, *Carnegie Rochester Conference Series on Public Policy*, **31**, 303–44.

Youssef, M.I. (1986) Global oil price war is expected to affect the industry for years, *Wall Street Journal*, February.

Index